Population Trends in
New Jersey

Population Trends in New Jersey

JAMES W. HUGHES AND DAVID LISTOKIN

Rutgers University Press

New Brunswick, Camden, and Newark, New Jersey, and London

Library of Congress Cataloging-in-Publication Data

Names: Hughes, James W. author. | Listokin, David, author.
Title: Population trends in New Jersey / James W. Hughes and David Listokin.
Description: New Brunswick: Rutgers University Press, [2022] |
    Includes bibliographical references and index.
Identifiers: LCCN 2021011641 | ISBN 9780813588315 (paperback) |
    ISBN 9780813588308 (hardback) | ISBN 9780813588322 (epub) | ISBN 9780813588339 (pdf)
Subjects: LCSH: New Jersey—Population—History—21st century. |
    Population forecasting—New Jersey—History—21st century. |
    New Jersey—Census, 2020. | Cities and towns—Growth—History—21st century.
Classification: LCC HB3525.N5 H84 2022 | DDC 304.609749—dc23
LC record available at https://lccn.loc.gov/2021011641

A British Cataloging-in-Publication record for this book is available from the British Library.

References to internet websites (URLs) were accurate at the time of writing. Neither the author
nor Rutgers University Press is responsible for URLs that may have expired or changed since
the manuscript was prepared.

♾ The paper used in this publication meets the requirements of the American National
Standard for Information Sciences—Permanence of Paper for Printed Library Materials,
ANSI Z39.48-1992.

www.rutgersuniversitypress.org

Manufactured in the United States of America

Contents

Preface and Acknowledgments ix

1 Overview and Summary: A State of Unrelenting Change 1

2 New Jersey Population from the Colonial Period to
the Early Republic 14

3 The Long-Term Decennial Growth Picture 75

4 The People of New Jersey: Long-Term Diversity in Racial,
Ethnic, and National Origin 88

5 Population, Geography, and the "Big Six" Cities 132

6 Components of Population Change 155

7 The Generational Framework 167

8 The Baby Boom Generation's Enduring Legacy 179

9 Generations X, Y, Z, and Alpha 188

10 Generations and Age-Structure Transformations 202

11 The Great Household Revolution 218

12 Demographics and Income 236

13 Recent Dynamics and the Future 246

Appendix A: Population by County in New Jersey in
the Colonial Era (1726, 1738, 1745, 1772, and 1784) and
as a State (1790–2018) 259

Appendix B: The Business Cycle and Demographics 269

Appendix C: Historic Black Population, "Great Migration,"
    and "Reverse Great Migration" Nationwide and in New Jersey   273
Appendix D: The Demographics of New Jersey
    Residential Housing   292
Appendix E: New Jersey Population Density and Urban
    and Metropolitan Residence   300
Notes   315
References   335
Index   359

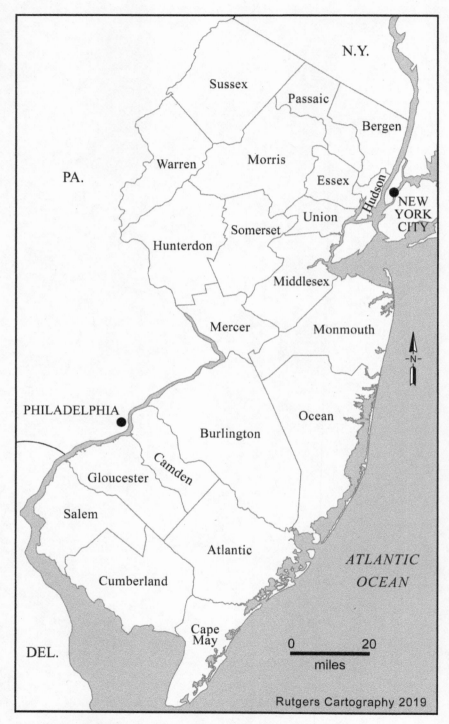

MAP 1 The State of New Jersey: Regional Context and Counties

Preface and Acknowledgments

New Jersey is a state strategically located in the northeastern United States, graphically described in a phrase usually credited to Benjamin Franklin as a "barrel tapped at both ends" vis-à-vis the major cities of New York and Philadelphia. It is also at the heart of the so-called megalopolis, the cohesive integrated region stretching from Boston to Washington, DC. Although it is socioeconomically entwined with this multistate interurban (New York City–Philadelphia axis) and megalopolitan (Boston-Washington corridor) footprint, it is also a distinct entity that sets itself apart.

Throughout its history, New Jersey has had a multifaceted character: it is the nation's fourth-smallest state in area, but it has the nation's highest population density (persons per square mile); it has long been an immigration gateway; it stands as one of the nation's leading examples of everchanging racial and ethnic diversity; its sprawling twentieth-century suburbs coexist with its twenty-first-century resurgent cities; and its vibrant evolving postindustrial economy is only the latest stage of its many industrial transformations over time. Nonetheless, its historical moniker of "Garden State" has not lost its legitimacy.

Ultimately, the character of a place is largely its people, and that subject is at the center of this book. We present significant features of the demography of New Jersey, focusing on the historic and contemporary dynamic interplay of the nation's and New Jersey's population, economic and societal forces, as well as technological advancement. Our efforts attempt to isolate the macrotrends that promise to dominate the 2020s, establishing the contextual frameworks from which to analyze the voluminous data that are emanating from Census 2020.

This work can be viewed as a product of nearly a century of combined efforts by the two authors. Its origins are in the many research projects of the Center for Urban Policy Research (CUPR) at Rutgers, which was one of the Ford Foundation's ten original urban studies centers created in 1958. Under the dynamic leadership of George Sternlieb, demographic change was integrated into CUPR's extensive portfolio of urban planning and urban public policy research. This book is dedicated to him for his extraordinary foresight.

The authors are indebted to a number of individuals who have supported this effort. Connie O. Hughes, at one time the state's demographer at the New Jersey Department of Labor, provided superb guidance throughout the book's long gestation. The Bloustein School's Marc D. Weiner (associate research professor) and William Irving (research associate) provided extensive basic research support and data preparation. A big debt of gratitude is owed to Jamie Berger (research associate) who helped in immeasurable ways; we also acknowledge the research assistance provided by Wee Siang Tay. Almost all the maps and figures were prepared by Michael Siegel, staff cartographer of the Rutgers University geography department; we applaud his skills and professional advice. The manuscript was greatly improved by one of the foremost editors in the Garden State, Marilyn Campbell, and we appreciate her impeccable work.

All errors and misinterpretations of the data and trends are solely those of the authors.

Population Trends in
New Jersey

1

Overview and Summary

•••••••••••••••••••••

A State of Unrelenting Change

Demographic observations abound in today's Garden State narrative. Some reflect profound insights ("Racial and ethnic diversity *is* New Jersey"), while others take the form of sarcastic quips/Jersey wisecracks ("Baby boomers used to rock around the clock; now they struggle to limp around the block"). The inventory of such insights, statements, sentiments, and platitudes expands almost daily:

- "Once dominant, suburban-centric baby boomers are yesterday's generation."
- "Boomer nation is no more."
- "Move over, boomers." "Oft-neglected 'stuck-in-the-middle' Gen Xers are now taking your place in the leadership ranks of all organizations."[1]
- "Oft-maligned digitally savvy millennials now rule."
- Oft-mocked millennials: "Generation avocado toast." "Generation rent."
- Millennial geographic movements: "Sprawl withdrawal."
- "Will urban-centric millennials continue to forsake the 'burbs' when they have children?"
- "Or will they weary of today's preferred 'live-work-play (LWP)' environments?"
- "Where will empty-nester boomers settle as they downsize and resize in the housing market?"

- "If you're suffering millennial fatigue, and tired of bashing millennials, you'll soon have a new generation to complain about—Gen Z (post-millennials)."
- "Gen Z: access and connectivity to everything, everywhere, instantaneously, all the time."
- "Domestic outmigration: Will the last person to exit New Jersey please turn off the lights?"

Many more comments and questions such as these reveal a larger phenomenon: the pervasive recognition of, and concern about, the profound changes taking place in the state's population and the ramifications of these impending changes.

Except perhaps for its intensity, this is nothing new. The 2020s will be the twenty-fifth decade that New Jersey has passed through since its inception as a state.[2] One constant within the multicentury time line that can be documented with the decennial U.S. Census—the official once-in-a-decade national headcount—has been relentless population change.[3] Among the dimensions of change are the fluctuating scale and rate of population increases; shifts in racial, ethnic, and immigration diversity; patterns of natural increase (driven by birth booms and birth busts); dual migration flows (international and domestic) into and out of the state; generational successions and disruptions; continuous age-structure transformations; geographic population movements (concentration, decentralization, and reconcentration); and evolving economic and technological drivers. Analyses of these changes serve as our major foci in the chapters that follow.

In particular, generations will receive extended analysis since they incorporate many other aspects of change that are in the demographic pipeline. Generational successions raise many of the issues that will shape New Jersey in the 2020s. Moreover, it will be possible for demographers to extrapolate their defining age contours through the next decade. Unless there are major scientific breakthroughs, the relentless aging of the population is an intractable reality and cannot be suspended; the biological time clock will remain a fundamental of duration. Thus, the aging of generations through their successive stages of the life cycle can be anticipated with a considerable degree of certainty, providing at least a partial blueprint of what is in store for New Jersey in the decade ahead.

Another overarching objective of the book is to provide the deep historical context that envelops current trend analysis. New Jersey's twenty-first-century demography is not simply a recent phenomenon but is the result in some cases of a transformative long-term odyssey that has taken place over centuries, and in many other cases over just several decades. One of our tasks is to answer the question of how we got to where we are today and to document, where feasible, the various quantitative metrics that provide underlying explanations. In this context, another general focus is to detail both the long-term demographic trends that have transformed New Jersey as well as shorter-term movements that are not aberrations but that give evidence of becoming more substantial in scope and duration. Thus, in addition to longer-term statistics, we use current metrics to fully flesh out emerging demographic directions.[4]

Overarching New Jersey Frameworks

Obviously, population change in New Jersey is not immune to broader demographic and economic forces. Thus, a synopsis of major global and national parameters provides a useful starting point for subsequent statewide analyses. The next section of this chapter will first examine what can be called the encompassing macro trends. Then the specific impact of the economy on demography is presented, which provides an analytical perspective that is employed throughout this volume. With this background completed, a final orientation for the reader is provided: an explanation of the composition of each of the chapters and appendixes of the book.

Prominent Twenty-First-Century Global Macro Trends

New Jersey and the United States are fully enmeshed in global population trends. These are summarized effectively in a 2019 United Nations report as well as in a Pew Research Center synopsis.[5] Key among the expected trends is the slowing world population growth, driven by falling global fertility rates. As the global fertility rate falls below replacement levels, the world's population is projected to stop growing by the end of the twenty-first century.

Leading this development are the advanced industrial nations. Europe and the United States, for example, are projected to have declining populations by 2100. Until that point is reached, migration from the rest of the world will be a major driver of continued population growth not only in the United States but also in the entire North American region. And migration will be a force inhibiting more precipitous drops when population declines unfold.

Moreover, decreasing fertility, in concert with increasing life expectancy, will lead to a general aging of the global population—a phenomenon already evident in the United States.[6] Fewer young people, more old people, and international migration flows—key global demographic trends—have already been reshaping the nation, and New Jersey will certainly be instrumental in continuing to transform them in the decade ahead. Although these strong global tendencies trends are not immutable (major unanticipated events can cause major societal disruptions), the likelihood is that they have significant traction and should persist.

Major National Forces

In attempting to decipher where New Jersey's population is going, it is also useful to isolate the specific national patterns of overarching demographic change. Although a number of these have been presented in the above discussion of global forces, the following profile of national parameters has significant ramifications for analyzing New Jersey.

Overall Demographic Stagnation

Consistent with its global counterparts, overall demographic stagnation is starting to characterize the United States, with the national rate of population growth in 2018 the lowest since the Depression year of 1938—eighty years earlier. Much of this slower growth is due to the aging of American society, driven by lower levels of natural increase (the number of births minus the number of deaths). And much of the latter is driven by fewer births and lower reproductive activity.

Contracting Fertility

The year 2018 marked the lowest level of fertility in the history of the United States. The total fertility rate—the number of births each woman is expected to have during her childbearing years—fell to a record low (below 1.73).[7] The year 2018 also had the lowest number of births in the nation in any year since 1986, thirty-two years earlier. The trend of lower births and record-low fertility rates is reflected by the decline in the under-eighteen-years-of-age population since the 2010 census.

The New Demographic Disconnect: A More Old-than-Young Society

One of the major ramifications of the aging of America is a growing gap between the two inexorably changing demographic forces that are positioned at opposite ends of the age spectrum: the huge growing cohort of aging baby boomers (the accelerating "elder boom") and the decline in the number of young people and young members of the labor force.[8] Not only is a broad labor-force shortage possible in the 2020s, but in particular there will be a shrinking pool of eldercare workers. Although the scale of this disconnect will depend on national immigration policies, a more old-than-young demography inexorably appears to be America's destiny—a future with more seniors than children.

Immigration

Population growth will depend increasingly on immigration as fertility rates remain below replacement levels. Immigration is now a fundamental demographic bulwark sustaining population growth. New Jersey stands as the leading-edge microcosm of "immigration nation." International population inflows into the state are already a force inhibiting absolute population contraction in an era of depressed fertility. The importance of these international population inflows is heightened in New Jersey since, within the United States, the state has been experiencing substantial net domestic outmigration to the rest of the country—that is, far more people leaving New Jersey relative to those entering New Jersey from the rest of the United States.

Increasing Diversity

As a result of the sustained immigration to the United States at relatively high levels for nearly one-half century, and the low fertility rates that have recently trended even lower, the nation's population is experiencing what the Brookings Institution calls a diversity explosion (Frey 2015, 2019b). The proportion of the population that is foreign-born now rivals that of a century ago, when the great waves of immigration from Europe were at their peak. Racial minorities are now "the primary demographic engine of the nation's future growth, countering an aging, slow-growing, and soon-to-be-declining white population" (Frey 2018). Diversity is even more pronounced in younger age groups. The dynamic of youthful diversity and aging whites will increasingly characterize America.

Regional Population Growth Differentials

Long-term shifts in regional population flows over the past two centuries have characterized the nation. This has resulted in differential regional and state growth patterns. The past four decades have been characterized by the South and West regions of the United States dominating the nation's population growth, with the mature Midwest and Northeast regions the geographic laggards. General internal population flows within the United States have been in a southern and western direction. National demographic stagnation is most pronounced in those regions that serve as the origin of the primary migration flows—the Northeast and Midwest.

The Great Migration Reversal

Contributing to regional growth differences have been the shifts in Black migration within the United States. The once-powerful Great Migration of Blacks from the South to the northern industrial states, with their then-lure of economic advancement, has been supplanted by a substantial reverse migration—from the North to southern metropolitan areas and their perceived potential for a better economic and social future. This has made a discernible impact on regional population patterns.

Metropolitan Dispersion, Concentration, and Redispersion

The suburbanization and dispersion of the American population dominated the second half of the twentieth century and the early pre–Great 2007–2009 Recession years of the twenty-first century. Initially catching demographic observers by surprise, urban population reconcentration quickly became the dominant national theme in the early 2010s. However, this turnaround appears not to have been long lived, based on end-of-decade annual population estimates. Equally surprising, "Americans are spreading out again into suburbs, exurbs, and smaller towns and rural areas.... The latest data reveal that broad-based population 'concentration' toward large urban areas in the early 2010s was an aberration related to the post-recession economy and housing crunch" (Frey 2019a). However, this renewed population deconcentration has not yet yielded workplace redispersion—that is, the urban economic centralization that characterized much of the aftermath of the Great Recession has not yet been reversed.

Emerging Dominant Global Superstar Cities

Although widespread urban demographic reconcentration in the United States may have been a Great Recession–spawned event of limited duration, the emergence of a few favored superstar cities—powerful innovation-based urban economic agglomerations—may be a more lasting spatial force. This is one demographic result of the latest global economic transformation that is drawing the nation's (and world's) technologically "elite" population to a select few favored geographical nodes (see the section below on demography and the economy). New York City stands atop the superstar rankings.

The Incredible Shrinking Household

The twentieth century was characterized by households dramatically shrinking in size: young adults in successive generations increasingly had the means to flee the parental hearth and establish their own households. This long-term structural change abated with the Great Recession. Multigenerational households became much more prevalent as economic conditions necessitated many young adults to continue to live at home. The cyclical/recessionary effect inhibiting household size shrinkage may recede fully at some point, but there may also be a downside limit to contracting size: How low can they go?

The Great Household Revolution

The second half of the twentieth century witnessed the radical reshaping of America's household composition. Married-couple (or husband-wife) families, particularly those with dependent children—often referred to as nuclear families—lost substantial proportional household share. In contrast, male and female householder families, as well as nonfamily households, experienced major increases in proportional representation. The nation's households thus have become much more diverse in structure, as an increasingly varied array of living arrangements and lifestyle preferences experience much greater presence.

Generational Transformations

The post-2010 era is experiencing one of the greatest age-structure transformations in the nation's history. The massive baby boom generation, the demographic centerpiece of the twentieth century, has been retiring and exiting the societal leadership positions that it had long dominated. Their labor market "outflow" has been mirrored by the labor market "inflow" of the millennial generation. In between, Gen X is ascending to the upper rungs of organizational leadership. In concert with an accelerating shift to a new innovation-based economy, discussed subsequently, the generational protocols of the past are fast becoming obsolete as new ones rapidly emerge.

The Faltering Income Trajectory

Median household and median family incomes are metrics that attempt to gauge the economic well-being and capacity of households and families. The long-term trajectory has shifted over time due to both structural and cyclical factors. In the decades following World War II, unprecedented income gains were achieved as a peacetime consumption economy developed and thrived. But following the structural economic shifts that stemmed from global competition and the energy crises of the 1970s, sustained income gains were supplanted by shorter-term advances and retreats corresponding to business cycle shifts—that is, expansions and recessions. Cumulative gains since the turn of the twenty-first century (2000) have been only modestly positive.

Demography and the Economy: A Basic Reference Framework

The evolution of the demography of the United States and New Jersey has been fully intertwined with long-term structural economic transformations. The analysis of this interplay is undertaken in a number of chapters. However, structural economic change has usually been tempered or accentuated by short-term cyclical factors: the expansionary and contractionary (recessionary) stages of the business cycle. The business cycle (*cyclical* change) and demographics are discussed more fully in appendix B. This discussion will be limited to the linkage between *structural* economic change and demographic change.

The state's ever-evolving population geography over the past two centuries stands as one prominent impact of structural economic shifts. The first (pre–Civil War) and second (post–Civil War) Industrial Revolutions in the nineteenth century were driven by machine and factory production—powered by coal, steam, and rail—replacing manual home production by artisans and craftspeople. The result was statewide economic agglomeration driving population concentration. The rise of New Jersey's densely populated industrial cities supplanted a rural, dispersed, largely agricultural-based society. Urban New Jersey reigned by century's end.

The widespread introduction of electricity at the beginning of the twentieth century—New Jersey was quickly wired up, plugged in, and turned on—was linked to the rise of the industrial metropolis. This was the early demographic overflow into previously undeveloped areas adjacent to the formal political boundaries of the city. The initial enabling force was the electric-powered streetcar, subsequently followed by the automobile. But industrial concentration still reigned as early residential suburbs proliferated.

A third industrial revolution unfolded by the mid-twentieth century, producing a postindustrial economy. An increasingly automobile-centric population, the rise of the computer, an emerging white-collar workforce, and a fading urban manufacturing ecosystem led to economic and demographic decentralization. Thus, the third industrial revolution spawned a suburban, white-collar, office-driven ecosystem and the decline of urban New Jersey. A dispersed suburban demography reigned at century's end.

The fourth industrial revolution characterizes the current twenty-first century: the emergence of an increasingly sophisticated knowledge-dependent, innovation-based economy, underpinned by surging information technology, a mobile internet, the Internet of Things, advanced automation, and artificial intelligence (AI).[9] Many of these economic forces were supposed to erase distance and diminish the power of geography, leading to a further dispersion of populations and workforces. Instead, a repeat of the nineteenth-century dynamic appears to be emerging—economic and demographic reconcentration centered on the imperative of sustained innovation.

Nationally, this reflects a key economic and research belief that real-life, face-to-face collaboration and intense face-to-face intellectual collisions are increasingly necessary to fuel rapid-fire innovation. The end result of the fourth industrial revolution is an economy where superstar employees work for superstar firms that are agglomerated into superstar cities. New Jersey does not yet have a superstar city, but fortunately it is in the gravitational orbit of New York City, the nation's leading superstar, innovation-based, urban economic agglomeration. The state's twenty-first-century population geography has been reconcentrating under the powerful force of New York City's economic gravity.

These current and historical structural economic shifts, along with seismic social forces such as the ebb and flow of international immigration, are what shaped and continually reshaped New Jersey's population trajectory during the past two centuries. They are particularly important in understanding the spatial patterns, but they are also tied to many other dimensions of demographic change.

Organizational Framework

The composition of the remaining chapters of this volume is presented below.

Chapter 2: New Jersey Population from the Colonial Period to the Early Republic

It is important to set the stage for subsequent analyses by presenting the key population growth metrics and the demographic profiles of what was ultimately to become the state of New Jersey within the United States in its formative colonial to Early Republic period (1600s to the first national decennial census in 1790). New Jersey's population grew from approximately 1,000 persons in 1670 to 14,000 in 1700, 71,000 in 1750, and 184,000 by 1790. During the eighteenth century, the state's population grew by 33 percent per decade, a rate of growth that would never again be equaled. Also considered are the specific demographic characteristics of New Jersey's colonial-era population, including race (about 92 percent white, with the Black population largely enslaved), gender (disproportionately male), age (disproportionately young), high fertility and large families (e.g., household size approaching seven members), and nationality (e.g., disproportionately of English, Scotch-Irish, and Dutch origins).

Chapter 3: The Long-Term Decennial Growth Picture

The broad decennial-based sweep of total population change in New Jersey and the United States is documented starting from the first U.S. Census (1790). By 2010, New Jersey's population had reached approximately 8.8 million people, almost forty-eight times greater than the 184,000 people counted in 1790, 220 years earlier. The chapter examines in detail the various structural and cyclical forces that have driven and shaped population growth in the state during key decade/decennial intervals in the nineteenth, twentieth, and twenty-first centuries. Growth rates peaked during three periods: the intersection of the first two Industrial Revolutions (1840–1870), the great European immigration waves (1890–1930), and unprecedented postwar suburbanization (1950–1970). In contrast, a distinct growth lull now characterizes New Jersey.

Chapter 4: The People of New Jersey: Long-Term Diversity in Racial, Ethnic, and National Origin

New Jersey has been a literal crossroads of different people, nationalities, racial and ethnic minorities, and immigrant and migrant groups over its history. This chapter profiles New Jersey's residents, starting with the original Native American inhabitants, and then considers the numerous racial and ethnic groups that continuously reshaped the state. The origins of New Jersey's major immigrant populations are then presented, not only those from abroad but also from within the United States, with attention directed to Black migration from the rural South—the "Great Migration"—and then its subsequent countertrend—the "Reverse Great Migration." Asians are currently the state's fastest-growing minority group, rising from a trace level (0.3 percent) population share in 1970 to 9.9 percent in 2017. In tandem, there has been a surge in the Hispanic share of New Jersey's total population, from 6.7 percent in 1980 to 20.4 percent in 2017. Further reflecting New Jersey's growing diversity is the significant increase of the foreign-born share of its population, from 8.9 percent in 1970 to 22.8 percent in 2017.

Chapter 5: Population, Geography, and the "Big Six" Cities

In the context of the overarching population change that has taken place in New Jersey since its inception, detailed in the preceding chapters, the internal distribution of the population within the state is examined in this chapter. New Jersey's basic settlement patterns have evolved over time as a result of changing economic, technological, and other forces. Successive developmental stages of urbanization, metropolitanization, suburbanization, re-urbanization, and de-suburbanization of the population are examined with particular reference to the growth patterns—the rise, fall, and rebirth—of the state's "Big Six" cities: Camden, Elizabeth, Jersey City, Newark, Paterson, and Trenton, as well as their encompassing counties.

Chapter 6: Components of Population Change

The overall population change presented in the preceding chapters was a consequence of broad cyclical and structural forces. But such changes can be disaggregated and refined into their distinct causal parts—what demographers have labeled the components of population change. The two broad components are net natural increase (births minus deaths) and net migration (the number of people moving into an area minus the number of people moving out of an area). Net migration is further partitioned into its domestic and international components. Swings in these components have driven changes in the magnitude of growth (or decline) in the state's overall population and that of its internal geographic parts. This chapter details the sharp shifts that have taken place in New Jersey's components of change during two transformative time periods: the postwar era of massive domestic in-migration versus the heavy domestic outmigration that has characterized the twenty-first century.

Chapter 7: The Generational Framework

Generations reflect a process of demographic disaggregation into specific groups that is intended to help understand large population blocs for a wide range of purposes. An underlying assumption is that a generation is an identifiable age-defined cohort of people shaped by the social, economic, and technological experiences of a particular period of time. This chapter explores early and more recent conceptualizations of generational frameworks leading to the final definitions employed in the analyses of this book: pre–baby boom, baby boom, Generation X, millennials (Generation Y), Generation Z (postmillennials), and Generation Alpha. Exploring these generations proves useful in helping to add structure to the analyses of past changes in New Jersey's population as well as to the changes and disruptions that are in the demographic pipeline.

Chapter 8: The Baby Boom Generation's Enduring Legacy

The post–World War II baby boom generation, born 1946 to 1964, was the most influential age-related demographic event of the twentieth century. Because of its sheer size—and its outsized needs and demands—and because New Jersey in the immediate postwar period was under-capacity in all of its manifold infrastructure dimensions from schools to roads, the baby boom not only shaped yesterday's and today's social, economic, and political landscape but also sculpted the physical landscape and built environment that now characterizes much of the state. This expansive footprint—a product of the baby boom life-cycle odyssey—still has an outsized impact on New Jersey as the third decade of the twenty-first century unfolds. Thus, extensive attention to this fabled generation is warranted.

Chapter 9: Generations X, Y, Z, and Alpha

Following in age-related sequence are four generations, each of which is more diverse than its immediate predecessor, and each of which will continue to shape population change in New Jersey. Immediately following the baby boom is Generation X, the undersized population cohort born between 1965 and 1980, originally termed the baby bust, a less-compelling term that is fading in use. Nonetheless, Gen X replaced concerns of expansion with concerns of shrinkage. Generation Y, most commonly called millennials, is the digital age's first generation, born between 1981 and 1996, and the current focus of many institutions trying to manage and accommodate its members. Generation Z (postmillennials) comprises the mobile internet's first generation, born between 1997 and 2012. Generation Alpha, born post-2012, is the first generation born totally in the twenty-first century and one that will come of age in the era of AI and robotics.

Chapter 10: Generations and Age-Structure Transformations

Closely intertwined with generational partitions is the age structure of the population—that is, the disaggregation of the overall population into specific age segments. Shifts in age structure impact many societal dimensions, such as changing school enrollments and growing/contracting housing market sectors. Moreover, generational change is directly reflected in age-structure profiles and age-structure changes. For example, between 1970 and 1980, the maturing baby boom generation caused a vast rate of increase in the population between twenty-five and thirty-four years of age, while Gen X caused a significant rate of decline in the population under ten years old—resulting in a distinct bulge and a distinct indentation in the state's age-structure profile. Age-structure analysis has a long tradition of being a key tool of demographers and planners in forecasting age-related service needs and market demands. Thus, age-structure profiles of the state over time are presented in detail.

Chapter 11: The Great Household Revolution

In addition to generational and age-structure divisions, overall populations can be partitioned into households and discrete household types—that is, the distinct ways in which people arrange themselves in housing units, which reflect lifestyle preferences and choices of specific living arrangements. Both nationwide and in New Jersey, the long-term trends have been household growth rates far in excess of population growth rates, sustained declines in the size of households, and the increasing diversity in the anatomy of household types—that is, household diversification. The latter has been the result of a powerful post–World War II household revolution in America that totally redefined living and lifestyle configurations. American and New Jersey households have departed significantly from the 1950s' predominant template of the married couple with male head of household and a brood of children. Considerable attention is given to each of these three household-change parameters at both the national and New Jersey levels.

Chapter 12: Demographics and Income

Income is one measure of the economic capacity and the economic well-being of people and households. Income, in its many statistical dimensions, could easily be the subject of a separate comprehensive book. In this work, however, simply household and family incomes will be the primary focus. The chapter begins with the long-term family income trajectory in the United States in the postwar era, detailing its early major advances (unprecedented affluence) and the subsequent moderate, at best, gains (cyclical stagnation) that were achieved. Substantial income variations across the household types and configurations that were presented in chapter 11 are then analyzed. What the data suggest is that economic well-being often requires a household or family team comprising more than a single earner. Incomes are further analyzed according to age of householders and the race and ethnicity of households.

Chapter 13: Recent Dynamics and the Future

This concluding chapter attempts to weave together the myriad dimensions of change in sketching out a New Jersey that will be reshaped in many dimensions during the 2020s. A "slow-go" demographic growth condition may well approach "no-go" status as the decade matures. International migration will be either the engine inhibiting population decline or achieving modest growth. It will also be a prime asset in maintaining the state's economic competitiveness. Racial and ethnic diversity will continue, while the household revolution may yield to household evolution. Age-structure variations may produce a young-old population divide that will challenge policymakers and planners. Generational evolution and disruptions will interact with all of these unrelenting changes to produce a New Jersey in the 2020s that will be radically different from the state that existed in 2000 when the new millennium unfolded.

Appendixes

The extensive appendixes of this volume have been compiled with a number of objectives in mind. One is to provide an essential toolkit for planners, policymakers, and housing specialists regarding the linkage of housing types and household configurations. The questions of what types of households dwell in what types of housing units, and the number of school-aged children that are generated by new housing developments, are contentious issues that have long bedeviled municipalities in the state when confronted by new development. The extensive baselines necessary to answer these questions are presented in appendix D.

Other objectives center on providing long-term historical demographic data—supplementing that provided in main chapters of this volume—that will be useful to readers and analysts who are deeply interested in exploring the antecedents of present-day New Jersey. In many cases, these data compendiums were not easily accessible and were not easily compiled. Hopefully, the result of our historical demographic "treasure hunt" will bring to light important documents and sources of data that rarely see the light of day. Also provided are other supplementary materials—such as business-cycle dates—that are linked to demographic change and provide important reference points. In total, the appendixes should provide a useful set of baselines helping to further understand New Jersey's population and the ramifications of demographic change.

2

New Jersey Population from the Colonial Period to the Early Republic

• •

We start our study of the population and demography of New Jersey at the area's historical beginning. This chapter presents in summary form key population and demographic profiles of what was ultimately to become the state of New Jersey in the United States from its formative colonial period to independence, roughly from the mid-1600s to the first national census in 1790. To do justice to New Jersey's demography over this approximate century-and-a-half span could itself require its own stand-alone monograph, but here we will only touch on demographic highlights of these early New Jersey years.

Also to be acknowledged is the considerable uncertainty regarding precise population counts and demographic profiles of this era, because population enumerations of this seventeenth- to eighteenth-century period were inchoate. The first European national census was conducted by Sweden in 1749, neither England nor France followed suit until 1801, and Austria, Italy, and Russia in 1818, 1861, and 1897, respectively (Lord 1997, 68; Wells 1975, 7). (By contrast, China's Han dynasty conducted a census in 2 CE and enumerated fifty-eight million persons; Population Reference Bureau, n.d.) Further, the English colonies balked at population enumerations, fearing they were a pretext or prelude for increased taxation (not unfounded) or being pressed into the militia (again, not unfounded), believing they violated religious tenets (i.e., biblical prohibitions against head counts), and understanding they were costly in terms of time and resource commitments (Sutherland 1966, vii). Even when conducted, supposed colony-wide population censuses were sometimes far from geographically complete. To illustrate, a 1772 census in New Jersey covered only half the colony (West Jersey) because of local intransigence against this mandate from the then-existing central authority, the royal governor (Wells 1975, 134). (Strong home rule sentiments would continue to bedevil the Garden State.) Finally, there was uneven treatment of how African Americans in the colonial era, almost entirely enslaved, were enumerated in census counts of the era. John McCusker (2006a, 5-654) observed that "[colonial] population estimates for blacks, both enslaved and free, are thought to be especially prone to inaccuracy." In short, the population figures and demographic profiles of the early years presented in this chapter have acknowledged uncertainties and represent only best available estimates. Apt is the following observation: "Little quantitative evidence from the seventeenth or eighteenth century comes down to us in a form we wish. We must, for all that, build our historical edifices with the bricks at hand" (J. Price 1976, 701, originally cited by McCusker 2006a, 5-628).

Early New Jersey History

To set the context for the presentation of early New Jersey populations, let us first consider the history of this period. Lengthy scholarly monographs have been written on this subject; we are indebted in our historical snapshot and later demographic presentation in this chapter to such seminal historic and demographic sources as those by Richard McCormick (1964), John McCusker (2006a, 2006b), W. S. Rossiter (1909), and Peter Wacker (1975).[1]

A 1765 history of colonial New Jersey described the province as an area where "harmony reigns in a considerable degree in all branches of the legislature; the publick business is consequently dispatched with ease, and at small expense" (S. Smith 1890, 448). Would that positive assessment were fully the case then (as well as today). In fact, New Jersey's early years were tumultuous. There were competing national interests by multiple colonizing European powers, including Sweden versus Holland, and Holland versus England (Craven 1965; Dahlgren and Norman 1988; Leiby 1965). There was early seventeenth-century Dutch presence, including a 1618 fortification on the site of what became Jersey City (additional Dutch settled at Pavonia,[2] later Jersey City, in 1630) and a 1624 Dutch settlement at Fort Nassau (near contemporary Gloucester City). The main Dutch settlement in what they called New Netherlands was New Amsterdam (contemporary New York City), settled 1626, and New Amsterdamers often crossed the river seeking larger and less expensive homesteads. (That attraction of New Jersey continues until today.) Dutch settler Cornelius Van Vorst, living circa 1630 in today's Jersey City, is referred to as "the first Jersey-man" (Wacker 1975, 123). In 1664, however, an English fleet forced the Dutch to surrender New Netherlands. The English Crown conveyed these conquered lands to titled English nobility—the area east of the Hudson River was renamed New York while that west of the Hudson was renamed New Jersey, the latter under the control of two so-called proprietors:[3] Sir George Carteret and Sir John Lord Berkeley. (These proprietors and the naming of New Jersey are described shortly in greater detail.) Settlements soon followed:[4] Middletown and Shrewsbury in 1665 and Newark, Piscataway, and Woodbridge in 1666 (Wacker 1975, 125). (New Jersey's first English settlement had been founded earlier in 1664 at Elizabeth-Town,[5] today's Elizabeth [Wacker 1975, 125].)

Somewhat earlier, there was a Swedish outpost (including settlers from Finland) in New Jersey in the 1640s at Fort Elfsborg (near present-day Salem) and infamously tagged with the moniker of Mosquito Castle (Leiby 1965, 33).[6] This settlement was part of a larger Swedish effort to colonize the region on both banks of the "South River" (Leiby 1965, 24), later called the Delaware River, including the southernmost counties of New Jersey (Clement 1893), northern Delaware (Swedes built Fort Christina in 1637 near today's Wilmington), and eastern Pennsylvania (Carney 1987). Although the Swedish settlement in New Jersey was not populous and faced daunting conditions (e.g., Fort Elfsborg was abandoned in 1652 due to the swarming mosquitoes; Sebold and Leach 1966, 6), the area had strategic value.

As the Dutch and English coveted the same New Jersey lands as the Swedes, not surprisingly frictions and worse ensued between these European groups. In fact, Fort Elfsborg was built on the site of the former English settlement of Varken Kill, and into the mid-1600s there was armed conflict between the Swedes and Dutch (Covart, n.d.; Leiby 1965; J. Snyder 1969, 4). A historian has described "the peopling of British North America" as the "conflict of civilizations" (Bailyn 2012), and that aptly describes New Jersey in that formative era.

In addition, there were inherent frictions and not infrequent armed conflict between the settlers of all nationalities and the original Native American inhabitants. In just one example, the early 1630s colonial settlement at Pavonia had to be abandoned repeatedly in the 1640s and 1650s as a result of "savage warfare . . . between the Dutch and Indians" (McCormick 1964, 10–11); "the west bank of the Hudson was laid waste by the aborigines, except for the Van Vorst residence" (Wacker 1975, 123), and there were unfortunate massacres by the combatants on both sides (Lurie and Veit 2016, 13). Serial revenge killing were not uncommon; after Thomas Quick Sr. was killed in an Indian raid in West Jersey in the 1750s, his son, Tom Jr., in a hell-bent vendetta, killed possibly a hundred natives (Cunningham 1966, 23).

Besides conflicts between the English, Dutch, and Swedish nations and between Europeans and Indians, within the English settlement there was considerable strife. Because of frequent acrimonious jockeying between the colonists and the proprietors, New Jersey was described as the "Rebellious Proprietary" (Lurie 2010; Pomfret 1962); indeed, the very nature of New Jersey's convoluted proprietary arrangement (it was described as the "Unique Proprietary"; Lurie 1987) fostered "political disorder and confusion" (Lurie 1987, 81) and "an element of uncertainty destined to disturb its political life" (Craven 1964, 46). Not helping matters was colonial New Jersey's "desperate configuration including land titles and property rights" (Grabas 2014, 17).

There were tensions between regions of the New Jersey colony, most notably between East and West Jersey (the colony was formally divided in 1676 by the Quintipartite Deed) and friction resulting from the sharp elbows of the New York and New Jersey colonies, both claiming hegemony. As summarized in one study, the proprietor's grant "not only created New Jersey, but also perplexities . . . for the next 40 years" (Federal Writers' Project 1939, 37) as the colonial leaders on both sides of the Hudson jostled for control. In 1680, the New York royal governor, Edmund Andros, arrested the royal governor of New Jersey, Philip Carteret (cousin of original proprietor George Carteret), and forcibly brought him to New York where he stood trial for alleged abuse of authority; Andros claimed only he had the right to tax and regulate East Jersey (McCormick 1964, 28). Although Philip Carteret was ultimately acquitted of the charges, the incident was nonetheless ignoble and humbling to both him personally and East Jersey writ large.

How the Colony and State Were Named

We can obtain a better sense of these multifold tensions, and more generally a better grasp of the history of early New Jersey, by examination of how New Jersey was named. After the English Civil War and the Cromwellian revolution of the seventeenth century, Charles II was restored to the British throne in 1660. In 1664, Charles conveyed to his brother, James, Duke of York, a large grant or patent of land in a portion of the New World in the Americas that extended between the Connecticut and Delaware Rivers and included other lands, such as portions of Maine and Long Island and ultimately the west side of the Delaware River as well (McCormick 1964, 16).

A British fleet was sent to take control of Dutch-controlled New Netherlands and the latter's most important settlement, New Amsterdam, surrendered to the British in September 1664. Shortly thereafter, James, Duke of York, conveyed a portion of his larger land grant (the segment that would ultimately become the state of New Jersey) to two royal confidants who had supported the throne during the seventeenth-century Civil War: Sir George Carteret and Sir John, Lord Berkeley. The grant to Carteret and Berkeley, who were both invested as proprietors, read, "Said tract of Land is hereinafter to be called by the name or names of Nova Caesarea or New Jersey" ("The Duke of York's Release 1664").

The origins of *New Jersey* are better known, so we will start there. Sir George Carteret was native to and had defended for the British throne the Isle of Jersey (the largest of the Channel Islands in the English Channel off the coast of France) during the English Civil War. It was commonplace in this era of settlement to name newly claimed lands after European nobility (e.g., New York) or European places of origin, such as New Netherlands, New Amsterdam, and in our case, New Jersey.

But what about *Nova Caesarea*, named in the land grant to Carteret and Berkeley—what were its origins? Very simply, Caesarea was another name for the Isle of Jersey (Myers 1945, 44). Its nomenclature harkens back to Roman times when the island was named after the Emperor Caesar (Caesarea Insula or Island of Caesar) (Rosetta 2014). Over time, Caesarea was anglicized to "Jersey": "*Jer* is a contraction of Caesar and *ey* signifies island" (Pomfret 1964, 8; Rosetta 2014).

Besides the designation in the original land grant to Berkeley and Carteret, Nova Caesarea was referred to early on in New Jersey's history. It continued to be used in some early legal and political framing documents in the colony, such as the 1672 "Proprietors Declaration to the Adventurers and Planters" concerning governmental organization and land allotments ("A Declaration of the True Intent" 1672). One of the earliest detailed accounts of New Jersey settlement, written by Samuel Smith and published in 1765, was titled *The History of the Colony of Nova-Caesaria, or New Jersey . . . to the Year 1721* (S. Smith 1890). One side of state-minted coins in colonial New Jersey (until 1790) proudly proclaimed Nova Caesarea (Rosetta 2014). One of the most important early cartographic studies of the Garden State, published in 1834 by Thomas F. Gordon, New Jersey's first gazetteer, was titled *Nova Caesarea: A Cartographic Record of the Garden State* (Snyder 1969, 1). Gordon's important work and the occasion of the 350th anniversary (1664–2014) of New Jersey's naming were acknowledged by John Delaney when in 2014 he authored the similarly named *Nova Caesarea: A Cartographic Record of the Garden State, 1666–1888*. Over time, however, the strange-sounding Nova Caesarea was largely forgotten except in history and related scholarly books and pamphlets (Peck 2013, 8; J. Snyder 1969, 7; Sutherland 1966, 92; Walker et al. 1929) with few exceptions (e.g., a unit of Daughters of the American Revolution in Newark calls itself the Nova Caesarea chapter).

The vagaries of history are evident in accounts of other possible names for New Jersey and, interestingly, how New Jersey might have been given instead as a name for a minor island off the coast of Virginia by no less than Sir George Carteret. Charles II gave the island off the Virginia coast to Carteret, who intended to colonize it and call it New Jersey. (Recall that Carteret was native to the Isle of Jersey.) However, the expeditionary force that Carteret sent to seize and colonize the island off Virginia was captured by Cromwellian forces who opposed Charles II (McCormick 1964, 18). So no island named New Jersey off Virginia's coast.

Although the Virginia island anecdote is an interesting historical footnote, other "might-have-been" names for the state of New Jersey are more significant and telling in the march of history.

Scheyichbi or Lenapehoking

The original inhabitants of what was to become the state of New Jersey were Native Americans who had lived there for millennia. They called themselves Lenni-Lenape ("Original People") and were later referred to by Europeans as Delaware Indians (after the Native American–inhabited Delaware Bay and River, geographies themselves named by the English in 1610 after Virginia's first governor, Lord de la Warre). The Lenni-Lenape (who, in fact, inhabited areas far broader than the Delaware watershed) were part of the larger Eastern Algonquin Indian Confederacy. They termed the New Jersey area Scheyichbi, "Land of the Shell Wampum" or "Land Bordering the Ocean" (Snyder 1969, 1). Others say the Delaware Indian term for the area was Lenapehoking, "Land of the Lenape" (Connolly 2018; Kraft 1986, xi). So, under an alternate history, New Jersey might have been called Scheyichbi or Lenapehoking.

In fact, many places in New Jersey, over two hundred according to one study (Becker 1964), kept their Native American names or derivatives, such as the communities of Absecon, Hackensack, Passaic, and Weehawken and such New Jersey mountains and lakes as Ramapo, Watchung, and Hopatcong (Cunningham 1966, 25). The city of Perth Amboy combines antecedents: the Native American name for the site, "Ambo" (native for "point"), with the English Earl of Perth who was one of the New Jersey proprietors (Randall 1975, 8; S. Smith 1890, 489). (Indian antecedents for today's place names apply elsewhere as well, such as the Lenape term for a long trail through Manhattan—Wickquasgeck, which was transliterated by the Dutch to "Bredeweg" and later morphed into "Broadway"; Connolly 2018.) Sadly, these place names endured for longer than the Lenni-Lenape people; they and their kin were largely obliterated by disease, starvation, warfare, and other harmful intrusions by the European colonists and were dispersed in a far-ranging geographical diaspora (Lurie and Veit 2012, 26–27). (The historical-to-current Native American presence and population in New Jersey is described in more detail in this book's chapter 4.)

What else might New Jersey been called? We present the illustrative list below, which reflects the vagaries of history and the many peoples and forces that coveted the Garden State (and nearby areas).

New Albion

This refers to a large 1634 grant of land in the New World, including what would have become New Jersey, that was given by Charles I to Sir Edward Plowden, scion of an ancient Saxon family (F. Lee 1902, 75). Although Plowden visited Delaware settlements in 1642, New Albion was never realized (McCormick 1964, 15; Snyder 1969, 6). (He also had his eye on settling Long Island, which he envisioned would be called Isle Plowden; F. Lee 1902, 75.) Plowden had a fanciful imagination (he dreamed New Albion would attract noble English knights who would convert Indian kings to their fold) and even touted a fanciful publication titled *Description of the Province of New Albion* upon his return to England (McCormick 1964, 15). New Albion was stillborn by 1650 (Snyder 1969, 6).

New Sweden

As noted earlier, settlers from Swedish domains (including inhabitants from Finland and the Low Countries) arrived on both sides of the Delaware River (in what became the states of Delaware, New Jersey, and Pennsylvania) starting in the early to mid-1600s (Hoffecker et al. 1995; F. Lee 1902, 85–101). To illustrate, on the east side of the Delaware, Burlington Island was settled by Swedes in 1626 (Wacker 1975, 122) and Fort Elfborg (near today's Salem) and Swedesboro (named the same today) were settled in the 1640s. Other Swedish settlements (and their approximate origin dates) included New Stockholm (1670s), Helms Cove (1676), and Repaupo (1684) (Wilson et al. 1950, 16). A history of this early Swedish presence identified settlements "from Gloucester County along the river and bay coast into Burlington, Cumberland, Salem, and Cape May Counties" (Hansen 1932, 392). New Sweden was sparsely populated with only a total of ninety adult males as of 1664 (Wacker 1975, 123–124). This was not for lack of territorial ambition—the "Swedes sought to extend their control up the [Delaware] valley as far as present-day Trenton" (McCormick 1964, 12–13). However, this same area had been claimed by the Dutch, and in 1655 a Dutch military force, with seven armed ships carrying four hundred soldiers and sailors, led by Peter Stuyvesant (of New Amsterdam), forced the Swedes, who could muster only seventy-four soldiers and armed farmers, to surrender their claims (Bailyn 2012, 296; McCormick 1964, 13). Yet the Swedish (and Finnish) legacy would remain in southwestern New Jersey and beyond, not only in the area's town names, such as Swedesboro, but in the form of the Scandinavian-inspired log cabin and rail fence construction found in New Jersey and more broadly on the America frontier (Lurie and Veit 2012, 35).

New Amsterdam or New Netherlands

Sailing for the Dutch, the Briton Henry Hudson sailed through Newark Bay and other areas in 1609 and claimed the region as New Netherlands. If the Dutch had not surrendered to the British in 1664, then the land that would form current New Jersey might have been just a portion of the larger Dutch settlement in the region and named as such.

New York

For many years in the eighteenth century, New Jersey shared a royal governor with New York. This overarching arrangement ended in 1738 with the appointment of the first New Jersey royal governor (Lewis Morris). For many years, the New York royal governor claimed only he had the right to both tax and govern on the west side of the Hudson River, especially in East Jersey (McCormick 1964, 28, 34). (Recall the earlier described trial of New Jersey governor Philip Carteret on that basis.) The colony of New York coveted the fertile lands of New Jersey, schemed to further the economic interests of the residents on the east side of the Hudson River (e.g., "Officials of the colony of New York sought to prevent the development of ports in neighboring New Jersey before 1700"; Lurie 2010, 45), and may have in time simply annexed New Jersey to an expanded New York colony. And in fact, New Jersey was absorbed in the "Dominion of

New England" (which included New York) between 1688 and 1692. (A footnote to history: the local English sometimes referred to New Jersey as "Albania"; Klett 2014, 3.)

East and West Jersey

As the states of Virginia and West Virginia were during the Civil War, the current state of New Jersey might have been permanently divided into East and West. Between 1676 and 1702, proprietary New Jersey consisted of East Jersey (oriented toward Hudson River) and West Jersey (oriented toward Delaware River). The exact boundary between East and West Jersey changed over time and was often hotly disputed (Snyder 1969, 8–9). Roughly, the boundary between East and West Jersey ran from Egg Harbor in the southeast to the Delaware River in the far northwest. East Jersey, comprising about 3,000 square miles, was considerably smaller than West Jersey (about 4,600 square miles and with full possession of the Delaware River's eastern bank; Craven 1964, 62; A. Taylor 2001, 264). (See appendix A for maps of New Jersey over the centuries including the East and West Jersey demarcation.) East and West Jersey were more than just a geographic or mapmaker's divide, for as noted by Wacker (1975, 158), "a major cultural divide in New Jersey was between East Jersey and West Jersey, a cleavage that persisted well beyond the colonial and early national periods."[7] Walter De Angelo (2007, 20) summarized that in the colonial era, "East and West Jersey were quite different," with the former tending to have "larger plantations (often slave-holding)" as opposed to the latter area's "smaller family farms." These differences (along with others) underlie the East Jersey–West Jersey variations in colonial racial composition and slavery's prevalence, discussed later in this chapter.

Pennsylvania

This a mite or more fanciful as a historical "might-have-been." Although first the colony and later the state of Pennsylvania is his actual namesake, William Penn had an early and important association in New Jersey. In brief, after original proprietor Sir John Berkeley sold his rights to Quakers John Fenwick and Edward Byllynge in 1674, the latter went bankrupt and William Penn and several others, seeking a haven for Quakers, secured Byllynge's rights for £3,400 (Myers 1945, 51). Penn and two hundred other Quakers arrived in West New Jersey in 1677; Penn himself established a 12,000-acre estate near today's Salem. Penn helped write and signed the 1677 "Laws, Concessions, and Agreements" (a combination colony constitution and bill of rights), which among other clauses granted religious freedom and guaranteed trial by jury (Wilson et al. 1950, 17). Not long afterward, after the death of Sir George Carteret in 1689, Penn and others secured the rights to East Jersey as well—in other words, now controlling the entire colony, both West and East. Had he remained in New Jersey, Penn would likely have been an influential figure, possibly even earning the area's naming rights and perhaps strengthening the state's Quaker legacy (Moretta 2007). In fact, however, Penn's interest shifted to the west of New Jersey to the area that would become known as Pennsylvania because "just two months after obtaining rights to East Jersey, he transferred his interest in the two Jerseys to other Quakers" (Doak and McConville 2005, 47).

A further reflection of the tumult of New Jersey's early history is manifest in its changing and multiple capital cities. Elizabethtown (named after the wife of Sir George Carteret, later shortened to Elizabeth), settled in the 1660s, was declared the colony's first capital in 1668. However, shortly after the division of the then-single proprietorship into East Jersey and West Jersey (in 1676), Perth Amboy became East Jersey's capital (in 1683) and Burlington (founded 1677) was named West Jersey's capital in 1681 (J. Walton 2010, 1). Even though the dual proprietorships were joined into a single Crown Colony in 1702, the two capitals were inefficiently retained until the Revolutionary War. During the hostilities, Princeton served as a de facto capital; it was not until 1790 that Trenton claimed the mantle as the new state's final capital city.[8]

Even though New Jersey's early colonial days were indeed tumultuous, like a teenager is, it simultaneously held many virtues. Long before contemporary New Jersey license plates were emblazoned with the moniker Garden State, a historian wrote, "By the time of the Revolution, New Jersey was the admiration of all who saw it. A English nobleman found it verdant and beautiful . . . pleasant, open, and well cultivated . . . the garden of America" (Leiby 1965, 1). In a similar vein, a Swiss botanist, Peter Kalm, visiting eighteenth-century New Jersey, spoke admiringly of the state's rich soil[9]—yielding corn "eight feet high, more or less," and unlike in Sweden, "every countrymen had an orchard full of peach trees" (quoted in Cunningham 1966, 79).

How many people lived in this colonial-era New Jersey "garden" and what were their demographic characteristics? With this snapshot of the early New Jersey history, we have the context within which to consider the people of New Jersey's early years.

New Jersey and All Colonies Colonial Population Estimates

An 1887 article in the *Report of the Council of the American Antiquarian Society* bemoaned the dearth of "systematic collection . . . of trustworthy population statistics [for] America under the colonial regime" (Dexter 1887). This dearth would end in time, for the subject was too important to neglect.

An exemplary 1932 feat of scholarship compiled all extant population enumerations for each of the American colonies before the 1790 national census as well as the numerous estimated population totals for all the colonies (Greene and Harrington 1932). Table 2.1 presents these estimates for New Jersey and all the colonies from the 1600s to the first federal census in 1790. It is readily apparent how varied and unlikely some of these figures are, a reflection of the many

Table 2.1
Varying Estimates of the Population of New Jersey and Total All Colonies from European Settlement through the 1790 Census

Year	New Jersey Colony	All Colonies
1625		1,980[a]
1641		50,000[b]
1663		200,000[c]
1665	137[d]	
1673	469[e]	
1682	3,450	
1688	10,000	200,000
1700		250,000
1701	15,000	
1702	8,000	270,000[f]
1715	22,500	434,600
1726	32,442	
1727		502,000[f]
1738	47,369	
1745	61,383	
1747	70,000	
1749	60,000	1,046,000
1750	50,000	1,260,000
1754	81,500	1,485,634[g]
1755	60,000	1,471,000[f]
1758	60,000	
	70,000–80,000	
1759	102,000	
1760	70,000	1,695,000
1765	80,000	2,240,000
1766	131,000	
1770	122,806	2,312,000
1773	168,000	
	120,000	2,141,307
1774		2,600,000
	130,000[b]	3,026,678[b]
1775	130,000	2,418,000
1776	150,000[b]	
1780	215,000	
1782	175,000[g]	
1783	130,000	2,389,300
1784	140,435	
1786	150,000	3,102,670
1787	138,000	2,776,000
1790 (Census)	184,139	3,929,214

SOURCE: Greene and Harrington 1932, 3–8 and 105–108.
NOTES: Two or more population counts in same year reflect multiple discrete estimates for that year. Unless otherwise indicated, all numbers refer to "people," "inhabitants," or "population."
[a]Colonists; [b]English inhabitants ("Mannen"); [c]English; [d]Males; [e]Men; [f]White inhabitants; [g]Souls; [h]Congressional estimate

uncertainties of this early era's population enumerations mentioned earlier in this chapter. To illustrate, for the New Jersey colony, a 1701 count estimated 15,000 persons while a year later the estimate was 8,000. In a parallel fashion, there was a 1747 New Jersey colony population estimate of 70,000 as against 60,000 in 1749; 81,500 in 1754 versus 60,000 in 1755; 102,000 in 1759 as against 70,000 in 1760. A nascent national congress estimated New Jersey's colonial population in 1776 at 150,000 but only four years later produced a much higher estimate of 215,000. Whereas a 1787 population estimate for New Jersey was 138,000, that count was clearly questionable in light of the 1790 federal census for New Jersey (the first national enumeration), which was conducted in a more rigorous fashion, indicating a much higher statewide head count of 184,139. The tremendous unevenness and wide ranges for New Jersey's population are paralleled by similar variations at the national level for the total colonies' population presented in table 2.1 (e.g., a 3.0 million national population estimate in 1774 versus 2.4 million in 1775, and a 2.8 million population estimate in 1787 versus the 1790 federal national census count of 3.9 million). The quick takeaway from table 2.1 is lots of population estimates with questionable empirical grounding.

Yet, population estimates for this early historical period are not as unreliable as it at first appears. Although there are many diverse estimates as compiled by Evarts Greene and Virginia Harrington in 1932 and summarized in table 2.1, over time these many counts have coalesced to a smaller set of generally accepted best estimates. We report here on two such estimates, the first conducted in 1909 under the supervision of William Rossiter and the second nearly a century later by John McCusker (2006b). Their work is found in two notable publications that are often referred by demographers: *A Century of Population Growth from the First Census of the United States to the Twelfth, 1790–1900* (Rossiter 1909) and "Colonial Statistics" (McCusker 2006a) contained in the larger and seminal *Historical Statistics of the United States, Millennial Edition* (Carter et al. 2006). Rossiter (then–chief clerk of the U.S. Census Bureau) and McCusker (a distinguished professor of American history and economics) drew on their own considerable expertise as well as the research of others (McCusker 1971, 1981, 2001; McCusker and Menard 1991). For example, McCusker's (2006b) colonial-era population estimates by colony and area cite scores of prior compilations on the subject, including that of Rossiter (1909), this chapter's previously referenced Greene and Harrington (1932), and much other research by Stella Sutherland (1966), among others. (Rossiter's 1909 study was also important in identifying the national stocks of the United States and New Jersey population in 1790, a topic referred to later this chapter.)

The Rossiter and McCusker population figures for both New Jersey and all the colonies (hereafter "all-colony") for the years from settlement in the early 1600s to the first 1790 federal census are summarized in table 2.2. Although there are differences in the Rossiter (1909) versus McCusker (2006b) population estimates for any given point in time, these differences are much narrower in

Table 2.2
All Colonies and New Jersey: Estimated Population from the Colonial Era to the 1790 Census

Year	All Colonies		New Jersey		New Jersey
	Rossiter Estimate	McCusker Estimate	Rossiter Estimate	McCusker Estimate	Colony Census
1610	210	350			
1620	2,499	2,302			
1630	5,700	4,646			
1640	27,947	26,634			
1650	51,700	50,368			
1660	84,800	75,058			
1670	114,500	111,935	2,500	1,000	
1680	155,600	151,507	6,000	3,400	
1690	213,500	210,372	9,000	8,000	
1700	275,000	251,444	14,000	14,010	
1710	357,500	327,360	20,000	19,872	
1720	474,388	467,465	26,000	29,818	
1726					32,442
1730	654,950	636,045	37,000	37,510	
1737					46,676
1740	899,000	912,742	52,000	51,373	
1745					61,403
1750	1,207,000	1,186,408	66,000	71,393	
1760	1,610,000	1,593,625	91,000	93,813	
1770	2,205,000	2,165,076	110,000	117,431	
1772					71,025 (West Jersey only)
1780	2,781,000	2,797,854	137,000	139,627	
1784					149,435
1790 Census	3,929,214	3,929,214	184,139	184,139	

SOURCES: McCusker 2006a, 5-651; Rossiter 1909, 9; New Jersey Colony Census from Wacker 1975, 413–416 and table A.1; 1790 decennial census.
NOTE: For 1770 and 1780, the McCusker-indicated population for Florida (17,000 in 1770 and 15,000 in 1780) is included in the all-colony population.

magnitude than the often widely divergent multiple estimates compiled by Greene and Harrington (1932). For example, Rossiter estimated an all-colony total population of 5,700 in 1630, as against a not-so-distant 4,646 by McCusker for that same year. Their 1650 all-colony population estimates were again similar: 51,700 (Rossiter) and 50,368 (McCusker). We see a same order-of-magnitude correspondence in the all-colony population tallies in later years; for example, in 1700, 275,000 (Rossiter) and 251,444 (McCusker) and 1750, 1,207,000 (Rossiter) and 1,186,408 (McCusker). By 1790, the first federal census, the total national population stood at 3,929,214. The country was clearly growing rapidly, a point to which we return shortly.

Similarly, for New Jersey there is an order-of-magnitude correspondence between population estimates given by Rossiter and McCusker and this colony, like its colonial peers, grew rapidly in its formative years. The first population estimates they present for New Jersey date to 1670: Rossiter claimed 2,500 persons and McCusker 1,000. English settlement in other areas of what was to become the United States started considerably earlier, at the dawn of the seventeenth century, in Jamestown, Virginia, in 1607 and Plymouth, Massachusetts, in 1620. Given this head start, the total colonial population in 1670 was about 110,000–115,000 persons as against only a few thousand persons in New Jersey at this date. The mere trace habitation of New Jersey would not last long, however, as this colony realized rapid growth. In 1700, New Jersey was home to about 14,000 persons (Rossiter—14,000; McCusker—14,010); by 1750, New Jersey claimed about 66,000–70,000 residents (Rossiter—66,000; McCusker—71,393). Just forty years later, the 1790 federal census population count for New Jersey stood at a much larger 184,139.

These total population tallies for both all the colonies and for New Jersey over the seventeenth and eighteenth centuries command notice for their rapidity of growth. That growth is explicitly expressed in table 2.3, which shows both the absolute and percentage change in population by decade. As in table 2.2, table 2.3 draws from both the Rossiter and McCusker population estimates; however, the narrative summary below on the population changes does not differentiate between the two because the results are roughly parallel.

At the all-colony level, the absolute population increment by decade over the eighteenth century numbered in the low thousands in the 1610s and 1620s, grew to a five-figure increment by decade in the 1630s to 1700s, rose to an increasingly larger six-figure population gain in the 1710s to 1770s, and then scaled upward to a seven-figure increment (about 1.1 million person gain) just in the 1780s. The New Jersey colony exhibits a similar pattern of population change, albeit at an understandably lower absolute magnitude than the more encompassing all-colony aggregate. New Jersey's absolute population increment by decade numbered in the low thousands in the decades from the 1670s through 1710s, and climbed to an increasingly larger five figures in the decades from the 1720s through the 1780s (see table 2.3 for details).

Table 2.3 also shows the percentage population gains by decade over the seventeenth and eighteenth centuries for both all the colonies and then separately for New Jersey. In the time series for both geographical areas, there were huge percentage increases in the earliest decades shown because the starting population base was so modest. After stabilization, so to speak, the decade-by-decade population percentage increases understandably decline yet are still very significant. The percentage decade increase in the all-colony population from 1700 through 1790 (the date of the first federal census) ranged mostly between about

Table 2.3
All Colonies and New Jersey: Estimated Decennial Population Increase from Colonial Era to the 1790 Census

| Decade | Decennial Population Increase (No.) | | | | Decennial Population Increase (%) | | | |
| | All Colonies | | New Jersey | | All Colonies | | New Jersey | |
	Rossiter	McCusker	Rossiter	McCusker	Rossiter	McCusker	Rossiter	McCusker
1610–1620	2,289	1,952			1,090.0	557.7		
1620–1630	3,201	2,344			128.1	101.8		
1630–1640	22,247	21,988			390.3	473.3		
1640–1650	23,753	23,734			85.0	89.1		
1650–1660	33,100	24,690			64.0	49.0		
1660–1670	29,700	36,877			35.0	49.1		
1670–1680	41,100	39,572	3,500	2,400	35.9	26.1	140.0	240.0
1680–1690	57,900	58,865	3,000	4,600	37.2	38.9	50.0	135.3
1690–1700	61,500	41,072	5,000	6,010	28.8	19.5	55.6	75.1
1700–1710	82,500	75,916	6,000	5,862	30.0	30.2	42.9	41.8
1710–1720	116,888	140,105	6,000	9,946	32.7	42.8	30.0	50.1
1720–1730	180,562	168,580	11,000	7,692	38.1	36.1	42.3	25.8
1730–1740	244,050	276,697	15,000	13,863	37.3	43.5	40.5	37.0
1740–1750	308,000	273,666	14,000	20,020	34.3	30.0	26.9	39.0
1750–1760	403,000	407,217	25,000	22,420	33.4	34.3	37.9	31.4
1760–1770	595,000	571,451	19,000	23,618	37.0	35.9	20.9	25.2
1770–1780	576,000	632,778	27,000	22,196	26.1	29.2	24.5	18.9
1780–1790	1,148,214	1,131,360	47,139	44,512	41.3	40.5	34.4	31.9

SOURCES: McCusker 2006a, 5–651; Rossiter 1909, 9; New Jersey Colony Census from Wacker 1975, 413–416 and table A.1; 1790 decennial census.

30–40 percent *every ten years*, a Malthusian pace. We also call specific attention to a 41 percent gain in the national all-colony population in the 1780–1790 period, the highest decade population increase ever realized by the United States in the almost twenty-five decades of its entire existence to date. Had the United States subsequent to 1790 grown at the torrid 41 percent decade increase it experienced between 1780 and 1790, then its 2019 population would amount to about 48,000 trillion, trillion, trillion—many multiples the actual 2019 national population of 0.3 trillion (329 million). Also of note, the 41 percent national population jump of the decade of the 1780s was noticeably higher than the below 30 percent national population gain (Rossiter 26.1 percent; McCusker 29.2 percent) of the previous decade, one of the more modest decade national population increments on a relative basis of the entire eighteenth century (see table 2.3 for details).

The very different national population increments for the decade of the 1770s (slower growth) versus that of the decade of the 1780s (faster growth) is likely linked to the colonies' quest for independence from Great Britain.[10] The American Revolutionary War was fought from 1775 to 1783, and there were earlier hostilities with the Mother Country (e.g., the Boston Tea Party in 1773). In short, most of the decade of the 1770s was a period of tension and worse that dampened population increase in the colonies. By contrast, much of the decade of the 1780s was past that imbroglio with England and as such the newly independent country experienced a postwar boom (Gemery 2000, 151), reflected by stellar national population growth in the 1780s. (The United States would experience subsequent postwar population gains later in its history after the Civil War and World Wars I and II, population changes noted later in chapter 3.)

What about New Jersey's decade-by-decade percentage population change in the eighteenth century? As detailed in table 2.3, the ten-year-cycle population changes described above for the nation were for the most part paralleled in New Jersey. For most of the decades of this period, New Jersey's population grew by a sizzling approximate 20–40 percent every ten years. As in the nation, there was a dampening of decade-cycle population growth in New Jersey as friction with England grew (in the 1760s and 1770s) and there was some rebound of population growth in the decade that followed in the 1780s, perhaps again due to the postwar peace dividend.

Thus far, we have focused on the population of the two geographies—New Jersey and all the colonies that would become the United States in their respective early histories. We can delve further by expanding our lens to consider the population dynamic of this early colonial era by the tripartite regions settled at that time—namely, the New England colonies (Connecticut, Maine, Massachusetts, New Hampshire, Rhode Island, and Vermont), middle colonies (Delaware, New Jersey, New York, and Pennsylvania), and southern colonies (Georgia, Kentucky, Maryland [and District of Columbia], North Carolina, South Carolina, Tennessee, and Virginia), as well as by the individual constituent colonies of these regions. To better understand the New Jersey colonial-era context, with respect to population magnitude and change, we examine the population dynamic of colonial New Jersey set in larger perspective against the population dynamic occurring by colonial region (New England, middle, and southern colonies) as well as individual colonies. We focus on the population for all of these areas as of the eighteenth century alone, because it is a more "stabilized" population period as opposed to the early formative seventeenth century (recall New Jersey's minuscule population in the seventeenth century). Over the eighteenth century, we examine population for all the areas decade by decade from 1700 through the first federal census in 1790. For brevity's sake, the population analysis for the eighteenth century refers only to the McCusker (2006b) population tallies, which were compiled much more recently than the much earlier Rossiter (1909) estimates. Recall as well there were only minor differences between the Rossiter and McCusker colonial population estimates.

The eighteenth-century population analysis is presented in tables 2.4–2.6. To briefly overview, table 2.4 shows the numerical population (in thousands) for individual colonies and regions, table 2.5 shows the colony and regional population percentage distribution, and table 2.6 quantifies the decennial population changes in percentage terms, both by individual decade and for the full 1700–1790 period.

This series of tables shows various population profiles and changes over time. For example, in 1700, somewhat more than one-third (36.8 percent) of the total colonial population lived in New England, slightly over four-tenths (41.8 percent) dwelled in southern colonies, and about one-fifth (21.3 percent) were found in the middle colonies of which New Jersey was a member (table 2.5). Concerning the population contribution to each of the regions, Massachusetts dominated New England, Virginia dominated the South, but within the middle colonies there was no such population dominance by any one colony, albeit New York and Pennsylvania were in the lead, followed by New Jersey and distantly by Delaware.

Over the eighteenth century, New England's share of the total population fell to about one-quarter (25.7 percent) in 1790. (Regional shift in the American population thus started early in the era of settlement and continued in the centuries that followed, as traced in this book's chapter 3 and elsewhere.) Massachusetts's capture of the total colonial population declined especially significantly from about one-fifth (22.2 percent) in 1700 to approximately one-tenth (9.6 percent) by 1790. (This is explained in part by the formation of Maine from what had been part of Massachusetts in this period.) Connecticut's population share of the colonies' total was almost halved over this period (i.e., 10.3 percent in 1700 versus 6.1 percent in 1790). This drop is understandable as these early settled colonies soon lost their dominance as the range of settlements expanded. Related and in contrast, the middle colonies increased their share of the total colonial population from about one-fifth (21.3 percent) in 1700 to about one-quarter (25.9 percent)

Table 2.4

National, Individual Colony, and Regional Distribution of Population (Persons in 000s), 1700–1790

Colony/Region	1700	1710	1720	1730	1740	1750	1760	1770	1780	1790
New England Colonies										
Maine							20.0	31.3	49.1	96.5
New Hampshire	5.0	5.7	9.4	10.8	23.2	27.5	39.1	62.4	87.8	141.9
Vermont								10.0	47.5	85.4
Massachusetts	55.9	62.4	91.0	114.1	151.6	188.0	202.6	235.3	268.6	378.8
Rhode Island	5.9	7.6	11.7	17.0	25.3	33.2	45.5	58.2	52.9	68.8
Connecticut	26.9	39.5	58.8	75.5	89.6	111.3	142.5	183.9	206.7	237.9
New England Subtotal	92.8	115.1	170.9	217.4	289.7	360.0	449.6	581.0	712.8	1,009.4
Middle Colonies										
New York	19.1	21.6	36.9	48.6	63.7	76.7	117.1	162.9	210.5	340.1
New Jersey	14.0	19.9	29.8	37.5	51.4	71.4	93.8	117.4	139.6	184.1
Pennsylvania	18.0	24.5	31.0	51.7	85.6	119.7	183.7	240.1	327.3	434.4
Delaware	2.5	3.6	5.4	9.2	19.9	28.7	33.3	35.5	45.4	59.1
Middle States Subtotal	53.5	69.6	103.1	147.0	220.5	296.5	427.9	555.9	722.9	1,017.7
Southern Colonies										
Maryland	29.6	42.7	66.1	91.1	116.1	141.1	162.3	202.6	248.0	319.7
Virginia	58.6	74.5	87.8	120.6	180.4	236.7	339.7	447.0	538.0	747.6
North Carolina	10.7	15.1	21.3	30.0	51.8	73.0	110.4	197.2	270.1	393.8
South Carolina	6.3	10.3	18.3	30.0	54.2	74.0	94.1	124.2	180.0	249.1
Georgia						5.2	9.6	23.4	56.1	82.5
Kentucky								15.7	45.0	73.7
Tennessee								1.0	10.0	35.7
Southern States Subtotal	105.1	142.7	193.5	271.7	402.5	529.9	716.1	1,011.1	1,347.2	1,902.1
Total All Colonies	251.4	327.4	467.5	636.0	912.7	1,186.4	1,593.6	2,148.1	2,782.9	3,929.2

SOURCES: McCusker 2006a, 5-651; 1790 decennial census.

NOTE: For 1770 and 1780, the McCusker-indicated population for Florida (17,000 in 1770 and 15,000 in 1780) is not added to the total all-colony population. Of further note, Maine in the colonial era was part of Massachusetts and Vermont was part of New York.

Table 2.5

National, Individual Colony, and Regional Distribution of Population (Percentages), 1700–1790

Colony/Region	1700	1710	1720	1730	1740	1750	1760	1770	1780	1790	Average 1700–1790
New England Colonies											
Maine							1.3	1.5	1.8	2.5	1.7
New Hampshire	2.0	1.7	2.0	1.7	2.5	2.3	2.5	2.9	3.2	3.6	2.4
Vermont								0.5	1.7	2.2	1.5
Massachusetts	22.2	19.1	19.5	17.9	16.6	15.8	12.7	11.0	9.7	9.6	15.4
Rhode Island	2.3	2.3	2.5	2.7	2.8	2.8	2.9	2.7	1.9	1.8	2.5
Connecticut	10.3	12.1	12.6	11.9	9.8	9.4	8.9	8.6	7.4	6.1	9.7
New England Subtotal	36.8	35.2	36.6	34.2	31.7	30.3	28.2	27.0	25.6	25.7	31.1
Middle Colonies											
New York	7.6	6.6	7.9	7.6	7.0	6.5	7.4	7.6	7.6	8.7	7.4
New Jersey	5.6	6.1	6.4	5.9	5.6	6.0	5.9	5.5	5.0	4.7	5.7
Pennsylvania	7.1	7.5	6.6	8.1	9.4	10.1	11.5	11.2	11.8	11.1	9.4
Delaware	1.0	1.1	1.2	1.4	2.2	2.4	2.1	1.7	1.6	1.5	1.6
Middle States Subtotal	21.3	21.3	22.1	23.1	24.2	25.0	26.9	25.9	26.0	25.9	24.1
Southern Colonies											
Maryland	11.8	13.1	14.1	14.3	12.7	11.9	10.2	9.4	8.9	8.1	11.5
Virginia	23.2	22.8	18.8	19.0	19.8	19.9	21.3	20.8	19.3	19.0	20.4
North Carolina	4.3	4.6	4.6	4.7	5.7	6.2	6.9	9.2	9.7	10.0	6.6
South Carolina	2.5	3.1	3.9	4.7	5.9	6.2	5.9	5.8	6.5	6.3	5.1
Georgia						0.4	0.6	1.1	2.0	2.1	1.2
Kentucky								0.7	1.6	1.9	1.4
Tennessee								0.0	0.4	0.9	0.4
Southern States Subtotal	41.8	43.6	41.4	42.7	44.1	44.7	44.9	47.1	48.4	48.4	44.7
Total All Colonies	100.0	100.0	100.0	100.0	100.0	100.0	100.0	100.0	100.0	100.0	100.0

SOURCES: McCusker 2006a, 5-651: 1790 decennial census.

Table 2.6

National, Individual Colony, and Regional Decennial Percentage Increase in Population, 1700–1790

Colony/Region	1700–10	1710–20	1720–30	1730–40	1740–50	1750–60	1760–70	1770–80	1780–90	Average 1700–1790
New England Colonies										
Maine			15	116	18	NA	56	57	96	70
New Hampshire	15	65				42	60	41	62	48
Vermont							NA	376	79	228
Massachusetts	12	46	25	33	24	8	16	14	41	24
Rhode Island	28	54	45	49	31	37	28	–9	30	33
Connecticut	52	49	28	19	24	28	29	12	15	29
New England Subtotal	24	48	27	33	24	25	29	23	42	31
Middle Colonies										
New York	13	71	32	31	20	53	39	29	62	39
New Jersey	42	50	26	37	39	31	25	19	32	33
Pennsylvania	36	27	67	66	40	54	31	36	33	43
Delaware	48	48	70	117	44	16	7	28	30	45
Middle States Subtotal	30	48	43	50	34	44	30	30	41	39
Southern Colonies										
Maryland	44	55	38	27	22	15	25	22	29	31
Virginia	27	18	37	50	31	44	32	20	39	33
North Carolina	41	41	41	73	41	51	79	37	46	50
South Carolina	65	78	64	81	37	27	32	45	38	52
Georgia						84	144	140	47	104
Kentucky								187	64	125
Tennessee								900	257	578
Southern States Subtotal	36	36	40	48	32	35	41	33	41	38
Total All Colonies	30	43	36	44	30	34	35	30	41	36

SOURCES: McCusker 2006a, 5-651; 1790 decennial census.
NA = Not Applicable.

by 1790. Southern colonies' capture of the total population also gained from 41.8 percent in 1700 to 48.4 percent in 1790.

Within the middle colonies, New York and Pennsylvania were the big gainers in national population capture (e.g., 7.1 percent of the total colonial population resided in Pennsylvania in 1700 and 11.1 percent by 1790, and New York's share rose somewhat from 7.6 percent in 1700 to 8.7 percent by 1790), while New Jersey captured a near constant roughly 5–6 percent of all residents in the colonies throughout the decades of the 1700s. (We will see later in this book the lingering population competition among New Jersey, New York, and Pennsylvania.) Of the southern colonies, the bellwether pioneer colony of Virginia lost national population share (declining from 23.2 percent in 1700 to 19.0 percent in 1790), in contrast to the burgeoning population growth of the newer settled North Carolina and South Carolina (see table 2.5).

There are understandably some parallel trends concerning the average decade percentage population increase over the 1700s by region and for individual colonies (table 2.6). As against a significant average all-colony population gain by decade of 36 percent over the eighteenth century, New England lagged with an average decade 31 percent gain over this time span, with Massachusetts being especially slow-growing (average 24 percent gain). The middle colonies region realized a torrid average decade population increase of 39 percent, driven in large part by the extremely high average decade growth over the eighteenth century in both Pennsylvania (43 percent) and New York (39 percent); New Jersey's average 33 percent decade growth over the 1700s just about mirrored the average for all the colonies (36 percent) over this time period. The average decade growth of the southern colonies over the 1700s was significant as well, averaging 38 percent every ten years, with the relatively more recently settled North Carolina (average 50 percent decade gain) and South Carolina (average 52 percent decade gain) being the pacesetters, while Virginia's growth abated somewhat but still remained high (average 33 percent decade gain) over the eighteenth century.

Although the all-colony average decade population growth over 1700 through 1790 averaged 36 percent, not surprisingly there was some unevenness over this period, with relatively lower ten-year-span population increases in some of the decades, such as the 1700s, 1740s, and 1770s (30 percent in all three decades), and higher in other decades, most notably the 1780s (41 percent). Some of this unevenness was related, as noted earlier, to the vagaries of the colonies' relations with England; it was thus understandable that population growth overall in all the colonies would slow in the 1770s (30 percent), with the Revolutionary War under way, followed by a population spurt in the 1780s (41 percent) when hostilities ended and.the newly free country experienced a postwar boom. All regions experienced slower growth in the wartime decade of the 1770s (e.g., New England's growth dropped to 23 percent and the middle colonies to 30 percent) with some rebound in the decade of the 1780s when hostilities ceased (e.g., New

England's population grew by 42 percent in that decade and the middle colonies by a similar 41 percent).

As elsewhere in the new country, the colony of New Jersey experienced some uneven decade-by-decade population growth in the eighteenth century. As against a 1700-through-1790 decade average 33 percent population gain for this colony, New Jersey's population growth was considerably greater in some early "growth-spurt" decades of this period (gaining 40–50 percent per decade in the 1700s and 1710s) and fell to a low of 19 percent population gain in the decade of the 1770s. (The colony of New Jersey experienced a disproportionate share of the Revolutionary War's armed conflicts.) Unlike the country as a whole, however, New Jersey interestingly did not experience as large a post–Revolutionary War population boom in the 1780s, for its growth over this 1780s decade (32 percent) was essentially the same as its decade average for the full 1700 through 1790 period (33 percent). Perhaps this was due in part to outsized 1780s decade population growth in New Jersey's neighboring states, such as that experienced by New York (62 percent population increment in the 1780s).

More broadly, it warrants mentioning that New Jersey in the sixteenth and seventeenth centuries routinely attracted settlers moving from other colonies.

Immediately after the establishment of English rule, New Englanders began to settle in the present-day counties of Essex, Union, Middlesex, and Monmouth, while English Quakers settled in the Southern part of the State. Migrating from settlements in Pennsylvania, Swedes and Finns also moved into the Southern part of the State. Later in the 17th century, the existing Dutch population in Northeastern New Jersey was augmented by Dutch farmers relocated from Long Island to the area of present-day Somerset and Northern Monmouth Counties. At the turn of the 18th century, German and Scots-Irish Pennsylvanians relocated into the Northern part of the State, especially present-day Hunterdon County, and New Englanders settled Cape May as well as other fishing communities. (New Jersey Office of State Planning 1988, 1–2)

What was the lure of New Jersey for people from other colonies? Relatively more plentiful and fertile land and lower taxes in the colony of New Jersey were given as an explanation in 1708 by Edward Hyde, Lord Cornbury (governor of both New York and New Jersey between 1702 and 1708; Bonomi 1998) as luring migrants from King's County in the New York colony (Brooklyn–Long Island area) to beckoning close-by New Jersey: "Many [Husbandman] are Removed lately, especially from King's County on Long Island; And the reasons why they remove are of two kinds: The first is because King's County is but small and full of people.... The land in the Eastern Division of New Jersey is good, and not very far from King's County, there is only a bay to crosse; the other reason that induces them to remove into New Jersey is because there they pay no taxes nor no duties" (Cornbury 1708; cited in Sutherland 1966, 109; and Wacker 1975, 135).

In a similar vein, a 1700 account of why New York colony farmers resettled in New Jersey derisively spoke of high land rents and the difficulty of owning land outright in their former abode ("What man will be such a fool to become a base tenant [in New York]") as opposed to better opportunities in New Jersey ("When for crossing Hudson River, that man can for a song purchase a good freehold in the Jersies") (1700 source cited by Hansen 1932, 371).

To be sure, New Jersey's colonial neighbors had lures of their own with, for example, Lord Cornbury in 1705 observing that rising New Jersey land expenses caused "several people who would settle in New Jersey [to] go over in Pennsylvania and settle there" (quoted in Wacker 1975, 135). In addition, Wacker (1975, 135) describes New Jersey losing potential settlers to neighboring Pennsylvania in the colonial era because of the former's relatively higher taxes. This eighteenth-century lower land, housing (farm), and tax costs lure of Pennsylvania foreshadows later twentieth-century population movement for similar reasons to the Keystone State and more broadly to the Sunbelt, as discussed later in this book's chapter 3 and elsewhere. Even in colonial times, New Jersey sometimes lost population to that era's booming frontier states and regions, the "sunbelts" of that day. In that vein, Governor William Franklin, New Jersey's last royal governor (1763–1776), lamented that people have "quit the colony for Virginia, North Carolina, the Ohio, and the Mississippi" (*New Jersey Archives*, 1st ser. X, 446; cited in Sutherland 1936, 109).

It is appropriate to conclude this section with a "big picture" perspective.[11] The American colonies in the seventeenth and eighteenth centuries, including New Jersey, had remarkable population growth. It is instructive to place that torrid colonial-era population growth in context with the population increases of the Mother Country, England. In the early 1600s (the first permanent English settlement in Virginia was founded in 1607), the total English population was about 4.3 million and it stood at 5.0 million by 1650 (plagues and poor harvests limiting population gains), rose to 5.3 million by 1700, 5.7 million by 1750, and 8.6 million by 1800 (Wells 1992, 89). In other words, England's population over the course of the seventeenth and eighteenth centuries doubled, or a gain of 100 percent. In contrast, the American colonies in the early seventeenth century (Jamestown was founded in 1607) rose from a minuscule about 300 persons to about 50,000 in 1650, 250,000 by 1700, 1.2 million by 1750 (all McCusker 2006b estimates; see table 2.2), 3.9 million by the nation's first census in 1790, and about 5.3 million in 1800. As summarized and put in context by Robert Wells (1992, 90), "By 1800, 5.3 million people lived in the newly established United States, almost as many as lived in England in 1750. Although growth fluctuated from decade to decade, after 1670, the colonial population seems to have come close to Franklin's estimate of doubling every 25 years. The population in 1800 was over twenty times larger than in 1700, and one hundred times that of 1650. Had England grown as a rapidly during the same century and a half, she would have contained half a billion people in 1800." Benjamin Franklin was indeed an astute demographic observer; the English American colonies, New Jersey included, were in fact growing at a rate that would double or yet more rapidly increase their population every twenty-five years, as is evident from table 2.6. An important question is why this high growth rate, especially in contrast to the main population-sending country of England? For that answer, we again return to the astute period observer Benjamin Franklin. In his masterful 1751 essay "Observations concerning the Increase of Mankind, and Peopling of Countries," Franklin credited favorable economic conditions in the American colonies, such as more readily available land (indeed, the population density of Europe in the 1500s was twenty times America's density in the colonial period; Engerman and Margo 2010, 292; McEvedy and Jones 1978), which encouraged early marriage ("Marriages in America are more general and more generally early that in Europe"), and subsequent fecund reproduction ("If in Europe they have but 4 births to marriage, [many of their marriages being late] we may here reckon 8"). In short, Franklin saw the state of the economy and demography in the form of accelerated population growth (with a favorable economy) or population stasis or decline (with a weak economy) as being inexorably intertwined.

In the same vein, the previously cited Swiss botanist Peter Kalm, who traveled to the colony of New Jersey in the eighteenth century, also observed some of this colony's favorable economic forces that fostered fecundity:

> It does not seem difficult to find out why the people multiply here more than in Europe. As soon as a person is old enough, he may marry in these provinces, without any fear of poverty; for there is such a tract of good ground yet uncultivated, that a new-married man can, without difficulty, get a spot of ground, where he may sufficiently subsist with his wife and children. The taxes are very low, and he need not be under any concern of their account. The liberties he enjoys are so great that he considers himself as a prince in his possessions. (Quoted in Cunningham 1966, 79)

More broadly, as McCusker (2006a, 5-639) has observed, "demographic and economic cycles coincided." The English American colonies, New Jersey included, grew rapidly, fostered by favorable land availability and more broadly good economic times; these colonies' per capita income by the time of the American Revolution exceeded that of the Mother Country as well as all other then-existing nations (McCusker 2006a, 5-630).

To be sure, there are continuously reinforcing economic and demographic cycles. Favorable colonial economic conditions did indeed foster rapid population growth, but in turn, the population ascendency helped enhance the economy and so on in repeated cycles. As observed by McCusker and Menard (1991, 9), "The economy of British America grew impressively in the century and one-half before 1775, if only because the population grew so fast." The above-described colonial-era demographic and economic nexus foreshadows later periods of

American history with these same interacting forces. These mutual associations are described later in this book's chapters 3, 12, and elsewhere (the "generations" analysis of chapters 7–10). As there noted, periods of societal economic bounty, such as the post–World War II booming 1950s, begot a subsequent "baby boom," while the hard economic times of the 1930s Depression and more recent mid-2000s Great Recession dampened subsequent births, family size, and population growth.

With these broad demographic and economic forces presented, we turn now to New Jersey's specific colonial censuses and what they show us about the number and profile of people living in this colony over the course of the eighteenth century.

Colonial-Era Census Enumerations in New Jersey

Between 1623 and 1775, there were 124 population censuses in the British colonies in the Americas (68 in North America and 56 in the West Indies; Wells 1975, 14). Of that total, there were five census counts of the New Jersey colony's population in 1726, 1737–1738 (hereafter, this enumeration is more simply dated 1738), 1745, 1772, and 1784. (See Wacker 1975 for an overview of these multiple enumerations and their respective tallies, and this book's appendix A for the tallies.) The 1726, 1738, 1745, and 1784 censuses were colony-wide whereas the 1772 enumeration was for West Jersey only, for as earlier noted, East Jersey balked at counting its residents in that year. All the enumerations were admittedly far from complete in counting all residents: there were likely higher undercounts of New Jersey's women, Blacks, and other minorities. (Contemporary census counts face lingering challenges in this regard; see Cressie 1988; Skerry 2000.) Native Americans, New Jersey's original inhabitants, were almost never included in multiple census efforts in the eighteenth century, reflecting the colonists' larger disregard of the rights, needs, and even more fundamentally, the presence of the area's Lenni-Lenape Indians. (See Wacker 1975, 144–145 for a discussion of how Native Americans and Blacks were treated in New Jersey colonial censuses.) Although New Jersey created the English colonies' first and only Indian reservation, called Brotherton, in 1758 (in today's Shamung Township), treatment of its original Native American inhabitants was the antithesis of "brotherly," and the Lenni-Lenape were largely exterminated in the seventeenth and eighteenth centuries. New Jersey's Native Americans warrant much more than a demographic footnote; accordingly, chapter 4 describes in some detail the Lenni-Lenape/Delaware history and population in New Jersey from the colonial era until contemporary times.

Moving past the demographic limitations of New Jersey's colonial-era censuses, which admittedly were legion, what were the head counts at the various points in time? These New Jersey populations are summarized in table 2.7 and table A.1 in appendix A and amounted to 32,442 in 1726, 46,676 in 1738,

Table 2.7
Population Count and Selected Demographic Profile of New Jersey in Five Colonial-Era State Census Enumerations (1726, 1738, 1745, 1772, and 1784)

	1726	1738	1745	1772	1784
I. Total Population					
Number					
Total Colony	32,442	46,676	61,403		149,435
East Jersey	18,062	25,776	29,472		
West Jersey	14,380	20,900	31,931	71,025	
Percentage					
Total Colony	100.0	100.0	100.0		
East Jersey	55.7	55.2	48.0		
West Jersey	44.3	44.8	52.0	100.0	
II. Racial Profile					
Total Colony					
% White	92.0	91.5	92.5		
% Black	8.0	8.5	7.5		
East Jersey					
% White	89.4	88.1	89.2		
% Black	10.6	11.9	10.8		
West Jersey					
% White	95.4	95.6	95.5	95.3	
% Black	4.6	4.4	4.5	4.7	
III. Gender (Adult Male to Adult Female Ratio)					
White					
Total Colony	1.14	1.08	1.10		
East Jersey	1.09	0.96	1.09		
West Jersey	1.20	1.24	1.11	1.10	
Black					
Total Colony	1.38	1.36			
East Jersey	1.42	1.35			
West Jersey	1.28	1.39		1.33	
IV. Age (% below 16)					
White					
Total Colony	48.6	47.6	49.3		
East Jersey	48.6	49.0	49.4		
West Jersey	48.6	46.1	49.3	49.3	
Black					
Total Colony	41.8	40.8			
East Jersey	42.1	41.2			
West Jersey	41.0	39.6		44.6	
V. Age (% above 16)					
White					
Total Colony	51.4	52.4	50.7		
East Jersey	51.4	51.0	50.6		
West Jersey	51.4	53.9	50.7	50.7	

(continued)

Table 2.7

Population Count and Selected Demographic Profile of New Jersey in Five Colonial-Era State Census Enumerations (1726, 1738, 1745, 1772, and 1784) (continued)

	1726	1738	1745	1772	1784
Black					
Total Colony	58.2	59.2			
East Jersey	57.8	58.8			
West Jersey	59.0	60.4		55.4	
VI. Children per Woman					
White					
Total Colony	2.02	1.90	2.04		
East Jersey	1.98	1.89	2.04		
West Jersey	2.08	1.91	2.04	2.04	
Black					
Total Colony	1.71	1.63			
East Jersey	1.76	1.65			
West Jersey	1.59	1.56		1.88	
VII. Household Size					
West Jersey				6.6	
VIII. Crude Birth Rate (CBR), Crude Death Rates (CDR), and					
Percentage of Natural Increase (PNI)					
White					
West Jersey					
CBR (per 000)				30.43	
CDR (per 000)				10.05	
PNI				2.04	
Black					
West Jersey					
CBR (per 000)				35.61	
CDR (per 000)				15.66	
PNI				1.99	

SOURCES: Wells 1975, 135, 137, 139, 140; for section VII and 1784 population, Wacker 1975, 161, 415. Population for 1772 reflects the corrected figure from Wacker.

61,403 in 1745, 71,025 in 1772 (recall this is for West Jersey alone), and 149,435 in 1784.

In considering these colonial-era New Jersey census counts over time, Wells (1975, 134–135) observed a changing rate of increase of 3.2 percent per year for the entire colony from the 1726 through 1738 enumerations, 3.7 percent for the entire colony from 1738 to 1745, and a tad slower 2.9 percent annual population gain for West Jersey alone over the 1745 through 1772 span. Wells (1975, 135) hypothesizes that one possible reason for this relative slowing of growth in New Jersey in this mid- to later eighteenth-century period was due to New Jersey's competition for settlers with the colony of New York, which, Wells observed, grew rapidly in the mid- to later eighteenth century. (See also table 2.6.) Further to this hypothesis, Wells (1975, 135) notes, "Given their geographic proximity, it is interesting to find that New Jersey's peak growth came during the slowest increase in New York's history, and vice versa. This seems to suggest that migration between New York and New Jersey may have had some effect on the population of both colonies in the middle of the eighteenth century." Competition for population between New Jersey and its neighbors (e.g., New York) and between New Jersey and other regions of the country (e.g., the South and West) would continue as a demographic dynamic in the centuries that followed the colonial era, as is discussed in chapter 3 and elsewhere in this book.

Returning to colonial-era New Jersey, besides containing the total population counts in the multiple New Jersey colonial-era censuses, table A.1 (in appendix A) further shows the population by *county* at these five periods of time. The reader is cautioned, however, that the existence, number, and boundaries of New Jersey's counties in the eighteenth century were far different than the number and boundaries of the state's twenty-one counties today. To aid in the proper interpretation of the New Jersey county population data in the colonial era, figure A.1 presents maps of the evolving New Jersey counties in the colonial period (and later eras) and further shows the boundaries of East Jersey versus West Jersey.[12] The changes depicted in these series of maps explain why certain counties are or are not presented in table A.1. For example, the population for Morris County is not shown until the 1745 New Jersey colony census because Morris County was not formed from an originally larger Hunterdon County until 1739. Similarly, Cumberland and Sussex Counties are not shown in the colonial-era census counts until 1772 because Cumberland was formed from a larger Salem County in 1748 and Sussex the same from Morris County in 1753.

Since there is an apples-versus-oranges challenge in considering New Jersey's population by county over the colonial era, given alternations in the number of counties and their changing boundaries over time, we shall for the moment consider the results of the censuses by the larger and less variable subcolony geographies for East Jersey versus West Jersey, with these results shown in table 2.7. Besides competing for population with other colonies in the eighteenth century, within New Jersey there were population shifts by region. In the 1726 colonial census, of the 32,442 total New Jersey population, 18,062 (55.7 percent) resided in East Jersey and 14,380 (44.3 percent) in West Jersey. There was a near identical population division in the 1738 census (55.2 percent East Jersey and 44.8 percent West Jersey). By the 1745 census, however, there was a shift, and the majority of the colony's population resided in West Jersey (52.0 percent) with less than half in East Jersey (48.0 percent). There would continue to be intraregional population shifts in New Jersey in the postcolonial era, such as the variations in contemporary population in inner-ring versus outer-ring counties, a subject considered later in chapter 5.

The Demographic Profile of New Jersey's Colonial-Era Population: Racial Composition

Let us move beyond the raw head counts of New Jersey's colonial-era population and consider some critical population characteristics. We start this review with the racial composition—namely, the percentage of New Jersey's colonial-period population that was white or Black. This white and Black distribution is available from many of these New Jersey colonial censuses and reflect a fairly consistent pattern—namely that the overwhelming share, more than nine-tenths, of New Jersey's colonial population was white (92.0 percent in 1726, 91.5 percent in 1738, 92.5 percent in 1745, and 95.3 percent in the 1772 solely West Jersey enumeration). How does this compare with racial composition in other colonies? It was (1) higher than the all-colony average white share of the population (84.7 percent in 1730, 82.7 percent in 1740, 78.8 percent in 1750, and 78.3 percent in 1770—four decades roughly comporting with the timing of the New Jersey colonial enumerations); (2) understandably higher than the white share of all residents in southern colonies, where slavery (and hence Black presence) was more dominant (71.4 percent in 1730, 68.0 percent in 1740, 60.3 percent in 1750, and 60.5 percent in 1770); and (3) closely resembles the average white share of the total population in the middle colonies as a region (91.9 percent in 1730, 92.8 percent in 1750, and 93.6 percent in 1770).

While the discussion above has focused on the white share of the total population, the Black share would essentially be 100 percent less the white share. So in the New Jersey eighteenth-century colonial censuses, the Black share of the total population would thus be between about 5–10 percent (8.0 percent in 1726, 8.5 percent in 1738, 7.5 percent in 1745, and 4.7 percent in 1772, the last for West Jersey alone). These are not value-free metrics because "to be black in eighteenth century New Jersey meant one was a slave" (Wells 1975, 136) and slaveholding was common in New Jersey's colonial history.[13] (Appendix C in this book considers in greater detail the Black and slave population of New Jersey from its colonial founding through 1860, just before the start of the Civil War; see also Carter 2006.)

Where racial data are available for both East Jersey and West Jersey, such as in the 1726, 1738, and 1745 New Jersey colonial censuses, it is apparent that the white percentage of the total population is lower in East Jersey versus West Jersey and in tandem that the Black percentage (and in parallel the slavery incidence) was higher in East Jersey versus West Jersey. For example, in the 1738 census, the racial breakout of the population was 88.1 percent white and 11.9 percent Black in East Jersey versus 95.6 white and 4.4 percent Black in West Jersey. Almost identical white-versus-Black racial ratios are found in both the 1726 and 1745 censuses, and clearly the Black population (and slavery) incidence was about twice as high in East Jersey versus West Jersey over the eighteenth century. "The reasons for the regional variations in racial composition (and presumably slave holding) are not clear" (Wells, 1975, 136). One explanation could be differing religious persuasion and antislavery sentiments. In brief, West Jersey had a higher share of Quakers relative to East Jersey. For example, in 1745, 19 percent of West Jersey's total population were "Quakers or reported Quakers" versus a lower 12 percent of East Jersey's total population in that year (Wacker 1975, 415). With many, albeit not all Quakers more opposed to slavery than the general population (Soderlund 1985), the dominance of this sect might have influenced the lower Black population and slavery incidence in West Jersey. According to Wells (1975, 136), this possible chain of influence does not hold up on closer empirical examination, though other researchers, such as Wacker, disagree on this point. Conversely, a more significant Dutch settler presence in East Jersey might have contributed to higher Black slave presence in the region, for the Dutch were prominent in the eighteenth-century slave trade (G. Wright 1988, 18), a possible connection discussed in this monograph's appendix C. Wacker (1975, 189–205) explored national origin (e.g., Dutch settler share), religious orientation, soil condition (and the related nature and scale of farm operations), and other influences on the varying Black population and incidence of slavery in colonial New Jersey and concluded that "in general, the largest numbers of blacks were associated with areas of Dutch or non-Quaker British population and with the fertile soils of the Inner Coastal Plain and the Piedmont" (Wacker 1975, 189).

There were also noticeable racial differences by county in New Jersey's colonial era. For example, while the Black percentage of the total East Jersey population was 10.6 percent in the 1726 census, 11.9 percent in the 1738 census, and 10.8 percent in the 1745 census, the Black share of East Jersey's Bergen County's population at these three census enumerations was considerably higher at 18.4 percent, 19.7 percent, and 20.5 percent, respectively (Wacker 1975, 190). In contrast, the West Jersey county of Gloucester had a relatively low percentage of Black population (and slavery)—3.2 percent in 1726, 3.7 percent in 1738, 5.8 percent in 1745, and 3.6 percent in 1772. (Recall only West Jersey had a New Jersey colonial-era census in 1772.) Numerous reasons encompassing religious orientation, national origin, and soil conditions may underlie these county variations, as they might have regional variations (Wacker 1975, 189–205). For example, Bergen County had a relatively large share of Dutch and Barbadian settlers—groups generally familiar and comfortable with Black slavery (Wells 1975, 136). Additionally, Bergen County had relatively rich and productive soils (Wacker 1975, 12), which were generally supportive of larger and more intensive farm operations benefiting from slave labor. Finally, considering that the Quaker religion discouraged slaveholding, Bergen County's white population had the lowest estimated Quaker presence of all New Jersey counties in 1745 (Wacker 1975, 183). In contrast, Gloucester County had some of the lowest shares of Dutch-origin settlers of all New Jersey colonial-era counties (Wacker 1975, 162); its soils were relatively less productive (Wacker 1975, 12) and therefore its farms would not benefit as much from slave labor; and finally it had the second highest

Quaker presence (e.g., 43 percent of its white settlers in 1745; Wacker 1975, 183) of all of New Jersey's colonial-era counties. We acknowledge, however, that a full complex, intertwined explanation of regional (East versus West Jersey) and county variations by race and slaveholding in colonial-era New Jersey is beyond our scrutiny here.

The Demographic Profile of New Jersey's Colonial-Era Population: Gender

What about the gender profile of the colonial-era New Jersey population? By way of background, Wacker (1975, 138) notes that as adult males "were in theory at least more able and more likely to migrate to areas of economic opportunity than were white females, a heavy imbalance in the ratio between the sexes in favor of males probably signifies in-migration." Outmigration is suggested in the reverse situation (higher female gender ratio) (Wacker 1975, 138). In colonial New Jersey, there was generally a higher adult male–to–adult female ratio evident over time in the different censuses. For the entire colony, this adult male–to–adult female gender ratio for whites was 1.14 in 1726, 1.08 in 1738, and 1.10 in 1745. Frequently, however, there were differing gender ratios in the different regions of the colony, with West Jersey typically having the greater excess of white adult males versus white adult females (1.20 in 1726, 1.24 in 1738, and 1.11 in 1745) compared to East Jersey (1.09 in 1726, 0.96 in 1738, and 1.09 in 1745). For Blacks, the excess of adult males to adult females was especially high; for the entire New Jersey colony, the Black adult gender ratio was 1.38 in 1726 and 1.36 in 1738; and this skewed Black gender ratio characterized *both* East and West Jersey. Wacker (1975, 146) further studied the sex ratios by county and found vast variations; for example, whereas Essex County in 1726 "was most in balance, with a slight majority of females . . . [suggesting] slight out-migration," in Cape May and Gloucester Counties, the male-to-female ratio in 1726 was about 1.3, signaling significant in-migration.

In a broader view, gender imbalance between men and women typified most of the colonies. According to one study (Moller 1945), this overall colonial-era imbalance may have been as high as 150 men to every 100 women for those over sixteen years old. One contributor to this gender imbalance was the disproportionate share of males migrating to the American colonies, especially in its formative years. For example, 86 percent of 2,010 immigrants from London to Virginia in 1635 were males, and 65 percent of a group of the 1,960 persons who migrated to Massachusetts before 1650 (Galenson 1996, 179). The male-to-female imbalance in the overall colonial population was most pronounced for the middle and southern colonies as opposed to New England, with one analysis concluding that "marked male surpluses would be the norm for nearly all areas south of the Hudson at least for the first half of the [eighteenth] century" (R. Thompson 1974, 161). Why less of a male-to-female imbalance in New England? As with many other demographic phenomena, there is no simple, singular explanation. One possible reason was that a disproportionate share of New England males later migrated to the middle and southern colonies, seeking land and economic advancement, a migration flow suggested when we consider the overall topic of colonial-era migration examined shortly in more detail.

If most of the American colonies, especially those south of the Hudson River, had a male-to-female imbalance, with a disproportionate share of males, did England, the source of the majority of those immigrating to the colonies, have a reverse imbalance (i.e., disproportionate female)? That indeed appears to be the case, with one analysis estimating that as of the late seventeenth century, there were in England 2.8 million women as against 2.7 million men (King 1936; cited in R. Thompson 1974, 162).

The Demographic Profile of New Jersey's Colonial-Era Population: Household and Age Characteristics

Chapter 11 in this book details that the contemporary household size in New Jersey is barely above two members. The New Jersey colonial-era household size, in contrast, was magnitudes higher (e.g., 6.6 according to the 1772 census). Household size ranged from 5.8 in Cumberland County to 6.9 in Burlington County (Wells 1975, 140).

Large family size was prevalent elsewhere in the American colonies (Lotka 1927). A meta-analysis by Wells (1992, 93) of prior conducted demographic studies of numerous colonial-era communities concluded, "In America, the average [mean family size] seldom fell below six and often reached eight or more." Contributing to a large family size in both New Jersey and the colonies overall was a high number of children per family and related a high fertility rate.

New Jersey colonial-era women had many children, especially by today's standards (and stands in contrast to a contemporary New Jersey "baby bust" examined later in chapters 6 and 11). In discussing the subject of New Jersey's colonial stupendous birth rate, Wacker cites the following telling 1787 narrative from an English immigrant woman, Mary Capnerhurst, who resided in Flemington in 1787. She said of her neighbors' families: "They was telling the number of children several women had. Some thirteen, one seventeen, by one husband. At her death there was pains taken to find out how many descendants she had and the number was three hundred and sixty odd. I asked Mrs. Grosses Mother how many children she had. She answered but eight" (quoted in Wacker 1975, 152).

The "but eight" children situation was found elsewhere. Jemima Condict, born 1754, who wrote a diary about living in Revolutionary-era New Jersey, was one of nine children (Worth-Baker 2014). Large colonial-era broods of children were found throughout the colonies, such as an 8.8 average in colonial Sturbridge, Massachusetts (Osterud and Fulton 1976). One-third of colonial Quaker women studied had eight or more children, with a handful bearing as many as fourteen (Wells 1971). Recall as well the earlier cited observation from Benjamin Franklin that marriages in America produced eight children as against four in England (Franklin 1751). The Wells meta-analysis of extant studies concerning demography in numerous colonial-period communities found high fertility rates across the board, such as 9.4 in North Hampton, Massachusetts (1700–1749), 9.2 in Sturbridge, Massachusetts (1730–1759), 8.8 in Nantucket, Massachusetts, and 9.9 in Philadelphia (1700–1775) (Wells 1992, 92).

Later chapters in this book trace the contemporary decline in household size and fertility, in New Jersey and nationally. Interestingly, there is a foreshadowing of this contemporary downward trend over the course of the seventeenth into the eighteenth centuries in colonial America, as documented by the Wells (1971) meta-analysis. In Northampton, Massachusetts, for example, the mean family size was 8.2 before 1700, 6.9 in 1700–1749, and 5.7 by 1750–1799. In Deerfield, Massachusetts, total fertility, which stood at 6.6 in 1721–1740, had dropped to 4.9 by 1775–1850 (Wells 1992, 92). Yet even at these lowered family size and fertility rates over the course of the eighteenth century, it nonetheless stands that colonial America was characterized by large families with many children, especially relative to later demographic epochs.

The high number of children per women and sky-high fertility, contributing in no small measure to the American colonies' meteoric colonial-era population gain that was described earlier in this chapter, caught the attention of Thomas Malthus ("the [American] population has been found to double itself in twenty-five years"; Malthus 1926, 105; cited in Potter 1965, 631–632), a geometric increase that Malthus feared could ultimately strain society's food supply, which was believed to at best increase only arithmetically (Malthus 1926, 106–107; cited in Potter 1965, 632). Thus, colonial-era American demographics was one impetus to the Malthusian population theory and challenge.

With colonial families having many children, it is not surprising that the New Jersey colonial-era population was relatively young, with just about half between the ages of zero and fifteen. This is spelled out in more detail in table 2.7 (see also McCusker 2006c, 5-662). The youth of the population is consistent in all of the New Jersey colonial-era censuses and generally holds true for both East and West Jersey and for both whites as well as Blacks, albeit Blacks tended to be somewhat incrementally older than their white counterparts (i.e., Blacks had a higher share of persons above sixteen years of age; see table 2.7). Further age detail is available from the New Jersey 1772 census, which admittedly is limited to West Jersey. Wells (1975, 137) observes that as of 1772, "43.6% of people were between the ages of sixteen and fifty; 6.9% were at least fifty but not yet eighty; while only three out of every 1,000 inhabitants had reached eighty." Studies of American colonies other than New Jersey similarly point to the relatively younger age of the inhabitants (D. Smith 1972). For example, in Rhode Island in 1755, there was roughly an even distribution of whites under sixteen years of age (49.4 percent) as opposed to those over sixteen (50.6 percent). There was almost an exact distribution for whites in Maryland in that same year, with 49.3 percent of that colony's population under sixteen and 50.7 percent over sixteen (Wells 1975, 102, 152). In summary, the New Jersey and broader colonial population was disproportionately younger as opposed to older in age, which is in stark contrast to today's "more old-than-young society," a contemporary elder boom discussed later in chapter 10.

The Demographic Profile of New Jersey's Colonial-Era Population: Components of Population Change—Births, Deaths, and Migration

What were the underlying drivers of the very rapid population growth experienced by New Jersey in the colonial period, a phenomenon experienced as well in other American colonies (Vinovskis 1979)? Although we have earlier alluded to the high colonial birth rate as one influence, that is just a piece of the puzzle. To answer definitively what drove New Jersey's torrid population gain in this colony's formative years would require a detailed analysis of the complicated multiple components of population change, encompassing not only births and deaths but also migration. Chapter 6 applies detailed analysis of population change in the Garden State in the more contemporary span of the nineteenth and twentieth centuries. Would that we could replicate that in the colonial era as well, but that is impossible because the full requisite data for this period are inchoate. We can, however, intuit a sense of the overall dynamic of the components of population change for New Jersey in its early history from research conducted by Rutgers University geography professor John Brush (1956) some seven decades ago and summarized here in table 2.8. According to Brush, New Jersey's rapid population increase over the 1726–1790 period was driven by

1 a very high birth rate of possibly over 50 per 1,000 population (a fecundity rate [Klein 2004, 3] paralleled in other colonies; Wells 1971, 73);
2 a death rate that although high—about 25–30 per 1,000 population in the 1726–1790 period—was more than offset by the extremely high birth rate just noted of possibly over 50 in this period, thus implying a very high rate of natural increase of about 20 per 1,000 persons; and
3 further acting as a steroid to fuel New Jersey's large population gain in the 1726–1790 period was a very high New Jersey net rate of migration (in-migrants less outmigrants) in this time period of about 20 per 1,000 persons.

Brush's research is further informative because he shows how these colonial-period components compare with those of later eras (1790–1840, 1840–1930, and 1930–1950). These changing components over time are detailed in table 2.8. The long-term trend from the colonial era to 1950 is a rapidly declining New Jersey birth rate and a death rate that went down over time but not as fast as the plummeting birth rate, thus dramatically lowering New Jersey's rate of natural increase. A further dampening of New Jersey's population growth over time was a rapidly falling net rate of migration. Brush's fine research is a preview of this

Table 2.8
New Jersey Rates of Natural Increase and Net Migration per 1,000 Persons by Periods, 1726–1950

Period	Birth Rate	Death Rate	Rate of Natural Increase	Average Rate of Growth	Net Rate of Migration
1726–1790	Possible over 50	About 25–30	About 20	39	+ 19–20
1790–1840	Probable range 45–50	Probable range 20–30	20–30	15	Loss of 5–15
1840–1930	Probable range 22–40; probable mean 29 +/–1	Probable range 11–25; probable mean 16 +/–1	11–15	29	+ 14–18
1930–1950	Range 13–24; mean 17	Range 10–12; mean 11	3–11; mean 6	10	+4

SOURCE: Brush 1956, 24.

monograph's detailed population-change analysis in the contemporary era presented in chapter 6.

The rapid natural increase (births less deaths) that Brush detailed for colonial New Jersey is echoed in other studies. From the 1772 New Jersey colonial census (recall this was limited to West Jersey), Wacker calculated birth rates, death rates, and the ensuing percentage of natural increase. His findings for West Jersey are shown in table 2.7 and depict a significant natural increase. While the crude death rate in West Jersey in 1772 was high (10.05 for whites and 15.66 for Blacks) by later historical standards, West Jersey's crude birth rate per 1,000 population was yet higher (30.43 for whites and 35.61 for Blacks), thus contributing to a significant approximate 2 percent natural increase for both whites and Blacks (Wacker 1975, 152, 161). Interestingly, Wacker further found that the percentage of natural increase for whites in 1772 was higher in the newer settled counties of West Jersey, such as Sussex (2.65 percent), Morris (2.40 percent), and Hunterdon (2.21 percent) as compared to West Jersey's relatively longer-settled counties where the percentage of natural increase per 1,000 persons was noticeably lower, such as Salem (1.36 percent) and Burlington (1.70 percent) (Wacker 1975, 152, 161).

The American colonial-era demographic dynamo (more population gain from the excess births over deaths, an overage that exceeded the population increment due to migration) was alluded to by no less than Benjamin Franklin (1751): "There are supposed to be now upwards of one million English souls in North America (though it is thought scarce eighty thousand have been brought over by sea)." Franklin then humorously observed that through the American colonies' doubling of population every twenty-five years, "in another century the greatest number of Englishman will be on this side of the water." (Franklin's views on the significant population growth in the American colonies influenced Thomas

Malthus.) A contemporary of Franklin, Edward Wigglesworth (1775, 1), observed in parallel that "this rapid population of the Americas arises, partially from the great accession of foreigners, but principally from the natural increase of the inhabitants."

Although natural increase (births less deaths) was a significant contributor to the rapid colonial-era population gains of both New Jersey and the colonies overall, migration was also important (Bailyn and DeWolfe 1986b; Fogleman 1992). To illustrate, Wacker (1975, 132–133) observed that based on natural increase alone, New Jersey's population would not have grown nearly as rapidly as it actually did between 1680 and 1726; the factor that contributed to the actual and significant 1680–1726 population increment was in-migration. Wacker (1975, 133) further observed differences in estimated in-migration by New Jersey county, such as a much higher in-migration flow to Burlington/Hunterdon Counties between 1680 and 1726 (Hunterdon was set off from a larger Burlington in 1714; see appendix A), and a much lower dynamic in Cape May County, which "experienced very little growth beyond natural increase alone" in that 1680 through 1726 span. These county differences in migration foreshadow later variations in this demographic feature and others (e.g., share of the population that is foreign-born) that are discussed in this book's later chapters.

More generally, and returning to our colonial-period analysis, migration was important throughout the American colonies, albeit it varied by colonial region and time period.[14] Henry Gemery (2000) examined the components of population change of the white population of the colonial United States over the seventeenth and eighteenth centuries including both natural increase and migration. For the seventeenth-century period (1620–1700), the all-colony migration totaled 171,000; for the eighteenth-century period (1700–1790), migration to the colonies increased to a cumulative 618,000. Clearly, by the eighteenth century, the American colonies were a more attractive place and many more made the passage. Total migration to all the colonies over the seventeenth and eighteenth centuries (1620–1790) studied by Gemery totaled just shy of 800,000 (789,000).

Besides differing migration tallies to the American colonies by century, the immigration magnitude calculated by Gemery varied by decades of higher and lower inflows. To illustrate, in the troubled revolutionary decade of the 1770s, total migration to the colonies was a scant 21,000 and then rose nearly twenty-fold to 395,000 migrants in the postwar boom decade of the 1780s. This chapter earlier identified a large increase in the all-colony population in the 1780s (gaining about 1.1 million from 2.8 million in 1780 to 3.9 million by 1790) and clearly migration was not a small contributor to this gain.

Also interesting is Gemery's calculation of migration by region—there are marked differences. Of the total 789,000 total migration to American colonies between 1610 and 1790, the New England colonies secured 61,000 migrants, middle colonies 211,000, and southern colonies the lion's share of 517,000. In the

New England colonies, which as a region were an original beacon to migrants (e.g., between 1620 and 1650, this region received about four-tenths of all the migration), that attraction soon paled (Klein 2004, 58). In fact, the New England colonies experienced many decades of negative migration (more residents leaving as opposed to newcomers arriving), such as 1690–1700 (–18,200 migrants in New England), 1740–1750 (–12,400 migrants), 1750–1760 (–12,000 migrants), and the war strife years of 1770–1780 (–29,200 migrants) (Gemery 2000, 171). No wonder, then, that New England's colonial population growth, especially after the middle of the seventeenth century, was fueled more by natural increase (which was significant with high fertility rates; D. Smith 1972) as opposed to migration (Main 2001). Interestingly, in the 1770s conflict decade, while New England had negative migration, the middle colonies did see some positive migration of 7,600 persons and the southern colonies managed to attract 42,300 migrants. As noted earlier, the colonies as a whole bounced back with respect to attracting migrants, some 395,000, in the post–Revolutionary War boom decade of the 1780s, but the migrant gains then were also uneven by colonial region. The New England colonies in the 1780s secured 83,800 migrants, the middle colonies 68,600, and the southern colonies 242,500. These colonial-era migration shifts by region and time period foreshadow later era demographic changes considered in subsequent chapters (e.g., Sunbelt population ascendency and the Black Great Migration and Reverse Great Migration).

It bears mentioning, although not doing the subject justice, that a significant share (Grubb 1985), an estimated one-half to two-thirds, of all the white immigrants who came to the American colonies were indentured servants (A. Smith 1947, 336). Indentured servants would often have to pay the cost of their passage (a daunting sum that could amount to one-half or more of an immigrant's annual European income; Grubb 1985, 316) in the form of many years, often four to seven, of unpaid labor, with this specific term and other labor conditions detailed in a servitude contract or "indenture" (Galenson 1984, 2; Klein 2004, 47; Rosenbloom, n.d.). Although work conditions for indentured servants could be harsh, those so contracted would ultimately become free, in contrast to the typically horrific life of enslaved Blacks in the colonies shackled to perpetual bondage. Sadly, although the first Blacks arriving in America in Virginia in 1619 were technically treated as indentured servants, their status soon changed to that of slaves ("Indentured Servants in the U.S.," n.d.).

The Demographic Profile of New Jersey's Colonial-Era Population: Density

Less complicated than the components of change (births, deaths, and migration) is the gross measure of density, typically calibrated as the number of persons per square mile. Although in time, as reviewed later in this book (appendix E), New Jersey would claim the title as the nation's most densely populated state, it did not start that way in the colonial period.

Interesting data on this subject are available from research conducted by Thomas Purvis (1999, 17), who quantified density from various sources (e.g., Greene and Harrington 1932 and Sutherland 1966) by (1) region of the colonies (New England, middle, and southern), (2) each individual colony (e.g., New Jersey), (3) smaller-scaled geographic areas within a given colony (such as for the seacoast versus interior counties of Massachusetts and the New York City–Long Island [NY-LI] versus Hudson Valley areas of New York State), and (4) the total-ity of the thirteen colonies overall. Purvis measured density by two metrics: acres per family and persons per square mile (our review here focuses on the lat-ter, more conventional persons-per-square-mile measure of density) for three time periods: 1650, 1700, and 1760.

In 1650, the New Jersey population density according to Purvis was an inher-ently low 0.1 persons per square mile. (Further reference to this density measure will not repeat this per square mile base.) For context, the average density for all thirteen colonies (within their modern boundaries) as of 1650 was an identical 0.1; however, the density within the coastal districts of all thirteen colonies as of that year was a higher 0.5. For further context, New Jersey's neighboring col-ony of New York had an overall colony density of 0.1 in 1650 (identical to New Jersey's), with a much higher 0.8 density in New York's NY-LI region as opposed to 0.2 in New York's more sparsely settled Hudson Valley. Massachusetts's over-all colony density in 1650 was 2.0, with a much higher density of 4.5 in this state's seacoast counties. It is no wonder, then, that the colony of New Jersey would attract migrants from such places as New York's NY-LI region (much like contemporary New Yorkers seeking a suburban haven with a larger lot in New Jersey—a subject discussed in this book's chapter 3) and Massachusetts's seacoast counties. Further conveying the lure of more plentiful land in the colony of New Jersey is the additional acres-per-family metric developed by Purvis (1999). In 1650, New Jersey on average offered 57,600 acres per family as opposed to a lower 11,400 acres per family in New York's NY-LI region and a much lower 1,241 acres per family in Massachusetts's seacoast counties.

By 1700, New Jersey's density rose to 1.9—higher than the overall all-colony density of 0.7 (within modern boundaries) yet lower than the 2.3 density aver-age of the coastal districts of all the colonies. Of more immediate context, the New Jersey 1700 density of 1.9, although exceeding the overall New York den-sity in that year of 0.4, was far less dense than the persons per square mile in New York's NY-LI area (7.2) and Massachusetts's seacoast counties (14.2). Relatively more plentiful and fertile land and the ability to own farmland (and not just till the soil as a tenant) as well as lower taxes in the colony of New Jersey were described earlier in this chapter as luring migrants in the eighteenth century from King's County in the New York colony (NY-LI area) and elsewhere to beckon-ing close-by New Jersey.

By 1760, New Jersey's density had risen to 12.6—now higher than the aver-age density of both all areas in the thirteen colonies (4.3) as well as the coastal districts of the colonies (10.7). At the same time, however, New Jersey's 12.6 density in 1760 was about half of the density of New York's NY-LI area (28.1) and about a quarter that the population per square mile of Massachusetts's coastal colonies (43.8). As mentioned earlier and as shall be further illustrated later in this chapter when the voices of New Jersey's colonial population are heard, settlers migrated to New Jersey for the relatively more available land and better economic opportunities.

Further information on the population density of New Jersey in the colonial era is presented by Wacker (1975, 138), who identified the density for New Jersey at the juncture of this colony's multiple censuses in the eighteenth century. Wacker calculated the rising numbers of persons per square mile in New Jersey at 5 in 1726, 6 in 1738, 8 in 1746, and 20 in 1784. Furthermore, Wacker shows the densities by county throughout the eighteenth century. (Again, the reader is referred to figure A.1 in appendix A showing the changing county boundaries over New Jersey's early history.) Taking just one example for illustrative purposes, the density of Essex County identified by Wacker (1975, 138) was 9 in 1726, climbed to 13 in 1738, increased to 26 in 1745, and reached 56 in 1784. From 1745 onward, Essex was the most densely settled county in New Jersey, and it has retained a high density standing up to contemporary times (see appendix E).

The Demographic Profile of New Jersey's Early Republic Population: National Origins

A final characteristic we will present concerning New Jersey's population in its early era concerns its residents' nationality (or country of origin). This characteristic is only available for the white population and then only as of 1790 (initial statehood) as opposed to the earlier New Jersey colonial-era censuses. Before presenting this nationality profile as of America's first census, it is important to stress that these data, as much other information in this chapter, are far from definitive; the 1790 nationality estimates have been in flux over time and in fact have been subject to considerable revision.

At the onset concerning this topic, it must be clearly stated that the 1790 census did not at that time quantify the nationality of the population; in fact, it was not until 1850 that the census queried whether respondents were even foreign-born, let alone from where immigrants came. But even though a direct data path to clearly ascertaining the nationality profile of America's white population quantitatively was unavailable, researchers turned to indirect means for estimating this information as of 1790. The most common indirect data analysis on this subject consisted of first identifying the surnames of the respondents to the 1790 census and then, through further linguistic, genealogical, and other research, painstakingly crosslinking the names to a presumed nationality, whether English, Irish, German, Dutch, and so on.

Although this description oversimplifies the analysis, it conveys the overall gist of the approach. This section describes three major studies conducted over nearly the span of a century that all worked to estimate the national origins of the country as of 1790, including New Jersey. The three studies and their publication dates are as follows:

1   William S. Rossiter (1909), then–chief clerk of the United States Census (We previously referred in this chapter to other 1909 research by Rossiter concerning the population of the American colonies over the seventeenth and eighteenth centuries.)
2   American Council of Learned Societies (1932)
3   Thomas Purvis (1984), then a history professor at the University of Georgia

In quantifying the nationality of America's population as of 1790, the Rossiter-directed research

1   Assembled all the census enumerator records ("schedules") of surnames from the 1790 census that were extant as of the early twentieth-century period of research. The schedules were available for most but not all states, a subject we consider momentarily.
2   From the available extant schedules from the first 1790 census, Rossiter (1909) identified nearly 30,000 different surnames. The most popular surname was Smith with 5,932 families, comprising 33,245 persons (Rossiter 1909, 115). Variations in the spelling of surnames, not uncommon, were noted as well. For example, the surname Hughes had multiple spelling variations (Heugh, Hewes, Hews, Hues, Hugh, Hughe, Hughs, Huse, and Huws). The surnames were then crosslinked through linguistic and other research to likely nationalities.
3   Further nationality research was conducted in states that did not have extant schedules of the 1790 surname information, census data that were likely lost when the British burned Washington, DC, when they invaded this city in the War of 1812 (U.S. Census Bureau, n.d.a). These states included Delaware, New Jersey, Georgia, Kentucky, Tennessee, and Virginia (Rossiter 1909, 48–49, 119–121). The Rossiter research then tried to address the lack of surname data for these states with lost schedules as best it could. For example, for Delaware, it tapped the surname information as of the second census in 1800, which was available for this state, under the assumption that only minor changes in surnames (and nationality) would have occurred in the ensuing ten years. For Virginia, the Rossiter research examined state-implemented enumerations that had been implemented over 1782 to 1785, in this case assuming that these 1780s Virginia schedules approximated 1790 conditions closely enough (Rossiter 1909, 119).

The New Jersey case was particularly challenging for the surname data sched-ules for this state were not available until the fifth census in 1830, and that was deemed far too distant from 1790 as to be relied upon. Consequently, the Ros-siter research asked the New Jersey Historical Society (NJHS), under the direc-tion of its responding secretary, William Nelson, to ascertain the nationality of New Jersey's residents as of 1790. This Nelson-directed NJHS study painstak-ingly examined the history and resident names associated with each of New Jer-sey's then-thirteen counties in 1790 to estimate nationality origins by county. An excerpt from the Nelson study for Bergen County follows (as reported by Rossiter 1909, 119):

> *Bergen.*—This county was originally settled by Dutch, with a very small admixture of Danes. Prior to 1680 there was a strong infusion of French settlers from Harlem [in New York City]. There was at no times any indepen-dent immigration from France. Some of the families having Dutch names, as the "Van Buskirks," were of German origin. . . . As early as 1700 there was a considerable infusion of German population from New York City and from German settlements north of New Jersey. About 1765 there was a consider-able importation of German miners. . . . There were Scotch settlers also at a very early period, say 1725 and later, who perhaps worked in the Dutch flax industry, and through affiliations with or acquaintance with Dutch settlers came to this county. I would say that in 1790 the population was about as follows: French, 15 percent; Germans, 20 percent; Scotch, 5 percent; Irish (principally in the iron mines), 5 percent; English, 15 percent; Dutch, 40 percent.

This county-by-county research was then summed to a statewide total, where the nationality of just shy 170,000 (169,954) white residents of New Jersey as of 1790 were quantified. According to Rossiter and based on Nelson, New Jersey white population as of 1790 had the following nationality distribution: English and Welsh, 58.0 percent; Dutch, 12.7 percent; German, 9.2 percent; Scotch, 7.7 percent; Irish, 7.1 percent; Swedish (includes Finnish), 2.9 percent; and unas-signed, 0.1 percent.

In sum, the Rossiter 1909 research estimated the nationality distribution of all the states as of 1790 from the surname schedule data available from the first census, and where that information was not available (Delaware, New Jersey, Georgia, Kentucky, Tennessee, and Virginia) from other means (e.g., the Nel-son New Jersey study). Bearing in mind these differences in state data, tables 2.9 and 2.10 summarize the 1790 nationality distribution from the Rossiter 1909 research for the entire white population of the United States as of 1790 (3,172,444) as well as the country's then-inclusive three regions (New England, middle states, and southern states).

Table 2.9
Percentage of the 1790 National and New Jersey White Population by Nationality according to Rossiter, American Council of Learned Studies (ACLS), and Purvis

National and Linguistic Stock	Percentage of the Population by Nationality					
	National (Total U.S.)			New Jersey		
	Rossiter	ACLS	Purvis	Rossiter	ACLS	Purvis
English and Welsh	82.0	60.9	64.0	58.0	47.0	54.2
Scotch and Irish	8.9	18.0	21.6	14.8	17.2	14.3
German	5.6	8.7	8.9	9.2	9.2	6.5
Dutch	2.5	3.4	3.1	12.7	16.6	20.1
French	0.6	1.7	2.1	2.1	2.4	3.8
Swedish (and Finnish)	0.2	0.7	0.3	2.9	3.9	1.1
Other	0.3	6.6	–	0.1	3.7	–
Total	100.0	100.0	100.0	100.0	100.0	100.0

The 1790 nationality composition (percentage of the population) for the individual components of the Scotch and Irish aggregate shown above for both the nation (entire U.S.) and New Jersey were:

National and Linguistic Stock	Percentage of the Population by Nationality					
	National (Total U.S.)			New Jersey		
	Rossiter	ACLS	Purvis	Rossiter	ACLS	Purvis
Scotch	7.0	8.3		7.7	7.7	
Irish	1.9	9.7		7.1	9.5	
Scotch-Irish			10.5			6.8
Scottish			5.3			3.4
Irish			5.8			4.1
Total Scotch-Irish Aggregate	8.9	18.0	21.6	14.8	17.2	14.3

SOURCES: Rossiter 1909, American Council of Learned Societies 1932, and Purvis 1984.

In 1790, according to Rossiter, the national origins of the U.S. white population were overwhelmingly English and Welsh (82 percent), followed by Scotch (7.0 percent), German (5.6 percent), and more distantly by other groups (2.5 percent Dutch, 1.9 percent Irish, 0.6 percent French, 0.2 percent Swedish, and 0.3 percent all other) (table 2.10). There were, however, distinct differences by region. While the nationality profile of the southern states was a near mirror of the national distribution (see table 2.10), the New England states had a much higher English-Welsh population (95 percent) according to Rossiter compared to the English-Welsh representation nationally (82 percent). The middle states were the most diverse, having a much lower English-Welsh share (66.1 percent) according to Rossiter, but having a higher incidence of settlers from other nationalities such as German (13.3 percent) and Dutch (7.8 percent). Within the middle

Table 2.10

Percentage of the 1790 National White Population by Nationality and Region According to Rossiter and Purvis

| National and Linguistic Stock | Percentage of the Population by Nationality | | | | | | | |
| | New England | | Middle States | | Southern States | | National (Total U.S.) | |
	Rossiter	ACLS	Rossiter	ACLS	Rossiter	ACLS	Rossiter	ACLS
English and Welsh	95.0	72.1	66.1	44.1	84.0	65.0	82.0	60.9
Scotch	3.5	4.3	8.0	7.9	9.0	11.6	7.0	8.3
Irish	0.9	5.0	2.6	11.4	2.0	12.1	1.9	9.7
German	–	0.0	13.3	19.2	4.0	7.3	5.6	8.7
Dutch	0.2	0.0	7.8	9.7	–	0.4	2.5	3.4
French	0.2	0.1	0.9	2.5	1.0	1.8	0.6	1.7
Swedish	–	–	0.5	1.6	–	0.4	0.2	0.7
Other	–	17.1	0.7	3.6	–	0.1	0.3	6.6
Total	100.0	100.0	100.0	100.0	100.0	100.0	100.0	100.0

SOURCES: Rossiter 1909 and American Council of Learned Societies (ACLS) 1932.
NOTES: For both Rossiter and ACLS, the total 1790 white population for which the national origins were estimated were 992,384 for New England, 954,003 for the middle states region, 1,226,057 for the southern states region, and 3,172,444 for the entire nation. For both Rossiter and ACLS, the total white population for which the New Jersey national origins were estimated was 169,954.

states, the German origin share of the population according to Rossiter's detailed tables (not reproduced here) was particularly high in Pennsylvania (26.1 percent) and the Dutch in New York (16.1 percent). New Jersey in 1790 was particularly diverse with a relatively much lower English-Welsh population origin (58 percent) compared to the national 1790 average for this group (82 percent), but New Jersey's 1790 Irish, Dutch, and German populations (7.1 percent, 12.7 percent, and 9.2 percent, respectively; see table 2.9) were far higher than the national average incidence for these three groups (1.9 percent, 2.5 percent, and 5.6 percent, respectively; see table 2.9). Additionally, whereas Rossiter estimated a scant 0.2 percent of the national population as of 1790 had Swedish roots, that group comprised 2.9 percent of New Jersey's population in that year—a reflection of its "New Sweden" past described earlier in this chapter. For all areas the United States as of 1790 including New Jersey, however, the national origin of the population was overwhelmingly from northern and western Europe.

It was no accident that that Rossiter 1909 research was conducted at the start of the twentieth century, because as will be detailed later in chapter 4, the late nineteenth century to the early twentieth century saw a tremendous upsurge in immigration to the United States, especially from southern and eastern Europe, which heretofore had not figured prominently as immigrant-sending regions to American soil. Given these marked changes, there was growing interest in quantifying the American nationality profile at its origins to benchmark the paradigm shift. Relatedly, the momentous Johnson-Reed Act of 1924, also detailed in chapter 4, established quotas for immigrants from different sending countries that were supposed to reflect in part the national origins of America's existing population. And what better way to do that than by researching the national origins of America's population as of the first census in 1790?

The legislators behind that 1924 Johnson-Reed Act knew of the 1909 Rossiter and related research but sought an expanded and refined study on 1790 national origins. The American Council of Learned Societies (ACLS) responded to this charge and appointed in 1927 a Committee on Linguistic and National Stocks in the Population of the United States. The committee involved numerous researchers, including primarily Howard Barker (an expert in the field of family names and descent over time) and Marcus Hansen (an expert in U.S. immigration history). Barker prepared a lengthy appendix to the ACLS study on the national stocks in the population of the United States as indicated by surnames. Hansen prepared another appendix on so-termed minor stocks of the 1790 American population (Dutch, Swedish-Finnish, and French), a subject of particular importance to New Jersey as we shall soon detail. The committee acknowledged the momentous importance of its research charge, for under the 1924 Johnson-Reed national origins plan, "the size of the immigrant quotas allotted to the different countries . . . would depend in part upon the attempted division of the white population of the United States among the various national or linguistic stocks from which it had sprung" (American Council of Learned Societies 1932, 107).

The ACLS initially reported its findings in the *Annual Report of the American Historical Association* for 1931; further information was compiled and released a year later in a U.S. government publication (American Council of Learned Societies 1932). The ACLS 1790 nationality research for the entire country and the tripartite regions (New England, middle states, and southern states) is summarized in tables 2.9 and 2.10. According to the ACLS, the 1790 national white population was estimated at 60.9 percent English and Welsh, 9.7 percent Irish, 8.7 percent German, 8.3 percent Scotch, 3.4 percent Dutch, 1.7 percent French, 0.7 percent Swedish, and 6.6 percent unassigned. Although both Rossiter (1909) and the ACLS (1932) found the English stock (English and Welsh) to dominate 1790 America, the English share claimed by Rossiter (82 percent) was noticeably higher than the English incidence (60.9 percent) identified by ACLS. In turn, the ACLS versus Rossiter study claimed a higher German incidence (8.7 percent versus 5.6 percent), higher Dutch representation (3.4 percent versus 2.5 percent), greater French (1.7 percent versus 0.6 percent), and Swedish presence (0.7 percent versus 0.2 percent), and a much higher unassigned group (6.6 percent versus 0.3 percent). These ACLS versus Rossiter differences were present by region as well. For example, whereas according to Rossiter, the incidence of Irish, German, and Dutch in the middle states region in 1790 were 2.6, 13.3, and 7.8 percent of the total regional white population, respectively, according to the ACLS these three nationality presences in the middle states were considerably higher: 11.4 percent (Irish), 19.2 percent (German), and 9.7 percent (Dutch), respectively.

The nationality distribution of the state of New Jersey in 1790 was unsurprisingly different as well under the Rossiter versus ACLS studies. According to Rossiter, the 1790 New Jersey white population (169,954) was estimated at 58 percent English and Welsh whereas it was a lower 47 percent according to the ACLS. Both Rossiter and the ACLS were in agreement that the Scotch presence in the 1790 New Jersey population stood at 7.7 percent; however, Rossiter estimated the Irish share at 7.1 percent while the ACLS estimate for this nationality was a higher 9.5 percent. Rossiter estimated the 1790 Dutch, Swedish, and French representation in the New Jersey population at 12.7 percent, 2.9 percent, and 2.1 percent, respectively, while the ACLS estimates were a higher 16.6 percent (Dutch), 3.9 percent (Swedish), and 2.4 percent (French). The ACLS unassigned nationality share for New Jersey as of 1790 (3.7 percent) was much higher than the Rossiter estimate (0.1 percent) in this regard.

The Rossiter 1909 nationality findings for New Jersey particularly differed from the 1932 ACLS findings when the estimates are compared at a county level. To recap, the Rossiter New Jersey findings relied on Nelson from the NJHS, while Hansen's research on "minor stocks" was particularly of value to the ACLS concerning New Jersey. The stark county differences in these populations are illustrated by the Rossiter (based on Nelson) estimate for the 1790 population of Bergen County as 40 percent of Dutch nationality while the ACLS (based on Hansen) estimated a much higher 74.2 percent Dutch share. In a similar vein, the ACLS estimate of a 79.8 percent Dutch nationality share of Somerset County's population was more than double the Rossiter Dutch share estimate of 30 percent for this county. In a reverse shift, the Rossiter estimate of a 25 percent Dutch share of the 1790 Hunterdon County population was multiple times higher than the ACLS estimate of a 10.7 percent Dutch origin for this county. Rossiter estimated that half (50 percent) of Cape May's 1790 population had Swedish roots, as opposed to a much lower 8.3 percent Swedish presence according to the ACLS. These vast differences reflect in part the inherent difficulty of the overall research objective and protocol—namely, estimating nationality from surnames—as well as the fact that greater errors and hence differences are expected at micro rather than larger macro geographies, such as individual counties versus the state overall.

The last 1790 nationality origin study considered here is the 1984 Purvis analysis, which is part of a larger contemporary revisiting of this subject of who lived in the United States at its founding (McDonald and McDonald 1980). Purvis (1984, 87, 89) carefully reviewed the 1932 ACLS investigation and its inclusive Barker and Hansen research, noting, for example, that "Barker's underlying procedures were sound, but as often happens in pioneering studies, his implementation suffered from several deficiencies. . . . [Hansen's] conclusions were largely impressionistic." Purvis carefully explored how improvements could be made to the ACLS approach to ascertaining the 1790 European ancestry of the American population. Part of that involved addressing the missing data for the six states, New Jersey included, where the original 1790 census schedules were lost. For example, Purvis used tax lists to replace missing census information. For New Jersey, Purvis utilized this state's extant property assessment rolls of the later eighteenth century (1770–1780) as a means to discover the names of household heads as of 1790.

Through a series of detailed calculations not described here, Purvis estimated the European ancestry (national or linguistic stock) of each state in the United States as of 1790 as well as for the country as a whole. From the manner in which these data were presented in the Purvis-authored journal article (1984), we cannot readily calculate the 1790 European ancestry by region of the United States; therefore, we show in table 2.9 the Purvis finding for only two geographies: the entire United States and New Jersey. For ready comparison, that table also shows the 1790 nationality estimates for these same two areas from the previously described Rossiter (1909) and ACLS (1932) studies in a common nationality typology through which all three studies can be compared (e.g., Scotch and Irish are combined in the top portion of table 2.9).

According to Purvis, the 1790 American national white population was estimated at 64 percent English and Welsh (59.7 percent English and 4.3 percent Welsh); 21.6 percent Scotch-Irish overall aggregate (10.5 percent Scotch-Irish, 5.3 percent Scottish, and 5.8 percent Irish); 8.9 percent German, 3.1 percent Dutch, 2.1 percent French, and 0.3 percent Swedish. For New Jersey, the Purvis estimate for 1790 was 54.2 percent English and Welsh (50.6 percent English and 3.6 percent Welsh), 14.3 percent Scotch-Irish overall aggregate (6.8 percent Scotch-Irish, 3.4 percent Scottish, and 4.1 percent Irish), 6.5 percent German, 20.1 percent Dutch, 3.8 percent French, and 1.1 percent Swedish. The Purvis (1984) estimates have both similarities and differences from the previous ACLS (1932) and Rossiter (1909) research (table 2.9). For example, using enhanced techniques, Purvis does not have an unassigned or other nationality category as do the two others (for the nation—Rossiter 0.3 percent and ACLS 6.6 percent). Of the three studies, Rossiter estimated at the national level the highest share of English and Welsh origin (82.0 percent) compared to the ACLS (60.9 percent) and Purvis (64.0 percent). Conversely, at the national level, the ACLS and Purvis had higher shares of Scotch-Irish origin (18.0 percent and 21.6 percent, respectively) compared to Rossiter (8.9 percent).

There are also differences between the three studies concerning the 1790 national origins for New Jersey. For example, Purvis estimated that approximately one-fifth (20.1 percent) of New Jersey's white residents in 1790 were Dutch, as opposed to about one-sixth (16.6 percent) for the ACLS and a yet lower about one-eighth share (12.7 percent) for this nationality according to Rossiter. Conversely, the Purvis estimate of German stock for New Jersey as of 1790 (6.5 percent) is lower than that of both the ACLS and Rossiter (both 9.2 percent).

The same is true concerning the Purvis estimate of Swedish nationality in New Jersey as of 1790 (1.1 percent), which is again lower than the ACLS and Rossiter figures for this nationality (3.9 and 2.9 percent, respectively).

Of broader note, the colony of New Jersey has variously and similarly been described as "the most culturally diverse of any of the North American colonies" (New Jersey Office of State Planning 1988, 1); "exhibit[ing] the maximum cultural diversity of any American colony or state before 1800" (Wacker 1975, 158); "enjoy[ing] unusual diversity in the origins of its population" (Wacker 1975, 158); "extremely heterogeneous" (Frankel 1937, 91), and a "melting pot" (Myers 1945, 57). New Jersey's greater diversity relative to the nation as a whole as of 1790 is borne out by all three—Rossiter, ACLS, and Purvis—studies as summarized in tables 2.9 and 2.10. The middle states as a region was relatively more diverse compared to other regions, and within the middle states region, New Jersey was a bellwether state with respect to diverse nationality, as can be ascertained from the Rossiter, ACLS, and Purvis studies. (Colonial New Jersey was also religiously diverse, encompassing numerous denominations; see Jamison 1964.) As detailed in chapter 4 and elsewhere in this book, New Jersey's greater relative population diversity would continue into contemporary times.

A Demographic and Socioeconomic Profile of New Jersey, the United States, and Regions in 1790

Although this chapter has focused on New Jersey and sister colonies in the colonial era preceding the creation of the United States, it is instructive to consider a snapshot of the demographic and socioeconomic profile of New Jersey in an early postcolonial period—namely, at the nation's first federal census in 1790. It is further illuminating to place the New Jersey population and socioeconomic profile as of 1790 in context with other areas, both nationally and regionally. These parallel data for 1790 are presented in table 2.11.

Before considering the detailed demographic and socioeconomic data from the 1790 census, it is instructive to first briefly describe this census and indeed the United States constitutional charge that a decennial census be taken. Much of this book's data are derived from the census over more than a two-century span, so knowing more about this seminal demographic source provides needed background.

Article I, section 2, of the Constitution of the United States mandates that congressional "Representatives and direct taxes shall be apportioned among the several states . . . according to their respective number," with a census to be taken every ten years (Eschner 2017). Interestingly, some members of the Constitutional Convention that preceded the Constitution's adoption in 1788 argued that the congressional representation and federal taxes should be proportioned according to state wealth, but this wealth-based proportionality was rejected in favor of a proportional head count (Rossiter 1909, 42). Reflecting the societal mores of its era, the first federal census counted free persons (including

Table 2.11
1790 Profile of the National United States, Census Regions, and New Jersey

Profile	United States	Census Regions			New Jersey
		New England	Southern States	Middle States	
Total Population (in 000s)	3,930	1,009	1,903	1,018	184
Percentage of U.S.	100.0	25.7	48.4	25.9	4.7
Race and Slavery					
% White	80.7	98.3	64.4	93.8	92.3
% Black	19.3	1.7	35.6	6.2	7.7
% Slave	17.8	0.4	34.1	4.4	6.2
% Free	1.5	1.3	1.5	1.8	1.5
Number of Slaves (in 000s)	697.6	3.8	648.7	45.2	11.4
Number of Slaves to 100 White Persons	22		53	5	7
% of Slaveholding Families	17.2	2.8	35.8	9.8	16.0
Value of Slaves (in 000s)	$104,644	$565	$97,298	$6,782	$1,713
Density					
Persons per Square Mile	9.4	16.3	7.5	10.0	24.7
Family Household Profile					
Average Persons per Private Family	5.7	5.7	5.7	5.8	5.8
White Persons per Dwelling	7.0	7.1	6.9	7.0	7.0
Ratio White Children to Adult White Females	1.9	1.7	2.0	2.0	2.0
Gender and Age Profile					
Number of Males per 1,000 White Population	509	498	515	514	510
% White Persons under 16 Years of Age	49.0	47.0	50.2	49.4	48.7

Table 2.11

1790 Profile of the National United States, Census Regions, and New Jersey (continued)

Profile	United States	Census Regions				New Jersey
		New England	Southern States	Middle States		
Economic Profile						
Aggregate Wealth (in $millions)	$522.4	$138.7	$272.4	$141.3		
% of U.S.		26.6	52.1	27		
Per Capita Wealth (in $millions)	$171	$138	$217	$145		
Ratio to U.S.	1	0.81	1.27	0.85		
Tonnage of Vessels Entering U.S. Ports (in 000s)						
Total	766	257	295	214		5.9
U.S. Flag	503	230	157	115		5.5
Foreign Flag	263	27	138	99		0.4
Governmental and Civil Society Profile						
Total Minor Civil Divisions (MCDs)	1,591	937	436	654		94
Average Population per MCD	1,273	1,077	4,365	1,555		1,959
Total Counties	292	41	199	52		13
Average Population per County	13,459	24,610	9,563	19,577		14,154
Total Post Offices	75	22	34	19		5
Post Offices per 1,000 Population	.019	.022	.018	.019		.027
Total Newspapers	103	37	24	42		3
Newspapers per 1,000 Population	.026	.037	.013	.041		.016

SOURCE: Rossiter 1909, 9, 25, 30, 32, 57, 58, 60, 77, 82, 93, 94, 96, 102, 105, 133, 135, 139, 141, and 144.

NOTE: New England region includes Maine, New Hampshire, Vermont, Massachusetts, Rhode Island, and Connecticut. Middle states include New York, New Jersey, Pennsylvania, and Delaware. Southern states includes Maryland (and District of Columbia), Virginia and West Virginia, North Carolina, South Carolina, Georgia, Kentucky, and Tennessee.

indentured servants), excluded Native Americans (they were not counted until 1870), and enumerated Blacks but on a fractional basis (the infamous three-fifths ratio).

The nation's first census commenced in 1790 and was conducted by U.S. marshals. (The latter took the national census every decade until 1870.) Only a handful of questions were posed in this first enumeration (U.S. Census Bureau, n.d.b). The enumerators ascertained the name of the family head, limited to white males (this schedule became the basis of the 1790 nationality studies described earlier) and further ascertained the number of persons differentiated by a few categories, such as free versus slave, age (under sixteen and sixteen and older for free white males only) and gender (for free whites only).

When completed, the 1790 census data or "schedules" were filed at the U.S. State Department, but as noted earlier, the 1790 census returns for six states, including New Jersey, were "destroyed when the British burned the capital at Washington during the war of 1812" (U.S. Census Bureau, n.d.a). Although rare, this was not the only time census information was lost, for most of the 1890 census population schedules were destroyed in a 1921 fire at the federal Commerce Department, which then housed this information (U.S. Census Bureau, n.d.d).

The 1790 census was conducted under the direction of Thomas Jefferson (then secretary of state) and both he and President George Washington were skeptical when this first national enumeration counted 3.9 million persons, as both of these founding fathers believed that the nation's population was greater than that official tally (U.S. Census Bureau, n.d.b). This was the first but surely not the last time that observers of the census believed it undercounted (e.g., as discussed in chapter 4, contemporary minorities especially may not be fully enumerated; Cressie 1988).

The 1790 census, not including the enumerators' full schedules of surnames and other collected raw detail, was a fifty-six-page document ("Return of the Whole Number of Persons" 1793), with the New Jersey portion summarized on four pages. A total of two hundred copies of this document were printed and distributed (Eschner 2017). The New Jersey information was arrayed by the then-existing thirteen New Jersey counties presented in the following order: Hunterdon, Sussex, Burlington, Essex, Monmouth, Morris, Middlesex, Gloucester, Bergen, Somerset, Salem, Cumberland, and Cape May. The above county presentation followed neither an alphabetical nor geographical (e.g., north versus south) array but was rank-ordered by size, so Hunterdon, then having the largest county population (20,153), was presented first, and Cape May, with the smallest county population (2,571), presented last. Each county's inclusive towns were arrayed as well, with the state then having a total of sixty-nine towns listed in the 1790 census (a far cry from today's 565 municipalities). The number of towns by county varied from a low of three in Essex and Cape May Counties to a high of twelve towns in Sussex County.

Table 2.12

Population Enumeration in the 1790 Census for New Jersey and the Total United States

Population Category	Total 1790 Population New Jersey	Total 1790 Population All U.S. States and Southwestern Territories
"Free white males 16 years and upwards, including heads of families"	45,251	813,365
"Free white males under 16 years"	41,416	802,127
"Free white females, heads of including families [not differentiated by age]"	83,287	1,556,628
"All other free persons"	1,762	59,511
"Slaves"	11,421	697,697
"Total number"	184,139	3,929,326

SOURCE: "Return of the Whole Number of Persons within the Several Districts of the United States according to 'An Act Providing for the Enumeration of the Inhabitants of the United States,'" 1793.

As elsewhere in this chapter, it is important to keep in mind that the number and boundaries of New Jersey's counties have changed markedly since the eighteenth century, with the reader referred to the appendix A county maps. Local community names have also sometimes changed—for example, Elizabethtown shortened to Elizabeth and Acquacknack no longer in existence; it must be further recognized that municipal boundaries have also altered over time. (The definitive source on the latter topic is John Snyder's masterful 1969 *The Story of New Jersey's Civil Boundaries, 1606–1968*.)

The 1790 census for New Jersey (as well as other states) presented in tabular form the number of persons by six categories. These categories and their respective statewide tallies for New Jersey (and for the overall nation for perspective) follow.

By individual listed town, Amwell in Hunterdon County had the state's largest population (5,201) and Wallpack in Sussex County had the smallest (496). By singular town, Lower Freehold in Monmouth County had the largest number of slaves (627) and Stafford in the same county the lowest slave total (2). In numerous instances, the different population tallies were not quantified by individual town but were only available on a county-wide aggregate basis. For instance, for Essex County, there was no separate tabulation for Newark, Elizabethtown, or Acquacknack, only the aggregate sum from these three communities (e.g., 17,785 total persons including 1,171 slaves). There was similar only county-wide population tallies for Bergen, Burlington, Cape May, Cumberland, Gloucester, Morris, and Sussex Counties.

Before leaving our overview of the 1790 census, it is instructive to compare its scope to the last U.S. census conducted in 2010. This side-by-side comparison

Table 2.13
Comparison of the 1790 and 2010 United States Census

	1790 Census	2010 Census
U.S. Resident Population (in millions)	3.9	308.7
Cost (in $000s)	$44	$12,900,000
Cost per Capita (cents)	1.1	4,778
Number of Enumerators (est.)	650	635,000

SOURCE: U.S. Census Bureau, "History—Decennial Census" n.d.

that follows (U.S. Census Bureau, n.d.c) speaks for itself and reflects the country's growth and the expansion of the population characteristics incorporated in the census, which has made it an indispensable demographic source.

With this 1790 census background (with a brief foray to the 2010 census), let us examine a demographic and socioeconomic snapshot as of 1790 (table 2.11) of the country, its three formative-era regions (New England, middle states, and southern states), and New Jersey. This snapshot is mainly derived from the Rossiter 1909 study, which in turn was based on 1790 census information and other sources.

In 1790, New Jersey's some 184,000 residents comprised 4.7 percent of the total nation's 3,930,000 persons. At that point in time, the lion's share, about one-half, of the country's total population was in southern states (1,903,000 persons; 48.4 percent of the total), followed in near equal shares by New England (1,009,000 persons; 25.7 percent) and the middle states (1,018,000; 25.9 percent).

In 1790, about eight-tenths (80.7 percent) of the nation's population was white and about one-fifth (19.3 percent) was Black. A much lower share of persons in southern states was white (64.4 percent) and a much higher portion was Black (35.6 percent). In both New England and the middle states, whites predominated the total population (98.3 percent and 93.8 percent, respectively) and Blacks in these two regions comprised just a sliver of all persons (1.7 percent and 6.2 percent, respectively). The racial composition of New Jersey at this initial census, 92.3 percent white and 7.7 percent Black, very closely resembled the 1790 middle states profile.

Almost all (92.2 percent—17.8 percent of the total 1790 national Black population share of 19.3 percent) of the nation's Blacks were enslaved. This percentage was highest in the South (95.8 percent—34.1 percent of the total southern Black population share of 35.6 percent) and lower in other regions: 23.5 percent in New England (0.4 percent of the total New England Black population share of 1.7 percent) and 71.0 percent in the middle states (4.4 percent of the total middle states' Black population share of 6.2 percent). The share of New Jersey's 1790 population that was enslaved (80.5 percent—6.2 percent of the total New Jersey Black population share of 7.7 percent) was lower than the then-national average (92.2 percent), much lower than slavery's incidence in the South

(95.8 percent), yet was noticeably higher than the middle states' 1790 average share of the enslaved Black population (71.0 percent). The important topic of slavery in the United States—for the nation, region of country, and New Jersey—over the full pre–Civil War period of 1790 through 1860 is considered in depth in this book's appendix C.

Further slave data contained in table 2.11 point to the tremendous 1790 regional differences concerning this institution of human bondage, which would culminate in the nation's Civil War some seventy years later. The nation in 1790 contained 698,000 slaves, with the lion's share (649,000), or more than nine-tenths, in southern states. New England contained almost no slaves (3,800) with more found in the middle states (45,200) and with 11,400 in New Jersey, or one-quarter of its host region's total tally of slaves.

Further reflective of the stark geographical differences of slavery's incidence in 1790 is the much varying ratio of slaves per 100 white persons. That ratio was 22 nationally: essentially 0 in New England, a high 53 in southern states, a tenth that in the middle states (5), with New Jersey's ratio in this regard (7) somewhat higher. Similarly, while 17.2 percent of the nation's families in 1790 were slave-holders, that share was a scant 2.8 percent in New England, stood at double the national average in the South (35.8 percent), and was 16.0 percent in New Jersey, which was noticeably higher than the 9.8 percent of its host middle states region. Slaves sadly constituted important capital in the nation's formative years and beyond (Beckert and Rockman 2016). The estimated value of slaves in the United States as of 1790 was $105 million (in 1790 dollars), almost all of that sum, $97 million, concentrated in southern states. In contrast, the aggregate value of slaves in New England in that year was only $0.6 million, stood at $6.8 million in all the middle states, $1.7 million of that regional tally (25 percent) in New Jersey.

Compared to Europe, the population density in the United States was far less, and indeed the availability of relatively more land per household attracted many from Europe to come to America in the seventeenth and eighteenth centuries. Indeed, as noted earlier, Benjamin Franklin (1751) attributed the American colonies' more rapid population growth relative to England in part because in the former, land was more plentiful, and thus marriages were more frequent and hence larger family size.

What was America's density as of its first census? As with many other characteristics considered here, it varied by location. The New Jersey density in 1790 of 24.7 persons per square mile was about two and one half times the national average (9.4 persons per square mile) and was higher than the persons per square mile in New England (16.3), the middle states as a whole (10.0), and the South (7.5). As discussed later in this book, New Jersey's claim in time to the title of the state with the highest population density was foreshadowed in 1790.

In 1790, household size averaged nationally 5.7 persons per private (nonslave) family and 7.0 white persons per dwelling. (Reflecting the mores of the time, the

1790 census concentrated almost exclusively on the white population.) The New Jersey profile was near identical (5.8 average persons per private family and 7.0 white persons per dwelling) and there was very little difference in these metrics between the new nation's regions. In 1790, the national average ratio of white children to adult white females was 1.9, a ratio that was closely approximated across different geographies considered here (e.g., 2.0 for both the middle states and New Jersey).

Reflecting a gender ratio imbalance discussed earlier in this chapter, there were slightly more males than females per 1,000 white population in 1790 in both the nation (509) and New Jersey (510). That high male ratio per 1,000 white population was somewhat more pronounced in the southern states (515) and the middle states (514). In New England, in contrast, the number of white males per the 1,000 white population (498) were less than half. Although there were numerous influences on this gender ratio, as discussed earlier, perhaps New England was losing males to other regions, with male émigrés in the vanguard of those departing from New England.

Table 2.11 presents illustrative facets of governmental and civil society as of 1790. The nation at that time contained 1,591 minor civil divisions (MCDs), with the New England, southern, and middle states regions containing 937, 436, and 654 MCDs, respectively. Due to the regions' different population sizes, however (recall the South being more populous), the number of persons per MCD was 1,077 in New England, 4,365 in the South, and 1,555 in the middle states. From its onset, then, New England trended to relatively smaller population MCDs, a structure encouraging its heralded participatory town meetings. New Jersey in 1790 contained 94 MCDs averaging 1,959 persons apiece, about a quarter larger than the average MCD size for the middle states region, and more population intensive than the 1790 national average persons per MCD (1,273).

The nation in 1790 contained 292 counties with an average of 13,459 persons apiece. In a not coincidental reversal of the MCD pattern described above, New England, containing only forty-one counties, averaged the most people per county (24,610) compared to the average county population in the middle states and southern regions (19,577 and 9,563, respectively). New Jersey's thirteen counties in 1790 averaged 14,154 persons apiece, about one-quarter smaller than the middle states average.

What about the availability of post officers and newspapers? These resources can best be compared on a normalized per 1,000 population basis. In this regard, New Jersey's .027 post office facilities per 1,000 persons in 1790 was relatively high, or more available, as shown in table 2.11 (e.g., it was .019 in the middle states). In contrast, New Jersey's .016 newspapers per 1,000 population in 1790 was relatively sparse (e.g., considerably less than the .037 and .041 newspaper ratios in New England and middle states, respectively). The limited availability of eighteenth-century newspapers in New Jersey, along with the more general communication and transportation challenges of that era, led one historian to humorously observe that "if New Jersey has paused to observe its centenary in 1764, provincial fathers would have been hard pressed to inform the widespread populace" (J. Cunningham 1966, 78).

Last presented in this section is the 1790 economic profile on an absolute and relative basis. We begin with two measures for 1790: aggregate wealth and per capita wealth, both measured in 1790 dollars. (These data were not available from Rossiter [1909] for New Jersey.) As evident from table 2.11, the southern states led the nation in wealth. Somewhat more than one-half of the total national wealth in 1790 ($522.4 million in 1790 dollars) was concentrated in southern states ($272.4 million), with near one-quarter shares apiece captured by New England ($138.7 million) and the middle states ($141.3 million). More telling is wealth per capita, because recall the different regional populations, with the South then containing almost twice the number of persons relative to both New England and the middle states. Per capita wealth per person in 1790 was $217 in southern states, about 30 percent higher than the 1790 national per capita wealth average ($171) and exceeding the near equivalent per capita wealth in both New England ($138) and the middle states ($145). There are many underlying causes and influences concerning variations in wealth and likely one contributor to the relatively higher southern affluence was slave ownership, which in that era was economically valuable in its own right (slaves were valued at a total of $97 million in the South) and allowed for heightened agricultural production and land values. McCusker (2006a, 5-672), based on previous research (e.g., Jones 1968), found that of total physical wealth in the South as of 1774, 40.5 percent was derived from land holdings and a slightly larger 42.1 percent share from servants and slaves.

What about the inequality of wealth in the colonial era? Then, as in contemporary American society, there was considerable wealth inequality. The latter can be measured statistically through what is referred to as a Gini coefficient (where 0 expresses perfect equality and 100 percent expresses total inequality), as well as through more popularly presented measures, such as the percentage of total societal wealth held by a top given percent (e.g., top 10 percent or 1 percent) of all people. In 1774, the Gini coefficient of the entire thirteen colonies was 0.66 and the richest 10 percent owned 50.7 percent of total wealth (Jones 1980, 165). In other words, there was considerable wealth inequality at America's founding. Interestingly, of the three colonial-era regions, New England, middle colonies, and the South, the middle colonies had "the lesser degree of inequality ... which may have been a result of the prosperity of the middle colonies' agriculture relative to that of New England, but without the considerable scale made possible by the large plantations that appeared in the South" (Galenson 1996, 204). The middle states' economic characteristics pertain in large part to colonial New Jersey as well, and thus conjecturally, this colony may have had less wealth inequality relative to the New England and southern colonies. One observer related in a nonstatistical fashion that "[colonial] inhabitants of New Jersey were said to enjoy 'near equality of wealth,' because most townships 'divided and then again subdivided [their land]' into two and three hundred separate, proper creditable estates" (Bobrick 1997, 38).

New Jersey's economy in this early era was largely agriculture based.[15] As observed in one study, "By 1775, the typical development form ... was an agricultural landscape" (New Jersey Office of State Planning 1988, 2). In 1784, New Jersey (with a 1780 population of about 140,000) contained 2,032,587 acres of improved land, 52,488 horses, and 102,221 horned cattle. For context, Massachusetts, with a 1780 population of 269,000, near double that of New Jersey at that time, contained in 1784 a total of 921,563 acres of improved land, 43,969 horses, and 237,993 horned cattle (McCusker 2006a, 5-700). A study of the occupation of 1,028 New Jersey persons named in wills over the period 1670–1730 (Whitehead 1880, cited in Purvis 1999, 112) (admittedly such persons were not fully representative of the overall population) found that 519, or 50.5 percent, were farmers, with the remaining 509 persons having diverse various craft occupations such as, in rank order, carpenters (4.8 percent), ropemakers (4.7 percent), smiths and tailors (4.4 percent), weavers (3.4 percent), mariners (3.2 percent), coopers (3.0 percent), and twenty-two other categories (e.g., masons, saddlers, hatters, and vintners).

New Jersey was not then doing much manufacturing, though that activity was nascent, such as the 1674 (estimated origin date) ironworks furnace in Tinton Falls, 1710 Whippany River Forge in Morristown, 1725 Black Creek Forge in Bordentown, 1730s Basto ironworks, and 1760s Long Pond Ironworks in Greenwood Lake (Bayley 1910; Boyer 1931 cited in Purvis 1999, 104; "Colonial New Jersey Bog Iron" 1963; Jasch, n.d.; Veit 2009b, 157). There were New Jersey copper mines as far back as in the 1660s (Pahaquarry Delaware River Water Gap Mine), 1710s (Schuyler mine in North Arlington), 1730s (Soho Mine in Belleville and Black Hill Mine in Griggstown), and 1740s (French Mine, New Brunswick) (Mulholland 1981, cited in Purvis 1999, 110; Veit 2009b 157; Weiss and Weiss 1963; Woodward 1944). Glassmaking existed in colonial New Jersey, mainly in its southern environs (G. Taylor 2006), such as the Alloway Creek glass furnace that operated in Salem starting in the 1730s (McKearin and McKearin 1941, cited in Purvis 1999, 107; Palmer 1976; Veit 2009b, 167). This Wistarburgh Glass Manufactory (named for its German immigrant founder Caspar Wistar) is credited with becoming the first successful glass company in America (La Gorce 2014). More broadly, South Jersey glassmaking was an important influence on the larger glass manufacturing industry in America (La Gorce 2014; Palmer 1976). Colonial-era water-powered mills operated in, for example, Bradford (1720s), Elizabeth (1730s) and Spotswood (1750s) (D. Hunter 1952 cited in Purvis 1999, 109). The growth of these nature-powered water mills coupled with settler ingenuity was near geometric in New Jersey's colonial era (about "a dozen ... by 1670, between 80 and 100 in 1717, and approximately 1,000 by the mid-1790s" [R. Hunter 2009, 170]).

Merchants and farmers participated in the shipping of goods inter- and intra-state and beyond (Levitt 1981). For example, Conestoga wagons would bring flour "down the Amwell and River roads to New Brunswick, whence their produce was shipped down the Raritan" (Sutherland 1966, 118). However, New Jersey was not then a leader in ship production or ship-based international shipping. While all the colonies over the 1769 through 1771 period had manufactured 1,212 sailing vessels of an aggregate 64,793 tonnage, New Jersey's boat production over these three years barely registered at 6 vessels of aggregate 153 tons (McCusker 2006a, 5-705, citing previous research). New Jersey captured a very small share of shipping from (outward-bound) and to (inward-bound) its ports. In 1769, for all the thirteen colonies outward-bound shipping amounted to a total of 339,302 tons (worth 2,852,441 pounds);[16] all the colonies had aggregate inward-bound shipping in that year of 332,146 tons (worth 2,623,412 pounds) (McCusker 2006a, 5-717, citing previous research). The 1769 shipping tallies for New Jersey were minuscule: 1,093 tons outward-bound (worth 2,532 pounds) and 936 tons inward-bound (worth 1,991 pounds).[17] In a similar vein, of the total 766,000 tonnage of vessels entering all U.S. ports in 1790, only a sliver of 5,900 tons were captured by New Jersey ports (see table 2.11). So New Jersey's economy in the late eighteenth century was primarily agricultural with relatively minor nonagricultural pursuits, such as nascent manufacturing (New Jersey Office of State Planning 1988, 2) and mostly local and regional shipping. That economic template would dramatically reverse later in this state's history as New Jersey shifted from an agricultural emphasis to at first manufacturing of all types (e.g., "Trenton makes, the world takes") and later postindustrial endeavors (Hughes and Seneca 2004a, 234–236; 2009, 152–155), a shift explored in this book's chapters 3, 5, and elsewhere. The postindustrial sector encompasses and capitalizes on information and education, and in this regard, it merits mentioning that of the nine pre–Revolutionary War colleges founded in American, only one colony—New Jersey—was the home of two (Princeton, originally the College of New Jersey, and Rutgers, originally Queens).

An interesting economic characteristic of the New Jersey economy concerns the sources of revenue for its colonial government. From 1704 through 1775, the total colonial government financial revenues (total yearly resources in hand) amounted to about 571,000 New Jersey pounds (£NJ). Of that total, 381,000 £NJ (67 percent) was raised from debt ("bills of credit"), 66,000 £NJ (12 percent) came from property tax collection, 63,000 £NJ (11 percent) from British Crown cash transfers, 39,000 £NJ (7 percent) from interest income, and 23,000 £NJ (4 percent) from duty on imported slaves (Grubb 2015, 146). Thus, from its origins, the New Jersey public sector tapped property taxes, credit instruments, and multiple other sources to fund its public expenditures. New Jersey in colonial times had legally licensed lotteries to raise public funds (e.g., in 1759, 1761, and 1762; Ezell 1960, cited by Purvis 1999, 302) and the state taps lotteries today as well. (Early in its history, Rutgers raised revenue from a lottery, as did almost all colleges founded before the Revolutionary War [Lukac 1966].) Surely, however, not all contemporary New Jersey public finance characteristics harken back to colonial roots. Purportedly, "down to the end of the Revolutionary War, there were no official government buildings in New Jersey" (Randall 1975, 9) and that is not the case today.

In an interesting historical footnote, following the Revolutionary War, British merchants argued in 1791 they were owed about 5 million pounds, presumably for goods shipped to the former colonies that remained unpaid for (Walton and Shepard 1979, 107). Certain colonies were most in arears with respect to these so-called claims of debt submitted to the British government by the British merchants, such as Virginia which was 2.3 million pounds in the red (Walton and Shepard 1979, 107). The least amount owed by far was that of New Jersey with a minuscule 524-pound debt claim (Walton and Shepard 1979, 107). For context, the second lowest debt claim was 21,796 pounds for New Hampshire. So either New Jersey as a colony was by far the most diligent in remitting owed payments or, more likely, was not as significant an importer of goods from Great Britain as some other former colonies such as Virginia.

Voices of Early New Jersey

Thus far, this chapter has been mainly quantitative in nature, presenting the population totals and demographic characteristics of New Jersey from the colonial era to initial statehood. To add a qualitative dimension, we conclude with short extracts from early New Jerseyans about their lives, concerns, and accomplishments. The persons chosen are purposely diverse and include Native Americans, the colony's governor, a founder of Elizabeth (then called Elizabethtown), some settlers of Raritan Landing (precursor to New Brunswick), women of various economic stations, and enslaved as well as freed and runaway Black slaves.

Original Inhabitants—Native Americans

Differing ideas about property ownership and land use led to misunderstandings and conflicts with the original inhabitants of New Jersey.

> You claim all the wild creatures, and will not let us come on your land to hunt after them. You will not so much as let us peel a "single tree": This is hard, and has given us great offence. The cattle you raise are your own, but those which are wild, are still ours, or should be common to both; for when we sold the land, we did not propose to deprive ourselves of hunting the wild deer, or using a stick of wood when we should have occasion. We desire the governor to take this matter into his care, and see that justice be done in it.
>
> —Indian spokesman for the Delaware at a meeting of the royal governor of the Province of New Jersey and the Indians to settle Indian land claims, 1758 (Quoted in O'Reilly 2012, 25)

Brotherton, in today's Shamong Township, was created in 1758 as a reservation for New Jersey's Native Americans (Lurie and Veit 2012, 25; 2016, 15; J. Snyder 1969, 1; Thomas 2013). Governor Francis Bernard praised the effort:

> It is a tract of Land Very suitable for this purpose, having soil good enough, a large hunting country and a passage by water to the Sea for fishing... & has a saw mill upon it which serves to provide them with timber for their own use & to raise a little money for other purposes. We laid out the plan of a town to which I gave the Name of Brotherton & saw an house erected being one of ten that were ready prepared. (*New Jersey Archives*, 1st ser., 9:174–175; cited in Williams 2010, 113–114)

However, as with other reservations, Brotherton's land was soon encroached on by white settlers, protested in "The Brotherton Indians' Agreement to Oppose White Settlement" of January 6, 1780: "Be it known by this, that it has been in our consideration of late about settling of White People on the Indian Lands. And we have concluded that it is a thing which ought not be, & a thing that will not be allowed by us" ("The Brotherton Indians of New Jersey, 1780" n.d.; see also Thomas 2013). Alas, this declaration did not stop the white settlers' encroachment, and the Brotherton Reservation, for which the Lenape "relinquished all rights to New Jersey except for fishing and hunting privileges" (Cunningham 1966, 23), was disbanded in 1802. The Brotherton Indians suffered for lack of "food and raiment" (Lurie and Veit 2002, 25).

Some Lenape assimilated to European society and even intermarried.

> Princess Ann was the daughter of a Unami Sachem (Chief) living in the area of Goose Creek, which fed into the inlet and the sound now known as Barnegat Bay.... [She married] a young Englishman named Thomas Luker, who had emigrated to New England in 1685, [then] came to Shrewsbury in quest of a whaling license to pursue that trade off the New Jersey coast. [They lived] in a wigwam on a triangular piece of land ... [with] ... two large trees ... —both still used by surveyors of the twentieth century. This homesite is thought to have been located on property where the present-day First National Bank now stands. (Lyttle et al. 1978, 57)

Some Early European Settlers

Elizabethtown was settled in the 1660s and soon became a significant city in the early colony.

> Among the eighty Elizabethtown Associates ... were Nathaniel Bonnell and Issac Whitehead.... Nathaniel Bonnell (Bunnell, Bonnell, Bonnel) was born in New Haven Connecticut in 1636 [and] ... he married Susanna Whitehead [daughter of Issac Whitehead] ... [in] ... 1665. Nathaniel was granted a farm

of sixteen acres and a six-acre town-house lot in an area with others who had come from Connecticut. Before 1682 he had built a house, which is still standing (1045 East Jersey Street; headquarters of New Jersey Society of Sons of the Revolution), in Elizabeth.

The Bonnells had seven children. . . . Nathaniel died in 1711 and was buried at the First Presbyterian Church of Elizabeth. . . . After his death Susanna moved, probably to the family farm, in the area of Elizabethtown called Connecticut Farms (now Union). Susanna Bonnell died . . . 1733. (Ogden 2016, 75)[18]

In the early days of the colony, there were many conflicting property claims. The royal governor of New York, Sir Edmond Andros, even arrested the governor of East New Jersey, Philip Carteret, in a jurisdictional dispute in 1675. Carteret was eventually released and resumed his post.

[Andros] sent a Party of Soldiers to fetch me away Dead or alive, so that in the Dead Time of Night broke open my Doors and most barbarously and inhumanly and violently hailed me out of my Bed, that I have not Words enough sufficiently to express the Cruelty of it; and Indeed I am so disabled by the Bruises and Hurts I then received, that I fear I shall hardly be a perfect Man again. (Whitehead 1880, citied in Lurie 2010, 44)

In West Jersey, Quakers began to question the morality of slavery. A leading advocate for emancipation was a minister named John Woolman.[19] Woolman recounts in his diary one encounter where he persuaded a neighbor to renounce slavery.

A neighbor received a bad bruise in his body, and sent for me. . . . He desired me to write his will. I took notes, and amongst other things he told me to which of his children he gave his young Negro. . . . I wrote his will, save only that part concerning the slave, and carrying it to his bedside read it to him. I then told him in a friendly way that I could not write any instruments by which my fellow-creatures were made slaves, without bringing trouble on my own mind. . . . We then had a serious conference on the subject; at length, he agreeing to set her free. I finished his will. (Quoted in Doak and McConville 2005, 72)

Women in the Colonial Era

Women, like most settlers, mostly worked on family farms. But there were exceptions.

Patience Lovell Wright of Bordentown ranks as America's first professional women sculptor . . . the most outstanding New Jersey women artist of the eighteenth century. . . . Born in 1725 in Bordentown, Patience was the daughter of John Lovell, a Quaker so strict that he required his six daughters and one son to dress in pure white from head to foot. As a result, the Lovell children enjoyed mixing colors, painting pictures, and modeling figures in dough and clay. Patience displayed her talents for sculpting at an early age. . . . In her early twenties, impatient Patience fled to Philadelphia where, in 1748, she married Joseph Wright, a cooper from Bordentown. [She] moved . . . to New York where she opened a studio and wax museum [and later moved to England]. Patience's crowning achievement in England was a life-size wax figure of William Pitt. . . . The Pitt statue is the only one sculptured by an American to be displayed in the Museum of Westminster Abbey, where it can still be seen. (Lyttle et al. 1978, 134–135)

And once the American Revolution began, numerous women sacrificed for the cause.[20] Some examples of these brave women include "The Ladies of Trenton," who raised money to support Washington's army (e.g., Annis Stockton, wife of Richard Stockton, a signer of the Declaration of Independence, who resided in Morven, a Princeton estate that later served as a residence for New Jersey's governors); Edus Richards, who voluntarily paid a revolutionary supply tax; and Theodeia Johnes Ford, a widow providing various material support (Hunold, n.d.). These women have been rightfully recognized as "Patriots" by the Daughters of the American Revolution (Hunold, n.d.). Their many contributions may explain the fact that women were granted the right to vote in New Jersey's 1776 state constitution (Klinghoffer and Elkis 1992).[21] Alas, this suffrage was rescinded in 1807 and would not be regained until passage of the Nineteenth Amendment in 1920.

The Diverse Inhabitants of Raritan Landing in Central New Jersey

Raritan Landing—settled c. 1700—was nearly destroyed when occupied by the British in the Revolutionary War and was dismantled and abandoned in late 1800s. The narratives below, extracted from the masterful *Voices from Raritan Landing* (Yamin 2013), are from this settlement's early years.

Bill (Slave)

I was a good baker so I knew I could get work somewhere else, if they would have me, but I couldn't stay with Cornelius Clopper anymore. He taught me the baking trade, but he made me wear an iron collar. I didn't want to wear that collar so I left with only the clothes on my back: an old red cloth jacket and a pair of homespun trousers. . . . I was young and strong and would settle wherever possible, as long as I could be free. That's what mattered most—and not to have to wear that collar. (Yamin 2013, 23)

Jean Blair

I outlived my husband by a good twenty years. . . . I didn't have any children, but there was plenty of work to do and when I made my will in 1784 I left my negro servant, Harry, to my friend Mary Covenhoven of Somerset County. I gave my mulatto slave his freedom forever. . . . I wonder what the villagers thought of that. (Yamin 2013, 25)

John Dumont

I had a big farm of 650 acres in Somerset County. . . . Like almost all the Dutch farmers in Somerset, we had slaves to work the land, nine in all when I made my will in 1759, valued at 265 pounds sterling. We couldn't have done the work without those slaves and they lived right in the house with us, not in separate quarters like in Virginia or the Carolinas. We sent the grain to Raritan Landing for export as wheat was the main crop. (Yamin 2013, 18)

Adolphus Hardenbrook

I came to Raritan Landing—well, actually the place didn't have a name—in 1719. . . . I was the first New Yorker at the Landing and it's due to me that the Lows and Duyckincks came to that growing place soon after. We were all in the shipping business. The Raritan Valley wasn't so different than the Hudson Valley where our fathers had been shippers. (Yamin 2013, 6)

Johanna Gouverneur Low

I chose Cornelius Low among my many suitors. He came from a landed family and had dreams of making the Raritan Valley as important to New York as the Hudson Valley had always been. We moved to the little village of Raritan Landing in 1730 and no sooner settled in than my first son was born. He died . . . [and later] . . . ten [children] lived—four girls and six boys, quite a houseful. . . . It was a good life at Raritan Landing once we were settled in the "house on the mountain." We had a cluster of family houses up there and pretty much kept apart from the villagers who were less familiar with fashionable New York ways. (Yamin 2013, 12)

Charles Suydam

You couldn't just build a mill in those days. I had to get permission from the New Jersey Assembly to put up a mill dam. That I did, and by 1750 I had the only mill on the north side of the river. That's why my friend, John Duyckinck, and I sponsored the project to build a new bridge across the river [the first Landing Lane Bridge] in 1772. With the bridge, the grain came from two directions, that is, along the Road Up Raritan and over the bridge from Somerset County. It was a lucrative operation, that is, until the British destroyed it. (Yamin 2013, 20)

3

The Long-Term Decennial Growth Picture

•••••••••••••••••••••

The broad sweep of overall population growth in New Jersey since its admission into the Union in 1787 as a state is documented by the decennial censuses starting in 1790. In the intervening decades, New Jersey's population change did not simply happen in a vacuum. It was continually driven and shaped by the forces of global immigration, domestic migration flows (internal to the United States), generational transformations, macro and regional economic swings, and technological change. In the nineteenth century, the state's basic demographic growth was influenced and determined by the westward geographic expansion of the territorial reach of the United States and the resulting migration of people; the first and second Industrial Revolutions; urbanization and the rise of technology-driven, industrial-manufacturing clusters; major waves of immigration, largely from Europe; and national and global economic cycles—that is, business-cycle expansions and contractions.

In the twentieth century, New Jersey's demography was further reshaped by two world wars, the rise of New Jersey's manufacturing enterprises to global preeminence and then their precipitous fall, their eventual late-century replacement by leading-edge postindustrial economic activities, the Great Depression, reversals of the forces of urbanization and suburbanization, fluctuations in fertility, changing immigration flows, advanced globalization, and regional interstate competition.

In the twenty-first century, intensification of the forces of both globalization and regional competition, introductions of advanced information technologies,

Table 3.1
Census Population Trends: United States and New Jersey, 1790–2010

Year	United States Population	New Jersey Population	Share of Nation (%)	Rank among States
1790	3,929,214	184,139	4.69	9
1800	5,308,483	211,149	3.98	10
1810	7,239,881	245,562	3.39	12
1820	9,638,453	277,575	2.88	13
1830	12,866,020	320,823	2.49	14
1840	17,069,453	373,306	2.19	18
1850	23,191,876	489,555	2.11	19
1860	31,443,321	672,035	2.14	21
1870	38,558,371	906,096	2.35	17
1880	50,189,209	1,131,116	2.25	19
1890	62,979,766	1,444,933	2.29	18
1900	76,212,168	1,883,669	2.47	16
1910	92,228,496	2,537,167	2.75	11
1920	106,021,537	3,155,900	2.98	10
1930	123,202,624	4,041,334	3.28	9
1940	132,164,569	4,160,165	3.15	9
1950	151,325,798	4,835,329	3.20	8
1960	179,323,175	6,066,782	3.38	8
1970	203,302,031	7,171,112	3.53	8
1980	226,545,805	7,365,011	3.25	9
1990	248,709,873	7,730,188	3.11	9
2000	281,421,906	8,414,350	2.99	9
2010	308,745,538	8,791,894	2.85	11

SOURCES: Data for 1790–2000: New Jersey State Data Center 2001. Data for 2010: U.S. Census Bureau 2011.

new corporate locational proclivities, generational successions, the Great Recession, and a range of national and state public policies proved influential. Many of these issues will be examined subsequently in more detail. They will be briefly highlighted in this section as they relate to the broad sweep of population change.

The Beginnings

In 1790, the nation's first decennial census encompassed the thirteen original colonies.[1] As shown in table 3.1, New Jersey ranked ninth in population size among the thirteen states;[2] its 184,000 people at the time accounted for 4.69 percent of the nation's total population (3.9 million people).[3] This share was to be the state's all-time historical high. Nonetheless, waves of population growth, fluctuating between faster and slower rates, continued to engulf New Jersey for the next 220 years and beyond.

Providing sharp contrast to this diminutive 1790 past are the final years of the second decade of the current century. New Jersey's population was just over

Table 3.2
Decadal Change: United States and New Jersey, 1790–2010

Time Period	New Jersey		United States	
	Population Growth	Rate of Change (%)	Population Growth	Rate of Change (%)
1790–1800	27,010	14.7	1,379,269	35.1
1800–1810	34,413	16.3	1,931,398	36.4
1810–1820	32,013	13.0	2,398,572	33.1
1820–1830	43,248	15.6	3,227,567	33.5
1830–1840	52,483	16.4	4,203,433	32.7
1840–1850	116,249	31.1	6,122,423	35.9
1850–1860	182,480	37.3	8,251,445	35.6
1860–1870	234,061	34.8	7,115,050	22.6
1870–1880	225,020	24.8	11,630,838	30.2
1880–1890	313,817	27.7	12,790,557	25.5
1890–1900	438,736	30.4	13,232,402	21.0
1900–1910	653,498	34.7	16,016,328	21.0
1910–1920	618,733	24.4	13,793,041	15.0
1920–1930	885,434	28.1	17,181,087	16.2
1930–1940	118,831	2.9	8,961,945	7.3
1940–1950	675,164	16.2	19,161,229	14.5
1950–1960	1,231,453	25.5	27,997,377	18.5
1960–1970	1,104,330	18.2	23,978,856	13.4
1970–1980	193,899	2.7	23,243,774	11.4
1980–1990	365,177	5.0	22,164,068	9.8
1990–2000	684,162	8.9	32,712,033	13.2
2000–2010	377,544	4.5	27,323,632	9.7
Change: 1790–2010	8,607,755	4,674.6	304,816,324	7,757.7

SOURCES: Data for 1790–2000: New Jersey State Data Center 2001. Data for 2010: U.S. Census Bureau 2011.

8.9 million people in 2018 (see note 20 of this chapter), up very modestly from the preceding decennial census in 2010, when it approached nearly 8.8 million people. The decennial 2010 total was nearly forty-eight times greater than that (184,000 people) of the first census (1790). Although the state's multicentury growth could be considered monumental, the nation overall grew much faster than New Jersey during this 220-year time span. The population of the United States in 2010 (309 million people) was nearly seventy-nine times greater than that of 1790 (3.9 million people). As further detailed at the bottom of table 3.2, the nation's 1790–2010 growth rate (7,757.7 percent) far eclipsed that of New Jersey (4,674 percent). As a result of long-term slower growth, the state's share of the total U.S. population in 2010 had declined to 2.85 percent from its 1790 peak of 4.69 percent (table 3.1).

Since New Jersey was limited in its geographic and developable area, and since it was the oldest, first-settled part of the country, it is not surprising that New

Jersey has been a demographic growth laggard when benchmarked from the first census;[4] nonetheless, there were intervening periods when the state achieved significantly above-average population growth rates (table 3.2). These occurred during the midst of the two Industrial Revolutions (1840–1870), during the subsequent rise to prominence of the great immigration-fueled industrial-manufacturing city in the late nineteenth/early twentieth centuries (1890–1910), and during the great post–World War II surges of residential suburbanization, particularly 1950 to 1960.

The Early Period of the Nineteenth Century

At the time of the first census in 1790, the economies of the United States and New Jersey were predominantly agricultural- and natural resources–based. The state's and nation's populations were largely rural and dispersed, with the largest settlement concentrations, albeit modest in scale, situated mostly at ocean shipping ports such as New York City and Philadelphia, located along the Atlantic seaboard.[5] But as the nineteenth century unfolded, a nascent industrial economy began to emerge at the same time as the population of the United States started to shift westward.

Outmigration from many coastal states followed directly with the sustained westward expansion of the nation's geographic footprint. A signature event was the 1803 Louisiana Purchase, which doubled the size (land area) of the United States. Less than four decades later, four out of ten Americans lived in the trans-Appalachian West. Thus, New Jersey and many eastern states began to lose population share during the first half of the 1800s due simply to the increasing territorial size of the nation, which created new economic opportunities and new settlements that attracted coastal migrants. By 1850, New Jersey's share of the nation's total population had slipped to just 2.11 percent, a historic low (table 3.1). While the state's population more than doubled between 1800 and 1850—from 211,000 people to 490,000 people in one-half century—that of the nation more than quadrupled—from 5.3 million in 1800 to 23.2 million in 1850. New Jersey's decennial population rank among the states slipped from tenth in 1800 (out of a total of sixteen states) to nineteenth in 1850 (out of a total of thirty states).[6]

The Industrial Revolutions

But New Jersey's declining share, and its below-national-average population growth, would have been even greater during this fifty-year-long period if it were not for the state's prominent role in the first Industrial Revolution, where manual home production by artisans and craftspeople was replaced by machine and factory production.[7] Modest immigration from Europe helped replace, although not fully, those people lost to westward migration. But the economic and settlement foundations were set in place for the era of city building that would emerge just before, during, and after the Civil War, an event that was a major impetus for the technological innovation that spurred the second Industrial Revolution.

Urbanization and Demographic Resurgence

Between 1850 and 1870, as a result of the full emergence of the second Industrial Revolution—an era that was spurred by more sophisticated technological advances leading to the rise of the industrial city—New Jersey's population grew faster than that of the United States for the first time since the advent of the first decennial census (table 3.2).[8] Its six-decade-long (1790–1850) shrinkage in national population share was halted as it increased from a low of 2.11 percent in 1850 to over 2.35 percent in 1870 (table 3.1). Concurrently, New Jersey's population rank among the states increased from nineteenth (out of thirty states) in 1850 to seventeenth (out of thirty-seven states) in 1870 (see note 6).

The rising cities of New Jersey, fed by rural-to-urban migration within the state and international migration into the state, became focal points of the industrialized economy. The core business of the Garden State shifted from strictly growing things to making things. The advance of industrialization was the start of the first major economic transformation of the state. Population began to mass in tight, dense, interdependent urban-industrial agglomerations. By 1870, the population of New Jersey had reached 906,000 people, up from 490,000 people in 1850, a remarkable 85 percent increase in just twenty years. This would prove to be the highest two-decade rate of population growth in the state's history (table 3.2).[9]

But difficult national and global economic conditions in the 1870s interrupted the economic ebullience of the Civil War decade and impacted international population flows. According to the Dating Committee of the National Bureau of Economic Research (2010), what has been called the Long Depression started in October 1873, lasted a record-long sixty-five months, and finally ended in March 1879. New Jersey's two-decade-long increase in population share was halted, although just modestly, from 2.35 percent in 1870 to 2.25 percent in 1880 (table 3.1).

Nonetheless, the state's population growth then became more competitive with the nation for the balance of the century. The state's population topped one million for the first time in 1880 (1.1 million people), approaching two million by 1900 (1.9 million people). This represented a two-decade (1880–1900) period when New Jersey's "Big Six" cities—Camden, Elizabeth, Jersey City, Newark, Paterson, and Trenton—all evolved into technology-driven, urban-manufacturing dynamos. These powerful urban industrial agglomerations were the key drivers of New Jersey's population growth. In addition, a web of nation-leading commuter railroad and trolley systems spurred the development of New Jersey's early suburban communities linked not only to the state's cities but also to the economic behemoths of New York City and Philadelphia. By the turn of the century (1900), the state's share of the nation's population had increased to 2.47 percent, up from 2.25 percent in 1880 (table 3.1). This increase in decennial share—the obvious result of faster population growth relative to the nation (table 3.2)—would continue for the next seventy years (1900–1970), interrupted only briefly during the decade of the Great Depression (1930–1940). That would be the second major national and global economic setback to influence the demographic trajectory of New Jersey.

The broad sweep of population growth between 1850 and 1900 was linked to two principal factors. The first (generally pre-1860) and second (generally post-1860) Industrial Revolutions constituted the first factor. These revolutions required labor forces beyond those extant in New Jersey and the United States. The first wave of immigration to satisfy the needs of early industrialization started around 1815 and originated in northern and western Europe. The second factor was the wave of population from central, eastern, and southern Europe, which then serviced the post–Civil War second Industrial Revolution. As will be explained in chapter 4, significant population growth in New Jersey stemming from immigration would be replicated again in the late twentieth and early twenty-first centuries.

Early Twentieth Century

During the first three decades of the twentieth century (1900–1930), New Jersey and its cities thrived economically, led by such nation- and global-leading manufacturing industries as Singer Sewing Machine in Elizabeth and RCA–Radio Victor in Camden. So, too, did the economies of New York City and Philadelphia thrive. Both phenomena spurred the further development of suburban communities, aided by the introduction and proliferation of the internal combustion engine and the private automobile. "The city was still the dominant focus of the New Jersey economy, but a host of contiguous territories became a viable and functional part of the daily urban system" (Hughes and Seneca 2015, 36). Thus, a process of "metropolitanization" ensued in New Jersey—the geographic spread and spillover of population and some economic functions beyond the cities' political boundaries—a result of sustained urban viability and the development of adjacent suburbs, tightly linked to, and highly dependent on, urban viability.

New Jersey continued to be enveloped by overlapping suburbanization stemming not only from internal-state population movements from its own cities but also from external-state movements originating in New York City and Philadelphia. By 1910, the state's population had jumped to over 2.5 million people, up from 1.9 million people ten years earlier (table 3.1). This represented, at the time, the largest absolute decade (1900–1910) population increase (over 650,000 people) in New Jersey since the state's inception (table 3.2). As a result, the state's 1910 share of the nation's population increased to 2.75 percent (table 3.1). At this point, New Jersey ranked eleventh among the forty-six states enumerated in the 1910 census, compared with sixteenth (out of forty-five states) in 1900 and nineteenth (out of thirty-eight states) in 1880.

A similar scale of growth (+620,000 people) continued for the next ten years (1910–1920) as the state's population approached 3.2 million people; consequently, New Jersey's share of the nation's population in 1920 reached 2.98 percent, the highest since 1810 (3.39 percent) more than a century earlier. And it moved up one place—to tenth (out of forty-eight states)—in the national state rankings.

But a new decade growth record was quickly set. Between 1920 and 1930—the Roaring Twenties—New Jersey gained over 885,000 people (table 3.2), and its population soared past 4.0 million people, or 3.3 percent of the nation (table 3.1). Thus, the first three decades of the twentieth century saw the state's population more than double—from just below 1.9 million in 1900 to over 4.0 million in 1930. The state's share of the nation's 1930 population increased to 3.28 percent, and its ranking improved to ninth place (out of forty-eight states). At the time, this was the highest national state rank ever achieved in the history of New Jersey. Sustained industrialization and urbanization, and then increased metropolitanization and suburbanization, drove the population boom and transformed New Jersey.

The Great Depression

But there has yet to be a boom that lasts forever. The Great Depression definitively halted all of the dynamics that had underpinned the state's eight-decade-long upward demographic trajectory. During the 1930s, economic growth collapsed, immigration plummeted, and fertility declined markedly, leading to what demographers today have labeled the Depression-era birth dearth. Nationwide, population growth slowed markedly; it almost halved, falling from an increase of seventeen million persons between 1920 and 1930 to just nine million persons between 1930 and 1940 (table 3.2).

New Jersey's negative change was even more dramatic. The state's population had expanded by almost 900,000 people between 1920 and 1930. However, between 1930 and 1940, its growth virtually halted: it gained fewer than 119,000 people, just 13 percent of the gain of the 1920s. Nonetheless, New Jersey still maintained its ninth-place ranking among the states, and its share of the nation's population diminished only slightly, from 3.28 percent in 1930 to 3.15 percent in 1940 (table 3.1).

With the national and state slowdowns persisting through the World War II years, many demographers were led to believe—and forecast—a slow-growth postwar population future for the United States. But this expectation was quickly shattered as the first postwar years actually unfolded.

The Post-World War II Boom

Initially confounding the "experts," the explosion of births in 1946 was just the start of an eighteen-year-long (1946–1964) phenomenon now known as the baby boom, the largest generation ever produced in the nation's history (see chapters 7 and 8). In conjunction with postwar consumer affluence and a decade and one-half (1930–1945) of deferred expectations—when the forces of household and family formation were fully held in check—America underwent one of the most dramatic transformations in its history. Rampant automobile-centric suburbia defined the 1950–1970 era.

In 1950, New York City (7.9 million people), on New Jersey's eastern border, was the largest city in the country, while Philadelphia (2.1 million people), on the state's western border, was the third largest. Thus, the Garden State comprised the suburban geographic commuter shed of two of the three largest cities in America.[10] As a result, it was quickly engulfed again by the sustained outward demographic flows from these two giants. Repeating earlier patterns, these interstate movements overlaid the suburban flows from New Jersey's own cities. Moreover, the truck-dependent suburban manufacturing infrastructure that was erected during this period in order to produce the bounty of postwar consumer goods hastened the obsolescence of the historic urban manufacturing concentrations. Thus, jobs and economic opportunities were also decentralizing at a rapid pace. Consequently, tract house suburban New Jersey flourished under these multiple movements, representing a national icon of this new way of life that was sweeping across America.

Between 1940 and 1950, the state's population increased by over 675,000 people, more than five times the growth (119,000 people) of the Depression-era decade, with most of this growth taking place in the postwar years (post-1945). By 1950, the state's population had approached five million people and its rank among the states grew to eighth, its highest ranking ever. And this was just a prelude of what was to come. Between 1950 and 1960, the state gained over 1.2 million people, and its total population surpassed 6.0 million people (tables 3.1 and 3.2). New Jersey's 1960 share of the nation's population jumped to 3.38 percent, compared with 2.47 percent in 1900 at the beginning of the century. Its eighth-place state ranking remained the same, but it was among fifty states, not forty-eight.

Strong growth continued during the ensuing decade. Between 1960 and 1970, the state grew by an additional 1.1 million people, and its total population approached 7.2 million people. It maintained its eighth-place ranking among the states, but its national population share actually increased to over 3.53 percent, its second-highest decennial share in history, lagging only the all-time high achieved during the 1790 census (4.69 percent).

So between 1950 and 1970, New Jersey's population increased by almost half (48.3 percent). During this twenty-year period, it gained more than 2.3 million people, the greatest period of absolute growth in the state's history. New Jersey thrived in the great era of suburbanization. In fact, New Jersey became the most suburban of states, its most defining characteristic for the balance of the twentieth century.

The 1970s: Regional and Global Reckoning

But this powerful growth trajectory was not to be maintained. America's postwar economic ebullience came to an end as the decade of the 1970s advanced. Within the country, an economic reordering commenced. The aging Northeast and Midwest regions were quickly rebranded, labeled the Rust Belt or the Frost Belt.[11] The nation's Sunbelt, with its affordability, lower business-cost structures, and more temperate climate, began to gain critical demographic and economic mass within the United States.[12] This was accentuated by multiple energy crises, the most negative impact of which was on the energy-consuming states. Moreover, emerging global economic competitors began to chip away at U.S. global economic hegemony, with the nation's aging and lagging industries most affected. New Jersey felt the brunt of this emerging economic storm, experiencing a sustained diminution of its manufacturing preeminence.

Between 1970 and 1980, the state's population growth tumbled to just 194,000 people, less than 20 percent of the average decade gain (over 1.1 million persons) of the 1950–1970 period (table 3.2). New Jersey became the ninth most populous state, dropping from its previous eighth-place high. And its share of the nation's population fell from 3.53 percent to 3.25 percent (table 3.1), the start of a sustained decline that would persist to the present day.

However, even during the manufacturing hemorrhage of the troubled 1970s, a foundation was being laid for the emergence of a postindustrial, information-age economy in the state, which was the second major technology-driven transformation of the New Jersey economy. Just as manufacturing replaced agriculture in the nineteenth and early twentieth centuries, white-collar, knowledge-based economic functions supplanted blue-collar manufacturing activities in the late twentieth century. Once again, replicating the pattern of the immediate postwar years, the seemingly unrelenting forces of suburbanization played a major transformative role.

The 1980s and 1990s Rebounds

The driving economic locational force of the final two decades of the twentieth century was reflected by New Jersey's great 1980s office building boom, which completely reinvented again the state's economic landscape. By 1990, 80 percent of all of New Jersey's commercial office inventory had been erected during the decade of the 1980s (Hughes and Seneca 2015). Much of it was located in auto-dependent, highway-oriented suburban growth corridors. This became the state's core economic specialization and core spatial competency. It was a reflection of a national dynamic: suburbanization of the knowledge-based economy.

New Jersey's suburban tract house model had become the country's standard dominant form of residential development between 1950 and 1970. Similarly, the state's post-1980 vast complex of suburban office corridors and agglomerations became the nation's archetypical symbol of what was supposed to be the future shape of a rapidly suburbanizing American economy (Garreau 1991). A national buzz again enveloped New Jersey.

Nonetheless, despite this new economic force, the state's population growth continued to lag that of the United States. Although the state's 1980–1990 population gain (+365,000 people) did eclipse that of the 1970s (+194,000 people), its share of the nation's population slipped from 3.25 percent in 1980 to 3.11 percent in 1990 (tables 3.1 and 3.2). This was the lowest share since 1920 (2.98 percent).

The state's absolute growth continued to pick up substantially during the century's final decade, with population increasing by 684,000 persons between 1990 and 2000. Thus, the multidecade trend was certainly positive again: from a growth of 194,000 persons in the 1970s, to 365,000 persons in the 1980s, and to 684,000 persons in the 1990s. However, each decade's growth rate lagged significantly behind those of the nation (table 3.2). This resulted in the sustained decline in share of the nation's population, which fell to 2.99 percent in 2000, down from 3.11 percent in 1990 and 3.25 percent in 1980 (table 3.1).

The resumption of stronger—but still below national-average—population growth in New Jersey was driven not only by the emergence of the "new" office-centric suburban economy but also by more substantial immigration. This reflected the impact of the Immigration and Nationality Act of 1965, which, among its many provisions, increased the overall scale of immigration in the United States. New Jersey again became an immigration gateway, a role it performed a century earlier. It enabled the state to maintain its ninth-place size ranking among the fifty states.

The New Millennium: 2000–2010

As the new century unfolded, the state's demographic growth trajectory again faltered. New Jersey's 2000–2010 population gain (378,000 persons), though still positive, was only 55 percent of the size (684,000 persons) of the 1990–2000 decade (table 3.2). Its share of the nation's population fell to 2.85 percent in 2010, down from 2.99 percent ten years earlier, and its size ranking among the states fell to eleventh place (table 3.1).

This was the result of several factors that fundamentally disrupted what had once been considered twentieth-century certainties. First, the overwhelming suburbanization forces that had pervaded postwar America in general and New Jersey in particular started to abate. Aging suburban-centric office inventories no longer represented the national crest-of-the-wave growth model. Resurgent urban areas such as New York City became the new centralized focal points as postsuburban economic forces started to dominate. Technological and age-structure/generational changes (chapter 7) also put twentieth-century suburban-dominated economies and demographies at distinct twenty-first-century disadvantages. And the 2007–2009 Great Recession, at that time the worst economic downturn in the nation since the Great Depression, hastened the pace of transformational change.

A Review of Recent Economic Cycles and Demographic Destiny

Looking forward, as has been the case in both the nineteenth and twentieth centuries, demographic destiny will be shaped by economic destiny.[13] The future course of the economy continues to be highly uncertain, shaped by both short-term cyclical conditions and long-term structural changes. As a result, as the second decade of the twenty-first century comes to an end, trends in the spatial distribution of the population, though not yet set in concrete, are unlikely to revisit the past. Let's take a brief short-term glance again in the economic rear-view mirror.

New Jersey and the United States entered the twenty-first century at the tail end of what can be called the Great Transmillennial Economic Expansion, which started in March 1991 and ended in March 2001. At that time, it was the longest expansion in the nation's history—120 months in length, or a full ten years. It defined a decade (1990s) of economic prosperity in the nation and New Jersey that unleashed substantial optimism about the seemingly unbridled prospects about the new millennium to come. The cyclical "high" at the time was accompanied by two long-term structural contours then still in force: sustained twentieth-century post–World War II suburbanization and the coming of age of demographic dominance by the fabled baby boom generation.

In 2000, the suburban-centric baby boom was between thirty-six and fifty-four years of age, furiously raising families, trading up in the suburban housing market, and ascending to the top-line workforce (see chapters 7 and 10). However, the late-1990s segment of the great expansion was actually fueled by a high-technology, dot-com bubble, which ultimately caused its demise. In 2000 and 2001, dot-com became dot-bomb, leading to the short-lived March 2001 to November 2001 recession, which lasted just eight months because of the extraordinary actions of the Federal Reserve. Although these actions would ultimately fuel a subsequent bubble, they did ensure that economic recovery would quickly ensue. The resulting 2001–2007 economic expansion started in November 2001 and lasted seventy-three months, obscuring the beginning of the end of many of the structural forces that had once dominated New Jersey. Moreover, this expansion was also propelled by an economic bubble—an unprecedented credit bubble that fueled a wild housing party. However, the credit bubble ultimately burst and terminated the expansion in December 2007. The world was soon staring into the economic abyss as the credit crisis and the Great Recession unfolded.

There is an old adage that proclaims that economic wild parties are often followed by prolonged economic hangovers. And America and New Jersey both had very prolonged credit-party hangovers. What is now called the Great 2007–2009 Recession turned out to be the worst downturn since the Great Depression. It lasted eighteen months, starting in December 2007 and ending in June 2009. In many dimensions, New Jersey came to a standstill. As it exited this stupor, the state would be confronted by a whole new set of locational parameters and fundamental generational change.

Post-2010

The second decade of the century was characterized by a maturation of the forces that started to fundamentally reshape New Jersey in the first decade. National economic growth resumed from the depths of the Great 2007–2009 Recession starting in June 2009. By July 2019, the national expansion reached 121 months in length and became the "new" longest in history, surpassing the 120-month-long March 1991 to March 2001 Great Transmillennial Economic Expansion.

Despite this positive national economic growth environment during the "second" decade, what we now call disruptive forces began to reshape New Jersey. These contributed to seemingly endemic below-national-average employment and population growth conditions in the state. An urban-centric millennial generation became the overall driving demographic force, replacing the suburban-centric baby boom generation (see chapters 9 and 10). New York City and Philadelphia, from which the baby boom and its parents once fled, became powerful population magnets drawing millennials from New Jersey and beyond. In addition, advancing information technology fully replaced routine standardized white-collar work processes, which provided the very rationale for erecting New Jersey's vast suburban office inventory. The central economic function of office buildings became innovation, hosting creative work activities. Corporate America found the most "creative" dynamic environments in which to locate their innovation hubs were dense, multifunctional, interactive urban areas preferred by millennials, the generation they viewed as the critical workforce of both the present and future. Isolated, insulated, one-dimensional suburban office campuses were considered the central part of yesterday's standardized economy.

Moreover, within the suburban-driven economies of the end of the twentieth century, New Jersey had always been regarded as a high-cost place of doing business in a national context. At the same time, it was considered the low-cost place of doing business in the multistate regional context surrounding New York City. But this favorable regional business-attractive position eroded as the twenty-first century advanced, driven by state fiscal imperatives and practices, as well as public policy shifts. Diminishing economic attractiveness led to slower employment growth, which, in turn, led to constrained population growth.

In addition, lower living-cost regions of the country increased their attractiveness for baby boom retirees, whose sheer numbers flooded the ranks of "sixtysomethings" as the first decade (2000–2010) came to an end and was then about to engulf the legions of "seventysomethings" as the second decade (2010–2020) came to a close (see chapter 10). The aging of this huge generational cohort, and its retirement shelter decisions, became a growing force of outmigration inhibiting population growth.

These generational and economic issues will all be discussed in depth in later chapters of this book. Suffice it to say, despite these many inhibitors, New Jersey remained firmly established as the nation's eleventh-ranked state in size in 2018 with a population of just over 8.9 million people.[14] Although its national share continued to retreat, from 2.85 percent in 2010 to 2.72 percent in 2018, New Jersey's current ranking remains secure for the foreseeable future. Sitting twelfth in the country in 2018 is Virginia, with a population just above 8.5 million people. It is followed by the states of Washington (7.5 million people) and Arizona (7.2 million people). Virginia has the potential to surpass New Jersey during the 2020s. The other two, Washington and Arizona, are not likely to challenge New Jersey in size until after the 2030 decennial census.

4

The People of New Jersey

• •

Long-Term Diversity in Racial, Ethnic, and National Origin

More Revolutionary War armed conflicts took place in New Jersey than in any other colony ("New Jersey and the Revolution," n.d.), earning this state the moniker "Crossroads of the American Revolution" (Keane 2016). More broadly and in the long term, New Jersey has been a historical crossroads in another sense: of different people, nationalities, and ethnic, minority, and immigrant groups. This chapter profiles New Jersey's diverse residents over time, starting with the original Native American inhabitants and then other racial groups, including whites, Blacks, and Asians, that made the state their home. Next, it examines the state's ethnic groups (e.g., Hispanics). We then segue to a review of New Jersey's major immigrant populations from at first Ireland, Germany, and Italy and then later Mexico, Central and South America, Asia, and other places. The intersection of all these peoples have made New Jersey a dynamic social crossroads. The many different people who have converged on and lived in the Garden State over the centuries have defined the diverse demographic character of New Jersey. In many respects, diversity is imbued in New Jersey's demographic DNA. Peter Wacker's (1975, 158) masterly observation on colonial history, that "New Jersey exhibited the maximum cultural diversity of any American colony or state before 1800," remained germane for the next more than two centuries.

It is important to acknowledge before commencing our presentation that the federal Census Bureau identification of race in the United States has changed repeatedly over time with respect to both the means of assignment (by a census enumerator or by the census respondent) and the definition of and nomenclature for different racial groups (Cohn 2010; Jersey Promise 2019; Rastogi et al. 2011). Of particular note, there was a marked change in the racial identification before and after the 2000 census (Cohn 2014). Before the 2000 census, the enumeration identified one race only, for example, white or Black. From the 2000 census onward, more than one race could be identified (e.g., Black in combination with other races). There have also been changes concerning how ethnicity, such as Hispanic and Latino heritage, have been measured. A good summary source of the many changes in the Census Bureau racial and ethnic enumeration and terminology over time is available from this bureau (U.S. Census Bureau, n.d.e), the Pew Research Center (Brown 2015), and other references (Humes and Hogan 2009; Prewitt 2005), and we recommend those interested to consult these sources as this chapter considers racial, ethnic, and related data over a more-than-two-century span from 1800 to 2017.

Additionally, racial and ethnic minorities are in general likely to be undercounted in census enumerations (Cressie 1988, 123; Haines 2000; Skerry 2000). Thus, for the many reasons, caution is in order when considering census-based racial data over time (especially pre- and post-2000); the census-derived racial information presented below is best viewed on an order of magnitude and relative basis, such as the overall population size of one racial group versus another. The same caveat applies to ethnic data. In all instances, to provide context to the different racial and ethnic populations in New Jersey, the national racial and ethnic profile is presented in tandem; the same approach is followed in presenting immigration information.

The racial, ethnic, and immigration data presented below is derived from multiple sources. Primarily, we tap the decennial census on population for both the United States and New Jersey. As the last decennial census was conducted in 2010, and more current data is imperative, we also draw from the annual American Community Survey (ACS) implemented by the Census Bureau, specifically unless otherwise indicated, the 2017 ACS 1-Year Estimates. Further, unless otherwise noted, in presenting and discussing racial data from the census and the ACS, we focus in the text that follows on the "race alone" enumeration and not the mixed racial counts ("race alone and in combination"). Detailed tables in this chapter, however, do contain both the "race alone" and "race in combination" population. Additionally, besides census and ACS, other sources of information, both quantitative and qualitative (e.g., data from surveys of different racial groups in New Jersey as well as oral histories of some of their members), are incorporated in order to present a multifaceted profile of the people of New Jersey. Finally, as many inherently complicated racial, ethnic, nationality, and other subjects for both the nation and New Jersey are examined in just this single chapter, we acknowledge that our treatment of any one topic is inevitably abbreviated to highlights.

Native American Racial Profile

The first inhabitants of what was to become the United States and New Jersey were Native Americans; in New Jersey, these were the Lenape (Kraft 1986; Wacker 1975, 57–119). The Lenape have also been called the Lenni-Lenape, Delaware, and other names (Kraft 1986; Lurie and Veit 2016), but in this chapter, we will use Lenape.[1]

In 1524, Giovanni da Verrazano, sailing for France, explored the mouth of the Raritan River (De Angelo 2007, 15). (There had been earlier North American native contact with Europeans following John Cabot's voyage in 1497 to the coasts of Newfoundland and Labrador [Kraft 1986, 195].) Verrazano was the first European to report contact with the native Lenape inhabitants. In 1609, Henry Hudson sailed into the area under contract to the Dutch East India Company, looking for a northwest passage to Asia. His reports of fertile land and amicable natives ("We found the country on its banks well peopled"; quoted in Philower 1931, 24) encouraged the Dutch government and other trading companies to explore and chart the area. Settlers soon followed in the 1600s into what was to become New Jersey and established the beginnings of a European-based community. These early European explorers "encountered a coastline littered with large oyster shells and a handsome and fertile countryside marked by salt marshes, meadows, and forests of pine, oak, chestnut, and hickory" (Slesinski 2014, 9). Such a bucolic landscape was of course already occupied by the Lenape.

The ancestors of the Lenape are believed to have migrated from Asia about ten thousand to twenty thousand years ago (these estimated dates by archaeologists and other scientists are in flux; Montaigne 2020) across a then-existing land bridge to North America across the current Bering Strait ("Beringia"); others hypothesize voyage by sea and other means (Montaigne 2020). The original inhabitants migrated to the Middle Atlantic region more than ten thousand years ago (Cohen 2006, 1; Norwood 2007; Thornton 2000, 9). These dates and origins must be viewed cautiously, however (as indeed more broadly should other descriptions of the earliest Indians and their descendants), for "who were the first humans in the Americas, and how and when did they get there" remains one of "archaeology's greatest mysteries" (Adovasio and Page 2002, book subtitle).

The Lenape territory stretched from the Delaware Bay in the south through all of present-day New Jersey, western Long Island, New York Bay, the Lower Hudson Valley in New York, and other areas. "Lenape," from the Algonquin language, can be translated to mean "Original People." Among the Algonquian-speaking tribes on the East Coast, the Lenape were considered the "grandfathers" from whom other groups originated. Although it was believed for many years that the Lenape were divided into three clans—the Minci (Wolf), Unami (Turtle), and Unilachtigo (Turkey) (De Angelo 2007, 12; Hess 1973, 35), this claim has been debunked by later scholars (Kraft 1986, xv). Lenape villages were semipermanent. The Lenape moved with the seasons, retreating to the cooler shore areas in the heat of the summer, much like the annual tradition of many New Jersey residents today. In the autumn, the Lenape would return to their villages and harvest their crops (De Angelo 2007, 14–15). At the time of European contact, the Lenape practiced agriculture alongside hunting and fishing. It is said that the Lenape would annually "feast on succulent oysters at the present site of... busy Newark Airport" (Cummings 2004, 1).

Prior to the arrival of European colonists, the Lenape contributed to a vast network of footpaths used by Algonquian- and Iroquoian-speaking tribes. Known as the Great Trail, these routes connected the areas of New England, eastern Canada, the mid-Atlantic region, and the Great Lakes region. Although these trails started out as single-file footpaths, they were eventually expanded and widened, later becoming the template for major highways in the northeastern United States (De Angelo 2007, 15). Such a transportation network dispels the notion that early explorers were encountering "untouched wilderness"; indeed, in many ways, America was already a "humanized landscape," and Native Americans offered "much valuable information about its contents" (Zelinsky 1973, 16).

Sadly, and despite their often generous assistance to European settlers, the fate of the Lenape was not much different from that of other Native American tribes: a sequence of disease, famine, death, disenfranchisement, and eventually displacement; the Lenape as a tribe were displaced to many places (e.g., New York, Canada, and Oklahoma; Kraft 1986, 234). A foreshadowing of the horrific manner in which the American colonists in general brutalized their Native American neighbors is evidenced by how quickly the Plymouth Colony's 1621 supposed bonhomie at the first "Thanksgiving" gathering with local tribes morphed not long after into a war of extinction with these very same Native Americans.[2] The colonists of New Jersey were little better and its estimated American Indian population "quickly dwindled to between twenty-four hundred and three thousand in 1700, to less than one thousand in 1763, and to fewer than two hundred by 1800" (Lurie 2010, 3). A century later, the 1900 the census enumerated only 63 American Indians in New Jersey,[3] a minuscule native population in this state and a demographic count we return to shortly. The Lenape sadly "watched their world dwindle and their children grow hungry" (Townsend 2016, 7).

The decimation of the native population in New Jersey after European colonial settlement was not unique but reflected a larger literal holocaust of Native Americans in North, South, and Central America following Christopher Columbus's Spanish-sponsored voyage in 1492 to various Caribbean islands, including Hispaniola (today's Haiti and the Dominican Republic). Columbus called the inhabitants he encountered "Indians" ("los Indios") under the mistaken belief that he had reached the East Indies in Asia with its fabled riches (Adovasio and Page 2002, 1; Kraft 1986, xiii). Columbus's perspective of "discovery" was as flawed as his geographic bearing and nomenclature because for eons before Columbus's so called discovery, Asian migrants passed over to North

America (Lepore 2018, 8). Over time, they migrated southward and inhabited the Americas in large numbers.

The exact size of the native population in the Americas in 1492 is "one of the most hotly, and in occasions bitterly debated issues in New World history" (Newson 1993, 248). There are different camps of historians with widely divergent estimates of this population. (For a good metastudy summary, including interviews with some of the principal researchers, see Mann 2005; see also Thornton 2000.) One group, labeled the skeptics (Newson 1993, 249) because their population estimates are at lower magnitudes than those of other researchers, pegged the pre-Columbian native population in the Americas at about 10–15 million, with the following estimates from this group of demographic historians as examples: 8.4 million (Kroeber 1934, 1939), 13.4 million (Rosenblat 1954), and 15.6 million (J. H. Stewart 1949). At the other end of the scale was a significantly higher pre-Columbian Indian population of 90–112 million estimated by H. F. Dobbyns (1966). Editing an entire book on the subject (*The Native Population of the Americas in 1492*), William Denevan (1992a) estimated 54 million, noting as well other estimates ranging between 8 and 112 million. One chapter in an edited volume on North American population history (Haines and Steckel 2000b) listed in a summary table twenty-three estimates of the aboriginal population of North America (Thornton 2000, 13) ranging from 1.1 million (James Mooney) to 12.3 million (Dobbyns); another chapter listed eighteen Native American aboriginal population estimates of a similar wide range (Ubelaker 2000, 53). In a similar vein, just one footnote in a 2015 scholarly article on the subject by Benjamin Madley (2015, 98) cited the following diverse Native American estimates for North America alone (north of Mexico): 1.0 million (Kroeber), 1.2 million (Mooney), 3.8 million (Denevan), 16 million (George Catlin), 16–17 million (Emmanuel Domenech), and 18 million (Dobbyns). The higher tallies dovetail with Bartolomé de las Casas's contemporaneous observation in the mid-1500s that the Native Americans were as populous as a "hive of bees" (quoted in MacNutt 1909). In a widely cited article, Denevan (1992b, 369) summarized that while a "myth persists that in 1492 the Americas were a sparsely populated wilderness . . . substantial evidence [says] that the Native American landscape of the early sixteenth century was a humanized landscape almost everywhere." This myth was unfortunately echoed by otherwise astute observers, such as Alexis de Tocqueville, asserting that "America before Columbus was 'an empty continent . . . awaiting its inhabitants'" (quoted in Lord 1997, 18). De Tocqueville's Eurocentric view of the Americas was hardly atypical and was paralleled by the nineteenth-century's Romantic notion of a near uninhabited forest primeval illustrated in that era's panoramic landscapes by such painters as Albert Bierstadt and Frederick Church, with hardly a Native American soul depicted. Fortunately, the erroneous perspective of a New World with scant Native American presence has been debunked by many studies, some noted above, that document a precontact New World population in the millions with a commensurate sophisticated societal structure (Mann 2005).

In parallel with the debate concerning in the size of the hemispheric-wide pre-Columbian Indian population are widely divergent native population estimates in different portions of the Americas. Just in Hispaniola alone, estimates of the 1492 population range from 8 million (Cook and Borah 1971) to 3 million (Sauer 1966) to 1–4 million (de las Casas estimates in Denevan 1996), and as low as about 0.1 million (Rosenblat 1967). (Further perspective on the variability of the native population estimates is that J. H. Stewart [1949] concluded that the entire Caribbean area before Columbus contained only 0.2–0.3 million original inhabitants.) In what was to become the continental United States, the pre-European settlement native population has been generally estimated as between roughly one and six million (Shoemaker 1999; Snipp 1986; Thornton 1987, 2000; Ubelaker 1976), with some estimates as high as eleven million (Adovasio and Page 2002).

To place some of these Indian population numbers in context, the Roman Empire at its full glory in the first century AD contained an estimated fifty-four million persons, twenty-three million in its European dominion (Russel 1958, 7). In the sixteenth century, a period of intensive European colonization of the Americas, the entire European population (excluding European Russia) was estimated at sixty-two million (Durand 1977, 256). Spain, the sponsor of Columbus's voyages, had a 1492 population of about six to seven million (Elliot 1963). Thus, even at the lower bounds of the estimate of the pre-Columbian Indian population, the number of native inhabitants of the Americas before Columbus looms large on both an absolute as well historical and relative basis.

Although we will never know the exact pre-Columbian Indian population, it is clear that European settlement and conquest decimated the original inhabitants of the Americas. A generation after Columbus "discovered" Hispaniola, its population, ravaged by disease (Ubelaker 2000), slavery, and other Spanish onslaughts, was estimated to have declined to only sixty thousand by the early 1500s (Denevan 1996; Sauer 1966) and possibly below eleven thousand (Lord 1997, 4). By 1650, only about six million Indians were left in most of the Americas (Lord 1997), albeit estimates on this count vary as much as the original pre-Columbian counts. In the continental United States, the pre-Columbian native population, which was generally estimated in the millions (1–6 million), had dwindled four centuries later to a nadir of less than a quarter of a million Native Americans nationally enumerated in the 1900 census, with less than one hundred of this population found in New Jersey.[4] Clearly, "European settlement of the Americas initiated a devastating decline to the native population" (Shoemaker 1999, xi). The precipitous drop of the Native American population was a result of a number of factors, including disease, famine, warfare, and genocide, removal to reservations, and changes in traditional ways of life (Thornton 1987, 91). Not surprisingly, this tremendous loss of Native American life has been described in such horrific terms as *genocide* (Lemkin 2012; Madley 2015, 1), *cataclysm* and *disaster* (Madley 2015, 98), *American holocaust* (Stannard 1992), *American Indian holocaust* (Thornton 1987), and *The Earth Shall Weep* (Wilson 1999).

Over time, the Native American population (technically encompassing both those identified as American Indians and Alaskan Natives or AIAN) has grown both nationally and in New Jersey. Nonetheless, Native Americans still comprise a small share of the total population, especially in the Garden State. We consider below data on the number of Native Americans both nationally and in New Jersey (tables 4.1 and 4.2) from 1900 until 2017. As elsewhere in this chapter, this information is derived from Census Bureau sources (Norris, Vines, and Hoeffel 2012), and we caution the reader that the enumeration of Native Americans over time has been particularly challenging and far from consistent.[5] A reflection of America's lacuna in counting its original inhabitants is the late and half-hearted start of such enumeration. Until 1860, the Census Bureau did not designate or count Native Americans as a separate racial category (these were limited to white and Black) and only in 1890 did the census count Native Americans living in reservations or Indian Territory (later Oklahoma) (Kraft 1986, 239).

The 1900 census counted 237,196 Native American nationally or 0.3 percent of the total U.S. population. This racial group grew to 343,410 persons in 1950 (0.2 percent of the national population), increased to 2,475,956 by 2000 (0.9 percent of the national population), and reached 2,726,278 by 2017 (0.8 percent of the national population). (Note again: here and elsewhere the racial enumerations from 2000 onward are for one "race alone" and not the larger "race alone or in combination." Tables 4.1 and 4.2 contain as well the "race alone and in combination" enumerations from 2000 onward. For Native Americans especially, their "race alone and in combination" population is substantially larger than their "race alone" count—for example, 5.6 million versus 2.7 million nationally in 2017.)

The census tallies of Native Americans in the Garden State from 1900 through 2017 are very modest in numbers. (There were only sixty-three in 1900.) There were a scant few hundred Native Americans in New Jersey in the decades from 1900 to 1950, comprising a minuscule share of the state's total population over this span (0.006 percent or less). The number of New Jersey Native Americans reached four figures and then a low five figures over the 1960, 1970, 1980, and 1990 censuses (1,699, 4,706, 8,394, and 14,970, respectively), but those numbers again represented only a small fraction of this total state's population (0.2 percent or less). The count of Native Americans in New Jersey ("race alone") from 2000 onward (19,492 in 2000, 29,026 in 2010, and 17,843 in 2017) was larger than in previous periods but never exceeded a minuscule 0.3 percent of the state's total population. (As at the national level, the "race alone and in combination" tally of New Jersey's Native American population is substantially higher—for example, 54,873 in 2017, or 0.6 percent of this state's total population.)

Table 4.1
Racial Composition (No.) of the United States and New Jersey, 1800–2017

Racial Group (One Race Only)—Number of Persons

Year	White		Black		American Indian and Alaskan Native (AIAN)		Asian and Pacific Islander (API)		Some Other Race (SOR)	
	United States	New Jersey	United States	New Jersey	United States	New Jersey	United States	New Jersey	United States	New Jersey
1800	4,306,446	195,125	1,002,037	16,824						
1850	19,553,068	465,509	3,638,808	24,046						
1900	66,809,196	1,812,317	8,833,994	69,844	237,196	63	114,189	1,445		
1910	81,731,957	2,445,894	9,827,763	89,760	265,683	168	146,863	1,345		
1920	94,820,915	3,037,087	10,463,131	117,132	244,437	100	182,137	1,581		
1930	110,286,740	3,829,663	11,891,143	208,828	332,397	213	264,766	2,630		
1940	118,214,870	3,931,087	12,865,518	226,973	333,969	211	254,918	1,894		
1950	134,942,028	4,511,585	15,042,286	318,565	343,410	621	259,397	3,602	110,240	956
1960	158,831,732	5,539,003	18,871,831	514,875	523,591	1,699	877,934	8,778	218,087	2,427
1970	177,748,975	6,349,908	22,580,289	770,292	792,730	4,706	1,369,412	20,537	720,520	22,721
1980	188,371,622	6,127,467	26,495,025	925,066	1,420,400	8,394	3,500,439	103,848	6,758,319	200,048
1990	199,686,070	6,130,465	29,986,060	1,036,825	1,959,234	14,970	7,273,662	272,521	9,804,847	275,407
2000	211,460,626	6,104,705	34,658,190	1,141,821	2,475,956	19,492	10,641,833	483,605	15,359,073	450,972
2010	223,553,265	6,029,248	38,929,319	1,204,826	2,932,248	29,026	15,214,265	728,769	19,107,368	559,722
2017	235,502,457	6,112,238	41,393,491	1,217,572	2,726,278	17,843	18,823,547	890,032	16,552,940	538,371

Racial Group (Race Alone or in Combination with One or More Other Races)—Number of Persons

Year	White		Black		American Indian and Alaskan Native (AIAN)		Asian and Pacific Islander (API)		Some Other Race (SOR)	
	United States	New Jersey	United States	New Jersey	United States	New Jersey	United States	New Jersey	United States	New Jersey
2000	216,930,975	6,261,187	36,419,434	1,211,750	4,119,301	49,104	12,773,242	534,421	18,521,486	583,527
2010	231,040,398	6,210,995	42,020,743	1,300,363	5,220,579	70,716	18,546,051	808,162	21,748,084	660,171
2017	244,691,364	6,295,783	45,789,188	1,332,592	5,631,945	54,873	23,053,166	978,774	18,346,638	593,903

SOURCES: 1800–2010: Decennial census for indicated years. See also Gaquin and Ryan 2015, 7, 31–34; Campbell Gibson, n.d., chap. 4; and Hobbs and Stoops 2002, A-2 to 29, 2017: American Community Survey 2017 ACS 1-Year Estimates.

Table 4.2
Racial Composition (% Population) of the United States and New Jersey, 1800–2017

Racial Group (One Race Only) as Percentage of Total Population

Year	White US	White NJ	Black US	Black NJ	AIAN US	AIAN NJ	API US	API NJ	SOR US	SOR NJ
1800	81.1	92.1	18.9	7.9						
1850	84.3	95.1	15.7	4.9						
1900	87.9	96.2	11.6	3.7	0.3		0.2	0.1		
1910	88.9	96.4	10.7	3.5	0.3		0.2	0.1		
1920	89.7	96.2	9.9	3.7	0.2		0.2	0.1		
1930	89.8	94.8	9.7	5.2	0.3		0.2	0.1		
1940	89.8	94.5	9.8	5.5	0.3		0.2			
1950	89.5	93.3	10.0	6.6	0.2		0.2	0.1	0.1	
1960	88.6	91.3	10.5	8.5	0.3		0.5	0.1	0.1	
1970	87.5	88.6	11.1	10.7	0.4	0.1	0.8	0.3	0.4	0.3
1980	83.1	83.2	11.7	12.6	0.6	0.1	1.5	1.4	3.0	2.7
1990	80.3	79.3	12.1	13.4	0.8	0.2	2.9	3.5	3.9	3.6
2000	75.1	72.6	12.3	13.6	0.9	0.2	3.8	5.7	5.5	5.4
2010	72.4	68.6	12.6	13.7	0.9	0.3	4.9	8.3	6.2	6.4
2017	72.3	67.9	12.7	13.5	0.8	0.2	5.8	9.9	5.1	6.0

Racial Group (Race Alone or in Combination with One or More Other Races)—as Percentage of Total Population

Year	White US	White NJ	Black US	Black NJ	AIAN US	AIAN NJ	API US	API NJ	SOR US	SOR NJ
2000	77.1	74.4	12.9	14.4	1.5	0.6	4.5	6.3	6.6	6.9
2010	74.8	70.6	13.6	14.8	1.7	0.8	6.0	9.1	7.0	7.5
2017	75.1	69.9	14.1	14.8	1.7	0.6	7.0	10.9	5.6	6.6

SOURCES: 1800–2010: Decennial census for indicated years. See also Campbell Gibson, n.d., chapter 4; Gaquin and Ryan 2015, 7, 31–34; and Hobbs and Stoops 2002, A-20–29. 2017: American Community Survey, 2017 ACS 1-Year Estimates.

Although clearly modest, these headcounts do not do justice to the continued presence of Native Americans in the Garden State (New Jersey Committee on Native American Community Affairs 2007). As proclaimed on the cover of a publication from New Jersey's Nanticoke and Lenape Indian tribe, "We Are Still Here!" (Norwood 2007). Excerpts from "Voices of New Jersey's Contemporary American Indian Groups" as profiled in a publication from the New Jersey State Museum (O'Reilly 2012) follow:

CHIEF MANN OF THE RAMAPOUGH LUNAAPE NATIONS
(MUNSEE-DELAWARE) NJ/NJ
The Ramapough Lunaape (Munsee Delaware) are living descendants of the great Lunaape tribes that existed in the area. . . . We have been able to survive in the Ramapo Mountains for nearly 13,000 years. . . . We carry on our traditions. . . . We are the oldest surviving family—Native or not—to exist in our same homelands since the first settlers came here. (35–36)

CLAIRE GARLAND, DIRECTOR, SAND HILL INDIAN
HISTORICAL ASSOCIATION
Sand Hills Indians of Monmouth were composed of local Lenape Indians and Cherokee Indians who migrated to New Jersey from Georgia in the late 19th century. . . . Knowing one's roots makes history more understandable. . . . It is important to share our ancestor's traditional ways with our Sand Hill descendants and those who are interested in Native culture. (35–36)

PASTOR NORWOOD, SPOKESPERSON, NANTICOKE LENNI-LENAPE,
BRIDGETON, NJ
The Nanticoke Lenni-Lenape remain in the area of their ancient homeland by the Delaware Bay. . . . [We are not] mere footnotes of history, relegated to the distant past and declared to no longer be part of the fabric of modern life. . . . An appreciation for tribal culture, and a sensitivity to the ongoing plight of tribal people are vital for both the Nanticoke Lenni-Lenape and the future of the state. (37)

White and Black Racial Profile

In tandem with the burgeoning total population of both the entire United States and New Jersey discussed in chapter 3 of this book has been the significant growth of the two largest racial groups in both the country and this state—whites and Blacks (Haines 2000; Steckel 2000). Tables 4.1 and 4.2 detail the number and percentage of total population of whites and Blacks in the United States and New Jersey from 1800 to 2017. (As with all Census Bureau racial enumerations, how whites, and especially Blacks, have been counted and referred to over time have varied. Current information on white and Black racial identification in the census is available from Hixson, Helper, and Kim 2011 and Rastogi et al. 2011.) We overview highlights of these data below.

Nationally, the number of whites in the United States grew from 4.3 million in 1800 to 66.8 million in 1900, 211.5 million in 2000, 223.6 million in 2010, and 235.5 million by 2017. Whites in New Jersey stood at just shy of 0.2 million (195,125) in 1800, 1.8 million in 1900, and hovered at the 6.0–6.1 million level in 2000 (6,104,705), 2010 (6,029,248), and 2017 (6,112,238).

The number of Blacks in the United States increased from 1.0 million in 1800 to 8.8 million in 1900, 34.7 million in 2000, 38.9 million in 2010, and

41.4 million by 2017. Persons identified as Black in New Jersey grew from 16,824 in 1800 to 69,844 in 1900, 1.1 million (1,141,821) in 2000, and stood at about 1.2 million in both 2010 (1,204,826) and 2017 (1,217,572). (All white and Black data are for "race alone.")

More telling than just the raw headcounts is the white and Black racial group share of the total population. Nationally, as detailed in table 4.2, the white population share of the total population in the United States generally grew (with some fluctuation) during the period from 1800 (81.1 percent) to 1940 (89.8 percent), and it has shrunk in almost all periods since (89.5 percent in 1950, 87.5 percent in 1970, 80.3 percent in 1990, 75.1 percent in 2000, 72.4 percent in 2010, and 72.3 percent in 2017). The white proportion of New Jersey's population, on the other hand, grew from 1800 (92.1 percent) to 1850 (95.1 percent), then remained relatively stable from 1850 (95.1 percent) to 1920 (96.2 percent), before beginning to decline at a faster rate than the national proportions. New Jersey's white population share dropped below the national average for the first time in 1990 (79.3 percent for the Garden State versus 80.3 percent for the nation) and has remained lower in New Jersey in the periods since (72.6 percent in 2000, 68.6 percent in 2010, and 67.9 percent in 2017).

The portion of the population identifying as Black from 1800 to 2017 varies significantly for the United States and New Jersey, reflecting divergent migration patterns and other trends. For the United States as a whole, the Black population declined as a portion of total population from 1800 (18.9 percent) to 1930 (9.7 percent), before beginning a period of moderate but steady growth from 1940 (9.8 percent) to 2000 (12.3 percent), 2010 (12.6 percent), and to 2017 (12.7 percent). The Black population share in New Jersey, on the other hand, was historically much smaller than in the United States as whole (e.g., 7.9 percent Black share for the state in 1800 compared to 18.9 percent Black population portion for the country), but it has generally seen growth in the period from 1910 to 2017. In 1910, New Jersey's Black population share was 3.5 percent compared to 10.7 percent for the United States as a whole. The Black portion of the New Jersey population then substantially grew in the decades following World War I and for some time after World War II (e.g., 5.2 percent in 1930, 6.6 percent in 1950, 8.5 percent by 1960, and 10.7 percent by 1970). By 1980, the Black population share in New Jersey (12.6 percent) had surpassed that in the United States overall (11.7 percent), and it has remained higher every period since. Since 1990, the Black population share in the Garden State has hovered at about 13.5 percent (13.4 percent in 1990, 13.6 percent in 2000, 13.7 percent in 2010, and 13.5 percent in 2017). The above counts are for the "race alone" enumerations of white and Blacks nationally and New Jersey, and the number and presence of Blacks and whites in these two geographies are yet greater if the higher tallies for the "race alone or in combination" enumerations are considered (see tables 4.1 and 4.2 for details).

The growth of New Jersey's Black population is considerably a result of migration from the rural South, which explains its sustained growth even during

Table 4.3

"The Great Migration" to and the "Reverse Great Migration" from New Jersey, 1900–2017

Year	Total NJ Black Population	"Great Migrants"— Blacks Living in NJ Emigrating from Southern States	"Reverse Great Migrants"— Blacks Born in NJ Living in Southern States	"Net Great Migrants"— Great Migrants Less Reverse Great Migrants	Black "Great Migrants" as % of Total NJ Black Population	Black "Reverse Great Migrants" as % of Total NJ Black Population	Black "Net Great Migrants" as % of Total NJ Black Population
1900	69,844	30,795	961	29,835	44.1	1.4	42.7
1910	89,760	46,178	1,761	44,417	51.4	2.0	49.5
1920	117,132	58,380	2,790	55,590	49.8	2.4	47.5
1930	208,828	123,565	3,128	120,437	59.2	1.5	57.7
1940	226,973	114,482	4,675	109,807	50.4	2.1	48.4
1950	318,565	159,803	6,495	153,308	50.2	2.0	48.1
1960	514,875	208,340	12,800	195,540	40.5	2.5	38.0
1970	770,292	233,500	19,300	214,200	30.3	2.5	27.8
1980	925,066	303,120	51,460	251,660	32.8	5.6	27.2
1990	1,036,825	254,556	82,742	171,814	24.6	8.0	16.6
2000	1,141,821	200,952	144,103	56,849	17.6	12.6	4.9
2010	1,204,826	150,552	206,987	−56,435	12.5	17.2	4.7
2017	1,217,572	120,694	236,949	−116,255	9.9	19.6	9.6

SOURCE: Irving 2019. (Analysis of Integrated Public Use Microdata Series [IPUMS] National Historical Geographic Information System [NHGIS] data for indicated years. The IPUMS USA database is attributed to Ruggles et al., n.d.) See appendix C for further description and detail of the analysis underlying the Great Migration results contained in this table.

periods when the Black proportion of the total U.S. population declined. World War I and World War II catalyzed major Black movements to the North and other promising locations in the Midwest and West; in the blunt words of one historian, Blacks "packed up and left" the South (Lepore 2018, 371). In turn, New Jersey absorbed a sizable number of these migrants. These movements by Blacks from the South to more promising regions of the United States for most of the decades of the twentieth century following World War I is more broadly referred as the Great Migration. With its burgeoning factories and relatively stronger civil rights protections for minorities in the twentieth century, New Jersey was a prime destination for these Great Migrants. This was one demographic contribution to the rapidly rising New Jersey Black population and growing Black share of this state's population in the decades following both World Wars.

As the Great Migration is critical for understanding the Black demographic racial patterns in both the nation and New Jersey, this subject is explored in greater detail in appendix C in this book. Table 4.3 distills from that appendix the number of Great Migrants in New Jersey—that is, Blacks living in this state who emigrated from southern states over the decades from 1900 onward to 2017.

Table 4.3 also shows side-by-side the total number of New Jersey resident Blacks in these same time periods. Clearly evident is the importance of the Great Migration to New Jersey's total Black population over much the twentieth century and beyond. For the first half of the twentieth century, the decades 1900–1950, Black Great Migrants to New Jersey comprised roughly 45–60 percent of the total Black population in the state. While this share trends downward by decade in the latter half of this century to about 30–20 percent from 1980 to 2000, and then to one-tenth by 2017, it nonetheless remains a not inconsequential portion of the Garden State's total Black residents over much of the twentieth century and beyond.

Demographic influences do not stand pat, however, and the exodus from the South slowed in recent decades both nationally and in New Jersey. In fact, there has been an uptick recently of Blacks in the North, Midwest, and West moving South, a phenomenon referred to as the Reverse Great Migration; they are returning South for economic, familial, and other reasons. As with other states that once were magnets for migrating southern Blacks, New Jersey has recently experienced this Reverse Great Migration, a subject explored in appendix C in this book—with the analytic results summarized in table 4.3. In brief, for the first eight decades of the twentieth century, there was minuscule to modest Reverse Great Migrants in New Jersey—that is, Blacks born in New Jersey who immigrated to southern states. That minor scale is especially evident in comparing the magnitude of the New Jersey Reverse Great Migrants to the New Jersey Great Migrants, the latter encompassing Blacks living in New Jersey who had emigrated from southern states. For example, in 1960, there were 12,800 New Jersey Reverse Great Migrants as against 208,340 New Jersey Great Migrants. In time, however, the number of New Jersey Reverse Great Migrants steadily grew (e.g., 51,460 in 1980, 144,103 in 2000, 206,987 in 2010, and 236,949 in 2017). This dramatic growth in New Jersey Reverse Great Migrants occurred, not coincidentally, in a period of declining New Jersey Great Migrants (e.g., 303,120 in 1980, 200,952 in 2000, 150,552 in 2010, and 120,694 in 2017). The difference in the number of New Jersey Black Great Migrants versus this state's Black Reverse Great Migrants is shown in table 4.3 as "Net Great Migrants," and it is evident that the demographic trend lines have crossed. In recent years, there have been more Blacks born in New Jersey who have emigrated South compared to Blacks living in New Jersey who had come from southern states, with the difference (termed Net Great Migrants) amounting to at first five figures and then climbing to six figures (e.g., 56,435 in 2010 and 116,255 in 2017). For context, those tallies of Net Great Migrants are about 5 and 10 percent, respectively, of New Jersey's total Black population in 2010 and 2017 (table 4.3).

Thus far, our analysis of white and Black racial groups in New Jersey has been solely numeric in nature. It is appropriate to conclude this section by briefly noting the broader human dimensions and interactions affecting and reflecting these racial populations over time.

Black slavery surely looms large as an influence and was present from the inception of European settlement (Wacker 1975, 190–200); august institutions such as Rutgers University were stained by human bondage (Boyd, Carey, and Blakey 2016; Fuentes and White 2016; White 2016), and tellingly, New Jersey was the last northern state to abolish this practice. (The demographics of the Black population, both free and slave, in the nation and New Jersey from the colonial era to 1860 are considered in detail in appendix C to this book.) Yet, while some in New Jersey embraced or at least tolerated human servitude, others worked assiduously to help Blacks in the period before the Civil War, such as facilitating the Underground Railroad, which brought enslaved southern Blacks northward to freedom. (Chillingly, there was also a Reverse Underground Railroad where free northern Blacks were kidnapped to the South and then enslaved; Bell 2019.) In the pre–Civil War period, New Jersey residents, often Quakers, helped many hundreds, if not thousands, escaping southern slaves cross the state on this clandestine network (J. Cunningham 1966, 171) to New York, Canada, and other northern destinations where slaves would legally be free from harm. The escaping slaves had to cross through New Jersey furtively because this was the only northern state that enforced the Fugitive Slave Act, which empowered seizing and returning escaping slaves to the South (J. Cunningham 1966, 171). A common Underground Railroad route led from the South to Philadelphia and southeastern Pennsylvania, followed by a perilous journey to southwestern New Jersey, then overland across New Jersey to Jersey City and then finally to freedom in New York (B. Cunningham 1977). "Thousands of frightened runaways first sensed hope when they saw . . . signal lights set by sympathizers on Salem and Cumberland shores. . . . [Then finding their] way to Quaker helpers and others who set them on the road to liberty" (J. Cunningham 1966, 171).

Examples of some of these helpers were two elderly Quaker teachers (Sarah Grimké and Angelina Grimké Weld) who opened the doors of Englewood Academy in Perth Amboy to shelter fleeing Blacks (B. Cunningham 1977, 75). Free Blacks in such New Jersey communities as Lawnside (Camden County) and Macedonia (Monmouth County) also offered much needed shelter. A Black clergyman, the Reverend Thomas Clement Oliver, served as a prominent Underground Railroad "conductor" through Salem and Camden Counties (B. Cunningham 1977, 75; New Jersey Historical Commission 2002, 10); a famous 1898 study of the Underground Railroad featured an oral history interview about Oliver's experiences (New Jersey Historical Commission 2002, 10; Siebert 1898). William Still, a free Black in New Jersey, was vigorously active in the Philadelphia–through–New Jersey Underground Railroad, in one poignant instance helping a Black fugitive from the South who turned out to be his brother "from whom he had been separated since boyhood" ("The Underground Railroad," n.d.). Still later went on to recount his work in 1870s and 1880s publications he authored, which are unique in heralding the role and heroism of Blacks in their hazardous Underground Railroad trek, as opposed to just focusing on white abolitionists

(Still 1879, 1886). Harriet Tubman is one of the most famous Blacks associated with these momentous events. Enslaved in Maryland, at age thirty she escaped North in 1849 with the "North Star as her guide" (New Jersey Historical Commission 2002, 10). She made it to Philadelphia and then Cape May, New Jersey. She did not then remain content enjoying her personal freedom, but this true heroine subsequently "used her own innate intelligence and courage to make 19 trips into Maryland and help over 300 slaves escape to freedom in the North" (New Jersey Historical Commission 2002, 11).

Traversing New Jersey was very hazardous because many of this state's larger communities, notably Trenton, Newark, and Jersey City, were "especially hostile to abolitionists and escaped slaves" (B. Cunningham 1977, 75). Underground Railroad "conductors" were wary of New Brunswick also, for "fugitive-slave agents lurked about the Raritan River ferry landings" (J. Cunningham 1966, 171) and this city was the headquarters of southern agents seeking slave runaways (Armstead et al. 2016, 94; B. Cunningham 1977, 75).

Some three generations later, there was angst as well as hope for Blacks trekking the Great Migration from the South to New Jersey. We can get a sense of the tribulations of Blacks traveling to New Jersey in the Great Migration and some of their later achievements from remarkable research done by the Newark Krueger-Scott Cultural Center and exhibited at the Newark Public Library in 2016, with Samantha Boardman as a guest curator (Newark Public Library 2016). This research is presented in more detail in appendix C. Here, we briefly excerpt some of the oral histories. Zaundria Mapson recalled that in leaving Florida to come to New Jersey in the late 1940s her family was "not able to stay in hotels." Mageline Little's journey from North Carolina in the late 1950s to New Jersey entailed packing food in advance and hoping for safe rest stops. In coming to Newark in the 1940s from Georgia, Bill Stubbs's family had to endure a racially segregated train ride until Washington, DC. One Great Migrant family (a mother and a nine-year-old) coming to Newark from Jacksonville, Florida, in 1936 endured as their first residence a one-room apartment with no indoor plumbing and only a potbellied stove for heat.

In time, however, conditions improved and opportunities beckoned for the Great Migrants. For instance, the nine-year-old described above was Sharpe James; he ultimately served as a New Jersey state senator and as Newark's thirty-fifth mayor. (Sadly, James was later convicted of fraud and served time in prison.) There were many other Great Migration success stories. A son of Georgia sharecroppers, Bill Stubbs ultimately served in prominent political roles. Another southern sharecropper's child coming to Newark overcame much adversity and achieved later success: "Annie Rose Johnston was born in Burke County, Georgia in 1911. Growing up as one of thirteen on a farm, she learned to pick cotton as a child, despite being blind. Mrs. Johnston came north by train with her family in 1922 and went on to work as an educator under the Works Progress Administration teaching at schools for the deaf and the blind. In 1944 she got a job in a Newark factory and stayed through 1947 when she returned to school for her Masters" (Newark Public Library 2016).

Although Newark surely posed tribulations to Black Great Migrants, it also offered new experiences. Zaundria Mapson came to Newark in 1947 from Florida and reveled in attending public school with white children (in contrast to the strictly segregated Florida schools); she also took childhood delight in the cultural attractions available in her new home: "I enjoyed activities—the museum, the library—and it seemed that Newark was a very exciting place [and] had everything" (Newark Public Library 2016). Martha Gaynor contrasted having to make do with a single-room schoolhouse in rural Georgia with a more modern school building available to her in Newark. Another Black migrant extolled the area's trolleys and streetlamps. Mildred Arnold

> came to Newark with her mother, brothers, and sister in 1924 ... migrating from ... South Carolina. ... My father and uncle met us at the [Newark] Pennsylvania Railroad Station. We came on the trolley. ... Oh lord, to come up South Orange avenue on that trolley car, that was something. ... Everything was amazing. ... You had a lot of gaslights in Newark. When they came on in the nighttime, ... the streets lit up. We had never seen anything like that. Down south, when the sun went down there was only darkness. (Wright 1986, 15–16)

Asian Racial Profile

Before presenting the Asian racial group numbers and profile for both the nation and New Jersey, we will outline changing immigration policy because that bears significantly on the numbers of this racial group. About 60 percent of all Asian Americans nationally are immigrants and a higher two-thirds of this group in New Jersey are (Budiman, Cilluffo, and Ruiz 2019; Jersey Promise 2019). As we shall see shortly, the Asian population in the United States has soared or plummeted depending on how the federal government has opened or closed its borders to outsiders. Also, meriting some discussion before considering the count of Asians over time is changing Census Bureau enumerations and classifications of this group.

From its earliest history forward, Americans were decidedly unreceptive to Asians in their midst. The nation's first Nationality Act of 1790 barred Asians from citizenship and the nation's immigration laws were inhospitable to this group to say the least (Hsu 2015, 1). Chinese did not arrive in the United States in any noticeable numbers until the 1848–1855 California gold rush and the 1860s building of America's first intercontinental railroad, which especially in its western leg, employed many Chinese laborers—as high as 90 percent of the Central Pacific's laborer workforce (Kennedy 2019). These Chinese laborers, estimated at about fifteen thousand to twenty thousand immigrants, were tasked with the most dangerous railroad-building work and were paid much less than their white counterparts (Kennedy 2019).[6] The nation did not respond with gratitude but "boiling resentment towards Chinese immigrants" (Okrent 2019, 44). In 1875, Chinese women immigrants were curtailed by the Page Act (Urban, n.d.). In 1878, Chinese and other Asian immigrants were disqualified from attaining citizenship by no less than the U.S. Supreme Court (Okrent 2019, 44). Four years later in 1882, the U.S. Congress passed the Chinese Exclusion Act restricting the immigration of Chinese laborers, which was interpreted strictly to exclude almost all Chinese (Hsu 2015, 7). The 1882 act was renewed ten years later by the Geary Act of 1892 (Urban, n.d.) and then in 1902 became a permanent exclusion. A euphemistically termed gentlemen's agreement curbed immigration from Japan (Hsu 2015, 7). Then the Immigration Act of 1917 barred immigration from most of Asia, excluding Japan.

More draconian was the Immigration Act of 1924, which dramatically reduced the volume of permitted immigration to the United States, drastically changed the countries from which immigration would be permitted, and had a particularly egregious impact on Asian immigration as it

> impos[ed] on the Japanese a quota so low it could only be considered ridiculous: the same minimum quota of one hundred immigrants a year allotted to the tiniest countries of Europe was applied to every Asian nation, no matter how large. Worse, because Asians not born in the United States were excluded from citizenship, the hundred-person-per country limit improbably accommodated only whites (or blacks) from Asian nations; [a U.S. Senate sponsor of the 1924 restrictive immigration law said] he liked the idea because "it could eliminate Japanese and other Orientals without the use of any words specifically targeting them." (Okrent 2019, 349)

In a similar vein, an analysis of the Immigration Act of 1924 bluntly concluded that it "effectively banned . . . immigration from much of Asia" (King 2019, 113). There were other subsequent restrictions against Asians immigrating to the United States, albeit with minor exceptions (e.g., the 1882 Chinese Exclusion Act was repealed in World War II as the U.S. allied with China during that conflict). For example, the 1952 Immigration and Nationality Act (McCarran-Walter) set a total immigration quota for Asia at a paltry annual 2,900 persons as compared to 149,667 for Europe (Chan 1991, 146). (The 1952 law similarly barred entry from other parts of the globe other than Europe, with the annual quota of all of Africa set at a minuscule 1,400.)

In time, the United States reversed immigration course and the Immigration Act of 1965 allowed for a much greater volume of immigration from a much broader swath of the globe, including Asian countries. The dramatically different 1924 and 1965 immigration laws are described in more detail later in this chapter. These changing laws affected not only the size of the Asian population but also influenced the presence of other demographic groups, such as Hispanics and the foreign-born generally, subjects also shortly discussed.

In considering the headcount of Asians, it is further instructive to briefly review the evolving enumeration of this group by the Census Bureau. Chinese were first counted by the census in 1870 and Japanese were added in 1890. In 1910, an "other" (nonwhite or Black) racial group was added by the census and the vast majority of persons included were Koreans, Filipinos, and Asian Indians. For example, the 1910 census for New Jersey revealed that of the state's 2.5 million population, there were 168 Asian Indians. This group was scattered throughout the state's communities, such as twelve Indians in Newark and six in Jersey City. (Reflecting later immigration law changes, these numbers would dramatically increase—27,000 Asian Indians called Jersey City home in 2010.) From 1920 to 1940, Asian Indians were tabulated in the census as Hindus regardless of their religion; Asian Indians were later counted as white between 1950 and 1970. The census did not begin to classify Asian as a racial category until 1990 when it included ten groups under this racial designation (e.g., Chinese, Japanese, Indian, and Korean). Ultimately, about twenty groups were included with the following as examples: Asian Indian, Chinese (without Taiwanese), Japanese, Korean, Pakistani, Taiwanese, and Vietnamese. Asians, according to the census, are people having origins in the Far East, Southeast Asia, or the Indian subcontinent (Hoeffel et al. 2012, 2), including the detailed associated Asian groups enumerated above. Of further note, Asians are identified regardless if respondents also report Hispanic origin. Starting in 1980, Native Hawaiians and Pacific Islanders were categorized as belonging to the same group as Asian Americans and the overarching group was referred to as "Asian and Pacific Islander" (API). Then the census in 2000 reclassified "Pacific Islander" as a separate category (Jersey Promise 2019, 11), but there is still common reference to Asians and Pacific Islanders as a combined racial group, a convention we continue here in presenting the API headcounts over time. (We shorten the API reference to a shorthand "Asian.") Thus, the Asian population tallies we present below for the nation and New Jersey over more than a century's span must be viewed through a cautionary lens, given the many Census Bureau changes in designating this racial group over time.

The number of Asians in the United States barely grew from about 0.1 million to 0.9 million from 1900 to 1960 (table 4.1). Moreover, given the nation's significant growth over this time span from a total population of 76.2 million to 179.3 million (see chapter 3), the Asian share of the full country's population (table 4.2) from 1900 to 1960 never exceeded 0.5 percent and for most decades in this six-decade period never exceeded 0.2 percent. In New Jersey, the Asian headcount was yet fainter with at most only a few thousand Asians present per decade in this state from 1900 to 1960 (table 4.1) and the Asian share of this state's total population over this span stood at a bare trace level of typically 0.1 percent (table 4.2). Herein was the end result of the restrictive national immigration policies against Asians discussed earlier.

With immigration law change in the 1960s, the number of Asians in the country soared to 3.5 million in 1980, more than doubled to 7.3 million in 1990, and climbed yet again to 10.6 million in 2000, 15.2 million in 2010, and 18.8 million by 2017. The percentage gains of the national Asian population far exceeded the increases in the country's total population traced in this book's chapter 3, climbing significantly from 0.8 percent in 1970 to 1.5 percent in 1980, 3.8 percent in 2000, 4.9 percent in 2010, and 5.8 percent by 2017 (table 4.2). These data fully support Asians earning the title of "America's fastest growing minority" (Jersey Promise 2019; Lopez, Ruiz, and Patten 2017; Ramakrishnan and Ahmad 2014).

There is a parallel, if not greater, Asian demographic ascendency in New Jersey. The headcount of this group in this state soared from 20,537 in 1970 to 103,848 in 1980, reached 483,605 in 2000, 728,769 in 2010, and 890,032 by 2017. As the New Jersey total population was not growing at anywhere near this pace over this time span (as traced in chapter 3), the Asian share of the total population in this state soared from 0.3 percent in 1970 to 1.4 percent in 1980, 5.7 percent in 2000, 8.3 percent in 2010, and 9.9 percent by 2017. As at the national level, Asians are by far the fastest growing racial group in the Garden State (table 4.2). Almost sixth-tenths (56 percent) of the nation's 2017 Asian population is clustered in a handful of states (California, Hawaii, New Jersey, Texas, and Washington) and in only two states (California and Hawaii) do Asians constitute a higher percentage of state residents than in New Jersey (Jersey Promise 2019, 7).

The data in the above paragraphs is for "race alone": the Asian enumeration with the more encompassing "race alone or in combination" is yet higher. This count in 2017 identified 23.1 million Asians nationally, with just shy of one million (978,774) in New Jersey. These Asian "race alone or in combination" tallies represent 7.0 percent and 10.9 percent, respectively, of the nation's and New Jersey's total residents in 2017.

Asians comprise many component groups both in the nation and New Jersey. Of the total New Jersey "race alone" Asian population in 2017 (not including Native Hawaiians and Pacific Islanders), the biggest component by far is Asian Indian (45.9 percent) followed by Chinese (18.9 percent), Filipino (12.2 percent), Korean (10.6 percent), and then others (e.g., Vietnamese with 2.3 percent and Japanese with 1.7 percent). The national 2017 Asian population has proportionally much fewer Asian Indians (22.5 percent), higher Chinese (23.9 percent), higher Filipino, and lower Korean (16.0 percent and 8.1 percent, respectively) and much higher shares of Japanese (4.2 percent) and Vietnamese (10.0 percent). The 2010 Asian population group component pattern for both New Jersey and the nation is similar to that traced above for 2017. For example, in 2010, the four largest Asian groups of the New Jersey population as a share of this racial category were Asian Indians (40.3 percent), Chinese (18.3 percent), Filipino (15.1 percent), and Korean (12.9 percent) while these four groups comprised 19.4 percent, 22.8 percent, 17.4 percent, and 9.7 percent of the national 2010 Asian population.

What has drawn Asian Americans to New Jersey? A 2019 survey by Jersey Promise found the following:

- 33.1 percent moved for employment
- 18.1 percent moved for quality of life
- 12.8 percent moved with parents
- 8.3 percent moved for quality of schools
- 7.9 percent moved because they were born there
- 5.6 percent moved because it is affordable
- 14.3 percent moved for other reasons

We conclude our numeric review of the Asian racial group by the following vignettes of the life story experiences of a few illustrative Asians in New Jersey, with the notes to this chapter containing more detail on these individuals.

KUSAKABE TARO

A young samurai, Kusakabe came to Rutgers University in 1867 to study with the ultimate goal of improving relations between Japan and Western nations (Rutgers University Libraries 2017, 1). In part because of its ties to the Dutch Reform Church, Rutgers in that era was the "most popular 'first institution'" (Perrone 2017, 456, citing Conte 1977, 90) of higher learning for young Japanese. A brilliant student, Kusakabe finished first in his class and Phi Beta Kappa, but sadly died before commencement and was posthumously granted his degree. Kusakabe's college friend and tutor, William Elliot Griffis, subsequently became a leading East Asian scholar, fostering continued academic research on Japan, Korea, and China.[7]

THEODORA YOSHIKAMI, IDDY ASADA, AND PAUL NOGUCHI AT SEABROOK FARMS

Japanese Americans interned after the start of World War II were given the option of working at Seabrook Farms in Upper Deerfield Township, New Jersey. Theodora Yoshikami persevered there with her family and ultimately she started a theater company. Iddy Asada left the scorching heat of an Arizona detention camp and, as a self-described "tomboy," played on the Seabrook Farm's softball and basketball teams. Paul Noguchi made the best of having to pick beans at Seabrook for forty cents a basket in the not infrequent heat and rain, yet he also has some positive recollections of his time at Seabrook Farms (Asada 1994; City University of New York 2018; Noguchi 1993).[8]

VICTORIA

When Victoria meets new people, they may think she is a Latina American or Filipina American or mixed-race American. But Victoria is a Jersey Girl, a third generation Japanese descendent born in Peru. . . . [Her parents left Peru] after a violent incident, [then] settled in Queens where . . . life was very hard. As a result, when a friend offered her mother a job in NJ, they gladly moved, found a better life and have never looked back. Victoria now works for a Fortune 500 company and has an entrepreneurial spirit. She raises her two daughters as Jersey Girls who are proud of their heritage. (Jersey Promise 2019, 18)

PHAM CO

A Vietnamese refugee, Pham Co immigrated first to California in 1975 and later made New Jersey his home. In the Garden State, he encountered both travails (e.g., a broken car transmission forced him for some time to walk thirty miles back and forth to work), neighborly empathy (an American family that shared food and car rides), and economic and social enhancement. Co worked many years with different New Jersey firms and his children adjusted well to American life (Co 2002).[9]

ASIAN AMERICANS IN NEW JERSEY POLITICAL OFFICE

Upendra Chivukula came to the United States from India in 1974, finished graduate school in 1976, and began working as an engineer (Chivukula 2002). He was elected mayor of Franklin Township in 2000 and became the first Asian American member of the New Jersey Legislature in 2002. Others have followed his pioneering Asian American political involvement (Rizzo 2019). Born in Passaic, New Jersey, to Indian immigrants, Ravinder Bhalla, a Sikh by heritage, was elected as mayor of Hoboken in 2017 after earlier serving on this community's city council. Hoboken has long been a city of "firsts" (first organized baseball game played in 1846, and the cloth zipper was invented there) and the election of Bhalla was also a milestone—"first Sikh elected mayor of New Jersey and one of only a few Sikh to become mayor of an American City" (Otterman 2017).

Some Other Race

In addition to the racial groups already discussed in this chapter—white, Black, American Indian and Alaska Native (AIAN), and Asian (Asian and Native Hawaiian or Other Pacific Islander—API), the Census Bureau has yet another category labeled Some Other Race (SOR). This additional taxonomy was added "to capture respondents who didn't identify with any of the other categories" (Ashok 2016). Reflecting the complexity of race (and ethnicity) in America and the challenges of pigeonholing individuals into separate racial (and ethnic) silos, there has been an increase in the number of people identifying as SOR and the

SOR's share of the total population. In 1980, about 6.8 million persons in the entire United States identified as SOR, 3.0 percent of the total population. In that year in New Jersey, about 0.2 million flagged their race as SOR, comprising a roughly similar 2.7 percent of all state residents. By 2010, those flagging SOR rose to 19.1 million persons nationally, with a number approaching 0.6 million (559,722) in New Jersey. (As elsewhere in this chapter, our narrative focuses on the "one race only" category as opposed to the larger "race alone or in combination" enumeration.) In 2010, the SOR share of the total national population had doubled from 1980 to about six in every hundred category and was the third largest national racial group after white and Black and the fourth largest in New Jersey after white, Black, and Asian. The results for 2017 are not that much different (see tables 4.1 and 4.2). No wonder one observer described this SOR trend as "The Rise of the American 'Others'" (Ashok 2016).

It bears mentioning that demographers have misgivings about the SOR racial category, as admittedly they do about other racial and ethnic specifications in census and related surveys. Indeed, of the 19.1 million persons who identified nationally as SOR in 2010, the majority were Hispanic (Krogstad and Cohn 2014). What we have with SOR and with census racial and ethnic categories writ large is the challenge of such identification given the complexity and variability of these subjects; census officials acknowledge that "increasingly Americans are saying they cannot find themselves" in the census-specified forms (Krogstad and Cohn 2014). That cautionary acknowledgment especially applies to the SOR category and that caveat bedevils the broader array of census-specified racial groups, and ethnicity identifications such as Hispanic, discussed next.

Hispanic Ethnic Profile

In addition to race, ethnic composition is an important demographic characteristic, and in turn, Hispanic identity is a key ethnic trait. A history of Hispanic North America observed, "The Hispanic past of the United States predates the arrival of the Pilgrims by a century and has been every bit as important in shaping the nation as it exists today" (Carrie Gibson 2019, book jacket). Despite their importance to the United States, Hispanics until recently have not been given their demographic due concerning their identification, enumeration, and profile. There was a one-time effort in the 1930 census to identify persons who were "Mexican" (Cohn 2010; Haines 2006b). This stillborn effort was further clouded by the method of such identification, namely that census enumerators decided who was or was not "Mexican"—a clearly difficult, if not impossible, charge. More broadly, until 1970, Hispanic determination by federal statisticians was made in a crude, indirect fashion (e.g., flagging individuals with Spanish surnames or those proclaiming Spanish as their "mother tongue") (Hobbs and Stoops 2002, 73). Matters improved some by the 1970 census, which included a specific Hispanic origin or descent question, but this probe was applied to only

Table 4.4

Hispanic Population (of Any Race) of the United States and New Jersey, 1850–2017

	Hispanic Population			
	Number		Percentage of Total Population	
Year	United States	New Jersey	United States	New Jersey
1850	116,943	360	0.5	0.1
1900	503,189	4,718	0.7	0.3
1950	3,231,409	33,639	2.1	0.7
1980	14,608,673	491,883	6.4	6.7
1990	22,354,059	739,861	9.0	9.6
2000	35,305,818	1,117,191	12.5	13.3
2010	50,477,594	1,555,144	16.3	17.7
2017	58,846,134	1,840,433	18.1	20.4

SOURCES: 1850, 1900, and 1950: Irving 2019. (Analysis of Integrated Public Use Microdata Series [IPUMS] National Historical Geographic Information System [NHGIS] data for indicated years. The IPUMS USA data base is attributed to Ruggles et al., n.d.). 1980, 1990, 2000, and 2010: Decennial census for indicated years. See also Gaquin and Ryan 2015, 35–56; Campbell Gibson, n.d., chapter 4; and Hobbs and Stoops 2002, A-34–35. 2017: American Community Survey, 2017 ACS 1-Year Estimates.

a modest 5 percent of census respondents. As one Pew Research Center demographer bluntly observed, "This question did not work very well" (Cohn 2010), and another observer called the 1970 effort a "half-hearted attempt" (Florido 2017). It was only at the 1980 census that Hispanic origin was collected from all households (Hobbs and Stoops 2002, 73; Haines 2006b, 1–23). Further, as one astute demographer notes, "The history of Census data on race and Hispanic origin is extremely complex with many issues of comparability" (Campbell Gibson, n.d., chap. 4, 17).

With these caveats in mind, table 4.4 identifies the number of Hispanics in both the United States and New Jersey from 1850 to 2017. Pre-1980 crude national estimates are 0.1 million Hispanics in 1850, 0.5 million in 1900, and 3.2 million in 1950, representing a very small yet growing 0.5 percent, 0.7 percent, and 2.1 percent, respectively, of the total United States population. For New Jersey, the Hispanic population over this century span was yet more modest. In 1850, only 360 Hispanics are estimated to have been living in the Garden State, amounting to just 0.1 percent of this state's mid-nineteenth-century population of just shy of half a million (489,555). The New Jersey Hispanic population was a scant 4,718 in 1900 and 33,639 in 1950, comprising only 0.3 and 0.7 percent, respectively, of the state's total residents in these years.

Let us focus more on the contemporary—1980 and later—Hispanic population enumeration, which as noted earlier has a firmer statistical foundation. The census in contemporary times defines Hispanic or Latino as "persons of Cuban,

Mexican, Puerto Rican, South or Central American, or other Spanish culture or origin regardless of race" (Ennis, Rios-Vargas, and Albert 2011, 2).

Nationally, the number of Hispanics in the United States has grown significantly from 14.6 million in 1980 to 22.4 million in 1990 (53 percent increase), reached 35.3 million in 2000 (58 percent gain), stood at 50.5 million in 2010 (43 percent increase), and was 58.8 million in 2017 (16 percent rise). These Hispanic percentage increases far exceed that realized by the nation's overall population over these same time periods as detailed in chapter 3 (i.e., 10 percent gain between 1980 and 1990, 13 percent between 1990 and 2000, and 6 percent between 2010 and 2017), reflecting the smaller starting numerical base of the Hispanic population relative to the nation's total population as well as the patently swelling Hispanic population over this period. In tandem, the Hispanic share of the country's total population has grown significantly, from just 6.4 percent in 1980 to 9.0 in 1990, 12.5 percent in 2000, 16.3 percent in 2010, and 18.1 percent by 2017 (table 4.4).

Since 1980, the growth of the Hispanic population share in New Jersey has very closely followed that in the United States as a whole, with the New Jersey Hispanic share of the total population standing at 6.7 percent in 1980, 9.6 percent in 1990, 13.3 percent in 2000, 17.7 percent in 2010, and 20.4 percent by 2017 (table 4.4). In absolute population counts, the number of Hispanics in New Jersey grew substantially from just shy of 0.5 million (491,883) in 1980 to 0.7 million (739,861) in 1990 (50 percent increase), climbed to 1.1 million (1,117,191) in 2000 (51 percent gain), stood at 1.6 million (1,555,144) in 2010 (39 percent rise), and climbed once again to 1.8 million (1,840,433) in 2017 (18 percent increase). These Hispanic population percentage gains from 1980 onward resemble on an order of magnitude the increases realized by this ethnic group nationally. As with the nation, and for similar reasons, these New Jersey Hispanic percentage increases far exceeded those of the growth of the state's total population. As observed by one New Jersey demographer, "Hispanic residents . . . form one of the fastest growing minority populations in the state" (Wu 2011, 1).

Unlike New Jersey's Black population growth, which is driven primarily by domestic migration, the state's Hispanic population growth has historically been propelled by a combination of immigration and internal migration. The first wave of Hispanic migrants to New Jersey consisted of Puerto Ricans leaving economic turmoil in that U.S. territory after World War II. This group laid the groundwork for future emigration from the island. Puerto Ricans would continue to come to New Jersey as well as other states (e.g., Florida and New York) in the decades that followed (Wang and Rayer 2018). During the 1960s, Cubans immigrated to New Jersey in large numbers following Fidel Castro's revolution. By 1980, about 80 percent of New Jersey's Hispanic population was either Puerto Rican or Cuban, and less than 4 percent was Mexican (Shaw 1994). By 2010, of the state's 1,555,144 Hispanics, 217,715 (14 percent) were Mexican; a large contingent was, as in the past, Puerto Rican (434,092, 27.9 percent) or Cuban (83,362, 5.4 percent); and Hispanics in New Jersey further hailed from many other places in the Americas and beyond in 2010 including the Dominican Republic, 197,922 (12.7 percent); Central America, 176,611 (11.4 percent); South America, 325,179 (20.9 percent); and other Hispanic, 120,263 (7.7 percent). Further detail of the national affiliations of Hispanics in New Jersey as of 2010 is available. For example, of the 176,611 Central American Hispanics in this state, 56,532 (3.6 percent of all Hispanics) were Salvadoran, 48,869 Guatemalan (3.1 percent), and 36,556 (2.4 percent) were Honduran. Of the 325,179 South American Hispanics in New Jersey in 2010, slightly over 100,000 were either Colombian (101,593, 6.5 percent of all Hispanics) or Ecuadorian (100,480, 6.5 percent), followed by 75,869 (4.9 percent) Peruvian.

For larger perspective, let us compare the national origins of New Jersey Hispanics components of this group for the nation overall. There are differences as well as some similarities. The top-ranked contemporary Hispanic groups for both the nation and New Jersey are a seemingly similar Mexican, Puerto Rican, Cuban, Dominican, and Colombian, but that masks the very different proportions of these groups. More than six-tenths (63.0 percent) of Hispanics nationally in 2010 were Mexican as against a much smaller one-seventh (14.0 percent) Mexican representation in New Jersey. It stands to reason that states closer to Mexico (e.g., Arizona, California, New Mexico, and Texas) and hence the nation overall would likely attract a much higher share of Mexican Hispanics compared to more distant New Jersey. Geography and historical cultural connections also explain why a much higher share of New Jersey's Hispanics in 2010 were either Puerto Rican (27.9 percent) or Cuban (5.4 percent) relative to the Puerto Rican (9.2 percent) and Cuban share (3.5 percent) of the national Hispanic population. Dominican is ranked a nominally similar third and fifth most important component of the total Hispanic population, respectively, in New Jersey and nationally in 2010, but the percentages they comprise of the respective total Hispanic headcounts at these two geographies are far different (12.7 percent in New Jersey versus 2.8 percent in nationally). Colombians are a component of the Hispanic population but at different 2010 proportions for New Jersey (6.5 percent) compared to the nation (1.8 percent). More broadly, somewhat more than a fifth (20.9 percent) of New Jersey's Hispanics in 2010 were South American, almost four times that continent's share nationally (5.5 percent) in that year. In short, Mexicans dominate the Hispanic population nationally, while New Jersey's Hispanic affiliations are heavily Puerto Rican, Mexican, Dominican, and South American.

As with the other "People of New Jersey" sections in this chapter, we add to our numeric presentation some illustrative "voices of the people." In this instance, we first extract some oral histories from the pathbreaking "The Latino New Jersey History Project" of the Rutgers Department of Latino and Caribbean Studies[10] and then recount a narrative of the Hispanic presence in New

Brunswick,[11] a city with one of the highest Hispanic proportions of its total local population (about half) in the state.

ELSA PEREZ, IMMIGRANT FROM ECUADOR TO PLAINFIELD, NEW JERSEY

Raised in Ambato, Ecuador, in the 1940s, Elsa Perez's husband first immigrated to New York City and she later joined him, first living in Brooklyn and then moving to Plainfield, New Jersey. She was attracted to Plainfield because her niece lived there and neighboring South Plainfield offered factory jobs for employment. In Plainfield, she first lived on West South Seventh Street and found that "living in the neighborhoods of Plainfield is a rewarding experience. Elsa was making a living for herself and her family" (Roserio, n.d.).

BENITO RODRIGUEZ, IMMIGRANT FROM PUERTO RICO TO NEWARK AND THEN KEANSBURG, NEW JERSEY

Benito Rodriguez migrated to the United States at age eighteen to find work and financially help his family in Puerto Rico. He first came to Newark (where his sister lived) and subsequently worked in a flower shop, then a restaurant located on Route 22, and finally a paper company, where he operated a forklift for forty-four years. Benito is a proud father and was overjoyed at his daughter's birth, yet experienced "some sadness at not being able to show her to the rest of his family back in Puerto Rico" (Rosado, n.d.).

MANUEL REY, IMMIGRANT FROM CUBA TO NEWARK, NEW JERSEY

Born in Havana in 1951, Manuel Rey's family fled Cuba with the coming of power of the Castro regime. The family first moved to Miami and then came to Newark, drawn by better job opportunities. "[Manuel] . . . passes down Cuban culture and traditions to his [family] and [celebrates American traditions as well, such as] Thanksgiving with a turkey . . . for the past 35 years" (Sandoval, n.d.).

Hispanics in New Brunswick

The first wave of Latino settlement in New Brunswick can be traced back to the family of Otilio Colon, which emigrated from Puerto Rico in 1948 (Colon 1982; Sanchez and Gutierrez 1982, 57). Early arrivals established grocery stores, barbershops, furniture stores, and repair shops. In 1959, the first two Puerto Rican students graduated from New Brunswick High School (Colon 1982). In the 1960s, Latinos began working in the public sector in New Brunswick as fire fighters and police officers and in the school system. Eventually, New Brunswick mayor Patricia Sheehan appointed Blanquita Valenti to the board of education, the first Latina in the state to hold such a position.

In the 1970s, Parque Bolivar, a new park by the city's Spanish Outreach Center, was created and a lead speaker at this facility's dedication, Jose Oyarzun, a member of the park board of directors, noted the Latino diversity in the city and the opportunity for unity: "Here in New Brunswick we have many Latin Americans—Puerto Ricans, Chileans, Argentineans, Cubans, Costa Ricans, and many more.... The dream of Bolivar was to unite all these people. Hopefully, the park can help do this" (quoted in Ledesman 1976). In 1977, the Spanish American Civic Association sponsored a flag-raising ceremony in front of city hall to observe the twenty-sixth anniversary of the constitution of the Puerto Rican Commonwealth. The city's recreation director raised the Puerto Rican flag and heralded the community's demographic diversity.

Indeed, New Brunswick's Hispanic population is highly diverse—in 1981, a Hispanic festival at a New Brunswick church flew the flags of twenty-two Latin American countries (Rojas 1981)—and the profile of that community has changed over time. New Brunswick's Hispanic population in the 1980s was composed primarily of Puerto Ricans and Dominicans; there were relatively few Hispanics from Mexico (the 1980 census enumerated just 23 residents born in Mexico, and the 1990 census counted just 332 among the city's foreign-born). Yet over time, many Mexicans arrived in New Brunswick, with the majority coming from the Oaxaca area of Mexico.

As of 2010, of New Brunswick's 55,181 total population, 27,553 (50 percent) were Hispanic and in turn 14,104, or slightly more than half (51 percent) of all Hispanics were Mexican. No wonder the Mexican president visited New Brunswick in 2008 and this community is now home to one of the largest Mexican populations in the tristate area. Other major components of New Brunswick's Hispanic population in 2010 included 4,139 Dominicans (15 percent), 2,832 Puerto Ricans (10 percent), and 1,103 South Americans. Rebecca Escobar, formerly of the city's Puerto Rican Action Board, reflected, "We have a diverse, vibrant community" (Escobar, n.d.).

National and New Jersey Immigration and Foreign-Born Profile

Historical and Legislative Context

Before commencing this section, which considers immigration and foreign-born trends in the United States over a nearly two-century span, the limitations of the data on these subjects must be acknowledged. There were no official statistics on international immigration before 1819, and when data were later kept, it was a far from universal tabulation of all those coming to the United States. For example, enumerations were often limited to those coming by ship through major ports, with first-class passengers excluded; land crossings, such as from Canada, were not always fully counted (Haines 2000, 311–314, 344).The census from 1850 onward did, however, query place of birth and from 1870 onward ascertained "the nativity of the respondent's parents" (Haines 2000, 344). In short, as with the racial and ethnic population counts described earlier, there are acknowledged gaps in the information on immigrants and the foreign-born. With this caveat noted, we can speak of broad-brush and long-term trends in the presentation that follows.

The United States has been described as a "Nation of Immigrants" (Haines 2000, 344) and indeed this country has long been a mecca for those seeking a better life (DeParle 2019). "Of the estimated fifty million [worldwide] immigrants who relocated during the hundred years of so preceding the 1920s, approximately 60 percent [30 million] came to the United States" (Barde, Carter, and Sutch 2015, 1–523). About one-quarter of the tremendous United States population growth from 1790 through 1920 identified in chapter 3 was due to international immigration (Haines 2000, 344).

There were both "pull" and "push "factors underlying this. The "pull" factors were land, farm, and homeownership; religious, social, and political liberties; and other attractions of living on American soil. There were as well strong "push" factors; the many immigrants coming to the United States were fleeing physical and social oppression of many stripes, from the Irish famine to Eastern European pogroms and mayhem that would morph ultimately into "Blood Lands" (T. Snyder 2010).

Carrying immigrants was also a very profitable enterprise. Shipping companies, such as the Hamburg American Line, coming to American shores to transport timber and other products back to Europe abhorred empty ships on the American-bound westward leg of this journey; people packed into steerage traveling eastward provided excellent ballast for the trip across the Atlantic (Okrent 2019, 69). Additionally, immigrant fares were a huge profit center in their own right, costing the shipping companies about $2 per person as against a fare that exceeded $20 per head in the currency of the day (Okrent 2019, 70). (This suggests a profit margin of about 10:1, far exceeding the touted approximate 60 percent gross margin by Apple on its iPhone [Miller 2017].) Also of note in encouraging immigration was that "trans-Atlantic passenger fares became cheaper" over the 1800s and the travel time was reduced by about one-third with the improving ship technology from sail to steam (Haines 2000, 353).

Despite improvements, immigrant travel to the United States did have its travails. Those packed into the windowless steerage hulls faced many challenges of crowding, disease, and seasickness (Shaw 1994, 35), and more than some were terrified, for as one immigrant wrote in a plaintive letter, "As all were crossing the ocean for the first time, they thought their end had come" (Bishop 1853, citied in Shaw 1994, 35). Many, however, braved these travails and millions came in the many decades from the mid-nineteenth to early twentieth centuries when America largely welcomed immigrants.

Although legally accepted, immigrants faced hostility and scorn upon their arrival in the United States. Xenophobic nativists often smoldered with resentment. Discrimination and even anti-immigrant riots occurred. Even historical luminaries over the centuries would sometimes rail at the incoming "not like us, inferior-class" immigrants. For example, the 1753 observation by one of America's notables of the day, Benjamin Franklin, that those immigrating (referring to Germans) "are generally the most stupid sort of their own nation" (Franklin cited by Okrent 2019, 41) echoes the 1902 charge by Woodrow Wilson (then a Princeton University professor) that those multitudes emigrating from southern and eastern Europe were "of the lowest class" (Wilson cited by Hochschild 2019, 30). In a similar vein, Madison Grant, born in 1865 and an embodiment of the American plutocracy of the day, railed in a 1910 letter to President Howard Taft that the Eastern European immigrants nested in lower Manhattan were an "invasive species," and shortly thereafter he wrote a best seller titled *The Passing of the Great Race* (Grant 1916), which warned of the immigrants' threat to white Nordic hegemony (C. King 2019, 87–90; Spiro 2008). (The theme of the pernicious invasive immigrant would sadly repeat in later dystopian books, such as *The Camp of the Saints* in which author Jean Raspail [1973] depicts subcontinent Indians invading France and eventually overrunning the European continent [Peltier and Kulish 2019].)

Yet, the history of immigration to the United States is not linear, for over the centuries, the waves of immigrants have ebbed and flowed (Easterlin 2000, 651; Haines 2000, 353) related to both conditions overseas and varying underlying sentiments on Miss Liberty's open-door policies. The following illustrative numbers show some peaks and valleys in the volume of immigrants to the United States in the twentieth century, which often coincided with fluctuating economic conditions of both the United States and Europe (Haines 2000, 352). From 1900 to 1909, when the golden door was wide open, about 8.2 million immigrants arrived. This figure plummeted to about 2.5 million total immigrants between 1950 and 1959 (the lingering effects of the previously mentioned 1920s immigration restrictions) and soared to just under 10 million total immigrants arriving between 1990 and 2000. (Recall the more flexible 1960s immigration framework.) Expressed as a share (percentage) of the total United States population, the annual flow of immigrants to this country was roughly 0.1 percent of all residents in 1820, 1.5 percent in 1850 (many a transportation, manufacturing, and other economic endeavors needing laborers in the prosperous period before the Civil War), 0.3 percent in 1880 (the dampening aftermath of the 1870s economic depression), 1.5 percent in 1910 (when Ellis Island had a wide-open portal), dropped to less than 0.1 percent in 1930 and 1940 (stifled by immigration restrictions, economic depression, and war), hovered at about 0.2 percent in 1950 and 1960 (better economic times but immigration restrictions), reached 0.7 percent in 1990 (immigration flexibility and economic prosperity), and has subsequently stood at about 0.3–0.4 percent (Abramitzky and Boutan 2017, 1315; Haines 2000, 352). Daniel Okrent (2019, 41) trenchantly observed in *The Guarded Gate* that "attitudes towards immigrants [in the United States] formed a perfect sine wave, periods of welcoming inclusiveness, alternating with years of scowling antipathy."

Okrent's alternating sine wave metaphor is illustrated by two drastically changing twentieth-century laws regulating the volume and composition of immigration to the United States. These two laws, mentioned earlier, warrant more detailed description and consist of (1) the Immigration Act of 1924 (popularly referred to after its Senate cosponsors as the [Albert] Johnson–[David] Reed Act) and (2) the Immigration and Nationality Act of 1965 (popularly referred to as the [Philip] Hart–[Emanuel] Celler Act).

The Johnson-Reed Act was a product of its time, a reaction against the burgeoning immigration to America at the turn of the twentieth century, especially from central, eastern, and southern European countries as opposed to the heretofore dominant immigration from northern and western Europe. As summarized by Haines, "For the decades between 1821 and 1890, 82% of all immigrants originated in northern and western Europe. For the three decades 1891 to 1920, the situation had altered dramatically; only 25% of the migrants came from northern and western Europe. Contemporaries described this as the shift from the 'old' to the 'new' immigration" (Haines 2000, 354).

Inflamed by such writings as Grant's *The Passing of the Great Race* and given credence by then-esteemed academics who railed against such "new" immigration (e.g., Harvard professor William Ripley [1899] wrote of the threat of the "Mediterranean" to the higher order "Teutonic" and "Alpine" races; C. King 2019), America's plutocracy deemed it time for an immigration paradigm change. In 1907, the U.S. Congress initiated a U.S. Immigration Commission (Haines 2000, 354) chaired by Senator William Dillingham and including such nationally famous and influential members as Senator Henry Cabot Lodge. After spending almost $1 million (roughly $30 million in current dollars) and hearing from some of the most heralded scientific minds of that era, the Dillingham Commission issued a forty-one-volume report that in its essence embodied the racial stereotyping of Grant, Ripley, and others. Ironically, one of the most prominent consultants to this effort, anthropologist Franz Boas, had empirically debunked the chimera pseudoscience of immutable racial differences, but his voice was not heard amid the clamor of other scientists claiming a genetically based racial hierarchy that elevated the "old" immigrants over the "new" immigrants (King 2019). The message of the Dillingham Commission was clear and blunt: it decried the spike of immigration from the "less progressive and advanced countries of Europe" that were "essentially unlike" the earlier superior immigrants from western and northern Europe (King 2019). With the imprimatur of an august congressional commission, the die was now cast to make over America's immigration policy. In an associated historical note, given the tenor of the Dillingham era, it is no wonder that William S. Rossiter (cited in chapter 2), then–chief clerk of the federal Bureau of the Census, wrote a study released in 1909 (*A Century of Population Growth from the First Census of the United States to the Twelfth, 1790–1900*) that examined how America had changed since 1790. This 300-page report included chapters on the national origin of the 1790 U.S.

population, which Rossiter documented as primarily England and other western European countries, and the growth of the foreign-born residents over time. Reflecting the zeitgeist of the day, Rossiter (1909, 116), in the opening paragraph of his study on national origin, spoke of a "classification . . . in the nature of blood, or what may be termed nationality strain."

In a celebrated 1929 Chicago Forum Council debate between nativist Madison Grant and celebrated Black sociologist W.E.B. Du Bois on the topic of Blacks and social equality, the crowd's consensus was that Du Bois easily trumped Grant's feeble arguments (Frazier 2019). Nevertheless, in the 1920s policy arena, Grant and his ilk, decrying immigrants and Blacks, ruled supreme. The Ku Klux Klan, with a 1920s membership of about five million, rode roughshod over many an American community (e.g., ten thousand Klan members marched in 1924 in Hamilton Township, New Jersey, and there was a cross-burning in Kenilworth a year later; Adomaitis, n.d.; Blackwell, n.d.). On the national front, the Johnson-Reed Act slammed the door on those seeking refuge on America's shores.

The Johnson-Reed Act radically changed and limited immigration to the United States. It set a numerical annual cap on the number of allowed immigrants at about 160,000 (for context, in the five years preceding World War I, immigration to the United States averaged slightly over one million annually; Okrent 2019, 287), and the 1924 law further established country-by-country quotas set at 2 percent of the number of foreign-born (or derived population) as of 1890 (Okrent 2019, 336). The 1890 benchmark was deliberately chosen as it *preceded* the surge of immigration from southern and eastern Europe that occurred just afterward (Shaw 1994, 49). In short, under the new law, "new immigrants were to be admitted in a rough ratio with those already here" (Shaw 1994, 94), and the law's "arcane framing was meant to tilt the country's demographic makeup back to what is had been" (C. King 2019, 113).

There were other 1920s roadblocks to immigration. A literacy test was imposed in 1917. Shortly thereafter, the State Department introduced a system of mandatory visas to monitor and restrict would-be immigrants. American women marrying certain immigrants (those not eligible for citizenship because of their national origin or race) could face the forfeiture of their own citizenship, a cupid-squelching policy implemented by the 1922 Married Women's Act (C. King 2019, 113–114).

The Johnson-Reed Act and other era restrictions had a draconian effect on who could immigrate to the United States. For example, whereas before Johnson-Reed in 1921, there were 189,198 immigrants from the Russian Empire (encompassing the latter-day Soviet Union, Poland, and Lithuania) and 222,260 Italian immigrants; in 1925, the number of Russian and Italian immigrants plummeted to 7,346 and 2,662, respectively (Okrent 2019, 344). Johnson-Reed had strong and enduring nativist ethnocentric supporters; for example, Prescott Hall, a cofounder of the Immigration Restriction League and strong advocate of Johnson-Reed, declared, "Enough! Enough we want no more of ye immigrant from a foreign shore" (Okrent, 2019, 67), and Grant praised the new law as "one of the greatest steps" in America's history because it "closed the doors just in time" (C. King 2019, 8).

Others, however, criticized the severe mid-1920s to early 1960s American immigration restrictions that trampled the Emma Lazarus's uplifting inscription on the Statue of Liberty of "Give me . . . your huddled masses yearning to breathe free." The Johnson-Reed Act especially was the target of opprobrium with, for example, one U.S. senator (Emanuel Celler of Hart-Celler fame) decrying its "rankest kind of discrimination," a charge bolstered by the odious citation by Nazis (including Adolf Hitler in *Mein Kampf*) that Germany's racial and citizenship restrictions saw "American immigration law as a model for Germany" (Okrent 2019, 361, 394). It was telling that Hitler kept a leather-bound German translation of Grant's *The Passing of the Great Race* (which had influenced Johnson-Reed) in his personal library (C. King 2019, 306) and even wrote the author a laudatory "fan letter, calling the book 'My Bible'" (Frazier 2019).

More broadly, American racism served as a useful template for a receptive Germany. For example, the infamous German 1930s classifications of Jews, such as *Mischlinge* (persons of mixed Jewish and Aryan blood), were foreshadowed by the U.S. Census Bureau's designation of persons of mixed Black and white blood (mulatto for one-half Black and quadroon for one-quarter Black) (C. King 2019, 307–308). Related to immigration restrictions based on "race" was contemporary advocacy for eugenics, policies that encouraged reproduction by the "fit" and limited reproduction by the "unfit." In both the United States and Germany before World War II, many supported the idea that "inferior" human groups should be sterilized or even more harshly excised (Garland 2002; Nicosia and Huener 2002). Not surprisingly, Madison Grant was associated with the American Eugenic Society (Frazier 2019). As one historian commented, Johnson-Reed "selectively restricted immigration from the very regions the eugenicists claimed harbored the most degenerative germ plasm" (Garland 2002, 25).

History, however, moves in a thesis-antithesis fashion, for in time, the United States reversed immigration course starting in the mid-1960s with passage of the Immigration and Nationality (Hart-Celler) Act of 1965. In signing this act into law, President Lyndon Johnson declared that it was "not . . . revolutionary" (quoted in Gjelton 2015), but in fact it was (E. Lee 2015, 285). It upended the Johnson-Reed restrictions, abolished the "national origins" quota system, and established a preference system for would-be immigrants based on their relationships with relatives who were already citizens of the United States or had permanent resident status. The Hart-Celler Act also gave immigration preference to those having employment skills useful to American business and society (Chan 1991, 146; Jersey Promise 2019, 12; E. Lee 2015, 286). The new law allowed for much greater immigration from Asian countries as well as other places that heretofore had been restricted, such as Latin America and Africa. The immigrants from these "new" places are sometimes referred to as "new new" immigrants (Easterlin 2000, 651)—in distinction from both the "new" immigrants (from central, eastern, and southern Europe) and the " old" immigrants (from western and northern Europe) that had previously come in large numbers to America.

To be certain, the Hart-Celler Act had its detractors when first proposed, such as negative testimony before Congress on the proposed changes from a group in New Jersey, New Jersey Coalition, who protested, "Are we prepared to embrace so great a horde of the world's unfortunate?" (Hacker 1965, cited in Kammer 2015). However, these and other criticisms were overcome; the Hart-Celler Act was signed into law in October 1965 (it was fully implemented by June 1968; Chan 1991, 146) and has had a momentous impact on the volume and profile of American immigration (e.g., immigrant-origin countries and world region of birth) from the mid-twentieth into the early twenty-first century. As observed by one author, "The United States is once again in the midst of an age of immigration" (Hirschman 2014, 69). That statement is bolstered by the following immigration data in the immediate period before and after Hart-Celler's 1965 passage. From 1945 to 1965, the net number of immigrants to the United States averaged about three million per decade. After Hart-Celler, that immigration tally rose to seven million in the 1980s, the highest decade increment since the eight million who came through the "open door" in first decade of the twentieth century (Easterlin 2000, 651). To be certain, as Easterlin (2000, 651) points out, the 1980s Hart-Celler uptick in immigration, when set in context to all those living in the United States in the 1980s (3.2 immigrants per 1,000 population), was substantially (about one-third) lower than the immigrant-to-native-born population ratio of 1901–1910. Nonetheless, Hart-Celler was an immigration sea change. In its aftermath, millions more would come to the United States and from more diverse places.

The Origins and Fluctuating Numbers of the Foreign-Born

Immigrants are the demographic stock of the foreign-born population in the United States. In this section, we examine changing tallies of foreign-born residents from 1850 to 2017 and their varying share of total residents (Dews 2013; Gibson and Jung 2006) over this more-than-one-and-a-half-century span (table 4.5).

From 1850 to 1910, the total foreign-born population in the United States grew from 2.2 million in 1850, to 6.7 million in 1880, to 13.5 million in 1910. In tandem, the foreign-born percentage of the total population rose as well, from 9.7 percent in 1850 to 13.3 percent in 1880, to 14.7 percent in 1910. From that high percentage, the foreign-born population leveled out and declined in percentage over the next two decades—13.9 million in 1920 and 14.2 million in 1930, representing 13.2 percent and 11.6 percent, respectively, of the total national population. Immigration restrictions in the 1920s discussed earlier resulted in a decline of the country's foreign population in both absolute terms (it dropped to

Table 4.5

Foreign-Born Population: Number and Percentage of Total Population for the United States and New Jersey, 1850–2017

	Foreign-Born Population							
	United States				New Jersey			
Year	Number (in 000s)	% Total Population	Change from Previous Period (in 000s)	% Change	Number (in 000s)	% Total Population	Change from Previous Period (in 000s)	% Change
1850	2,245	9.7	NA	NA	60	12.2	NA	NA
1860	4,139	13.2	1,894	84	123	18.3	63	105
1870	5,567	14.4	1,428	35	189	20.9	66	54
1880	6,680	13.3	1,113	20	222	19.6	33	17
1890	9,250	14.8	2,570	38	329	22.8	107	48
1900	10,341	13.6	1,091	12	432	22.9	103	31
1910	13,516	14.7	3,175	31	661	26.0	229	53
1920	13,921	13.2	405	3	742	23.5	81	12
1930	14,204	11.6	283	2	850	21.0	108	15
1940	11,595	8.8	−2,609	−18	699	16.8	−151	−18
1950	10,347	6.9	−1,248	−11	635	13.2	−64	−9
1960	9,738	5.4	−609	−6	615	10.1	−20	−3
1970	9,619	4.7	−119	−1	635	8.9	20	3
1980	14,080	6.2	4,461	46	758	10.3	123	19
1990	19,767	7.9	5,687	40	967	12.5	209	28
2000	31,108	11.1	11,341	57	1,476	17.5	509	53
2010	39,956	12.9	8,848	28	1,845	21.0	369	25
2017	44,526	13.7	4,570	11	2,055	22.8	210	11

SOURCES: 1850–2010: Decennial census for indicated years. See also Dews 2013; CampbellGibson, n.d., chaps. 11 and 12; Gibson and Jung 2006; Gaquin and Ryan 2015, 8, 35. 2017: American Community Survey 2017 ACS 1-Year Estimates.
NA = Not Applicable.

11.6 million in 1940, 10.3 million in 1950, and then to under 10 million by the 1960s and 1970s) and as a percentage of the total population. From a high of 14.7 percent of the total national population comprised of the foreign-born in 1910, that share dropped to 11.6 percent in 1930, 8.8 percent in 1940, 6.9 percent in 1950, and reached a low of 4.7 percent in 1970. As previously noted, the 1965 Hart-Celler immigration law removed many barriers to legal immigration, and the foreign-born population nationally has subsequently climbed over time. From a modern-day-era low of 9.6 million foreign-born residents in 1970, the national tally of this group grew to 19.8 million in 1990, 31.1 million in 2000, 40 million in 2010, and 44.5 million in 2017. In tandem, from the low of 4.7 percent of the national population comprised of the foreign-born in 1970, that share increased to 7.9 percent nationally in 1990, 11.1 percent in 2000, 12.9 percent in 2010, and 13.7 percent in 2017 (table 4.5).

Table 4.6
Foreign-Born Population in the United States by World Region of Birth (1850–2017)

Year	Percentage Foreign-Born Population	Percentage of Foreign-Born Population from World Region of Birth						
		Europe	Northern America	Latin America	Asia	Africa	Oceania	Total
1850	9.7	92.2	6.7	0.9	0.1			100.0
1860	13.2	92.1	6.0	0.9	0.9		0.1	100.0
1870	14.4	88.8	8.9	1.0	1.2		0.1	100.0
1880	13.3	86.2	10.7	1.3	1.6		0.1	100.0
1890	14.8	86.9	10.6	1.2	1.2		0.1	100.0
1900	13.6	86.0	11.4	1.3	1.2		0.1	100.0
1910	14.7	87.4	9.0	2.1	1.4		0.1	100.0
1920	13.2	85.7	8.2	4.2	1.7	0.1	0.1	100.0
1930	11.6	83.0	9.2	5.6	1.9	0.1	0.1	100.0
1940	8.8	85.3	9.3	3.9	1.3		0.1	100.0
1950	6.9	82.3	9.9	5.6	1.8	0.2	0.3	100.0
1960	5.4	75.0	9.8	9.4	5.1	0.4	0.4	100.0
1970	4.7	61.7	8.7	19.4	8.9	0.9	0.4	100.0
1980	6.2	39.0	6.5	33.1	19.3	1.5	0.6	100.0
1990	7.9	22.9	4.0	44.3	26.3	1.9	0.5	100.0
2000	11.1	15.8	2.7	51.7	26.4	2.8	0.5	100.0
2010	12.9	12.1	2.0	53.1	28.2	4.0	0.5	100.0
2017	13.7	10.8	1.8	50.4	31.2	5.1	0.6	100.0

SOURCES: 1850–2010: Decennial census for indicated years. See also Abramitzsky and Boustan 2017, 1315–1316; Campbell Gibson, n.d., chap. 13; and Gaquin and Ryan 2015, 8. 2017: American Community Survey 2017 ACS 1-Year Estimates.

Further revealing of the fluctuating waves of the foreign-born in the United States is the decade-by-decade change of this population shown in table 4.5. For example, the country's number of foreign-born increased by 2.6 million between 1880 and 1890, and there was a yet larger 3.2 million gain from 1900 to 1910. That was followed by significant decade reductions in the foreign-born (e.g., 2.6 million diminishment between 1930 and 1940) as the impact of the 1924 legal changes and economic depression and war discouraged immigrants. Then, better economic times and, most importantly, vastly changed immigration policy led to significant decade-by-decade increases in the United States foreign-born at the end of the twentieth century and the beginning of the next century (e.g., an 11.3 million gain in the foreign-born between 1990 and 2000, followed by an 8.8 million increase between 2000 and 2010 and a 4.6 million increase between 2010 and 2017).

Despite a return to foreign-born percentages as a share of the total population not seen since the late 1800s and early 1900s, the national composition of the foreign-born population has changed dramatically (Grieco et al. 2012). Consider first the world region of birth of this population (table 4.6). From 1850 to

1950, roughly 85–90 percent of the national foreign-born population came from Europe; that share dropped to 75 percent by 1960. (Recall earlier in the chapter we examined European origins of these immigrants.) With significant alteration of national quotas in immigration laws in the 1960s, the composition of the foreign-born population in the United States noticeably changed. The dominant European origin of the foreign-born in the country dropped from 75 percent in 1960, to 39 percent in 1980, 22.9 percent in 1990, 15.8 percent in 2000, 12.1 percent in 2010, and stood at 10.8 percent by 2017. In contrast, has been a dramatic rise in immigrants nationally from Latin America as well as Asia. From 1850 to 1900, only about 1 percent of the foreign-born in the United States came from Latin America. That Latin American share rose to about 4–6 percent in the 1920–1950 span and reached 9.4 percent in 1960. Then, following immigration law changes in the 1960s, the Latin American portion of the foreign-born in the United States increased dramatically to 33.1 percent in 1980, 44.3 percent by 1990, and has exceeded 50 percent in 2000, 2010, and 2017.

Immigrants born in Asia have been the other major component of the foreign-born population in America's recent history, a departure from the past. Reflecting the nativist immigration restrictions, many targeted specifically at Asians, earlier described, for much of the century between 1850 and 1950, only about 1–2 percent of the foreign-born in the United States came from Asia and this portion only rose somewhat to 5.1 percent by 1960. The Asian share nationally of the foreign-born then increased dramatically to 19.3 percent by 1980, 26.3 percent by 1990, 26.4 percent by 2000, 28.2 percent by 2010, and 31.2 percent by 2017.

The leading countries of origin for the U.S. foreign-born population have also shifted dramatically over the last more than century and a half from the mid-nineteenth century onward. From 1850 to 1870, Ireland supplied the largest number of immigrants nationally, followed by Germany with the largest foreign-born contribution from 1880 to 1920, and by Italy as the top country of origin of the U.S. foreign-born from 1930 to 1970. Other major countries of origin of the U.S. foreign-born from 1850 to 1970 included Canada, Great Britain/United Kingdom, Poland, and Russia/USSR. Since 1980, Mexico has remained the leading country of origin, with also significant contributions to the U.S. foreign-born in this period by immigrants from China, India, the Philippines, and other places (e.g., El Salvador, Dominican Republic, Vietnam, and Cuba).

While Europe, Latin America, and Asia combined dominate as the places of origin of America's foreign-born, also deserving mention are other global contributions (table 4.6). Immigrants have come from Northern America (Canada and other Northern America) at first (1850–1880) being the original home of between roughly 7–11 percent of the foreign-born in the country, but in recent years, the share from Northern America has declined to a much more modest level nationally (e.g., 4.0 percent in 1990, 2.7 percent in 2000, 2.0 percent in 2010, and 1.8 percent in 2017). Immigrants to the nation from Africa have gone from a trace percentage (less than 1 percent of the national foreign-born in the period 1970 and earlier) to a rising, albeit still modest, contribution more recently (1.9 percent in 1990, 2.8 percent in 2000, 4.0 percent in 2010, and 5.1 percent in 2017). From a very low base, the number of African-born immigrants "has been doubling in every decade of the past half-century: census officials . . . [in 2018] estimated the stock has reached 2.4 million from just 80,000 in 1970" ("The Other African Americans" 2019).

In New Jersey, overall foreign-born trends have generally followed national trends, though accounting for a higher proportion of the state population (Shaw 1994) and having other differences (e.g., the absolute magnitude of the foreign-born, a lower share of this population coming from Northern America and specific top countries of origin). As with the nation, there have been varying waves of immigration since 1850, which are reflected in the changing number of foreign-born in New Jersey and the fluctuating foreign-born proportion of this state's population from the 1850s onward (table 4.5). From 1850 to 1920, the total foreign-born population in New Jersey increased from 60,000 in 1850, to 222,000 in 1880, 661,000 by 1910, and 742,000 by 1920. Whereas in the period between 1860 and 1880, New Jersey experienced an average decade increase in the foreign-born of 54,000, the decade gains of this population essentially doubled to 107,000 between 1880 and 1890 and more than doubled yet again to 229,000 between 1900 and 1910 (table 4.5). In parallel was a considerable increase in the percentage of New Jersey's population that were immigrants. The foreign-born share in the Garden State's population rose from 12.2 percent in 1850, to 19.6 percent in 1880, and reached about a one-quarter share in both 1910 (26.0 percent) and 1920 (23.5 percent).

Then, 1920s national immigration restrictions led to a reduction of both the number of foreign-born in New Jersey as well as the foreign-born share of this state's total population. Whereas in 1930, there were 850,000 foreign-born in New Jersey, that number tumbled to 615,000, or a reduction of 28 percent, by 1960. For perspective, the state's total population had increased in that time period by slightly over 2 million, from 4.0 million in 1930 to 6.1 million in 1960—a significant increase of about 50 percent. Not surprisingly given the falling numbers of immigrants, there was a significant reduction of the foreign-born share in New Jersey from 21.0 percent of the total population in 1930 to 13.2 percent in 1950, and reached a low of 8.9 percent by 1970. National immigration law changes that broadened entry to the United States then reversed this downward trend and the number of foreign-born in New Jersey rose to 967,000 in 1990, 1,476,000 in 2000, 1,845,000 in 2010, and 2,055,000 in 2017. In parallel was a continuing increase in the foreign-born share of the total New Jersey population that reached 12.5 percent in 1990, 17.5 percent in 2000, 21.0 percent in 2010, and 22.8 percent by 2017.

In short, as with the United States as a whole, and reflecting immigration law revisions, the New Jersey foreign-born population as a component of the total

Table 4.7

Foreign-Born Population in New Jersey by World Region of Birth (Selected Years 1850–2017)

Year	Percentage Foreign-Born Population	Percentage of Foreign-Born Population from World Region of Birth						
		Europe	Northern America	Latin America	Asia	Africa	Oceania	Total
1850	12.2	97.4	1.5	1.1				100.0
1910	26.0	97.6	1.6	0.4	0.3			100.0
1950	13.2	94.3	2.5	1.4	1.6	0.1	0.1	100.0
2000	17.5	23.9	1.1	43.0	27.8	4.1	0.2	100.0
2010	21.0	17.2	1.0	46.2	30.8	4.5	0.2	100.0
2017	22.8	13.8	0.8	46.2	33.3	5.7	0.1	100.0

SOURCES: 1850, 1900, and 1950: Irving 2019. (Analysis of Integrated Public Use Microdata Series [IPUMS] National Historical Geographic Information System [NHGIS] data for indicated years. The IPUMS USA database is attributed to Ruggles et al. 2019.) 1980, 1990, 2000, and 2010: Decennial census for indicated years. 2017: American Community Survey 2017 ACS 1-Year Estimates.

population increased from 1850 to 1910, declined from 1920 to 1970, and has grown continually since. Yet while these changing foreign-born share patterns were observed earlier at the national level, the share of New Jersey's population that is foreign-born (table 4.5) has been roughly 1.5 to 2.0 times greater than the national share from 1850 to 2017. For example, in 1910, when the foreign-born as a share of the total population reached a historical high for both the United States (14.7 percent) and New Jersey (26.0 percent), the New Jersey–to–national foreign-born percentage ratio was 1.8. The ratio was 1.7 in 2017 in comparing the New Jersey foreign-born share (22.8 percent) to that of the nation (13.7 percent). New Jersey's proximity to the major immigrant gateway of New York City has always been a primary contributor to the state's large foreign-born population.

As with the nation, the places of origin of New Jersey's foreign-born population has changed dramatically (table 4.7). The share of immigrants from Europe has gone from a dominant to a modest contribution. From 1850 to 1950, the lion's share, about 95 percent or more, of New Jersey's foreign-born persons emigrated from Europe. Reflecting the 1960s change in national immigration beyond a Eurocentric focus, the share of the foreign-born in New Jersey originating from Europe declined dramatically from 94.3 percent in 1950, 23.9 percent in 2000, 17.2 percent by 2010, and 13.8 percent by 2017. Also in parallel with the nation has been a dramatic increase in the share of New Jersey's foreign-born population originating from Latin America and Asia. In 1910, when about one-quarter of New Jersey's total population that was foreign-born (26 percent), only 0.4 percent of New Jersey's foreign-born came from Latin America and only 0.3 percent originated in Asia. This bare trace level from these two regions changed dramatically after 1960s national immigration law broadened acceptance of immigrants from other parts of the globe. By 2000, the shares of New

Jersey's foreign-born from Latin America and Asia were 43.0 and 27.8 percent, respectively. This increased to 46.2 percent (Latin America) and 33.3 percent (Asia) by 2017. These trends very much resemble in both magnitude and percentage the data on regional origins earlier observed for the nation as a whole (table 4.6).

Although the lion's share of New Jersey's foreign-born hail from the three world regions of Europe, Latin American, and Asia, with the latter two areas gaining ascendency in recent years, also deserving mention are other global area contributions. Emigrants from Northern America (Canada and other Northern America) have come to the Garden State but not in large numbers, contributing about 2 percent of this state's foreign-born in both 1850 and 1910 as examples. For context, the Northern America share of the national-level foreign-born was far higher during this time span, about 7 percent in 1850 and 9 percent in 1910. Yet for both the nation and New Jersey, immigrants coming from Northern America are at a trace level in recent years (i.e., about 1–3 percent in 2000 and 2017). As in the nation, there is a growing but still modest share of New Jersey's foreign-born hailing from Africa. In 1950, only 0.1 percent of the foreign-born in this state hailed from this continent. The share of New Jersey's foreign-born coming from Africa grew to 4.1 percent in 2000 and 5.7 percent by 2017.

The top ten countries of origin of the foreign-born in New Jersey have dramatically changed over time. In 1850, the top countries were Ireland, Great Britain, and Germany, which together comprised an overwhelming 95 percent of foreign-born that year. Other top ten countries of origin in New Jersey in 1850 included France (ranked fourth), Canada (ranked fifth), and Mexico (ranked tenth). Soon, there was a rising tide of immigrants from southern and eastern European countries. In 1910, for example, Germany ranked first as the country of origin of New Jersey's foreign-born; however, Italy and Russia were now ranked a close second and third. Ireland was now ranked fourth, Great Britain ranked fifth, and other top ten countries of origin of New Jersey's foreign-born in 1910 included Hungary and Austria. This 1910 pattern was largely maintained for many subsequent decades into the mid- to late twentieth century with some exceptions. For example, in 1980, the top two countries of origin of New Jersey's foreign-born were Italy and Cuba, respectively. While Italy has perennially been a top country of origin of New Jersey's foreign-born, Cuba had emerged as a leading source as well by 1980 as a result of the Freedom Flights from Cuba to the United States in the 1970s and the Mariel boatlift exodus that soon followed. We also see by 1980 the beginning of immigration from India and Colombia to New Jersey, with these two countries ranked ninth and tenth, respectively, as the countries of origin of the New Jersey foreign-born in that year. As we shall soon see, immigration from India, Colombia, and other countries in Asia and Latin America to the Garden State would soon surge. This was foreshadowed by our earlier review of the rising hegemony of Latin America and Asia as the regions of the world supplying many of New Jersey's immigrants.

With the 1960s revision in national immigration laws, the top ten countries contributing to New Jersey's foreign-born changed drastically. For example, in 2000, the top five countries in rank order were India, the Dominican Republic, the Philippines, Mexico, and Colombia; Italy fell to seventh place in that year. By 2017, the top five countries (India, the Dominican Republic, Mexico, China, and Colombia, respectively) very much resembled the 2000 rank order and Italy was no longer in the top ten—as were almost none of the top-ten countries that had contributed to New Jersey's foreign-born population in 1850.

World region or country of origin is not the only measure of the "roots" of a population. A broader term employed by the federal Census Bureau since 1980 is *ancestry*,[12] defined as "a person's ethnic origin, heritage, descent, or 'roots,' which may reflect their place of birth, place of birth of parents or ancestors, and ethnic identities that has evolved with the United States" (Brittingham and de la Cruz 2004, 1). When the New Jersey population was asked to identify "ancestry" in the 2016 ACS (2012–2016 five-year estimates), the top five responses were as follows:[13]

1 Italian (16.1 percent)
2 Irish (14.1 percent)
3 German (10.6 percent)
4 Polish (5.7 percent)
5 English (4.7 percent)

For context, the national population response to the "ancestry" question from this same 2016 ACS source was as follows:

1 German (14.4 percent)
2 Irish (10.4 percent)
3 English (7.7 percent)
4 American (6.9 percent)
5 Italian (5.4 percent)

In short, although there is some resemblance in the declared ancestry of the national and New Jersey populations, there are differences as well, such as Italian looming as a much larger ancestral identification in the Garden State. It also underscores that while in contemporary times there are relatively few foreign-born residents in New Jersey who have come to this state from countries that once dominated immigration here (e.g., Italy, Ireland, and Germany), there remain prominent Italian, Irish, and German and other largely European ancestral associations in the state.

As with previous sections of this chapter, we conclude our statistical presentation of New Jersey's diverse immigrants and foreign-born with illustrative vignettes of those who came from abroad to this state over time.

JEREMIAH O'ROURKE AND DOMINIC CASSIDY—IRISH IMMIGRANTS

Born in 1833, Jeremiah O'Rourke was a Dublin native and immigrated to the United States at age eighteen. Trained as an architect, he was a master of the Gothic Revival style and had many important and enduring commissions (e.g., Seton Hall College Chapel and Sacred Heart Cathedral in Newark) (Quinn 2004, 110).

Dominic Cassidy left Ireland in 1927, came to Harrison (where his sister lived), and subsequently moved to Kearny. Harrison and Kearny at that time attracted many immigrants from Scotland and Ireland "because of the linen mills and the thread mills, the type of work they had left back in the old country. [There were,] for example, the Clark Thread Mills in East Newark and Harrison" (Wright 1986, 24). Cassidy recounted that coming to the area was "like coming to the old country, like coming to Belfast" (24).

GERMANS HELP SEED INDUSTRY IN CENTRAL NEW JERSEY IN THE MID-1800S

A shipowner, James Bishop, imported raw rubber from South America, which was used by Horace Dey and other Germans operating rubber factories (Maugham 1982). Christopher Meyer found his way from Hanover, Germany, in 1838 (Garmm 1938), worked for Dey, and went on to invent "most of the machinery and processes used for the manufacture of rubber goods" (Maugham 1982, 53). In 1853, together with a partner, Meyer formed the Novelty Rubber Company, which recruited workers from Germany. James Neilson opened a prominent cotton mill. Other Germans operated shoe, hosiery, and carriage factories (Listokin, Berkhout, and Hughes 2016, 46–47).

MARY DEFALCO—ITALIAN IMMIGRANT

My father got here [from Italy] when he was twenty-one years old. My mother was sixteen when [her family] came. [My mother's] aunt had come before [and] had written and told them they would be able to find a little farm and make a living here. She met them in New York, and they came to live in Vineland. . . . Then my father and mother met and they were married. They lived on Vine Road, where they bought a little farm. My father was a farmer. My mother did housework and took care of us. (G. Wright 1986, 26)

The Changing Hungarian Presence in New Brunswick

Hungarians fled to this city from unsettled conditions back home seeking a better life, many drawn to the area's burgeoning factories. At one point, two-thirds of Johnson & Johnson factory employees in New Brunswick were of Hungarian descent, and the corporation acquired the colloquial nickname Hungarian University (Gurowitz 2006–2008, chap. 57; Karasik and Aschkenes 1999, 100).

By 1910, the 2,463 immigrants in New Brunswick (four-tenths of all this community's foreign-born) earned it the title as "the most Hungarian city in the United States" (Gurowitz 2006–2008, chap. 57). Portions of New Brunswick became largely Hungarian enclaves where "one would hardly find property owners other than Magyars" (Laky 1921). James Borbely, born in the United States in 1921 to Hungarian immigrants and raised in New Brunswick, praised the "close social network" of a Hungarian-affiliated church (Borbely 2009, 3), and others from Hungary appreciated similar cultural institutions. That also was the draw for Hungarians flocking to New Brunswick after the failed Hungarian Revolution of 1956. Camp Kilmer, near New Brunswick, took in thirty-two thousand Hungarian refugees. Eventually, three thousand of them settled in the New Brunswick area, about one thousand of them in New Brunswick itself (Karasik and Aschkenes 1999, 102). These new residents helped to revive a Hungarian culture in the city that had been slowly dying out. But the revival was short-lived: by 1980, there were only 561 Hungarian-born residents, and this dwindled to 140 in 2000 and a scant 43 in 2010. They were replaced by Hispanics from many countries; so this city, as others in New Jersey, became the home of changing racial, ethnic, and immigrant groups over time (Listokin, Berkhout, and Hughes 2016, 47–49).

Racial, Ethnic, and Foreign-Born Differences within New Jersey

Thus far, we have examined the racial, ethnic, and foreign-born profile of New Jersey from the 1800s to today and have contextualized these three characteristics against that of the nation. It is important to realize that even though the overall national–versus–New Jersey tableau is instructive, there is considerable *within-state* variation as well.

Starting first with the 2017 racial profile ("one race alone and not in combination"), whereas the state overall was about seven-tenths (67.9 percent) white in that year, in some counties the white representation was about nine-tenths or greater (Cape May, Hunterdon, Ocean, Sussex, and Warren) as against approximately half or less in other counties (Essex and Hudson). Related, although about one-seventh (13.5 percent) of New Jersey's total state population was Black in 2017, fewer than about one in twenty of those living in Cape May, Hunterdon, Morris, Ocean, Sussex, and Warren were Black, while Essex had a four-tenths Black representation. There were marked differences as well concerning where Asians resided. As against one-tenth (9.9 percent) Asian population statewide in 2017, this group comprised about one-quarter of Middlesex's residents and stood at about one-sixth in Bergen, Hudson, and Somerset; in contrast, Asian residents were about one-in-twenty or less in ten New Jersey counties. There are similar widespread differences in the intrastate distribution of Hispanics. Although this ethnic group comprises about one-fifth (20.4 percent) of the state's total residents in 2017, it is about two-fifths in Hudson and Passaic, about three-tenths in Cumberland and Union, and less than one-tenth in Burlington, Cape May, Gloucester, Ocean, Salem, Sussex, and Warren.

In parallel are variations in the share of the population that is foreign-born—somewhat more than one-fifth (22.8 percent) statewide in 2017, but more than four-tenths in Hudson; about three-tenths to one-third in Bergen, Middlesex, Passaic, and Union; and only roughly one-in-twenty in Cape May, Gloucester, and Salem. The world region of birth of the foreign-born is also quite different in different areas of the state. For example, whereas about one-third (33.3 percent) of all the state's foreign-born came from Asia in 2017, that share was about one-half in Middlesex and Somerset and was about one-eighth in Union. While somewhat less than one-half (46.2 percent) of New Jersey's total foreign-born population hailed from Latin America in 2017, almost two-thirds of the foreign-born in both Passaic and Union originated from Latin America, and in contrast about one-third or less in Bergen, Burlington, Middlesex, and Somerset.

It is further instructive to consider both recurring a well varying patterns regarding the demographic profile of the people of New Jersey over time. Some pundits refer to the rising share of this state's foreign-born as a marked departure from the past. That is myopic: it is true that the recent 2000 and onward foreign-born share of New Jersey's population (about one-fifth climbing to nearly one-quarter) is roughly double that in the 1960s and 1970s (about one-tenth), the recent foreign-born composition of this state's residents in fact mirrors the longer New Jersey historical pattern from 1860 to 1930 (about one-fifth to one-quarter foreign-born).The low 1960s and 1970s foreign shares of the population in New Jersey were in fact the outliers rather than the state norm. Thus, the current New Jersey foreign-born representation is a reversion to, rather a departure from, the historical foreign-born profile of this state over the mid-nineteenth to early twentieth centuries (see table 4.5).

In some cases, the racial profile of portions of the state today is not that different from what it was in the past. For example, in 1920, Blacks comprised 15.0 percent of the population of Atlantic County, 1.1 percent of Hunterdon, and 8.5, 2.3, and 2.6 percent in Monmouth, Morris, and Ocean Counties, respectively. This Black share is not that much different in 2017 for these same counties: Atlantic (14.4 percent), Hunterdon (2.5 percent), Monmouth (6.9 percent), Morris (3.5 percent), and Ocean (3.1 percent). Of course, there have been notable differences regarding other dimensions of the "People of New Jersey" over time. Take, for instance, the Asian racial group. In the 1920 census, the Asian share of the total population (Chinese, Japanese, and Indians) in Bergen, Hudson, Middlesex, and Somerset Counties were a barely trace level—0.06 percent, 0.04 percent, 0.04 percent, and 0.09 percent, respectively. Fast forward to 2017 and the Asian share of the residents of these four counties is far higher: 17.1 percent in Bergen, 15.7 percent in Hudson, 25.1 percent in Middlesex, and 18.6 percent in Somerset.

Many New Jersey municipalities have seen waves of immigrants and other newcomers. As referenced earlier, in New Brunswick, Germans, Irish, Hungarian, Italian, and other immigrants were followed by Hispanics from Puerto Rico and later immigrants from Mexico and diverse Latin and South American countries. Newark has seen an ebb and flow of different inhabitants (S. Lee 2008; Tuttle 2009). For example, in 1870, there were only 257 Italians in the entire city, which then had a population of about 105,000. With surging immigration, Newark grew to 415,000 population by 1920, and at that point, its Italian community had grown to about 28,000 (S. Lee 2008, 71). In 2015, the Newark population of approximately 202,000 has a minuscule Italian presence (about 4,300 persons of Italian ancestry), and Italians, similarly with other ethnic groups that were once prominently represented in the city such as Germans, Irish, and Jews, have been succeeded by a rainbow of many diverse racial and ethnic groups from literally around the world.

Paterson, America's first planned (by Alexander Hamilton) city of industry, "has always been a melting pot with a diverse population depending on the neighborhood. Irish, Germans, Dutch, and Jews settled in the city in the 19th century. Italian and Eastern European immigrants soon followed. As early as 1890, Syrian and Lebanese immigrants also arrived in Paterson. The African American population increased during the Great Migration of the 20th century but then decreased. . . . The city [now] is marked as an important destination for Latinx immigrants" (Castillo, n.d.). In a like vein, Union City, given the moniker in 1872 as the "embroidery capital of the world," welcomed in the mid-eighteenth-century Dutch immigrants, then somewhat later persons from Irish and Italian shores, followed by Cubans who first arrived in large numbers in the 1960s, and today is the home of many diverse Hispanics, including Dominicans, Puerto Ricans, Ecuadorians, and Colombians. In short, Union City has served, "for the past century, as an ethnic enclave for incoming immigrants" (Ortega, n.d.). Thus, the demographics of the "People of New Jersey" reflect a complex dynamic and admixture of stasis, change, and reversion. Diversity personifies New Jersey's demographic DNA.

5

Population, Geography, and the "Big Six" Cities

••••••••••••••••••••

The internal distribution of New Jersey's population within the state since its colonial origins has been continually shaped and configured by technological, economic, immigrational, and generational changes. These factors have already been cited as determinants of the overall population size of the state relative to the nation, but they have also been responsible for the changing settlement patterns across the state. As this chapter will document, the long journey to the present started from a rural (agricultural-based) to urban (industrial-based) transformation of New Jersey in the nineteenth century, followed by growing suburbanization and metropolitanization beyond the political boundaries of the state's industrial cities in the early twentieth century, successive massive waves of demographic and economic decentralization along with urban decline later in the twentieth century, and finally the beginnings of population/economic recentralization and resurgence in the twenty-first century. However, the potential of the comeback of the "burbs" will be a question permeating the 2020s in New Jersey.

The Early Industrial-Based Transformation

The first (pre–Civil War) and second (post–Civil War) Industrial Revolutions, which spanned the entire nineteenth century, were initially spawned by the steam engine (i.e., the shift from waterpower to steam power), the canal and the railroad, the telegraph, and the sewing machine. This led to the rise of machine and factory production during the first Industrial Revolution and the increasing population concentration in the state's nascent urban centers. The physical expression on New Jersey's landscape of this stage of economic development was the beginning of the rise of the concentrated industrial city.

The second Industrial Revolution, underpinned by steam-powered shipping, more comprehensive railroad systems, the telephone, and other technological advances, facilitated the further centralization of the state's population into its rapidly expanding industrialized urban areas. The actual scale of this massed population would not have been possible were it not for the vast waves of European immigration that helped satisfy the seemingly insatiable demand for labor to staff the state's rapidly growing urban manufacturing ecosystems. As a result, rural low-density population dispersion at the start of the nineteenth century was supplanted by high-density population concentrations at the end of the century. "The cities' populations—fed by rural-to-urban and international migrations—massed around emerging factory structures and were dependent on close pedestrian linkages. A tight, dense, interdependent urban complex evolved, with residences closely linked to workplaces, and service facilities clustering near their residential markets. The urban way of life began to secure critical mass in New Jersey" (Hughes and Seneca 2015, 14). This set the stage for the opening of the twentieth century.

The Rise of New Jersey's Cities, 1860–1900

Consequently, as the Industrial Revolution traversed the nineteenth century, New Jersey's population increasingly began to cluster in or close to its emerging urban economic agglomerations. The basic demographic story was the growing domination of New Jersey's cities. By 1860, what today are the state's "Big Six" cities—Camden, Elizabeth, Jersey City, Newark, Paterson, and Trenton—had already accounted for nearly one out of four (24.4 percent) residents of New Jersey (table 5.1). Of the state's total population of 672,035 people, these six cities housed 163,906 individuals. The largest city at the time, by far, was Newark (71,941 people). A distant second in size was Jersey City (29,226 people), followed by third-place Paterson (19,586 people). Although still modest in scale by today's standards, the emerging population centers of 1860 were just the start of an unprecedented transformation to come.

Four decades of intense urban industrialization immediately followed. Growing economic concentrations were paralleled by growing population concentrations, bolstered by waves of immigration from central, eastern, and southern Europe. By 1900, the overall population of the Big Six had increased by 363.1 percent since 1860, more than double the rate of increase (180.3 percent) of the state's total population (table 5.1). The Big Six's overall growth totaled 595,140 people, as their population soared from 163,906 people in 1860 to 759,046 people by 1900. Their share of the state's total 1900 population (1,883,669 people) exceeded four out of ten (40.3 percent), up from one out of four (24.4 percent) in 1860.

Table 5.1
Population of New Jersey's Big Six Cities, 1860–1900

	1860	1900	Change: 1860–1900	
			Number	Percent (%)
Camden	14,358	75,935	61,577	428.9
Elizabeth	11,567	52,130	40,563	350.7
Jersey City	29,226	206,433	177,207	606.3
Newark	71,941	246,070	174,129	242.0
Paterson	19,586	105,171	85,585	437.0
Trenton	17,228	73,307	56,079	325.5
TOTAL	163,906	759,046	595,140	363.1
TOTAL NJ	672,035	1,883,669	1,211,634	180.3
Big Six Share	24.4%	40.3%		

SOURCE: U.S. Census Bureau, decennial census for indicated years.

Leading this late nineteenth-century population growth surge in both absolute number and rate of increase was Jersey City, although Newark maintained its top-ranked position. Jersey City's population increased by an extraordinary 606.3 percent, from 29,226 people in 1860 to 206,433 people in 1900 (table 5.1). Its absolute gain of 177,207 people during this period just edged out that of Newark (+174,129 people). Nonetheless, Newark's population was approaching a quarter of a million (246,070) people at the beginning of the new century, up from 71,941 people forty years earlier (1860). Paterson maintained its distant number three position with a total 1900 population of 105,171 people.

Not included in this tabulation was Hoboken, which briefly had replaced Elizabeth as the sixth-ranked city in the 1880, 1890, and 1900 censuses. But Elizabeth regained its position in the Big Six by 1910, never to relinquish it again.[1] In any case, the combination of the Big Six and other burgeoning manufacturing cities of lesser scale, such as New Brunswick and Perth Amboy, pushed the urban share of the state's population to approximately one-half. The great transformation of New Jersey from an agrarian, natural resources–dominated economy to a nation-leading industrial state was virtually complete by the dawn of the twentieth century. "Paterson became known as Silk City USA. 'Trenton Makes, the World Takes' and 'On Camden Supplies, the World Relies' were not mere slogans, but economic reality. New Jersey was a technology-driven, urban manufacturing dynamo by the time the twentieth century arrived, and was at the leading edge of global industrialization" (Hughes and Seneca 2015, 35).

Metropolitanization: The Early Twentieth Century, 1900–1930

By the start of the new century, manufacturing establishments had firmly agglomerated in the state's urban areas. These locations were bulwarked by their unique technological advantages: rail- and water-based transportation infrastructure, roads (for emerging vehicles using internal combustion engines), electrical energy systems, and water supply and sanitation networks. The demographic imperative was the need for ample concentrated pools of skilled and unskilled labor necessary to staff the industrial economy.

The geographic spread within the state's urban centers had been severely constrained by the dependence on pedestrian accessibility to the workplace, thus the dense clustering of multifamily housing around factory structures. But the advent of streetcar systems enabled crowded cities to spread out within existing urban boundaries and to spill over into adjacent territories and political units. Streetcar systems were more instrumental to the economy and labor force needs of the state's urban centers than slowly accelerating, steam-powered commuter railroads, which mainly benefited New York City and Philadelphia, although the latter cities were instrumental in the development of a number of early New Jersey suburbs that were directly linked to them.

The growth and advance of transportation technology spawned a new population geography in the first three decades of the twentieth century: the early industrial metropolis. Suburban residential communities developed outside of the formal boundaries of the state's cities, but they were still highly dependent on the latter's economic and social functions. The metropolitan pattern internal to New Jersey—the suburbs linked directly to the state's cities—was overlapped by broader regional dynamics—suburbs linked directly to New York City and Philadelphia. The end result, however, was the same in both cases: demographic decentralization adjacent to and linked to the urban concentrations.

The earliest suburbs were also constrained in geographic size themselves since they were highly linked to streetcar systems and commuter rail lines. Feasible walking distance to commuter stations limited the geographic spread of suburban development and produced a highly disciplined growth pattern. But the rise of the internal combustion engine, private automobile ownership, and the early development of the state highway system (in the 1920s) spawned further suburban residential development. New Jersey had established one of the earliest state highway departments in America. A state highway commission was established in 1909, with a highway department approved in 1917, followed by an initial designation of a statewide system comprising thirteen highways. The highly disciplined development pattern of the earliest rail-dependent suburbs was gradually lost as transportation constraints to outlying growth were eased.

The new metropolitan dimension of New Jersey's population geography is revealed by the 1900–1930 growth of the Big Six cities in the context of the overall state (table 5.2). In total, they added close to one-half million (495,164) people, growing from 759,046 people in 1900 to 1,254,210 people in 1930, a strong rate of increase (65.2 percent). Newark was the growth leader (+196,267 people, or +79.8 percent), followed by Jersey City (+110,282 people, or +53.4 percent). The impressive 1930 population totals of Newark (442,337 people) and Jersey City

Table 5.2
Population of New Jersey's Big Six Cities, 1900–1930

	1900	1930	Change: 1900–1930	
			Number	Percent (%)
Camden	75,935	118,700	42,765	56.3
Elizabeth	52,130	114,589	62,459	119.8
Jersey City	206,433	316,715	110,282	53.4
Newark	246,070	442,337	196,267	79.8
Paterson	105,171	138,513	33,342	31.7
Trenton	73,307	123,356	50,049	68.3
TOTAL	759,046	1,254,210	495,164	65.2
TOTAL NJ	1,883,669	4,041,334	2,157,665	114.5
Big Six Share	40.3%	31.0%		

SOURCE: U.S. Census Bureau, decennial census for indicated years.

(316,715 people) would actually turn out to be their all-time peaks; as will be detailed subsequently, they would never surpass these levels for the balance of the twentieth century and beyond.

Despite their sustained and robust demographic expansion, the six cities' share of the total state population contracted, declining from 40.3 percent in 1900 to 31.0 percent in 1930. During this time frame, New Jersey's population surged by 2,157,665 people (+114.5 percent), more than four times the absolute growth (+495,164 persons) of the Big Six.

Reflecting the process of suburbanization and metropolitanization, the most significant population growth increases that did occur took place in the counties hosting the major cities or the counties tied to them economically. This is shown in table 5.3 and figure 5.1, which partitions New Jersey's counties into regional areas. These areas were deployed previously in analyzing New Jersey's postsuburban economy, and this book is designed to facilitate direct demographic-economic comparisons. The following are brief descriptions (Hughes and Seneca 2015, 68–71).

> *Core Metropolis* consists of Bergen, Essex, Hudson, Union, and Passaic Counties. This region encompasses the older industrial heartland of New Jersey and its allied suburbs, which experienced some of the state's earliest and rapid suburban growth. The region also contains part of the core of the broader metropolitan region centered on Manhattan.
>
> *Rural North/Exurban* includes Sussex and Warren Counties, both bordering the Delaware River in the northwest corner of the state. Once primarily agricultural, they became accessible to the suburban job-growth clusters that emerged in the 1980s.

Table 5.3
New Jersey Regional and County Population, 1900–1930

	1900	1930	Change: 1900–1930		Share of New Jersey (%)	
			Number	Percent (%)	1900	1930
New Jersey	1,883,669	4,041,334	2,157,665	114.5	100.0	100.0
Core Metropolis	1,078,097	2,496,558	1,418,461	131.6	57.2	61.8
Essex	359,053	833,513	474,460	132.1	19.1	20.6
Hudson	386,048	690,730	304,682	78.9	20.5	17.1
Union	99,353	305,209	205,856	207.2	5.3	7.6
Bergen	78,441	364,977	286,536	365.3	4.2	9.0
Passaic	155,202	302,129	146,927	94.7	8.2	7.5
Rural North/ Exurban	61,915	77,149	15,234	24.6	3.3	1.9
Sussex	24,134	27,830	3,696	15.3	1.3	0.7
Warren	37,781	49,319	11,538	30.5	2.0	1.2
Central	389,795	756,865	367,070	94.2	20.7	18.7
Hunterdon	34,507	34,728	221	0.6	1.8	0.9
Mercer	95,365	187,143	91,778	96.2	5.1	4.6
Middlesex	79,762	212,208	132,446	166.1	4.2	5.3
Monmouth	82,057	147,209	65,152	79.4	4.4	3.6
Morris	65,156	110,445	45,289	69.5	3.5	2.7
Somerset	32,948	65,132	32,184	97.7	1.7	1.6
Metro South	197,789	416,655	218,866	110.7	10.5	10.3
Camden	107,643	252,312	144,669	134.4	5.7	6.2
Burlington	58,241	93,541	35,300	60.6	3.1	2.3
Gloucester	31,905	70,802	38,897	121.9	1.7	1.8
Southern Shore	79,350	187,378	108,028	136.1	4.2	4.6
Atlantic	46,402	124,823	78,421	169.0	2.5	3.1
Cape May	13,201	29,486	16,285	123.4	0.7	0.7
Ocean	19,747	33,069	13,322	67.5	1.0	0.8
Rural South	76,723	106,729	30,006	39.1	4.1	2.6
Cumberland	51,193	69,895	18,702	36.5	2.7	1.7
Salem	25,530	36,834	11,304	44.3	1.4	0.9

SOURCE: U.S. Census Bureau, decennial census for indicated years.

Central comprises Hunterdon, Mercer, Middlesex, Monmouth, Morris, and Somerset Counties, all located in the suburban midsection of the state. Generally, these six counties define a key part of the broad suburban perimeter of the metropolitan area centered on Manhattan. In the 1980s and 1990s, it was labeled New Jersey's Wealth Belt.

Metro South consists of three counties centered on the city of Camden, once the manufacturing colossus of southern New Jersey—Camden,

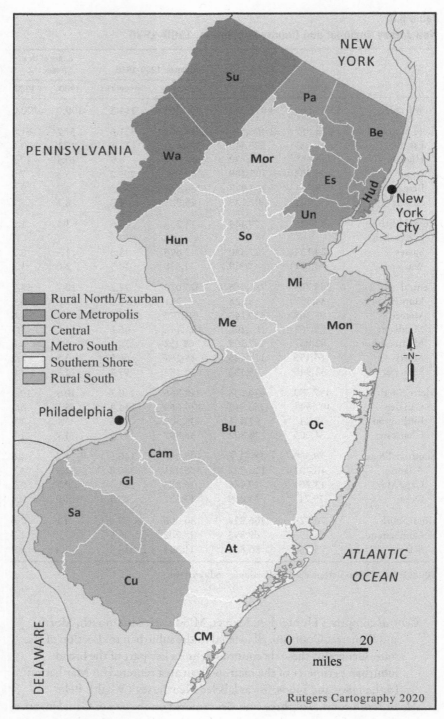

FIG. 5.1 New Jersey Regions

Burlington, and Gloucester Counties. This region contains a number of early and maturing inlying suburban municipalities, as well as the developing suburban perimeter/edge city of the Camden-Philadelphia-centered metropolitan area.

Southern Shore incorporates within it the three southeastern counties of New Jersey bordering the Atlantic Ocean: Atlantic, Cape May, and Ocean. It is functionally heterogeneous—currently including a mix of bedroom, retirement, resort, seasonal, and gambling communities. Its dominant orientation is the Jersey Shore, although the northern sectors are linked to the north-central New Jersey economy.

Rural South consists of Cumberland and Salem Counties in the southwest parts of the state. This is still a rural, agriculturally focused region falling mostly outside of the commuter sheds of the job-growth areas of New Jersey.

The five-county Core Metropolis stood positioned as the epicenter of New Jersey (table 5.3). By 1930, it accounted for 61.8 percent of the state's total population (2,496,557 people out of 4,041,324 people). The process of metropolitanization is clearly illustrated by Essex County, which emerged as the largest county (833,512 people) in the Core Metropolis by 1930, surpassing Hudson. It also had the largest county share (20.6 percent, or more than one out of five) of the state's population that year. Essex had a total 1900–1930 population growth of 474,459 people, more than double that (196,267 people) of the city of Newark, its major employment center. Areas of the county adjacent to Newark either industrialized as a result of economic activity spillover, or became bedroom communities, or both.

Similarly, Hudson County's 1900–1930 growth (+304,682 people)—ranked only second to Essex—was nearly triple that (+110,282 people) of Jersey City, its major municipality, indicating the scale of geographic population spread. But Hudson's growth was not sufficient to forestall Essex County's ascension to the most populous county. Hudson's share of New Jersey's population fell from 20.5 percent (number one ranked) in 1900 to 17.1 percent (number two ranked) in 1930.

In contrast to these spreading urban-suburban concentrations were the state's then-mostly rural areas, such as western Sussex and Warren Counties (which constituted the Rural North/Exurban region) and Hunterdon, the farthest west county within the Central region. Although still growing, all were characterized by minimal population gains (table 5.3). But their share of the state's total population contracted markedly: Sussex County's population fell from 1.3 percent in 1900 to 0.7 percent in 1930, Warren's from 2.0 percent to 1.2 percent, and Hunterdon's from 1.8 percent to 0.9 percent. The rural fringes of the state were seemingly becoming backwaters.[2] As subsequent analyses will reveal, these counties would come under intense growth pressures in the late twentieth century, only to revert to population stagnation and absolute decline in the twenty-first century.

Nonetheless, before the Great Depression, New Jersey was still in the intense process of city building. The state's population was centralizing into its urban areas and adjacent suburbs as nascent metropolitan areas were emerging. In "the then new twentieth century, New Jersey could boast proudly of the mammoth Singer Sewing Machine plant in Elizabeth—one of the largest sewing machine facilities in the world, which at its peak employed 10,000 workers; the RCA Radio-Victor factory in Camden, one of the largest of its type in the world; and Western Electric in Kearny—the world's leading telephone manufacturing complex" (Hughes and Seneca 2015, 35). The state's global manufacturing prowess was undeniable. However, the development of what eventually would be called global cities and superstar cities did not fully materialize.

The Limited Status of New Jersey's Major Cities

Despite their substantial 1900–1930 growth documented above, the state's Big Six cities not only lagged the state's overall growth but also lost ground to their surging national peers. Of New Jersey's top three cities in 1900, Newark's population ranked sixteenth among the nation's biggest cities, Jersey City ranked seventeenth, and Paterson ranked thirty-seventh. They were the only New Jersey representatives in the nation's top fifty. By 1930, Newark's position fell to eighteen, Jersey City to twenty-three, and Paterson to sixty. One part of this positional decline may have been due to the more limited geographic areas of New Jersey's cities because of the multiplicity of small municipalities in the state. Growth that was functionally part of the state's geographically constrained cities spilled out beyond their formal political boundaries.

The other part of positional decline may have been the result of the sheer scale of the urban behemoths bookending New Jersey. To the immediate east, New York City's 1930 population (6,930,446 people), ranked number one nationally; its population was approximately 60 percent greater than that of all of New Jersey (4,041,334 people) and more than fifteen times greater than Newark (442,337 people). To the immediate west was the nation's third largest city, Philadelphia, whose 1930 population (1,950,961 people) was more than quadruple that of Newark. The sheer scale of these competitors led to their amassing unique concentrations of wealth, power, culture, and amenities, putting New Jersey's urban places at a distinct competitive disadvantage and limiting their full potential.

Wilbur Thompson's (1974, 189) national observations, made more than four decades ago, would prove prescient for New Jersey: "We did not, for the most part, build great cities in this country; manufacturing firms agglomerated in tight industrial complexes and formed labor pools of half a million workers. This is not the same as building great cities. We sort of woke up one day and there was

Cleveland. There was Detroit . . . the biggest factory town on earth." Similarly, the state's process of city building also involved assembling large labor forces to feed ever larger plants, while the highest-order urban functions were largely established outside of the boundaries of New Jersey in the two leading urban giants. As will be discussed subsequently, this situation reasserted itself in the twenty-first century.

Unprecedented Suburbanization, 1950–1970

The Great Depression and World War II proved to be potent inhibitors of the spatial dynamics that had been under way prior to 1930. However, there were several unique events that took place during this widespread development hiatus that would impact postwar population shifts. The first was New Jersey's advancing state highway system, one of the nation's most comprehensive, which began bypassing the state's urban centers as well as providing easy accessibility to undeveloped and outlying territories. The system set in place during the Great Depression would become the dominant framework of development in the postwar era. The second was a national policy of deconcentration of new wartime production facilities away from dense urban areas, making them less vulnerable to potential aerial bombing by wartime foes. An oft-cited example was the long-departed Hyatt Bearing plant in Clark (Union County), now a golf course. Postwar consumer manufacturing facilities would follow this model.

The end of World War II released a number of pent-up forces: deferred household formation and housing investment, pent-up consumer demand, and returning veterans yearning to embrace a normal civilian life. Single-family housing quickly emerged as the centerpiece of the American dream. All of this led to unprecedented automobile-centric residential suburbanization and metropolitan expansion, urban population contraction, and the development of a robust consumer economy whose products were increasingly produced in newly erected suburban production facilities. The geography of the state's economy and population was dramatically transformed.

The shift from wartime to peacetime consumer-led production bolstered the absolute size of New Jersey's manufacturing base, which increased from 756,400 jobs in 1950 to 860,700 jobs in 1970 (Hughes and Seneca 2004b).[3] However, manufacturing's share of total state employment fell from 45.6 percent in 1950 to 33.0 percent in 1970. Service-producing (private-sector) employment, in contrast, increased from 38.9 percent (644,200 jobs) in 1950 to 47.9 percent (1,247,100 jobs) in 1970. A goods-producing economy was starting to be supplanted by a service-producing economy. This was the start of the second great transformation of the New Jersey economy, paralleling the rise of the state's suburban population.

As presented in table 5.4, between 1950 and 1970, New Jersey's total population increased by 2,335,783 people, or nearly one-half (48.3 percent). Approximately one million housing units were added during this twenty-year period,

Table 5.4
Population of New Jersey's Big Six Cities, 1950–1970

	1950	1970	Change: 1950–1970	
			Number	Percent (%)
Camden	124,555	102,551	(22,004)	(17.7)
Elizabeth	112,817	112,654	(163)	(0.1)
Jersey City	299,017	260,350	(38,667)	(12.9)
Newark	438,776	381,930	(56,846)	(13.0)
Paterson	139,336	144,824	5,488	3.9
Trenton	128,009	104,638	(23,371)	(18.3)
TOTAL	1,242,510	1,106,947	(135,563)	(10.9)
TOTAL NJ	4,835,329	7,171,112	2,335,783	48.3
Big Six Share	25.7%	15.4%		

SOURCE: U.S. Census Bureau, decennial census for indicated years.

the greatest housing construction surge in the state's history. Much of this new construction focused on sheltering the fabled baby boom generation, located in a newly suburban New Jersey made accessible not only by the excellent prewar state highway system but also by the opening of the state's toll roads.

However, much of this developmental activity bypassed the Big Six cities, whose aggregate population declined by 10.9 percent (−135,563 people). Their share of the state's population plummeted from 25.7 percent in 1950 to 15.4 percent in 1970. Newark (−56,846 people) and Jersey City (−38,667 people) experienced the largest absolute declines while Trenton (−18.3 percent) and Camden (−17.7 percent) experienced the largest rates of decline. In contrast, as shown in table 5.5, counties with triple-digit growth rates were Ocean (+268.2 percent), Burlington (+137.8 percent), Morris (+133.3 percent), Sussex (+125.2 percent), Middlesex (+120.4 percent), Monmouth (105.0 percent), and Somerset (+100.3 percent). All were characterized by vast swaths of easily developable land not encumbered by today's environmental strictures and protection laws. The most urban of states was becoming the most suburban of states.

The six suburban counties of the Central region increased their share of the state's population to 27.9 percent in 1970, up from 21.2 percent twenty years earlier (table 5.5). In contrast, the Core Metropolis experienced a significant decline in share to less than one-half—to 48.0 percent in 1970 from 58.5 percent in 1950. Nonetheless, the Core had the two largest counties in 1970: number one Essex (932,526 people), and fast-rising number two Bergen (897,148 people), displacing Hudson (607,839 people), which fell into third place.

Again, two dimensions of suburbanization/decentralization overlapped—population movements stemming from New Jersey's urban centers and those originating from New York City and Philadelphia. When the state's cities were

Table 5.5

New Jersey Regional and Country Population, 1950–1970

	1950	1970	Change: 1950–1970		Share of New Jersey (%)	
			Number	Percent (%)	1950	1970
New Jersey	4,835,329	7,171,112	2,335,783	48.3	100.0	100.0
Core Metropolis	2,827,756	3,441,411	613,655	21.7	58.5	48.0
Essex	905,949	932,526	26,577	2.9	18.7	13.0
Hudson	647,437	607,839	(39,598)	(6.1)	13.4	8.5
Union	398,138	543,116	144,978	36.4	8.2	7.6
Bergen	539,139	897,148	358,009	66.4	11.1	12.5
Passaic	337,093	460,782	123,689	36.7	7.0	6.4
Rural North/ Exurban	88,797	151,488	62,691	70.6	1.8	2.1
Sussex	34,423	77,528	43,105	125.2	0.7	1.1
Warren	54,374	73,960	19,586	36.0	1.1	1.0
Central	1,026,139	2,001,322	975,183	95.0	21.2	27.9
Hunterdon	42,736	69,718	26,982	63.1	0.9	1.0
Mercer	229,781	304,116	74,335	32.4	4.8	4.2
Middlesex	264,872	583,813	318,941	120.4	5.5	8.1
Monmouth	225,327	461,849	236,522	105.0	4.7	6.4
Morris	164,371	383,454	219,083	133.3	3.4	5.3
Somerset	99,052	198,372	99,320	100.3	2.0	2.8
Metro South	528,380	952,104	423,724	80.2	10.9	13.3
Camden	300,743	456,291	155,548	51.7	6.2	6.4
Burlington	135,910	323,132	187,222	137.8	2.8	4.5
Gloucester	91,727	172,681	80,954	88.3	1.9	2.4
Southern Shore	226,152	443,067	216,915	95.9	4.7	6.2
Atlantic	132,399	175,043	42,644	32.2	2.7	2.4
Cape May	37,131	59,554	22,423	60.4	0.8	0.8
Ocean	56,622	208,470	151,848	268.2	1.2	2.9
Rural South	138,105	181,720	43,615	31.6	2.9	2.5
Cumberland	88,597	121,374	32,777	37.0	1.8	1.7
Salem	49,508	60,346	10,838	21.9	1.0	0.8

SOURCE: U.S. Census Bureau, decennial census for indicated years.

booming, it was international immigration that was an instrumental part of their growth. But as the suburbs exploded in the 1950–1970 period, it was domestic migration flowing into the state that was a major contributor to suburban growth. New Jersey's overall net migration—the difference between people moving into the state and those moving out of it—approached a positive 1.1 million in the two-decade period (Hughes and Seneca 2000). Most of this gain came from inside the United States, not from international immigration.[4]

Table 5.6
Population of New Jersey's Big Six Cities, 1970–1980

	1970	1980	Change: 1970–1980	
			Number	Percent (%)
Camden	102,551	84,910	(17,641)	(17.2)
Elizabeth	112,654	106,201	(6,453)	(5.7)
Jersey City	260,350	223,532	(36,818)	(14.1)
Newark	381,930	329,248	(52,682)	(13.8)
Paterson	144,824	137,970	(6,854)	(4.7)
Trenton	104,638	92,124	(12,514)	(12.0)
TOTAL	1,106,947	973,985	(132,962)	(12.0)
TOTAL NJ	7,171,112	7,365,011	193,899	2.7
Big Six Share	15.4%	13.2%		

SOURCE: U.S. Census Bureau, decennial census for indicated years.

The 1970s: Demographic Stagnation

Chapter 3 reviewed New Jersey's demographic deceleration during the decade of the 1970s in the context of the reordering of the nation's regional growth trajectories. This was reflected economically by the start of the state's long-term manufacturing employment hemorrhage. This sector, once the dynamic centerpiece of the New Jersey economy, experienced an employment loss of 79,700 jobs (−8.0 percent). Much of this took place in the mature industries located in the older urban manufacturing concentrations in the Big Six cities. At the same time, the service-producing sector of the economy continued to grow, increasingly located in the suburbs and increasingly staffed by the early waves of baby boomers entering the labor force.

Overall, New Jersey's total population growth came to a near standstill as it gained only 193,899 people (+2.7 percent) between 1970 and 1980 (table 5.6). During the two previous decades (1950–1970), it had gained almost 1.2 million people per decade. In this new slow-growth context, the population of the Big Six cities continued to trend downward. They lost 12.0 percent of their population (−132,962 people) between 1970 and 1980, as their total fell below one million people (from 1,106,947 people to 973,985 people). This was the first time in eighty years, since the 1900 decennial census, that their combined populations failed to reach the one-million-person threshold.[5] Urban manufacturing's rise had led to the growth of New Jersey's major cities; urban manufacturing's decline led to their contraction. Newark (−52,682 people) and Jersey City (−36,818 people), the state's historic manufacturing epicenters, accounted for the bulk of the state's urban losses.

Not surprisingly, the declines in these two cities were evident in the encompassing Core Metropolis region (table 5.7), which had a population loss of 236,071 people during the decade, led by Essex County (−81,222 people). Overall, the

Table 5.7
New Jersey Regional and County Population, 1970–1980

	1970	1980	Change: 1970–1980		Share of New Jersey (%)	
			Number	Percent (%)	1970	1980
New Jersey	7,171,112	7,365,011	193,899	2.7	100.0	100.0
Core Metropolis	3,441,411	3,205,340	(236,071)	(6.9)	48.0	43.5
Essex	932,526	851,304	(81,222)	(8.7)	13.0	11.6
Hudson	607,839	556,972	(50,867)	(8.4)	8.5	7.6
Union	543,116	504,094	(39,022)	(7.2)	7.6	6.8
Bergen	897,148	845,385	(51,763)	(5.8)	12.5	11.5
Passaic	460,782	447,585	(13,197)	(2.9)	6.4	6.1
Rural North/ Exurban	151,488	200,548	49,060	32.4	2.1	2.7
Sussex	77,528	116,119	38,591	49.8	1.1	1.6
Warren	73,960	84,429	10,469	14.2	1.0	1.1
Central	2,001,322	2,105,049	103,727	5.2	27.9	28.6
Hunterdon	69,718	87,361	17,643	25.3	1.0	1.2
Mercer	304,116	307,863	3,747	1.2	4.2	4.2
Middlesex	583,813	595,893	12,080	2.1	8.1	8.1
Monmouth	461,849	503,173	41,324	8.9	6.4	6.8
Morris	383,454	407,630	24,176	6.3	5.3	5.5
Somerset	198,372	203,129	4,757	2.4	2.8	2.8
Metro South	952,104	1,034,109	82,005	8.6	13.3	14.0
Camden	456,291	471,650	15,359	3.4	6.4	6.4
Burlington	323,132	362,542	39,410	12.2	4.5	4.9
Gloucester	172,681	199,917	27,236	15.8	2.4	2.7
Southern Shore	443,067	622,423	179,356	40.5	6.2	8.5
Atlantic	175,043	194,119	19,076	10.9	2.4	2.6
Cape May	59,554	82,266	22,712	38.1	0.8	1.1
Ocean	208,470	346,038	137,568	66.0	2.9	4.7
Rural South	181,720	197,542	15,822	8.7	2.5	2.7
Cumberland	121,374	132,866	11,492	9.5	1.7	1.8
Salem	60,346	64,676	4,330	7.2	0.8	0.9

SOURCE: U.S. Census Bureau, decennial census for indicated years.

Core's share of the state's population fell from 48.0 percent to 43.5 percent over the decade. Population growth continued to decentralize statewide but at a diminished pace compared with the earlier postwar decades. The Central region's share of the state's population increased only modestly during the 1970s, from 27.9 percent to 28.6 percent. The parade out of New York City and Philadelphia of households and families seeking child-rearing environments in the state's suburban counties began to run its course. And the baby boom, entering the housing market in full force, seemingly refused to reproduce itself, resulting in a baby bust that permeated the population growth totals for most of the decade.

The absolute growth leader in both absolute and percentage terms (+137,568 people, or +66.0 percent) was Ocean County in the Southern Shore region, increasingly the recipient of significant internal state migration from the Core Metropolis (table 5.7). This continued Ocean's meteoric rise established in the 1950s and 1960s, when it first became a retirement destination.

Two other outlying counties experienced state-leading growth rates: Sussex (+49.8 percent) and Hunterdon (+25.3 percent). The leading edge of the tidal wave of metropolitan expansion started to inch closer to the lesser populated, lesser developed western border of New Jersey along the Delaware River across from Pennsylvania.

Suburban Economic Growth Corridors, 1980–2000

Two dynamics began to reshape New Jersey's economic and demographic geography in the final two decades of the twentieth century: the great 1980s office building boom—concentrated in suburban growth corridors and agglomerations, and discussed in chapter 8—and the surge in immigration stemming from the Immigration and Nationality Act of 1965, discussed in chapter 4.

Despite the economic decentralization that accompanied the full rise of the postindustrial, knowledge-based economy, the state's Big Six cities virtually halted their three-decade-long population decline. After losing 268,525 people between 1950 and 1980 (tables 5.4 and 5.6), they contracted by only 25,287 people between 1980 and 2000 (table 5.8). Although Newark continued its long-term decline (−55,702 people), the populations of Jersey City (+16,523

Table 5.8
Population of New Jersey's Big Six Cities, 1980–2000

	1980	2000	Change: 1980–2000	
			Number	Percent (%)
Camden	84,910	79,904	(5,006)	(5.9)
Elizabeth	106,201	120,568	14,367	13.5
Jersey City	223,532	240,055	16,523	7.4
Newark	329,248	273,546	(55,702)	(16.9)
Paterson	137,970	149,222	11,252	8.2
Trenton	92,124	85,403	(6,721)	(7.3)
TOTAL	973,985	948,698	(25,287)	(2.6)
TOTAL NJ	7,365,011	8,414,350	1,049,339	14.2
Big Six Share	13.2%	11.3%		

SOURCE: U.S. Census Bureau, decennial census for indicated years.

people), Elizabeth (+14,367 people), and Paterson (+11,252 people) rebounded, bolstered by international immigration. Jersey City also benefited from New York City's resurgence, which started in the 1990s, ultimately spilling across to what would eventually be labeled New Jersey's Hudson River Gold Coast. Nonetheless, the six cities' share of the state's population continued to contract, from 13.2 percent in 1980 to 11.3 percent in 2000 (table 5.8). One hundred years earlier (1900), their share had reached 40.3 percent (see table 5.1).

The five counties comprising the Core Metropolis also experienced a reversal. After losing 236,071 people between 1970 and 1980 (table 5.7), they gained 92,976 people between 1980 and 2000 (table 5.9). However, the Core's loss in state population share continued during the latter two-decade period, declining from 43.5 percent (1980) to 39.2 percent (2000). Seven decades earlier (1930), its share had reached 61.8 percent (table 5.3). Its two largest counties in total, Essex and Hudson, had accounted for 39.6 percent of the state's population in 1900 (table 5.3). By 2000, their combined share had dropped to 16.6 percent (table 5.9).

In contrast, the six suburban counties of the Central region, whose office-based economic development during this period resulted in their declaration as New Jersey's "Wealth Belt" (spanning the narrow midsection, or "waistline" of the state), gained 500,866 people (table 5.9). This represented nearly half of the state's total population increase (+1,049,339 people) and more than five times that of the Core Metropolis (+92,976 people). The leading growth county in this region was Middlesex, which added 154,269 people. However, its gain was eclipsed by Ocean County (+164,878 people) of the Southern Shore, the leading growth county in the state as the twentieth century came to a close.

The broad suburban arena was characterized by a baby boom generation trading up in the housing market and producing a new large birth cohort that was originally called the baby boom echo but is now popularly known as millennials (see chapters 7–9). While Bergen (884,118 people) and Essex (793,633 people) remained the two most populous counties in 2000, suburban Middlesex (750,162 people) and Monmouth (615,301 people) Counties moved up into third and fourth place, respectively, in the state rankings. Hudson County (608,975 people) dropped to fifth.

Outward metropolitan growth pressures continued. The population gains of Hunterdon (+39.6 percent), Sussex (+24.2 percent), and Warren (+21.3 percent) Counties all exceeded the state's overall rate of growth of 14.2 percent. Growing employment opportunities within the state's newly ascendant automobile-centric office growth corridors brought all three of these counties into their expanding suburban-exurban commuter sheds.

Big Six City Turnaround, 2000–2010

The ultimate demographic fate of the first intercensal period of the twenty-first century—the decade of the "oughts" (2000–2010)—was given shape by two

Table 5.9
New Jersey Regional and County Population, 1980–2000

	1980	2000	Change: 1980–2000 Number	Change: 1980–2000 Percent (%)	Share of New Jersey (%) 1980	Share of New Jersey (%) 2000
New Jersey	7,365,011	8,414,350	1,049,339	14.2	100.0	100.0
Core Metropolis	3,205,340	3,298,316	92,976	2.9	43.5	39.2
Essex	851,304	793,633	(57,671)	(6.8)	11.6	9.4
Hudson	556,972	608,975	52,003	9.3	7.6	7.2
Union	504,094	522,541	18,447	3.7	6.8	6.2
Bergen	845,385	884,118	38,733	4.6	11.5	10.5
Passaic	447,585	489,049	41,464	9.3	6.1	5.8
Rural North/ Exurban	200,548	246,603	46,055	23.0	2.7	2.9
Sussex	116,119	144,166	28,047	24.2	1.6	1.7
Warren	84,429	102,437	18,008	21.3	1.1	1.2
Central	2,105,049	2,605,915	500,866	23.8	28.6	31.0
Hunterdon	87,361	121,989	34,628	39.6	1.2	1.4
Mercer	307,863	350,761	42,898	13.9	4.2	4.2
Middlesex	595,893	750,162	154,269	25.9	8.1	8.9
Monmouth	503,173	615,301	112,128	22.3	6.8	7.3
Morris	407,630	470,212	62,582	15.4	5.5	5.6
Somerset	203,129	297,490	94,361	46.5	2.8	3.5
Metro South	1,034,109	1,186,999	152,890	14.8	14.0	14.1
Camden	471,650	508,932	37,282	7.9	6.4	6.0
Burlington	362,542	423,394	60,852	16.8	4.9	5.0
Gloucester	199,917	254,673	54,756	27.4	2.7	3.0
Southern Shore	622,423	865,794	243,371	39.1	8.5	10.3
Atlantic	194,119	252,552	58,433	30.1	2.6	3.0
Cape May	82,266	102,326	20,060	24.4	1.1	1.2
Ocean	346,038	510,916	164,878	47.6	4.7	6.1
Rural South	197,542	210,723	13,181	6.7	2.7	2.5
Cumberland	132,866	146,438	13,572	10.2	1.8	1.7
Salem	64,676	64,285	(391)	(0.6)	0.9	0.8

SOURCE: U.S. Census Bureau, decennial census for indicated years.

unique factors: the housing and credit bubbles that buoyed the economy of the 2000s until they burst in 2007 and the severity of the Great 2007–2009 Recession that followed—the worst economic downturn since the Great Depression. These national and global factors were strongly evident in New Jersey and its geography. The state's recessionary employment losses fully erased all of the job gains that had been achieved in the preceding economic expansion. The prolific job opportunities that were in place at the end of the first decade of the

Table 5.10

Population of New Jersey's Big Six Cities, 2000–2010

	2000	2010	Change: 2000–2010	
			Number	Percent (%)
Camden	79,904	77,344	(2,560)	(3.2)
Elizabeth	120,568	124,969	4,401	3.7
Jersey City	240,055	247,597	7,542	3.1
Newark	273,546	277,140	3,594	1.3
Paterson	149,222	146,199	(3,023)	(2.0)
Trenton	85,403	84,913	(490)	(0.6)
TOTAL	948,698	958,162	9,464	1.0
TOTAL NJ	8,414,350	8,791,894	377,544	4.5
Big Six Share	11.3%	10.9%		

SOURCE: U.S. Census Bureau, decennial census for indicated years.

twentieth century, one hundred years earlier, were not to be found at the end of the first decade of the twenty-first century.

Nonetheless, the Big Six cities managed to eke out a positive intercensal population gain for the first time since the 1940s.[6] In total, they added 9,464 people between 2000 and 2010 (table 5.10), with Jersey City (+7,542 people) the top gainer, followed by Elizabeth (+4,401 people) and Newark (+3,594 people). In fact, Newark snapped a five-decade-long period of sustained population declines.

Immigration, whose magnitude paralleled that of a century earlier, was certainly a contributing factor to New Jersey's urban demographic stabilization and revival, particularly in the prerecession years. In addition, in the case of Jersey City, the shelter spillover from an increasingly expensive New York City—as well as that stemming from maturing New Jersey baby boomers resizing in the housing market—further bolstered the Hudson River Gold Coast. Nonetheless, the Big Six in total still lost state population share, albeit slightly, declining from 11.3 percent of New Jersey's total population in 2000 to 10.9 percent in 2010 (table 5.10). In 1900, their share had been 40.3 percent (table 5.1).

Surprisingly, in the context of the prerecessionary national and state housing and homeownership bubbles, the regional distribution pattern of New Jersey's population remained remarkably stable during the 2000–2010 period, with minimal state-share changes in each of the six regions (table 5.11). Ocean (+65,651 people) and Middlesex (+59,696 people) were again the county population growth leaders between 2000 and 2010, just as they were in the 1980–2000 period. Middlesex's growth was sufficient in scale to make it New Jersey's second largest county. Its 2010 population (809,858 people) just surpassed that of Essex (783,969 people), which dropped to third place. Bergen County (905,116

Table 5.11
New Jersey Regional and County Population, 2000–2010

	2000	2010	Change: 2000–2010		Share of New Jersey (%)	
			Number	Percent (%)	2000	2010
New Jersey	8,414,350	8,791,894	377,544	4.5	100	100.0
Core Metropolis	3,298,316	3,361,076	62,760	1.9	39.2	38.2
Essex	793,633	783,969	(9,664)	(1.2)	9.4	8.9
Hudson	608,975	634,266	25,291	4.2	7.2	7.2
Union	522,541	536,499	13,958	2.7	6.2	6.1
Bergen	884,118	905,116	20,998	2.4	10.5	10.3
Passaic	489,049	501,226	12,177	2.5	5.8	5.7
Rural North/ Exurban	246,603	257,957	11,354	4.6	2.9	2.9
Sussex	144,166	149,265	5,099	3.5	1.7	1.7
Warren	102,437	108,692	6,255	6.1	1.2	1.2
Central	2,605,915	2,750,820	144,905	5.6	31.0	31.3
Hunterdon	121,989	128,349	6,360	5.2	1.4	1.5
Mercer	350,761	366,513	15,752	4.5	4.2	4.2
Middlesex	750,162	809,858	59,696	8.0	8.9	9.2
Monmouth	615,301	630,380	15,079	2.5	7.3	7.2
Morris	470,212	492,276	22,064	4.7	5.6	5.6
Somerset	297,490	323,444	25,954	8.7	3.5	3.7
Metro South	1,186,999	1,250,679	63,680	5.4	14.1	14.2
Camden	508,932	513,657	4,725	0.9	6.0	5.8
Burlington	423,394	448,734	25,340	6.0	5.0	5.1
Gloucester	254,673	288,288	33,615	13.2	3.0	3.3
Southern Shore	865,794	948,381	82,587	9.5	10.3	10.8
Atlantic	252,552	274,549	21,997	8.7	3.0	3.1
Cape May	102,326	97,265	(5,061)	(4.9)	1.2	1.1
Ocean	510,916	576,567	65,651	12.8	6.1	6.6
Rural South	210,723	222,981	12,258	5.8	2.5	2.5
Cumberland	146,438	156,898	10,460	7.1	1.7	1.8
Salem	64,285	66,083	1,798	2.8	0.8	0.8

SOURCE: U.S. Census Bureau, decennial census for indicated years.

people) remained firmly ensconced in first place—not likely to be challenged as the state's most populous county, as demonstrated by the post-2010 trend lines.

Post-2010: New Urbanism

The aftershocks of the Great Recession and the bursting of the housing bubble continued to reverberate through the early and intermediate parts of the second

Table 5.12
Population of New Jersey's Big Six Cities, 2010-2018

	2010	2018	Change: 2010-2018	
			Number	Percent (%)
Camden	77,344	73,973	(3,371)	(4.4)
Elizabeth	124,969	128,885	3,916	3.1
Jersey City	247,597	265,549	17,952	7.3
Newark	277,140	282,090	4,950	1.8
Paterson	146,199	145,627	(572)	(0.4)
Trenton	84,913	83,974	(939)	(1.1)
TOTAL	958,162	980,098	21,936	2.3
TOTAL NJ	8,791,894	8,908,520	116,626	1.3
Big Six Share	10.9%	11.0%		

SOURCE: U.S. Census Bureau, decennial census for indicated years.

decade of the new century. Lingering postrecession financial constraints—joined by a great generational shift (driven by an ascendant millennial generation), a national economic expansion of record-setting length, and a booming New York City—underpinned New Jersey's changing spatial demography. Between 2010 and 2018, the state's Big Six cities' population growth accelerated as they gained a total of 21,936 people (table 5.12). Their composite rate of growth (2.3 percent) was more than half again as high as New Jersey's (1.3 percent)! As a result, their share of the state's population actually increased, from 10.9 percent to 11.0 percent.

Leading this resurgence was a booming Jersey City (+17,952 people), which saw its population increase by 7.3 percent, more than five times faster (1.3 percent) than that of the state as a whole. In terms of growth rates, both Elizabeth (+3.1 percent) and Newark (+1.8 percent) also outpaced New Jersey as a whole. In terms of absolute growth, Newark (+4,950 people) ranked second to Jersey City (+17,952 people), continuing the population gains first registered in the preceding decade (2000–2010).

As noted earlier, Jersey City's population had peaked in 1930 at 316,715 people (table 5.2). After bottoming out at 223,532 people in 1980 (table 5.6), its population rebounded to 265,549 people by 2018 (table 5.12). If Jersey City's current growth trajectory were to continue unabated, it is entirely possible for it to come close to matching its historic 1930 population peak by 2030! In contrast, Newark—whose population stood at 282,090 people in 2018 (table 5.12)—must traverse a much longer road in order to replicate its 1930 peak of 442,337 people (table 5.2), despite its recent resurgence.

The post-2010 regional and county population changes reflect this new demographic centralization. The Core Metropolis was by far the regional growth pacesetter in both absolute and relative terms (table 5.13). Its 2010–2018 population

Table 5.13
New Jersey Regional and County Population, 2010–2018

	2010	2018	Change: 2010–2018		Share of New Jersey (%)	
			Number	Percent (%)	2010	2018
New Jersey	8,791,894	8,908,520	116,626	1.3	100	100.0
Core Metropolis	3,361,076	3,473,897	112,821	3.4	38.2	39.0
Essex	783,969	799,767	15,798	2.0	8.9	9.0
Hudson	634,266	676,061	41,795	6.6	7.2	7.6
Union	536,499	558,067	21,568	4.0	6.1	6.3
Bergen	905,116	936,692	31,576	3.5	10.3	10.5
Passaic	501,226	503,310	2,084	0.4	5.7	5.6
Rural North/ Exurban	257,957	246,578	(11,379)	(4.4)	2.9	2.8
Sussex	149,265	140,799	(8,466)	(5.7)	1.7	1.6
Warren	108,692	105,779	(2,913)	(2.7)	1.2	1.2
Central	2,750,820	2,770,956	20,136	0.7	31.3	31.1
Hunterdon	128,349	124,714	(3,635)	(2.8)	1.5	1.4
Mercer	366,513	369,811	3,298	0.9	4.2	4.2
Middlesex	809,858	829,685	19,827	2.4	9.2	9.3
Monmouth	630,380	621,354	(9,026)	(1.4)	7.2	7.0
Morris	492,276	494,228	1,952	0.4	5.6	5.5
Somerset	323,444	331,164	7,720	2.4	3.7	3.7
Metro South	1,250,679	1,243,870	(6,809)	(0.5)	14.2	14.0
Camden	513,657	507,078	(6,579)	(1.3)	5.8	5.7
Burlington	448,734	445,384	(3,350)	(0.7)	5.1	5.0
Gloucester	288,288	291,408	3,120	1.1	3.3	3.3
Southern Shore	948,381	959,640	11,259	1.2	10.8	10.8
Atlantic	274,549	265,429	(9,120)	(3.3)	3.1	3.0
Cape May	97,265	92,560	(4,705)	(4.8)	1.1	1.0
Ocean	576,567	601,651	25,084	4.4	6.1	6.8
Rural South	222,981	213,579	(9,402)	(4.2)	2.5	2.4
Cumberland	156,898	150,972	(5,926)	(3.8)	1.8	1.7
Salem	66,083	62,607	(3,476)	(5.3)	0.8	0.7

SOURCE: U.S. Census Bureau, decennial census and Current Population Survey for indicated years.

increase (+112,821 people) was more than five times that of the second-place Central region (+20,136 people). The Core also accounted for 96.7 percent of the total state population increase (112,821 people out of 116,626 people). As a result, its share of the state's population increased from 38.2 percent in 2010 to 39.0 percent in 2018 (table 5.14). Four of the five Core Metropolis counties—Bergen, Essex, Hudson, and Union—had growth rates eclipsing that of the state. Three of the four (Bergen, Hudson, and Union) bordered directly on New York City, while Essex was in close proximity.

Table 5.14

New Jersey Regional and County Population: Distributional Profile, 1900–2018 (Percentage)

Year	1900	1930	1950	1970	1980	2000	2010	2018
New Jersey	100	100	100	100	100	100	100	100
Core Metropolis	57.2	61.8	58.5	48.0	43.5	39.2	38.2	39.0
Essex	19.1	20.6	18.7	13.0	11.6	9.4	8.9	9.0
Hudson	20.5	17.1	13.4	8.5	7.6	7.2	7.2	7.6
Union	5.3	7.6	8.2	7.6	6.8	6.2	6.1	6.3
Bergen	4.2	9.0	11.1	12.5	11.5	10.5	10.3	10.5
Passaic	8.2	7.5	7.0	6.4	6.1	5.8	5.7	5.6
Rural North/ Exurban	3.3	1.9	1.8	2.1	2.7	2.9	2.9	2.8
Sussex	1.3	0.7	0.7	1.1	1.6	1.7	1.7	1.6
Warren	2.0	1.2	1.1	1.0	1.1	1.2	1.2	1.2
Central	20.7	18.7	21.2	27.9	28.6	31.0	31.3	31.1
Hunterdon	1.8	0.9	0.9	1.0	1.2	1.4	1.5	1.4
Mercer	5.1	4.6	4.8	4.2	4.2	4.2	4.2	4.2
Middlesex	4.2	5.3	5.5	8.1	8.1	8.9	9.2	9.3
Monmouth	4.4	3.6	4.7	6.4	6.8	7.3	7.2	7.0
Morris	3.5	2.7	3.4	5.3	5.5	5.6	5.6	5.5
Somerset	1.7	1.6	2.0	2.8	2.8	3.5	3.7	3.7
Metro South	10.5	10.3	10.9	13.3	14.0	14.1	14.2	14.0
Camden	5.7	6.2	6.2	6.4	6.4	6.0	5.8	5.7
Burlington	3.1	2.3	2.8	4.5	4.9	5.0	5.1	5.0
Gloucester	1.7	1.8	1.9	2.4	2.7	3.0	3.3	3.3
Southern Shore	4.2	4.6	4.7	6.2	8.5	10.3	10.8	10.8
Atlantic	2.5	3.1	2.7	2.4	2.6	3.0	3.1	3.0
Cape May	0.7	0.7	0.8	0.8	1.1	1.2	1.1	1.0
Ocean	1.0	0.8	1.2	2.9	4.7	6.1	6.6	6.8
Rural South	4.1	2.6	2.9	2.5	2.7	2.5	2.5	2.4
Cumberland	2.7	1.7	1.8	1.7	1.8	1.7	1.8	1.7
Salem	1.4	0.9	1.0	0.8	0.9	0.8	0.8	0.7

SOURCE: U.S. Census Bureau, decennial census and Current Population Survey for indicated years.

Hudson (+41,795 people) came out on top of the county-growth rankings on both the state and regional levels (table 5.13). Its 2010–2018 growth rate (+6.6 percent) was close to that (+7.3 percent) of Jersey City, as most of the Hudson River coastal communities boomed. Bergen County (+31,576 people), with significant Hudson River frontage, was in second place in absolute growth in terms of both its regional and state positions.

The fourth-ranking county (following third-place Ocean) was Union (+21,568 people), also located in the Core Metropolis and also bordering New York City, directly to the west of the Borough of Staten Island (Richmond County). And just below Union (geographically and rank-wise) stood fifth-place Middlesex (+19,827 people). Thus, four of New Jersey's five leading growth counties post–Great Recession were clustered closely around New York City. In contrast, those regions farthest from New York slipped into absolute population decline. The two counties comprising the Rural North/Exurban Region—Sussex (−8,466 people) and Warren (−2,913 people)—both started to experience population declines between 2010 and 2018; this was a dramatic reversal from the demographic growth pressures evident in earlier decades. Again, both are situated along the Delaware River, the state's western border.

Hunterdon County (−3,635 people), just south of Warren, is similarly situated on the western border across from Pennsylvania. In the 1990s, it had been one of the fastest-growing counties of the state (table 5.9). The once ever-expanding perimeter of the broad metropolitan region centered on New York City suddenly began to contract as the twenty-first century advanced. This is reminiscent of the pattern of rural population growth lag and stagnation in the early part of the twentieth century. The broader Central region, which includes both declining Hunterdon County and rapidly growing Middlesex County, also experienced a shrinking share of the state's total population (table 5.13). Despite growing by 20,136 people between 2010 and 2018, its share of the state's population fell from 31.3 percent to 31.1 percent (table 5.14). This was a pattern that replicated that of the 1900–1930 period (table 5.3)—modest growth but shrinking share.

Ocean County (+25,084 people) remained a potent growth node, ranking third among the counties (table 5.13). At the same time, the two other counties of the Southern Shore Region—Atlantic (−9,120 people) and Cape May (−4,705 people)—suffered population declines, as did both counties of the Rural South—Cumberland and Salem. The population of the Metro South Region, clustered near Philadelphia, also declined (−0.5 percent). While Gloucester County did grow, both Camden and Burlington experienced population declines. A rebounding Philadelphia was not nearly as powerful an economic or demographic magnet as New York City.

For more than two centuries, New Jersey's population geography has constantly evolved. From dispersed rural and international locations, populations flocked into concentrated settlements, marking the first major spatial transformation. The powerful forces of centralization and urbanization underlying it were ultimately supplanted by powerful forces of decentralization and suburbanization, the second major transformation. Yet the beginnings of another reversal appear to be emerging, as centralization and re-urbanization seemingly have started to take hold, portending the unfolding of a process of de-suburbanization. The full strength and sustainability of this latest transformation remains an open book, however, as the latest metrics raise questions. Further discussion and evaluation will be made as generational shifts, economic change, and migration patterns are explored in subsequent chapters.

6
Components of Population Change
•••••••••••••••••••

Population change by decade and for longer time intervals was the subject of chapters 3–5. The cyclical and structural macro forces underlying the shifts in growth patterns in both the United States and New Jersey were particularly noted where relevant. For example, the Great Depression and the allied recessions that took place during the decade of the 1930s—which were potent cyclical economic factors, both globally and nationally—had the effect of slowing both national and state population growth. International migration flows into the United States and New Jersey were reduced to a trickle, while the economic capacity to produce families and children had diminished markedly. Thus, economic swings between boom and bust stand as cyclical forces influencing population growth.

In contrast, during the decade of the 1970s, broad structural shifts—particularly the globalization of manufacturing and the economic rise of the Sunbelt in the United States—were prominent contributors to the state's population-growth malaise. For the first time in the post–World War II era, New Jersey experienced a net outflow of people between 1970 and 1980 as the state underwent a fundamental economic reshaping. Thus, economic and societal structural changes also stand as influential factors influencing the scale of population growth.

Within the geographic divisions of New Jersey, cyclical events have also been influential, paralleling those impacting the nation and the state as a whole. But long-term structural shifts—such as the rise and fall of urban industrial agglomeration and the decentralization and recentralization of postindustrial economic functions—have also been key forces driving the changing growth fortunes of the state's individual counties and regions. Thus, population changes at all geographical levels do not happen in a vacuum but are the consequences of a broader set of cyclical and structural factors.

Their specific impact can be discerned and refined when the specific components of population change are examined—that is, disaggregating overall quantitative population increase or decrease into its distinct causal parts. Population in a geographic area can change depending on the balance between the number of people being born, the number of people dying, and the migratory flows of people moving into and out of it. Demographers have termed these three elements as the components of population change: births, deaths, and migration.

The difference between births and deaths in a population is alternatively labeled natural increase, natural increment, or natural change. Natural increase occurs when births exceed deaths, while natural decrease happens when the number of people dying exceeds the number of babies being born. (In census tabulations, births and deaths are also called vital events.) Natural decrease usually occurs in areas that are characterized by aging populations with an insufficient number of young adults in their prime childbearing years. This is a rare but not unprecedented condition in the United States. In the post-2010 period, only West Virginia and Maine among the fifty states experienced natural decrease (or negative natural increase).

Migration is the flow of people moving from one jurisdiction to another. The Census Bureau usually employs "net migration" in its tabulations, which is the difference between the number of people moving into an area and the number of people moving out of an area. The bureau also partitions net migration into its domestic and international components. Net domestic migration tabulates only movements whose origins are internal to the United States and whose destinations remain within the United States. In the case of New Jersey, net domestic migration is the balance between the number of people moving from New Jersey to the rest of country versus the number of people from the rest of the country moving to New Jersey. In the post-2010 period, the Garden State domestically has had far more people moving out than moving in—that is, negative net migration. An alternative expression for this condition is "net domestic outmigration." On a regional basis, the South has been the post-2010 clear-cut net domestic migration "winner," being the primary destination of United States internal (domestic) population movements.

Net international migration is the difference between the number of people moving into the United States from foreign countries versus those moving from the United States to other countries.[1] In-movers are largely foreign-born individuals, supplemented by such population subsectors as returning U.S. citizens who had been working abroad and returning members of the U.S. military who had been serving or stationed in other countries. International in-movers have been far greater than out-movers. Over time, international migration has become a greater component of population growth for the United States, particularly as the relative importance of net natural increase declined as the twenty-first century advanced. As we will see, this has been particularly the case for New Jersey and its encompassing Northeast region, where positive net international migration exceeds the magnitude of net natural increase and has helped to partially counterbalance negative net domestic migration.

The National Framework

To set the basic reference framework for the region and New Jersey, a brief glance at the national totals on the tops of tables 6.1 and 6.2 proves instructive.[2] The

Table 6.1

U.S. and Regional Components of Population Change, 1950–1960

| | Base Population | Components of Change: 1950–1960 | | |
		Net Population Change	Net Natural Increase	Total Net Migration
United States Total	151,325,798	27,997,377	25,337,000	2,660,000
Region				
Northeast	39,477,986	5,199,833	4,864,000	336,000
North Central (Midwest)	44,460,762	7,158,377	7,280,000	(121,000)
South	47,197,088	7,776,025	9,180,000	(1,404,000)
West	20,189,962	7,863,142	4,013,000	3,850,000

SOURCE: U.S. Census Bureau, decennial census.
NOTE: Base population is April 1, 1950.

Table 6.2

U.S. and Regional Components of Population Change, 2010–2018

| | Base Population | Components of Change: 2010–2018 | | | | |
| | | Population Change 2010–2018 | Net Natural Increase | Net Migration | | |
				Total	International	Domestic
United States Total	308,758,105	18,409,329	10,714,959	7,694,370	7,694,370	—
Region						
Northeast	55,318,430	792,649	1,234,219	(425,095)	1,786,346	(2,211,441)
Midwest	66,929,743	1,379,001	1,833,582	(441,750)	1,065,306	(1,507,056)
South	114,563,045	10,190,903	4,038,394	6,117,386	3,082,344	3,035,042
West	71,946,887	6,046,776	3,608,764	2,443,829	1,760,374	683,455

SOURCES: U.S. Census Bureau, decennial census and Current Population Survey.
NOTE: Base Population is April 1, 2010.

comparison periods are the high-fertility-rate intercensus decade of the 1950s (ten years) and the low-fertility-rate 2010–2018 period (eight years). From a 1950 base of 151.3 million people, the population of the United States increased by 28.0 million people (+18.5 percent) between 1950 and 1960 (table 6.1). Net natural increase (+25.3 million people) accounted for 90.5 percent of the nation's total population growth (+28.0 million people).[3] Net migration accounted for only 2.7 million people. This was the old mid-twentieth-century demographic normal.

Shifting to the second decade of the twenty-first century (table 6.2), the scale of absolute growth was considerably smaller. Starting from a base in 2010 of 308.8 million people—double the base (151.3 million people) of six decades earlier (1950)—the nation's population increased by only 18.4 million people (+6.0 percent) between 2010 and 2018. Net natural increase (+10.7 million people) accounted for just 58.2 percent of the total population growth (+18.4 million people). Net migration (international) had soared to 7.7 million. Much slower growth (both absolutely and relatively), less dependence on net natural increase, and much greater reliance on international migration are the new demographic normals.

Now and Then: The Regional Setting

Twenty-first-century metrics reveal distinct regional disparities within the United States in population growth and migration tendencies, as well as in many other measurable socioeconomic characteristics. The current regional situation generally stands in sharp contrast to those fundamentals of mid-twentieth-century America. As noted in chapters 3 and 5, the decade of the 1950s was a time of U.S. global manufacturing hegemony, of resurgent postwar personal consumption, and of increased mobility. These were the conditions producing a unique positive demographic storm. But this earlier period also had precursors of how the nation would ultimately be reshaping itself during the post-2000 era.

As shown in table 6.1, absolute population growth between 1950 and 1960 was relatively evenly distributed among the four regions of the nation. Three of the four regions had total population gains greater than seven million people—the West (+7.9 million people), the South (+7.8 million people), and North Central (+7.2 million people). The Northeast, while lagging behind the other regions, still gained 5.2 million people. In aggregate change, then, most parts of postwar America were seemingly advancing in demographic lockstep, each building on their prewar population bases and resurgent civilian-based economies. However, the West still represented the frontier in 1950, as it was approximately one-half the population size of the other three regions.

By 2010 (table 6.2), the West had long since surpassed the Northeast and Midwest (formerly North Central) regions in population size, but it was the South that became the dominant regional leader—and the Northeast the laggard. Thus, a new demographic regional order had been set in place. The post-2010 census estimates confirm that sharp regional differences in growth had become firmly established. Between 2000 and 2018, the population gains of the South (+10.2 million people) and West (+6.0 million people) regions were both far in excess of those of the lagging Midwest (+1.4 million people) and Northeast (+793,000 people) regions. The critical mass of the population of the United States continued to dramatically shift to the South and West, away from the far more mature and developed midwestern and northeastern states.

The differences in the components of change in the two periods underscore the long-term transformations that have been taking place. Between 1950 and 1960 (table 6.1), Americans were mainly flocking westward across the country. The West region, the national leader, had a positive net migration increase of nearly 3.9 million people. In contrast, the Northeast region was the beneficiary of only a modest migration gain (+336,000 people), while the North Central region experienced a modest loss (−121,000 people). But it was the South region that was afflicted with the most substantial migration losses (−1.4 million people), driven by Black migration to the economic opportunities of the thriving northern industrial cities of that era (see chapter 4 and appendix C).

The post-2010 period could not be more different. The South was firmly established as the primary destination of population movements (table 6.2). The total net migration gain of the South between 2010 and 2018 (+6.1 million people) was more than double that registered by the West (+2.4 million people), while the Midwest (−441,750 people) and Northeast (−425,095 people) suffered total net migration losses. The disparities become even more apparent when migration is partitioned into its domestic and international components. Domestically, strong population flows out of the Northeast (−2.2 million people) and Midwest (−1.5 million people) to the South (+3.0 million people) predominate.

Particularly relevant to New Jersey is the Northeast region's dependence on international migration as a source of population growth. The region's net international migration gain between 2010 and 2018 (nearly 1.8 million people) was greater than the region's overall population growth (+792,649 people). Had positive international migration not compensated for domestic migration losses, the region would have an overall population loss approaching 1.0 million people.

Then and Now: New Jersey

Interperiod differences in New Jersey's components of population change exhibit far more variation than the Northeast region in total. In particular, the state's net domestic migration has been uniquely influenced by the presence of two extraordinarily large bordering cities—New York City and Philadelphia. New Jersey's immediate postwar demographic destiny was shaped by the massive

Table 6.3

New Jersey Components of Population Change, 1950–1960, 1960–1970, 1970–1980, and 2010–2018

		Components of Population Change		
	Base Population	Net Population Change	Net Natural Increase	Total Net Migration
Period 1				
1950–1960	4,835,329	1,231,453	654,032	577,421
1960–1970	6,066,782	1,104,330	508,685	495,645
Period 2				
1970–1980	7,171,112	193,899	311,602	(117,703)
Period 3				
2010–2018	8,791,894	116,558	256,493	(140,088)

SOURCES: U.S. Census Bureau, decennial census and Current Population Survey.
NOTES: The intercensal periods (1950–1960, 1960–1970, and 1970–1980) are measured from April 1 of each census year. The 2010–2018 period is measured from the April 1, 2010 census base to the July 1, 2018 estimate.

The net population change from 2010 to 2018 (116,558 persons) is calculated from a revised 2010 estimates base of 8,791,962 persons, which is 68 persons greater than the 2010 decennial population of 8,791,894 persons. The 2010–2018 change in this table differs slightly from the change (116,626 persons) in tables 5.12 and 5.13 of chapter 5.

household exodus to the suburbs from these two urban behemoths. In the early twenty-first century, these two cities began attracting young—and less young—New Jersey adults.

It should be pointed out again that the breakdown/partition between international and domestic migration is not available for the interdecennial census decades following World War II. However, this does not constitute a major analytical impediment. In general, international migration was a less significant source of population growth in the early postwar period. And its importance to New Jersey was further lessened by the sheer scale of domestic suburbanization flows into the state up until 1970.

Table 6.3 details the components of population change for three distinct periods. The first comprises the two high-growth postwar decades (1950–1960 and 1960–1970) that immediately followed World War II; the second (1970–1980) period reveals the transition to a slow-growth New Jersey population environment; and the third (2010–2018) represents the new slow-growth demographic normal of an advancing century.

In the initial decade (1950–1960) of the first period, the state's population surged by more than 1.2 million people (+25.5 percent), with a robust total net migration gain (+577,421 people) almost matching an equally robust net natural increase (+654,032 people). It should be emphasized that this positive net migration (+577,421 people) into New Jersey was far in excess of the total positive net migration (+336,000 people) experienced by the entire Northeast region (table 6.1). The next intercensal decade (1960–1970) of this period closely repli-cated the first (table 6.3). The state had a population gain in excess of 1.1 million people (+18.2 percent), a positive net natural increase of 508,685 people and a net migration gain of 495,645 people. Thus, the two-decade 1950–1970 period was one of strong population gains (+2.3 million people) driven by vigorous growth in both of the components of change: net natural increase (+1.2 million people) and net migration (+1.1 million people). Controlling growth—and confronting its costs—began to emerge in public policy discussions.

However, the components of change shifted remarkably in the second period (1970–1980) under discussion. The end result was a single-decade population increase of just 193,899 people. As the baby boom was fully supplanted by the baby bust (chapter 7), net natural increase plummeted to just 311,602 people, approximately one-half that of the decades of the 1950s and 1960s. And the great waves of demographic suburbanization came to a virtual halt: net population in-migration was transformed into net outmigration (−117,703 people) despite the national increase of international migration initiated as a result of the Immigra-tion and Nationality Act of 1965.

The 1970–1980 population experience—transformative shifts in growth dynamics—revealed an ominous potential future for New Jersey: population stagnation leading to potential decline. But international immigration amelio-rated the potentially harsh consequences of diminished net natural increase and a shift to net domestic outmigration. A comparison of the ebullience of the 1950–1960 intercensal decade with that of the 2010–2018 period proves instructive.

In the eight years between 2010 and 2018, the state's population increased by only 116,558 people, less than 10 percent of the overall population gain of 1.2 mil-lion people experienced in the full decade of the 1950s (table 6.3). The entire growth between 2010 and 2018 was due to net natural increase (+256,493 people), even though it was less than one-half of the net natural increase (+654,032 people) of the 1950–1960 period. Adding further significance to the importance of this diminished scale of natural increase was post-2010 total net migration, which turned negative (−140,088 people). The contrast with the huge net in-migration (+577,421 people) of the 1950s could not be more striking. New Jersey has become the origin of demographic outflows rather than the destination of demographic inflows.

This new reality has come into being despite the emergence of large-scale pos-itive international migration. As shown in the top line of table 6.5, New Jersey had a net international migration gain of 302,522 people between 2010 and 2018. The latter was not sufficient to counterbalance huge domestic migration losses (−442,610 people). As a result, the state had a total net migration loss of 140,088 people. Without the benefit of international migration, New Jersey's 2010–2018 population growth (+116,558 people) would have been transformed into a popu-lation decline of 185,964 people—116,558 people (actual overall growth) minus 302,522 people (positive net international migration).

Table 6.4

New Jersey County Components of Population Change, April 1, 1950 to April 1, 1960

Area	April 1, 1950 Population	Cumulative Estimates of the Components of Population Change, April 1, 1950 to April 1, 1960		
		Total Population Change	Net Natural Change	Migration Total
New Jersey	4,835,329	1,231,453	654,032	577,421
County				
Atlantic	132,399	28,481	9,738	18,743
Bergen	539,139	241,116	88,269	152,847
Burlington	135,910	88,589	27,194	61,395
Camden	300,743	91,292	46,405	44,887
Cape May	37,131	11,424	1,798	9,626
Cumberland	88,597	18,253	11,881	6,372
Essex	905,949	17,596	92,524	(74,928)
Gloucester	91,727	43,113	16,275	26,838
Hudson	647,437	(36,703)	61,540	(98,243)
Hunterdon	42,736	11,371	4,189	7,182
Mercer	229,781	36,611	29,021	7,590
Middlesex	264,872	168,984	56,943	112,041
Monmouth	225,327	109,074	35,907	73,167
Morris	164,371	97,249	28,693	68,556
Ocean	56,622	51,619	9,470	42,149
Passaic	337,093	69,525	42,157	27,368
Salem	49,508	9,203	7,556	1,647
Somerset	99,052	44,861	17,491	27,370
Sussex	34,423	14,832	4,800	10,032
Union	398,138	106,117	56,705	49,412
Warren	54,374	8,846	5,476	3,370

SOURCE: U.S. Census Bureau, decennial census.

Within New Jersey

The dramatic shifts that have taken place over time in New Jersey's components of population change are matched by those that have taken place within the boundaries of the state during equivalent periods of time. Again, the 2010–2018 period stands in vivid contrast to the 1950–1960 decade of rampant suburbanization. The detailed components of each of these periods are shown in tables 6.4 and 6.5.

The migration component of change between 1950 and 1960 for each county was dominated by two "losers" and two "winners" (table 6.4). Of the former, Hudson County had the largest total migration loss (−98,243 people)—as well as a total population loss of 36,703 people. Hudson was the only county in New Jersey to lose population during the 1950s, a time when the state was seemingly

Table 6.5
New Jersey County Components of Population Change, April 1, 2010 to July 1, 2018

| Area | 2010 Population | Total Population Change | Net Natural Increase | Cumulative Estimates of the Components of Population Change: April 1, 2010 to July 1, 2018 | Net Migration | |
				Total	International	Domestic
New Jersey	8,791,894	116,558	256,493	(140,088)	302,522	(442,610)
County						
Atlantic	274,549	(9,092)	3,661	(12,869)	8,665	(21,534)
Bergen	905,116	31,549	18,364	13,791	31,662	(17,871)
Burlington	448,734	(3,346)	4,810	(8,010)	4,996	(13,006)
Camden	513,657	(6,641)	13,664	(20,458)	9,612	(30,070)
Cape May	97,265	(4,701)	(3,409)	(1,206)	1,070	(2,276)
Cumberland	156,898	(5,661)	4,384	(10,118)	3,234	(13,352)
Essex	783,969	15,882	36,423	(20,918)	35,778	(56,696)
Gloucester	288,288	2,838	3,698	(685)	1,820	(2,505)
Hudson	634,266	41,816	52,736	(11,148)	64,621	(75,769)
Hunterdon	128,349	(2,643)	176	(2,855)	746	(3,601)
Mercer	366,513	2,300	10,672	(8,539)	16,749	(25,288)
Middlesex	809,858	19,761	30,811	(11,410)	45,945	(57,355)
Monmouth	630,380	(9,020)	4,629	(13,645)	5,360	(19,005)
Morris	492,276	1,914	7,734	(5,743)	11,355	(17,098)
Ocean	576,567	25,105	9,615	16,078	2,572	13,506
Passaic	501,226	1,701	26,899	(25,562)	22,118	(47,680)
Salem	66,083	(3,459)	(384)	(3,096)	392	(3,488)
Somerset	323,444	7,731	8,548	(757)	9,415	(10,172)
Sussex	149,265	(8,110)	496	(8,719)	382	(9,101)
Union	536,499	21,500	23,110	(1,511)	24,732	(26,243)
Warren	108,692	(2,866)	(144)	(2,708)	1,298	(4,006)

SOURCES: U.S. Census Bureau, decennial census and Current Population Survey.

being overwhelmed by a demographic tidal wave originating from outside its borders. But in terms of net migration losses, Hudson County was joined by Essex County (−74,928 people), although Essex did experience overall population growth (+17,596 people) because of the rapid suburban expansion taking place in its western territories. In any case, these two jurisdictions—Hudson and Essex, both perched adjacent to New York City—were the only counties to experience net population outmigration during this postwar decade. The other nineteen counties experienced net migration gains.

Leading the 1950–1960 migration "winners" were the net inflows into Bergen County (+152,847 people) and Middlesex County (+112,041 people), both of which also led the state in overall population growth. (Bergen's total population increased by nearly one-quarter of a million [+241,116] people while

Middlesex's expanded by 168,984 people.) These two counties were the prized suburban destinations of the migration flows of this era. Among the counties in the United States that experienced a net in-migration of 100,000 people or more, Bergen ranked seventeenth nationally while Middlesex ranked twenty-sixth. Following these two statewide county leaders were the net migration gains of Monmouth (+73,167 people), Morris (+68,556 people), and Burlington (+61,395 people) Counties. Areas distant from yesterday's (and today's) primary commuter sheds surrounding the state's primary employment nodes had minimal migration gains: Salem (+1,647 people), Warren (+3,370 people), and Cumberland (+6,372 people).

The migration totals in the 1950–1960 period—reflecting older immigration policies and constraints—can be construed to be approximately similar to the domestic migration component of change of the 2010–2018 period. In contrast to the overwhelmingly positive numbers of the 1950s, which occurred in nineteen of twenty-one counties (table 6.4), the post-2010 years are characterized by overwhelmingly negative net domestic migration numbers, which occurred in twenty of twenty-one counties (table 6.5). Even Hudson, which had the highest county population growth (+41,816 people) between 2010 and 2018, had domestic migration losses. In fact, it experienced the highest net domestic migration outflow (−75,769 people) of any county. This loss was mitigated by its county-leading net international migration inflow (+64,621 people), though it did not fully counterbalance it. Despite the booming Hudson River waterfront, a regional demographic magnet, the county still had a total migration loss of 11,148 people (domestic minus international).

This is not unique, as Hudson replicates the general pattern for New Jersey as a whole. As noted earlier, the state's high net international migration (+302,522 people) was insufficient to fully counterbalance its net domestic migration outflow (−442,610 people). This was also the case for nineteen of the twenty-one counties. Only Bergen and Ocean Counties had unique experiences. Bergen, the county with the second highest total population growth (+31,549 people), was bolstered by international inflows (+31,662 people) eclipsing the magnitude of domestic outflows (−17,871 people). Ocean was the only county that experienced positive net domestic migration (+13,506 people), driven by the booming growth of a singular religious community in Lakewood. This unique positive domestic migration experience was given added impetus by modest yet positive gains in international migration (+2,572 people).

In general, international migration became a powerful determinant of the overall demographic fortune of the state's individual counties (except for Ocean). Those areas of strong population growth—led by Hudson (+41,816 people) and Bergen (+31,549 people)—also had strong international migration gains (table 6.5). The same was true of Union, Middlesex, and Essex, the next three population growth leaders. All five were clustered close to New York City, the heart of the broader multistate metropolitan region.

The ten counties that lost population during the 2010–2018 period generally fared poorly as destinations for international migration inflows. For example, the international migration gains of outlying Sussex (+382 people) and Salem (+392 people) totaled far less than 500 people, while that of Hunterdon (+746 people) failed to reach 1,000 persons. Cape May (+1,070 people) and Warren (+1,298 people) Counties had international gains that barely exceeded 1,000 people.

The impact of differential migration flows on the demographic fortunes of the state's outer-edge counties is illustrated by Sussex County (northwestern New Jersey) and Salem County (southwestern New Jersey). Sussex's net domestic outflow (−9,101 people) was almost twenty-four times greater than its international inflow (+382 people)—that is, there was only one international replacement for each twenty-four domestic out-movers. Salem's net domestic outmigration (−3,488 people) was nearly nine times greater than its net international gain (+392 people)—that is, nine domestic out-movers were replaced by only one international in-mover. In sharp contrast, inlying northeastern Bergen County had almost two international arrivals (+31,662 people) for every domestic departure (−17,871 people).

In the 1950s (table 6.4), all twenty-one counties experienced positive net natural increase, with the largest gains experienced by either the largest or most rapidly developing counties—Essex (+92,524 people), Bergen (+88,269 people), Hudson (+61,540 people), Middlesex (+56,943 people), and Union (+56,705 people). The smaller, rural outlying counties such as Cape May (+1,798 people), Hunterdon (+4,189 people), and Sussex (+4,800 people) had the lowest net natural increase.

Six decades later (post-2010), many parts of this pattern were replicated, with the rural outlying counties showing the weakest net natural increase (table 6.5). In fact, between 2010 and 2018, three counties experienced negative net natural increases—that is, more deaths than births, led by Cape May County (−3,409 people), followed by Salem County (−384 people) and Warren County (−144 people). Concurrently, Hunterdon (+176 persons) and Sussex (+496 persons) narrowly achieved positive net natural increases.

The combination of negative or marginally positive net natural increases, high net domestic migration losses, and marginal international migration gains has been reflected in declining school enrollments in the outer suburban/exurban/perimeter counties of the state. Just the opposite conditions generally prevail in those counties positioned closely to New York City—such as Hudson, Bergen, Union, and Middlesex—where school enrollments are growing. Thus, significant disparate experiences characterize New Jersey's population geography post the Great 2007–2009 Recession in the state.

To summarize, examining aggregate population change via its contributing components helps to clarify not only national demographic change but also New Jersey's evolving population shifts and those of its constituent counties. The state's slow growth, particularly post-2010, is a consequence not only of declining birth and fertility rates, leading to a diminished role for net natural increase, but also due to out-movers outnumbering in-movers—that is, net outmigration. Internal United States population flows show that many more people leave New Jersey than move into it, yielding substantial statewide net domestic migration losses that even high international migration gains fail to fully counter.

Nineteen of twenty-one counties reflect this condition: total net migration losses driven by high net domestic population outflows (table 6.5). Every county had net international migration gains, but those ten counties that lost population generally had the minimal international inflows. Negative net natural change also impacted three of the counties that had overall population losses. The county growth leaders were those with the largest international population inflows, which tended to concentrate in the counties bordering New York City.

7

The Generational
Framework

••••••••••••••••••••

The purpose of this chapter is to provide and explain the generational delineations that are employed and detailed throughout this book. The generational definitions that have been chosen reflect planning, public policy, and economic market perspectives—that is, an applied demographic vantage point—rather than a purely scholarly frame of reference. Generations reflect a process of segmentation and differentiation that is intended to help understand large population blocs for a wide range of purposes. The six generations that are mainly used in subsequent analyses are as follows (see also table 7.3):

Pre–Baby Boom—a broad generation (1930–1945) that comprises within it the often referred to Depression-era birth dearth (1930–1940) and then the temporary mini–World War II upswing (1942–1944), often called war babies or goodbye babies.

The Baby Boom—the fabled oversized population cohort born between 1946 and 1964, largely the children of returning GIs, and intensively marketed to during the suburban 1950s.

Generation X (Gen X)—the undersized population cohort born between 1965 and 1980, originally termed the baby bust, a less-compelling term that is fading in use.

Millennials (Gen Y)—the digital age's first generation, born between 1981 and 1996, and the current focus of many institutions trying to manage and accommodate its members.

Postmillennials (Gen Z)—the internet's first generation, born between 1997 and 2012 (tentative definition), with its full differentiation from millennials still a work in progress.

Generation Alpha—born post-2012. This could also be called the What Comes Next? generation. Alpha is just a suggested name for a cohort that will come of age in the era of artificial intelligence and robotics.[1]

During the early and mid-twentieth-century decades, sharp variations in births and fertility in the context of economic and societal shifts were instrumental in specifying generational boundaries. This is particularly the case for the starting and end points of the baby boom generation. Thus, this chapter also provides the historical baseline birth and fertility data for the United States that underlie these determinations. This baseline further provides a reference framework for subsequent analyses on the components of population change as well as for other historical population shifts. However, as the data demonstrate, sharp variations in births and fertility diminished in the late twentieth and early twenty-first centuries, lessening their value in generational identification. In their stead, changes/disruptions in societal, economic, and technological environments gained increasing prominence.

General Overview

The term *generation* as employed in this book is used as a flexible means of demographic organization in order to partition the state's (and nation's) populations into specific age cohorts or segments. An underlying assumption is that a generation is an identifiable group of people shaped by a particular period of time— by the social, cultural, and political experiences of that temporal increment. Thus, certain unique events and conditions at a specific time can have outsized impacts on a generation's world views. Nonetheless, there are also generalized behaviors that apply to all groups. In many cases, these are linked to stage in the life cycle, such as living/working in exciting environments as young adults, but then yielding to suburban environments when family-raising becomes a priority.

According to the Pew Research Center (2015), which focuses on measuring public attitudes and differences in attitudes among demographic groups, "Age cohorts give researchers a tool to analyze changes in views over time; they can provide a way to understand how different formative experiences interact with the life-cycle and aging process to shape people's view of the world. . . . Generations are one way to group age cohorts. A generation typically refers to groups of people born over a 15–20 year span." Moreover, "generations provide the opportunity to look at Americans both by their place in the life cycle—whether a young adult, a middle-aged parent, or a retiree—and by their membership in a cohort of individuals who were born at a similar time" (Pew Research Center 2018b). In addition, particularly in the decades before and after World War II, changes in social, cultural, and economic experiences were also reflected in threshold changes in fertility and birth patterns, which produced different size population cohorts that helped define the generations spawned in that era.

Although it may be possible to make broad generalizations about identifiable groups, it should also be recognized that there may not be substantial homogeneity across an entire generational spectrum. For example, the baby boom is that fabled generation born between 1946 and 1964, a period broadly characterized by post–World War II economic optimism. But despite the power of this unifying generational factor, there were other distinctions. For example, the oldest boomers, born in the late 1940s, had to confront the military draft and participation in the Vietnam War as they reached adulthood. This turned out to be a formative experience in their lives. In contrast, the youngest boomers, born in the early 1960s, became adults in the post–Vietnam War, post–military draft era, giving them a different influential background. Thus, there may not be a set of overwhelmingly uniform cross-generational formative experiences shaping a specific population cohort. Similarly, under the generational definition suggested here, the first millennial was born in 1981. Is this first-born millennial more similar to a 1996 last-born millennial, or to a 1980 last-born Gen Xer? Most likely the latter, illustrating the potential variability and weaknesses of rigid beginning and end points.

This possibility should not reduce the analytical value of the generalization lens but simply raises caution as to the dangers of attempting over-generalization or over-precision. Moreover, it should also be pointed out that the specification of generational boundaries is not fixed but may be quite fluid and can change over time as research and analyses advance. And at any one time, there may not be unanimous consensus on precise boundary points. Nonetheless, despite these caveats, the generational concept hopefully proves useful in helping to add structure to the analyses of past change in New Jersey's population and the exploration of changes to come in the future.

Cohort Size Variation and the Generations

A key demographic force that was recognized during the decades preceding and following World War II centered on the sharp changes in the size of sequential age groups within the overall population. This was premised on the wide variations in the annual number of births over time. What emerged were different age-defined population cohorts that stemmed from fluctuations in fertility and birth patterns. For example, following the "fallow" birth years of the Great Depression (often referred to as the Depression-era birth dearth) and a brief uptick during World War II, the explosion of births starting in 1946 (the fabled baby boom) initiated sharp changes in America's age structure, with an extraordinarily large population cohort (baby boom) following a particularly small cohort (birth dearth). In addition to changing societal conditions, those two generations were defined and partitioned by the scale of births—and the resulting population sizes—of each cohort.

The data in table 7.1 show these variations. For example, prior to 1930 in the United States, the annual number of births generally fluctuated between 2.6 and 3.0 million. But births in the 1930s fell to below 2.4 million per year at the lowest points during that decade. This led to the term the *Depression-era birth dearth*, a generational determinant linked to the economic severity of the Great Depression. But both the lower birth years of the 1930s and the higher birth totals of the preceding decades were quickly eclipsed by those registered during the postwar baby boom. At the peak of the boom, births exceeded 4 million per year for eleven straight years (1954–1964), and during the highest portions of that eleven-year period exceeded 4.2 million for six straight years (1956–1961). Similarly, the total fertility rate—the average number of children born to women during their reproductive years—reached a low point below 2.2 in 1936 (table 7.2).[2] In 1957 and 1958, the total fertility rate had soared above 3.7.

Of all the possible generational partitions, 1946 as the starting date of the postwar baby boom has probably achieved the greatest consensus due both to the sharp increase in the number of births that was tallied that year (table 7.1) and the sharp jump in the total fertility rate (table 7.2). However, as pointed out at the beginning of this chapter, a mini–baby boom of "war babies" or "goodbye babies" had occurred during the early years of World War II (1942–1944). Many soldiers about to be deployed overseas, and not knowing when or whether they would return, hastily started families, and a spike in births resulted. This subsequently tapered off after victory was assured. As can be seen in table 7.1, births jumped from 2.7 million in 1941 to 3.1 million in 1943 and then retreated to 2.9 million in 1945. Births then exploded to 3.4 million in 1946, as the baby boom commenced. But the societal motivations that produced the mid-war mini-boom and postwar baby boom were quite different. The first reflected wartime uncertainty and insecurity, while the latter reflected postwar optimism about a more prosperous future.

An Early Conceptualization of Today's Generations

An early generational framework emerging during the 1980s was heavily premised on birth and fertility fluctuations. As was described in 1999 and based on pre-1998 data patterns, "the resulting slowdowns and surges in the population since the 1920s have yielded five broad generations of varying sizes, each of which underpins significant changes in American society. Sequentially, these generations have assumed the conventional labels of the Depression-era birth dearth, the post–World War II baby boom, the great baby bust, the baby boom echo, and the baby-bust echo.... Demographically, we have gone from bust to boom to bust to boomlet to bustlet" (Hughes and Seneca 1999, 1–2). At that time, it was change in size (because of birth fluctuations) that was an important

Table 7.1
Births by Decade and Year, United States, 1924–2018 (numbers in thousands)

Total

1920s Year	Births	1930s Year	Births	1940s Year	Births	1950s Year	Births	1960s Year	Births	1970s Year	Births	1980s Year	Births	1990s Year	Births	2000s Year	Births	2010s Year	Births
1924	2,979	1930	2,618	1940	2,559	1950	3,632	1960	4,258	1970	3,731	1980	3,612	1990	4,158	2000	4,059	2010	3,999
1925	2,909	1931	2,506	1941	2,703	1951	3,820	1961	4,268	1971	3,556	1981	3,629	1991	4,111	2001	4,026	2011	3,954
1926	2,839	1932	2,440	1942	2,989	1952	3,909	1962	4,167	1972	3,258	1982	3,681	1992	4,065	2002	4,022	2012	3,953
1927	2,802	1933	2,307	1943	3,104	1953	3,959	1963	4,098	1973	3,137	1983	3,639	1993	4,000	2003	4,090	2013	3,932
1928	2,674	1934	2,396	1944	2,939	1954	4,071	1964	4,027	1974	3,160	1984	3,669	1994	3,953	2004	4,112	2014	3,988
1929	2,582	1935	2,377	1945	2,858	1955	4,097	1965	3,760	1975	3,144	1985	3,761	1995	3,900	2005	4,138	2015	3,978
		1936	2,355	1946	3,411	1956	4,210	1966	3,606	1976	3,168	1986	3,757	1996	3,891	2006	4,266	2016	3,946
		1937	2,413	1947	3,817	1957	4,300	1967	3,521	1977	3,327	1987	3,809	1997	3,881	2007	4,316	2017	3,856
		1938	2,496	1948	3,367	1958	4,246	1968	3,502	1978	3,333	1988	3,910	1998	3,942	2008	4,248	2018	3,792
		1939	2,466	1949	3,649	1959	4,286	1969	3,600	1979	3,494	1989	4,041	1999	3,959	2009	4,131		

SOURCE: National Center for Health Statistics, Centers for Disease Control and Prevention.

Table 7.2
Total Fertility Rate by Decade and Year, United States, 1933–2018

1930s Year	Rate	1940s Year	Rate	1950s Year	Rate	1960s Year	Rate	1970s Year	Rate	1980s Year	Rate	1990s Year	Rate	2000s Year	Rate	2010s Year	Rate
1933	2.210	1940	2.301	1950	3.091	1960	3.654	1970	2.480	1980	1.840	1990	2.081	2000	2.056	2010	1.931
1934	2.274	1941	2.299	1951	3.269	1961	3.620	1971	2.267	1981	1.812	1991	2.063	2001	2.031	2011	1.895
1935	2.235	1942	2.628	1952	3.358	1962	3.461	1972	2.010	1982	1.828	1992	2.046	2002	2.021	2012	1.881
1936	2.193	1943	2.718	1953	3.424	1963	3.319	1973	1.879	1983	1.799	1993	2.020	2003	2.048	2013	1.858
1937	2.225	1944	2.568	1954	3.543	1964	3.191	1974	1.853	1984	1.807	1994	2.002	2004	2.052	2014	1.863
1938	2.280	1945	2.491	1955	3.580	1965	2.913	1975	1.774	1985	1.844	1995	1.978	2005	2.057	2015	1.844
1939	2.232	1946	2.943	1956	3.689	1966	2.721	1976	1.738	1986	1.838	1996	1.976	2006	2.108	2016	1.821
		1947	3.274	1957	3.767	1967	2.558	1977	1.790	1987	1.872	1997	1.971	2007	2.120	2017	1.766
		1948	3.109	1958	3.701	1968	2.464	1978	1.760	1988	1.934	1998	1.999	2008	2.072	2018	1.730
		1949	3.110	1959	3.670	1969	2.456	1979	1.808	1989	2.014	1999	2.008	2009	2.002		

SOURCES: National Center for Health Statistics, Centers for Disease Control and Prevention; Federal Reserve Bank of St. Louis.

NOTES: Replacement level = 2.100; since 1971, it has been above that only twice (2006 and 2007).
2017 fertility is the lowest since 1978; 2018 the lowest in history.

contributing organizing element. As will be shown, the definition of subsequent generations has yielded to more sophisticated concepts centered on the impact of changing socioeconomic and technological conditions, particularly digital information technology advances, that are helping to define and reformat age-structure partitions. The above working generational protocols were employed by the Center for Urban Policy Research (CUPR) at Rutgers University by the late 1990s.[3] Their specific age boundaries, premised mainly on the cohort size metric, were as follows (from youngest to oldest):

The Baby Bust Echo—born 1996 and later, a smaller generational cohort anticipated because of the smaller generation (Gen X or baby bust) producing it. This is similar to what is now called postmillennials (Gen Z).

The Baby Boom Echo—born 1977 to 1995, a larger generation cohort premised on the very large size of the generation (baby boom) producing it. This definition corresponds loosely to Gen Y as used in this book.

The Baby Bust—born 1965 to 1976, a small generation whose end point was the last year (1976) of a four-year-long birth trough, after which births began to increase substantially. The term *baby bust* subsequently was largely supplanted by *Gen X*.

The Post–World War II Baby Boom—born 1946 to 1964, this definition has received the widest consensus of any generational partition.

The Depression-Era Birth Dearth—born 1930 to 1945, a very loose formulation primarily used to set the stage for the baby boom.

Newer Conceptualizations

As noted above, early groupings such as those used by CUPR were still largely premised on birth and fertility fluctuations. The more recent generational formulations—particularly post–baby bust—were subsequently modified (and less strictly defined by annual changes in births) because of increased immigration flows bolstering individual age cohorts and significant powerful formative experiences surrounding each of them.

Typical of the new generational protocols as the twenty-first century advanced are those originally defined by the Pew Research Center in 2015, which the center suggests are somewhat imprecise but useful cultural grouping of Americans by age. These are as follows:

The Millennial Generation—born 1981 to 1997.
Generation X—born 1965 to 1980.
The Baby Boom Generation—born 1946 to 1964.
The Silent Generation—born 1928 to 1945.
The Greatest Generation—born before 1928.

It should be noted that the CUPR-defined Depression-era birth dearth largely corresponded to the silent generation but without any of the cultural underpinnings used by Pew. Subsequently, in 2018, modifications were set down by Pew (2018b). Most important was the change in the final millennial year (1997–1996), the addition of an open-ended postmillennial generation, and the grouping together of the silent and greatest generations. Then, in 2019, Pew reiterated its generational boundaries and also replaced the term *postmillennial*, which it had been using as a "placeholder." Because Pew observed that the term *Gen Z* had taken hold and gained momentum in popular culture and journalism, it adopted this term.

> *Generation Z (Postmillennial Generation)*—born 1997 and later.
> *Millennial Generation*—born 1981 to 1996.
> *Generation X*—born 1965 to 1980.
> *The Baby Boom Generation*—born 1946 to 1964.
> *Silent and Greatest Generations*—born 1945 or earlier.

Certainly, there are other partitions. For example, the U.S. Census Bureau (2015) loosely defines millennials as being born between 1982 and 2000. This is also the starting year for millennials specified by Neil Howe and William Strauss (2000). In contrast, the Urban Land Institute in several studies defines Generation Y as being born in the period encompassing 1978 and 1995 (Lachman and Brett 2011, 2013). Others consider the boundary years to be 1980 and 2000 (CNN 2019). For example, William Emmons (2014) of the Federal Reserve Bank of St. Louis has used the following generational boundaries:

> *The Greatest Generation*—born 1900 to 1924 (including people who fought in World War II).
> *The Silent Generation*—born 1925 to 1945 (Depression and World War II).
> *Baby Boomers*—born 1946 to 1964.
> *Generation X*—born 1965 to 1980.
> *Generation Y* (also called "Millennials" or "Echo Boomers")—born 1981 to 2000.
> *Postmillennial Generation*—born after 2000.

Recognizing that these alternatives have validity, we are nonetheless adopting the 2018 Pew formulation to be used in the following chapters of this book. These are the same as presented at the beginning of this chapter. Again, it should be noted that an end point has been added by the authors to the Pew postmillennial generation, assuming the fifteen-year length of the Gen X and Gen Y (millennial) generations. We also added Generation Alpha starting in 2013 (post-2012), and pre–baby boom—what came before—for those born before 1945.

Table 7.3

Generations by Population and White Non-Hispanic Share for New Jersey, 2017

Generation	Birth Years	Age Range	Total	Share of Population (%)	White, Non-Hispanic	Percentage White, Non-Hispanic (%)
Pre–Baby Boom	Pre-1946	>71	809,948	9.0	598,704	73.9
Baby Boom	1946–1964	53–71	2,094,487	23.3	1,389,215	66.3
Gen X	1965–1980	37–52	1,928,130	21.4	1,002,588	52.0
Millennials (Gen Y)	1981–1996	21–36	1,869,103	20.8	889,605	47.6
Gen Z	1997–2012	5–20	1,782,258	19.8	856,583	48.1
Gen Alpha	2013–2017	<5	521,718	5.8	225,775	43.3
Total			**9,005,644**	**100.0**	**4,962,470**	**55.1**

SOURCE: Data derived from the American Community Survey by Will Irving, Rutgers University, 2019.

Pre–Baby Boom—born 1930 to 1945.
The Baby Boom—born 1946 to 1964.
Generation X (Gen X)—born 1965 to 1980.
Millennials (Gen Y)—born 1981 to 1996.
Postmillennials (Gen Z)—born 1997 to 2012.[4]
Generation Alpha (Alphas)—born post-2012.

However, the substance of the analyses that follow would not be appreciably changed if alternative definitions were used. And it is recognized that these boundaries are not set in concrete and could be modified in the future if subsequent research, rationales, and events so warrant. Moreover, as noted earlier, individuals who are positioned at one of these boundaries—or fringes—may not feel kinship with those located at the opposite boundary, nor with the cohort as a whole.

The Generational Framework of the Book

For orientation purposes, the abbreviated snapshots of the generations that are being used in this book are presented below. As will be detailed subsequently, diversity has increased with each successive generation. Table 7.3 shows the generational population totals for 2017 and the share of each that comprises the white, non-Hispanic population.

Pre–Baby Boom (1930–1945). This generally corresponds to Pew's greatest and silent generations. It comprises a period that is generally characterized by low births but really has two components. The first is the Depression-era birth dearth (1930–1940), which reflected Depression-inspired economic conservatism in reproduction behavior. The result was a moving, distinctly visible indentation in the state's age-structure profile as the "dearth" moved through its life-cycle stages. The second was the mini–World War II generation (1942–1944)—the war babies or "goodbye" babies. It comprised a modest upswing in births that peaked in 1943 (table 7.1), foreshadowing the huge baby boom upswing that would follow. This mini generation is not featured prominently in subsequent analyses of the book. It is noted mainly for historical perspective, but it is visible in the state's age structure, as it is visible between the "dearth" and the "boom." The birth dearth is what is given attention as it provides a sharp contrast to the postwar fertility upswings that followed and the resultant baby boom explosion.

The *Baby Boom* (1946–1964) is the oversized population cohort defined by the huge surge of births following World War II. The fertility rate surged from 2.491 in 1945 to 2.943 in 1946 (table 7.2), an unprecedented increase in a single year. Births increased by 553,000 (19.3 percent) between 1945 and 1946 (from 2.8 million to 3.4 million), the largest jump in both absolute and relative terms in history (table 7.1).[5] The peak birth years of the boom then took place in the late 1950s. As shown in tables 7.1 and 7.2, births peaked at 4.3 million in 1957 as did the total fertility rate (3.767) the same year. Subsequent declines in these metrics then began; however, they tumbled following 1964, leading to the widely accepted end of the boom. Interestingly, this is the one generational cohort that is definitively identified (1946–1964) by the U.S. Census Bureau (Colby and Ortman 2014).

Gen X (1965–1980) is the undersized baby bust cohort—as it was often called originally—that was produced during the low-birth era following the baby boom. The largest single drop in annual births (−267,000) in American history took place between 1964 and 1965 (table 7.1). Similarly, the largest drop in total fertility also took place (−0.278), from 3.191 in 1964 to 2.913 in 1965 (table 7.2). Thus, the starting point (1965) of the baby bust is relatively clear. The leanest birth years then took place in the mid-1970s. As shown in table 7.1, births fell below 3.2 million per year for four straight years (1973–1976). As shown in table 7.2, the total fertility rate also bottomed out over a four-year period, but it occurred somewhat later. The fertility rate fell below 1.8 between 1975 and 1978, inclusively, before increasing again. These shifting reproduction patterns underpinned the earlier assumed end to the bust (1976). But taking other societal shifts into consideration, particularly those that initiated Gen Y/millennials, Pew then determined that 1980 was the appropriate end point. As will be analyzed in chapter 9, 1981 marked the point where the technological advance of the desktop personal computer gained critical momentum.

Gen Y (1981–1996) reflects the baby boom reproducing itself (baby boom echo) as well as the impact of increasing immigration. Although it represents a bounce back from the baby bust, the rebound was not characterized by a repeat of the baby boom 1950s' fertility-rate surge but by the sheer scale of women in their childbearing years. The "echo" is now characterized as being the first cohort raised in the digital age and achieving adulthood in the era of the internet.

The total fertility rate essentially stabilized during the creation of Gen Y, at least in comparison to the sharp baby boom to baby bust variations. Between 1981 and 1988, it varied only between 1.8 and 1.9 (table 7.2). In 1989, it increased marginally, reaching 2.0, and stayed in that general range (below 2.1) through 1994. In 1995 and 1996, it slipped again to just below 2.0.

Births did grow substantially, however, despite this stabilization in fertility rates. They increased steadily from 3.6 million births in 1981 to nearly 4.2 million in 1990 (table 7.1), before trending downward below 4.0 million for the balance of the 1990s. In retrospect, the 1989–1993 years, when annual births surpassed 4 million, may represent the true "echo"—the peak of the baby boom reproducing itself. In 1990, for example, the baby boom was between twenty-six and forty-four years of age—fully encompassing the peak family-raising stage of the life cycle.

Gen Z/Postmillennials (1997–2012) are characterized as being the first population cohort born into the internet age and then coming of age in the post-2007 era of social media and instantaneous mobile information accessibility. As presented in table 7.1, annual births started to increase modestly in 1998 and then during the first decade of the twenty-first century topped 4.0 million for ten straight years (2000–2009). The peak year was 2007 (4.32 million births), when the United States finally broke the post–World War II baby boom record of 4.30 million births that had been achieved in 1957, fully fifty years earlier. The new 2007 peak, however, coincided with the onset of the Great 2007–2009 Recession. Births then slipped and fell below 4.0 million by 2010, where they have remained ever since.

The earlier, once–highly expected baby bust echo—a decline in births resulting from a smaller-size Gen X concentrating in its prime reproduction years— did not materialize. For example, in 2007, when the new peak birth year took place, Gen X was between twenty-seven and forty-two years of age, its peak childbearing years. The occurrence of a peaking in the number of births rather than the onset of a birth trough was the result of two factors: a slight rise in the total fertility rate, which peaked in 2007 at just above 2.1 (table 7.2), and the impact of international immigration, which greatly increased the number of people of childbearing age. Thus, Gen Z certainly turned out not to be an undersized population cohort tied to its Gen X antecedents.

Births and fertility rates continued to fall even as economic recovery gathered momentum in 2010. In that year, births fell below 4.0 million and continued to decline during the final two postmillennial years (2011 and 2012). By 2018, the total number of births fell to 3,792,000; this was the lowest level since 1986, thirty-two years earlier (table 7.1). Similarly, by 2018, the total fertility rate fell to 1.730, the lowest on record, just below the previous low (1.738) experienced in

1976 (table 7.2). Both of these trends have implications not only for future generational sizes but also for the overall population growth dynamics of the United States and New Jersey.

Generation Alpha/Alphas (born post-2012) is a generation that started in 2013. Its specific name has yet to receive the unanimity of its predecessors, but Generation Alpha is the top candidate at this time, which leads to its members being labeled alphas.[6] Certainly that has attractiveness, but other options exist. If current birth trends continue downward, one of the defining elements of this newly named generation may well be its smaller size. So size may regain some of the generation-defining legitimacy that was lost following the baby bust. That may potentially contribute to a naming possibility: "Baby Bust 2.0." Whatever the contributions made by the size dimension, diversity increases may also help to shape and define the emerging generation, as diversity will ratchet up to higher levels than its predecessors. A name linked to this attribute could certainly have some appeal.

But other defining factors remain elusive. Certainly, the first members of this generation were born into the longest economic expansion in the nation's history, a status the expansion achieved in July 2019 when it reached 121 months in length. However, the end of the first quarter of 2020 heralded the onset of a severe economic downturn whose depth and duration have yet to be determined. How this transition from economic advancement to economic retrenchment will shape this generation is still unknown. In addition, the definitional role and impact of technological advancement—particularly how it changes the way people interact and communicate with one another—is also uncertain, but it is destined to continue to be important in generational shaping. Although millennials were the digital age's first tech-savvy cohort and Gen Z was the mobile internet's first totally connected cohort, what technology will shape the next generation? Will alphas—or another creative designation—be the first cohort shaped in childhood and post-childhood by artificial intelligence and advancing robotics? Undoubtedly, during their infancy and toddlerhood—more so than their predecessors—alphas were virtually immersed in technology, immersed in smartphones (introduced in 2007), and immersed in tablets (introduced in 2010). The long-term future impact on alphas by these and future technologies undoubtedly will be intensively documented as they unfold.

8

The Baby Boom Generation's Enduring Legacy

• •

The profound twentieth-century phenomenon known as the post–World War II baby boom was the most influential age-related demographic event of the twentieth century, one that has left an expansive imprint on twenty-first-century New Jersey. It has been nothing less than a pivotal force throughout every single phase of its life cycle, shaping the state's economy, its built environment, and its geography during the second half of the twentieth century. Much of today's age-specific demographic attention, however, is focused on the outsized impact of millennials.[1] Although the latter's impact is proving to be very powerful, it is just starting to replicate the widespread multidimensional power displayed by the baby boom.

The Baby Boom's Unprecedented Imprint

If there has ever been a demographic tidal wave in America, it was the baby boom, the generation born 1946 to 1964. Significantly, much of current New Jersey still stands as its enduring legacy. But its origins and the life-cycle trajectory leading to its lasting imprint have not received sufficient attention. In fact, many of today's young *post*millennial New Jerseyans may simply consider the baby boom—even if they are cognizant of the historic demographic meaning of the term—as "ancients," creatures from an earlier century now long past their prime. Nonetheless, as the third decade of the twenty-first century unfolds,

New Jersey still bears a deep legacy of a generation that was initiated in 1946, more than seven decades earlier. The baby boom has not only shaped today's social and political landscape but also sculpted the physical landscape and the built environment of the state. Its physical impression was particularly vast because it was placed onto a state that had severe and widespread capacity limitations. Much of New Jersey had been a relatively blank slate as World War II came to a close. It had minimal suburban infrastructure in place—both human/organizational as well as physical—to accommodate the needs and demands of a huge new generation. Thus, at each of its life-cycle stages, vast new capacity had to be constructed for baby boomers, such as educational facilities/systems and housing inventories, because the preexisting bases were so shallow.[2] Although it is now aging—sometimes badly—this once–newly constructed capacity remains an integral part of New Jersey.

Residual Living Environments

In a postwar period of widespread housing shortages, the sprawling post–World War II suburban subdivisions (comprising Cape Cod, ranch, and split-level dwellings set on pedestrian-unfriendly street patterns dominated by cul-de-sacs) were essential to conceiving and raising many of the baby boomers. Such shelter configurations had to be quickly set in place in less than one-quarter of a century, causing a vast geographic transformation of New Jersey. Many examples of such early tract house developments still starkly dominate large swaths of suburban New Jersey that were either historically tied to New York City and Philadelphia or were located within the commuter sheds of the state's major cities. Similarly, the newly constructed garden apartments of the 1960s and 1970s facilitated baby boom household formations. Subsequently, the townhouses/condominiums that burst on the statewide scene in the 1980s and early 1990s facilitated homeownership entry. Both formats are still highly visible working parts of the state's suburban housing supply system, standing as physical residuals of the early phases of the baby boom life cycle from birth through early adulthood.

Also still prominent on the landscape stands the next historic stage of baby boom shelter consumption—the geographically dispersed array of large-lot, trade-up single-family units, the most extreme of which were outsized McMansions; many of these behemoths served as upscale millennial-centered family-raising environments. This is where turn-of-the-century "living large" excesses were concentrated, symbols of baby boom suburban shelter overconsumption that many millennials fled from as they came of age. Left behind were empty-nester baby boomers rattling around in what are now highly visible housing market laggards desperate for buyers.

Now the latest visible housing-market sectors catering to late-stage baby boomers are twenty-first-century age-restricted and life plan communities.[3] Thus, the baby boom has permanently stamped its successive phases of housing consumption on every geographic part of New Jersey.

Residual Work-Play Environments

The baby boom successively not only dominated New Jersey's multiple living environments as it traversed its life cycle but also produced lasting footprints of its favored twentieth-century work-and-play environments. At the extreme are the rapidly aging—and in some cases, the carcasses of—automobile-centric suburban office campuses that were erected in the 1980s and 1990s largely to house legions of suburban-centric baby boom white-collar workers. This office inventory now stands—if indeed it is still standing—as obsolete early postindustrial workplaces internally structured and shaped by what today are considered primitive first-stage information technology systems.

Similarly, New Jersey still has the aging—and in some cases, the forlorn—remnants of a vast landscape of impenetrable shopping fortresses known as enclosed superregional malls. The brick-and-mortar residuals of these once-vibrant cathedrals of consumption are monuments to the shopping and consumption protocols of the baby boom past.

This physical evidence—and many societal norms of today—makes it difficult to refute the fact that the baby boom was the most influential demographic event shaping the second half of the twentieth century. Much of New Jersey today—and perhaps what needs to be surmounted—is a product of the baby boom life-cycle odyssey. Thus, a historical retrospective of this expansive generation is warranted.

The Demographic Rearview Mirror: How We Got Where We Are

The era of the Great Depression—the decade of the 1930s—was not quite a demographic Death Valley, but it encompassed a period where both overall population growth and fertility in the United States and New Jersey faltered badly due to dire economic conditions. Suffice it to say that attitudinally widespread pessimism reigned, with little hope for a prosperous future.

During World War II—even though the U.S. economy had rebounded markedly due to the unprecedented scale of wartime production—the conventional economic wisdom predicted that the cessation of hostilities and the termination of massive wartime spending would cause widespread recessionary conditions to return to the United States, perhaps even depressionary conditions. Instead, the unleashing of pent-up demand for consumer goods—which had been stifled by the Depression and wartime rationing—quickly emerged, bolstered by wartime savings buildups and then by government programs such as the GI Bill.[4] This provided much more than a smooth transition to a peacetime economy. What has been called the postwar miracle ensued, one of the greatest periods of economic growth that the United States ever experienced.[5]

Similarly, demographers predicted that there would be only modest postwar population growth (Thompson and Whelpton 1943). However, paralleling the unexpected upward course of the economy, a great population growth surge ensued. Births erupted in 1946, completely overwhelming America's unprepared hospital delivery systems. Over the next eighteen years, an event of epic proportions unfolded: the fabled postwar baby boom. In retrospect, the baby boom was the collective offspring of perhaps the greatest period of fertility increases in American history.

The baby boom was vitalized by a phenomenon labeled *compression.* Those Americans who postponed marriage and children due to the tribulations of the Great Depression and World War II started to make up for lost time. This was often linked to women who, while postponing births, had become successful participants in wartime occupations. But many of their ranks were subsequently displaced or "demobilized" from such jobs when hostilities ended. In addition, their potential working futures in the civilian economy were put in jeopardy as they had to make way for returning servicemen; thus, many became available to pursue family raising, accounting in part for the immediate 1946–1947 postwar spike in births. More significantly, in many cases younger women decided not to enter the postwar labor force—or were strongly inhibited from doing so by the competition stemming from the flood of returning servicemen swelling the labor force. They married at a younger age than historically and began to start raising families immediately.[6] Such decisions by the young and less young were facilitated by a general confidence that the postwar future was destined to be one of prosperity and advancement.

Whatever the precise causal factors, the vastly oversized population cohort born between 1946 and 1964—nearly 77 million people nationwide—was the largest generation ever produced in U.S. history. It was often visually described as the "pig in the demographic python"—a huge outcropping on the nation's age-structure charts. Approximately 2.8 million babies had been born in 1945.[7] This jumped by a remarkable 20 percent to approximately 3.4 million in 1946, the start of the boom. Then, beginning in 1954, births averaged over 4.0 million per year for ten straight years (through 1964; see table 7.1 in chapter 7).

During this time span, 1957 was the all-time peak birth year, when 4.3 million boomers were born in the United States. That translates into 11,781 births per day, or 491 per hour. Drilling down further, every seven and one-half seconds another baby boomer entered America's postwar world—or eight per minute that year. If the average woman that year experienced all of the age-specific birth rates of 1957 throughout her reproductive years, which is measured by the total fertility rate, she would produce nearly 3.8 children during her lifetime.[8] To put that in perspective, the total fertility rate in the United States in 2018 was less than one-half of that—well below 1.8 (see table 7.2 in chapter 7) (Hamilton et al. 2018).

But peaks—years or periods—rarely last forever. Births then started to trend downward in 1958. Seven years later, in 1965, births fell below 4.0 million, where they would remain until 1989. When the boom technically ended in 1964—the last of the 4.0 million or more birth years—its total product represented about 40 percent of the nation's total population. This was an enormous population share—an unprecedented population bulge.

Compositionally, compared with succeeding generations—such as Gen X and millennials (Gen Y)—the baby boom was the least diverse cohort when viewed by today's more complex multiracial, multi-continent-of-origin parameters. Most baby boomers were descendants (grandchildren) of the late nineteenth- or early twentieth-century European immigration waves. Early baby boom subpopulations were often differentiated by their primary European nationalities—for example, Irish versus Italian versus German. Such metrics have less direct relevance or application in the context of today's more complex diversity segments. In retrospect, although the fertility upsurge was pervasive across many societal subgroups, the baby boom looks far more homogeneous than any successor generation.

Twentieth-Century Baby Boom Life-Cycle Stages

As the baby boom commenced, housing was immediately shaped by the requirements of child-rearing. As a result, tract house suburbia spread across America, with New Jersey one of its epicenters. This started a tidal wave of metropolitan expansion that pushed development ever outward from urban America for more than half a century.

Throughout each of its life-cycle stages, the baby boom dominated America, sending tidal waves through the economy and society. As noted earlier, one legacy of the sheer size of the population bulge was its lasting physical imprint on the state's landscape. In addition, boomers became a core marketing demographic for a vast array of consumer products as it passed through each of its life-cycle phases.

The baby boom generation lived the good life through much of its rise to full adulthood. These are some of the popular images of its twentieth-century life-cycle odyssey:

- It was originally the "hula hoop" generation in the 1950s, which overwhelmed the nation's school systems and educational plant.
- It then became the "Woodstock" generation in the 1960s, which began to inundate America's colleges and universities.
- It eventually swamped most housing and labor markets in the 1970s and then formed the "yuppie"—young upscale/urban professional—brigades as the 1980s commenced.
- "Dinks"—double (dual) income no kids—and then "dewks"—dual employed with kids—successively became widespread consumer market targets.
- "Grumpies"—grown-up mature professionals—then supplanted "yuppies" as the 1990s unfolded and the century came to an end.

Although the reality was certainly much more complex than these popular snapshots, the baby boom did dominate the changing economic and lifestyle fabric of the nation.[9] For example, as it formed households and entered the housing market, it produced what has been labeled *household differentiation*. Although this process will be discussed more fully in chapter 11, suffice it to point out here that the boomers created what were then considered unconventional living arrangements. One result was that the Census Bureau in the late 1970s designated certain unmarried couples living together as "POSSLQs"—"Persons of the Opposite Sex Sharing Living Quarters"—as it attempted to describe cohabitating households.[10] What was radical then, quickly became today's conventional/standard issue.

In any case, the baby boom was the long-standing centerpiece of a postwar suburban nation. It was largely born and then reared in automobile-centric suburbia, formed households there, worked in the newly built office agglomerations there, shopped and consumed in enclosed regional malls there, traded up in the housing market there, and ultimately reached the peak of its housing consumption there. But this suburban-centric twentieth-century legacy is now fading into history.

Shelter Eras

As noted earlier in this chapter, the baby boom left a vast residual on the built landscape of New Jersey. The dynamics of its advance through the second half of the twentieth century produced three distinct demographically driven housing eras in America, followed by a fourth in the twenty-first century. All of these were instrumental in successive transformations of the Garden State. The first era emerged in the immediate post–World War II years and lasted through about 1970. The shelter produced during this era was purchased by a population cohort that can be loosely termed The Post–World War II Nesting Generation or The Original Levittowners, which serve as defining labels for this era. "Immediately after the war, GI Joe and Rosie the Riveter married, mated, and nine months later the baby boom erupted, commencing its historic eighteen-year run. The baby boom roared; tract house suburbia emerged. Housing was largely shaped by the requirements of child-rearing. The nesting generation and its offspring transformed not only shelter configurations but housing geography as well" (Hughes and Seneca 2015, 95). Environmentally unrestricted tract house suburbia swept across New Jersey's farmlands, green fields, and woodlands.

During this era (1950–1970), young families moved into Levittown-style houses at the approximate rate of one thousand per week across New Jersey for more than one thousand straight weeks. Nothing less than a homebuilder's bacchanalia took place—nearly fifty thousand units per year were erected. The 1950s and 1960s defined the state's golden housing production era— approximately one million new housing units erected in twenty years.[11] This peak housing-production rate would never be seen again. The great engine of baby boom demography drove the high-volume production of standardized family-raising shelter for two decades, resulting in a vast homogeneous mass middle market.

The second era—"Direct Baby Boom Housing Demand"—can be partitioned into two stages. The first can be labeled First-Generation, Entry-Level Demand. By the beginning of the 1970s, the baby boom itself began to enter the housing market directly and in full force. Thus, the broad second era was powered by the offspring of the first. But the market impact of this generation's direct housing consumption was far different from that of their parents. The mass middle market of the first housing era was supplanted by market segmentation. Emerging new social values and lifestyle aspirations—including the deferral of producing offspring—generated household diversification and fragmentation. A new set of what were then considered eclectic household configurations gained prominence. Singles, mingles (that is, unmarried couples, or POSSLQs), single-parent families, and yuppies are just a few of the demographic partitions that emerged as market forces. A great household revolution redefined shelter in America and New Jersey, as new housing alternatives to detached single-family dwellings emerged to satisfy demand profiles that were no longer dominated by the imperatives of child-rearing.

During the first sub-era, garden apartments penetrated deep into the suburbs and began to change their once-dominant child-centric focus. The Garden State seemingly became the Garden Apartment State. But, the baby boom–driven transformation of suburbia did not abate. Soon, the second sub-era unfolded: "Baby Boom First-Time Homeownership." Townhouses and condominiums invaded suburbia, as housing developers began to follow a strategy of baby boom life-cycle riding—that is, catering to changing housing needs as the generation traversed successive life-cycle stages. Homeownership aspirations soared as the 1980s unfolded.

"Maturing Housing Demand" is the third era, driven by a maturing baby boom fully engaged in reproductive activities. After blazing new and revolutionary paths to first-time household formation and then to first-time homeownership, a rapidly maturing baby boom created a huge web of single-family trade-up markets in the late 1980s and 1990s. Family-rearing accommodations appropriate in scale, amenities, and ingenuity to a population cohort advancing through its peak earning years were the favored destination. Nothing less than finished machines for living were produced. In these increasingly expansive domiciles—the most commodious labeled McMansions—the baby boom produced a replica of itself; as noted earlier, their offspring originally became known as the baby boom echo, now supplanted by the overarching millennial nomenclature. Although this third housing era was mainly a late twentieth-century phenomenon, it extended into the early 2000s as America underwent an unprecedented housing and credit bubble.

Thus, each housing era of the second half of the twentieth century was driven by the successive life-cycle stages of the baby boom: birth and adolescence, young adulthood, and middle aging. Massive waves of residential construction in response to each stage's specific living requirements underpinned the sustained suburbanization of the state. So, too, with baby boom–driven ancillary work-and-play environments. Much of New Jersey's land use at the unfolding of the new century/millennium can be attributed to this fabled generation. But the legacy continued.

The Twenty-First Century

It has often been quipped that the baby boom's national pastime was trying to postpone middle age—and that it desperately tried to recast "middle age" as "middle youth." But despite such efforts, serious middle age fully landed with a vengeance in the 2000s, when boomers became increasingly seasoned. At the turn of the century, the oldest boomer had already turned fifty-four years of age. Thus, the new millennium heralded a generation whose leading edge was starting to evolve into the next life-cycle stage: mature childless households repositioning and resizing in the housing market.

By 2006, when the baby boom's leading edge reached sixty years of age, a fourth housing era—"Fully Mature Housing Demand"—was already well under way. "While mid-century boomers were still living large and driving the housing bubble of the 2000s, graying, longer-in-the-tooth leading-edge boomers started to face grandparenthood in large empty nests surrounded by big fast-growing lawns. Thus, empty nesterhood arrived in full force" (Hughes and Seneca 2015, 98). Many started to realize that their suburban shelter dream machines—their supersized McMansions—were yesterday's shelter excesses, and new accommodations were in order. Anticipating a new baby boom phase of shelter demand, builders had already started producing large inventories of suburban, age-restricted, active-adult communities. This reflected a continuation of the baby boom's long-held attachment to suburbia.

But a new geographic phase of changing boomer lifestyle preferences started to gain substantial traction in the aftermath of the Great 2007–2009 Recession—demand for less automobile-centric, more walkable residential locations with access to a wide range of activities and public transportation options. Many such locations are found in the older, developed portions of the state, not only in such urban communities that lie along the Hudson River in Hudson and Bergen Counties but also in select older suburbs with walkable downtowns and rail stations.

The post-2010 period of the twenty-first century marked the seventh decade—starting with the 1950s—of a baby boom still profoundly shaping the state's housing landscape. "Between 2010 and 2020, seniors (sixty-five years of age and older)—encompassing about one-half of the baby boom generation—will account for nearly one-half (47 percent) of the nation's total population growth. They will constitute 59 percent of the growth of the adult population (eighteen years of age and older) during this period. These percentage shares will actually increase during the subsequent decade. . . . Such shares of future population growth suggest that the baby boom will continue to flex its considerable size" (Hughes and Seneca 2015, 99).

Thus, the baby boom has not yet finished its shelter impact. Drilling down deeper into the post-2010 period, the first boomers turned sixty-five years of age in 2011, a traumatic event for them. This became popularly known as the year of the "big bang." Then, in 2016, the first boomers turned seventy years of age, an event that was far more than traumatic; in fact, it was considered a disaster of biblical proportions. Although the youngest were "just" fifty-two years of age in 2016, America's entire "sixtysomething" population cohort comprised boomers. By the end of 2018, one half of the baby boom was sixty-three years of age or older. The median age of retirement in the United States that year was sixty-three years of age. That implied that one-half of the entire baby boom generation was in retirement. Increasingly, it was starting to represent the workforce of the past—slowing down, getting more cautious, trying to adapt to cutting-edge technologies, facing retirement, and actually retiring. Paralleling this postwork transformation is the beginning of the proliferation of life plan communities, previously labeled continuing care retirement communities, as described earlier. A baby boom–*less* demographic-housing future will still not have arrived.

The aging of the entire baby boom into the senior sectors of the life cycle brings with it many other current issues that will be discussed further in chapter 13. First, a lifetime of cognitive skills has been accrued by senior boomers. Their experience, wisdom, institutional memory, and interpersonal and knowledge-based skills will not easily be replaced. It is probably little exaggeration to suggest that the aging of the baby boom out of the workforce represents one of the greatest brain drains in the nation's history. How to capture and retain the wealth of retiring boomer accumulated knowledge is a critical issue for all organizations over the decade of the 2020s.

An equally critical issue will be the sheer scale of the nation's resources that will be consumed by a baby boom in full retirement. It will have an insatiable appetite for benefits and public assistance. The potential scale of intergenerational support will be unprecedented. The baby boom will continue to exert its outsized influence.

The building of the twentieth century's modern economic engine can largely be credited to the baby boom. But that economic engine, though not yet fully obsolete, has started to be significantly disrupted. It will be reshaped and reinvented by succeeding generations. Nonetheless, the baby boom residuals will still remain, not likely to fade away anytime soon.

9

Generations X, Y, Z, and Alpha

• •

The profound shifts taking place in the age structure of the population, detailed in chapter 10, are dominated by the movements of the two generational behemoths, both of which are perched on opposite ends of the adult age spectrum. At one end is the unrelenting maturation of the baby boom. Reviewed in chapter 8, it is driving the rampant growth in America's and New Jersey's senior populations. As this inexorable aging process continues and the ranks of the retired elderly soar, the baby boom's exodus from the workforce—particularly from its leadership cadre—becomes ever more apparent. So, too, does its withdrawal from large single-family homes as it resizes itself in the housing market. In these and other sectors of the economy, voids are opening that must look to younger age cohorts as replacements.

At the other end of the age spectrum is the simultaneous maturation of millennials (Gen Y) into young and full adulthood and their full entry into the labor, housing, and other economic markets. In the first instance, the labor market, this represents a vast replenishing of the entry and mid-level workforce. From a macro labor-force perspective, the millennial inflow is roughly counterbalancing the massive baby boom outflow at the exit levels. Similarly, in aggregate housing-market terms, this represents a vast replenishment by young (destined-to-grow) rental and ownership households that is more or less supplanting mature (destined-to-shrink) households entering the final stages of the housing consumption life cycle. Similar transformations are at play in other sectors of the economy.

Although macro-level perspectives may give the impression that these are one-for-one direct substitutions keeping the overall market whole, the reality is obviously far more complex. For example, in the labor market, young millennial employees are certainly not providing direct replacements for vacancies left in the senior management ranks by retiring baby boomers. Similarly, new millennial housing-market entrants are not consuming the large single-family dwellings being vacated by baby boomers resizing to less expansive shelter. It is the intervening age cohorts that represent significant parts of the demographic transformation process. This chapter looks at these broader movements in the context of the four generations that follow the baby boom.

Generation X (Gen X)

The baby boom is just one segment of the great age-structure transformation taking place in the nation and New Jersey. But as detailed previously, this massive demographic bulge came to an end at the close of 1964 after a nineteen-year run. During 1964, the oldest baby boomers, born in 1946, turned eighteen years old, the beginning of a massive population movement into adulthood. Then, in 1965, births plummeted, a seeming paradox in the context of the vast sexual revolution that was beginning to fully unfold in America. One contributing factor to this seeming contradiction was effective birth control, facilitating the pursuit of alternative lifestyles by newly adult baby boomers. In this broader milieu, "the total fertility rate declined by nearly 50 percent between 1960 and 1973, from 3.6 to 1.9 births per woman, and changed little from then until 1982. It would appear that growing use of the pill, the IUD, and sterilization—but principally the pill—is the prime factor in the dramatic decline in unwanted and mistimed births among married couples" (Mosher 1988, 207). In addition, the Supreme Court ruled in *Griswold v. Connecticut*, a 1965 landmark case about access to contraception, that it was unconstitutional for the government to prohibit married couples from using the pill (Garrow 2011).

It was in this encompassing environment that a baby bust supplanted a baby boom. In fact, the generational result was initially called the baby bust, an undersized population cohort produced during the low-birth era from 1965 through 1980. Originally, it comprised mainly offspring of pre–baby boomers and baby boomers, but its small size in subsequent decades was bolstered by immigration. It has sometimes been called the *Sesame Street* Generation, the age group for whom an original children's television program, *Sesame Street*, was introduced in 1969 (NPR 2008). This age-defined population sector is now more commonly referred to as Gen X or Generation X. In contrast to the baby boom "outcropping," this cohort of contraction initially became a moving indentation on America's and New Jersey's age-structure charts, trailing in the wake of the huge older baby boom bulge and followed by the huge younger millennial bulge. In contrast to the baby boom, whose sheer size unleashed the dynamics of sustained expansion to accommodate it at each of its life-cycle stages, the baby bust unleashed the dynamics of shrinkage.

Expansion versus Shrinkage

For example, baby boom–inspired school-expansion issues that took place in many communities in the 1960s and 1970s were supplanted by baby bust–inspired school closing issues in the 1980s and 1990s. This is but one example of excess supply/over-capacity issues associated with the baby boom to baby bust transformation. It is also the reason why Gen X's physical impact on the state's landscape has been far less than that of the baby boom. The vast infrastructure set in place to harbor the oversized baby boom was more than sufficient to accommodate an undersized Gen X. This disparity was subsequently ameliorated somewhat by the impact of sustained international immigration following the Immigration and Nationality Act of 1965, which increased the ranks of Gen Xers in subsequent decades. It also served to ultimately increase the diversity of Gen X far beyond that of the baby boom, many of whom served as the parents of the baby bust as it was conceived.

As observed by the Pew Research Center, Gen X is America's neglected "middle child," sandwiched between those two "media-dominating" heavyweights—the huge baby boom (largely white) and millennial (far more diverse) generations. "Generation X has a gripe with pulse takers, zeitgeist keepers, and population counters. We keep squeezing them out of the frame. . . . Gen Xers are book-ended by two much larger generations—the Baby Boomers ahead and the Millennials behind—that are strikingly different from one another. And in most of the ways we take stock of generations—their racial and ethnic makeup; their political, social, and religious values; their economics and educational circumstances; their technology usage—Gen Xers are a low-slung, straight-line bridge between two noisy behemoths" (Taylor and Gao 2014).

Move Over, Boomers

But stuck-in-the-middle Gen Xers finally may have gotten their due at the tail end of the 2010s. An emerging task of vital importance to the state and nation started to fall to them: the direct replacement of boomers leaving the many societal roles that they had extensively performed since the turn of the century. More assertive members of this generation will increasingly be able to proclaim, "Move over, boomers—it's our time." In 2015, the first Gen Xers turned fifty years old, maturing into the top-line workforce. They were then poised to assume the leadership ranks left open by exiting boomers, although younger baby boomers still in their fifties were not fully ready to yield their positions to replacements at that time. Nonetheless, in organizations across New Jersey as well as in the nation, by the late 2010s older Gen Xers were starting to ascend to the C-suite, which gets its name from the titular letter *C* usually attached to the three highest-level executives in senior management—CEO (chief executive officer), CFO (chief financial officer), and COO (chief operating officer).[1] This was increasingly the case by 2020, when the leading-edge Gen Xers became fifty-five years of age and will be entirely the case during the decade that follows.[2] Succession planning in both the private and public sectors is becoming an increasing concern. A key question is how Gen X's leadership and management styles will differ from that of their baby boom predecessors.

Gen Xers and the Business Cycle

Gen X's early ascension to the top tier of the workforce occurred at a fortuitous stage of the national business cycle. Following in the wake of the Great 2007–2009 Recession, the subsequent economic expansion became the longest in American history by July 2019 (121 months at that time). So Gen X began taking the reins of the economy when business conditions had turned highly positive. Although expansions ultimately yield to recessions, the postrecession economic upswing was simply the latest intersection of Gen X and the business cycle.

The childhoods of older Gen Xers, born between 1965 and 1970, progressed through the troubled decade of the 1970s—or the "gloomy" '70s—when the nation's global economic hegemony began to be challenged, manufacturing industries declined, and two energy crises ripped the nation. But just as this troubled period followed the ebullient postwar prosperity of the 1950s and 1960s, it in turn was followed by two decades—the 1980s and 1990s—of robust employment growth. It was during this period that Gen Xers advanced through their life cycle and fully entered adulthood. Nationally, the two great expansions—1982–1990 and 1991–2001—were punctuated only by the very short and very mild 1990–1991 recession. Between 1982 and 2001, the nation's total employment increased by almost 44 million jobs.[3] Not to overstate the case, but youth, business advancement, and rising affluence led to the popular term *yuppie* to characterize successful, highly educated, professional Gen Xers. This was the proliferating demographic of that era.

So the formative years of Gen X were encapsulated by an extraordinary nineteen-year-long period of almost unwavering job growth and the full emergence of a knowledge-based, information-age economy. This period technically ended in March 2001, when another shallow recession was experienced.[4] But the economy quickly resumed growth until the advent of the Great 2007–2009 Recession. This suggests that Gen X had traversed much of its march into adulthood and beyond during an even longer period—more than one-quarter of a century (1981–2007)—that was characterized by only inconsequential economic setbacks and seemingly unrelenting positive economic news.[5] This probably accentuated and deepened the shock to Gen X that the severity of the Great Recession caused. Even a "normal" sharp downturn would have been fully uncharted territory that this group would have had to confront. Nonetheless, however it weathered the great economic storm, it subsequently was moving up through the workforce ranks in a postrecession economic expansion whose length was not only reminiscent of that of the 1980s and 1990s but surpassed it. But the economic downturn of 2020 has the potential to be a major disrupter of all previous economic expectations.

Concurrently, during the post-2009 period, Gen Xers were firmly entrenched in the family-rearing stage of the life cycle. In terms of housing dynamics, they represented the core of trade-up buyers, which led to market mismatches and distortions. This ascending cohort of contraction—even bolstered by international immigration—may not have been of sufficient size to fully absorb by itself the baby boom's expansive pool of preowned (used) suburban housing. This suggests again another example of excess capacity that may be beneficial to Gen Xers but is confronting society at large (and in this case, suburban baby boom home-sellers in particular) with problems of relative degrees of difficulty.

Millennials/Gen Y

If there were a formal set of "demographic laws," the first would probably be that "the baby boom always moves on." The Gen Y/millennial cohort was activated by what looked like the delayed discovery of procreation by baby boomers.[6] As young adults, baby boomers seemingly refused—totally and absolutely—to reproduce themselves. But eventually, they began pairing, nesting, reproducing, and parenting in earnest. What started as a baby "boomlet" exploded into a very real secondary baby boom as the 1980s matured. A potent baby boom echo resulted, with suburban New Jersey again invaded by what could be called the stroller people, replicating the streetscape phenomenon of three decades earlier.[7] This broad generation represents the second great population bulge of the twentieth century, first called echo boomers—another term retreating into history— then subsequently termed Gen Y or millennials, now the most popular usage. Like the original baby boom, they came of age in a period of rapid economic advancement. But more so, this was an age (1980–2000) when digital information technologies began to significantly reshape the workplace.

Digital-Age Advances and Demographics

The very definition of Gen Y/millennials, as noted earlier, has been predicated on the logic that this was the first population cohort born and raised in the rapidly advancing digital age (1980–2000). Indeed, the informational- and computational-technology progress made during this two-decade period has proved to be nothing less than transformative to all dimensions of society, and it has been instrumental in shaping the population cohort now known as the millennial generation. These achievements thus warrant a brief overview.

By 1980, the Apple II—the first highly successful mass-produced personal computer—was already three years old. But the next year (1981), the IBM PC was introduced; it was the IBM brand that further legitimized the placement of the personal computer on corporate America's desktops.[8] At its heart was the Intel 8088 microprocessor chip, which had a transistor count of 29,000. To put that in perspective, it is useful to fast forward to 2017, when the Apple iPhone X had a microprocessor with 4.3 billion transistors.[9] But however quaint and limited was the power of the 8088 microprocessor by today standards, 1981's IBM PC ultimately proved metamorphic and laid the foundational groundwork of a revolution that would reshape workplace and American life.

In 1986, Intel surpassed itself and introduced the 80386 microprocessor, which contained 275,000 transistors and more than one million electronic components. This increased capability led to the first major advance in desktop functionality, driven by the widespread adoption of the first killer application (or killer app) tailored specifically to the IBM PC—the Lotus 1-2-3 spreadsheet.[10] This quickly became the industry standard, further propelling the success of the IBM PC and further changing and refining basic white-collar work processes.[11]

Then, in 1995, Intel's Pentium Pro microprocessor—containing 5.5 million transistors—provided another advance in desktop personal computer capability.[12] Along with the implementation of widespread fiber-optic cabling throughout America, Pentium-based computers became a window onto the internet. Concurrently, Microsoft released Windows 95, then its latest operating system, and introduced Internet Explorer, which became many people's first web browser. These advances turned out to be another game changer. By 2000, increasingly powerful desktop computers were disrupting and reshaping the very structure of knowledge-based work.[13]

It was this two-decade period of remarkable digital advances that millennials were born into and were subsequently raised in. Compared with their somewhat reluctant baby boom elders, they embraced this new information technology world as it continued to progress. After the turn of the century, when the first millennials began to enter the labor force, they were technologically attuned to evolving workplaces that were adapting to the new digital frontiers.

But the relentless odometer of technological history never pauses or stops. When the mobile-untethered smartphone era unfolded in 2007 with the introduction of the iPhone, millennials constituted the first vast number of adopters. They were the digital front-runners of an era that suddenly started to fully unshackle workers from fixed-in-place information-technology systems. It was the Pentium 4 microprocessor, containing 125 million transistors, that initially shaped this mobile-internet-untethered period. Subsequently, in the years that immediately followed, such digital advances as tablets and iPads (2010), successively more powerful laptops and ultrabooks (2011), and 4G LTE (2011–2012) high-speed wireless broadband communications capabilities further disrupted the workplace of the past as they helped reshape knowledge-based work protocols and where that work can take place. Demographically, many baby boomers initially struggled to adapt to these disruptions, while most millennials flourished and thrived.[14] But baby boomers were no strangers to technological advancement and change. In fact, a closer look suggests that the digital age's origins can be found decades earlier.

A Possible Baby Boom Rejoinder

Intergenerational tensions have always been an ever-present reality. And the baby boom is probably not sanguine about any assumptions or assertions of millennial digital distinctiveness. In fact, it is not impossible for the baby boom to claim it was the first generation impacted by the digital revolution, not millennials. The more stalwart baby boom advocates could make the argument that what millennials actually experienced was digital era 2.0 and that it was the baby boom generation that was enmeshed earlier in what could be considered digital era 1.0. Whatever the full merits of such assertions, the digital world did first open during the baby boom's peak birth years. But what opened up was a much earlier revolution—a period of digital infancy.

The first portable transistor radio was introduced when the oldest boomers were turning eight years of age, almost three decades before the introduction of the IBM PC. On October 18, 1954, the Regency TR-1 transistor radio hit the consumer market and launched the portable electronic age, marking a turning point from analog to digital. The TR-1 was a handheld device that was five inches high by four inches wide, and it weighed just twelve ounces. It could be considered the distant ancestor of today's iPods and iPhones, an earlier technological breakthrough, even though its scale was extremely modest. The TR-1 had a total of only *four* transistors compared with the billions in the latest smartphones. Still, it was the cutting-edge, advanced product in 1954, utilizing printed circuit boards and then-state-of-the art micro-components.

With the transistor radio, music and information suddenly became mobile. News of the world was available anyplace, and young baby boomers could listen to music and news unrestricted by controlling adults and elders. The subsequent proliferation of transistor radios helped spark a music revolution known as rock and roll and helped spawn subsequent cultural movements. "In a burst of post–World War II innovation, the transistor radio with music for your pocket fueled a teenage social revolution" (Romm 2014).[15]

Thus, this first stage of the digital revolution influenced the basic fabric of baby boom life, just as its later stages influenced millennial life. But its impacts on the workplace, on a nascent knowledge-based economy, and on white-collar work processes prove difficult to find. Then, in the 1970s, when the baby boom was entering the labor force en masse, the introduction of the first handheld portable pocket electronic calculator expanded the math capabilities of everyone and provided mobile computational capabilities.[16] This had a more substantial impact on work processes ("Electronic Calculators—Handheld" n.d.). And although empirical evidence is lacking, baby boomers probably were the leading adopters of this digital technology.

So the baby boom may have a legitimate claim as being the first generation shaped by the unfolding of the digital age. The parallels between the iPhone and the transistor radio (and then handheld digital calculators) are substantial, with both untethering users from fixed-in-place systems. This "lends credence to the old adage 'the more things change, the more they stay the same'" (Romm 2014). Still, the baby boom struggled to keep pace with millennials as digital era 2.0 transpired.

The Garden State Effect

As a complete aside, the early digital era—and the advances that followed—had unique ties to the Garden State. It was in December 1947 that the transistor was successfully demonstrated at the Bell Labs headquarters in Murray Hill, New Jersey. As a result, the three scientists at Bell Labs credited with the transistor's discovery/invention received the Nobel Prize in Physics in 1956. Bell Labs was the research and development wing of American Telephone and Telegraph (AT&T); its many facilities in New Jersey were often dubbed genius factories. "In the decades before the country's best minds began migrating west to California's Silicon Valley, many of them came east to New Jersey, where they worked in capacious brick-and-glass buildings located on grassy campuses.... At the peak of its reputation in the late 1960s, Bell Labs employed about fifteen thousand people, including some twelve hundred PhDs. Its ranks included the world's most brilliant (and eccentric) men and women. In a time before Google, the Labs sufficed as the country's intellectual utopia. It was where the future, which is what we now happen to call the present, was conceived and designed" (Gertner 2012, 1). The transistor, the laser, digital communications, and cellular telephony all emerged from Bell Labs and are the technological foundations of the information age that ultimately shaped millennials. Thus, suburban New Jersey can take credit as being instrumental in transforming, nationally and globally, twentieth- and twenty-first-century digitally influenced demographics.

Millennials and the Business Cycle

The emergence of millennials and the rapid advancement of the digital age occurred during the robust employment-growth periods of the 1980s and 1990s. Subsequently, the oldest millennials entered college age and adulthood during the 2001–2007 economic expansion. Thus, relatively smooth economic sailing was the constant to that point. But in December 2007, the Great 2007–2009 Recession began its harsh journey. Many millennials were entering the labor market during the worst economic downturn since the Great Depression, which set back some career trajectories. Household formation, marriage, and family-rearing were also deferred.

The Great Recession ultimately translated into long-lasting wealth impacts across all age cohorts, but they were most severe for young families, households, and individuals. According to analyses by the Federal Reserve Bank of St. Louis (2018), "the 1980s cohort is at greatest risk of becoming a 'lost generation' for wealth accumulation."[17] A key question is whether the economic trauma that unfolded in 2008 and lasted well past its official end in 2009 will have the same long-term impact on millennials as the 1929 stock market crash and the Great Depression had on the 1930s' population cohorts that experienced it directly. The latter may or may not have lost substantial wealth during the Great Depression; nonetheless, they may have lagged in accumulating assets during the boom years of the 1950s and 1960s, perhaps due to lingering doubts about the stock market and ultraconservative financial choices.

Lost recession/postrecession earning years experienced by millennials, or post-recession under-earning years, may have spawned lasting economic insecurity and hindered asset accumulations necessary to ultimately pursue homeownership. Added to this impediment are the issues of student debt, covered extensively in the popular media, and stricter postrecession lending standards, both of which may also have underpinned delayed millennial household formation and homeownership (Kitroeff 2018). All of these factors contributed to the surging postrecession growth of rental households and stagnation of owner households at both the national and state levels.

Post–Great Recession Millennials

By 2014—five years into the postrecession economic expansion—millennials (then between eighteen and thirty-three years of age) surpassed the baby boom in share of the American workforce (aged eighteen and over); by 2015, they surpassed Generation X as the largest sector of the workforce. (In 2012, Gen Xers had surpassed boomers in workforce share [Fry 2015]. But their dominance proved to be short-lived.)

During this period (the 2010s), millennials had become the prized labor force commodity, eagerly sought by a corporate America that increasingly required digital talent. Increasingly, where that talent wanted to be started to drive corporate locational decision-making. Millennials have been totally reinventing New Jersey's economic and shelter landscapes—redefining the workplace, reshaping workplace location, and transforming the geography of housing demand. They have been replicating the impact—although quite differently—that the predecessor baby boom had made when it entered adulthood.

In contrast to automobile-centric suburban environs, many millennials prefer 24/7 live-work-play (LWP) environments—not plain-vanilla suburban domiciles but often edgy, authentic, and experiential environments. Developers and locational specialists labeled the most talented and highly skilled millennials as the "digerati," who were at the forefront of the new lifestyle preferences. In contrast to the baby boom, which was instrumental in establishing twentieth-century suburban locational preferences, millennials have been instrumental in fundamentally reinventing the geographic norms of the twenty-first century.

Throughout the second decade of the twenty-first century—despite the rise in the number of young adults living with their parents (Fry 2017)—millennials' spatial movements across the state could be described simply as sprawl withdrawal, exiting rural, exurban, and suburban jurisdictions for the millennial-cool, urban-centric environments. But as the decade came to a close, older millennials were getting married and starting to reproduce. In fact, the era of millennials in the family-rearing stage of the household life cycle has commenced, an era that will prevail during the third decade of the century. Their postrecession shelter choices and workplace locational preferences have already been restructuring the state and region. Will their preferences change in the unfolding era? Will their financial capabilities be sufficient to vigorously pursue homeownership, particularly in relationship to student debt levels (Chakrabarty et al. 2017)? Will the burbs bounce back? Will there be sharp suburban differentiation, as millennials may want a different type of suburban landscape (Berger 2017)? These are key questions that remain to be answered.

Moreover, millennials have also reshaped, and are continuing to reshape, the economy in other profound ways. One dimension is the shift in the nation's consumer spending behavior—the choosing of experiences over goods, a trend that has been driven by millennials. "Personal-consumption expenditures (PCE) on experience-related services—such as attending spectator events, visiting amusement parks, eating at restaurants, and traveling—have grown more than 1.5 times faster than overall consumption spending and nearly 4.0 times faster than consumer goods. . . . Consumers of all ages are opting for experiences, with millennials leading the charge" (Goldman, Marchessou, and Teichner 2017).

There has been a vast proliferation of such market analyses detailing the shift to the experiential economy. Not surprisingly, the sometime passionate search for unique experiences by millennials has given rise to the acronym YOLO (You Only Live Once) generation (Ganatra 2017). It may be an over-generalization, but it has been asserted by marketers that the goods-accumulation passion of earlier generations has been supplanted by millennial-led experience-accumulation passion. Such behavioral shifts, along with information technology facilitation, underscore the severe problems afflicting brick-and-mortar retailing during the second half of the second decade of the current century. While the baby boom was once one of the driving forces of the "malling" of New Jersey, millennials have become one of the driving forces of the "demalling" of New Jersey.

As the third decade of the twenty-first century unfolds, the great age-structure transformation will increasingly be dominated by the many decisions and choices made by millennials. Along with the sustained diversification of the state's population, detailed in chapter 4, this will be a primary determinant of New Jersey's demographic and economic future.

Postmillennials/Gen Z

As noted in chapter 7, this book has adopted the 2018 Pew determination of postmillennials, which specifies 1997 as the starting year of this generation. But Pew has yet to establish a definitive year when it ended. To be consistent with the sixteen-year age span of Gen X and Gen Y, the year 2012 has been adopted as the "work-in-progress" end point for postmillennials, with the full recognition that further research may serve to alter this selection.

It is often observed that older generations tend to complain about younger generations and that the latter must experience and submit to such rites of passage. Millennials suffered such indignities as to their "radical" choice of residence and their workplace habits and preferences. Such behaviors were initially very foreign to what many baby boomers considered "certainties," and uneasiness still lingers. For example, many baby boomers are still uncomfortable with the workplace accommodations that have been made for millennials. But their discomfort will not abate. They will soon have to make new accommodations, as Gen Z will eventually be the latest target of intergenerational bashing. "Eventually" will soon be arriving, as Gen Z becomes the current entry-level workforce.

In 1997, the first Gen Zer was born. This was when the proliferation of Pentium-based computers and the widespread adoption of the internet had already been under way for two years. Thus, the total Gen Z experience was a world where advancing digital information technology and the internet were intensifying their impact on all dimensions of society in the nation and in New Jersey. In 2007, when the smartphone and mobile internet connectivity became the new innovative frontier, the oldest postmillennial was only ten years old, not long past the post-toddler stage of the life cycle. In the ensuing decade, despite the economic setbacks of the Great 2007–2009 Recession, adolescent—and younger—New Jerseyans could not avoid being engulfed by an era of mobile digital technology and an era of social media.[18] Gen Y has thus grown up with access and connectivity to everything, everywhere.

In the late 1980s, when birth and fertility fluctuations appeared to be principal factors in generation delineations, the collective offspring of a small Gen X (baby bust) was supposed to amount to a baby bust echo—a secondary small generation. This would have been a parallel development to the baby boom producing Gen Y (millennials)—a baby boom echo. But due to immigration and a slight bump in fertility, this size expectation did not materialize. Thus, the term *baby bust echo* was rendered obsolete. Instead, another peaking of births occurred in the first decade of the twenty-first century, the core years of Gen Z.

In 2010, when economic recovery and expansion gained momentum, the first postmillennials became teenagers (thirteen years old), while the last had yet to be born. For the balance of the decade of the 2010s, when economic growth prevailed throughout the nation and state, all postmillennials were passing through, or had just passed through, the state's K–12 educational system. Certainly, school systems have had to continually adapt since the onslaught of the baby boom more than sixty years earlier. But the more recent imperative is to adapt to the widespread presence of smartphones in their classrooms and their students' seemingly habitual need to socially connect via digital technology, as well as to a new threshold level of racial and ethnic diversity.

The introduction of the smartphone and unfettered connectivity represents fundamental structural—and perhaps disruptive—change, the latest in a series of technological shocks. In contrast, racial and ethnic diversity represents more of a long-term transformation with many antecedents. Most educational systems are not confronting major short-term diversity shocks but instead are adapting to gradual, sustained change in their constituent student bodies for more than one-half century. Sequentially, Gen X was more diverse than the baby boom, millennials were more diverse than the members of Gen X, and most recently, postmillennials are/were more diverse than millennials. Thus, there has been—or should have been—a multidecade period of adjustment to the long-term trajectory of racial and demographic change.

Unlike the baby boom, Gen X, and millennials, the generational essence of postmillennials has yet to be fully distilled, if there is such a thing as a singular generational essence, nor has one been scholarly determined. They are still the least defined and scholarly analyzed of the many generations under scrutiny here. As noted above, millennial behavior and preferences—in the context of the impact of digital advances—did instigate fundamental change in the workplace, workplace location, and residential geography. This represented a radical departure from earlier baby boom protocols that dominated the twentieth century. A key question is whether Gen Z (postmillennials) will ultimately spawn equivalent fundamental changes as the twenty-first century advances, or whether they will initiate only modest changes that largely follow in the footsteps of the new "norms" established by millennials. In the latter case, after drastically reinventing themselves to cope with intersecting millennial and digital-technology challenges, will workplaces find it much easier to adapt to potentially more muted postmillennial essentials?

One of the most influential societal changes associated with millennials was highly visible on New Jersey's physical demographic landscape: millennial-driven higher-density urban resurgence and lower-density suburban malaise. This represented another major disruption to twentieth-century baby boom norms. Is it possible that Gen Z will ultimately return to the suburban-centric posture of the baby boom, or will it maintain the urban-centric preferences of millennials?

As was the case for earlier generations, severe business-cycle swings occurring at specific life-cycle stages have had the ability to shape long-term economic frames of reference and future attitudes and behaviors. How influential was, and will be, the Great Recession on impressionable young Gen Z postmillennial children if they closely observed its negative impact on their parents and/or older siblings? What will this mean to their lifetime thinking on the economy, and their resulting workplace behavior? As noted several times in this book, the Great 2007–2009 Recession, as the second decade of the twenty-first century came an end, was the worst global economic downturn since the Great Depression. The children of the Great Depression exhibited economic conservatism and financial reticence during much of their lifetimes, despite some extraordinary long and powerful economic expansions. Will history repeat itself? Or, since postmillennials were still some distance from entering the workforce and their career trajectories—unlike those of their millennial predecessors—were not directly interrupted by the Great Recession, will its long-term impact be far more muted? A related question is whether the economic downturn of early 2020 will prove to be another "game-changing" event.

Generation Alpha

This is the first demographic cohort where every member was born in the twenty-first century. Thus, the tentative name of alpha—the first letter of the Greek alphabet—certainly serves as an appropriate, if preliminary, moniker. Since alphas were born in the second decade of the twenty-first century (post-2012), the receding twentieth century will probably seem like ancient history to them. This is not surprising, since many alphas will be children of millennials—the last generation born totally in the twentieth century—and they will also be either grandchildren (oldest alphas) or even great-grandchildren (youngest alphas) of the increasingly "ancient" baby boom, the mid-twentieth-century colossus.[19]

Gen Alpha's cutting-edge position in the extended post–World War II generational pantheon will certainly give it a different and unique frame of reference. For example, the time gap (forty-five years) between Gen Alpha in 2020 and the end of the Vietnam War (1975) is greater in length than the gap (forty-two years) between the baby boom in 1960 and the end of World War I (1918). Even the tragic events of the terrorist attacks of 9/11 (2001) will be as distant (nineteen years) from alphas in 2020 as the end of World War II (1945) was to the baby boom in 1964 (nineteen years). Thus, events that may have great relevance to one generation can be historical footnotes to a following generation.

When the first alpha was born (2013), births and fertility rates in the United States were strongly trending downward (see tables 7.1 and 7.2 in chapter 7). In 2018, for example, births nationally fell below 3.8 million (down from over 4.3 million in 2007), and the total fertility rate fell to 1.7 (down from over 2.1 in 2007). Consequently, Gen Alpha is destined to be the smallest generation since the baby bust (Gen X), and it will be immersed in a new demographic era—a more "old-than-young" society. In 2019, a transformational demographic event took place: The number of Americans over sixty years of age surpassed the number of people under eighteen years of age. How will the new "minority young" be impacted by the dawn of a grayer America? Will alphas be viewed as a scarce commodity that will be generously nurtured in order to challenge a workforce-short economic future? Or will the needs of alphas be overshadowed by an older America consuming a disproportionate share of society's resources? At a minimum, the prospect of a new era of population growth stagnation, if realized, and a complementary period of an aging America, have the potential to help forge and mold Gen Alpha as the century advances.

Another notable first for this cohort is that it is the first generation that was not alive when smartphones, tablets, and always-on instantaneous connectivity did not exist. While Gen Y and Gen Z quickly adapted to this new technological world as it emerged, it was already Gen Alpha's encompassing world at birth. What was once cutting edge and "new" quickly became commonplace and "assumed." But the subsequent era of artificial intelligence, robotics, and even more advanced interconnectiveness, just under way, is destined to define the new "new," which will further shape Gen Alpha as it proceeds through its early life-cycle stages.

Other generational-molding events are in force, but their impact is not yet fully realized or defined. An even higher level of diversity will characterize Gen Alpha, continuing a long-established trend of successively more diverse generations. And the business cycle, an instrumental force shaping the lives of past generations, will not be abolished anytime soon. Alphas, through the end of 2019, experienced only positive economic times, being enveloped by the longest upcycle in American history—that is, an expansion that, as noted earlier, reached a then-record 121 months in length in July 2019. But a downcycle of undetermined magnitude started early in 2020. Future analysts will have to make the determination of how such an economic event will shape this generation. So, too, will future analysts have the task of specifying its full temporal span. Any attempt to calibrate even an approximate terminal boundary of Gen Alpha and the emergence of its successor is still way too premature. To say the least, Generation Alpha remains a work in progress.

10

Generations and Age-Structure Transformations

• •

The age structure of a population is simply the division of the total population into specific age segments/sectors at a specific point in time. These age segments are not uniform in size since they reflect different historical reproduction rates and migration patterns.[1] To cite the obvious examples, surging fertility rates following World War II produced the outsized baby boom cohort which, as it matured, sequentially moved through the age-structure sectors, causing bulges in each.[2] Similarly, post-boom plunges in the fertility rate yielded a baby bust (Gen X) that, as it matured, generated a moving, undersized age cohort. The bulge and indentation caused by these two generations became permanent, moving age-structure features over time, modified by migration flows into and out of the state. Thus, age-structure analyses historically have had reasonable predictive capacity for planning and policy purposes—future growth or decline of different age groups was readily apparent.

Shifts in age structure over time impact many societal dimensions, such as K–12 school enrollments, demand for higher education, workforce size and its age composition, age-linked housing market sectors, age-dependent commercial/consumption markets, and innumerable others. The earliest (now oldest) postwar generations—the baby boom and Gen X—dominated the largest age-structure disruptions that took place in New Jersey, as they did in the nation, during the second half of the twentieth century and beyond.

Thus, the generations presented in this book are captured in the age profiles presented in this chapter, and generational aging is revealed by changes in those profiles over time.[3] To return to the obvious example cited above, this was particularly evident during the decade of the 1970s when the aging of the baby boom (born 1946 to 1964) into adulthood swelled the ranks of the population between twenty-five and thirty-five years of age, while at the same time Generation X or baby bust (born 1965 to 1980) sharply reduced the size of the young, under-ten-years-old population (see table 10.3). These firmly established cohorts subsequently journeyed over time through successively older population age brackets with significant ramifications for society and the economy. In this chapter, these shifts will be examined decade by decade, along with brief commentary on how they have impacted New Jersey.

The 1950–1960 Period

Unprecedented growth in the state's youngest population dominated the decade of the 1950s. The principal culprit was the baby boom (chapter 8); the vast scope of its impact was immediately apparent. Between 1950 and 1960, the state's decadal population growth (more than 1.2 million people, or 25.5 percent) was and remains an all-time historical record (table 10.1). As was detailed in earlier chapters, this growth had two key dimensions. The first was the great wave of suburbanization out of New York City and Philadelphia to New Jersey's burgeoning child-rearing environments, less affectionately known as tract house suburbia. The second, of greater magnitude, was the baby boom itself, produced in the new shelter accommodations.

In 1960, the baby boom's oldest member was fourteen years of age while the youngest had yet to be born. Thus, every member of the state's population under fifteen years old was a baby boomer. The three youngest age brackets in table 10.1—under five years, five to nine years, and ten to fourteen years—were the only sectors in 1960 to contain more than one-half million persons. The 1950–1960 growth of the three sectors combined totaled 627,513 people, slightly more than one-half of the state's total population increase (1,231,453 people). At the leading edge was the ten-to-fourteen-years-old sector; it had not only the greatest absolute (233,836 people) increase but also an unprecedented 80.5 percent rate of increase. The attendant stress on New Jersey's education system caused by this age-structure bulge had reached nothing less than a fever pitch.

The Depression-era birth dearth (those born between 1930 and 1945) was between twenty and thirty years of age in 1960.[4] During the preceding decade (1950–1960), the population in the age sectors between twenty and twenty-four years (−8.4 percent) as well as between twenty-five and twenty-nine years (−11.6 percent) had contracted between 1950 and 1960, yielding a reduction in the state's young adult population. This decline in "normal" times would have

Table 10.1
New Jersey Age Structure, 1950–1960

	1950	1960	Change: 1950–1960	
			Number	Percent (%)
New Jersey Total	4,835,329	6,066,782	1,231,453	25.5
Under 5 years	458,906	642,197	183,291	39.9
5–9 years	371,826	582,212	210,386	56.6
10–14 years	290,544	524,380	233,836	80.5
15–19 years	295,859	396,363	100,504	34.0
20–24 years	350,403	321,054	(29,349)	(8.4)
25–29 years	409,890	362,373	(47,517)	(11.6)
30–34 years	409,434	435,080	25,646	6.3
35–39 years	393,917	472,429	78,512	19.9
40–44 years	357,760	446,139	88,379	24.7
45–49 years	318,504	406,721	88,217	27.7
50–54 years	305,235	350,531	45,296	14.8
55–59 years	263,516	304,112	40,596	15.4
60–64 years	215,546	262,777	47,231	21.9
65–69 years	164,921	222,457	57,536	34.9
70–74 years	109,441	163,149	53,708	49.1
75–84 years	101,632	146,832	45,200	44.5
85 years and over	17,995	27,976	9,981	55.5

SOURCE: U.S. Census Bureau, decennial census.

received overwhelming attention; however, it was overshadowed in a decade when the intense focus was generally directed at the extraordinary growth in young school-aged children. Nonetheless, it was noticeable in its labor market impact. The size of the entry-level workforce pool—which included potential young teachers and others who would service the baby boom—contracted as the economy boomed.[5] To the benefit of the young adult "birth dearth," which was born during the severe economic travails of the 1930s, the huge baby boom–driven economic expansion of the 1950s did provide great—but previously unanticipated—employment opportunities.

The Decade of the 1960s

Teenagers and young adults dominated demographic change during the 1960s. Overall, this ten-year period marked the second straight decade of extraordinary population increases in New Jersey (table 10.2). The absolute 1960–1970 population gain (+1.1 million people) nearly matched that achieved during the 1950s (+1.2 million people), although the 1960s' growth rate was about one-quarter less (18.2 percent versus 25.5 percent) because of the expanding population base. Highly visible within this continued growth surge was the baby boom bulge unabashedly exiting toddlerhood and marching into young

Table 10.2
New Jersey Age Structure, 1960–1970

	1960	1970	Change: 1960–1970	
			Number	Percent (%)
New Jersey Total	6,066,782	7,171,112	1,104,330	18.2
Under 5 years	642,197	589,266	(52,931)	(8.2)
5–9 years	582,212	692,648	110,436	19.0
10–14 years	524,380	710,409	186,029	35.5
15–19 years	396,363	611,831	215,468	54.4
20–24 years	321,054	509,198	188,144	58.6
25–29 years	362,373	463,164	100,791	27.8
30–34 years	435,080	403,475	(31,605)	(7.3)
35–39 years	472,429	413,929	(58,500)	(12.4)
40–44 years	446,139	465,492	19,353	4.3
45–49 years	406,721	477,978	71,257	17.5
50–54 years	350,531	439,103	88,572	25.3
55–59 years	304,112	380,677	76,565	25.2
60–64 years	262,777	314,045	51,268	19.5
65–69 years	222,457	245,757	23,300	10.5
70–74 years	163,149	194,112	30,963	19.0
75–84 years	146,832	209,210	62,378	42.5
85 years and over	27,976	47,910	19,934	71.3

SOURCE: U.S. Census Bureau, decennial census.

adulthood. By 1970, the baby boom was between six and twenty-four years of age. The four largest age-structure sectors in the state that year were those five to nine years old (692,648 people), ten to fourteen years old (710,409 people), fifteen to nineteen years old (611,831 people), and twenty to twenty-four years old (509,198 people). A highly visible "protrusion" in the structural profile had been set in play.

In contrast, the 1960–1970 age-structure changes also revealed the emergence of a second undersized generation in the state: the baby bust (Gen X)—born between 1965 and 1980. During the decade of the 1960s, the earliest members of Gen X caused an 8.2 percent decline (−52,931 people) in the under-five-years-of-age sector. Similarly, the aging of the Depression-era cohort—all "thirtysome-things" by 1970—resulted in the shrinkage in the thirty-to-thirty-four-years-old (−7.3 percent) and thirty-five-to-thirty-nine-years-old (−12.4 percent) age sectors between 1960 and 1970. Standing in sharp contrast were the age groups that the baby boom had matured into, with the highest growth rates registered by the fifteen-to-nineteen-years-old (+54.4 percent) and twenty-to-twenty-four-years old (+58.6 percent) sectors. Thus, the three generations—the Depression-era birth dearth, the baby boom, and Gen X, whose very definitions were premised by his-torical changes in fertility rates and birth totals—were firmly embedded in the state's age-structure data by 1970.

The decade saw leading-edge boomers enter their college-age years. Generational-linked expansionary pressures once felt most heavily by K–12 education systems in New Jersey were now starting to be felt by its institutions of higher education.[6] The oldest boomers were also beginning to enter and subsequently swell the labor force; they also started to directly enter the housing market in full force as they began to move into the household-formation stage of the life cycle.

The Challenging 1970s

The age-structure changes in the 1970s were marked by a surging young adult population between twenty and thirty-four years of age, sandwiched between two contracting sectors—the youngest New Jerseyans under fifteen years old and a more mature population group approaching middle age (forty to forty-nine years old). Three generations began to more fully shape the demography of the state and the many issues confronting it.

As described in earlier chapters, the decade of the 1970s subjected New Jersey to many economic challenges which had significant demographic repercussions. The overall population growth rate of the state between 1970 and 1980 plummeted to just 2.7 percent (table 10.3). After New Jersey grew by more than

Table 10.3
New Jersey Age Structure, 1970–1980

	1970	1980	Change: 1970–1980 Number	Change: 1970–1980 Percent (%)
New Jersey Total	7,171,112	7,365,011	193,899	2.7
Under 5 years	589,266	463,289	(125,977)	(21.4)
5–9 years	692,648	508,447	(184,201)	(26.6)
10–14 years	710,409	605,481	(104,928)	(14.8)
15–19 years	611,831	670,665	58,834	9.6
20–24 years	509,198	614,828	105,630	20.7
25–29 years	463,164	574,135	110,971	24.0
30–34 years	403,475	563,758	160,283	39.7
35–39 years	413,929	479,749	65,820	15.9
40–44 years	465,492	400,074	(65,418)	(14.1)
45–49 years	477,978	394,038	(83,940)	(17.6)
50–54 years	439,103	432,520	(6,583)	(1.5)
55–59 years	380,677	430,048	49,371	13.0
60–64 years	314,045	367,660	53,615	17.1
65–69 years	245,757	303,670	57,913	23.6
70–74 years	194,112	227,037	32,925	17.0
75–84 years	209,210	256,833	47,623	22.8
85 years and over	47,920	72,231	24,321	50.8

SOURCE: U.S. Census Bureau, decennial census.

2.3 million people between 1950 and 1970 (tables 10.1 and 10.2), fewer than 200,000 people were added between 1970 and 1980 (table 10.3). Within the United States, New Jersey went from one of its demographic dynamos (1950–1970) to one of its demographic laggards (1970–1980)—from "go-go" to "slow-go"! Positive net migration into the state withered, while births and fertility rates plunged to postwar lows.

Within this new slow-go environment, Gen X (the baby bust) began to etch deeper into the state's demographic fabric. By 1980, the age span of this generation was between "just born" and sixteen years old; everyone in the first three youngest categories of table 10.3 was what was then called a buster. Their decline between 1970 and 1980 produced a marked age-structure indent: The population under five years of age declined by 21.4 percent, the five-to-nine-years-old population fell by 26.6 percent, while the ten-to-fourteen-year-olds lost 14.8 percent (table 10.3). In total, the number of New Jerseyans under fifteen years old dropped by 415,106 people during the decade. Suddenly, there were empty "pupil stations" (desks and chairs) in many of the state's elementary schools. Excess capacity became a new postwar phenomenon. This caused a fundamental reset of the growth mentality that had prevailed in the two preceding decades. The emerging problems centered on redundant infrastructures, previous capacity over-expansions, and shrinking economic sectors.

The loss in population in the state's youngest tiers took place despite the burgeoning of the most fertile age sectors of the population—that is, the maturing baby boom was settling into its prime reproductive years. But surprisingly at the time, it was neglecting to reproduce itself. In 1980, the baby boom was between sixteen and thirty-four years of age. Between 1970 and 1980, the thirty-to-thirty-four-years-of-age sector expanded by 39.7 percent, the twenty-five-to-twenty-nine-years-of-age sector gained 24.0 percent, and the twenty-to-twenty-four-years-of-age sector grew by 20.7 percent. The three combined experienced a population increase of 376,884 people. Thus, the state's entry-level and young labor force was expanding rapidly, placing pressure on the state's economy to absorb a baby boom almost entirely of workforce age. Concurrent was pressure on New Jersey's housing industry to provide appropriate shelter for surging household formations and for first-time homeownership.

The aging of the Depression-era birth dearth—between forty and fifty years old in 1980—was also evident in the contracting middle portions of the age structure (table 10.3). Between 1970 and 1980, those forty to forty-four years old declined by 14.1 percent (−65,418 people) and those forty-five to forty-nine years old fell by 17.6 percent (−83,940 people). The pool of aspirants for upper-level positions in the economy was thus becoming shallower. This contrasted sharply with an expanding young labor force supply (the baby boom) confronting a slow-growth economy (see chapters 3, 5, and 8). Most evident during the challenged economy of the 1970s was a shrinkage in demand for more teachers in the state's elementary schools as the decade advanced.

Table 10.4
New Jersey Age Structure, 1980–1990

	1980	1990	Change: 1980–1990	
			Number	Percent (%)
New Jersey Total	7,365,011	7,730,188	365,177	5.0
Under 5 years	463,289	532,637	69,348	15.0
5–9 years	508,447	493,044	(15,403)	(3.0)
10–14 years	605,481	480,983	(124,498)	(20.6)
15–19 years	670,665	505,388	(165,277)	(24.6)
20–24 years	614,828	566,594	(48,234)	(7.8)
25–29 years	574,135	668,917	94,782	16.5
30–34 years	563,758	691,734	127,976	22.7
35–39 years	479,749	622,963	143,214	29.9
40–44 years	400,074	573,696	173,622	43.4
45–49 years	394,038	466,481	72,443	18.4
50–54 years	432,520	376,528	(55,992)	(12.9)
55–59 years	430,048	355,677	(74,371)	(17.3)
60–64 years	367,660	363,521	(4,139)	(1.1)
65–69 years	303,670	340,232	36,562	12.0
70–74 years	227,037	269,960	42,923	18.9
75–84 years	256,833	326,286	69,453	27.0
85 years and older	72,231	95,547	23,316	32.3

SOURCE: U.S. Census Bureau, decennial census.

The 1980–1990 Transformation

Robust growth in the number of pre-middle-aged adults between thirty and forty-four years of age, contraction in the number of more mature middle-aged adults fifty to fifty-nine years old, and shrinkage in the school-aged population defined the key demographic narrative of the decade of the 1980s (table 10.4). This took place while New Jersey experienced renewed total population growth (+5.0 percent) that was almost double the 2.7 percent increase of the 1970s (table 10.3), but it still paled behind the rates of the 1950s (25.3 percent) and 1960s (18.3 percent). The three generations—the Depression-era birth dearth, the baby boom, and Gen X—still dominated the 1980–1990 age-structure changes. Thus, the generational framework was still largely the province of the three cohorts defined by changes in reproductive activity, since there was just scant evidence of a baby boom echo (Gen Y) that was once highly anticipated. But this decade marked the start of the attenuation of such fluctuations, a process that would continue into the next century.

In 1990, the baby boom was between twenty-six and forty-four years of age; between 1980 and 1990, its maturation led to the number of people thirty to thirty-four years old increasing by 22.7 percent, thirty-five to thirty-nine years old by 29.9 percent, and forty to forty-four years old by 43.4 percent (table 10.4).

The three age segments combined grew by 444,812 people, a total far greater than the state's overall population increase of 365,365 people. These baby boom–driven increases were also given added impetus by international immigration into New Jersey, which was becoming a growing force of population change in the state. One of the results was the rapid expansion of the middle tier of the labor force and in the ranks of trade-up homeownership aspirants.

The Depression-era birth dearth was between fifty and sixty years old in 1990. It maintained its visibility in the age-structure charts as it negatively impacted the size of the fifty-to-fifty-four-years-old (−12.9 percent) and fifty-five-to-fifty-nine-years-old (−17.3 percent) segments between 1980 and 1990. Concurrently, a baby boom echo was just starting to appear but not nearly to the extent once envisioned. What are now known as millennials or Gen Y (born 1981–1996) were visible only in the modest growth (+15.0 percent) that took place in the under-five-years-of-age population. As detailed in chapter 7, the younger generations analyzed in this book would subsequently be distinguished and defined more by other societal factors.

Gen X (the baby bust) also continued to mature. In 1990 it was between ten and twenty-six years of age. Between 1980 and 1990, it was the ten-to-fourteen-years-old (−20.6 percent), fifteen-to-nineteen-years-old (−24.6 percent), and twenty-to-twenty-four-years-old (−7.8 percent) sectors of the population that experienced declines. The more-modest-than-expected decrease in those twenty to twenty-four years of age was due to the growing impact of international migration bringing additional population to this age sector.[7] Nonetheless, by 1990, high schools and higher education in New Jersey had to confront shrinkage in their prime market segments.

1990–2000: The Twentieth Century's Final Decade

The 1990s marked the return to growth of New Jersey's young population—constituting a mini-boom or mini-bulge—and the continued aging of the three primary generations under scrutiny (table 10.5). These moving cohorts continued to receive a positive boost from international immigration into the state; so, too, was the state's 1990–2000 overall population growth rate (+8.9 percent). This stronger pace surpassed that (5.0 percent) of the preceding decade (1980–1990), which in turn had surpassed that (2.7 percent) of the 1970s (tables 10.5, 10.4, and 10.3, respectively). The century did not quite end with a demographic "bang" in New Jersey, but the state's population growth was set on an upward trajectory. As noted in previous chapters, this trajectory faltered post-2000.

Millennials (Gen Y)—the modest smaller-than-anticipated baby boom echo—were between four and twenty years old in 2000, and they were largely evidenced by the growth in the school-aged population between five and nineteen years of age (table 10.5). Between 1990 and 2000, millennial growth was strongest in the five-to-nine-years-old (+22.6 percent) and ten-to-fourteen-years-old

Table 10.5
New Jersey Age Structure, 1990–2000

	1990	2000	Change: 1990–2000 Number	Change: 1990–2000 Percent (%)
New Jersey Total	7,730,188	8,414,350	684,162	8.9
Under 5 years	532,637	563,808	31,171	5.9
5–9 years	493,044	604,549	111,505	22.6
10–14 years	480,983	590,590	109,607	22.8
15–19 years	505,388	525,242	19,854	3.9
20–24 years	566,594	480,105	(86,489)	(15.3)
25–29 years	668,917	544,937	(123,980)	(18.5)
30–34 years	691,734	644,136	(47,598)	(6.9)
35–39 years	622,963	727,943	104,980	16.9
40–44 years	573,696	707,222	133,526	23.3
45–49 years	466,481	611,392	144,911	31.1
50–54 years	376,528	547,578	171,050	45.4
55–59 years	355,677	423,387	67,710	19.0
60–64 years	363,521	330,673	(32,848)	(9.0)
65–69 years	340,232	293,228	(47,004)	(13.8)
70–74 years	269,960	281,489	11,529	4.3
75–84 years	326,286	402,484	76,198	23.4
85 years and older	95,547	136,001	40,454	42.3

SOURCE: U.S. Census Bureau, decennial census.

(+22.8 percent) sectors. These gains replaced the declines that took place in the same age categories during the preceding (1980–1990) decade (table 10.4), which were then filled by Gen Xers. However, the 1990–2000 growth rates were far more modest than those caused by the baby boom when it was in the equivalent life-cycle stages. For example, between 1950 and 1960, the number of baby boomers between ten to fourteen years of age exploded by 80.5 percent (table 10.1), more than three times that (22.8 percent) of ten-to-fourteen-year-old millennials between 1990 and 2000 (table 10.5). Thus, despite being bolstered by international migration, millennials turned out to be a very modest echo of the original baby boom.

In 2000, the oldest baby boomer turned fifty-four years old (while the youngest was thirty-six years old), heading the march of this massive generation into full middle age. The aggregate 1990–2000 growth of the four age sectors between thirty-five and fifty-four years—which fully encompassed the baby boom in 2000—totaled 554,467 people (table 10.5). Thus, the baby boom accounted for approximately 80 percent of New Jersey's total decadal population increase (684,576 people). The oldest boomers (fifty to fifty-four years old) headlined this growth, increasing in number by 45.4 percent. A baby boom in middle age was driving the run-up in the trade-up single-family housing market, and it swelled the middle and upper tiers of the state's workforce.

Continuing to follow in the baby boom's wake, Gen X was twenty to thirty-five years old in 2000. As a result, the Gen X–driven age-structure indentation moved into the twenty-to-thirty-five-years-old sector during the decade, as all three of its subsectors contracted in size between 1990 and 2000, led by those between twenty-five and twenty-nine years old (−18.5 percent). Thus, the state's entry-level labor force was declining in size at century's end just at the time the 1991–2001 transmillennial economic expansion was approaching its peak (see appendix B).

The youngest population (under five years of age) demonstrated only modest growth (+5.9 percent) between 1990 and 2000. Three-quarters of this sector represented members of Gen Z (postmillennials), born between 1997 and 2012. Thus, Gen Z did not exactly burst onto the New Jersey demographic scene; it entered relatively quietly. At the other end of the age spectrum, the Depression offspring were between sixty and seventy years old by 2000. As a result, between 1990 and 2000, the sixty-to-sixty-four-years-old (−9.0 percent) and sixty-five-to-sixty-nine-years-old (−13.8 percent) populations had experienced decline between 1990 and 2000.

The New Century: The 2000–2010 Decade

The resumption of the decline in size of the state's most youthful population was the newest demographic feature of the first decade of the twenty-first century. Similarly, the bursting of the unprecedented housing/credit bubble and subsequent Great 2007–2009 Recession were the decade's signature economic events. The analytical untangling of the latter's short- and long-term implications has yet to be fully completed, but they certainly helped shape many dimensions of the decade, which in New Jersey was one of decelerating population growth. The overall rate of increase between 2000 and 2010—+4.5 percent (table 10.6)—was approximately one-half of the 8.9 percent rate of the preceding 1990–2000 decade (table 10.5). Despite births increasing at the national level during this period (see table 7.1 in chapter 7), New Jersey's population under five years old declined by 4.0 percent, those between five and nine years old declined by 6.6 percent, and those between ten and fourteen years old declined by 0.6 percent. Thus, under-sized Gen Z—thirteen years of age and younger in 2010—fostered a reduction of 65,842 people, or 11.2 percent, in the under-fifteen-years-of-age population sectors between 2000 and 2010.[8]

In contrast, millennials (Gen Y) swelled the state's population of high school and higher education age. The fifteen-to-nineteen-years-old sector increased by 13.9 percent, and the twenty-to-twenty-four-years-old sector grew by 12.7 percent. This provided a brief respite for the continuing enrollment challenges confronting New Jersey's colleges and universities.

The voids continually produced by the aging of Gen X shifted to the three sectors between thirty and forty-four years of age. Leading the declines in

Table 10.6
New Jersey Age Structure, 2000–2010

	2000	2010	Change: 2000–2010	
			Number	Percent (%)
New Jersey Total	8,414,350	8,791,894	377,544	4.5
Under 5 years	563,808	541,020	(22,788)	(4.0)
5–9 years	604,549	564,750	(39,799)	(6.6)
10–14 years	590,590	587,335	(3,255)	(0.6)
15–19 years	525,242	598,099	72,857	13.9
20–24 years	480,105	541,238	61,133	12.7
25–29 years	544,937	553,139	8,202	1.5
30–34 years	644,136	556,662	(87,474)	(13.6)
35–39 years	727,943	588,379	(139,564)	(19.2)
40–44 years	707,222	649,918	(57,304)	(8.1)
45–49 years	611,392	704,516	93,124	15.2
50–54 years	547,578	674,680	127,102	23.2
55–59 years	423,387	565,623	142,236	33.6
60–64 years	330,673	480,542	149,869	45.3
65–69 years	293,228	350,972	57,744	19.7
70–74 years	281,489	260,462	(21,027)	(7.5)
75–84 years	402,484	394,948	(8,074)	(2.0)
85 years and older	136,001	179,611	43,610	32.1

SOURCE: U.S. Census Bureau, decennial census.

population between 2000 and 2010 were those thirty-five to thirty-nine years old (−19.2 percent) and those thirty to thirty-four years old (−13.6 percent). As a result, the middle ranks of the state's labor force were decreasing in size, as was the pool of homeownership aspirants.

Concurrently, 2010 was a palindromic-type year for the baby boom: the generation born between 1946 and 1964 was between sixty-four and forty-six years old in 2010! All four of the specific age sectors between forty-five and sixty-four years old experienced significant growth between 2000 and 2010 (table 10.6), led by those sixty to sixty-four years old (+45.3 percent). The C-suites of New Jersey, largely occupied by baby boomers, had to contend with the organizational leadership repercussions of the Great Recession. The oldest boomers were also increasingly empty nesters confronting changes in their shelter needs and desires and concurrently beginning to face retirement. Most of their undersized Depression-era predecessors were already in retirement in 2010, as they aged to between seventy and eighty years old.

2010–2018: The Post–Great Recession Period

Modest losses in New Jersey's youngest population and significant expansion of its older population characterized the century's second decade—a trend marking

Table 10.7
New Jersey Age Structure, 2010–2018

	2010	2018	Change: 2010–2018	
			Number	Percent (%)
New Jersey Total	8,791,894	8,908,520	116,626	1.3
Under 5 years	541,020	518,628	(22,392)	(4.1)
5–9 years	564,750	533,562	(31,188)	(5.5)
10–14 years	587,335	558,614	(28,721)	(4.9)
15–19 years	598,099	557,815	(40,284)	(6.7)
20–24 years	541,238	551,030	9,792	1.8
25–29 years	553,139	583,053	29,914	5.4
30–34 years	556,662	572,786	16,124	2.9
35–39 years	588,379	581,487	(6,892)	(1.2)
40–44 years	649,918	557,813	(92,105)	(14.2)
45–49 years	704,516	602,340	(102,176)	(14.5)
50–54 years	674,680	633,534	(41,146)	(6.1)
55–59 years	565,623	646,773	81,150	14.3
60–64 years	480,542	572,558	92,016	19.1
65–69 years	350,972	451,916	100,944	28.8
70–74 years	260,462	358,182	97,720	37.5
75–84 years	394,948	426,136	31,188	7.9
85 years and older	179,611	202,293	22,682	12.6

SOURCE: U.S. Census Bureau, decennial census.

the emergence of young/old age disparities. Overall, the state's decelerating pace of growth continued deep into this period (table 10.7). Between 2010 and 2018, New Jersey's total population grew by only 1.3 percent. This translates approximately into a 2010–2020 growth rate of 1.6 percent. This will not only be lower than the record lows experienced during the troubled decades of both the 1970s (2.7 percent) and the 1930s (2.9 percent; see chapter 3), but it will be the lowest decade growth rate since the first census of 1790.

Within this unprecedented statewide growth hiatus, both Gen Z (six to twenty-one years of age in 2018) and Gen Alpha (born post-2012) caused decreases between 2010 and 2018 in all four of the age categories under twenty years of age (i.e., zero to nineteen years old), with the largest decline (−6.7 percent) exhibited by those fifteen to nineteen years old (table 10.7). The eight-year rates of decline for the under-twenty-years-of-age sectors were far less than the decade rates of decline caused by Gen X when it had traversed the same age sectors (see tables 10.3 and 10.4).[9] Thus, a young population growth "lull" rather than a full-scale "bust" may be the appropriate adjective for the post-2010 period.

Stagnant overall enrollments in the state's K–12 educational system reflected the demographic reality of the 2010–2020 decade to date, recognizing that geographical preferences of young family-raising households will still cause enrollment growth in selected municipalities and declines in others. Again, enrollment decreases are far milder than those that occurred in the 1970s and 1980s. The same holds true for higher education's shrinking enrollment pools.

Gen X—thirty-eight to fifty-three years old in 2018—was still causing shrinkage during the decade to date (2010–2018), this time most severely impacting the forty-to-forty-four-years-old (−14.2 percent) and forty-five-to-forty-nine-years-old (−14.5 percent) sectors. As a result, upper-level management aspirants among this generation do not have to confront an expanding reservoir of competition, a situation that has been endemic to this generation throughout its life-span.

The baby boom has started to swell the ranks of those sixty-five years and older, just as the Depression-era generation starts to vacate them. In 2018, the baby boom was fifty-four to seventy-two years of age. Most fell in the four fastest-growing age segments: fifty-five to fifty-nine (+81,150 people, or +14.3 percent), sixty to sixty-four (+92,016 people, or +19.1 percent), sixty-five to sixty-nine (+100,944 people, or +28.8 percent), and seventy to seventy-four (+97,720 people, or +37.5 percent). The growth in just these four sectors combined (+371,830 people) was more than triple the overall population growth of the state during this period (+116,626 people). The popular phrase of the time—"The baby boom still got game"—is borne out by this generation's continued dominance of New Jersey's age-structure shifts.

Changing Age-Structure Distributions

The result of the generations moving through their life-cycle progressions is the changing age profiles of the state's population over time. These are presented in table 10.8, which provides each age sector's percentage share of the total population for each decennial year from 1950 to 2010 as well as for 2018. In addition, the median age of New Jersey's population for each of these years is presented at the bottom of table 10.8. In order not to be too repetitive of the preceding decade-by-decade examinations, there will be just selective analyses for the balance of this chapter.

Not unexpectedly, between 1950 and 1960, the emerging baby boom is captured by the increasing population share in the three youngest age sectors: under five years (9.5 percent to 10.6 percent), five to nine years (7.7 percent to 9.6 percent), and ten to fourteen years (6.0 percent to 8.7 percent). This was the emergence of the classic bulge that would move through the age distribution charts for the next six decades and beyond. The boom also resulted in the decline in median age from 32.8 years to 32.3 years—the beginning of a more youth-oriented society in the postwar years.

The Depression-era birth dearth was also prominently visible—the classic age-structure indentation—revealed by declining shares in the twenty-to-twenty-four-years-old (7.2 percent to 5.3 percent) and twenty-five-to-twenty-nine-years-old (8.5 percent to 6.0 percent) sectors. As was noted earlier, the start of the postwar

Table 10.8

New Jersey Age Structure Profiles, 1950–2018 (Percentage of Population)

Decade	1950	1960	1970	1980	1990	2000	2010	2018
Total	100.0%	100.0%	100.0%	100.0%	100.0%	100.0%	100.0%	100.0%
Under 5 years	9.5	10.6	8.2	6.3	6.9	6.7	6.2	5.8
5–9 years	7.7	9.6	9.7	6.9	6.4	7.2	6.4	6.0
10–14 years	6.0	8.7	9.9	8.2	6.2	7.0	6.7	6.3
15–19 years	6.1	6.5	8.5	9.1	6.5	6.2	6.8	6.3
20–24 years	7.2	5.3	7.1	8.3	7.3	5.7	6.2	6.2
25–29 years	8.5	6.0	6.5	7.8	8.7	6.5	6.3	6.5
30–34 years	8.5	7.2	5.6	7.7	8.9	7.7	6.3	6.4
35–39 years	8.1	7.8	5.8	6.5	8.1	8.7	6.7	6.5
40–44 years	7.4	7.4	6.5	5.4	7.4	8.4	7.4	6.3
45–49 years	6.6	6.7	6.7	5.4	6.0	7.3	8.0	6.8
50–54 years	6.3	5.8	6.1	5.9	4.9	6.5	7.7	7.1
55–59 years	5.4	5.0	5.3	5.8	4.6	5.0	6.4	7.3
60–64 years	4.5	4.3	4.4	5.0	4.7	3.9	5.5	6.4
65–69 years	3.4	3.7	3.4	4.1	4.4	3.5	4.0	5.1
70–74 years	2.3	2.7	2.7	3.1	3.5	3.3	3.0	4.0
75–84 years	2.1	2.4	2.9	3.5	4.2	4.8	4.5	4.8
85 years and over	0.4	0.5	0.7	1.0	1.2	1.6	2.0	2.3
Median Age	32.8	32.3	30.1	32.2	34.5	36.7	39.0	40.0

SOURCES: U.S. Census Bureau, decennial census; Current Population Survey (for 2018 data).

suburban inflow of population to New Jersey from out-of-state origins amelio-
rated the scale of decline in these two age categories.

These two cohorts of markedly different size were joined by the reduced-scale
Gen X during the following two decades (1960–1980). All three of these generations remained highly discernible as they matured through the balance of the
century. For example, in the twenty years between 1960 and 1980, Gen X had
negative impacts on the size of the state's youngest population, with the age sectors under fifteen years old experiencing significant share declines. Concurrently
(1960–1980), the maturing baby boom caused the swelling of the fifteen-to-
thirty-four-years-old population, while the Depression-era birth dearth caused
share contractions in those aged between forty and fifty years.

By 1980, the median age of the population started to increase again because
of these shifts (table 10.8). After declining to a low of 30.1 years in 1970—down
from 32.8 years in 1950—the median age increased to 32.2 years by 1980. This was
the start of a sustained general aging of New Jersey's population that continued
through the first two decades of the twenty-first century. By 2000, the median
age had already reached 36.7 years.

The inexorable movement of these generational groups continued their impact
in the 2000–2010 age distribution changes. During this period, the baby boom
caused share increases in the four sectors between forty-five and sixty-four years,
while Gen X caused contractions in the population between thirty and forty-
five years old (table 10.8). This pattern continued in the post-2010 period as the
two generations continued their journey into successively older age brackets.
Moreover, the "failure to materialize" magnitudes in the once-anticipated baby
boom and baby bust (Gen X) echoes—now known as Gen Y (millennials) and
Gen Z—made the distributional shifts in the younger age sectors quite modest
compared with those spawned by the original baby boom and baby bust. As
pointed out in chapter 7, the delineation of these younger generations has been
predicated on non–birth fluctuation rationales.

Of significance in the entire 2000–2018 period is the steady decline in the
share of the state's population accounted for by those under fifteen years old, and
the additional decline that took place in the fifteen-to-nineteen-years-old share
between 2010 and 2018. This does not mean that young New Jerseyans are becoming an endangered species, but their presence is steadily diminishing. The
declines in national fertility and birth patterns underlying this development were
detailed in chapter 7. But the declines are also linked to population outflows from
the state (domestic migration losses), which were examined in the analysis of the
state's components of change in chapter 6.

The baby boom's unprecedented scale underpinned the emergence of the postwar youth society and the decline in median age in the decades following World
War II. Fast forward half a century to the decades following the turn of the
twenty-first century. The baby boom's powerful trajectory has been maintained,
but the game plan has irrevocably changed. The unrelenting force of its sheer size

has now started to underpin the emergence of an aged society—with the attendant increase in median age. Between 2000 and 2010, the median age in New Jersey increased from 36.7 years to 39.0 years. By 2018, it had reached 40.0 years (table 10.8).

The approaching more-old-than-young society in New Jersey is made evident by a direct comparison of the 1970 age distribution to that of 2018. In the former year, 27.8 percent of the state's population was under fifteen years of age. This was nearly triple the 9.7 percent share held by those sixty-five years of age and older. By 2018, a "young-old" parity was close to arriving: 18.1 percent were under fifteen years old compared with 16.2 percent who were sixty-five years old and over. This shift in age structure was reflected in median age. In 1970, the state's median age was 30.1 years; by 2018, it had climbed to 40.0 years, approximately one-third higher.

Again, New Jersey was at the leading edge of demographic change in the United States. The median Garden Stater was 1.8 years older than its national counterpart in 2010 (39.0 years versus 37.2 years); this 1.8-year edge was maintained in 2018 (40 years versus 38.2 years).[10] New Jersey's baby boom was once a front-runner in the emergence of the nation's and New Jersey's youth societies; it has now become an elder-boom front-runner in the nation's and New Jersey's senior societies.

11

The Great Household
Revolution
....

New Jersey's households, as those of the nation, have been fundamentally recast throughout the twentieth century, particularly in its later decades. These long-term changes continued into the twenty-first century, although tempered most recently by a vast cyclical economic downswing and its lingering aftereffects. These changes can be categorized into three broad partitions: the sheer rate of growth in the formation far in excess of the population growth rate, the sustained decline in the size of households, and the increasing diversity in the anatomy of household types. The latter (household diversity) was the result of a powerful post–World War II household revolution in America that totally redefined living and lifestyle configurations.

For each of these three household changes, and for each delineated time period, the powerful national dynamics enveloping New Jersey are first presented, followed by their manifestation in the state. In each national and state section, and for each successive time period, the initial focus is on the rapid growth and shrinking size of households. Changing household composition and increasing complexity of living arrangements are then examined.

American Households: The Twentieth Century

A household is simply defined as one or more people (all the persons) who occupy a housing unit as their usual place of residence.[1] The number of households equals the number of occupied housing units.[2] Not all people reside in households;

Table 11.1

Total Population and Households: United States, 1900 and 2000

	1900	2000	Change: 1900–2000	
			Number	Percent (%)
Total Population	75,994,575	281,421,906	205,427,331	270.3
Total Households	15,963,965	105,480,101	89,516,136	560.7

Household Size	% Distribution	
Total	100.0	100.0
1 person	5.1	25.8
2 person	15.2	32.6
3 person	17.8	16.5
4 person	17.2	14.2
5 person	14.4	6.6
6 person	11.2	2.5
7 or more person	19.2	1.8
Average Household Size (Persons)	4.60	2.59

Average Household Size		
	Year	Size
	1900	4.60
	1910	NA
	1920	NA
	1930	4.01
	1940	3.68
	1950	3.38
	1960	3.20
	1970	3.11
	1980	2.75
	1990	2.63
	2000	2.59

SOURCE: U.S. Census Bureau, decennial census for indicated years.
NOTES: Household size (persons per household) includes only population residing in households.
NA = not applicable.

people not living in households are classified as living in group quarters, such as college residence halls, military barracks, and correctional facilities. Persons per household (average household size) is obtained by dividing the number of persons living in households by the number of households (or occupied dwelling units).

As detailed in chapter 3, the nation's population grew rapidly throughout the 1900–2000 period, from almost 76 million people in 1900 to slightly over 281 million people in 2000 (table 11.1). The century-long rate of increase (270.3 percent), however, was less than one-half of that (560.7 percent) in the growth in the number of households. America entered the twentieth century (1900) with 16.0 million households. When it exited the century (2000), it had 105.5 million households (table 11.1).

Household Size

The sharply different scales of growth reflect the basic trend of higher proportions of the nation's population living in smaller households. In 1900, the average household size was 4.60 persons. By 2000, it had plummeted to 2.59 persons (table 11.1). Thus, during the twentieth century, the average household in the United States contracted by 2.01 persons.

This decline was continuous during the century. During the first four decades (1900–1940), the average size declined by nearly one person, from 4.60 persons to 3.68 persons, a 20 percent decrease. Then, during the next five decades (1940–1990), another person was lost, as the average household size dropped from 3.68 persons to 2.63 persons, a 28.6 percent decrease. The smallest decline then took place in the 1990s, just 0.04 persons, as the average size fell from 2.63 persons to 2.59 persons.

The steep declines that took place in the early decades of the century reflected declining fertility rates and increasing household formation as rapid urban and metropolitan economic growth fostered the expansion of the middle class, particularly in the 1920s. This was followed by even lower fertility rates during the Depression/pre–baby boom era (see chapter 7). Subsequently, the spiking of fertility rates that produced the baby boom (1946–1964) slowed the pace of household-size shrinkage during the 1950s and 1960s. But decline then accelerated in the 1970s, a result of the return of lower fertility rates that produced Gen X (the baby bust), rapid household formation by baby boomers, and still relatively low levels of immigration. As a result, the 1970–1980 period had the sharpest decade decline in size during the entire century, from 3.11 persons to 2.75 persons (table 11.1). The 1980s and 1990s then saw shrinkage turn more modest, a result of the huge baby boom reproducing itself and much greater levels of immigration.

The distribution of households by size (number of persons) in table 11.1 further illustrates the dramatic household-size transformation. In 1900, one out of five (19.2 percent) households comprised seven or more persons.[3] By 2000, fewer than one out of fifty (1.8 percent) had seven or more members. Similarly, the share of six-person households declined from 11.2 percent in 1900 to 2.5 percent in 2000—one in nine to one in forty. Larger American households (six or more persons) had become a rarity by the time the twentieth century ended.

At the other end of the age spectrum, in 1900 one out of twenty (5.1 percent) households contained just one person (table 11.1). By 2000, more than one out of four (25.8 percent) comprised a single person, a fivefold increase in share. Less dramatic but still highly transformational, the share of total households composed of just two people more than doubled between 1900 and 2000, from 15.2 percent to 32.6 percent. The latter figure represents the highest percentage share of any household-size segment in 2000. Thus, the most common household in America contained two people at century's end.[4] In contrast, the most common household one hundred years earlier (1900) contained seven or more persons (19.2 percent).

The decline in average household size has thus been a consequence of sharp declines in large households and sharp increases in small households. Much less important are the modest proportional shifts in middle-sized households. In 1900, 35.0 percent—over one-third—of all households comprised three or four persons (table 11.1). By 2000, this share declined to 30.7 percent.

Household Diversification: Second Half of the Twentieth Century

Household segmentation and life-cycle diversity crosscut the household-size trajectory described above as well as interacted with other demographic and economic dynamics. There has been a transformation in the way in which the nation's population arranges itself into specific household configurations and in the lifestyle choices inherent in these arrangements. America has been passing through a profound and long-term household transformation—the "great household revolution"—that intensified with the coming-of-age of the baby boom. Lifestyle and socioeconomic changes had been powering a furious process of household segmentation and diversification across the nation.

The major dynamic has been twofold. First, there has been the surging growth of single-parent families, one-person households (singles), and unmarried couples. The second has been complementary: the slow growth and contracting share of traditional married-couple (husband-wife) families. As noted above, the most dramatic increase was in one-person households. Before examining such household changes in detail, a definitional framework should prove useful.

Census Bureau Definitional Framework

A household consists of all the people who occupy a housing unit. A householder refers to the person (or one of the people) in whose name the housing unit is owned or rented (or maintained). The number of householders is equal to the number of households.[5] There are two major categories of households—"family and nonfamily." A family household is a household maintained by a householder who is in a family. A family is a group of two or more people (one of whom is the householder) who are related by birth, marriage, or adoption and residing together. (It can also include other members who are not related.) A nonfamily household consists of a householder living alone (a one-person household) or where the householder shares the home exclusively with people to whom he/she is not related (a two-or-more unrelated-individuals household).

Family households have two major subsets: a "married-couple family"—also termed "husband-wife households"—and "other family." A married-couple family consists of a household maintained by a husband and wife. Married-couple families may or may not have children living with them. Other families comprise two basic types. The first is "male householder, no wife present"—a family with a male householder that has no spouse of the householder present. The second is "female householder, no husband present"—a family with a female householder that has no spouse of the householder present.

As noted above, nonfamily households consist either of a householder living alone (a one-person household) or a householder that shares the home (housing unit) exclusively with nonrelatives (people to whom he/she is not related). The latter is often labeled as a nonfamily household comprising two or more members. Other often-used partitions classifying nonfamily households start with male and female householder groupings, each further broken down by living alone or not living alone. Another classification (or subgroup) within the two-or-more person (or not living alone) nonfamily category that is currently used is "unmarried-couple households," further subdivided into opposite-sex partners and same-sex partners.

The 1950–2000 Trendlines

Household compilations by detailed type were less comprehensive in the early censuses of the twentieth century. Thus, this section focuses on the second half of the century (1950–2000), when the most significant changes are captured by the available data. Between 1950 and 2000, the total number of households in the United States increased from 42.3 million to 105.5 million, a gain of 63.2 million or 149.6 percent (table 11.2). Although family households accounted for more than half (54.0 percent, or 34.0 million out of 63.2 million) of total household growth, their rate of increase was only 90.0 percent.

In contrast, although nonfamily households captured less than one-half (46.0 percent, or 29.2 million out of 63.2 million) of the nation's total household growth, their rate of increase was 652.7 percent, more than seven times greater than that (90.0 percent) of family households. Thus, the rate of increase of non-families far eclipsed that of families during this one-half-century period. Within the nonfamily sector, households with two or more members increased by 1,238.4 percent—the fastest of any household type (albeit from a very small base)—while one-person (single-member) nonfamily households increased by 581.9 percent.

Within the family sector, married couples with children (i.e., the "with own children under eighteen years" category) had the slowest overall increase (36.5 percent) of any household type. Families with the fastest growth rates were male householders (no wife present) with children (754.7 percent) and female householders (no husband present) with children (550.3 percent). (In subsequent census tabulations, the term *spouse* replaced *wife* and *husband*.)

As a result of this diverse growth pattern, the household structure of America was dramatically transformed during the second half of the twentieth century. This is evident in the percentage distribution of households by type (table 11.2). Married couples accounted for nearly four-fifths (78.1 percent) of all households in 1950; their share in 2000 (51.7 percent) was approaching one-half. Married couples with children (under eighteen years) experienced a decline in share from 43.1 percent to 23.5 percent. The classic mid-century image of the American

Table 11.2
Households by Type, United States Total, 1950–2000

	1950	2000	Change: 1950–2000		Percentage Distribution (%)	
			Number	Percent (%)	1950	2000
Households by Type						
Total Households	42,251,415	105,480,101	63,228,686	149.6	100.0	100.0
Family households	37,775,167	71,787,347	34,012,180	90.0	89.4	68.1
Married-couple families	33,019,225	54,493,232	21,474,007	65.0	78.1	51.7
With own children under 18 years	18,190,774	24,835,505	6,644,731	36.5	43.1	23.5
Female householder, no husband present	3,424,976	12,900,103	9,475,127	276.6	8.1	12.2
With own children under 18 years	1,162,811	7,561,874	6,399,063	550.3	2.8	7.2
Male householder, no wife present	1,330,966	4,394,012	3,063,046	230.1	3.2	4.2
With own children under 18 years	256,347	2,190,989	1,934,642	754.7	0.6	2.1
Nonfamily households	4,476,248	33,692,754	29,216,506	652.7	10.6	31.9
One member	3,993,399	27,230,075	23,236,676	581.9	9.5	25.8
Two or more members	482,849	6,462,679	5,979,830	1,238.4	1.1	6.1

SOURCE: U.S. Census Bureau, decennial census for indicated years.

family—mom, pop, three-point-something children, and pet entourage—was rendered fully obsolete by century's end, as married couples with children accounted for fewer than one out of four households.

In contrast, the nonfamily household share grew from one out of ten (10.6 percent) to nearly one-third (31.9 percent) during this fifty-year period (1950–2000). Nonfamilies consisting of one member (single-person households) comprised fully one-quarter (25.8 percent) of all households by 2000. In 1950, their share was less than one-tenth (9.5 percent). This new pattern of living continues to have significant implications for housing consumption and residential location. The suburban single-family home hegemony of the 1950s and 1960s had changed markedly by century's end.

American Households in the Twenty-First Century (2000–2010) by Size and Type

The significant interaction between demography and the combination of both long-term economic transformations and short-term business-cycle shifts has been pointed out several times. In this context, it appears that the Great 2007–2009 Recession's severity impacted the long-term pattern of household change

Table 11.3

Population Growth Rate versus Household Growth Rate, United States, 1900–2000 and 2000–2010

Period	Population (%)	Households (%)	Ratio: Household/ Population
1900–2000	270.3	560.7	2.07
2000–2010	9.7	10.7	1.10
Average Household Size 2000: 2.59 persons 2010: 2.58 persons			

SOURCE: U.S. Census Bureau, decennial census for indicated years.

in the United States. As noted above (and also presented in table 11.3), the overall household growth rate (560.7 percent) that took place throughout the entire twentieth century (1900–2000) was more than double the population growth rate (270.3 percent). More precisely, the ratio of the household growth rate to the population growth rate was 2.07 (table 11.3).

In contrast, in the first decade of the twenty-first century (2000–2010), the growth rates converged markedly. The household growth rate (10.7 percent) barely exceeded the population growth rate (9.7 percent), and the ratio between the two plummeted to just 1.10. As a result, the average household size contracted by just 0.01 persons, from 2.59 persons per household in 2000 to 2.58 persons in 2010. This followed the century-long period (1900–2000) where the average household size lost 2.01 persons, declining from 4.60 persons in 1900 to 2.59 persons in 2000 (see table 11.1). The revolutionary changes in average household size and household size distribution may be settling into a new postrevolutionary normal.

2000–2010 Household Size Distribution

Changes in the distribution of households by size between 2000 and 2010 were also quite minor (table 11.4) compared with past decades. The most significant shift was the increased share of one-person (25.8 percent to 26.7 percent) households. This was counterbalanced by decreases in three- (16.5 percent to 16.1 percent) and four- (14.2 percent to 13.4 percent) person households.

The stabilization in the average household size may be partially a consequence of that end-of-decade cyclical economic event: the Great 2007–2009 Recession. Many financially challenged young-adult millennials, just completing their undergraduate college years, were saddled with student debts and confronting hostile job markets. As a result, the parental hearth proved to be an attractive alternative rather than embarking on their own independent household journeys (see chapter 9). But other noncyclical factors were simultaneously at work, particularly the sheer number of baby boom households entering the empty-nester

Table 11.4
Total Households and Household Size, United States, 2000 and 2010

	2000	2010
Total Households	105,480,101	116,716,202
Household Size	% Distribution	
Total	100.0	100.0
1 person	25.8	26.7
2 person	32.6	32.8
3 person	16.5	16.1
4 person	14.2	13.4
5 person	6.6	6.5
6 person	2.5	2.6
7 or more person	1.8	1.9
Average Household Size	2.59	2.58

SOURCE: U.S. Census Bureau, decennial census for indicated years.

stage of the life cycle. Boomers would become more influential in instigating household size changes as the economic cycle turned into its expansionary phase, assuming the exit of their millennial children.

Moreover, the long-term trend of household size contraction will attenuate further as households get smaller and smaller. In the extreme, by very definition, household size cannot fall below 1.0 persons: a household size of 1.0 persons implies a nation where every single person lives alone.[6] Economic, life-cycle, and age circumstances permitting, most people will choose to live with others at some point in their life cycle, particularly when they desire to reproduce themselves, establishing some minimum floor to household size.

The age structure of the population also proves influential in determining household-size trends. Large population cohorts (such as the baby boom) entering their household-formation years suggest that many new, below-average-size households will be added to the overall household pool, pushing average sizes down. Conversely, small population cohorts (such as the baby bust/Gen X) entering adulthood imply a smaller number of newly formed, below-average-size households, thus having a lesser effect on the overall household size. At the other end of the age spectrum, the growing/shrinking size of the senior, empty-nester household cohort will influence the scale of additional smaller (childless) households. For example, the maturing baby boom cohort in their later life-cycle stages will continue to exert downward-size pressures throughout the decade of the 2020s. So, too, will changes in divorce rates influence the downward size of households, as divorce-driven household fragmentation can create two smaller households from a single larger one. In contrast,

Table 11.5
Households by Type, United States Total, 2000–2010

	2000	2010	Change: 2000–2010 Number	Change: 2000–2010 Percent (%)	Percentage Distribution (%) 2000	Percentage Distribution (%) 2010
Households by Type						
Total Households	105,480,101	116,716,292	11,236,191	10.7	100.0	100.0
Family households	71,787,347	77,538,296	5,750,949	8.0	68.1	66.4
Husband-wife households	54,493,232	56,510,377	2,017,145	3.7	51.7	48.4
With own children under 18 years	24,835,505	23,588,268	(1,247,237)	(5.0)	23.5	20.2
Female householder, no spouse present	12,900,103	15,250,349	2,350,246	18.2	12.2	13.1
With own children under 18 years	7,561,874	8,365,912	804,038	10.6	7.2	7.2
Male householder, no spouse present	4,394,012	5,777,570	1,383,558	31.5	4.2	5.0
With own children under 18 years	2,190,989	2,789,424	598,435	27.3	2.1	2.4
Nonfamily households	33,692,754	39,177,996	5,485,242	16.3	31.9	33.6
One member	27,230,075	31,204,909	3,974,834	14.6	25.8	26.7
Two or more members	6,462,679	7,973,087	1,510,408	23.4	6.1	6.8

SOURCE: U.S. Census Bureau, decennial census for indicated years.

new multigenerational households stemming from international immigration would produce the opposite effect. Thus, a complex range of factors are at work.

2000–2010 Household Configuration

The first decade of the current century also experienced a more muted continuation of the long-term trend of household diversification (table 11.5). Between 2000 and 2010, the share of nonfamily households continued to increase (from 31.9 percent to 33.6 percent) while that of family households continued to decrease (from 68.1 percent to 66.4 percent). Husband-wife households (or married-couple families) for the first time accounted for less than one-half (48.4 percent) of all households in 2010, while the share of husband-wife households (with own children under eighteen years) fell to just one out of five (20.2 percent). This loss in share was due not just to slower growth but also to absolute decline; the number of husband-wife configurations (with own children under eighteen years) contracted by more than 1.2 million (−5.0 percent) between 2000 and 2010. In contrast, the largest absolute growth (nearly 4.0 million) in any specific family or nonfamily household type was experienced by one-member nonfamily households (or single-person households), many of them maturing baby boomers and pre–baby boomers.

Table 11.6
Total Households and Household Size, United States, 2010 and 2017

	2010	2017
Total Households	114,567,419	120,062,818
Household Size	% Distribution	
Total	100.0	100
1 person	27.4	27.9
2 person	33.4	34.1
3 person	15.8	15.5
4 person	13.2	12.7
5 person	6.1	6.0
6 person	2.4	2.3
7 or more person	1.6	1.5
Average Household Size	2.63	2.65

SOURCE: U.S. Census Bureau, American Community Survey for indicated years.

Post-2010: Size and Configuration in the Second Decade

Both the economy and demography of the century's second decade were initially shaped by the Great Recession and its harsh aftereffects. This lingering negative environment was then gradually superseded by an increasingly positive one, dominated by what would turn out to be the nation's record-long economic expansion. As the decade matured, the significance of the expansion increased, while that of the recession decreased but did not entirely fade away. Thus, both transformative events continued to influence the nation's demographic contours as the 2020s came into focus.

To examine second-decade trendlines, American Community Survey data—which are not directly comparable to the decennial census—were employed to ensure data consistency;[7] therefore, the American Community Survey is used for both 2010 and 2017 (table 11.6). This does not impact trend analysis although there are numerical differences between the two sources in 2010. Thus, broad trend contours are the central analytical focus of the post-2010 period.

As shown in table 11.6, and further confirmed by alternative combinations of the various sources, the dominance of smaller households continued its increase.[8] This is evidenced by the increasing share achieved by both one- and two-person configurations; combined, their share increased from 60.8 percent in 2010 to 62.0 percent in 2017. Concurrently, the combined share of the other five (larger) size categories (three or more persons) fell from 39.1 percent to 38.0 percent.

Table 11.7
Households by Type, United States Total, 2010–2017

Households by Type	2010	2017	Change: 2010–2017 Number	Change: 2010–2017 Percent (%)	Percentage Distribution (%) 2010	Percentage Distribution (%) 2017
Total Households	114,567,419	120,062,818	5,495,399	4.8	100.0	100.0
Family households	76,089,045	78,631,163	2,542,118	3.3	66.4	65.5
Married-couple families	55,704,781	57,847,574	2,142,793	3.8	48.6	48.2
With own children under 18 years	22,924,853	22,334,270	(590,583)	(2.6)	20.0	18.6
Female householder, no husband present	14,998,476	14,896,928	(101,548)	(0.7)	13.1	12.4
With own children under 18 years	8,521,814	7,789,620	(732,194)	(8.6)	7.4	6.5
Male householder, no wife present	5,385,788	5,886,661	500,873	9.3	4.7	4.9
With own children under 18 years	2,585,091	2,723,009	137,918	5.3	2.3	2.3
Nonfamily households	38,478,374	41,431,655	2,953,281	7.7	33.6	34.5
One member	31,403,342	33,513,155	2,109,813	6.7	27.4	27.9
Two or more members	7,075,032	7,918,500	843,468	11.9	6.2	6.6

SOURCE: U.S. Census Bureau, American Community Survey for indicated years.

Thus, two-person households solidified their status as the most prevalent living arrangement (defined by size) in America, accounting for more than one-third (34.1 percent) of all households in 2017. In contrast, the diminishing presence of the largest (seven or more persons) households continued; in 2017, they accounted for just 1.5 percent of all households—approximately one out of sixty-seven. The modest increase in household size (0.02 persons) shown in table 11.6 is largely due to American Community Survey sample variations.

The post–2010 profile of household types (defined by family/nonfamily configuration) also showed a continuation of the fundamental changes that have characterized more than seven decades of post–World War II America (table 11.7). The mythic images of families and family life keep receding deeper into history. One-member (single-person) nonfamily households had the largest increase in configurational share between 2010 and 2017 (27.4 percent to 27.9 percent), as shown in table 11.7. Husband-wife households (with own children under eighteen years old) had the largest decrease (20.0 percent to 18.6 percent). These modest but consistent post-2010 configurational changes basically reflect what may be the final stages of two demographic revolutions: the long-term—but increasingly maturing—structural adjustments, reinforced by younger—but nevertheless increasingly permanent—post–Great Recession disruptions.

Table 11.8
Total Population and Households, New Jersey, 1900 and 2000

	1900	2000	Change: 1900-2000	
			Number	Percent (%)
Total Population	1,883,669	8,414,350	6,530,681	346.7
Total Households	321,032	3,064,645	2,743,613	854.6

Household Size	Percentage Distribution (%)	
Total	100.0	100.0
1 person	2.8	24.5
2 person	11.5	30.3
3 person	15.1	17.3
4 person	15.9	16.0
5 person	14.1	7.5
6 person	11.4	2.7
7 or more person	29.3	1.7
Average Household Size (Persons)	5.87	2.68

Average Household Size	Year	Size
	1900	5.87
	1910	6.23
	1920	6.16
	1930	5.60
	1940	3.78
	1950	3.39
	1960	3.28
	1970	3.16
	1980	2.84
	1990	2.70
	2000	2.68

SOURCE: U.S. Census Bureau, decennial census for indicated years.
NOTE: Household size (persons per household) includes only population residing in households.

New Jersey Households

The powerful household trajectory extensively detailed above was evident throughout every corner of the United States. New Jersey was no exception; in fact, it stood at the forefront of household change, closely mirroring the nation in terms of both size and configurational parameters.

The Twentieth Century

During the twentieth century (1900–2000), the rate of increase in the number of households in New Jersey (854.6 percent) was two and one-half times (2.46) the increase (346.7 percent) in population (table 11.8). This was somewhat higher

Table 11.9
Households by Type, New Jersey Total, 1950-2000

Household by Type	1950	2000	Change: 1950-2000 Number	Change: 1950-2000 Percent (%)	Percentage Distribution (%) 1950	Percentage Distribution (%) 2000
Total Households	1,395,667	3,064,645	1,668,978	119.6	100.0	100.0
Family households	1,272,135	2,154,539	882,404	69.4	91.1	70.3
Married-couple families	1,105,809	1,638,322	532,513	48.2	79.2	53.5
With own children under 18 years	612,768	776,205	163,437	26.7	43.9	25.3
Female householder, no husband present	114,221	387,012	272,791	238.8	8.2	12.6
With own children under 18 years	43,256	196,809	153,553	355.0	3.1	6.4
Male householder, no wife present	52,105	129,205	77,100	148.0	3.7	4.2
With own children under 18 years	14,185	52,542	38,357	270.4	1.0	1.7
Nonfamily households	123,532	910,106	786,574	636.7	8.9	29.7
One member	95,370	751,287	655,917	687.8	6.8	24.5
Two or more members	28,162	158,819	130,657	463.9	2.0	5.2

SOURCE: U.S. Census Bureau, decennial census for indicated years.

than the national household growth-population growth differential (2.07) shown previously in table 11.3. But the pattern of household formation rates far exceeding population growth rates prevailed in both instances.

As a result, not surprisingly, the path of New Jersey's sustained shrinkage in household size was similar to that of the nation (table 11.8). Structurally, a slight difference was the state's marginally higher shares of larger (seven-or-more-person) households and lower shares of smaller (one-person) households at the start of the century (1900), perhaps due to New Jersey's role as an immigration gateway and its greater level of urbanization/industrialization.[9]

But by the end of the century (2000), the national and state household profiles were tightly aligned (tables 11.1 and 11.8), with one-quarter of all households comprising a single person and more than one-half comprising two persons or less. New Jersey's average household size (2.68 persons) was just slightly higher than that of the nation (2.59 persons), reflecting the state's higher degree of post-war suburbanization—that is, a higher prevalence of family-raising environments (tables 11.1 and 11.8).

The same close national-state alignment was evident in household configuration (tables 11.2 and 11.9). In both cases, the 1900–2000 growth rates in nonfamily households far outdistanced the growth in family households. In New Jersey, nonfamily households grew by 636.7 percent, while family

Table 11.10
Total Households and Household Size, New Jersey,
2000 and 2010

	2000	2010
Total Households	3,064,645	3,214,360
Household Size	% Distribution	
Total	100.0	100.0
1 person	24.5	25.2
2 person	30.3	29.8
3 person	17.3	17.4
4 person	16.0	15.7
5 person	7.5	7.2
6 person	2.7	2.7
7 or more person	1.6	1.9
Average Household Size	2.68	2.68

SOURCE: U.S. Census Bureau, decennial census for indicated years.

households increased by just 69.4 percent (table 11.9). By 2000, families accounted for 70.3 percent of all households in the state, compared to 68.1 percent nationally; nonfamilies accounted for 29.7 percent compared with 31.9 percent nationally (tables 11.2 and 11.9). Only minor percentage point differences existed for each specific type of household. The broad twentieth-century household transformation was largely identical for New Jersey and the country as a whole.

The Twenty-First Century: New Jersey's First Decade

New Jersey's continued failure to keep pace with national population growth was reflected in diminished household growth in the state. Between 2000 and 2010, the number of households in the United States increased by 10.7 percent (tables 11.3 and 11.5); in New Jersey, the increase was less than one-half that— 4.9 percent (table 11.11). Despite this lag, there was still close national-state alignment in both size and compositional distributions and trends.

The century-long household size contraction moderated significantly in the post-2000 period, following the national pattern. The average size of New Jersey's households in 2010, comprising 2.68 persons, was exactly the same as that in 2000 (table 11.10) while the household size of the United States experienced a barely discernible decline of just 0.01 persons, from 2.59 persons to 2.58 persons (see table 11.4). In 2010, the difference between New Jersey's household size and that of the nation was just one-tenth (0.1) of a person.

The combined share of one- and two-person households in New Jersey in 2010 was 55.0 percent (table 11.10), virtually identical to that of 2000 (54.8 percent). At the other end of the size spectrum, the combined share of the two largest

Table 11.11
Households by Type, New Jersey Total, 2000–2010

	2000	2010	Change: 2000–2010		Percentage Distribution (%)	
			Number	Percent (%)	2000	2010
Households by Type						
Total Households	3,064,645	3,214,360	149,715	4.9	100.0	100.0
Family households	2,154,539	2,226,606	72,067	3.3	70.3	69.3
Married-couple families	1,638,322	1,643,377	5,055	0.3	53.5	51.1
With own children under 18 years	776,205	748,765	(27,440)	(3.5)	25.3	23.3
Female householder, no husband present	387,012	429,095	42,083	10.9	12.6	13.3
With own children under 18 years	196,809	213,744	16,935	8.6	6.4	6.6
Male householder, no wife present	129,205	154,134	24,929	19.3	4.2	4.8
With own children under 18 years	52,542	63,105	10,563	20.1	1.7	2.0
Nonfamily households	910,106	987,754	77,648	8.5	29.7	30.7
One member	751,287	811,221	59,934	8.0	24.5	25.2
Two or more members	158,819	176,533	17,714	11.2	5.2	5.5

SOURCE: U.S. Census Bureau, decennial census for indicated years.

categories (six and seven or more persons) increased slightly from 4.4 percent to 4.6 percent. In both cases, New Jersey's changes remained in alignment with what was happening in the nation.

This was also evident in the state's 2000–2010 shifts in household composition (table 11.11). The only configuration to numerically decrease comprised husband-wife households (with own children under eighteen years), which exhibited a 3.5 percent rate of decline in New Jersey (table 11.11) compared with a 5.0 percent decline nationally (table 11.5). Although still growing in absolute terms, family households in the state lost share (70.3 percent to 69.3 percent) between 2000 and 2010, while nonfamilies gained share (29.7 percent to 30.7 percent). New Jersey's profile continued to be weighted slightly higher proportionally in families (versus nonfamilies) compared with the United States.

The same was true for husband-wife households, in total and those with children. Total husband-wife households' share fell to 51.1 percent in 2010 from 53.5 percent in 2000, while the subcategory with children fell to 23.3 percent from 25.3 percent (table 11.11). Similar to the national pattern, the share of female householders (no spouse present) increased (from 12.6 percent to 13.3 percent), while male householders (no spouse present) increased from 4.2 percent to 4.8 percent. The process of New Jersey household diversification continued as the century's first decade came to a close.

Table 11.12
Total Households and Household Size, New Jersey,
2010 and 2017

	2010	2017
Total Households	3,172,421	3,218,798
Household Size	% Distribution	
Total	100.0	100.0
1 person	26.1	25.4
2 person	30.2	31.3
3 person	17.2	17.5
4 person	15.6	15.3
5 person	6.8	6.7
6 person	2.5	2.3
7 or more person	1.6	1.5
Average Household Size	2.72	2.74

SOURCE: U.S. Census Bureau, decennial census and American
Community Survey for indicated years.

Post-2010 in New Jersey

According to the American Community Survey, the pace of household growth
continued to abate as the nation and state exited the Great Recession, but New
Jersey fell even further behind the United States. In the seven years between 2010
and 2017, the number of households in New Jersey increased by 1.5 percent
(table 11.13), a rate less than one-third that (4.8 percent) of the nation (see
table 11.7).

This was reflected in the unexpected decline in percentage share of one-person
households in the state. Between 2010 and 2017, in contrast to that of the nation,
the share of one-person households in New Jersey declined from 26.1 percent to
25.4 percent, a marked break in trend (table 11.12). Nationally, one-person
households increased their share from 27.4 percent to 27.9 percent (table 11.6).

A potential causal factor was linked to New Jersey's high housing costs and
lagging economic recovery, which may have inhibited millennial household formation during this time period. A key question is whether this phenomenon
also contributed to the modest increase in share of three-person households—
from 17.2 percent to 17.5 percent—between 2010 and 2017 (table 11.12). This
increase contrasts with the national decrease in share of three-person
households—from 15.8 percent to 15.5 percent (table 11.6) during this period. The
tendency for millennials living with their parents in New Jersey may be under-
pinning this national-state differential.

Otherwise, two-person households in the state continued to increase
(30.2 percent to 31.3 percent), while those configurations with five or more persons continued to decline (table 11.12). This was the exact pattern of change

Table 11.13
Households by Type, New Jersey Total, 2010–2017

	2010	2017	Change: 2010–2017		Percentage Distribution (%)	
			Number	Percent (%)	2010	2017
Households by Type						
Total Households	3,172,421	3,218,798	46,377	1.5	100.0	100.0
Family households	2,185,732	2,235,231	49,499	2.3	68.9	69.4
Husband-wife households	1,614,230	1,654,129	39,899	2.5	50.9	51.4
With own children under 18 years	730,620	697,785	(32,835)	(4.5)	23.0	21.7
Female householder, no spouse present	417,466	418,074	608	0.1	13.2	13.0
With own children under 18 years	210,678	199,446	(11,232)	(5.3)	6.6	6.2
Male householder, no spouse present	154,036	163,028	8,992	5.8	4.9	5.1
With own children under 18 years	66,214	63,162	(3,052)	(4.6)	2.1	2.0
Nonfamily households	986,689	983,567	(3,122)	(0.3)	31.1	30.6
One member	827,294	818,713	(8,581)	(1.0)	26.1	25.4
Two or more members	159,395	164,854	5,459	3.4	5.0	5.1

SOURCE: U.S. Census Bureau, American Community Survey for indicated years.

experienced by the nation. Not surprisingly, by 2017 the most prevalent household size continued to be two persons—trending toward a one-third share in both New Jersey and the United States. So with the above exceptions, general national-state household-size alignments continued during the post–Great Recession years, in terms of both size distribution and direction of change.

Compositional congruence between the state and nation was generally maintained during the post-2010 period, despite some seemingly fundamental divergences. In contrast to the nation, nonfamily households in New Jersey declined (albeit minimally) in number between 2010 and 2017, and their share of total households fell from 31.1 percent to 30.6 percent (table 11.13). This was caused by the drop in one-member nonfamilies (26.1 percent to 25.4 percent), which is the equivalent to the decline in one-person households discussed above and detailed in table 11.12.[10] Also in contrast to the nation, family households increased their share of total households from 68.9 percent to 69.4 percent.

This family-nonfamily reversal marked not only a modest divergence from the national trend but also marked the end of a six-decade-long (1950–2010) ascension in the proportional representation of nonfamilies in New Jersey and the corresponding proportional descension of families. Nonetheless, there were two family configurations that avoided the trend reversal during the post-2010 period.

This was the continuing decline in the share of husband-wife households with children (23.0 percent to 21.7 percent) and the increasing share (4.9 percent to 5.1 percent) of male householder (no spouse present) families (table 11.13).

Full explanations for this break in trend, or trend abatement, remain elusive. As suggested above, millennial movements or nonmovements, harsh post–Great Recession economic realities, and unique housing cost impediments may be part of the equation. In addition, the American Community Survey may paint a slightly different picture during time intervals between decennial censuses. Or the data may merely represent a blip or a simple pause on the secular trend.

Whatever the case, the household revolution has vastly reconfigured living arrangements in the nation and New Jersey. A counterrevolution does not appear to be in the demographic cards, but a new postrevolutionary household normal may be settling into place, setting the stage for a future characterized by stabilizing size and compositional shifts.

12

Demographics and Income

• •

The investigation of the income of New Jersey's households and families benefits from an understanding of the longer-term trends and dynamics in the United
States.[1] Thus, this chapter starts with an analysis of the nation's income trajectory beginning in the mid-twentieth century (1950). It reveals economically
linked intervals of affluence and stagnation, starting with the glorious multidecade period following World War II.[2] This was the fabled era of the American
dream—epitomized by suburban homeownership—which was largely synonymous with the procreation of the baby boom generation. It was characterized
by the seemingly unfettered growth—in aggregate terms—in the economic well-
being of households and families in the United States. Unfortunately, it was
subsequently followed by more than four decades of more limited advances punctuated by both modest and severe setbacks.

Following this broad secular framework, New Jersey's changing incomes over
time in relation to those of the United States are then examined. Current (2017)
demographically linked variations in income are presented for both New Jersey
and the United States, with particular attention to the household types detailed
in the preceding chapter.[3]

Unprecedented Affluence

Real incomes in the United States, as measured by constant median family
income levels, experienced major advances in the immediate post–World War
II decades.[4] This was a time of unchallenged worldwide economic hegemony by
the United States. But the sustained parade of growing affluence proved not to

Table 12.1

U.S. Median Family Income, 1950–2017 (Current and 2017 Constant Dollars)

	Median Family Income	
	Current Dollars	2017 Dollars
1950	3,319	29,584
1970	9,867	55,743
1973	12,051	59,595
1980	21,023	59,711
1990	35,353	64,489
2000	50,732	72,417
2007	61,355	72,716
2010	60,236	67,869
2012	62,241	66,575
2017	75,938	75,938
Gains in Real 2017 Income		
1950–1973	$30,011	101.4%
1973–1980	116	0.2
1980–1990	4,778	8.0
1990–2000	7,928	12.3
2000–2007	299	0.4
2007–2012	(6,141)	(8.4)
2012–2017	9,363	14.1
1973–2017	16,343	27.4

SOURCES: Fontenot, Semega, and Kollar 2018; U.S. Census Bureau, "Real Median Family Income in the United States [MEFAINUSA672N]," accessed May 27, 2020 from FRED, Federal Reserve Bank of St. Louis, https://fred.stlouisfed.org/series /MEFAINUSA672N.

NOTE: Families as of March of the following year (CPI-U-RS Adjusted 2017 Constant Dollars, Current Population Survey data).

be everlasting. The widespread income gains of this period were never again replicated following the 1973 oil embargo, which marked the beginning of a global economic reordering.

Table 12.1 presents the nation's median family income as determined by the Census Bureau's Current Population Survey in real and constant dollars for the key benchmark years between 1950 and 2017.[5] The sheer scale of the growth in postwar affluence in the United States is made readily apparent by the increase in income between 1950 and 1973. In constant 2017 dollars, real median family incomes more than doubled—101.4 percent—in this twenty-three-year period, from $29,584 in 1950 to $59,595 in 1973. Just how extraordinary this postwar gain was is illustrated by a comparison with the meager 27.4 percent increase that occurred over the subsequent forty-four-year period (1973–2017)—from $59,595 to $75,938. In terms of absolute growth pre- and post-1973, real median family incomes increased by $30,011 between 1950 and 1973 (twenty-three years) compared with an increase of just $16,343 between 1973 and 2017 (forty-four years).

Post-Affluence Intervals

Within the overall post-1973 period (1973–2017) of tepid income growth are distinct time intervals that have been shaped by the start-stop patterning of the U.S. economy.[6] Following its 1973 peak, real median family incomes increased by just $116 (0.2 percent) between 1973 and 1980, from $59,595 in 1973 to $59,711 in 1980. The onset of two energy crises (1973 and 1979), the 1973–1975 recession, and the loss of global manufacturing hegemony characterized the troubled economic decade of the 1970s. However, the virtual disappearance of real income growth was largely masked by the impact of inflation. Unadjusted or current-dollar median incomes actually grew from $12,051 in 1973 to $21,023 in 1980, an increase of $8,972, or 74.5 percent in seven years (table 12.1). Families may have relished this robust nominal increase, but the reality in constant dollars (or purchasing power) was one of stagnation—running faster just to stay in place.

However, the emergence and rise to prominence of a postindustrial economy brought renewed real income growth to the United States in the 1980s and 1990s, albeit far from the robust increases of the ebullient postwar years. Between 1980 and 1990, despite a setback experienced during the 1981–1982 recession, the real median family income gain totaled $4,778 (or 8.0 percent), from $59,711 in 1980 to $64,489 in 1990. This modest real increase for families was again obscured by inflation. Nominal incomes grew from $21,023 in 1980 to $35,353 in 1990, a gain in current dollars of $14,330. The real-income increase of $4,778 was just one-third of that. The 1980–1990 rate-of-change differential was equally stark: 8.0 percent growth in real dollars versus 68.2 percent in nominal dollars. Thus, increases in nominal dollars in hand were again much greater than actual purchasing-power gains.

Moreover, the gains that were achieved were bolstered by the addition of more earners per family. Much greater levels of labor force participation by women took place during the final decades of the twentieth century. In 1970, the overall labor force participation rate for women stood at 43.4 percent. By the year 2000, the rate had reached 59.9 percent.[7] In the absence of growing multiple-worker families, modest income gains would have been even more moderate.

Nonetheless, reflecting an improved national economic performance, the decade of the 1990s experienced more substantial income gains compared with the 1980s.[8] Real median family incomes increased from $64,489 in 1990 to $72,417 in 2000, a gain of $7,928 (or 12.3 percent). Both in absolute ($7,928 versus $4,778) and relative terms (12.3 percent versus 8.0 percent), the 1990s surpassed the 1980s. Supported by this upward income trajectory, optimism abounded as the new millennium dawned.

The Twenty-First Century

However, the end-of-decade/century optimism proved to be of limited duration. The 2001 recession marked the start of another period of income stagnation (Kliesen 2003). Between 2000 and 2007 (the start of the Great 2007–2009 Recession), real median family income increased by only $299, or 0.4 percent (table 12.1). This seven-year period of early new-millennium stagnation was immediately followed by a substantial income retreat. Throughout the Great Recession and the three years that followed (2007–2012), real incomes declined by 8.4 percent or $6,141, from $72,716 in 2007 to $66,575 in 2012. The worst economic downturn since the Great Depression inflicted substantial monetary pain on families in the United States. As pointed out in chapter 9, millennials entering the job market, or stuck in their early career stages, were particularly affected.

From the 2012 trough, robust income growth then ensued. Between 2012 and 2017, real median family incomes increased by 14.1 percent, or $9,363, from $66,575 in 2012 to $75,938 in 2017. While large compared with previous growth periods, almost two-thirds (65.6 percent) of this increase—$6,141 out of $9,363—represented simply the recovery of the income losses of the Great Recession. Thus, only $3,222 out of the overall $9,363 advance represented an income increase beyond the 2007 income peak.[9]

During the entire new century/millennium, real median family incomes increased from $72,417 in 2000 to $75,938 in 2017 (table 12.1). This represents a gain of just $3,521 achieved during a seventeen-year period. It took the robust 2012–2017 growth—$9,363—to surmount and advance past two impediments: the 2000–2007 income stagnation—a barely perceptible gain of $299—and the extended recession/postrecession (2007–2012) income contraction—a $6,141 loss.

So although the-end-of-decade (2012–2017) trajectory was undoubtedly positive—a gain of $9,363 in five years—it should also be put again into the long-term post–World War II perspective. In the sixty-seven years between 1950 and 2017, the real median family income in the United States increased from $29,584 (1950) to $75,938 (2017), a growth of $46,354. Of this overall gain, $30,011 (64.7 percent) occurred in the twenty-three years between 1950 and 1973, while just $16,343 (35.3 percent) was achieved in the forty-four years between 1973 and 2017.

The reality of modest recent U.S. income growth taking place in fits and starts defines the basic economic environment that has been enveloping the demographics of New Jersey. The immediate post–World War II ebullience was an extraordinary experience but is now a historical footnote.

New Jersey and the Nation

New Jersey has generally traversed the same income growth journey that was experienced by the nation. However, it has been modified by the unique economic circumstances of the state. Table 12.2 details the median family incomes

Table 12.2

Median Family Income, United States and New Jersey, 1960–2017

	United States ($)	New Jersey ($)	Ratio: NJ/US
1960	5,660	6,786	1.20
1970	9,586	11,403	1.19
1980	19,917	22,906	1.15
1990	35,225	47,589	1.35
2000	50,046	65,370	1.31
2010	60,609	82,427	1.36
2017	73,891	97,300	1.32

SOURCES: U.S. Census Bureau, decennial census 1960–2000; American Community Survey 2010–2017.

for New Jersey and the United States determined by each of the decennial censuses between 1960 and 2000, and then the median income drawn from the American Community Survey for 2010 and 2017. In 1960, New Jersey was one of the nation's key manufacturing dynamos. The state's median family income ($6,786) was 20 percent higher than that of the nation ($5,660). This high-ranking, industrial-based position was still evident in New Jersey in 1970. Its median family income advantage over the nation was largely maintained—19 percent greater ($11,403 versus $9,586).

But manufacturing in New Jersey began its long secular decline during the 1970s, and the state's relative income position slipped. By 1980, its income ($22,906), though still higher, fell to 15 percent greater than that of the United States ($19,917). But this early adjustment to a new economic era set the stage for the 1980s, when New Jersey became a postindustrial economic front-runner. By 1990, the state's median family income was more than one-third (35 percent) higher than the nation's ($47,589 versus $35,225). New Jersey's incomes subsequently remained comfortably ahead of those of the United States in 2000, 2010, and 2017, as they consistently maintained a 30-percent-plus advantage.

Income and Household Configuration

Within the long-term trend of cyclical national income growth are substantial income differences by household and family type.[10] What the data suggest is that the good life in much of the United States often requires a household or family team comprising more than a single earner. The latter are most prevalent in married-couple families, which stand at the top of the income ladder, but are also present in nonfamily households comprising more than one member (not living alone). Other household formats have widely varying positions but all on the lower rungs of the income ladder. This is apparent in the data of table 12.3, which presents median incomes according to household type for the United States and

Table 12.3
Median Income by Household Type, United States and New Jersey, 2017

	United States ($)	New Jersey ($)	Ratio: NJ/US
Households by Type			
Total Households	60,336	80,088	1.33
Family households	73,891	97,300	1.32
Married-couple families	88,315	116,294	1.32
With own children under 18 years	96,057	127,504	1.33
Female householder, no spouse present	36,959	47,367	1.28
With own children under 18 years	27,894	32,707	1.17
Male householder, no spouse present	50,886	62,774	1.23
With own children under 18 years	42,500	50,752	1.19
Nonfamily households	35,980	44,186	1.23
Female householder	31,303	36,411	1.16
Living alone	27,339	32,263	1.18
Not living alone	62,872	83,040	1.32
Male householder	41,593	53,345	1.28
Living alone	35,700	46,943	1.31
Not living alone	69,545	91,679	1.32

SOURCES: U.S. Census Bureau, decennial census 1960–2000; American Community Survey 2010–2017.

New Jersey for 2017, as well as the income ratios between the state and the nation for each of the household categories.[11]

The 2017 median income (in 2017 dollars) for all households in the United States was $60,336; New Jersey's median household income ($80,088) was 33 percent higher, consistent with the median family income differentials reviewed in table 12.2. However, partitioning households into family and non-family configurations reveals wide variations. Nationally, the median income for all family households ($73,891) was more than double that of all nonfamily households ($35,980). So too in New Jersey, where the family income ($97,300) was also more than double that of nonfamilies ($44,186).

Within the family household sector in New Jersey, married couples had a median income of $116,294 (table 12.3), the highest of any major household type. Those married-couple families with children under eighteen years old had an even higher median income ($127,504). That stands in sharp contrast to the other major family types, where the median incomes were significantly lower ($62,774) for male householders (no spouse present) and even lower still ($47,367) for female householders (no spouse present).

Standing in even sharper contrast were the much lower incomes for those male and female householders (no spouse present) who had children. The greatest disparity was evident for female householders (no spouse present) with own children under eighteen years old. Their median income of just $32,707 was only a quarter (25.7 percent) of the income of married couples with children ($127,504).

Moreover, the severity of their lagging incomes—and the economic constraints that it implies—is emphasized by a comparison with their national counterparts. Although overall family household median income ($97,300) in New Jersey was 32 percent higher than that ($73,891) of the nation, the New Jersey "advantage" was far lower for female and male householders with children. For example, the median income ($32,707) of female householders (no spouse present) with own children under eighteen years old was only 17 percent higher than that ($27,894) of their national counterparts. This stands as an extraordinarily economic/income-constrained demographic sector.

Such disparities are also prevalent in the lagging incomes in the nonfamily householder sectors detailed in table 12.3. Female householders in particular had the greatest income shortfall. For example, the median income ($32,263) of female householders living alone in New Jersey was only 18 percent higher than that ($27,339) of their equivalents in the United States. And their income level ($32,263) was far less than half (only 40.2 percent) of that ($80,088) of all households in New Jersey. The income constraints facing such household arrangements, to say the least, are substantial.

Much more competitive in the income arena are nonfamily households comprising more than an individual living alone. The median incomes in New Jersey of both female householders not living alone ($83,040) and male householders not living alone ($91,679) were greater than the state's overall median income ($80,088) for all households. And both were 32 percent higher than their national counterparts. The likelihood of multiple-person nonfamily households having multiple earners is probably similar to that of married-couple families, yielding for these household segments the highest income levels—and the most significant "consumption power"—in both New Jersey and the United States.

The median income level for total households in table 12.3 certainly represents a legitimate measure of central tendency, with New Jersey maintaining its income "lead" in comparison to the nation. In this case, however, a single measure is not sufficient to reveal significant demographic variations. Household diversity/segmentation reveals a wide variety of income capacities and disparities, ranging from a high of $127,504 for married couples (with own children under eighteen years)—the highest perch on the income ladder—to a low of $32,263 for female householders living alone—the lowest rung on the ladder.

Race and Ethnicity

Similar disparities are evident in terms of race and ethnicity. As shown at the bottom of table 12.4, white alone (not Hispanic or Latino) households in New Jersey in 2017 had a median income of $91,454, considerably higher than all New Jersey households ($80,088), and 39 percent higher than that ($65,845) of their national equivalents. But this high position was easily eclipsed by fast-growing

Table 12.4

Median Income by Race/Ethnicity, United States and New Jersey, 2017

	United States ($)	New Jersey ($)	Ratio: NJ/US
All Households	60,336	80,088	1.33
One race	NA	NA	NA
White	63,704	85,715	1.35
Black or African American	40,232	50,395	1.25
American Indian and Alaska Native	41,882	51,027	1.22
Asian	83,456	118,917	1.42
Native Hawaiian and Other Pacific Islander	60,734	NA	NA
Some other race	47,219	46,572	0.99
Two or more races	56,519	71,547	1.27
Hispanic or Latino origin (of any race)	49,793	54,482	1.09
White alone, not Hispanic or Latino	65,845	91,454	1.39

SOURCES: U.S. Census Bureau, decennial census 1960–2000; American Community Survey 2010–2017.
NOTE: NA = not applicable.

Asian (one-race) households, whose median income ($118,917) in New Jersey was 30 percent higher than white (alone) households in the state, and 42 percent higher than Asians ($83,456) in the United States, the highest national/state differential.

In contrast, at the opposite end of the household income scale stand two large and growing sectors. The median incomes of Black or African American households in New Jersey ($50,395) and Hispanic or Latino origin (of any race) households ($54,482) lag significantly behind all households in the state. And in the case of Hispanic or Latino households, the lag behind their national counterparts is strikingly evident—New Jersey's Hispanic or Latino incomes are only 9 percent higher while the incomes of all households in the state are 33 percent higher. Thus, racial and ethnic income disparities are as wide as household-type income disparities.

Age of Householder

As households traverse their career trajectories and stage in life cycle, their incomes change accordingly. This is reflected in table 12.5, which presents 2017 median household incomes by household age. As is evident from the similar patterns exhibited by both the nation and New Jersey, young households (fifteen to twenty-four years of age) have the lowest incomes. This is not surprising as the leading edge of this age group would just be entering the labor market, holding

Table 12.5
Median Income by Age of Householder, United States and New Jersey, 2017

	United States ($)	New Jersey ($)	Ratio: NJ/US
All Households	60,336	80,088	1.33
15–24 years	31,867	35,648	1.12
25–44 years	65,879	86,472	1.31
45–64 years	72,443	98,073	1.35
65 years and over	43,735	52,620	1.20

SOURCES: U.S. Census Bureau, decennial census 1960–2000; American Community Survey 2010–2017.

Table 12.6
Median Income by Age of Householder, New Jersey, 2010 and 2017

	2010 ($)	2017 ($)	Ratio: 2017/2010
All Households	67,681	80,088	1.18
15–24 years	31,182	35,648	1.14
25–44 years	73,858	86,472	1.17
45–64 years	82,348	98,073	1.19
65 years and over	41,452	52,620	1.27

SOURCE: U.S. Census Bureau, American Community Survey.

entry-level positions that have (in general) the lowest levels of compensation. Incomes then rise as age advances, with the biggest jump taking place as households move into the twenty-five-to-forty-four-years-of-age sector, the age when career patterns become more firmly established. Incomes then reach their highest levels in middle age (forty-five to sixty-four years of age), when most careers generally peak. Incomes then retreat (sixty-five years old and over) as labor market participation contracts and retirement unfolds.

More specifically, in New Jersey, median household incomes in 2017 showed a sharp advance as age increased—the $35,648 income of the fifteen-to-twenty-four-years-old sector was far less than one-half that ($86,472) of the twenty-five-to-forty-four-years-of-age sector. Incomes then increased at a less intense pace to $98,073 (forty-five to sixty-four), and finally contracted substantially to $52,620 (sixty-five and over). And although the income of the state's young households had lowest relative advantage compared with the nation (the median household income of the fifteen-to-twenty-four-years-old sector was just 12 percent higher than the nation), the advantage grew substantially for the forty-five-to-sixty-four-years-old sector—35 percent higher. As New Jersey's generations mature in the years ahead, the issue of the continuance of this age-related pattern will assume greater importance.

Also relevant in this regard is the growth of age-specified income in the post–Great Recession period (2010–2017). As presented in table 12.6, the median income for all households increased by 18 percent from 2010 to 2017 ($67,681–$80,088). It was the senior population that had the greatest rate of growth. The income of the sixty-five-years-and-over household category increased from $41,452 in 2010 to $52,620 in 2017—a 27 percent gain. In contrast, the median income of the youngest group—fifteen to twenty-four years—grew by only 14 percent.

Thus, although not excessively divergent, the age-related household income gains post–2010 have not been distributed evenly. This is consistent with the pattern of income disparities according to household configuration, and race and ethnicity. New Jersey's growing demographic complexity and increasing diversity are reflected in household economic wherewithal, its manifold dimensions, and its many consequences.

13

Recent Dynamics
and the Future

● ● ● ● ● ● ● ● ● ● ● ● ● ● ● ● ● ● ● ●

Yogi Berra, the famous Garden Stater, was alleged to have once stated, "It's tough to make predictions, especially about the future." Similar statements have also been attributed to Mark Twain, movie producer Samuel Goldwyn, Groucho Marx, Casey Stengel, and others. All are probably modest variations or adaptations of an adage more often formally linked to the famous Noble Prize–winning physicist Niels Bohr: "It's difficult to make predictions, especially about the future." Whatever the precise source, it's an oft-stated demographic quip that illustrates the trepidation expressed by population specialists in making projections.

In this vein, we will admit that forecasting the future of New Jersey's population is obviously fraught with uncertainty, particularly since demographic change is dependent on many variables. Primary among them is its ability to adapt to the inevitable structural transformations of the global and national economies. New Jersey's competitive economic position will help not only to determine the long-term well-being of its people and households but will also stand as a magnet/repellant for the magnitude of population flows—international and domestic—into and out of the state. How well New Jersey copes in a future environment of relentless technological progress that is continuously reinventing and reconfiguring national and global economies is an ever-present question. Historically, as our analyses have shown, it has fared very well.

Two centuries ago, New Jersey was one of the epicenters of the two Industrial Revolutions of the 1800s. Manufacturing agglomerations facilitated the concentration of the state's population into its early industrial cities. The labor required to staff rapidly growing urban-manufacturing ecosystems was supplied by vast waves of European immigration. As a result, New Jersey's dispersed, low-density population at the start of the nineteenth century was replaced by high-density, more diverse population concentrations by the end of the century. An economic transformation yielded a totally reconfigured demographic reality.

This reigning order ultimately became unraveled by a set of sequential disruptions that took place in the twentieth century's post–World War II era. Mass residential suburbanization, industrial decentralization, the emergence of a postindustrial economy, and a second great immigration wave again transformed New Jersey. An even newer economic and demographic order came into being.

But a new set of disruptions is now serving to reconstruct the very foundation of twenty-first-century New Jersey. Increasingly sophisticated digital advances are now not only redefining the economy but have been instrumental in shaping the ever more diverse generational transitions that are well under way. This powerful combination of technological and generational forces is now driving further multidimensional change.

Despite ever-present uncertainties, there are discernible emerging factors that provide input into the anatomy of demographic change in New Jersey. Many of them are quite different from the assumptions and protocols that were promulgated at the end of the last century, which brings to mind another Yogi Berra observation: "The future ain't what it used to be." We would add: "The future, it will come, but it may be subject to change without notice." In any case, recent international population trends provide a starting point for the overriding factors influencing New Jersey's demographic future.

Contextual Dynamics

Powerful global and national demographic trends will increasingly exert their influence on the future contours of New Jersey during the 2020s. These are presented in chapter 1 and discussed throughout the chapters of this book—slower population growth due to declining fertility rates in much of the world, with most advanced industrial countries having sub-replacement rates. As a consequence, migration is securing a more prominent role in determining the scale of population growth. Moreover, a general aging of the population—fewer young people and more old people—is gaining traction as a result of lower levels of fertility, increasing longevity rates (globally), and the rapid aging of the massive baby boom into the ranks of seniors (nationally). Within this contextual environment, New Jersey's population change in the decade ahead will be shaped and characterized by a number of key parameters.

Slow-Go/Slow-Grow New Jersey

Following the tidal waves of suburban population inflows into New Jersey in the immediate postwar decades, and the concurrent birth surge that produced its expansive baby boom, the state has consistently lagged the nation in population growth rates. This sluggish demography is typical of the Northeast region and the older industrial states of the Midwest; at the same time, aggregate population-growth advances in the United States have increasingly been captured by the South and West. The momentum of this decades-long trend is substantial, with little likelihood of it being reversed in the third decade of the twenty-first century.

The final accounts tabulated in the 2020 decennial census will officially confirm that New Jersey's 2010–2020 decadal population growth rate will probably be the lowest since the first census was undertaken in 1790. Although the state will not have to confront depopulation in the near-term future, it will certainly continue to experience what could be termed an extended and severe growth lull. It is highly likely that a new decade-low growth rate will prevail in the 2020s in the Garden State.

International Migration: The Demographic Growth Engine

With continued low levels of births standing as a high probability on the 2020s' horizon, dueling migration flows will become the ever-increasing determinant of population growth in the state. Sustained domestic outmigration losses put New Jersey, as well as its neighboring northeastern states, at a severe competitive national growth disadvantage. It may be an exaggeration, but the "Great Garden State Exodus" may be gaining momentum, propelled by unrelenting net domestic outmigration. (The state's urban bookends—New York City and Philadelphia—exhibit the same tendencies.) The affordability of movers' out-of-state destinations is the magnet, while a livability crisis—extraordinarily high living costs in New Jersey's most attractive and competitive (urban and suburban) places—is the repellant. The Garden State is in danger of becoming the Great Departure State.

Given the likely scale of New Jersey's continued domestic population outflows, a slow demographic death spiral will be avoided only by robust immigration population gains. Consequently, international migration will become an increasingly important component of positive population change for New Jersey in a likely future of constrained net natural increase and heavy domestic outmigration.

The foreign-born represent increasingly important economic assets in a potentially labor-constrained nation and state in the 2020s. But immigration destinations have been spreading across the country, no longer concentrating on traditional gateways such as New Jersey. Thus, immigration can no longer be taken for granted. To avoid slipping into population contraction and severe labor-force shortfalls, the state must maintain its historic attractiveness for international arrivals.

Racial and Ethnic Diversity Marches On

New Jersey has been at the forefront of an increasingly diverse nation, with an extraordinarily high proportion of its current population foreign-born. The latter will approach and then probably exceed a one-out-of-four share during the 2020s if current migration patterns are maintained. This will represent a sustained evolutionary transformation in the racial and ethnic composition of the state's population. It is not a revolutionary condition in New Jersey but a long-standing part of the state's very "essence."

One quandary will be the impending change in New Jersey's African American population. The Great Migration of the twentieth century bolstered the ranks of the state's Black population. In contrast, the twenty-first century's Reverse Great Migration of Black Americans may produce the opposite effect, lessening this historic dimension of diversity.

Emerging Demographic Disconnects

The inevitable age-structure transformation of New Jersey's population will continue to reflect past fertility variations and the emergence of new ones, tempered by evolving migration patterns. The huge population cohort that emerged from the great postwar "birth surge" is now maturing into a massive "elder boom" that will dominate the decade ahead. Standing at the opposite end of the age spectrum are contracting young population cohorts that have resulted from post–Great Recession fertility declines. Thus, there are two inexorable demographic forces—contraction and expansion. Will this produce age-cohort disconnects or will cooperation prevail? Entry-level labor force—predominantly minority—shortages will have to coexist with retirement population growth—largely white—excesses.

Household Revolution Yields to Household Evolution

The twentieth century was characterized by households shrinking in size: young adults in successive generations increasingly had the means to establish their own households. In the post–World War II era, a virtual household revolution took place, with an increasingly diverse set of household configurations gaining prominence. Both phenomena were significant forces for robust housing demand and housing construction.

This trend abated with the Great Recession as multigenerational households became much more prevalent due to economic constraints leading to young adults living at home. It was also partially due to the living-arrangement preferences of households headed by the foreign-born. But even with sustained economic expansion in the 2020s, a retreat to the sustained change of the past is unlikely. There are trend limits. Households cannot shrink much smaller. And as what were once "revolutionary" household formats become mainstream and conventional, it will be increasingly difficult to invent newer radical configurations in their stead. It is highly probable that household change will be far less dramatic in the decade to come.

"Burbs versus Urbs": Is the Urban Revival Over?

For over two centuries, the internal geography of New Jersey's population was continuously reinvented. The state experienced successive phases of demographic repositioning that pervaded the nation: the rise of the industrial city, early suburbanization and metropolitanization, rampant suburbanization, and reurbanization. Throughout the nineteenth and twentieth centuries, New Jersey was a front-runner of each national transformation. Will that continue as the twenty-first century matures?

Nationally, the years immediately following the Great 2007–2009 Recession heralded an era of large cities growing faster than their suburbs, reversing the decentralization trends that long characterized post–World War II America. But during the second half of the second decade of the current century, another reversal of course took place: suburbanization renewed itself as a national force. This does not mean a "return to Mayberry" (a perfect utopia-like small-town place to live) nor does it mean a return to the urban dysfunctions of the 1970s and 1980s. But it does suggest fewer overall spatial growth disparities than were prevalent for many decades. The more-than-century-long era of dramatic spatial "flip flops" may be over.

More recently, New Jersey's suburban malaise tracked the nation quite closely. Will the scale of the state's re-suburbanization—just in its formative stages—similarly follow? The "burbs versus urbs" tension may still be present in 2020s' New Jersey, but similar to the nation, a more geographically balanced future appears likely. It will be shaped by infrastructure capacities, cost differentials, income disparities, and household stage-in-life-cycle and lifestyle preferences. Moreover, New Jersey will remain a vital suburban asset of the greater New York and Philadelphia metropolitan regions as they recalibrate their internal demographic composition during the 2020s and beyond.

Perhaps the key determinants of the internal geographic distribution of New Jersey's population will be the pattern of settlement choices made by new international arrivals—assuming they remain a positive growth force—along with the generational transformations that are destined to buffet the Garden State. Will generational disruptions spawn an "out-of-kilter" demography, or will generations moving through their life cycles be a stabilizing influence? The continuing generational odyssey may provide the most effective framework for viewing the future demography of New Jersey and its potential impact on societal institutions.

Generational Longwaves: Charting the Future

Based on the inexorable aging of the population, there are six key age-defined generational longwaves that will be instrumental in shaping life in the Garden State in the decade of the 2020s and beyond. These are the product of the extensively reviewed six generations—pre–baby boom, baby boom, Generation X, millennials (Gen Y), Generation Z (postmillennials), and Generation Alpha. What will they look like in New Jersey and the nation in the 2020s at the beginning and end of this new decade?

Although the future age boundaries of each generation can be forecast with some certainty (assuming new research does not provide compelling evidence to recalibrate them), the exact numerical future size of each generation is more uncertain. For example, every member of the six defined generations who will be resident in New Jersey in 2030 is already alive, though perhaps residing in another state or even outside the United States. Similarly, every member of the six classifications who is resident in New Jersey in 2020, and who will be alive in 2030, may have an out-of-state residence in 2030. Thus, future domestic and international migration flows during the decade will be instrumental in overall generational size determinations; so, too, will fertility-rate trends, which will determine the ultimate size of Generation Alpha (and any as-yet-to-be-determined succeeding generation born before 2030).

Moreover, the future behavioral attributes of each generation will undoubtedly be shaped by their advancing age and stage in the household life cycle; less certain will be the impact of the scale of national and state economic growth, the stage in the business cycle, changing lifestyle aspirations, and new potentials enabled by inevitable technological advancement as well as other unforeseen factors. Nonetheless, despite such uncertainties, some outlines of the generational future can be delineated.

The demographically driven workforce transformations that dominated the 2010s will continue to disrupt workplace conventions as generational successions continue. This will also be the case for New Jersey's housing market conventions. The traditional protocols of demographic cohorts marching through established life-cycle stages, each characterized by specific housing-consumption patterns, will face significant challenges as the new decade progresses. The six generational longwaves will likely evolve as follows, with the members of each sequentially being far more diverse than their immediate predecessor.

Pre–Baby Boom: The Oldest New Jerseyans

Pre–baby boomers (born 1930 to 1945) will have aged to between seventy-five and ninety years old in 2020, their numbers continuing to diminish steadily. Because the first two-thirds of this generation represents the "depressed" Depression birth totals, the number of "eightysomethings" will have already declined between 2010 and 2020. As they age further, to between eighty-five and one hundred years by 2030, the number of "ninetysomethings" will also markedly contract. This does not mean a shrinkage in the overall ranks of seniors during the 2020s, because the aging baby boom will be rapidly growing the younger senior segments (under eighty years of age).

The Baby Boom: Maturing Seventysomethings

In 2020, the baby boomers (born 1946 to 1964) were between fifty-six and seventy-four years of age, and a new gray dawn was rising in America: a more-old-than-young society, with more people over sixty years of age than young people under the age of eighteen years. A new age-based multigenerational world started to characterize New Jersey.

With a median age of sixty-five years in 2020, members of the baby boom will be evenly partitioned between retirees (older than sixty-five years) who have exited the workplace doors for the final time and active labor-force participants (younger than sixty-five years). Of the latter, many will still be in their peak earning years, perched on the upper rungs—both private and public—of the organizational ladder. Although many quips abound about the baby boom representing the workforce of the past, it still maintained its widespread leadership presence.

But the subsequent decade of the 2020s will see a mass exodus of baby boomers from the labor force and from their once-dominant societal positions. This will represent the greatest brain drain in the state's history. How to capture and retain the baby boom's expansive knowledge that was accumulated over a lifetime—encompassing experience, wisdom, cognitive skills, and institutional memory—will be a crucial issue confronting all public and private organizations in the state. Another key issue will be the sheer scale of the nation's resources that will be consumed by the exploding number of baby boom retirees. It is anticipated that their historical insatiable appetite of wants and needs will not abate. The potential scale of intergenerational support—or conflict—could be unprecedented.

Simultaneously, mass grandparenthood will also arrive in full force during the 2020s. Not surprisingly, the baby boom's residential preferences and movements will continue to reshape New Jersey's housing and economic markets as they have throughout each of its life-cycle stages. Starting from its early direct housing-market entry in the 1960s, the 2020s will mark the seventh decade wherein the baby boom has reinvented shelter in the Garden State, always exerting an outsized market footprint. The 2020s will see a vast proliferation of retirement, life-plan, and continuing care retirement communities, as baby boomers reinvent retirement and advanced senior living.[1] The sheer scale of this generation's departure from suburban single-family homeownership will represent a housing-supply excess whose sheer size may overwhelm the scale of demand exerted by younger generations. Huge buyers' markets in vast swaths of suburban New Jersey most likely will ensue. A key force—the baby boom life cycle—that had long driven the historic twentieth-century suburbanization of the Garden State will continue to retreat.

By 2030, all New Jerseyans in their seventies will be baby boomers. Overall, the generation's members will range in age between sixty-six and eighty-four years; the graying of America and New Jersey will be even more pronounced. The nation and state will be approaching the point where there will be more people—a great majority of them boomers—over sixty-five years old than under the age of eighteen years. A tidal wave of seventysomething baby boomers will be fully engulfing the Garden State.

Generation X: Maturing Fiftysomethings

Generation X (born 1965 to 1980) will continue to trail in the wake of the huge predecessor baby boom bulge. In 2020, Gen X was between forty and fifty-five years of age. This age span represents the peak family-raising stage of the life cycle and the age of peak housing consumption. But the single-family home market's robustness will be inhibited by generational-size disparities. A smaller Gen X market inflow will not be sufficient to fill the voids left behind by the exiting baby boom market outflow. Gen X will also be poised to ascend fully into the twenty-first-century top-line workforce by 2020; it will already be overwhelmingly dominating the mid-tier sectors of the economy and starting to move into the lower- and mid-level leadership ranks in the state's public and private organizations.

This generational transition will make succession an increasing concern during the subsequent decade of the 2020s. Increasing vacancies in leadership positions will lead to Gen X eventually fully dominating the C-suite. Its leading-edge members will continue to follow closely in the wake of their trailing-edge baby boom predecessors. They will be maturing into empty-nester status in the household and housing market.

By 2030, Generation X will be firmly set into advanced middle age—between fifty and sixty-five years of age. Every fiftysomething in New Jersey will be a Gen Xer. Depending on the state of the economy at that time, retirement will be on the radar screen of the oldest Gen Xers. But for the most part, their leadership positions in society and the economy will be peaking. To the likely dismay of the oldest Gen Xers, young postmillennial generation members will probably consider them as joining the ranks of the "ancients" as the 2030s are reached. Nonetheless, they will still be in full command of the economy and most of society's institutions.

At the same time, another generational shift out of the single-family home market beckons. The oldest Gen Xers will be empty nesters, facing entry into the first-stage, specialized post-single-family housing market sectors—such as age-restricted active-adult communities—pioneered by the baby boom earlier in the century. The youngest Gen Xers will still be in the late child-rearing sector of the life cycle, still trading up in the housing market—and consuming greater amounts of housing. The entire generation will happily be confronting buyers' markets, being the beneficiary of the baby boom's vast supply residual: Gen X–driven under-capacity demand meeting baby boom–driven over-capacity supply.

Millennials (Gen Y): Maturing Thirtysomethings/Fortysomethings

Millennials, or Gen Y (born 1981 to 1996), comprise the first generation where whites (non-Hispanic) constitute a minority. Long fixated on as the new, emerging demographic cohort in New Jersey, millennials will no longer be "youngsters" by 2020 and, like the nation, will have overtaken boomers in population size. Not quite yet "yesterday's generation," they will dominate the "thirtysomething" age bracket as their leading edge passed through their fourth decade of existence and were poised to enter their fifth.[2] Between twenty-four and thirty-nine years old in 2020, they will dominate the lower and lower-middle tiers of the labor market. They will have totally transformed the structure of the workplace and workplace location and reshaped housing demand.

One of the millennials' legacies was their pre-2020 role as a driving force in the emergence of a postsuburban New Jersey economy and demography. Millennial workplace and residential choices led the state's urban resurgence during the century's first two decades (2000–2020), a period when New Jersey's automobile-centric outer suburbs seemingly ran out of gas. It may be an overexaggeration to label them zones of suburban evacuation, but placid, low-density, outer-suburban territories had fallen out of millennial fashion. In contrast, exciting, higher-density, multidimensional urban activity centers were in. The latter could be labeled zones of urban millennial emergence. But lifestyle preferences tend to change with age and maturity.

Although leading-edge millennials had already moved into the family-raising stage of the life cycle by 2020, most of the remainder will do so during the ensuing decade, raising the possibility of significantly different spatial living-environment choices throughout the decade. The issue of the state's changing demographic geography during the 2020s will largely be framed by two boundary questions: Will maturing millennials decide to remain in car-free or car-light, amenity-rich, urban-style environments? Or will they prove not to be averse to human-driven personal vehicles, lower-density domiciles, and other suburban appurtenances? At a minimum, there should be some abatement of the de-suburbanization tendencies that dominated the 2010s.

Still, any suburban bounce back will not be a tidal wave but a differentiated transition. Select, suburban, family-raising environments that provide urban amenities will likely gain increasing favor as the decade advances. And surging costs in those locations that "suffered" intense millennial demand in the 2010s will act as a push factor into the new "zones of suburban millennial emergence." However, those areas that benefited earlier from millennial lifestyle preferences will probably counter with an array of millennial-retention strategies.

Much of the vast inlying suburban single-family housing stock built between 1950 and 1970 to accommodate the gestation and raising of the baby boom will be between sixty and eighty years old by 2030. Will millennials, many of them offspring of the baby boom, come full circle and reinhabit the now (mostly) obsolete suburban childhood homes of their parents? Or will they want suburban locales that replicate the amenity-laden live-work-play, higher-density environments and lifestyles they embraced as young adults? This is a fundamental question that many suburban New Jersey communities will have to confront: what strategies to follow in order to reinvent themselves. Although the ultimate outcome is still uncertain, one likely result is unprecedented suburban differentiation—communities either adopted or rejected by family-raising millennials.

The post–World War II trade-up dynamic—increasing moves to larger houses on bigger lots—was an overwhelming housing-market force perfected to an art form by the baby boom. But so far in this century, millennials have rejected many baby boom conventions. Will "upscaling" in place be the "new" trade-up model, with specific community (municipality) characteristics assuming a much more central role in residential decision making? Will a new normal emerge: trading up (renovating) in place instead of moving up and out, with "ideal" community supplanting "ideal" housing configuration? Will starter homes ultimately become the new "forever" homes? This would represent a disruption of the high rates of geographic mobility historically displayed by households moving through the life cycle. If so, urban "zones of millennial retention" may proliferate by 2030. Regardless, the new millennial-driven "zones of suburban emergence" will have made some imprint on the state's population geography. However, the full scale of this imprint is open to very real question.

By 2030, millennials will enter middle age and be between thirty-four and forty-nine years of age. Like their baby boom predecessors, they will probably attempt to recalibrate the biological clock by rebranding this age span "middle youth" instead of middle age. But again, it probably won't work. Nonetheless, with increased earning power, their lifestyle preferences will increasingly dominate New Jersey and the nation, although they may not yet have to cede their next-gen workforce designation to their postmillennial successors. Thus, another uncertainty arises: If a new suburban-based millennial residential pattern strongly emerges, what does that mean for a corporate sector that had repositioned itself in relation to their earlier locational preferences?

New Jersey's workforce will increasingly become millennial-centric by 2030. This technology-defined generation already helped to dramatically restructure the workplace, both functionally and spatially. But information technology, artificial intelligence, and machine learning will inexorably advance. Will the mantle of cutting-edge technological prowess and leadership be retained by millennials, or will it be captured by the next generation?

Gen Z (Postmillennials): Maturing Twentysomethings

Gen Z (born between 1997 and 2012), the second generation in the state that is majority-minority, will be eight to twenty-three years of age in 2020. Except in the very youngest grades, Gen Z will dominate most of the K–12 education system. This is almost exactly the same generational position held by the baby boom in 1970, one-half century earlier. Similarly, Gen Z will constitute most of the undergraduate enrollment ranks of colleges and universities in 2020, just as the baby boom did in 1970. However, racial and ethnic diversity characterizes postmillennials in the educational system; racial and ethnic homogeneity had characterized the baby boom when it was similarly positioned.

Gen Z to date has been subject to less analysis compared with the older generations under scrutiny here, leading to somewhat more speculation about their future behavioral attributes. But the implications of Gen Z's specific age- and life-cycle position are less speculative. During the 2020s, Gen Z will increasingly dominate the entry-level job market. "Move over, millennials" may be the new labor market catchphrase. Gen Z will probably be labeled the "post-gen" workforce, succeeding the millennial-based "next-gen" predecessor. If history is a guide, the emerging post-gen workforce will then become the prized corporate knowledge-based labor-force commodity. It will constitute the critical mass of the new talent foundation that will be essential for sophisticated technological leadership. Whatever technological advances unfold in the 2020s, Gen Z will be the first generation to have experienced them in New Jersey's classrooms.

As pointed out earlier, millennials constituted the first generation raised in the digital age, and their subsequent impact on the state's economy was profound. Postmillennials—the first generation raised in the mobile era of smartphones and social media, with access and connectivity to everything, everywhere, instantaneously—have the potential to have an equivalent transformative impact. Will this result in a paradigmatic economic shift, or will it simply be an evolutionary extension of now-established millennial-driven economic contours?

Moreover, in the 2020s, Gen Z will represent the most diverse generation born in the post–World War II twentieth/twenty-first centuries. It will also be the least suburban-/most urban-born demographic cohort in New Jersey. Will it discover the state's suburban arena to be an exciting new frontier as it forms households, or will it eschew the suburbs not only in residential terms but also in place of work?

By 2030, Gen Z postmillennials will be between eighteen and thirty-three years of age, with many still engaged in first-time household formation. Questions and uncertainties will abound. Will those geographic areas favored by millennials in the 2010s be saddled with out-of-reach cost levels, inhibiting the entrance of Gen Z? Will new, more affordable "cool" areas then emerge? Or will millennial outflows from their favored lifestyle-based haunts of the past to more conducive family-raising environments leave voids that can be filled by Gen Y? Alternatively, will "mature-in-place" millennials effectively post "no vacancy" notices inhibiting postmillennial inflows? Concurrently, will the corporate settlement patterns predicated on millennial preferences be adaptable to postmillennial realities?

Generation Alpha: First Twenty-First-Century Generation

Gen Alpha is the third post–World War II generation to be minority white, following Gen Y millennials and Gen Z. It is likely that in every successive generation in the twenty-first century, whites will become an increasingly smaller minority, particularly if immigration flows are maintained. New Jersey will be leading the nation in this continuing transformation.

Born post-2012, the oldest alpha was seven years old in 2020 and just entering the state's K–12 educational system. Gen Alpha will then begin its decade-long march through elementary and high school. By 2030, it will encompass almost all of the state's school-aged population when the oldest alpha turns seventeen years old. Although the majority of alphas will be children of millennials, some of the youngest—born post-2025—may well be offspring of Gen Z, since the oldest Gen Zer will turn twenty-eight years old in 2025. This assumes that a newly identified additional generation—post-alphas?—will not have been recognized before 2030.

Fertility-rate patterns in the 2020s will ultimately determine whether the final size of Gen Alpha represents simply a continuation of the birth "lull" evident during the post–Great Recession years or if it will reflect a potentially more robust birth "dearth." Certainly, its final size will also be linked to domestic and international migration patterns post-2020. Nonetheless, the decade of the 2020s will be one where school enrollment declines will be prevalent statewide, although wide variations will occur among the state's school districts. This will be a function of millennial preferences and choices with regard to family-raising environments.

The 2020s will represent the latest school system generational challenges, which started with the baby boom (system expansion), followed by Gen X (system contraction), millennials (Gen Y—increasing diversity and new digital technology environments), and Gen Z (further diversity and total immersion in the connected, mobile information/social media world). Gen Alpha brings size-contraction challenges back into the equation as well as further majority-minority dynamics. Gen Alpha also represents a cohort totally enveloped by all of the predecessor technologies since birth and additionally shaped by artificial intelligence/robotics and other advances yet to be fully unveiled. Sustained increases in educational complexity will continue to confront all of New Jersey's educational systems.

Summary

New Jersey continues to be beset by major structural transformations, vividly illustrated by sustained generational succession waves. Consequently, the shelf lives of many of our pre–Great Recession assumptions and certainties have finally reached their expiration dates. In fact, the world as we once confidently knew it has long since vacated today's Garden State premises.

Appendix A

• •

Population by County in
New Jersey in the Colonial Era
(1726, 1738, 1745, 1772,
and 1784) and as a State
(1790–2018)

Note on New Jersey Counties and County Boundaries

The existence, number, and boundaries of New Jersey counties have changed over the historical period presented in this appendix and referred to in chapters 2, 4, 5, and elsewhere in this book. To interpret the county population numbers presented in this appendix and elsewhere, the reader is referred to figures A.1 and A.2 and Wacker (1975). See also "Maps of New Jersey" (https://www.mapofus .org/newjersey/) and that site's "Interactive Map of New Jersey County Formation History." Choosing the "New Jersey County Formation Years" or the "New Jersey County Census Years" at this source displays in map form which New Jersey counties existed at different time periods and the boundaries of each county.

Note on Population Counts and Sources

There were four colonial-era state population enumerations in New Jersey that encompassed the entire colony in 1726, 1737–1738 (hereafter simply dated 1738), 1745, and 1784. (The 1772 enumeration covered only the then-eight counties in West Jersey.) The New Jersey colonial-era populations in this appendix are based

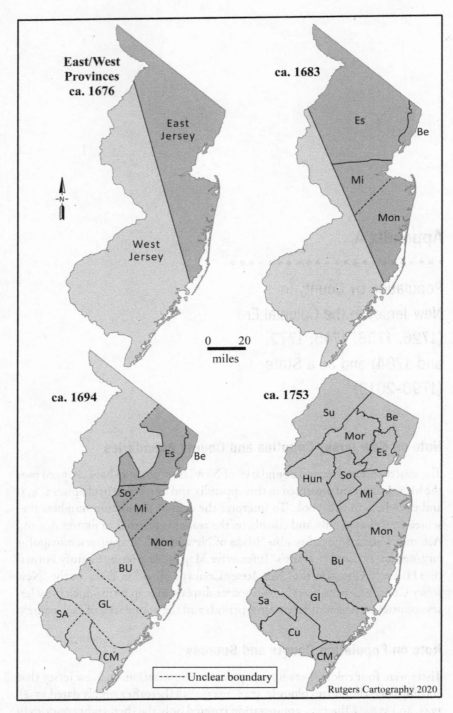

FIG. A.1 East-West Jersey and Evolving Counties in the Seventeenth and Eighteenth Centuries. (Source: © 2020 Rutgers, The State University of New Jersey. Map created from historical information contained in Walton 2010.)

Table A.1

Population by County in New Jersey in the Colonial Era

Year	1726 Number	1726 Percent (%)	1738 Number	1738 Percent (%)	1745 Number	1745 Percent (%)	1772 Number	1772 Percent (%)	1784 Number	1784 Percent (%)
State of NJ	32,442	100	46,676	100	61,403	100	71,025	100	149,435	100
Counties										
Atlantic	—	—	—	—	—	—	—	—	—	—
Bergen	2,673	8.2	4,095	8.8	3,006	4.9	—	—	9,356	6.3
Burlington	4,129	12.7	5,238	11.2	6,803	11.1	13,124	18.5	15,801	10.6
Camden	—	—	—	—	—	—	—	—	—	—
Cape May	668	2.1	1,004	2.2	1,188	1.9	1,759	2.5	2,231	1.5
Cumberland	—	—	—	—	—	—	5,059	7.1	6,300	4.2
Essex	4,230	13.0	6,326	13.6	6,988	11.4	—	—	13,430	9.0
Gloucester	2,229	6.9	3,267	7.0	3,506	5.7	8,754	12.3	10,689	7.2
Hudson	—	—	—	—	—	—	—	—	—	—
Hunterdon	3,377	10.4	5,507	11.8	9,151	14.9	15,605	22.0	18,363	12.3
Mercer	—	—	—	—	—	—	—	—	—	—
Middlesex	4,009	12.4	4,764	10.2	7,612	12.4	—	—	12,005	8.0
Monmouth	4,879	15.0	6,086	13.0	8,627	14.0	—	—	14,708	9.8
Morris	—	—	—	—	4,436	7.2	11,535	16.2	13,416	9.0
Ocean	—	—	—	—	—	—	—	—	—	—
Passaic	—	—	—	—	—	—	—	—	—	—
Salem	3,977	12.3	5,884	12.6	6,847	11.2	5,960	8.4	8,473	5.7
Somerset	2,271	7.0	4,505	9.7	3,239	5.3	—	—	10,476	7.0
Sussex	—	—	—	—	—	—	9,229	13.0	14,187	9.5
Union	—	—	—	—	—	—	—	—	—	—
Warren	—	—	—	—	—	—	—	—	—	—

SOURCES: These population enumerations are derived from Wacker (1975, 413–416) and include corrections to original sources indicated by Wacker.

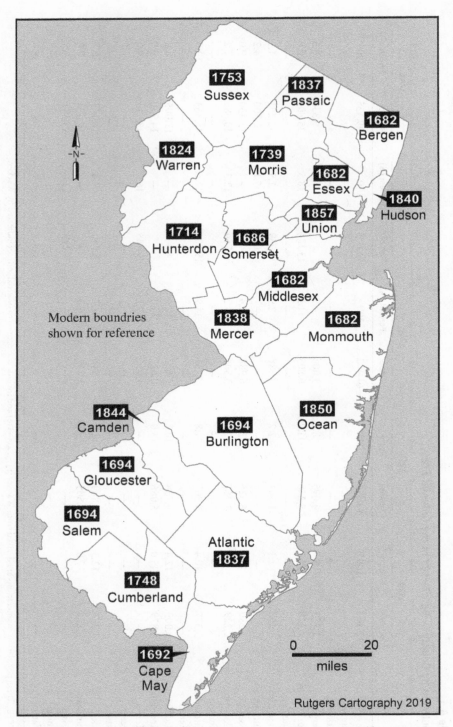

FIG. A.2 New Jersey County Map and Historical Data on County Formation (showing county seats, present boundaries, and dates of formation). (Source: New Jersey Department of State, "New Jersey County Map," https://www.nj.gov/state/archives/catctytable.html.)

FIG. A.2 New Jersey County Map and Historical Data on County Formation (showing county seats, present boundaries, and dates of formation)

County	Date Formed	County Seat	Historical Data
Atlantic	1837	Mays Landing	Formed from Gloucester County.
Bergen	1683	Hackensack	Original county in East Jersey; Passaic County set off, 1837; Hudson County set off, 1840.
Burlington	1681	Mount Holly	Original county in West Jersey; Court-established 1681; boundary set with Gloucester County, 1692; Hunterdon County set off, 1714; part of Mercer County formed from Burlington, 1838.
Camden	1844	Camden	Formed from Gloucester County.
Cape May	1685	Cape May Court House	Original county in West Jersey; Court-established 1685; boundaries set 1692.
Cumberland	1748	Bridgeton	Formed from Salem County.
Essex	1683	Newark	Original county in East Jersey; part of Passaic County formed from Essex, 1837; Union County set off, 1857.
Gloucester	1686	Woodbury	Original county in West Jersey; Court-established 1686; boundary set with Burlington County, 1692; Atlantic County set off, 1837; Camden County set off, 1844.
Hudson	1840	Jersey City	Formed from Bergen County.
Hunterdon	1714	Flemington	Formed from Burlington County; Morris County set off, 1739; part of Mercer County formed from Hunterdon, 1838.
Mercer	1838	Trenton	Formed from Burlington, Hunterdon, Middlesex, and Somerset Counties.
Middlesex	1683	New Brunswick	Original county in East Jersey; Somerset County set off, 1688; part of Mercer County formed from Middlesex, 1838.
Monmouth	1683	Freehold	Original county in East Jersey; Ocean County set off, 1850.
Morris	1739	Morristown	Formed from Hunterdon County; Sussex County set off, 1753.
Ocean	1850	Toms River	Formed from Monmouth County.
Passaic	1837	Paterson	Formed from Bergen and Essex Counties.
Salem	1681	Salem	Original county in West Jersey; Court-established 1681; formed from Salem Tenth, 1694; Cumberland set off, 1748.
Somerset	1688	Somerville	Formed from Middlesex County.
Sussex	1753	Newton	Formed from Morris County; Warren County set off, 1824.
Union	1857	Elizabeth	Formed from Essex County.
Warren	1824	Belvidere	Formed from Sussex County.

SOURCE: This material is excerpted verbatim from New Jersey Department of State, "New Jersey County Map," https://www.nj.gov/state/archives/catctytable.html.
NOTE: Some inconsistent county formation dates on the map and table of figure A.2 reflect differences by historians on these exact formation dates.

Table A.2
Population by County in New Jersey as a State, 1790–2018

Year	1790		1800		1810		1820		1830		1840		1850	
	Number	Percent (%)	Number	Percent (%)	Number	Percent (%)	Number	Percent (%)	Number	Percent (%)	Number	Percent (%)	Number	Percent (%)
State of NJ	184,139	100	211,149	100	245,562	100	277,575	100	320,823	100	373,306	100	489,555	100
Counties														
Atlantic	–		–		–		–		–		8,726	2.3	8,961	1.8
Bergen	12,601	6.8	15,156	7.2	16,603	6.8	18,178	6.5	22,412	7.0	13,223	3.5	14,725	3.0
Burlington	18,095	9.8	21,521	10.2	24,979	10.2	28,822	10.4	31,107	9.7	32,831	8.8	43,203	8.8
Camden	–		–		–		–		–		–		25,422	5.2
Cape May	2,571	1.4	3,066	1.5	3,632	1.5	4,265	1.5	4,936	1.5	5,324	1.4	6,433	1.3
Cumberland	8,248	4.5	9,529	4.5	12,670	5.2	12,668	4.6	14,093	4.4	14,374	3.9	17,189	3.5
Essex	17,785	9.7	22,269	10.5	25,984	10.6	30,793	11.1	41,911	13.1	44,621	12.0	73,950	15.1
Gloucester	13,363	7.3	16,115	7.6	19,744	8.0	23,089	8.3	28,431	8.9	25,438	6.8	14,655	3.0
Hudson	–		–		–		–		–		9,483	2.5	21,822	4.5
Hunterdon	20,153	10.9	21,261	10.1	24,556	10.0	28,604	10.3	31,060	9.7	24,789	6.6	28,990	5.9
Mercer	–		–		–		–		–		21,502	5.8	27,992	5.7
Middlesex	15,956	8.7	17,890	8.5	20,381	8.3	21,470	7.7	23,157	7.2	21,893	5.9	28,635	5.8
Monmouth	16,918	9.2	19,872	9.4	22,150	9.0	25,038	9.0	29,233	9.1	32,909	8.8	30,313	6.2
Morris	16,216	8.8	17,750	8.4	21,828	8.9	21,368	7.7	23,666	7.4	25,844	6.9	30,158	6.2
Ocean	–		–		–		–		–		–		10,032	2.0
Passaic	–		–		–		–		–		16,734	4.5	22,569	4.6
Salem	10,437	5.7	11,371	5.4	12,761	5.2	14,022	5.1	14,155	4.4	16,024	4.3	19,467	4.0
Somerset	12,296	6.7	12,815	6.1	14,725	6.0	16,506	5.9	17,689	5.5	17,455	4.7	19,692	4.0
Sussex	19,500	10.6	22,534	10.7	25,549	10.4	32,752	11.8	20,346	6.3	21,770	5.8	22,989	4.7
Union	–		–		–		–		–		–		–	
Warren	–		–		–		–		18,627	5.8	20,366	5.5	22,358	4.6

Table A.2

Population by County in New Jersey as a State, 1790–2018 (*continued*)

Year	1860		1870		1880		1890		1900		1910	
	Number	Percent (%)	Number	Percent (%)	Number	Percent (%)	Number	Percent (%)	Number	Percent (%)	Number	Percent (%)
State of NJ	672,035	100	906,096	100	1,131,116	100	1,444,933	100	1,883,669	100	2,537,167	100
Counties												
Atlantic	11,786	1.8	14,093	1.6	18,704	1.7	28,836	2.0	46,402	2.5	71,894	2.8
Bergen	21,618	3.2	30,122	3.3	36,786	3.3	47,226	3.3	78,441	4.2	138,002	5.4
Burlington	49,730	7.4	53,639	5.9	55,402	4.9	58,528	4.1	58,241	3.1	66,565	2.6
Camden	34,457	5.1	46,193	5.1	62,942	5.6	87,687	6.1	107,643	5.7	142,029	5.6
Cape May	7,130	1.1	8,349	0.9	9,765	0.9	11,268	0.8	13,201	0.7	19,745	0.8
Cumberland	22,605	3.4	34,665	3.8	37,687	3.3	45,438	3.1	51,193	2.7	55,153	2.2
Essex	98,877	14.7	143,839	15.9	189,929	16.8	256,098	17.7	359,053	19.1	512,886	20.2
Gloucester	18,444	2.7	21,562	2.4	25,886	2.3	28,649	2.0	31,905	1.7	37,368	1.5
Hudson	62,717	9.3	129,067	14.2	187,944	16.6	275,126	19.0	386,048	20.5	537,231	21.2
Hunterdon	33,654	5.0	36,963	4.1	38,570	3.4	35,355	2.4	34,507	1.8	33,569	1.3
Mercer	37,419	5.6	46,386	5.1	58,061	5.1	79,978	5.5	95,365	5.1	125,657	5.0
Middlesex	34,812	5.2	45,029	5.0	52,286	4.6	61,754	4.3	79,762	4.2	114,426	4.5
Monmouth	39,346	5.9	46,195	5.1	55,538	4.9	69,128	4.8	82,057	4.4	94,734	3.7
Morris	34,677	5.2	43,137	4.8	50,861	4.5	54,101	3.7	65,156	3.5	74,704	2.9
Ocean	11,176	1.7	13,628	1.5	14,455	1.3	15,974	1.1	19,747	1.0	21,318	0.8
Passaic	29,013	4.3	46,416	5.1	68,860	6.1	105,046	7.3	155,202	8.2	215,902	8.5
Salem	22,458	3.3	23,940	2.6	24,579	2.2	25,151	1.7	25,530	1.4	26,999	1.1
Somerset	22,057	3.3	23,510	2.6	27,162	2.4	28,311	2.0	32,948	1.7	38,820	1.5
Sussex	23,846	3.5	23,168	2.6	23,539	2.1	22,259	1.5	24,134	1.3	26,781	1.1
Union	27,780	4.1	41,859	4.6	55,571	4.9	72,467	5.0	99,353	5.3	140,197	5.5
Warren	28,433	4.2	34,336	3.8	36,589	3.2	36,553	2.5	37,781	2.0	43,187	1.7

(*continued*)

Table A.2

Population by County in New Jersey as a State, 1790–2018 (*continued*)

Year	1920		1930		1940		1950		1960		1970	
	Number	Percent (%)	Number	Percent (%)	Number	Percent (%)	Number	Percent (%)	Number	Percent (%)	Number	Percent (%)
State of NJ	3,155,900	100	4,041,334	100	4,160,165	100	4,835,329	100	6,066,782	100	7,171,112	100
Counties												
Atlantic	83,914	2.7	124,823	3.1	124,066	3.0	132,399	2.7	160,880	2.7	175,043	2.4
Bergen	210,703	6.7	364,977	9.0	409,646	9.8	539,139	11.1	780,255	12.9	897,148	12.5
Burlington	81,770	2.6	93,541	2.3	97,013	2.3	135,910	2.8	224,499	3.7	323,132	4.5
Camden	190,508	6.0	252,312	6.2	255,727	6.1	300,743	6.2	392,035	6.5	456,291	6.4
Cape May	19,460	0.6	29,486	0.7	28,919	0.7	37,131	0.8	48,555	0.8	59,554	0.8
Cumberland	61,348	1.9	69,895	1.7	73,184	1.8	88,597	1.8	106,850	1.8	121,374	1.7
Essex	652,089	20.7	833,513	20.6	837,340	20.1	905,949	18.7	923,545	15.2	932,526	13.0
Gloucester	48,224	1.5	70,802	1.8	72,219	1.7	91,727	1.9	134,840	2.2	172,681	2.4
Hudson	629,154	19.9	690,730	17.1	652,040	15.7	647,437	13.4	610,734	10.1	607,839	8.5
Hunterdon	32,885	1.0	34,728	0.9	36,766	0.9	42,736	0.9	54,107	0.9	69,718	1.0
Mercer	159,881	5.1	187,143	4.6	197,318	4.7	229,781	4.8	266,392	4.4	304,116	4.2
Middlesex	162,334	5.1	212,208	5.3	217,077	5.2	264,872	5.5	433,856	7.2	583,813	8.1
Monmouth	104,925	3.3	147,209	3.6	161,238	3.9	225,327	4.7	334,401	5.5	461,849	6.4
Morris	82,694	2.6	110,445	2.7	125,732	3.0	164,371	3.4	261,620	4.3	383,454	5.3
Ocean	22,155	0.7	33,069	0.8	37,706	0.9	56,622	1.2	108,241	1.8	208,470	2.9
Passaic	259,174	8.2	302,129	7.5	309,353	7.4	337,093	7.0	406,618	6.7	460,782	6.4
Salem	36,572	1.2	36,834	0.9	42,274	1.0	49,508	1.0	58,711	1.0	60,346	0.8
Somerset	47,991	1.5	65,132	1.6	74,390	1.8	99,052	2.0	143,913	2.4	198,372	2.8
Sussex	24,905	0.8	27,830	0.7	29,632	0.7	34,423	0.7	49,255	0.8	77,528	1.1
Union	200,157	6.3	305,209	7.6	328,344	7.9	398,138	8.2	504,255	8.3	543,116	7.6
Warren	45,057	1.4	49,319	1.2	50,181	1.2	54,374	1.1	63,220	1.0	73,960	1.0

Table A.2
Population by County in New Jersey as a State, 1790–2018 (continued)

Year	1980 Number	Percent (%)	1990 Number	Percent (%)	2000 Number	Percent (%)	2010 Number	Percent (%)	2018 Number	Percent (%)
State of NJ	7,365,011	100	7,730,188	100	8,414,350	100	8,791,894	100	8,908,520	100
Counties										
Atlantic	194,119	2.6	224,327	2.9	252,552	3.0	274,549	3.1	265,429	3.0
Bergen	845,385	11.5	825,380	10.7	884,118	10.5	905,116	10.3	936,692	10.5
Burlington	362,542	4.9	395,066	5.1	423,394	5.0	448,734	5.1	445,384	5.0
Camden	471,650	6.4	502,824	6.5	508,932	6.0	513,657	5.8	507,078	5.7
Cape May	82,266	1.1	95,089	1.2	102,326	1.2	97,265	1.1	92,560	1.0
Cumberland	132,866	1.8	138,053	1.8	146,438	1.7	156,898	1.8	150,972	1.7
Essex	851,304	11.6	778,206	10.1	793,633	9.4	783,969	8.9	799,767	9.0
Gloucester	199,917	2.7	230,082	3.0	254,673	3.0	288,288	3.3	291,408	3.3
Hudson	556,972	7.6	553,099	7.2	608,975	7.2	634,266	7.2	676,061	7.6
Hunterdon	87,361	1.2	107,776	1.4	121,989	1.4	128,349	1.5	124,714	1.4
Mercer	307,863	4.2	325,824	4.2	350,761	4.2	366,513	4.2	369,811	4.2
Middlesex	595,893	8.1	671,780	8.7	750,162	8.9	809,858	9.2	829,685	9.3
Monmouth	503,173	6.8	553,124	7.2	615,301	7.3	630,380	7.2	621,354	7.0
Morris	407,630	5.5	421,353	5.5	470,212	5.6	492,276	5.6	494,228	5.5
Ocean	346,038	4.7	433,203	5.6	510,916	6.1	576,567	6.6	601,651	6.8
Passaic	447,585	6.1	453,060	5.9	489,049	5.8	501,226	5.7	503,310	5.6
Salem	64,676	0.9	65,294	0.8	64,285	0.8	66,083	0.8	62,607	0.7
Somerset	203,129	2.8	240,279	3.1	297,490	3.5	323,444	3.7	331,164	3.7
Sussex	116,119	1.6	130,943	1.7	144,166	1.7	149,265	1.7	140,799	1.6
Union	504,094	6.8	493,819	6.4	522,541	6.2	536,499	6.1	558,067	6.3
Warren	84,429	1.1	91,607	1.2	102,437	1.2	108,692	1.2	105,779	1.2

SOURCES: The 1790 through 2010 New Jersey populations in this appendix are derived from the decennial census. (See also U.S. Census Bureau 1996.) The 2018 New Jersey population is from the U.S. Census Bureau's Population Estimates Program (PEP) for New Jersey: https://www.nj.gov/labor/lpa/dmograph/est/est_index.html https://www.census.gov/programs-surveys/popest.html.

on these colonial-period enumerations as presented by Peter Wacker (1975, 413–416; see also Wells 1975). After the federal United States was formed, there was a decennial census to date from 1790 through 2010. The 1790 through 2010 New Jersey populations in this appendix are derived from the decennial census (see also U.S. Census Bureau 1996). The 2018 New Jersey population in this appendix is from the U.S. Census Bureau's Population Estimates Program (PEP) for New Jersey (https://www.nj.gov/labor/lpa/dmograph/est/est_index.html https://www.census.gov/programs-surveys/popest.html).

Appendix B

• •

The Business Cycle and Demographics

Structural and Cyclical Economic Shifts

In the main text of this book, New Jersey's population change was linked to the broad, large-scale structural economic shifts that took place since the beginning of the nineteenth century: the shift from a preindustrial-, agricultural-, and natural resources–based economy to an urban industrial manufacturing one and then to a postindustrial, knowledge-based, information age economy.[1] The analysis of the demographic impact of these long-term structural economic transformations, particularly in the twentieth century, was tempered or accentuated by short-term cyclical factors: the expansionary and contractionary (recessionary) stages of the business cycle.[2] Moreover, the business cycle also helped to shape and define the post–World War II generational cohorts, as the nation's economic trajectory changed course twenty-three times since October 1945. Thus, it is useful to present the formal business cycle phases that have occurred since World War II; this provides a basic reference framework for the analyses and discussions that take place in several chapters.

Cyclical Economic Changes: Recessions (Contractions)

Starting with the 1948–1949 slump (the first postwar recession), there have been twelve recessions in the post–World War II era.[3] Starting with the 1945–1948 upswing, there have been twelve expansions, with the most recent—starting in June 2009—ending in February 2020. Table B.1 defines the month-to-month boundaries for these cyclical phases. The lengths of the recession and expansion

Table B.1
Post-World War II Expansions and Recessions

Business Cycle Stage	Dates	Duration (Length, in Months)
Expansion	October 1945–November 1948	37
Recession	November 1948–October 1949	11
Expansion	October 1949–July 1953	45
Recession	July 1953–May 1954	10
Expansion	May 1954–August 1957	35
Recession	August 1957–April 1958	8
Expansion	April 1958–April 1960	24
Recession	April 1960–February 1961	10
Expansion	February 1961–December 1969	106
Recession	December 1969–November 1970	11
Expansion	November 1970–November 1973	36
Recession	November 1973–March 1975	16
Expansion	March 1975–January 1980	58
Recession	January 1980–July 1980	6
Expansion	July 1980–July 1981	12
Recession	July 1981–November 1982	16
Expansion	November 1982–July 1990	92
Recession	July 1990–March 1991	8
Expansion	March 1991–March 2001	120
Recession	March 2001–November 2001	8
Expansion	November 2001–December 2007	73
Recession	December 2007–June 2009	18
Expansion	June 2009–February 2020	128
Recession	February 2020–[a]	–

SOURCE: National Bureau of Economic Research.
NOTE: [a] End date not determined.

periods for the United States are defined by the National Bureau of Economic Research (NBER). The boundary dates, which indicate cyclical peaks and troughs, are determined by a set of comprehensive economic metrics.[4]

The average length of America's eleven completed postwar recessions has been 11.1 months, just under one year. The shortest was only six months (1980), while the longest was triple that—eighteen months (2007–2009). The latter—now termed the Great Recession (December 2007 to June 2009)—was not only the longest but also by far the deepest in terms of absolute job loss. The second longest recession, which occurred twice, was sixteen months—the length of both the 1973–1975 and 1981–1982 downturns.

However, the recessions presented in table B.1 were deliberately limited to those of the "modern" or post–World War II era.[5] And in general, they pale in significance to the experiences of the prewar period. To most Americans and New Jerseyans who did not experience the Great Depression, the eighteen-month-long 2007–2009 Great Recession was the most traumatic—and unprecedented—economic setback in their lifetimes. But historically, a recession of that duration was not unusual. Between 1854 and the end of World War II, there were twelve downturns that lasted eighteen months or longer. The longest (65 months in length) was the result of the Panic of 1873, and was called the Long Depression, which started in 1873 and lasted until 1879.[6] The Great Depression (August 1929 to March 1933) was the second longest (43 months) according to NBER's determination, although the common perception is that the entire decade of the 1930s encompassed the Great Depression "period." This historical footnote, however, may be of little consolation to millennials whose economic trajectory was derailed by the 2007–2009 Great Recession.

The reality is that recessions have been getting shorter in the "modern" era due to the development and implementation of macroeconomic countercyclical public policy measures. Between 1854 and 1919 (16 cycles), the average contraction lasted 21.6 months. Between 1919 and 1945 (6 cycles), the average length fell to 18.2 months. Then, as noted above, between 1945 and 2009, the average postwar recession (11 cycles) lasted just 11.1 months. This "comforting" pattern, however, did not lessen the pain of the Great 2007–2009 Recession, which not only impacted millennial labor market aspirations but also the housing values that many baby boomers believed would carry them comfortably into retirement.

Cyclical Economic Changes: Expansions

The average length (63.8 months) of the twelve postwar economic expansions was just over five years. The longest among them was 128 months (June 2009 to February 2020). There were three great expansions during the past sixty years: the 1961–1969 expansion (106 months in length), the 1991–2001 expansion (120 months in length), and the post–Great Recession/Great Expansion (a record 128 months in length). All three were the only expansions since the first measured business-cycle phase starting in 1854 to exceed one hundred months in length, and all three were nearly double the average length of the postwar upswings.

Just as recessions have been getting shorter over time, expansions have been getting longer. Between 1854 and 1919 (16 cycles), the average expansion lasted 26.6 months. This was only five months greater than the average contraction (21.6 months) during this period. Thus, during the second half of the nineteenth century and the early twentieth century (to the end of World War I), the United States would see, approximately every two years, its economy continually shifting from expansion to recession to expansion and so forth. It was a very uncertain economic world from the perspective of today.

Between 1919 and 1945 (6 cycles), the average expansion length grew to thirty-five months, nearly double the length of the average (18.2 months) contraction that took place during the 1919–1945 period. Then, as noted above, between 1945 and 2020, the average postwar expansion (12 cycles) lasted 63.8 months. The latter was more than five times greater than the average contraction (11.1 months) that took place between 1945 and 2009.

Further Discussion

Historically, NBER's dating of national recessions and expansions—based on a comprehensive set of economic metrics—showed close correspondence to the dates of national employment peaks and troughs. However, this close relationship has seemingly weakened. During the last two contractions, employment continued to decline following the formal end of the recession. This led to the phrase "jobless economic growth." For example, the tenth post–World War II recession (2001) technically lasted just eight months, starting in March 2001 and ending in November 2001. However, total employment losses in the nation continued for an additional twenty-one months (to August 2003). So the total employment downturn lasted twenty-nine months, while "technically" the recession lasted only eight months. Similarly, the eighteen-month-long Great Recession technically ended in June 2009. Nonetheless, total employment continued to decline for another eight months, finally reaching a nadir in February 2010.

This new cyclical divergence has probably been caused by structural economic shifts. Historically, the blue-collar (goods-producing) industrial sector of the economy—dominated by manufacturing and construction—was the most cyclical and most interest rate sensitive, and it accounted for the great bulk of recessionary job losses. During contractions, layoffs in this sector were generally temporary, and rehires were common as the economic recoveries ensued. However, during the last two recessions—2001 and 2007–2009—employment losses were dominated by the white-collar (service-providing) sector of the economy. These two recessions could be considered the first postindustrial contractions dominated by a knowledge-based, information age economy, with white-collar job losses much greater in magnitude than blue-collar losses. Many of the white-collar employment declines did not constitute temporary layoffs but permanent structural changes in these economic sectors. This was particularly the case in the Great 2007–2009 Recession, whose severity drove many parts of corporate America to permanently restructure and reinvent themselves. Thus, the short-term cyclical dimension of economic change in many cases spurred and/or accelerated major long-term structural change. This was another unique condition that impacted the postrecession career trajectories of many millennials.

Appendix C

••••••••••••••••••••••

Historic Black Population, "Great Migration," and "Reverse Great Migration" Nationwide and in New Jersey

The early 1500s saw the first slave voyage from Africa to the Americas. The latter continent, "newly discovered" by Europeans, had near limitless demand for imported slaves, especially as the indigenous Native American population, who themselves had often been placed in servitude, was soon virtually wiped out. Approximately 36,000 total slaving expeditions to the Americas would be made from the 1500s to as late as the 1860s (McGinty 2019, A-2) carrying, in total, about 12.5 million Black men, women, and children ripped from their ancestral homes. Of that 12.5 million, major slave destinations included Brazil (5.5 million slaves); Caribbean, Dutch Guiana, and Danish West Indies (4.7 million); Spanish Americas (1.6 million); and mainland North America (0.5 million) (Emory University, n.d.). Of the 472,381 slaves who endured the "Middle Passage" to mainland North America, 253,028—or the majority (53.6 percent)—disembarked at Carolina/Georgia ports, followed by 158,427 (33.5 percent) offloaded at Chesapeake destinations, 33,103 (7.0 percent) in northern ports, and the remainder at other locations (Emory University, n.d.). These horrific slave passages brought a growing number of Blacks to the American colonies, including New Jersey. Table C.1 shows that growth by decade from the early seventeenth century to the late eighteenth century (1610–1780). In reviewing these numbers of Blacks

Table C.1

Black Population in All Colonies, Southern Colonies, and New Jersey, 1610–1780

Year	All Colonies		Southern Colonies		New Jersey	
	Number	Percent of Total Population (%)	Number	Percent (%)	Number	Percent of Total Population (%)
1610	0	0.0	0	0.0	—	—
1620	20	0.9	20	0.9	—	—
1630	60	1.3	50	2.0	—	—
1640	597	2.2	170	1.5	—	—
1650	1,600	3.2	720	3.1	—	—
1660	2,920	3.9	1,758	4.8	—	—
1670	4,535	4.1	3,410	6.4	60	6.0
1680	6,971	4.6	5,076	7.3	200	5.9
1690	16,729	8.0	13,389	14.9	450	5.6
1700	28,373	11.3	23,167	21.5	840	6.0
1710	42,698	13.0	34,395	23.5	1,332	6.7
1720	68,667	14.7	54,586	27.4	2,385	8.0
1730	97,621	15.3	80,298	28.6	3,008	8.0
1740	159,224	17.4	135,266	32.0	4,366	8.5
1750	252,068	21.2	221,846	39.7	5,354	7.5
1760	325,806	20.4	285,773	38.1	6,567	7.0
1770	468,822	21.7	420,362	39.5	8,220	7.0
1780	587,905	21.0	534,109	37.9	10,460	7.5

SOURCE: McCusker 2006a, 5-651–5-653.

NOTE: All colonies includes the area of Florida. The southern colonies and areas include Delaware, Florida, Georgia, Kentucky, Maryland, North Carolina, South Carolina, Tennessee, and Virginia.

in the colonies, it must be remembered that in this era Black race and enslaved status were largely synonymous, especially in the southern colonies. Also in this period, the counts of Blacks by decade are best available estimates, for these individuals, sadly viewed as less than human, were hardly the subject of accurate regular enumerations.

Keeping in mind the above caveats, we see a rising number of Blacks over the American colonial era. In 1650, there were an estimated 1,600 Blacks in all the colonies with 720, almost one-half, found in the southern colonies,[1] comprising in both instances about 3 percent of the total (Black and white) population. There were no reported (or at least counted) Blacks in New Jersey in this early 1650 period, and Blacks were not found (or again counted) in this colony until an estimated sixty in 1670. In 1700, the all-colonies Black population stood at 28,373 (11.3 percent of the total population), with the lion's share of this group, about eight-tenths, now in southern colonies (23,167 Blacks; 21.5 percent of that region's total population). New Jersey counted 840 Blacks that year, 6 percent of its total residents. By 1780, there was a total of 587,905 Blacks in all the colonies (21.0 percent of the total population), with again the preponderance of this group in the southern colonies (534,109 Blacks, or 37.9 percent of that region's total

Table C.2
United States: Black (Total, Free, and Slave) Population, 1790–1860

Year	Population Number		
	Total	Free	Slave
1790	757,181	59,557	697,624
1800	1,002,037	108,435	893,602
1810	1,377,808	186,446	1,191,362
1820	1,771,656	233,634	1,538,022
1830	2,328,642	319,599	2,009,043
1840	2,873,648	386,293	2,487,355
1850	3,638,808	434,495	3,204,313
1860	4,441,830	488,070	3,953,760

Year	Population Percentage		
	Total	Free	Slave
1790	100	7.9	92.1
1800	100	10.8	89.2
1810	100	13.5	86.5
1820	100	13.2	86.8
1830	100	13.7	86.3
1840	100	13.4	86.6
1850	100	11.9	88.1
1860	100	11.0	89.0

SOURCE: Haines 2006a, 1–48.

population). The number of Blacks in New Jersey first crossed five figures in 1780 (10,460), constituting 7.5 percent of this colony's total residents.

America had its first census in 1790. Whites and Blacks were both counted, along with identification of whether Blacks were enslaved or not. Although in 1790 almost all Blacks remained slaves, as was the case in the 1610 through 1780 period discussed above, at first a trickle and then a growing share of Blacks were freed, at least in northern states, in the pre–Civil War (PCW) period (1790–1860), reviewed below.

In the PCW period of the United States (1790–1860), there was a dramatic increase in the nation's Black population, growing from 757,181 in 1790 to 4,441,830 in 1860 (table C.2). High fertility, a decreasing death rate, and the importation of slaves contributed to the rapid gains of the Black population in the decades before the Civil War. Although the federal Act Prohibiting Importation of Slaves went into effect in 1807, illegal slave importing into the new country was far from totally ended (the last slave ship reached Mobile, Alabama, in 1860; Diouf 2007, 2020), and there were interregional slave shipments. The Black slave population "had grown, filling part of the labor needs to the new nation following the westward extension of the plantation south" (Horton and Horton 2001, 105).

Table C.3
Southern Region of the United States: Black
(Total, Free, and Slave) Population, 1790–1860

Year	Population Number		
	Total	Free	Slave
1790	690,061	32,523	657,538
1800	918,336	61,239	857,097
1810	1,268,499	107,658	1,160,841
1820	1,642,672	133,980	1,508,692
1830	2,161,885	181,501	1,980,384
1840	2,641,977	213,991	2,427,986
1850	3,352,198	235,569	3,116,629
1860	4,097,111	258,346	3,838,765

Year	Population Percentage		
	Total	Free	Slave
1790	100.0	4.7	95.3
1800	100.0	6.7	93.3
1810	100.0	8.5	91.5
1820	100.0	8.2	91.8
1830	100.0	8.4	91.6
1840	100.0	8.1	91.9
1850	100.0	7.0	93.0
1860	100.0	6.3	93.7

SOURCE: Carter et al., 2-375–2-377.
NOTE: The southern region includes Alabama, Arkansas, District of
Columbia, Delaware, Florida, Georgia, Kentucky, Louisiana,
Maryland, Mississippi, North Carolina, Oklahoma, South Carolina,
Tennessee, Texas, Virginia, and West Virginia.

The overwhelming number of United States Blacks lived in the South in the
PCW period, as was the case for much of the earlier seventeenth and eighteenth
centuries. For example, in 1790, of the nation's 757,181 total Blacks, 690,061 or
91 percent, lived in southern states (table C.3). The southern share of national
Blacks was a similar 92 percent in 1860.

During the PCW period, the lion's share of all Blacks nationally were slaves
(e.g., 92.1 percent in 1790, barely dropping to 89.0 percent in 1860; table C.2). Slave
status of Blacks was near universal in the South[2] (e.g., 95.3 percent in 1790 and
93.7 percent in 1860) (table C.3), a situation influenced by economic and other
forces (e.g., the region's tobacco and cotton agricultural economy was labor intensive, and indentured servants were more expensive and less reliable; Perkins 1988,
99–100). Although the majority of Blacks in the northeast[3] United States were
enslaved at the country's founding (i.e., 59.7 percent in 1790), slavery waned to
16.3 percent in 1820 and to 2.2 percent in 1830. It then essentially disappeared from
this region by the end of the PCW period (i.e., 0.2 percent in 1850; table C.4).

Table C.4

Northeast Region of the United States: Black (Total, Free, and Slave), Population, 1790–1860

| Year | Population Number | | |
	Total	Free	Slave
1790	67,120	27,034	40,086
1800	83,066	46,696	36,370
1810	102,237	75,156	27,081
1820	110,724	92,723	18,001
1830	125,214	122,434	2,780
1840	142,324	141,559	765
1850	149,762	149,526	236
1860	156,001	155,983	18

| Year | Population Percentage | | |
	Total	Free	Slave
1790	100.0	40.3	59.7
1800	100.0	56.2	43.8
1810	100.0	73.5	26.5
1820	100.0	83.7	16.3
1830	100.0	97.8	2.2
1840	100.0	99.5	0.5
1850	100.0	99.8	0.2
1860	100.0	100.0	0.0

SOURCE: Carter et al., 2-375–2-377.
NOTE: The northeast region includes Connecticut, Maine, Massachusetts, New Hampshire, New Jersey, New York, Pennsylvania, Rhode Island, and Vermont.

The overwhelming share of Blacks in the state of New Jersey were enslaved at the nation's founding: 80.5 percent in 1790. Slavery in this state diminished to 37.8 percent in 1820 and 11.0 percent in 1830; it then essentially disappeared by the end of the PCW period (i.e., 1.0 percent in 1850 and 0.1 percent in 1860; table C.5). Although the above-described New Jersey slavery pattern of at first commonplace and then an outlier practice over the PCW period broadly tracks slavery's evolution of the larger Northeast region, slavery's hold was much more persistent in New Jersey compared with the Northeast (table C.5). For example, whereas only about two in one hundred, or 2.2 percent of Blacks in the Northeast were enslaved in 1830, New Jersey's slavery share exceeded one-tenth (11 percent) in that year. In 1840, of the total remnant 765 Black slaves found throughout the Northeast, 674—or an overwhelming roughly nine-tenths— were in New Jersey. In 1850 and 1860, *all* of the 236 (1850) and then 18 (1860) slaves located in the Northeast were found in New Jersey. It is no wonder that a Connecticut traveler passing through New Jersey in the 1800s "expressed a common northern view and called New Jersey 'the land of slavery'" (G. Wright

Table C.5
New Jersey: Black (Total, Free, and Slave)
Population, 1790–1860

| Year | Population Number | | |
	Total	Free	Slave
1790	14,185	2,762	11,423
1800	16,824	4,402	12,422
1810	18,694	7,843	10,851
1820	20,017	12,460	7,557
1830	20,557	18,303	2,254
1840	21,718	21,044	674
1850	24,046	23,810	236
1860	25,336	25,318	18

| Year | Population Percentage | | |
	Total	Free	Slave
1790	100	19.5	80.5
1800	100	26.2	73.8
1810	100	42.0	58.0
1820	100	62.2	37.8
1830	100	89.0	11.0
1840	100	96.9	3.1
1850	100	99.0	1.0
1860	100	99.9	0.1

SOURCE: Carter et al., 2-375–2-377.

1988, 13). In a similar vein is the trenchant observation of the late Rutgers professor Clement Price that New Jersey's colonial-era support for slavery surpassed that of any other northern colony (Price cited in Hennelly 2015).

The Northeast consists of both the New England and Middle Atlantic geographic areas. New England includes the states of Connecticut, Maine, Massachusetts, New Hampshire, Rhode Island, and Vermont, while the Middle Atlantic area comprises the three states of New Jersey, New York, and Pennsylvania. Slavery had its weakest hold in New England. For example, in 1790, whereas about nine-tenths (92.1 percent) of Blacks nationwide were enslaved, bondage characterized a much lower share of Blacks in New England—about one-fifth (22.4 percent). Just a decade later in 1800, slavery shares of Blacks in the nation and New England were yet further apart at 89.2 percent and 7.2 percent, respectively. Black slavery essentially disappeared from New England from 1810 onward (i.e., 0.7 percent in 1820 and 0.2 percent in 1830).

Slavery was more strongly ingrained in the Middle Atlantic colonies, though it too would wane and then eventually cease. The share of Middle Atlantic Blacks that were enslaved stood at 72.2 percent in 1790, 54.4 percent in 1800, 32.4 percent in 1810, 19.9 percent in 1820, and a scant 2.6 percent in 1830. Compared with these Middle Atlantic slavery shares, with Middle Atlantic being the most comparable region to New Jersey proper, slavery's percentage incidence of Blacks in New Jersey was a quantum higher at 80.5 (1790), 73.8 (1800), 58.0 (1810), 37.8 (1820), and 11.0 (1830). In short, in the PCW period, slavery's hold endured far longer in New Jersey relative to both the Northeast and Middle Atlantic areas.

In the PCW period, there were at first nascent and then more significant efforts by nonsouthern states to improve the civil rights of Blacks, including some curbs on, and ultimately abolishment of, slavery (Holt 2010; Horton and Horton 2001). New Jersey followed suit in this regard but more than sometimes lagged in the protections it extended to slaves and ultimately the abolition of this practice. The ravages of the Revolutionary War, which hit New Jersey especially hard, may have contributed to slavery's lingering hold in this state. "The Revolutionary War battles fought in New Jersey had caused much destruction and pushed the state into a deep economic recession. White New Jerseyans decided that slavery could spur economic recovery and thus refused to advance abolition, even as it moved forward in other Northern states" (Boyd, Carey, and Blakley 2016, 51–52).

It is not known exactly when Black slaves were first brought to New Jersey. Although it is speculated that the earliest settlements in this colony, such as Fort Nassau (settled 1623 and near today's Gloucester City) "probably had slaves" (G. Wright 1988, 180), we do not know this for certain. By the mid- to somewhat later seventeenth century, Black slaves were most definitely pressed to service in New Jersey (an estimated sixty Black slaves by 1670; table C.1). Where did these first New Jersey slaves come from? Once again, exact records are unclear, but it is believed that the early arrivals were Africans who had first been shipped to the West Indies and then brought to New Jersey, because before 1750, New Jersey "had too little slavery to absorb full shiploads of African slaves" (G. Wright 1988, 22).

From the onset, the new colony of New Jersey embraced slavery. The original Dutch settlers carried the tradition of their country being "among the foremost slave traffickers of the seventeenth century" (G. Wright 1988, 18). The British Crown and settlers seamlessly carried on this pro-slavery mindset. For example, the 1664–1665 Proprietors "Concession and Agreement" awarded bounties of land for each slave imported by a New Jersey colonist. (Each imported slave would gain the settler from thirty to sixty extra acres.) The British Crown (Queen Anne) urged New Jersey's first Royal Government (Lord Cornbury) to promote slave importation (G. Wright 1988, 19). Especially in East Jersey, slave labor was embraced as proper and necessary. Indeed, throughout the burgeoning young colony, Black slaves materially contributed to New Jersey's growth and economy in agriculture, nascent industry, and other ways (e.g., domestic help). As an example, Lewis Morris, who built an early New Jersey ironworks and forge in 1680 (purportedly one of the first such manufacturing complexes south of New England), benefited from the brawn and skills of sixty or more Black slaves (Hennelly 2015).

Although some colonists early on in New Jersey's history resisted the institution of slavery, they were the distinct minority and had little material impact. For example, in part due to the colony's Quaker settlers, the West Jersey charter in 1676 declared that all persons would be free from oppression and slavery. Yet that declaration was stillborn, and slavery continued apace after East and West Jersey were united in 1702. In 1713, harsh penalties, including lashing and branding on the left cheek, were imposed for crimes committed by New Jersey slaves. In that same year, New Jersey acted to discourage manumission by the colony's slaveholders.

Slavery was ingrained in much of New Jersey's colonial-era society and history. One illustration of that was the slavery holding of many of the prominent individuals associated with Queens College (later Rutgers University), which was founded in 1766: "The charter trustees of Queens came from the most prominent slaveholding and slave trading families in the region.... The college sat in the Dutch slaveholding belt ... and its founding president ... and first tutor ... were slave owners. Its earliest graduates were from slaveholding Dutch families" (Wilder 2013, 186).

Similarly, a book on early Rutgers history—*Scarlet and Black* (Fuentes and White 2016), which focuses on the college's slavery ties, bluntly concluded that "the Rutgers connection to slavery was neither casual nor accidental—nor unusual" (White 2016, 1). Princeton University, originally named the College of New Jersey (and located first in Elizabeth, then Newark, and finally Princeton) was also implicated in the slave trade, as were most other colonial era–founded Ivy League colleges, as documented in *Ebony and Ivy* (Wilder 2013).

Colonial-era New Jersey law and custom perpetuated slavery. For instance, although other northern colonies imposed taxes on the importation of slaves, in part to raise revenues as well as to discourage this practice, New Jersey's slave importation was largely untaxed until the 1760s. The state legislature in 1786 did, however, prohibit bringing into New Jersey slaves who had been imported into the country after 1776. (Such slave importation was banned at the national level after 1808.) The year 1793 saw the formation of the New Jersey Society for Promoting the Abolition of Slavery. But abolition action came slowly in New Jersey, and New Jersey laws to realize that goal were often only partially successful in practice, as discussed below.

Although the New Jersey 1804 Act for the Gradual Abolition of Slavery freed children born of slaves after July 4 of that year, those so freed still had to remain the servant of the owner for some time (until age twenty-five for freed Black males and age twenty-one for their female counterparts). As described by one historian, "These [freed] children opened a fluid boundary between slavery and freedom that slaveholders exploited with little resistance. Therefore, instead of starting from a presumption of freedom ... anyone born to a slave after 1804 was a *slave for a term* (Gigantino 2014, 412; original emphasis). In a similar vein, although New Jersey enacted a law in 1846 to abolish slavery (the last northern state to do so), this law did not fully emancipate, as the former New Jersey slaves were now made "apprentices for life." A 2011 doctoral dissertation described the 1846 law denouement as "not quite free: slaves for a term in post-abolition New Jersey" (Gigantino 2010, ix). Notably, New Jersey was the only northern state to enforce the federal Fugitive Slave Act of 1850.

To be fair to the historical record, although many in New Jersey strongly supported Black servitude of different stripes, others saw it as morally evil and long overdue to be abolished. Reverend Jacob Green, allegedly the first person in New Jersey to go on public record to separate from England, declared that freedom for the colony should be paired with New Jersey's enslaved Blacks being freed as well (Hennelly 2015). In an act and declaration that was surely not quotidian for New Jersey in the eighteenth century, Moses Bloomfield, the father of New Jersey's fourth governor (Joseph Bloomfield), publicly freed his slaves on July 4, 1783, declaring that "as a nation we are free . . . and why should these, my fellow citizens, my equals, be held in bondage?" (G. Wright 1988, 23). But these and like-minded individuals were minority voices in much of New Jersey's early history. More common were such luminaries as Richard Stockton, who "did not seem to struggle with the inconsistency of owning people in bondage" while signing the Declaration of Independence (one of New Jersey's five signers), which heralded liberty (Morven Museum and Garden, n.d.). (The same inconsistency could be directed to the Declaration's author, Thomas Jefferson, who owned many slaves at his home in Monticello.) Multiple subsequent generations of the Stocktons, who lived in Morven (later the residence of many New Jersey governors and today a historic house museum) had their fields and residence tended to by slaves. In short, slavery in New Jersey was a scourge that was not fully exorcised until the aftermath of the Civil War.

Following the Civil War, both the nation and New Jersey enacted many parallel actions to enhance Black civil rights (New Jersey Historical Society 1992, 2). Initially, New Jersey sometimes lagged in this regard. For example, New Jersey was not among the original states ratifying the 1865 Thirteenth Amendment, which abolished slavery nationwide; it did not sign on to this sea change amendment until January 1866. In time, however, New Jersey became much more proactive in furthering the civil rights of Blacks, such as enacting a series of state Civil Rights Acts in 1884, the same year it outlawed school segregation. For context, it wasn't until the 1954 *Brown v. Board of Education* decision where the U.S. Supreme Court nationally prohibited school segregation. The landmark 1947 New Jersey State Constitution prohibited segregation and discrimination in schools and the militia. In 1954, New Jersey outlawed discrimination in housing, about a decade before this was done nationwide (New Jersey Historical Society 1992).

Improving civil rights protections to Blacks, and enhanced Black economic opportunities in New Jersey, not surprisingly attracted African Americans living in the South to come to this state as well as other states in the Midwest and

West with similar allure. This population movement, referred to as the Great Migration, is examined below.

The Great Migration and Reverse Great Migration Nationwide and in New Jersey

In the PCW period in the United States, many African Americans living in southern states, often in rural areas, faced the intertwined challenge of onerous discrimination and frequent poverty. Not surprisingly, in time, southern Blacks migrated to states and cities in the northern, midwestern, and western regions of the United States that offered better social and economic opportunities.[4] As poetically described by Richard Wright (1993), Blacks were "leaving the South" attracted "to the warmth of other suns." The Great Migration[5] is estimated to have encompassed millions of African Americans relocating from the South over much of the twentieth century (U.S. Census Bureau 2012). A magisterial book on the subject, echoing Richard Wright, was titled *The Warmth of Other Suns* (Wilkerson 2010) and denoted the Great Migration as an "epic story."

This population movement occurred in waves over time and was prompted by various forces. These "push and pull" factors included Blacks fleeing the restrictions of the Jim Crow South (and horrifically, about four thousand Black lynchings from Reconstruction through the twentieth century)[6] and a desire to improve their educational, housing, health, and other social conditions; burgeoning industrial and other job opportunities in northern, midwestern, and western cities (in part catalyzed by the defense needs of the two world wars and a growing need for workers as the United States limited immigration at the start of the twentieth century); and an understandable desire to join their friends and relatives who had earlier made the journey out of the South. As summarized by Henry Louis Gates and Nellie McKay (1997, 930), "As legal segregation made living conditions for blacks in the South more and more intolerable... migration to the North increasingly seemed an absolute necessity for blacks seeking a better life for themselves and their children." This population movement was recognized early on by demographers, economists, and others, with pundits dubbing it an "exodus" and massive migration ("Another Negro Exodus to the North" 1923; Baker 1917; "Exodus in America 1917"; Harris 1924; J. Hill 1924; Horwill 1918; "Migration of Negroes to Northern Industrial Centers" 1921; Motow 1923).

The above descriptions of the prompts to, and scale of, the Great Migration do not, however, do full justice to the human pathos of Black Americans upending their often rural southern roots to claim a better life elsewhere. These emotions were perhaps best expressed by the Black poet Langston Hughes, who penned his famous "One-Way Ticket" in 1949, which ended with the following stanza (Hughes 1979):

I pick up my life
And take it away
On a one-way ticket—
Gone up North,
Gone up West,
Gone!

With its growing economy and booming industrial jobs for much of the start of the twentieth century, New Jersey, in particular its cities, was not surprisingly a sought-after destination for migrating Blacks. Newark, for example, touted its industrial prowess. On celebrating its 250th anniversary in 1916, it boasted that the city "as a manufacturing center ranks ahead of thirty states in the value of its manufactured goods" (Newark Sales and Advertising Co. 1916). Its industries, such as the Newark naval shipbuilding yard, which was to employ twelve thousand workers in World War I, had a near-insatiable need for workers; this shipyard advertised in 1917 that "if you can use tools you are wanted" ("Great Ship Plant Needs Steel Men" 1917). Blacks in the South heeded such manpower calls and migrated to Newark (C. Price 2005). A book on this community's history by Brad Tuttle (2009, 147) noted that "by and large Newark's black population came to the city from the South," with this trek made for compelling economic reasons. As an example, Tuttle (2009, 147) describes that in the World War I era, Newark industrial workers were paid almost $3 daily compared with the less than $1 per diem wage that a Black farmhand made in the South for "a long grueling day laboring in the fields." (The experiences of some of these Black southern migrants to Newark is described below.) Other New Jersey industrial centers had a similar siren attraction to downtrodden Blacks in the South. The Great Migration of southern Blacks to New Jersey in the twentieth century was extensive demographically in terms of both the numbers of southern African Americans emigrating to the Garden State and the long-term duration of, and impacts from, this population movement.

Table C.6 details the number of Blacks living in New Jersey by decade over the twentieth century and beyond (1900–2017) who emigrated from the South. The number grew by decade and the march of history. It was at first a slow trickle of approximately 30,000 to 60,000 Black Great Migrants living in New Jersey per decade in the 1900 to 1920 period; increased to roughly 120,000 to 160,000 per decade over 1930 to 1950—a period spanning the economic cataclysm of the 1930s, the war years, and early postwar period; rose considerably by decade to about 200,000 to 300,000 Black Great Migrants in New Jersey in 1960 through 1980; trended downward in 1990 and 2000 to approximately 200,000 to 250,000 per decade; and then plummeted to about 150,000 by 2010 and 120,000 in 2017. (Table C.7, shortly explained, documents the Reverse Great Migration—Blacks leaving New Jersey and migrating South.)

Table C.6
Detailed Great Migration for New Jersey, 1900–2017

African Americans Living in NJ, Born in Southern States

State	1900	1910	1920	1930	1940	1950	1960	1970	1980	1990	2000	2010	2017	Total
Alabama	62	106	1,992	4,974	5,883	9,462	12,680	17,600	22,920	19,376	12,719	10,137	8,609	126,520
Arkansas	239	94	100	182	156	713	740	500	1,060	1,891	973	797	828	8,273
Delaware	1,638	1,997	2,960	3,172	1,358	1,101	1,940	1,000	2,560	2,445	2,440	3,070	2,532	28,214
District of Columbia	850	1,102	1,515	1,577	2,429	2,502	1,880	2,500	3,920	3,882	3,718	3,822	1,962	31,658
Florida	277	313	1,923	5,926	3,000	9,932	11,940	14,300	18,420	16,185	13,543	10,018	9,676	115,453
Georgia	279	1,061	7,483	22,241	23,897	33,958	40,660	41,100	56,080	42,914	32,059	19,532	14,846	336,110
Kentucky	60	195	402	404	500	642	640	1,700	1,520	1,334	1,285	967	325	9,974
Louisiana	60	94	200	264	200	1,195	1,480	2,100	3,220	3,718	3,182	3,748	2,525	21,986
Maryland	5,304	7,392	7,011	9,824	6,202	7,404	7,100	8,300	9,120	7,755	7,516	7,371	6,521	96,821
Mississippi	79	108	0	364	900	1,591	2,720	4,600	5,320	4,310	3,948	2,534	2,137	28,612
North Carolina	3,880	6,317	8,353	20,736	20,074	27,566	44,600	54,400	71,460	58,838	47,364	33,340	28,596	425,524
Oklahoma	0	0	0	81	200	198	420	200	480	700	517	346	769	3,911
South Carolina	1,112	2,772	3,815	14,826	16,924	23,738	36,000	40,600	54,300	46,616	39,054	26,597	20,072	326,426
Tennessee	20	101	210	1,094	1,000	1,344	2,040	2,100	2,700	2,976	2,016	1,754	1,457	18,811
Texas	61	206	102	466	200	1,007	1,680	2,500	2,800	3,598	3,014	3,435	2,820	21,889
Virginia	16,755	24,124	21,612	36,946	31,285	36,364	39,100	36,400	43,620	34,553	25,384	21,878	15,442	383,463
West Virginia	119	197	703	486	274	1,086	2,720	3,600	3,620	3,465	2,220	1,206	1,577	21,273
Total	30,795	46,178	58,380	123,565	114,482	159,803	208,340	233,500	303,120	254,556	200,952	150,552	120,694	2,004,917

SOURCE: Irving 2019 (analysis of Integrated Public Use Microdata Series [IPUMS] National Historical Geographic Information System [NHGIS] data for indicated years).

Table C.7
Detailed Reverse Great Migration for New Jersey, 1900–2017

African Americans Born in NJ, Living in Southern States

State	1900	1910	1920	1930	1940	1950	1960	1970	1980	1990	2000	2010	2017	Total
Alabama	0	0	0	80	0	33	280	400	1,920	2,246	3,619	4,019	4,006	16,603
Arkansas	0	94	0	0	0	0	40	0	160	32	521	70	737	1,654
Delaware	176	803	201	225	587	123	560	600	1,100	2,455	4,786	9,885	9,210	30,711
District of Columbia	213	0	316	574	759	1,733	1,980	2,300	2,960	3,173	3,044	2,111	2,001	21,164
Florida	0	0	0	0	0	231	2,000	1,900	6,740	11,829	20,924	35,634	34,648	114,299
Georgia	19	0	91	182	552	148	740	2,000	5,800	11,335	22,606	42,871	47,237	133,582
Kentucky	19	0	0	0	0	0	180	100	540	737	796	448	1,857	4,677
Louisiana	19	0	0	41	0	140	140	300	420	951	1,703	814	1,434	5,822
Maryland	157	0	1,045	768	863	896	1,660	2,900	5,900	9,354	14,463	18,265	27,697	83,967
Mississippi	0	0	0	0	0	0	0	300	480	633	844	384	682	3,403
North Carolina	39	102	339	181	470	341	1,260	2,800	9,600	14,475	25,918	40,678	47,381	143,583
Oklahoma	0	0	0	0	0	0	80	80	380	714	1,002	257	929	3,362
South Carolina	0	0	0	80	300	303	820	1,800	5,660	7,719	11,017	16,081	19,332	63,112
Tennessee	20	0	99	20	0	308	160	400	740	882	2,211	2,959	2,561	10,360
Texas	20	0	205	20	0	330	560	1,200	2,300	3,354	7,200	8,225	11,884	35,298
Virginia	279	762	495	755	600	1,939	2,100	2,200	6,440	12,504	22,911	23,322	24,689	98,996
West Virginia	0	0	0	81	274	110	160	100	320	349	538	964	664	3,560
Total	961	1,761	2,790	3,128	4,675	6,495	12,800	19,300	51,460	82,742	144,103	206,987	236,949	774,152
Net Outmigration	−29,835	−44,417	−55,590	−120,437	−109,807	−153,308	−195,540	−214,200	−251,660	−171,814	−56,849	56,435	116,255	−1,230,765
Outmigrants/ Immigrants	3.1%	3.8%	4.8%	2.5%	4.1%	4.1%	6.1%	8.3%	17.0%	32.5%	71.7%	137.5%	196.3%	38.6%

SOURCE: Irving 2019 (analysis of Integrated Public Use Microdata Series [IPUMS] National Historical Geographic Information System [NHGIS] data for indicated years).

It is instructive to place these numbers in perspective. One benchmark is to compare the number of Black Great Migrants living in New Jersey to the total number of African Americans living in the Garden State by decade. The total Black population in New Jersey at any point in time is affected by many demographic influences: birth, deaths, and in- and outmigrations. The Great Migration from the South is just one component. Yet, although only one piece of the story, the Black Great Migration contribution to New Jersey's total Black population over the twentieth century and beyond is considerable, as is evident from table 4.3 in chapter 4. For the first half of the twentieth century, for the decades 1900–1950, Black Great Migrants to New Jersey constituted roughly 45–60 percent of the total Black population in the state. Although this trended downward by decade in the latter half of the twentieth century from about 30 percent to 20 percent from 1980 to 2000, and then to about one-tenth by 2017, it nonetheless remains a not inconsequential portion of the Garden State's total Black residents.

Where did Black Great Migrants from the South to New Jersey come from? We can identify by decade these southern places of origin over 1900 through 2017. In the aggregate, over this century, there are two million such place identifications (Irving 2019). (Note: this does *not* mean there was a *total* of two million discrete Black Great Migrants to New Jersey in the 1900–2017 period; rather, this refers to the aggregate places of origin of New Jersey Black Great Migrants tabulated, decade by decade, over this time period.) Of the 2,004,917 such place identifications, a combined 1,471,523, or about three-quarters, were from the four states of North Carolina (425,524, or 21.2 percent), Virginia (383,463, or 19.1 percent), Georgia (336,110, or 16.8 percent), and South Carolina (326,426, or 16.3 percent). However, there was emigration (place identification) from many other southern states as well: 126,520, or 6.3 percent, from Alabama; 115,543, or 5.8 percent, from Florida; and 28,612, or 1.4 percent, from Mississippi.

New Jersey, and especially the urban areas of this state, were viewed as beacons of opportunity for many Blacks confronting poverty and rigid Jim Crow segregation in the South. A Newark pastor (Bonfield 1916) during World War I observed that "many of the newcomers are driven North by persecution in southern states as well as by the lure of high wages in the munitions factories." In a similar vein, in 1917 a Newark social worker, Helen Pendleton (1917), noted that due to a pressing labor shortage, "northern industries turned to the South and began to import Negroes by the thousands." Pendleton observed groups of these new migrants arriving in Newark's Pennsylvania Station on a daily basis "sitting patiently, surrounded by bundles and babies and shivering in cotton garments."

The numbers detailed in table C.6 and the above brief text description with respect to the Great Migration of Blacks to New Jersey do not do sufficient justice to the personal travails of the journey, the "push and pull" influence that influenced Blacks to leave the South and seek out New Jersey (and other northern states), and what happened once they came to their new home. For many decades—and especially south of the Mason-Dixon line—there was stark and cruel discrimination against Blacks in train, bus, and other travel modes and associated travel accommodations, such as motels, restaurants, and gas stations. In the mid-1950s, 3,500 white-owned motels nationwide allowed dogs to stay in their guest rooms compared with only fifty that would accommodate Black guests (Wallis 2014). We can secure a sense of the tribulations of Blacks traveling to New Jersey in the Great Migration from remarkable oral history and other research done by the Newark Krueger-Scott Cultural Center and exhibited at the Newark Public Library in 2016, with Samantha Boardman as a guest curator (Boardman 2016; Krueger-Scott, n.d.; Newark Public Library 2016).[7] Chapter 4 of this book briefly referred to this research; some of these Newark Great Migration oral histories are synopsized in table C.8.

The gauntlet of the journey North is evident from these Newark Great Migration histories. Food had to be packed for the long trip because restaurants were largely unavailable; migrants were barred from hotels too, and they hoped to find alternative safe rest stops. Public transportation, such as the trains north, were segregated for at least a portion of the journey (until Washington, DC), and there was further ignominy, such as fountains and restrooms with "white only" signs. A reflection of this unfortunate segregated era was publication for decades, between 1936 and 1966, of a guide popularly referred to as the Green Book (Green 1940). The Green Book listed nationwide the locations where Black travelers could secure essential services (hotels, tourist homes, restaurants, gas and service stations, and beauty salons and barber shops).

Further research conveys the motivations for the Great Migration to New Jersey and the often daunting challenges confronting Blacks coming north to the Garden State. A study completed in 1942 interviewed one hundred Black families in New Brunswick (N. Hill 1942). Of those families, twenty-six had been born in the city, and the remainder moved to New Brunswick, New Jersey (most often from Georgia, South Carolina, North Carolina, and Virginia) because of both "push and pull." The "push" came from poor educational opportunities and limited economic prospects in the South; the "pull" was hope for a better economic and social situation in New Brunswick. (Some of the families had been recruited by agents for factories in the New Brunswick area.) Among those interviewed, Black women worked mostly as domestics, and Black men held down industrial jobs. The survey revealed daunting problems in the community. The majority of the families "would not advise . . . other blacks . . . to locate in New Brunswick because of bad housing, lack of job opportunities, recreational facilities and poor race relations" (N. Hill 1942, 117).

Adverse conditions confronting the Black Great Migration to New Jersey were of course, not unique to New Brunswick. Social worker Helen Pendleton observed in 1917 that in Newark, "these humble newcomers . . . have been forced into finding lodging . . . in the worst parts of our city." A newspaper account in the *Atlanta Constitution* from the same period was dire in summarizing that

Table C.8
Illustrative Newark Black Great Migrants: Journey North and Life in the City

Martha Gaynor
"Martha Gaynor was born in Irwinville, Georgia, in 1916 and came to Newark in 1926. Her sharecropper father grew peanuts, potatoes and tobacco and she remembered her mother as being able to pick 300–400 pounds of cotton in a single day. While single-room schoolhouses were the norm in Georgia, in Newark she was put in the 1st grade and was such a diligent student she worked her way through 3rd grade by the summer. In high school she attended Barringer Evening School while working days in a factory manufacturing children's clothing."

Sharpe James
"The 35th Mayor of the City of Newark, Sharpe James was born in Jacksonville, Florida in 1936 and came to Newark with his mother at the age of nine. Their first residence in the city was a one-room apartment at Howard Street and Springfield Avenue that had no indoor plumbing and a potbellied stove for heat. Mr. James worked as an educator prior to entering politics, first as South Ward Councilman and later Mayor and State Senator."

Reather Boswell Johnson
"Reather Boswell Johnson was born in Wauchula, Florida and came to Newark in 1941. She traveled by train, an uncomfortable journey that took three days. Mrs. Johnson first worked at a thread company in Carney [sic], doing domestic work on her days off and working at a tailor shop on weekends. After returning to Florida for a time, Mrs. Johnson came back to Newark, where she met Madame Louise Scott who encouraged her to apply training she'd received in cosmetology to open a chain of beauty salons."

Mageline Little
"Mageline Little was born in 1932 in Tidewater, Virginia and migrated to Newark from Durham, North Carolina, in 1958. She and her husband made the journey by car and packed their own food for the trip, planning the route in advance to make sure their rest stops were in safe areas. A longtime school librarian and teacher, Mrs. Little earned a Master's Degree in Library Science.... [She served as] the Project Coordinator for the Krueger-Scott African-American Cultural Center and its oral history project."

Zaundria Mapson
"Came to Newark with her family from West Palm Beach, Florida in 1947.... We traveled by car.... At that time we could not stop in the South for overnight accommodations.... We were not able to stay in hotels.... I do remember fountains with the white only sign and colored sign.... In Newark I attended school with white children. If I had been in [Florida] I would not have been able to attend school with white children.... At the time I lived in Newark I was in school, I was growing up and I enjoyed school, I enjoyed activities—the museum, the library—and it seemed that Newark was a very exciting place. It had everything."

Bill Stubbs
"William (Bill) Stubbs was born in Georgia in 1918. Both of his parents were sharecroppers. Mr. Stubbs and his family came to Newark in 1944, riding in a train that was segregated until it reached Washington, D.C. A member of the Masons in Montclair, Mr. Stubbs was active in politics as Chairman of the Central Ward Republican committee and won the 1964 Republican nomination for Congress before losing in the general election. In addition to politics he frequently attended Board of Education meetings to advocate for greater black representation in Newark schools."

SOURCE: Boardman 2016. See note 7 in appendix C.

many Black emigrants to Newark "are dying . . . due to the unhealthy conditions in which they are compelled to live" (Bonfield 1916). A 1930s federal Works Progress Administration (WPA) report of the Black community in Newark's Third Ward described an extremely overcrowded neighborhood (half of this city's 44,000 Blacks were jammed into this compact area of fifty-six hundredth of a square mile) characterized by "sound and fury [and] replete with bad housing, delinquency and poor health" (Works Progress Administration, n.d., 1). Similarly, a Depression-era Newark Interracial Commission (n.d., 7) report bemoaned health, housing, and other challenges faced by Newark's Black population, mentioning that in 1930 "71 percent of this city's black residents were born in the South." The previously referenced graphic oral histories of Black Great Migrants to Newark poignantly depicted their tableau of various travails living in that city, challenges faced by Great Migrants in other New Jersey communities.

Over time, however, the living conditions for many Black Great Migrants to New Jersey improved, and opportunities beckoned. The oral histories depicted many cases of Black Great Migrants arriving penniless and ultimately rising to business, professional, educational, cultural, and political prominence. These migrants made New Jersey their home and contributed mightily to the state's social, cultural, and economic fabric.

But as observed many places elsewhere in this book, demographics are not static and often change over time. The same is true with respect to the Great Migration. Whereas for much of the twentieth century, many Blacks left the South in a Great Migration for northern, central, and western points in the United States, during the end of this century and accelerating in the beginning of the twenty-first century, increasing numbers of Blacks have reversed this movement and are disproportionately moving to the South from other regions of the country. This twist of Black Americans returning to the South is referred to as the New Great Migration, or sometimes the Reverse Great Migration, the latter term used here. Brookings Institution demographer William Frey (2004, 2) observed "that over the past three decades, the South has developed into a regional magnet for blacks." Frey (2004, 2–3) studied net migration trends (the difference between the number of in-migrants to an area minus the outmigrants from that area) and found that over time, the South was experiencing net Black migration gains from the other regions—Northeast, Midwest, and West—of the United States. More recent 2016 research on the subject concluded that the Reverse Great Migration "marks the unprecedented return for African Americans to the South" ("The Migrations" 2016, 11).

As with the original Great Migration of Blacks leaving the South, there are complex forces underlying the Reverse Great Migration (Hunt, Hunt, and Falk 2013). Blacks are increasingly seeking southern residence because of heightened southern economic opportunities (with fewer jobs, especially industrial employment, elsewhere), attractive southern climate, lessened southern racial discriminatory barriers (and the persistence of racial and social barriers elsewhere in the

United States), as well as the lure of cultural and family roots in returning to south of the Mason-Dixon line. A *New York Times* article on the Reverse Great Migration had the poignant title of "Racism Is Everywhere, So Why Not Move South?" and spoke of the personal histories of numerous Reverse Great Migrants (Allen 2017). Illustrative was Jasmine Owens, born in South Carolina, who then moved to New York for law school and built a legal career. Yet, she subsequently returned to Atlanta for the city's reputation as a "Black mecca" and much lower housing costs (Allen 2017). The multiple movements of one Black family over the generations is telling. Although Hardis White came to Chicago as a teen-ager from Mississippi (leaving the daily toil of picking up to 150 pounds of cotton), his granddaughter "left Chicago for job opportunities elsewhere. . . . She headed south, finding a career in Houston, a growing metropolis teeming with young transplants and opportunity" (Bosman 2020, A10).

Given these multifaceted and powerful influences, New Jersey not surprisingly is experiencing a Reverse Great Migration of increasing numbers of its Black population moving from the Garden State to points South. Table C.6 quantified the number of Blacks living in New Jersey from 1900 to 2017 who were originally born in southern states—the classic "Great Migration." In a reverse mirror image, table C.7 quantifies the number of Blacks born in New Jersey who were living in southern states—the Reverse Great Migrants—over the same 1900–2017 time span. Also indicated is the difference between these two population counts. From 1900 to 1970, there were hardly any Reverse Great Migrants from New Jersey (about 1,000 to 5,000 per decade from 1900 to 1940, and 6,000 to 19,000 per decade in 1950 to 1970), while the number of Great Migrants to New Jersey (about 31,000 to 234,000) per decade from 1900 to 1970 was magnitudes greater. From 1980 to 2000, there was a discernible uptick in Reverse Great Migrants (51,000, 83,000, and 144,000 in 1980, 1990, and 2000, respectively). However, as the number of Great Migrants to New Jersey (although declining) was still large over this time period (303,000, 255,000, and 201,000 in 1980, 1990, and 2000, respectively), the Great Migrants outnumbered the Reverse Great Migrants in New Jersey over this span, albeit by a declining number (252,000, 172,000, and 57,000 in 1980, 1990, and 2000, respectively). Starting in 2010, however, these trends reversed.

There were an increasing number of Reverse Great Migrants from New Jersey (207,000 in 2010 and 237,000 in 2017), a declining number of Great Migrants to New Jersey (151,000 in 2010 and 121,000 in 2017), and for the first time since the beginning of the twentieth century, Reverse Great Migrants of Blacks from New Jersey to the South *exceeded* the number of Great Migrants of Blacks from the South to New Jersey by a five-figure, and then a six-figure, count (56,000 in 2010 and 116,000 in 2017). (See table 4.3 in chapter 4 as well for these changing Black demographic migrations; tabulation of "Net Great Migrants"—the Great Migrants less Reverse Great Migrants over time; and the setting in context against the state's total Black population by decade of the Great Migrants, Reverse Great Migrants, and Net Great Migrants, respectively, over time.)

To paraphrase Langston Hughes, there are many reasons for an African American to be "Gone" from New Jersey as a Reverse Great Migrant. To paraphrase Richard Wright, Blacks are leaving New Jersey "to seek the warmth of other suns"—but now the orb is in a southern sky. For example, a thirty-six-year-old African American woman leaving Jersey City in 2006 for the Atlanta, Georgia, suburb of Stockbridge cited the lure of greater affordability, enhanced job opportunities, and cultural affinity. Simply put, she said, "The business and political opportunities are here" (Tavernise and Gebeloff 2011). Two twin Black sisters, once Alabama natives but then residents of New Jersey, "are counting down the days until they can leave the area, with one sister musing that she 'misses the stars at night' as well as 'black society in the South, which . . . is at a different level'" (Allen 2017). Black Reverse Great Migrants are altering the demographics of some New Jersey cities. For example, a study of Paterson observed that a recent influx of Hispanics to this city was accompanied by a fluctuating Paterson Black population, one that had increased early on by the Great Migration "but then decreased between the years 2000 and 2010 due to the returning African American migration to the South" (Castillo, n.d.).

Appendix D

•••••••••••••••••••
The Demographics of New
Jersey Residential Housing

Demographic Multipliers: Description and Derivation

How many people and schoolchildren are generated by newer housing in New Jersey? Government and citizens in general understandably are interested in these population figures because they affect the demand introduced by newer housing for public services and expenditures (e.g., operating and capital costs for education and transportation). These data are often referred to as residential demographic multipliers—the number and profile of people (including school-age and public school children) found in different categories of newer housing units. Chapter 11 examined the overall topic of household size and its change over time; this appendix extends that analysis by considering variations in household size (as well as differences in the number of children) in different types of housing.

As the profile of population in housing in New Jersey (and elsewhere) is a moving target over time—a mirror of the dynamic flux of America's households—it is important to obtain current demographic information. The stark changes in the demographic multipliers of New Jersey housing over the past few decades are found in table D.1. Over the decades, there has been a downward trend in the average household size (as noted in chapter 11) and the average number of pupils per housing unit. For instance, the number of public school children in the average newer built New Jersey four-bedroom single-family detached (SFD) home dropped from 1.21 in 1980 (units built 1970–1980) to 0.85 in 2016 (units built 2000–2016), a decline of about 30 percent. In other words, the introduction of

Table D.1
New Jersey Statewide Residential Demographic Multipliers for Newer Built Housing over Time (1980–2016)

Housing Type/Size	Household Size				School-Age Children				Public School Children			
	1980	1990	2000	2016	1980	1990	2000	2016	1980	1990	2000	2016
Single-Family Detached[a]												
3 Bedrooms	3.28	3.16	2.98	2.76	0.77	0.61	0.58	0.45	0.66	0.48	0.48	0.39
4–5 Bedrooms	4.12	3.84	3.77	3.78	1.43	1.08	1.08	1.04	1.21	0.84	0.87	0.85
Single-Family Attached[a] (Townhouse)												
2 Bedrooms	2.09	2.06	2.00	2.31	0.22	0.14	0.16	0.27	0.20	0.11	0.13	0.23
3 Bedrooms	3.06	2.76	2.66	3.00	0.76	0.44	0.44	0.57	0.70	0.37	0.38	0.48
Multifamily[a]												
0–1 Bedroom	1.52	1.48	1.53	1.45	0.03	0.06	0.08	0.08	0.02	0.05	0.07	0.06
2 Bedrooms	2.45	2.13	2.11	2.23	0.36	0.24	0.25	0.21	0.32	0.20	0.21	0.19

SOURCES: For 1980, 1990, and 2000, U.S. Census of Population and Housing, Public Use Microdata Sample for New Jersey. For 2016, 2012–2016, American Community Survey, Public Use Microdata Sample for New Jersey.

NOTES: Multifamily in 1990 and 2000 includes all units in buildings of five or more units; multifamily in 1980 includes new garden apartments (low-rise) only. (The 1980 census allowed specification of garden apartments.) Data for 1980 is for New Jersey housing built 1970 through 1980; data for 1990 is for housing built 1980 through 1990; data for 2000 is for housing built 1990 through 2000; and data for 2016 is for housing built 2000–2016.

[a] Owned and rented units of average value.

100 four-bedroom SFDs in New Jersey as of 2016 would generate only about 85 public school children compared with 121 pupils a few decades earlier. It is also observed that the downward trend in household size and pupils in New Jersey has generally moderated some in the past decade compared with earlier periods of time. Nonetheless, there is flux in these figures, and accordingly, current demographic information is essential.

To provide empirical updated information concerning "who lives in New Jersey housing," this appendix presents data on residential demographic multipliers that show the number and profile of the populations associated with different categories of housing in the Garden State.[1] Demographic profiles are presented for the vast majority of the occupied housing types in this state, including detached and attached, single and multifamily, and owned and rental. The demographic multipliers are derived from the American Community Survey (ACS), specifically the 2012–2016 five-year ACS Public Use Microdata Sample (PUMS). Demographic multipliers are derived for recently built (2000–2016) New Jersey housing (termed newer housing). The housing studied includes the more important categories and common configurations of newer housing built in the Garden State encompassing the following:

Single-Family Detached (SFD) homes of three and, separately, four or more bedrooms (BR).

Single-Family Attached (SFA, or "townhouses") of two and three BR.

Multifamily (attached housing of five or more housing units) differentiated into two building-size categories (five to forty-nine housing units and fifty or more housing units). In both size categories, the housing units encompass (studio–one BR[2] as well as two BR).

The SFD and SFA categories combine both owned and rental units. For the multifamily, a differentiation is made by the tenure of the housing units that is multifamily owned versus multifamily rental. All of these housing categorizations are guided by both practical as well as statistical criteria.[3]

For the full range of newer housing enumerated above, demographic multipliers are derived for the following:

1 *Household size* (HS): Total persons per housing unit.
2 *Age distribution* of the household members organized into the following age categories: 0–4 ("preschool"), 5–17 ("school-age"), 18–34 ("young adults"), 35–44 ("maturing adults"), 45–64 ("middle-age"), and 65+ ("seniors").
3 *Total school-age children* (SAC) or number of persons in the household of school age, defined as those five to seventeen years old. (The SAC is the same as the number of household members in the age five-to-seventeen category.)

4 *Total public school children* (PSC), or the SAC who attend public schools.
5 *SAC and PSC by school level and grade group* organized as follows: elementary (kindergarten through grade 5), junior high/middle school (grades 6–8), and high school (grades 9–12).

Summary of Key New Jersey Demographic Multipliers

The demographic multipliers of newer New Jersey housing (units built 2000–2016) are summarized in tables D.2–D.4.

Illustrative examples are provided (table D.2). For every one hundred three-bedroom newer SFD homes (both owned and rented), about 276 persons would be generated, including 45 school-age children, of whom 39 would likely attend public school. One hundred two-bedroom newer townhouses (both owned and rented) would generate approximately 231 persons, including about 27 school-age children, 23 in public school. One hundred two-bedroom newer multifamily condominiums in buildings of at least fifty housing units would contain about 201 persons, of whom 8 would be of school age, with 4 attending public school. One hundred two-bedroom newer rental housing in buildings of minimum fifty-housing-unit size would house about 224 persons, of whom 15 would be of school age, with 13 attending public school.

Table D.2
New Jersey Statewide Residential Demographic Household Size and School Multipliers (2016—Newer Units Built 2000-2016)

Housing Type	Housing Size (Bedrooms)	Household Size (HS)	School-Age Children (SAC)	Public School Children (PSC)
Single-Family Detached	3	2.762	0.446	0.385
(own and rent)	4–5	3.780	1.044	0.848
Single-Family Attached	2	2.311	0.274	0.226
(own and rent)	3	3.002	0.572	0.477
Multifamily (own)				
5–49 units	0–1	1.352	0.012	0.012
	2	1.796	0.086	0.058
50+ units	0–1	1.318	0.003	0.003
	2	2.011	0.078	0.039
Multifamily (rent)				
5–49 units	0–1	1.568	0.127	0.127
	2	2.512	0.368	0.339
50+ units	0–1	1.392	0.020	0.018
	2	2.243	0.148	0.130

SOURCES: See text.
NOTE: Housing units of all housing values built 2000–2016 as monitored by the 2012–2016 American Community Survey.

Table D.3
New Jersey Statewide Residential Demographic School (Grade Level)
Multipliers (2016—Newer Units Built 2000–2016)

Housing Type	Housing Size (Bedrooms)	School-Age Children			
		All (K–12)	Elementary (K–5)	Middle (6–8)	High School (9–12)
Single Family Detached	3	0.446	0.222	0.105	0.118
(own and rent)	4–5	1.044	0.481	0.259	0.304
Single Family Attached	2	0.274	0.164	0.042	0.068
(own and rent)	3	0.572	0.315	0.126	0.131
Multifamily (own)					
5–49 units	0–1	0.012	0.012	0.000	0.000
	2	0.086	0.062	0.015	0.008
50+ units	0–1	0.003	0.003	0.000	0.000
	2	0.078	0.070	0.005	0.004
Multifamily (rent)					
5–49 units	0–1	0.127	0.058	0.020	0.048
	2	0.368	0.220	0.057	0.090
50+ units	0–1	0.020	0.013	0.004	0.003
	2	0.148	0.072	0.028	0.048

SOURCES: See text.
NOTE: Housing units of all housing values built 2000–2016 as monitored by the 2012–2016 American Community Survey.

From the above and the more detailed data contained in table D.2, a number of demographic impact patterns are evident with respect to the number of people and number of schoolchildren associated with newer New Jersey housing. In general, detached housing currently produces the highest number of residents and pupils compared with attached homes. Detached homes with more (four to five) bedrooms have the relatively largest household size and pupil generation. Additionally, common types and configurations of attached housing, such as two- to three-bedroom townhouses and one- to two-bedroom multifamily units, have a relatively low demographic impact. It is sometimes erroneously assumed that each housing unit in New Jersey contains about one public school child. The current American Community Survey data indicates that is the case only for large (four-or-more-bedroom) SFD homes.

Further demographic information is provided by the current appendix. In addition to the total number of school-age and public school children, there is understandable interest in their grade or school level, such as elementary, junior high or middle school, and high school. The current investigation provides the breakout of the total school-age (SAC) and public school children (PSC) by three school categories—elementary, middle, and high school. Table D.3 shows this tripartite school distribution for SAC in newer New Jersey housing. Besides

Table D.4
New Jersey Statewide Residential Demographic Multipliers by Age Cohort (2016—Newer Units Built 2000–2016)

Housing Type	Housing Size (Bedrooms)	Housing Members by Age Cohort						
		All Ages	Preschool (0–4)	School Age (5–17)	Young Adults (18–34)	Maturing Adults (35–44)	Middle Age (45–64)	Senior (65+)
Single Family Detached (own and rent)	3	2.762	0.169	0.446	0.471	0.420	0.699	0.559
	4–5	3.780	0.266	1.044	0.548	0.651	1.021	0.249
Single Family Attached (own and rent)	2	2.311	0.218	0.274	0.499	0.420	0.542	0.358
	3	3.002	0.301	0.572	0.675	0.547	0.679	0.227
Multifamily (own)								
5–49 units	0–1	1.352	0.031	0.012	0.314	0.377	0.270	0.348
	2	1.796	0.104	0.086	0.356	0.280	0.356	0.614
50+ units	0–1	1.318	0.062	0.003	0.339	0.336	0.169	0.408
	2	2.011	0.207	0.078	0.469	0.417	0.357	0.483
Multifamily (rent)								
5–49 units	0–1	1.568	0.064	0.127	0.507	0.218	0.363	0.291
	2	2.512	0.263	0.368	0.865	0.420	0.415	0.181
50+ units	0–1	1.392	0.041	0.020	0.505	0.185	0.192	0.450
	2	2.243	0.178	0.148	0.896	0.398	0.291	0.332

SOURCES: See text.

NOTE: Housing units of all housing values built 2000–2016 as monitored by the 2012–2016 American Community Survey.

differences in the total SAC for the various housing types, sizes, and tenures, also evident from table D.3 are variations in the school-level distribution of the multipliers. For instance, whereas in the SFD and SFA homes about half of the SAC are in elementary school, in the multifamily owned homes, about three-quarters to all of the SAC are at the elementary level. This variation has implications for the demands placed on New Jersey school districts by new residential development.

Although schoolchildren rightfully garner a lot of attention with respect to demographic multipliers, other age groups are also significant. Table D.4 shows the household members by multiple age groups, such as preschool (0–4 years), middle-age (45–64 years), and seniors (65 years and older) for the different types and configurations of newer built New Jersey housing. These age cohort data are of interest to demographers, planners, social workers, and others with respect to the relevant demographic multipliers.

Take, for example, the senior (persons at least 65 years) population, which is expected to experience considerable growth into the future as baby boomers age. Accompanying that senior growth are valid social, health, and other concerns regarding needed accommodations. Although heretofore the most interest concerning demographic multipliers has typically focused on SAC and PSC, in light of the population trends just cited, much more attention needs to be paid to senior demographics. The senior and other age-cohort data in this appendix can help expand the age lens of the demographic multipliers to be consulted.

To illustrate further: How many persons and public school children are found in a newer two-bedroom townhouse (SFA unit) versus a newer four- to five-bedroom SFD home in New Jersey? From tables D.2–D.4, we would ascertain the following: One hundred of the two-bedroom townhouses would generate, on average, about 231 persons, of whom approximately 27 would be school-age children. For the four- to five-bedroom SFD homes, the 100 units would generate about 378 persons, with 104 school-age children.

Of these total school-age children, how many are likely to attend elementary (kindergarten–grade 5), junior high/middle school (grades 6–8), and high school (grades 9–12)? From table D.3, the analyst would estimate that of the 27 school-age children from the 100 two-bedroom townhouses, 16, 4, and 7 pupils would likely be found in elementary, junior high/middle school, and high school, respectively. For the 100 four-to-five-bedroom detached homes, generating 104 school-age children, the pupil distribution for the three school categories can be expected to be 48, 26, and 30 students, respectively.

What about the age distribution of all the persons generated by the townhouses versus the detached homes? From table D.4, detailed age-cohort information can be assembled. From that data, the analyst could estimate as an example that of the 231 persons from the 100 two-bedroom townhouses, about 22 (100 x 0.218) would be four years of age or under, while of the 378 population from the 100 detached four-to-five-bedroom homes, 27 persons (100 x 0.266) would fall into the youngest age cohort. The townhouses would proportionately contain relatively more persons of senior age—sixty-five years or older—than their detached counterparts. Of the 231 persons from 100 townhomes, 15.6 percent, or 36 (100 x 0.358) persons, would be expected to be at least sixty-five years old as contrasted with 6.6 percent, or 25 (100 x 0.249) persons (of the total 378 persons), for the SFD homes. These age differences imply differing social service needs.

Demographic Multipliers and Future New Jersey Demographic Change

This appendix provides residential demographic multipliers which, as described, are useful for ascertaining the population impact of development. It is important to place the application of demographic multipliers in a larger conceptual model context.

In considering how new housing development may impact population in a community, it is important to consider the broad changes in the New Jersey schoolchildren over time and projected changes in this population into the future. The New Jersey enrollment in public elementary and secondary schools stood at 1.090 million in 1990, rose substantially to 1.313 million by 2000, gained some to 1.403 million by 2010, and is projected to decline to 1.297 million by 2027 (National Center for Education Statistics 2016). In short, whereas the number of public school children in New Jersey grew significantly between 1990 and 2000, that growth has since abated in more recent years and is projected to decline into the future.

New Jersey in not unique in this changing school enrollment dynamic. For example, a study by the Massachusetts Metropolitan Area Planning Council (MAPC; Reardon and Philbrick 2017) observed that Massachusetts public school enrollment peaked in 2002 and has declined since then. The study also found that the school-age children population in metropolitan Boston (ages 5–19) was projected to decline by 8 percent from 2010 to 2040, even as the total population was projected to increase by 13 percent. Given these macro population forces, the report concluded, "At the district level, we observe no meaningful correlation between housing production rates and enrollment growth over a six-year period. . . . It appears that broad demographic trends, parental preferences, and housing availability now play a much larger role in enrollment growth and decline" (Reardon and Philbrick 2017, 1). Although New Jersey is surely not a mirror of either Massachusetts or metropolitan Boston, the Garden State does share some of the macro population forces that MAPC observed. Accordingly, policymakers in New Jersey need to better think how development adding population affects actual school enrollment growth. It may be time to consign the long-standing fear that New Jersey new residential development will overwhelm local New Jersey school district educational capacity to the dustbin of history. The school demographic dynamic has changed.

Appendix E

●●●●●●●●●●●●●●●●●●●●●●

New Jersey Population Density and Urban and Metropolitan Residence

A popular image of New Jersey is that of a highly urbanized state that packs a lot of people into a relatively small area. Demographers would agree—today, New Jersey leads the nation in population density (Rhode Island is second) and has one of the highest shares of residents living in an urban location, as categorized by the Census Bureau. These population attributes, however, as New Jersey's "Garden State" sobriquet implies, developed over time. We trace here the evolution of New Jersey's demographic density and urban status in the context of the entire United States.[1] We also briefly consider the designation of "metropolitan area" in New Jersey and the nation historically.

Population Density

Population density refers to the number of people in a given location. In the United States, density is typically expressed as the number of people per square mile of land area. Table E.1 shows the density of the United States and New Jersey from 1790 to 2018.

Our narrative begins in the nation's formative years. As described in chapter 2, relative to England, the American colonies had a low population density and "the opportunity to own land was the primary attraction for colonists to risk a trip across the Atlantic Ocean" (Virginia Places, n.d.). Land rights of the original Native American inhabitants were dismissed, if they were acknowledged

Table E.1
Population Density of the United States and New Jersey,
1790–2018

Year	Population Density	
	United States	New Jersey
1790	4.5	25.0
1800	6.1	28.7
1810	4.3	33.4
1820	5.5	37.7
1830	7.4	43.6
1840	9.8	50.8
1850	7.9	66.6
1860	10.6	91.4
1870	10.9	123.2
1880	14.2	153.8
1890	17.8	196.5
1900	21.5	256.1
1910	26.0	345.0
1920	29.9	429.1
1930	34.7	549.5
1940	37.2	565.7
1950	42.6	657.5
1960	50.6	824.9
1970	57.5	975.1
1980	64.0	1,001.5
1990	70.3	1,051.1
2000	79.6	1,144.2
2010	87.4	1,195.5
2018	92.6	1,211.3

SOURCES: U.S. decennial census for indicated years; Gaquin and Ryan 2015, 7; Hobbs and Stoops 2002, A-2; New Jersey Department of Labor and Workforce Development 2020a.

NOTES: There have been varying estimates for the land areas of the United States and New Jersey. The latest estimate of the land area for New Jersey is 7,354.22 square miles, a figure somewhat different from earlier estimates (e.g., 7,417.34 square miles that was assumed in the Census 2000 density calculation). The density figures shown in this table were calculated by dividing the New Jersey state population for the indicated years by a consistent 7,354.22 square miles. Since this calculation uses the latest land area for New Jersey (7,354.22 square miles), which is somewhat less than the previous land area assumed for this state (7,417.34), the population densities are somewhat higher than previous published data on this subject. Density is measured in persons per square mile of land area.

at all, by colonists who claimed preeminent "right of discovery" and "right of conquest."

The 1790 census, the first such decennial enumeration after the United States was formed, counted only 4.5 persons nationally per square mile[2]—a low density of settlement. For context, England at about that time (1800) had a rough count about 170 persons per square land mile.[3] (Hereafter, we will not repeat the "per square land mile" base.)

New Jersey's density in 1790 (25.0) exceeded the nation's overall density at that time (4.5) by fivefold. Other states,[4] however, had higher densities than New Jersey in 1790: Rhode Island (63.4), Connecticut (49.1), Massachusetts (47.1), Maryland (32.2), and Delaware (30.2) (Rossiter 1909, 58). These five states' higher densities were influenced by such factors as their earlier settlement than that of New Jersey (e.g., Massachusetts) as well as sheer physical size (e.g., Rhode Island and Delaware were the smallest colonies in land area). For various reasons, then, at the nation's first census in 1790, New Jersey had the sixth highest density of all states in the new country.

In time, New Jersey's density rank would climb. In 1820, the nation's overall density was 5.5, New Jersey's density was multifold higher at 37.7, and New Jersey was now the fifth most densely populated state, only exceeded by Rhode Island (76.5), Massachusetts (65.1), Connecticut (57.0), and Maryland (41.3).

The 1850 New Jersey density (66.6) was again multiples higher than the nation's overall density (7.9) and New Jersey now had the fourth highest density of all states, surpassed only by Rhode Island (200.3), Massachusetts (123.7), and Connecticut (76.5). The burgeoning New Jersey state population in the second half of the nineteenth century traced in chapter 3 soon upped this state's density ranking yet again to third place. The New Jersey 1870 density (123.2) was exceeded by only Rhode Island (200.3) and Massachusetts (181.2) and was almost twelve times the national average density (10.9) in that year.

In 1900, when the national average density was 21.5, New Jersey's density (256.1) was again about twelvefold higher. New Jersey's 1900 density, however, still ranked third—far behind Rhode Island (410.1) and Massachusetts (357.8). It was followed in fourth place by Connecticut (187.5). The four densest states in 1900 remained the four densest states in 2000 (Hobbs and Stoops 2002, 30), and that was true as well in 2018, although their rank order changed, as shall soon be detailed.

New Jersey would keep its title as the state with the third highest density until the middle of the twentieth century (1940—New Jersey density of 565.7), would climb to second rank in 1950 (New Jersey density of 657.5), and would become the nation's densest state in 1960 (New Jersey density of 824.9), a distinction it has held ever since. New Jersey over the course of these decades remained far denser in population relative to its host Northeast region, and the Northeast in turn kept its title as the most population-intensive region, albeit density rose considerably in the other regions over the course of the twentieth century and beyond, as shown in table E.2.

What were the underlying larger demographic forces influencing these changing metrics?

At the beginning of the twentieth century, the eastern half of the United States comprised all of the nation's more densely populated states. Sustained westward flows of population, joined by southward flows after World War II,

Table E.2
Population Density by Census Region, United States and New Jersey, 1900–2018

	1900	1950	2000	2010	2018
Northeast	129.7	243.3	330.3	341.7	346.6
Midwest	35.0	59.2	85.7	89.2	91.0
South	28.2	54.2	115.1	131.9	143.7
West	3.5	16.7	36.1	41.1	44.5
Total U.S.	25.7	50.9	79.6	87.4	92.6
New Jersey	256.1	657.5	1,144.2	1,195.5	1,211.3

SOURCES: U.S. decennial census for indicated years; Hobbs and Stoops 2002, A-2; New Jersey Department of Labor and Workforce Development 2020a.

subsequently reshaped the nation's population geography. Nearly two-thirds of the nation's 1900–2000 population growth took place in the South and West. Nonetheless, at the end of the twentieth century, despite its lagging long-term growth, the eastern half of the country still remained more densely populated than the western half. The four densest states in America in 2000 in rank order were New Jersey (1,144.2), Rhode Island (1,003.2), Massachusetts (809.8), and Connecticut (702.9). So New Jersey is the leading regional player of a broader national epicenter of massed demographic concentration.

It was forty years earlier, in 1960, when New Jersey became the most densely populated state in the United States according to the decennial census. This nation-leading position was the result of rapid population growth stemming from the great waves of suburbanization flowing into the state from New York City and Philadelphia in the 1950s and 1960s, as discussed in chapter 3. In 1950, Rhode Island's then-nation-leading population density (757.8) had far surpassed that of New Jersey (657.5), but for larger perspective, New Jersey then ranked as the state with the second highest density nationally. However, after the first decade of unprecedented suburbanization (1950–1960), the gap between the two states narrowed. In 1960, Rhode Island's density (822.5) was just below that of New Jersey (824.9). By 1970, following the second decade (1960–1970) of unrelenting suburbanization, New Jersey's soaring density (975.1) had relegated Rhode Island more distantly to second place (906.0). Despite slower population growth relative to the nation since 1970, New Jersey has firmly remained in first place, pulling further ahead of much slower-growing Rhode Island. For larger context, the average density nationally stood at 42.6 in 1950, 50.6 in 1960, and 57.5 in 1970.

In the 1980 census, New Jersey's population density reached 1,001.5, and New Jersey then became the first state in the United States to exceed more than 1,000 people per square mile. In the 1990 census (New Jersey density 1,051.1), it remained the sole member of this exclusive club; Rhode Island's density that year (960.3) approached but fell short of that four-figure population-intensity threshold. In Census 2000, when New Jersey's density reached 1,144.2, it was joined by Rhode

Island as the only two states to reach 1,000 people or more per square mile. That remained the case as well in 2010 as the New Jersey and Rhode Island densities were 1,195.5 and 1,018.1, respectively. Both states are not likely to relinquish this exclusive status anytime soon. As against the five-figure density of New Jersey and Rhode Island in the decades just discussed, the national average density was at a two-figure mark in this period—64.0 in 1980, 70.3 in 1990, 79.6 in 2000, and 87.4 in 2010.

By 2018, the national average density rose to 92.6. New Jersey continued as the state with the highest population density (1,211.3), followed once again and more distantly by Rhode Island (1,022.7). Since second-place Rhode Island's 2010–2018 population average rate (0.5 percent) was only about one-third that of New Jersey's population gain over this period (1.3 percent), the Garden State is assured of maintaining its number-one density position for the foreseeable future. The 2018 population density in Massachusetts (884.9) and Connecticut (737.8) ranked them in third place and fourth place, respectively, in that year. A graphic depiction of population density in New Jersey and states across the United States as of 2018 is shown in figure E.1.

It bears repeating that since density is measured by both the scale of population and land area, relatively less populous states that are physically compact will have a high density, while relatively populous states that also are physically large will rank lower on density (Hobbs and Stoops 2002, 30). Rhode Island personifies the former scenario and Texas the latter. In 2018, Rhode Island's population of 1.06 million ranked forty-fourth of all fifty states, but since its land area (1,033.8 square miles) was the smallest of all the states, its population density (1,022.7) was high. Matters were very different in Texas. In 2018, Texas had the second largest population (28.7 million) after California (39.6 million) of all fifty states. However, since this state is "Texas big" (261,232 square miles, the second physically largest state after Alaska's 570,641 square miles), the Texas population density of 109.9 in 2018 ranked only twenty-fourth of the fifty states. New Jersey's high density is driven by its physically compact size combined with a near top decile-scaled population. For example, in 2018, New Jersey's land area (7,354.2 square miles) was ranked fifth smallest of all fifty states (after Rhode Island, Delaware, Connecticut, and Hawaii) while its 8.9 million population was ranked eleventh largest of all the states, just shy of the top decile.

In broad perspective and in order-of-magnitude terms, the current (2018) national average density in the United States is nearing 100 (92.6) and is about 1,200 in this country's most population-intensive state, New Jersey. New Jersey, joined by Rhode Island, are the only two states north of 1,000 persons per square mile. Alaska in 2018 was the state with the lowest density (1.3) and Wyoming in the continental United States recorded the lowest density (6.0) in that year. Were the District of Columbia ever granted statehood, it would have the nation's highest population density, as its 2018 population per square mile (11,506.2) was almost tenfold greater than in New Jersey.

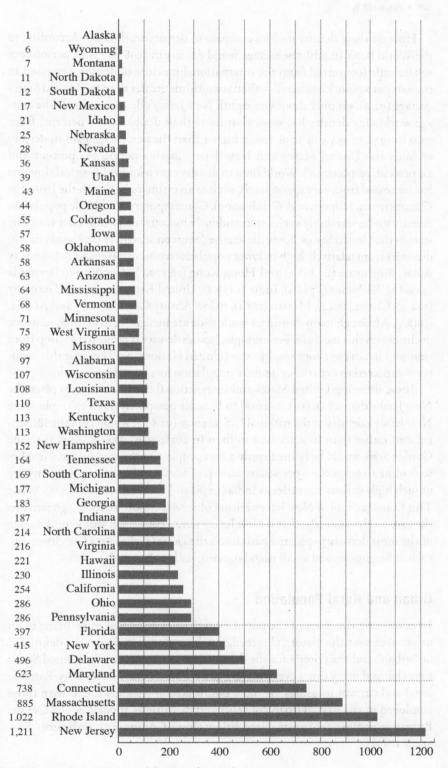

FIG. E.1 Population Density of the United States by State, 2018

How do these density metrics compare to density worldwide? According to the World Bank (n.d.b), the average world density in 2018 was 154.5 persons per square mile (converted from the international measure of density expressed in persons per square kilometer)[5]—about two-thirds greater than the United States average (92.6), yet only about one-eighth New Jersey's density (1,211.3). The average worldwide density has somewhat more than doubled (106 percent) from 74.9 in 1970 to 154.5 in 2018, much higher than the percentage gain in density of both the United States and New Jersey in this period (61 percent and 24 percent, respectively). World human density over a longer historical timeline has increased from very sparse levels, such as an estimated 3 to 6 in the Iron Age (Zimmerman, Hilpert, and Wendt 2009). Contemporary worldwide population density understandably varies tremendously by country, as indeed it varies by state in the United States. Some illustrative (not representative) 2018 world nation densities from relatively high to lower population concentrations were from very dense, Singapore (20,598.3) and Hong Kong (18,379.2), dropping to Bermuda (3,068.1), Barbados (1,726.5), India (1,178.2), United Kingdom (711.7), Germany (614.9), China (384.1), Mexico (168.1), to low density Canada (10.6) and Australia (8.3). Although many countries worldwide are increasing in density, some are declining on this measure. For example, Japan's density is projected to drop from near 900 in 2015 to about 500 by 2100 (United Nations, n.d.) because this country is expected to experience a severe population loss over these decades.

These differing United States and international density measures place the New Jersey density (1,211.3 in 2018) in broader perspective. For example, were New Jersey's density at the national U.S. average (92.6), it would contain 681,000 persons rather than its actual 8.9 million in 2018; at Alaska's density (1.3), the Garden State would be home to only 9,600 people. On the world stage, New Jersey's some 1,200 persons per square mile as of 2018 would put it in the company of such high-density countries as India (1,178) and the Netherlands (1,325). What Tim Evans (2010b) of New Jersey Future observed almost a decade ago remains the case today—namely, that if New Jersey were a country, it would rank as one of the most densely populated nations on the globe (excluding a few city-states, such as Singapore, and small island nations, such as Bermuda).

Urban and Rural Population

In examining the share of the population that is considered to be living in an urban area over the historical record, much caution is in order: the definition of "urban" and the criteria for the delineating urban areas in the United States have changed many times over time (Boustan, Bunten, and Hearey 2013; Ratcliffe 2015) and current measures are more multitiered and sophisticated than those employed in the past.[6] Urban concepts and definitions applied by the Census Bureau over time are summarized below (Iowa Community Indicators Program 2019):

- Urban Definition 1 (1940 urban concept, backcast to 1790): Urban comprised all territory in incorporated places of 2,500 or more. In addition, some areas were classified as urban under special rules relating to population size and density.
- Urban Definition 2 (1950 urban concept): Urban included all population in "urbanized areas" (densely settled territory with specific population thresholds), and incorporated places or Census Designated Places (CDPs) with population 2,500 or more located outside of urbanized areas.
- Urban Definition 3 (2000 urban concept): Urban included all population in urbanized areas and urban clusters (each with their own population size and density thresholds).

These changing definitions must be kept in mind in interpreting table E.3, which shows the urban share of the population in the United States and New Jersey from its founding until the contemporary period. "Rural," as Michael Commons (2018, 7) of the Census Bureau has described, "is defined as the residual.' This could be 'not urban,' . . . in a dichotomous classification, or what remains after all other categories in a multi-category classification have been defined." The following discussion focuses on the urban share of the population for both the United States and New Jersey from 1790 through 2010.

In 1790, the popular image of the United States as the bastion of the yeoman farmer was borne out by the fact that only 5.1 percent of the nation's population was urban (i.e., lived in a place then classified by the Census Bureau as "urban"). New Jersey's population at that time was entirely rural. Over time, the urban share of the population would grow both nationally and especially in New Jersey. By 1850, 15.4 percent of the nation's residents were urban and in that year for the first time (and hereafter) the share of New Jersey's population deemed urban (17.6 percent) exceeded that of the national average. The demographic and economic forces taking place in New Jersey over the latter half of the nineteenth century traced at chapters 3 and elsewhere in this book contributed to this state's growing urbanization. By 1880, for the first time the majority of New Jersey's population (54.4 percent) was urban as against a much lower urban share for the nation on average in that year (28.2 percent). (The nation's population did not turn majority urban until 1920.)

In 1900, as against about four-tenths (39.6 percent) of the nation's population that was urban, the New Jersey urban share had risen to about seven-tenths (70.6 percent). In that year, New Jersey was the state with the fourth highest urban share behind Rhode Island (88.3 percent), Massachusetts (86.0 percent), and New York (72.9 percent). The burgeoning industrialization and population of Providence, Boston, and New York and other cities in these three states contributed to their high urban population share at the dawn of the twentieth century. This population spurt parallels that of New Jersey's big six cities in the same epoch described in chapter 5.

Table E.3
Percentage Urban Population for the United States and New Jersey, 1790–2010

Year	% Urban Population	
	United States	New Jersey
Urban Definition 1		
1790	5.1	0.0
1800	6.1	0.0
1810	7.3	2.4
1820	7.2	2.7
1830	8.8	5.7
1840	10.8	10.6
1850	15.4	17.6
1860	19.8	32.7
1870	25.7	43.7
1880	28.2	54.4
1890	35.1	62.6
1900	39.6	70.6
1910	45.6	76.4
1920	51.2	79.9
1930	56.1	82.6
1940	56.5	81.6
1950	59.6	79.6
Urban Definition 2		
1950	64.0	86.6
1960	69.9	88.6
1970	73.6	88.9
1980	73.7	89.0
1990	75.2	89.4
Urban Definition 3		
2000	79.0	94.4
2010	80.7	94.7

SOURCES: U.S. decennial census for indicated years; Iowa Community Indicators Program n.d.

NOTE: See text for detail on these three urban definitions.

These patterns remained largely unchanged until 1950 when New Jersey's urban share (86.6 percent) was highest in the nation, just nosing out the urban population percentage in New York (85.5 percent), Massachusetts (84.4 percent), and Rhode Island (84.3 percent), and far greater the national urban population percentage (64.0 percent) in that year.

Other states, however, were rapidly urbanizing in the latter half of the twentieth century. In 1970, although about three-quarters (73.6 percent) of the U.S. population was classified as urban, that share was just under nine-tenths (88.9 percent) in New Jersey. In California, though, slightly more than nine-tenths of its population (90.9 percent) in 1970 was urban, so New Jersey was now the second-most urbanized state, the position it would continue to hold until 2000. After second-ranked New Jersey in 1970, the highly urbanized state stalwarts remained and included, in rank order, Rhode Island (87.1 percent), Massachusetts (84.6 percent), and New York (85.7 percent). Just below them, however, was a new group of rapidly urbanizing jurisdictions. In 1950, about six-tenths (57.2 percent) of Nevada's population was urban and about seven-tenths (69.0 percent) of Hawaii's. By 1970, more than eight-tenths of the persons living in these two states were urban (83.1 percent in Hawaii and 80.9 percent in Nevada)—a reflection of the tremendous growth of Honolulu and Las Vegas, among other burgeoning urban places in those states.

By 2010, the percentage of the New Jersey population that was urban (94.7 percent) was now second highest after California (95.0 percent), with Nevada's urban percentage (94.2 percent) claiming third place, just ahead of Massachusetts (92.0 percent). Thus, while New Jersey has relinquished its crown as the state with the highest share of its population living in a place defined as urban, it remains in the top handful of highly urbanized states in the country.

In sum, the population of both the United States and New Jersey have shifted from overwhelmingly rural to urban residence from the late eighteenth century until today. As of 2010, the vast majority, about eight-tenths of the U.S. population, was categorized as urban, that is true for almost all (95 percent) of New Jersey's population, and New Jersey for many decades has ranked in the top handful of the most urbanized states in the country. To set that in broader perspective, the world's population in general has become more urbanized, rising from about one-third (33.6 percent) urban in 1960 to more than one-half urban (55.3 percent) in 2018, and that urban share is projected to increase to two-thirds by 2050 (World Bank, n.d.a). Some illustrative (not representative) 2018 world nation urban population percentages from higher to lower shares were Singapore and Hong Kong (100 percent urban), Japan (92 percent), Canada (81 percent), Mexico (80 percent), China (59 percent), and Nepal (20 percent). (Note: Countries define urban in different ways.) As with density, were New Jersey a country, it is some 95 percent urban population share would rank in the top tier of the world's most urbanized nations (Evans 2010b).

Density and Urban Profiles within New Jersey

Thus far, we have examined the density and urban share of the New Jersey population over the long period of time from the 1790 census until today and have placed these characteristics in perspective against those of the nation and also briefly the international context. It is important to realize, however, that there is considerable *within-state* variation in these population characteristics. Density variations are illustrative.

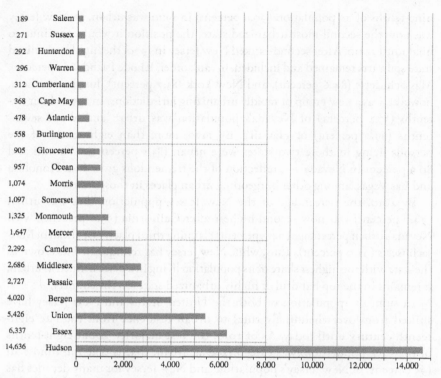

FIG. E.2 Population Density by New Jersey County, 2018

Although the state's overall density in 2018 was 1,211.3, densities that year were far higher in some counties, most notably Hudson (14,636.2) and Essex (6,336.7), as opposed to much lower densities in Salem (188.6), Sussex (271.3), Hunterdon (291.5), and Warren (296.4).

In parallel, there are vast differences in local population density within counties. To illustrate, while Burlington County in 2018 had an average 557.7 density, the population per square mile of its individual communities in that year ranged from a high of 5,261.3 (Riverside Township) to a low of 7.1 (Washington Township). Densities in Hudson County (14,636.2 average) in 2018 ranged from 57,882.6 (Guttenberg) to 3,562.8 (Secaucus); in Monmouth County (1,325.4 average) from 28,932.3 (Neptune) to 151.2 (Upper Freehold); and in one last example, in Ocean County (956.9 average density) from 31,689.0 (Barnegat Township) to 17.1 (Barnegat Light Boro).

With New Jersey's massive suburbanization from the 1960s through much of the twentieth century, earlier described in chapter 3, we would expect large density increases in these hotspots. That is indeed the case. For example, as against the 1950 densities of Cherry Hill (Camden County), East Brunswick (Middlesex County), Mount Laurel (Burlington County), and West Windsor (Mercer

Table E.4
Population Density of the New Jersey's Big Six Cities, 1950–2018

City	1950	1970	2000	2018
Camden	14,118	11,624	9,057	8,292
Elizabeth	9,231	9,218	9,866	10,462
Jersey City	20,047	17,454	16,094	17,950
Newark	18,438	16,050	11,495	11,663
Paterson	16,504	17,154	17,675	17,278
Trenton	16,718	13,685	11,154	10,979

SOURCES: U.S. Decennial Census of Population and Housing; New Jersey Department of Labor 2001; New Jersey Department of Labor and Workforce 2020b.

County) of 427.1, 259.6, 129.2, and 96.9, respectively, by 2018, their densities had climbed to 2,946.8, 2,212.6, 1,899.2, and 1,097.1, respectively. Fort Lee's high-rise construction boom saw this Bergen County community's density climb from 4,599.2 in 1950 to 14,924.8 by 2018. Interestingly, with all the construction that has taken place in Hoboken, this municipality's 2018 density (41,917.4) was only fractionally higher than its 1950 density (39,723.2). (In the interim, Hoboken's density had fallen to 30,239.2 in 2000.)

What about the density of New Jersey's Big Six cities studied in chapter 5? Their densities over the postwar period (1950, 1970, 2000, and 2018) are shown in table E.4. From 1950 to 2000, four of the six experienced sharp reductions in density—by approximately four-tenths in Newark, one-third in Camden and Trenton, and one-fifth in Jersey City. Interestingly, density in both Elizabeth and Paterson increased slightly by about 7 percent over this 1950-through-2000 span. From 2000 to 2018, there were small upticks in density in Elizabeth (6 percent) and Newark (2 percent), a larger increase in Jersey City (12 percent), Paterson's density remained essentially constant, and Camden and Trenton both continued to decline in density (–8 percent and –2 percent, respectively), but their hemorrhaging in this regard abated from prior years. These changes reflect the improving fortunes of New Jersey's Big Six cities due to some return to urban living by millennials and aging baby boomers. Additionally, New Jersey's surging immigrant populations often seek their first home in cities as did their immigrant predecessors.

Metropolitan Area

Besides density and urban designation, there are other population spatial designations that demographers consider (MacKum and Wilson 2011, 4; S. Wilson et al. 2012), and we will conclude here with just brief mention of one such designation—metropolitan area. This spatial area has been studied and designated by the Census Bureau since 1910 with various technical modifications. For our

Table E.5
Percentage Metropolitan Population for the United States and New Jersey, 1910–2010

	% Metropolitan Population	
Year	United States	New Jersey
1910	28.4	65.0
1920	34.0	73.9
1930	44.6	88.6
1940	47.8	88.3
1950	56.1	90.0
1960	63.3	88.4
1970	69.0	87.8
1980	74.8	91.4
1990	77.5	100.0
2000	80.3	100.0
2010	83.7	100.0

SOURCE: U.S. decennial census for indicated years; Hobbs and Stoops 2002, A-5; Wilson et al. 2012, 8.

conceptual purposes here, we use a general definition of metropolitan designation as described by the bureau's chief statistician "as area containing a large population nucleus together with adjacent communities that have a high degree of social and economic integration with that nucleus" (Wallman 2012, iii).

What are the national and New Jersey metropolitan trends? As is evident from table E.5, over the century from 1910 to 2010, the share of both the U.S. and the New Jersey population living in census-designated metropolitan areas has steadily grown. In 1910, somewhat more than one-quarter (28.4 percent) of the national population lived in metropolitan areas as against almost two-thirds (65.0 percent) in New Jersey. By 1950, the majority (56.1 percent) of the nation's population was metropolitan and that share in New Jersey had climbed to nine-tenths. By 2010, the metropolitan percentages for the United States and New Jersey were 83.7 percent and 100 percent, respectively. The entire New Jersey population since 1990 is categorized as living in a metropolitan area. For describing New Jersey's fully metropolitan status as of 2010, we refer to the good research of Tim Evans (2010a, 1) of New Jersey Future:

> New Jersey is an entirely metropolitan state (a distinction it shares only with much-smaller Rhode Island) in that every one of New Jersey's 21 counties is part of one metro area or another. In fact, all but four counties are contained in one [of the nation's] top 100 metro areas.
>
> 12 northern and central New Jersey counties are part of the New York metro area, the nation's largest—Bergen, Passaic, Sussex, Essex, Hudson, Union,

Morris, Middlesex, Somerset, Hunterdon, Monmouth, and Ocean; together these counties account for 73 percent of New Jersey's population.

4 southern NJ counties—Burlington, Camden, Gloucester, and Salem—are part of the Philadelphia metro area, the #5 most populous metro area in the country; these counties make up another 15 percent of the state's population.

Warren County is part of the #62 metro area, Allentown–Bethlehem–Easton, PA–NJ.

Mercer County constitutes the Trenton–Ewing metro area, #137 in population.

Atlantic County constitutes the Atlantic City–Hammonton metro area, #166.

Cumberland County constitutes the Vineland–Millville–Bridgeton metro area, #249.

Cape May County constitutes the Ocean City, NJ metro area, #349.

It is advantageous for New Jersey to be so closely nested in some of the nation's leading metropolitan areas, for these are hotspot locations of wealth and job creation. A Brookings Institution 2007 study found that the one hundred largest metropolitan areas in the United States comprised only a small share of the nation's land area (12 percent) yet contained 65 percent of the nation's population (and 74 percent of graduate-degree holders and 67 percent of research universities), 68 percent of the country's jobs (capturing a yet-higher 76 percent of knowledge economy jobs), secured the lion's share of technical and economic pump-priming funding (81 percent of research and development and 94 percent of venture capital financing), and generated 75 percent of total national wealth (Berube 2007, 7). As such, the Brookings report argued that these top metropolitan areas "fuel American prosperity," and fortunately, as noted earlier, New Jersey is located in the center of the nation's largest and leading metropolitan areas. In a similar vein, a European Union 2019 report observed that "metropolitan areas are 'engines' of development" (Dallhammer et al. 2019, 1), and that bodes well for the fully metropolitan New Jersey.

Although New Jersey's metropolitan identity has its pluses, that is accompanied by tension with New Jersey's home strong rule bent, with 565 separate municipalities making critical and largely independent economic and land use decisions, against a metropolitan model that envisions a high degree of social and economic integration of a region's population nucleus and adjacent communities. The imbroglio that accompanied the adoption and implementation of the New Jersey State Plan for development reflected those tensions. The search continues for the Aristotelian golden mean on this subject—namely, how to combine the best of regional metropolitan integration with individual New Jersey community character.

Notes

Chapter 1 Overview and Summary

1 Gen Xers are sandwiched age–wise and media attention–wise between the two much larger and more vociferous generations—older baby boomers and younger millennials (Gen Y).

2 Since New Jersey was admitted into the Union in 1787, it was technically a state during two decades in the eighteenth century (1780s and 1790s), ten full decades each in the nineteenth and twentieth centuries, and two full decades in the twenty-first century (2000s and 2010s). Thus, the third decade (2020s) of the current century is New Jersey's twenty-fifth in which it was constituted as a state. New Jersey's history did not begin in 1787. The geographic area that now constitutes the state has many demographic antecedents that are reviewed in chapter 2.

3 The first national census was taken in 1790. Decennial census data are continuously supplemented by less authoritative but still extraordinarily valuable annual estimates.

4 The data tabulations that focus on more recent events do not have a uniform end date. The analyses presented in the book were completed over a multiyear period. With the increasing availability of annual data estimates between decennial censuses—data that often are subject to subsequent revisions—we have attempted to steer clear of the always present temptation to repetitively update our tabular material with each new data release. This could prove to be an arduous and never-ending task, often with little value added. Moreover, since we have taken care to stress what we believe are secular trends and not short-term micro distortions or variations, we can avoid an excessive fixation on the absolute latest set of numerical releases. Nonetheless, we have continuously monitored the most recent available metrics to ensure that they are consistent with the data points we have used to establish longer-term demographic courses of events.

It should also be pointed out that decennial data through 2010 are essentially fixed, so there is little danger of any substantial revisions. Thus, the various decennial compendiums contained in the chapters and appendixes of the book should stand as long-term baseline reference points that can confidently be employed in future analyses of more recent data releases. Hopefully, that will be a useful facet of this book. Annual intercensal data estimates, however, have a much higher probability of being updated and modified in the future. Although they certainly are valuable in indicating population direction and movement, their specific numerical values may have limited shelf lives. Thus, their utility as firm data baselines for subsequent quantitative analyses is more limited than decennial census benchmarks.

5 The Pew Research Center has succinctly summarized the United Nations' report: https://www.pewresearch.org/fact-tank/2019/06/17/worlds-population-is -projected-to-nearly-stop-growing-by-the-end-of-the-century/?utm_source =Pew+Research+Center&utm_campaign=8c881f687d-EMAIL_CAMPAIGN _2019_06_21_03_07&utm_medium=email&utm_term=0_3e953b9b70 -8c881f687d-399493533.

6 A key implication is that an aging population leads to lower future economic growth as new investment is depressed. As will be pointed out subsequently, the massive post–World War II fertility upswing produced the oversized baby boom generation nationwide and in New Jersey. This resulted in massive societal invest-ment and robust economic development in the 1950s and 1960s. The opposite conditions may prevail in the 2020s.

7 As explained in chapter 7, the replacement-level fertility rate is 2.1. The total fertility rate referred to here is a synthetic measure that indicates the number of children that a woman would produce if she experienced all of the current age-specific birth rates during her lifetime.

8 Chapter 8 is devoted to the baby boom and its lasting imprint on New Jersey.

9 "Industry 4.0" is a concise term for the AI/robotics economy.

Chapter 2   New Jersey Population from the Colonial Period to the Early Republic

1 There are helpful historical time lines of New Jersey's colonial history: see Descen-dants of Founders of New Jersey, n.d.; Klett 2014, 3–6; and McCormick 1964, 179–180.

2 Pavonia means "Land of the Peacock" and is a variation of the name of Michael Reyniersz Pauw who was one of the first persons granted an estate on the west side of the Hudson River (Karnoutsos, n.d.).

3 There were other proprietary American colonies, including Delaware, Maryland, New York, North Carolina, Pennsylvania, and South Carolina (Purvis 1999, 188).

4 These new communities were prompted by economic, religious, and other motiva-tions. For instance, Newark was first settled in 1666 by Puritans leaving Connecti-cut who sought to form a "purer" theocracy in which only members of the Congregational church could vote or own property (Bilby, Madden, and Ziegler 2014, 11; Pomfret 1964, 13–14). The intended theocracy to be a "New Ark of the Covenant" was shortened to simply Newark. Shortly after its settlement, "Newark was a busy place" (Pomfret 1964, 14). Of the proverbial "Big Six" New Jersey cities (including Newark) discussed in this book's chapter 5, five were founded before the close of the seventeenth century (Wilson et al. 1950, 13).

   Understandably, the initial populations of these early New Jersey communities were modest. For example, the estimated 1680 population of Elizabeth and New-ark were 750 and 400, respectively (Wacker 1975, 130). For context, the estimated population of some of the larger communities in the American colonies in roughly that same late seventeenth-century period were 3,000–4,500 in Boston (1660–1680), 2,400–3,200 in New York City (1660–1680), 2,500 in Philadelphia (1685), and

2,500 in Newport, Rhode Island (1680) (McCusker 2006a, 5-655, citing previous research). America's largest cities started small and grew significantly over time. For example, Philadelphia's population was estimated at 4,659 in 1720, 14,750 in 1760, and 28,522 in 1790 (Nash and Smith 1975). That city grew to some 1.6 million persons by 2019.

5 The original Elizabethtown grant was huge, stretching southward from the Passaic to Raritan Rivers (Ogden 2016, 28) as well as ranging extensively—thirty-four miles—inland and encompassing some 500,000 acres (Craven 1964, 38).

6 In an interesting footnote to history, the first New Sweden voyage to the region in 1637 was led by no less than Peter Minuit, who had heretofore served as governor of New Netherlands and had famously purchased Manhattan from the Native Americans but was now disgruntled and sought a new European patron (Covart, n.d.).

7 There are modern-day echoes of the demarcation such as Province Line Road in Mercer County straddling the historical East Jersey–West Jersey division boundary (Myers 1945, 51).

8 Mahlon Stacy and other Quakers were attracted in 1678 to the area that was to become Trenton, in part because of the area's Delaware River waterfalls ("ye ffalles of ye De La Warr") and water access, important economic and transportation considerations in the seventeenth century. The area, then referred to as The Falls was renamed Trent's-town (or Trent-town) when William Trent bought Stacy's interest in 1714. This community's name was later shortened to Trenton (Shuman 1958; Walker et al. 1929).

9 Peter Kalm did, however, complain of swarms of New Jersey mosquitos, especially "in the greatest heat of the summer they are so numerous [and] are very trouble-some" (Kalm quoted in Weiss 1964, 42). As further noted in the current chapter text, Kalm observed 1700s soil conditions in New Jersey. There was early recognition that the New Jersey colony had varied soil conditions, with a 1776 account observing that of the province's claimed 4,800,000 acres "at least one-fourth (probably more) is poor barren land with respect to tillage" (S. Smith 1890, 485). For analysis of contemporary New Jersey's varying geological and soil conditions, see Wacker 1975 and Widmer 1964.

10 It bears mentioning that many but far from all of the residents in the American colonies supported the revolutionary break from England. John Adams estimated that about one-third of all colonists remained Loyalist or Tories and more than one hundred thousand fled the country during the revolutionary conflict (Bobrick 1997, 324). The colonial society split on this issue, often acrimonious, characterized New Jersey as well; for example, a Loyalist clergyman in Amwell in this state "arrived one Sunday morning at his church to find dangling over his pulpit a hangman's noose" (Bobrick 1997, 316).

11 Of further perspective, and not covered in the text, is the population of British colonies more broadly in the Americas, such as in the West Indies. In the seventeenth century, the West Indies were far from insignificant in size relative to the population of the American mainland colonies. However, the population of the American mainland colonies gained multifold thereafter and in time greatly exceeded that of the West Indies. In 1650, the population of the British settlements in the West Indies was 30,000 persons and there were 50,000 persons on the North American mainland and in 1680, 107,000 in the West Indies and 152,000 on the mainland. By 1700, population on the mainland had begun to grow much more rapidly: 251,000 in 1700, 467,000 in 1720, and 1,186,000 in 1750. At the same intervals, the population

of the West Indies was only 129,000 in 1700, 221,000 in 1720, and 343,000 in 1750, only about 30 percent of the North American mainland population. By 1770, the North American mainland population was 2,165,000, and the West Indies colonies had grown to only 436,000, only about 20 percent of the population of the thirteen mainland colonies (Purvis 1999, 130, for West Indies population and McCusker 2006b, 5-651, for American mainland colony population).

12 Further information on the existence, number, and boundaries of New Jersey's counties in the colonial era is available from such references as J. Snyder (1969, 5, 10–11, 20–21, 31, 35–36, 39, 49, 55), Wacker (1975, 122, 134, 139, 140), and Walton (2010, 4–6). See also Lurie and Wacker 2009 for seminal presentation on New Jersey maps.

13 See Armstead et al. 2016 and McMahon and Schriver 2000 for description of slaveholding in New Brunswick.

14 The same, of course, was true of the colonies' cities. For example, between 1710 and 1719, more than nine-tenths (93 percent) of Philadelphia's European population growth was due to migration. This considerable share declined over time to about four-tenths (40 percent) between 1720 and 1749, one-third (34 percent) between 1750 and 1759, and somewhat more than one-quarter (28 percent) between 1760 and 1769 (McDaniel, n.d.).

15 For overall discussion of the broader colonial-era economy, see, for example, Rosenbloom 2018; Rosenbloom and Weiss 2011; and Terrell 2017.

16 See Mancall, Rosenbloom, and Weiss 2008 for role of exports in the colonial-era middle colonies.

17 See Grubb 2013 for analysis of New Jersey's paper money between 1709 and 1775.

18 "In August 1665, Governor Carteret, whose brother had been granted the land of all East Jersey, arrived from England. He issued a proclamation promising land to the settlers. After Carteret's arrival, [an initial settlement from 1664 Achter Kol Plantation] was renamed Elizabethtown, after the wife of the Governor; and Carteret made the settlement the first capital of New Jersey" (Ogden 2016, 75).

19 "Born in New Jersey in 1720, Quaker minister John Woolman grew to detest slavery. A part-time writer of wills, Woolman refused to sign any documents that included the sale or transfer of slaves. From 1746 until his death in 1772, the Quaker minister traveled throughout the colonies, preaching against slavery and the mistreatment of Native Americans. Woolman was known as 'the Quaker saint'" (Doak and McConville 2005, 72).

20 As other colonies, far from all New Jersey colonial residents supported the break from England (see note 10). One notable naysayer was William Franklin (Benjamin Franklin's illegitimate son), who served as England's last royal governor of New Jersey and ultimately as an ardent Loyalist had to flee to England (Benjamin Franklin derogatorily called his son and others of similar ilk "Royalists"; Schiff 2005). In contrast, many from New Jersey were ardent supporters of the revolution, including many New Jersey women. In overdue historical recognition, these women have been given the moniker of Revolutionary Jersey Girls (Hunold, n.d.).

21 Perhaps in part because of yeoman service to the revolutionary cause in the break from England, women in New Jersey were allowed to vote in this state's elections from 1776 to 1807, a unique state constitutional suffrage that was available to women only in this state (Klinghoffer and Elkis 1992, 160; see also Schuessler 2020). The New Jersey 1776 state constitution was unique in this respect and granted the right to vote to "all inhabitants" meeting certain qualifications of age, financial capacity, and residence. (Initially, New Jersey Blacks meeting these requirements

could technically vote in New Jersey as well, again near unique to this state at the nation's founding; but Black suffrage was pared back in 1797 when New Jersey limited voting to "free inhabitants"; National Park Service, n.d.). Alas, New Jersey's constitution was "reinterpreted" in 1807, and suffrage was limited to white male tax-paying citizens. New Jersey women lost their voting rights until reclaimed by twentieth-century suffragettes with the passage of the Nineteenth Amendment in 1920. This came after a long fight for voting equality. The New Jersey Women Suffrage Association was founded back in 1867, and its founder, Lucy Stone, had ten years earlier refused to pay property taxes in Orange, New Jersey, "claiming taxation without representation" (New Jersey State Library, n.d.).

Chapter 3 The Long-Term Decennial Growth Picture

1 The nation's thirteen original colonies comprised Connecticut, Delaware, Georgia, Maryland, Massachusetts, New Hampshire, New Jersey, New York, North Carolina, Pennsylvania, Rhode Island, South Carolina, and Virginia.

2 Vermont was admitted in 1791, and the census was conducted there that year.

3 Two decimal places are being used to gauge New Jersey's share of the nation's population. Rounding off to a single decimal point at times obscures the actual change taking place between decennial censuses.

4 In total area (land plus water), New Jersey is the fourth smallest state—or forty-seventh out of fifty in size. Its 8,723 square miles size is larger than only three of its close neighbors: Connecticut (5,543 square miles), Delaware (2,489 square miles), and Rhode Island (1,545 square miles).

5 The five largest cities in 1790 were New York City (33,131 people), Philadelphia (28,522 people), Boston (18,320 people), Charleston (16,350 people), and Baltimore (13,503 people). They were the only five settlements in the country with more than 10,000 people.

6 The number of states enumerated in each census is available at www.census.gov />history>through the decades>fast facts.

7 The state's strategic position relative to two of the largest markets in the nation at the time—New York City and Philadelphia—made it an ideal location for early industrialization. In 1860, for example, New York City ranked number one in population, Philadelphia number two.

8 Between 1850 and 1860, New Jersey's population grew by 37.3 percent compared to 35.6 percent for the nation. Between 1860 and 1870, New Jersey increased its relative growth rate advantage (34.8 percent versus 22.6 percent) during a period also influenced by Civil War distortions.

9 Between 1850 and 1870, the state's population increased by 85.1 percent, eclipsing that of 1890 to 1910 (75.6 percent) and that of 1950 to 1970 (48.3 percent).

10 Chicago was second, with a population of 3.6 million people.

11 The terms rust and frost in this context described the phenomenon of deindustrialization of the nation's historic economic power regions and the net domestic outmigration of populations to more hospitable climates.

12 The term Sunbelt became widely used during the decade when the southeastern and southwestern tiers of the nation, stretching from Florida to Texas to California, achieved remarkable economic prosperity, challenging the historic dominance of the Northeast and upper Midwest.

13 See appendix B for a more detailed overview of the business cycle and demographics.

14 New Jersey's July 1, 2018, population estimate stood at 8,908,520 people; this accounted for 2.72 percent of the nation's total population (327,167,434 people).

Chapter 4   The People of New Jersey

1 From the early 1600s, arriving European settlers called the Lenape and other Native Americans living proximate to the Delaware River watershed (in what was to become the states of Delaware, New Jersey, New York, and Pennsylvania) Delaware Indians (Norwood 2007). Delaware, both state and river, were named after Sir Thomas West, third Lord de la Warr, Virginia's first provisional governor ("Native Americans," n.d.).

2 There is a popular image of the Plymouth Colony in 1621 meeting and sharing food with and thanking local Native Americans (the Wampanoags, led by their tribal leader Ousamequin) for ensuring the colony's survival through a harrowing winter. Yet, in a travesty of this supposed convivial gathering, not long afterward, "the Plymouth men mounted the head of Qusamequin's son . . . above their town on a pike, where it remained for two decades, while his dismembered and unburied body decomposed" (Deloria 2019, 70–71).

3 When the census counts Native Americans in New Jersey, it is not enumerating Lenape (or Delaware) descendants per se but rather includes all those considered to be Native American in race. That practically includes descendants from many tribes. In his masterly treatise *The Lenape: Archaeology, History, and Ethnography*, Herbert Kraft (1986, 240) notes that of the 8,394 Native Americans in New Jersey in 1980, fewer than 100 were descendants from the original Delaware or Munsee.

4 See note 3's clarification concerning the Native American census enumerations in New Jersey.

5 Although official enumeration of the American Indian population by the U.S. Census did not begin until 1890, the Bureau of Indian Affairs (BIA) did make earlier estimates. The BIA counts from the nineteenth century showed a severe decline in the American Indian population from 400,764 in 1850 to 306,543 in 1880. The same downward trend was observed when the census began its enumerations in 1890; the American Indian population dropped from 248,253 in 1890 to its nadir of 237,196 in 1900. From this 1900 low point, the American Indian population increased to 265,683 in 1910 but decreased again to 244,437 in 1920. That drop was due largely to the global influenza epidemic after World War I, which severely affected the American Indian population (Snipp 1986, 15). Shoemaker (1999, 4) also reports that "budgetary constraints on the 1920 Census collection meant that the Census Bureau took no special care to enumerate Indians as it had in the 1890 through 1910 Censuses and the 1930 Census." The American Indian population rebounded to 332,397 in 1930, but as in the United States as a whole, the Depression and war years dampened growth of the American Indian population; the number of American Indians, which stood at 333,969 in 1940, rose only slightly to 343,410 in 1950.

    The 1960 census showed a huge increase (explained shortly) in the national Native American population, reporting a total of 523,591 Native Americans—a gain of 52 percent from 1950, compared with a 19 percent growth rate over the decade for the nation's population as a whole. The 1970 through 1990 censuses also registered significant growth; the national Native American population was 792,730 in 1970, 1,420,400 in 1980, and 1,959,234 in 1990. (The contemporary American Indian population counts referred to here include American Indian and Alaskan Natives or AIAN.) In percentage terms, these Native American population gains far exceeded national population increases in the same time periods.

The 2000 census was the first to give respondents the option of selecting one race ("race alone") or one or more race categories ("race alone or in combination") in reporting their racial identity (Seneca 2001, 20). When the "race alone or in combination" identification is used, the 2000 census count of American Indians increases from 2,475,956 to 4,119,301. Thus, an additional 1.6 million respondents in 2000 reported American Indian and at least one other race. The "race alone or in combination" enumeration affected the 2000 census count of other racial groups in the United States as well (table 4.1). In a similar vein, the 2010 census counted 2,932,248 American Indians ("race alone") and 5,220,579 ("race alone or in combination"). The 2017 American Community Survey (2017 ACS one-year sample) enumerates 2,726,278 American Indians ("race alone") nationally and 5,631,945 ("race alone or in combination").

Why have the recent increases in the national American Indian population been so large? Much scholarly work has addressed this question, and we shall highlight only some of the underlying factors here. Demographic forces played an important role. Population growth based on demographics is influenced by fertility, mortality, and migration (Shoemaker 1999, 8). Migration is a minor influence in the case of American Indians; however, their relatively high fertility rate and declines in their mortality rate have contributed to their recent population gains (Sandefur, Rindfus, and Cohen 1996; Shoemaker 1999; Snipp 1986). Changes in the process of racial identification in the census from enumerator-assigned to self-identification also increased the count of the American Indian population (Eschbach 1993; Passel 1997). From 1910 to 1950, census enumerators counted as Indian those people who looked like Indians—clearly a difficult assignment as there is not a readily assignable Indian racial phenotype. The problem was compounded by changes in the instructions given to census enumerators. From 1960 onward, census respondents identified their own race, and in recent decades, "the American Indian population has grown dramatically as a result of increased numbers of persons choosing to claim American Indian as their racial identity" (Snipp 1986, 17). This growth by national American census respondents to self-identify as American Indian likely affects the growing count of this racial group in New Jersey in the last few decades as well (Kraft 1986, 240).

6 Historians have only recently begun to study in detail Chinese worker life in this railroad-building period through such efforts as the Stanford University Chinese Railroad Workers in North America Project (Kennedy 2019).

7 Born Yagi Yasohachi, near the Sea of Japan in what was later termed the Fukui Prefecture, but better known when he came to America as Kusakabe Taro, this young samurai arrived in New Brunswick in 1867 to study first at the Rutgers Grammar School (Rutgers then operated a high school) and later Rutgers College (Perrone 2017, 458–459). Kusakabe was part of a small contingent of young Japanese who studied in foreign universities, first European and then American, in the mid- to late nineteenth century as Japan sought to assimilate Western science and technology given the threat of "gunboat" interventions to both Japan and China (Perrone 2017, 460–461). A considerable portion of this small group of young Japanese seeking American education in this era came to Rutgers, described as "the most popular 'first institution' over Yale, Harvard, Amherst, and others" (Perrone 2017, 456, citing Conte 1977, 90). Rutgers served as a beacon to young Japanese men for various reasons, including that this college (and New Brunswick)

had long-standing ties with the Dutch Reform Church, which sponsored early missionary activities in Japan (Perrone 2017, 458–459). Kusakabe entered Rutgers College in the spring 1867 term with the goal of "fulfill[ing] my duty to the Imperial realm by clarifying defects in the relations between us Japanese and the foreigners in light of the international law of all nations and universal principles" (Rutgers University Libraries 2017, 1).

The small contingent of Japanese with Kusakabe at that time at Rutgers College were serious students, with one writing to a Rutgers professor that in contrast to the raucous, rambunctious, and gallivanting behavior of their American student counterparts, "we acted no part in the disorder created in your classroom" (Perrone 2017, 456). Kusakabe shone academically and realized notable honors: he ranked first in his Rutgers College class and was elected to Phi Beta Kappa. He was the first Japanese national to graduate from Rutgers College and one of the first two Japanese nationals to graduate from any American college (joined by a graduate from Amherst College; Lamiell 2008). Sadly, Kusakabe contracted tuberculosis, died at age twenty-five on April 13, 1870 (weeks before commencement), and was granted his Rutgers degree posthumously (Lamiell 2008). His legacy lives on, however, in numerous ways. A Rutgers classmate, tutor (in English and Latin), and friend, William Elliot Griffis, became enamored with East Asian culture, graduated Rutgers, then lived and taught in Japan for some years (one of the first Americans to do so). Upon returning home, Griffis became over the next half century before his death in 1928 one of the country's first and most preeminent and prolific East Asian scholars, writing many books, hundreds of articles, and delivering about three thousand lectures (Burks and Cooperman 1960, 62). Griffis's legacy was also bibliographical in the form of an important fifteen-thousand-item collection on Japan, Korea, and China, housed at Rutgers University (Burks and Cooperman 1960), with a second sixteen-hundred-item Griffis collection at Cornell University (Wolfe 1980). Yet another Kusakabe legacy is an enduring sister city relationship between New Brunswick, New Jersey, and Kusakabe's original home community, now the city of Fuki, Japan.

8 Theodora Yoshikami is a Japanese American who with her family lived and worked at Seabrook Farms in Upper Deerfield Township (Cumberland County) during World War II. This farm employed thousands of Japanese who had earlier been interned after Pearl Harbor. Yoshikami recounts, "It wasn't a great place to live," but she and her family persevered. Her siblings ultimately became a doctor, lawyer, and dentist and Yoshikami started a theater company and also was a dancer and choreographer. She recounts, "Let us just hope it is never repeated" (Japanese Americans put into camps). After the war, many of the camp's Japanese families settled in the area and it became a small Japanese community. Many became naturalized citizens, 127 alone on June 25, 1953, and the swearing-in of these new citizens that day occurred in the Seabrook Community House auditorium as that large a crowd exceeded the capacity of the county courthouse. Today, few such Japanese families remain behind, but their story is documented at the Seabrook Education and Cultural Center (City University of New York 2018).

Many other New Jersey Japanese Americans have Seabrook Farm recollections. Iddy Asada grew up in Salinas, California, then "WAR broke out [and] our family went through the horrible stages . . . of evacuation . . . [including a stay at] Poston, Arizona, [with July heat] exceeding 'over 100 degrees.' [When] the war was over, [her family] resettle[ed] to a place called Seabrook" and as a former tomboy she joined the Seabrook Farms "softball and basketball team" (Asada 1994). Paul Noguchi, who picked beans at Seabrook for "forty cents a basket," recalled both the travails of the experience ("I remember the anticipation of whether the sun would be hot or whether it would be cloudy. I remember how uncomfortable it was after a rainfall") and also "a feeling of accomplishment when I reached the daily quota" (Noguchi 1993).

9 Pham Co was born in North Vietnam, came to Saigon in South Vietnam in 1954, and immigrated to the United States in 1975, first to California, then Florida, and ultimately to New Jersey. He recounts:

> To be honest, with 3 kids, we did not know where New Jersey was located [and] relying totally on a map, we [drove] 24 hours [from Florida] without rest [to Florence, New Jersey]. [There was] difficulty [in getting] a job due to not only my broken English, but also my profession back in Vietnam, teaching of painting which was not suitable for any jobs offered here. . . . I got a job at a telephone company, 15 miles from my home . . . near Hamburg Route 23. . . . Unluckily for me, the transmission . . . of my car broke down. I had to walk every day for 30 miles back and forth for 5 weeks. . . . We were much impressed by an American man who brought our family a few food packages and drove me home.
>
> [Ultimately, I secured work at a] bottle firm. . . . I was busy as a bee . . . there for 9 and a half years. [Then] I worked at a firm dealing with aluminum phone parts for the next 15 years.
>
> [At home] we all speak Vietnamese to each other. When our kids were at school, they adapted to American life very well. . . . We find living in the U.S. is fine. (Co 2002)

10 For further details, see Rutgers University, Department of Latino and Caribbean Studies, n.d.

11 The New Brunswick Hispanic narrative is extracted from Listokin, Berkhout, and Hughes 2016. See also "A Latino History of New Brunswick, short video" (Mota, Sandoval, and Sandoval, n.d.) at the Rutgers University "Latino New Jersey History Project."

12 The census had earlier asked where a native (born in the United States) person's foreign-born parents came from. That earlier question was limited to people born in the United States with one or both parents born abroad, a much narrower frame than the current (since 1980) broader "ancestry" question from the census.

An illustration of the earlier-frame probe follows: in the 1930 decennial census, the native (born in the United States) white population with foreign parentage was asked to identify their parental countries of origin. For New Jersey native whites with foreign parents (either both parents foreign or one parent foreign), the top five responses were as follows:

1 Italy (22.4 percent)
2 Germany (16.4 percent)
3 Ireland (13.3 percent)
4 Poland (11.3 percent)
5 England (6.9 percent)

For context, the *national* response to this question in 1930 was as follows:

1 Germany (20.8 percent)
2 Ireland (11.2 percent)
3 Italy (10.0 percent)
4 Poland (8.2 percent)
5 Canada (8.1 percent)

13 This 2016 ancestral rank order by New Jersey residents closely resembles the ranking of ancestral ties by the population of this state in earlier somewhat analogous census probes. See footnote 12 regarding results from the 1930 census.

Chapter 5   Population, Geography, and the "Big Six" Cities

1 Hoboken's 1900 population (59,364 people) eclipsed that (52,130 people) of Elizabeth. But by 1910, Elizabeth's population (73,409 people) surpassed that (70,324 people) of Hoboken. The latter's limited geographic area inhibited its population growth in the ensuing decades of the twentieth century.

2 The Rural South's population share of the state also contracted markedly during the 1900–1930 period, declining from 4.1 percent to 2.6 percent.

3 The manufacturing sector was bolstered in the 1960s by extended Vietnam-era military production, whose termination was reflected in the 1970s.

4 The components of population change are discussed in chapter 6.

5 In 1900, the Big Six population total stood at 759,046 people. By 1910, it surpassed the one million level (1,005,610 people) for the first time, subsequently increasing to 1,179,883 people in 1920, and then topping out at 1,254,210 people in 1930.

6 The Big Six cities' population increased from 1,222,734 people in 1940 to 1,242,510 people in 1950, a modest increase linked to the return of World War II veterans, many of whom would mostly likely suburbanize in the post-1950 period.

Chapter 6   Components of Population Change

1 The Census Bureau published components of change for the four full decennial periods—measured from and to April 1—between 1950 and 1990. However, net migration was not partitioned into its domestic and international components. Subsequently, the components of change were measured by the annual estimates program, with periods ending July 1. Detailed migration estimates—international and domestic—were then provided. Most of the analyses of this chapter, in order not to become mired in complexity, primarily focus on the post-2010 estimates of components of change in comparison to the 1950–1960 intercensal statistics. These two periods represent fundamentally different demographic eras.

The exception is for the overall state analysis undertaken later in this chapter when we provide the components for the 1950–1960, 1960–1970, and 1970–1980 intercensal periods to show the dramatic change in New Jersey from extraordinary growth to virtual stabilization—led by a transformation from strong overall in-migration to outmigration and much lower levels of natural increase.

2 The census-defined decades are measured from April 1 to April 1. The post-2010 intercensal estimate period begins April 1, 2010 and ends on July 1, 2018.

3 According to the 1962 Current Population Report cited below, between the decennial censuses of 1950 and 1960, "net migration represents the difference between the number of persons migrating into a particular area and the number migrating from the area. It comprises, therefore, both net immigration from abroad and net internal migration." Net migrations for the decade were obtained as residuals by subtracting natural increase from the change in resident population between 1950 and 1960. Thus, international and domestic components of migration were not determined. In order to better understand the redistribution of the population during the 1950s, the Census Bureau undertook for the first time the compilation on the separate components of population change for counties. See U.S. Census Bureau 1962.

Chapter 7   The Generational Framework

1 Since Z is the end of the X-Y-Z generational alphabet road, the question is raised: What comes next? According to Mark McCrindle, many scientific disciplines often move to alpha, the first letter of the Greek alphabet, after exhausting the Roman alphabet or Arabic numerals (Sterbenz 2015).

2 The total fertility rate for a specific year hypothetically indicates the number of children born per woman assuming that she would experience the age-specific birth rates of that year throughout her childbearing years. Replacement-level fertility—the average number of children born per woman that would cause the population to exactly reproduce itself from one generation to the next—stands at 2.08 in the United States (Livingston 2019).

3 An earlier CUPR analysis focused heavily on the baby boom and baby bust. See Sternlieb, Hughes, and Hughes 1982.

4 Postmillennials have been popularly designated as Gen Z. But the *New York Times* reports that this generation is not happy with that label (Bromwich 2018a, 2018b). Nonetheless, Pew has adopted the Gen Z terminology based on its growing utilization.

5 Since the generations are national in scope, the national statistics on fertility and births are used here for analytical purposes. New Jersey closely followed and still follows the national metrics quite closely.

6 As noted earlier, this is a term proposed by Mark McCrindle, and it has its advocates. See Sterbenz 2015.

Chapter 8   The Baby Boom Generation's Enduring Legacy

1 As described in the preceding chapter, millennials comprise a generation that closely corresponds to a distinct population cohort that had first been termed the baby boom echo in the mid-1980s. This large cohort was originally composed mostly of children produced by the baby boom, hence the term *baby boom echo*. However, its current size has also been bolstered by immigration and the resulting foreign-born offspring.

2 In contrast, as the subsequent undersized baby bust generation proceeded through its life-cycle stages, it found excess capacity in many parts of the built environment that had been scaled to accommodate the oversized baby boom.

3 Life plan communities is a recent term created by the senior living industry to replace what had previously been called continuing care retirement communities. Reflecting historic baby boom sensitivities and challenges to older norms, the new name implies a vibrant community setting that supposedly fosters independence, new experiences, and growth and has the right plan for what the next stage in life has to offer. In contrast, "continuing care" implies dependence—a community setting where older adults are being cared for.

4 GI Bill of Rights was the popular name for the Servicemen's Readjustment Act of 1944 signed into law by President Franklin D. Roosevelt. Among its provisions were low-interest-rate insured mortgage loans administered by the Veterans Administration, and funds for higher education.

5 With much of Europe and Asia suffering widespread devastation, there was a marked absence of global competition for American industry. Thus, consumer markets were fully satisfied by U.S. production, with little economic leakage out of the country. This unique situation lasted until the start of the 1970s.

6 "The post–World War II marriage boom mainly affected people born between 1925 and 1949, who married younger than any previous generation" (Ruggles 2016, 4–5).

7 See chapter 7 for detailed birth and fertility tabulations.

8 The total fertility rate in 1957 was approximately 3.8. The total fertility rate in any specific year is the sum of all of the individual age-specific birth rates of that year. As defined by the Population Reference Bureau, it is "the average number of children that would be born alive to a woman during her child-bearing years if she conformed to the age-specific fertility rates of a given year." https://www.prb.org/humanpopulation/.

9 For example, the demand for baby products soared in the 1950s, bolstering the consumer durables and nondurables manufacturing sectors of the economy. Swelling school enrollments led to massive additions to the state's K–12 educational plant during this period. Still evident today are sprawling single-story school buildings, many of which have large aluminum classroom windows decorated with pastel-colored panels. This was followed by a higher education construction boom in the 1960s, much of which is now seen as architecturally challenged. These are just a few examples of the early baby boom stimulants to the economy.

10 Pronounced "possle-cues."

11 There were actually just 998,000 dwelling units authorized by building permit between 1950 and 1970. See Hughes and Seneca 2003, 9–11.

Chapter 9   Generations X, Y, Z, and Alpha

1 Increasingly, there are other "Cs"—chief information officer, chief diversity officer, and so on.

2 For example, in September 2019, the nation's largest steelmaker—Nucor Corp.—announced that its CEO would retire by the end of the year and be replaced by a veteran company executive. The CEO retiree was a sixty-seven-year-old baby boomer (born in 1952), while the veteran replacement was a fifty-one-year-old Gen Xer (born in 1968). Generational transitions such as this will be replicated extensively in the 2020s. See Tita 2019.

3 This period is measured from November 1982 (when total employment in the United States stood at 88,783,000 jobs) to March 2001 (when total employment reached 132,748.000 jobs). November 1982 was the start of the 1982–1990 expansion and March 2001 was the end of the 1991–2001 expansion. See appendix B.

4 It lasted only eight months and ended in November 2001.

5 The term *inconsequential* is used here relatively. The recessionary setbacks surely inflicted pain on those who lost their jobs or were otherwise negatively impacted by the broader economic transformation taking place. But the magnitudes of the 1990–1991 and 2001 recessions were far less impactful than those of the 1981–1982 recession, then the worst recession since the Great Depression, and the Great 2007–2009 Recession—the "new" worst recession since the Great Depression as the third decade of the twenty-first century began.

6 As discussed in chapter 7, what are today called millennials (or Gen Y) were originally termed echo boomers, children of baby boomers, who were born between 1977 and 1995—the boundaries defined by birth patterns. But the generational concept of millennials is linked to the encompassing era in which this cohort was born and raised—the digital age (1980 and 2000). Thus, this book uses the Pew-defined 1981–1996 Gen Y/millennial age boundaries.

7 Baby strollers or conveyances again became part of suburbia. Some of the early suburban residential subdivisions of the 1950s incorporated curb cuts/ramps to accommodate "stroller moms" lugging baby boomers in baby carriages. After the baby bust interregnum, increasingly upscale "new-generation" strollers were adopted by Gen X yuppies as the 1980s advanced. Streetscape activities—child hauling—began to replicate that of an earlier era, albeit with more sophisticated carriages. Subsequently, the Americans with Disabilities Act (ADA) in 1990 mandated that curb cuts be present on all sidewalks to enhance the mobility of disabled people and other users. Many post–baby boom subdivisions lacked such features.

8 It used an operating system called MS-DOS 1.0 made by a then-little-known thirty-two-person company located in Washington State named Microsoft. "Though not a spectacular machine by technological standards, the IBM PC brought together all of the most desirable features of a computer into one small machine. It offered 16 kilobytes of user memory (expandable to 256 kilobytes), one or two floppy disks and an optional color monitor" (IBM, n.d.).

9 The A11 Bionic, the iPhone10's processor, features 4.3 billion transistors (Kingsley-Hughes 2017). The iPhone11, containing Apple's A13 chip, has the highest transistor count that has ever powered the iPhone, with a total of 8.5 billion transistors (Zafar 2019).

10 It was produced by the Lotus Development Corporation and originally introduced in 1983. As a historical note, Rutgers University professor emeritus Richard K. Brail points out that the first killer app for the desktop computer was VisiCalc, a predecessor to Lotus 1-2-3, which came on the market in 1979 and ran on the Apple II. Professor Brail taught the first microcomputer class in the Rutgers planning department in 1980–1981, using the Apple II and VisiCalc. Subsequently, the IBM PC and Lotus 1-2-3 became the dominant replacement.

11 Microsoft's Excel spreadsheet, first introduced in 1987, gradually supplanted Lotus 1-2-3 in the 1990s.

12 The Pentium Pro's micro-architecture was an advanced departure from that of the original Pentium, which was introduced in 1993 and contained 3.1 million transistors.

13 The huge technological leaps—semiconductors, software, and desktop computing—that were made throughout this period finally translated into higher rates of productivity economy-wide by the second half of the 1990s. Prosperity reigned as the new millennium approached (Irwin 2018).

14 The developers of these advancing technologies were baby boomers and members of older generations. But the discussion here focuses on the broad generalized behaviors of populations/cohorts at large.

15 "Radio, once a family activity, where everyone gathered around a single static machine, could now become a solitary pursuit, one that followed a person wherever they went" (Romm 2014).

16 Integrated circuit development advances led to the "calculator on a chip."

17 For the full study, see Emmons, Kent, and Ricketts 2018.

18 An adolescent is considered to be between ten and nineteen years old—roughly the period between childhood and adulthood. This is consistent with the World Health Organization's definition of adolescence.

19 Obviously, baby boomers may be offended by the term *ancient*, just as they were by such descriptors as *aging* and *older*. What they prefer are adjectives such as *leading-edge, life-experienced, chronologically gifted*, and so on.

Chapter 10   Generations and Age-Structure Transformations

1 They also reflect survival rates as groups move through the age segments over time.

2 The term *cohort* as used here refers to a population group that sequentially moves through the age-structure sectors over time. Generations can be considered cohorts.

3 Another analytical or graphical presentation/technique used by demographers is called the population pyramid, or age-sex pyramid, which adds male and female partitions to the age-structure profile. A population experiencing replacement-level fertility will take the graphical shape of a pyramid over time, as each older age segment is smaller than its younger predecessor. The amount of shrinkage between segments varies with age-related survival rates.

4 The Depression-era birth dearth and its position within the pre–baby boom generation was detailed in chapter 7.

5 Expanding school systems faced a shortage of trained teachers, particularly in the developing suburbs. This was exacerbated by the declining pool of "twentysome-things" from which entry-level teachers are drawn, as well as alternative career paths for returning veterans who took advantage of the educational benefits of the GI Bill.

6 Higher education previously faced a postwar imperative to expand in order to accommodate returning veterans taking advantage of the GI Bill.

7 Between 1970 and 1980, the population between ten and fourteen years old declined by 104,928 people (table 10.3). This group aged into the twenty-to-twenty-four-years-old sector ten years later (1990). But this latter group declined only by 48,234 people (table 10.4), less than one-half of the loss that would have occurred in the absence of positive migration.

8 Only those born in the first thirteen years of Gen Z (born 1997–2012) were alive in 2010.

9 An eight-year period is being compared to a ten-year period in this case. Nonetheless, the differentials in growth rates would still be substantial correcting for this fact.

10 The 2010 national median age is from the 2010 census. The Census Bureau's 2018 Current Population Survey is the source of the 2018 median age.

Chapter 11   The Great Household Revolution

1 The Census Bureau classifies households into two broad groups: family and nonfamily households. Families consist of two or more related individuals. Nonfamilies consist of either singles, or two or more unrelated individuals. Families are further subdivided into married-couple families (with or without children) or other families (male or female householders without spouses, with or without children).

2 "A housing unit is a house, an apartment, a mobile home, a group of rooms, or a single room that is occupied (or if vacant, is intended for occupancy) as separate living quarters." https://www.census.gov/prod/cen2010/doc/sf1.pdf#page=504.

3 This understates the actual significance of this large household format in American life. When the total number of people residing in each household type is examined (not presented in table 11.1), approximately one-half of all Americans in 1900 lived in households of six or more persons. This difference is illustrated by the following example. Suppose an area is made up of six households—five one-person households and one five-person household. Thus, five of six, or 83.3 percent of all households, comprise a single person. But 50 percent of the population resides in one five-person household, and 50 percent resides in five single-person households.

4 The median (not mean) household size was below two persons, since 32.6 percent of all households comprised two persons and 25.8 percent comprised one person. Thus, 58.4 percent of all households were made up of two or one persons.

5 If the house is owned or rented jointly by a married couple, the householder may be either the husband or the wife. The number of family householders is equal to the number of families. https://www.census.gov/programs-surveys/cps/technical -documentation/subject-definitions.html.

6 An affluent single person could have multiple housing units, but only one would count as a principal residence place for census and other purposes.

7 Mixing the two different sources can be problematic since both have differing universe counts and specific times of measurement. Thus, the 2010 decennial census and the 2010 American Community Survey data are not directly comparable. In addition, the Current Population Survey is another interdecennial census data source that is used in this book. The reader is urged to use caution in examining different sources of data for comparative analyses.

8 This is confirmed by the authors' analyses of all combinations of the different sources.

9 This may have been due to the widespread presence of urban boarding houses, which were tabulated as single housing/dwelling units but internally provided single-room accommodations sheltering single people. The multiple residents may have created larger households if the entire boarding house were counted as a single housing unit.

10 One-person households (table 11.12) are exactly equivalent to one-member nonfamily households (table 11.13).

Chapter 12   Demographics and Income

1 "Census money income is defined as income received on a regular basis (exclusive of certain money receipts such as capital gains) before payments for personal income taxes, social security, union dues, Medicare deductions, and the like. Therefore, money income does not reflect the fact that some families receive part of their income in the form of noncash benefits, such as food stamps, health benefits, subsidized housing, and goods produced and consumed on the farm" (U.S. Census Bureau 2016).

Income is just one measure of the economic well-being of households. Net worth, another metric, is the value of assets such as houses and real estate, and financial and other investments minus mortgage and other debts. In the 2010s, the post–Great Recession asset boom passed by many less-affluent (measured by income) households, with wealth inequality in the United States increasing faster than income inequality. See Harrison 2019.

2 It was glorious in terms of the unprecedented gains in overall real median incomes. It was not glorious in terms of income disparities, white flight to the suburbs, urban decline, and racial discord.

3 Income trends established through 2017 continued for the balance of the decade. However, the coronavirus-driven 2020 economic downturn will have significant income ramifications, although these will not be known until the downturn runs its full course.

4 "Constant" or "real" dollars are terms describing incomes that are inflation adjusted. They provide a more accurate comparison of incomes over time by adjusting for changes in the cost of living (or purchasing power). In contrast, current, nominal,

or unadjusted dollars are interchangeable terms describing income in the year in which a person or household received it.

5 The Federal Reserve Bank of St. Louis provides historical data on real median family income in the United States. U.S. Census Bureau, "Real Median Family Income in the United States [MEFAINUSA672N]," FRED, Federal Reserve Bank of St. Louis, accessed May 27, 2020, https://fred.stlouisfed.org/series /MEFAINUSA672N.

6 Appendix B details the periods of recession and expansion. See also Hughes and Seneca 2015.

7 The data are from the Bureau of Labor Statistics. They are seasonally adjusted figures for December of each year. It should be pointed out that the participation rate for women in 2018 (57.5 percent) was actually lower than that of 2000 (59.9 percent).

8 The then-longest economic upswing in history—the 120-month-long March 1991 to March 2001 expansion—was a prime force in the improved income performance (Kliesen 2003).

9 In 2007, the real median family income was $72,716. Ten years later, the 2017 income was $75,938, just $3,222 higher.

10 The full elaboration of household types and configurations is presented in chapter 11.

11 The data in table 12.3 are from the American Community Survey and are consistent with the 2017 data of table 12.2.

Chapter 13   Recent Dynamics and the Future

1 As the 2010s came to a close, demographically savvy developers anticipated surging demand for such accommodations and may have overbuilt—creating excess market inventory. But according to the *Wall Street Journal*, they were still expecting the expansive fundamentals of senior living to fully assert themselves in the 2020s (Fung 2018).

2 By 2020, leading-edge millennials, born pre-1985 or so, had passed through four decades: 1980s, 1990s, 2000s, and 2010s. Thus, although in their late thirties by 2020, they entered their fifth decade of existence—the 2020s.

Appendix B

1 These macroeconomic structural changes in particular shaped demographic geography: population dispersal, to centralization, to suburbanization, recentralization, and then nascent re-suburbanization.

2 Most recently, the Great 2007–2009 Recession had significant impact on the rate of household formation during both the downturn itself and its aftermath.

3 During the immediate postwar period, the February 1945–October 1945 recession was still in effect. (It reflected the massive industrial demobilization of America's wartime "arsenal of democracy.") It started during the last stages of the war and ended during the early peacetime stages. It was followed by the first postwar economic expansion (October 1945 to November 1948). The first contraction that started in the postwar period was the November 1948–October 1949 recession.

4 The website of the National Bureau of Economic Research (nber.org) provides extensive information on the definition of a recession and how beginning and end points are determined. The Business Cycle Dating Committee of the National

Bureau of Economic Research makes this determination. The website also details the historic prewar recessions cited here.

5 The earliest reference dates determined by NBER's dating committee are for the 1854–1857 expansion and the 1857–1858 recession.

6 It was also called the Great Depression until the downturn of the 1930s took this label. It started in October 1873 and lasted until March 1879.

Appendix C

1 For the purposes of this colonial-era analysis, the South includes the following colonies: Delaware, Florida, Georgia, Kentucky, Maryland, North Carolina, South Carolina, Tennessee, and Virginia.

2 For the purposes of this pre–Civil War analysis, the southern region includes Alabama, Arkansas, Delaware, District of Columbia, Florida, Georgia, Kentucky, Louisiana, Maryland, Mississippi, North Carolina, Oklahoma, South Carolina, Tennessee, Texas, Virginia, and West Virginia.

3 For the purposes of this pre–Civil War analysis, the northeast region includes Connecticut, Maine, Massachusetts, New Hampshire, New Jersey, New York, Pennsylvania, Rhode Island, and Vermont.

4 There were, of course, migrations of Blacks from some portions of the South to southern areas of greater promise. For example, Bernadette Pruitt (2005, 49) refers to a "Great Migration to Houston," encompassing about 44,000 Blacks moving to this city between 1914 and 1945, with most of those Houston-bound coming from eastern Texas and southern Louisiana.

5 This is surely not the only "Great Migration" of Blacks fleeing persecution and seeking better opportunities elsewhere. See a recent Pew Research Center (2018a) study, "At Least a Million Sub-Saharan Africans Moved to Europe since 2010."

6 Although the exact number of lynchings of Blacks in the South from Reconstruction to the 1960s is a subject of continuing historical research, it is estimated at about 3,500 to 4,000. See Tolnay and Beck 1995; NAACP, n.d.; and Equal Justice Institute 2019.

7 These Newark Black Great Migration oral histories are extracted from pathbreaking research by the Krueger-Scott Cultural Center and an important 2016 Newark Public Library exhibition, with Samantha J. Boardman as a guest curator.

Between 1995 and 2000, the Newark-based Krueger-Scott Cultural Center conducted about 120 interviews of Newark residents, including Great Migrants, from the beginning to better part of the twentieth century (Boardman 2013). This oral history project, titled "The Lost Years Recovered: Oral History of African Americans in Newark, New Jersey, from 1910–1970, a Continuum," was made possible by the collaboration and participation (besides those interviewed) of Krueger-Scott Cultural Center leadership (then-director Catherine J. Lenix-Hooker), notable historians (Giles R. Wright Jr. and Clement Price), volunteers from the Newark Bethany Baptist Church and others (Boardman 2013).

The Newark Public Library, a vital historical and cultural institution in the heart of the city's downtown, has an annual Black History celebration exhibit. For 2016, this exhibit was titled "'We Found Our Way: Newark Portraits from Great Migrants." Besides tapping the invaluable Krueger-Scott oral histories, curator Samantha J. Boardman assembled and communicated multiple materials on the Great Migration to Newark including photographs, prints, digital audio collages, and short documentary videos (Boardman 2013; Krueger-Scott Oral History Collection, n.d.).

The Newark Black Great Migrant oral histories in chapter 4 of this book and appendix C are collectively extracted from the above-described Krueger-Scott, Newark Public Library, and Samantha Boardman materials and are collectively cited as Krueger-Scott/Newark Public Library/Boardman 2016.

Appendix D

1 The demographic data in this chapter are based on a larger study on this subject by Alexandru Voicu and David Listokin (2018).
2 The studio and one-bedroom units are combined because there is insufficient ACS PUMS data to study studio units alone.
3 For full detail and statistical analysis, see Voicu and Listokin (2018).

Appendix E

1 We acknowledge the limitations of the metrics presented in this appendix. For example, some observers view density and the designation of urban as linked rather than separate. As Malpezzi (2013, 183) opined, "The simplest definition of urbanization is the existence of above average density." The ability of the raw metrics to convey larger concepts is limited as well. Take, for instance, "density," which is a simple mathematical calculation of the number of persons per square land mile. Although that may seemingly imply connectedness, as in compact development versus sprawl, that misreads what density conveys. Thus, although the New Jersey population density is the highest in the nation, much of this state is characterized by what New Jersey Future terms as dense sprawl—that is, areas that have high residential densities but "are physically cut off from employment and shopping areas and are accessible only by car" (Evans 2011, 1). In a similar vein, although almost all of New Jersey's population is technically identified by the Census Bureau as "urban," we again refer the reader to New Jersey Future research, which in classifying New Jersey communities according to their "net activity density" (a multidimensional metric factoring population, employment, and developed acres), found only 34 of the state's then 566 municipalities with a level of net activity density that New Jersey Future deemed "urban" in nature (Evans 2017). Thus, the data in this appendix on New Jersey density and urban residence are useful from a historical view and relative to other areas, yet are a starting point on these subjects and surely not the last word.
2 In the Rossiter (1909) study referred to in chapter 2, the population density for the nation for 1790 was calculated based on a 1790 national population of 3,929,625 and a national land area ("area of enumeration") assumed to comprise 417,170 square miles. That yielded a national average density (persons per square mile of land area) of 9.4 and was reported as such in chapter 2, which summarized this and other findings from Rossiter.

In more contemporary density calculations for the nation as of 1790, a national population of 3,929,214 is assumed (almost identical to the Rossiter assumed 3,929,625 count for that year); however, the contemporary density calculations utilize a 1790 national land area of 864,746 square miles—almost double the Rossiter 1790 land area assumption. Hence, the contemporary national density calculation for 1790 is estimated at 4.5 persons per square miles (3,929,214/864,746) as opposed to the Rossiter 1909 estimate of the average national 1790 density of 9.4 persons per square mile (3,929,625/417,170).

This book's chapter 2 section on density and other national characteristics as of 1790, which largely derives from the Rossiter (1909) study, reports the Rossiter-indicated national average density of 9.4 persons per square mile. This appendix E, which considers the national and New Jersey population densities from 1790 to 2018, relies on contemporary data and calculations, and hence the average national 1790 density in this appendix E is indicated at 4.5 persons per square miles.

Similarly, in calculating the population density for New Jersey from 1790 to 2018, this appendix assumes for all of these decades that the New Jersey land area comprises 7,354.22 square miles. This is an update as of the 2010 census and is somewhat smaller than the earlier assumed land area for this state (e.g., 7,417.34 square miles in the 2000 census). Since population density is calculated by dividing population by land area, and the denominator utilized in this appendix is the slightly smaller New Jersey land area (7,354.22 versus 7,417.34 square miles), the New Jersey population densities reported in table E.1 and elsewhere in this appendix are somewhat higher than those reported elsewhere in previous studies (e.g., Hobbs and Stoops 2002, A-2).

A final comment concerning how density is reported in this appendix concerns how the Alaska and Hawaii land areas were incorporated. In brief, just before the 1960 census, in 1959, Alaska and Hawaii were added as the forty-ninth and fiftieth states to the United States. Table E.1 shows the national average density from 1900 to 1950 as if the land areas from Alaska and Hawaii were already included—to maintain consistency in how density is presented for the decades that followed. Were these two state land areas excluded, then the national average population density for these five decades would be higher than the densities reported in table E.1 because the denominator national land area would be smaller than that incorporated in the table E.1 calculations (Hobbs and Stoops 2002, 15). Without Alaska and Hawaii land areas, population densities for the United States would be 25.7 (1900), 31.1 (1910), 35.7 (1920), 41.5 (1930), 44.5 (1940), and 50.9 (1950).

3 We can only estimate the density of England in 1800 because that country did not conduct its first census until 1801. We quantify some order of magnitude of the 1800 density in England from research estimating that England's population in 1800 at about 8.6 million (Wells 1992, 89; see also Hyginus and Nusteling 1993) and then divide the 8.6 million by England's land area of about 51,000 square miles.

4 The 1790 population densities reported here for Rhode Island, Connecticut, Massachusetts, Maryland, and Delaware are as reported by Rossiter (1909, 58).

5 This conversion is accomplished by multiplying the density expressed in population per square kilometer by 2.59 to yield density expressed in square miles.

6 Also warranted is acknowledging cross-national and cultural differences in defining an "urban" place. For example, the United States has sometimes defined settlements of at least 2,500 inhabitants as "urban" while the Japanese have used a much higher 30,000-person minimum (National Geographic Society, n.d.).

7 The rural population (living in rural areas) is not the same as the farm population (living on a farm). For example, in 1890, 61 percent of the nation's rural residents was classified as farm population. By 1950, however, that farm population share of the total rural population had declined to 28 percent (Truesdell 1960, 7).

References

Abramitzky, Ran, and Leah Boustan. 2017. "Immigration in American History." *Journal of Economic Literature* 55, no. 4: 1311–1345.

Adomaitis, Greg. n.d. "A History of the Ku Klux Klan in N.J." *NJ.com*. Accessed November 26, 2019. https://www.nj.com/news/2017/02/a_history_of_the_ku_klux_klan_in_nj.html.

Adovasio, James M., and Jake Page. 2002. *The First Americans: In Pursuit of Archaeology's Greatest Mystery*. New York: Random House.

Allen, Reniqua. 2017. "Racism Is Everywhere, So Why Not Move South?" *New York Times*, July 9.

American Community Survey (ACS) implemented by the Census Bureau, the 2017 ACS 1-Year Estimates.

American Council of Learned Societies. 1932. *Report of the Committee on Linguistic and National Stocks in the Population of the United States*. Washington, DC: Government Printing Office. Reprinted from the *Annual Report of the American Historical Association* for 1931.

"Another Negro Exodus to the North." 1923. *Literary Digest* (February 17): 18.

Armstead, Shaun, Brenann Sutter, Pamela Walker, and Caitlin Wiesner. 2016. "'And I Poor Slave Yet': The Precarity of Black Life in New Brunswick, 1766–1835." In Fuentes and White 2016, 91–122.

Asada, Iddy. 1994. "I Remember Being a Tomboy." Seabrook Farms Oral History, July 20. https://rucore.libraries.rutgers.edu/rutgers-lib/2937/.

Ashok, Sowmiya. 2016. "The Rise of the American 'Others.'" *The Atlantic*, August 27. https://www.theatlantic.com/politics/archive/2016/08/the-rise-of-the-others/497690/.

Bailyn, Bernard. 2012. *The Barbarous Years: The Conflict of Civilization 1600–1675*. New York: Vintage Books.

Bailyn, Bernard, with Barbara DeWolfe. 1986a. *The Peopling of British North American: An Introduction*. New York: Knopf.

Bailyn, Bernard, with Barbara DeWolfe. 1986b. *Voyages to the West: A Passage in the Peopling of America on the Eve of the Revolution*. New York: Knopf.

Baker, R. S. 1917. "The Negro Goes North." *World's Work* (July): 314–319.

Barde, Robert, Susan Carter, and Richard Sutch. 2015. "International Migration." In Carter et al. 2006, 1–523.

Bayley, Williams. 1910. *Iron Mines and Mining in New Jersey*. Final Report Series of the State Geologist. Trenton: Geological Survey of New Jersey.

Becker, Donald William. 1964. *Indian Place-Names in New Jersey*. Cedar Grove, NJ: Phillips-Campbell.

Beckert, Sven, and Seth Rockman, eds. 2016. *Slavery's Capitalism: A New History of American Economic Development*. Philadelphia: University of Pennsylvania Press.

Bell, Richard. 2019. *Stolen*. New York. Simon & Schuster.

Berger, Alan M. 2017. "The Suburb of the Future, Almost Here." *New York Times*, September 15. https://www.nytimes.com/2017/09/15/sunday-review/future-suburb -millennials.html.

Berube, Alan. 2007. *Metro Nation: How U.S. Metropolitan Areas Fuel American Prosperity*. Washington, DC: Brookings Institution Press.

Bilby, Joseph G., James M. Madden, and Harry Ziegler. 2014. *350 Years of New Jersey History: From Stuyvesant to Sandy*. Charleston, SC: History Press.

Bishop, David. 1853. Letter to E. B. Earl, A. D. Wilson and J. W. Smith. February. Cited in Shaw 1994, 35.

Blackwell, Jon. n.d. "1924: Hatred Wore a Hood in Jersey." *Trentonian*. Accessed November 26, 2019. http://www.capitalcentury.com/1924.html.

Boardman, Samantha J. 2013. "Collard Greens All Year Long: African-American Migration Narratives and the Promise of Newark." *Aster(ix)*, June 18. https:// asterixjournal.com/collard-greens-all-year-long-african-american-migration -narratives-and-the-promise-of-newark-by-samantha-j-boardman/.

Boardman, Samantha J. 2016. "'We Found Our Way': Newark Portraits from the Great Migration." Newark Public Library Exhibition, February 4–April 7.

Bobrick, Benson. 1997. *Angel in the Whirlwind: The Triumph of the American Revolution*. New York: Simon & Schuster.

Bonfield, O. M. 1916. Quoted in "Penalties of Migration." *Atlanta Constitution*, December 14.

Bonomi, Patricia U. 1998. *The Lord Cornbury Scandal: The Politics of Reputation in British America*. Chapel Hill: University of North Carolina Press.

Borbely, James A. 2009. Oral History Interview, March 27, by Shaun Illingworth and Jordan Richman, Rutgers Oral History Archives. http://oralhistory.rutgers.edu /alphabetical-index/31-interviewees/820-borbely-james-a.

Bosman, Julie. 2020. "Black Families Helped Define Chicago. Why Are They Leaving?" *New York Times*, February 17, 1, A10–11.

Boustan, Leah P., Devin Bunten, and Owen Hearey. 2013. "Urbanization in the United States, 1800–2000." Working Paper 19041, National Bureau of Economic Research.

Boyd, Kendra, Miya Carey, and Christopher Blakey. 2016. "Old Money, Rutgers University, and the Political Economy of Slavery in New Jersey." In Fuentes and White 2016, 43–57.

Boyer, Charles S. 1931. *Early Forges and Furnaces in New Jersey*. Philadelphia: University of Pennsylvania Press.

Brittingham, Angela, and C. Patricia de la Cruz. 2004. "Ancestry: 2000." *2000 Census Brief*, June. Washington, DC: U.S. Census Bureau.

Bromwich, Jonah Engel. 2018a. "Tell Us What to Call the Generation after Millennials (Please)." *New York Times*, January 23. https://www.nytimes.com/2018/01/23/style /generation-names.html?module=inline.

Bromwich, Jonah Engel. 2018b. "We Asked Generation Z to Pick a Name. It Wasn't Generation Z." *New York Times,* January 31. https://www.nytimes.com/2018/01/31 /style/generation-z-name.html.

"The Brotherton Indians of New Jersey, 1780." n.d. Gilder Lehrman Institute of American History. Accessed September 5, 2019. https://www.gilderlehrman.org /sites/default/files/inline-pdfs/00540_FPS_0.pdf.

Brown, Anna. 2015. "The Changing Categories the U.S. Has Used to Measure Race." Pew Research Center, June 12. https://www.pewresearch.org/fact-tank/2015/06/12 /the-changing-categories-the-U-S-has-used-to-measure-race.

Brush, John E. 1956. *The Population of New Jersey.* New Brunswick, NJ: Rutgers University Press.

Budiman, Abby, Anthony Cilluffo, and Neil G. Ruiz. 2019. "Key Facts about Asian Origin Groups in the U.S." Pew Research Center, May 22. https://www.pewresearch .org/fact-tank/2019/05/22/key-facts-about-asian-origin-groups-in-the-u-s/.

Burks, Ardath W., and Jerome Cooperman. 1960. "The William Griffis Collection." *Journal of Asian Studies* 20, no. 1 (November): 61–69.

Carney, Leo H. 1987. "New Jersey Journal: Swedes in New Jersey." *New York Times,* April 19.

Carter, Susan B. 2006. "Black Population by State and Slave/Free Status: 1790–1860." In Carter et al. 2006, 2–377.

Carter, Susan B., Scott Sigmund Gartner, Michael R. Haines, Alan L. Olmstead, Richard Sutch, and Gavin Wright, eds. 2006. *Historical Statistics of the United States: Millennial Edition* (online version). New York: Cambridge University Press.

Castillo, Amy. n.d. "Paterson's Multiethnic Communities—Dominicans, Colombians, and Peruvians." The Latino New Jersey History Project, Rutgers University Department of Latino and Caribbean Studies. Accessed November 8, 2019. https://latcar.rutgers.edu/about-us/the-latino-new-jersey-history-project.

Chakrabarty, Rajashri, Andrew Haughwout, Donghoon Lee, Joelle Scally, and Wilbert van der Klaauw. 2017. "At the NY Fed: Press Briefing on Household Borrowing with Close-up on Student Debt." *Liberty Street Economics,* Federal Reserve Bank of New York, April 3. http://libertystreeteconomics.newyorkfed.org/2017/04/at-the-ny-fed -press-briefing-on-household-borrowing-with-close-up-on-student-debt.html.

Chan, Sucheng. 1991. *Asian Americans, An Interpretive History.* Boston: Twayne.

Chivukula, Upendra. 2002. Oral History Interview, December 6, by Renu Agarwal, New Jersey Multi-Ethnic Oral History Project. Accessed November 20, 2019. https://njdigitalhighway.org/portalResults?q1=oral+histories&q1field =mods%3Agenre&q1bool=AND&q2field=object&orderby=relevance&ppage =10&key=NJDH&numresults=1&start=16.

City University of New York. 2018. CUNY TV Digital Series, first aired August 7, 2018. https://www.youtube.com/watch?v=OpBXrtxqR0g.

Clement, John. 1893. "Swedish Settlers in Gloucester County New Jersey, Previous to 1684." *Pennsylvania Magazine of History and Biography* 17, no. 1: 83–87.

CNN. 2019. "American Generation Fast Facts." https://www.cnn.com/2013/11/06/us /baby-boomer-generation-fast-facts/index.html.

Co, Pham. 2002. Oral History Interview, August 14, by To-Thi Bosacchi, New Jersey Multi-Ethnic Oral History. Accessed November 20, 2019. https://rucore.libraries .rutgers.edu/rutgers-lib/3999/.

Cohen, David Steven. 2006. "The Lenape Village at Waterloo." Trenton, NJ: NNJ Public Television and New Jersey Historical Commission. http://www.nj.gov/state /historical/pdf/lenape-guide.pdf.

Cohn, D'Vera. 2010. "Race and the Census: The 'Negro' Controversy." Pew Research Center, Social and Demographic Trends. https://www.pewsocialtrends.org/2010/01/21/race-and-the-census-the-negro-controversy/.

Cohn, D'Vera. 2014. "Millions of Americans Changed Their Racial or Ethnic Identity from One Census to Another." Pew Research Center, Social and Demographic Trends. http://www.pewresearch.org/fact-tank/2014/05/05/millions-of-americans-changed-their-racial-or-ethnic-identity-from-one-census-to-the-next/.

Colby, Sandra L., and Jennifer M. Ortman. 2014. "The Baby Boom Cohort in the United States: 2002 to 2060." Current Population Reports (May), U.S. Census Bureau. https://www.census.gov/prod/2014pubs/p25-1141.pdf.

Colon, Otilio. 1982. "A Brief History of the Hispanic Community in New Brunswick, 1948–1980." In *The Tercentennial Lectures, New Brunswick, New Jersey,* edited by Ruth Patt, 57–59. New Brunswick, NJ: City of New Brunswick.

"Colonial New Jersey's Bog Iron." 1963. *Journal of Metals* 15:158.

Commons, Michael. 2018. "Defining Rurality." PowerPoint presentation, Geography Division, U.S. Census Bureau, June 20.

Connolly, Colleen. 2018. "The True Native New Yorkers Can Never Truly Reclaim Their Homeland." *Smithsonian.com,* October 5. https://www.smithsonianmag.com/history/true-native-new-yorkers-can-never-truly-reclaim-their-homeland-180970472/.

Conte, James Thomas. 1977. "Overseas Study in the Meiji Period: Japanese Students in America, 1867–1902." PhD diss., Princeton University.

Cook, Sherburne F., and Woodrow Borah. 1971. "The Aboriginal Population of Hispaniola." In *Essays in Population History,* Vol. 1, *Mexico and the Caribbean,* 376–410. Berkeley: University of California Press.

Cook, Sherburne F., and Woodrow Borah. 1979. "Royal Revenues and Indian Population in New Spain, ca. 1620–1646." In *Essays in Population History,* Vol. 3, *Mexico and California,* 1–128. Berkeley: University of California Press.

Cornbury, Edward Hyde, Viscount. 1708. *New Jersey Archives,* 1st ser., III, 333.

Covart, Elizabeth. n.d. "New Sweden: A Brief History." Penn State University Libraries. Accessed January 3, 2020. https://libraries.psu.edu/about/collections/unearthing-past-student-research-pennsylvania-history/new-sweden-brief-history.

Craven, W. Frank. 1964. *New Jersey and the English Colonization of North America.* Princeton, NJ: Van Nostrand.

Craven, W. Frank. 1965. *New Jersey and the English Settlement of North America.* Princeton, NJ: Van Nostrand.

Cressie, Noel. 1988. "Estimating Census Undercount at National and Subnational Levels." In *Fourth Annual Research Conference Proceedings,* 123–150. Washington, DC: Bureau of the Census.

Cummings, Charles F. 2004. *The People of New Jersey: Their Enduring Journey.* Exhibition catalog. Newark, NJ: Newark Public Library.

Cunningham, Barbara, ed. 1977. *The New Jersey Ethnic Experience.* Union City, NJ: Wm H. Wise.

Cunningham, John T. 1966. *New Jersey: America's Main Road.* Garden City, NY: Doubleday.

Cunningham, John T. 1994. *This Is New Jersey.* 4th ed. New Brunswick, NJ: Rutgers University Press.

Dahlgren, Stellan, and Hans Norman. 1988. *The Rise and Fall of New Sweden: Governor Johan Risingh's Journal 1654–1655 in Its Historical Context.* Stockholm: Almqvist & Wicksell.

Dallhammer, Erich, Martyna Derszniak-Noirjean, Roland Gaugitsch, Sebastian Hans, and Sabine Zillmer. 2019. *The Impacts of Metropolitan Regions on Their Surrounding Areas*. Brussels: European Union Committee of the Regions.

De Angelo, Walter A. 2007. *The History Buff's Guide to Middlesex County*. New Brunswick, NJ: Middlesex County Board of Freeholders. http://www.co.middlesex .nj.us/Government/Departments/BDE/Documents/history_buffsguide.pdf.

"A Declaration of the True Intent and Meaning of US the Lords Proprietors, and Explanation of There Concessions Made to the Adventurers and Planters of New Caesarea or New Jersey" (1672). In Thorpe 1909.

Delaney, John. 2014. *Nova Caesarea: A Cartographic Record of the Garden State, 1666–1888, Including the Frist Maps, Wall Maps & County Atlases, as well as Past & Current Views*. Princeton, NJ: Princeton University Library.

Deloria, Philip. 2019. "The Invention of Thanksgiving: Massacres, Myths, and the Making of the Great November Holiday." *New Yorker*, November 25, 70–74.

Denevan, William M. 1992a. *The Native Population of the Americas in 1492*. 2nd rev. ed. Madison: University of Wisconsin Press.

Denevan, William M. 1992b. "The Pristine Myth: The Landscape of the Americas in 1492." *Annals of the Association of American Geographers* 82, no. 3: 369–385.

Denevan, William M. 1996. "Carl Sauer and Native American Population Size." *Geographical Review* 86, no. 3: 385–397.

DeParle, Jason. 2019. *A Good Provider Is One Who Leaves: One Family and Migration in the 21st Century*. New York: Viking.

Descendants of Founders of New Jersey. n.d. "Historical Timeline of Early New Jersey." Accessed January 15, 2018. www.njfounders.org/history/historical-timeline-early -new-jersey.

Dews, Fred. 2013. "What Percentage of the U.S. Population Is Foreign Born?" *Brookings Now*, October 3. https://www.brookings.edu/blog/brookings-now/2013/10/03/what -percentage-of-u-s-population-is-foreign-born/.

Dexter, Franklin B. 1887. "Estimates of Population in the American Colonies." *Report of the Council of the American Antiquarian Society*, October, 22–50.

Diouf, Sylviane A. 2007. *The Slave Ship* Clotilda *and the Story of the Last Africans Brought to America*. Oxford: Oxford University Press.

Diouf, Sylviane A. 2020. "Journey of No Return." *National Geographic* (February):53–61.

Doak, Robin, with Brendan McConville. 2005. *Voices from Colonial America—New Jersey, 1609–1776*. Washington, DC: National Geographic Society.

Dobbyns, H. F. 1966. "Estimating Aboriginal American Population: An Appraisal of Techniques with a New Hemispheric Estimate." *Current Anthropology* 7:395–416.

Donald, H. H. 1921. "Negro Migrations of 1916–1918." *Journal of Negro History* (October):401–407.

Doyle, Theresa. 1996. "A History and Bibliography of the Lenni Lenape." Master's thesis, Rowan University. https://rdw.rowan.edu/etd/2153.

"The Duke of York's Release to John Lord Berkeley, and Sir George Carteret, 24th of June 1664." In Thorpe 1909.

Durand, John. 1977. "Historical Estimates of the World's Population: An Evaluation." *Population and Development Review* 3, no. 1 (September): 253–296.

Easterlin, Richard. 2000. "American Population in the Twentieth Century." In Haines and Steckel 2000, 631–675.

"Electronic Calculators—Handheld." n.d. National Museum of American History, Smithsonian Institution, Washington, DC. https://www.si.edu/spotlight/handheld -electronic-calculators/introduction.

Elliot, John. 1963. *Imperial Spain*. London: Penguin.

Emmons, William R. 2014. "Generations X and Y: In the Shadow of the Baby Boom." Federal Reserve Bank of St. Louis, March 6. https://www.stlouisfed.org/~/media /files/pdfs/hfs/assets/emmons-little-rock-mar-6-2014.pdf.

Emmons, William R., Ana H. Kent, and Lowell R. Ricketts. 2018. *The Demographics of Wealth: How Education, Race, and Birth Year Shape Financial Outcomes*. St. Louis, MO: Center for Household Financial Stability, Federal Reserve Bank of St. Louis.

Emory University. n.d. "Trans-Atlantic Slave Trade Database." Accessed February 27, 2019. https://www.salvevoyages.org/voyage/database.

Engerman, Stanley, and Robert Margo. 2010. "Free Labor and Slave Labor." In Irvin and Sylla 2010, 291–314.

Ennis, Sharon R., Merarys Rios-Vargas, and Nora G. Albert. 2011. "The Hispanic Population: 2010." *2010 Census Briefs* (May). Washington, DC: U.S. Census Bureau.

Equal Justice Institute. 2019. "Lynchings in America: Confronting the Legacy of Racial Terror." https://lynchingamerica.eji.org/report/.

Eschbach, Karl. 1993. "Changing Identification among American Indians and Alaska Natives." *Demography* 30, no. 4 (November): 635–652.

Eschner, Kat. 2017. "The First US Census Only Asked Six Questions." *Smithsonian Magazine*, August 2.

Escobar, Rebecca. n.d. "Oral History Interview." http:// mappingnewbrunsiwckmemories.org/exhibits.

Evans, Tim. 2010a. "Metro Areas Are the Key to America's—and New Jersey's—Future Economic Prosperity." *New Jersey Future–Future Facts*, April 22.

Evans, Tim. 2010b. "If New Jersey Were a Country." *New Jersey Future–Future Facts*, June 17.

Evans, Tim. 2011. "Density and Sprawl Are Not Mutually Exclusive." *New Jersey Future—Future Facts*. https://www.njfuture.org/2011/08/24/density-sprawl/.

Evans, Tim. 2017. "Where Are We Going? Implications of Recent Demographic Trends in New Jersey." *New Jersey Future* report, September.

"Exodus in America." 1917. *Living Age* (October 6):57–60.

Ezell, John S. 1960. *Fortune's Merry Wheel: The Lottery in America*. Cambridge, MA: Harvard University Press.

Federal Reserve Bank of St. Louis. 2018. "A Lost Generation? Long-Lasting Wealth Impacts of the Great Recession on Young Families." Center for Household Financial Stability, Federal Reserve Bank of St. Louis. https://www.stlouisfed.org/household -financial-stability/the-demographics-of-wealth/wealth-impacts-of-great-recession -on-young-families.

Federal Writers' Project of the Works Progress Administration for the State of New Jersey. 1939. *New Jersey: A Guide to Its Present and Past*. New York: Viking.

Florido, Adrian. 2017. "Here's Why the Census Started Counting Latinos, and How That Could Change in 2020." Code Switch, NPR, August 3. https://www.npr.org /sections/codeswitch/2017/08/03/541142339/heres-why-the-census-started-counting -latinos-and-how-that-could-change-in-2020.

Fogleman, Aaron. 1992. "Migrations to the Thirteen British North American Colonies, 1700–1775: New Estimates." *Journal of Interdisciplinary History* 22, no. 4: 691–709.

Fontenot, Kayla, Jessica Semega, and Melissa Kollar. 2018. *Income and Poverty in the United States: 2017*. U.S. Census Bureau, Current Population Reports, P-60–263. Washington, DC: U.S. Government Printing Office.

Frankel, Emil. 1937. "Crime Treatment in New Jersey—1668–1934." *Journal of Criminal Law and Criminology* 28, no. 1: 90–105.

Franklin, Benjamin. 1751. "Observations Concerning the Increase of Mankind, and Peopling of Countries." *Founders Online*. https://founders.archives.gov/documents /Franklin/01-04-02-0080.

Frazier, Ian. 2019. "When W.E.B. Du Bois Made a Laughing Stock of a White Supremacist." *New Yorker*, August 19. https://www.newyorker.com/magazine/2019/08/26 /when-w-e-b-du-bois-made-a-laughingstock-of-a-white-supremacist.

Frey, William H. 2004. "The New Great Migration: Black Americans Return to the South, 1965–2000." Brookings Institution, Living Cities Census Series, May.

Frey, William H. 2015. *Diversity Explosion: How New Racial Demographics Are Remaking America*. Washington, DC: Brookings Institution Press.

Frey, William H. 2018. "The US Will Become 'Minority White' in 2045, Census Projects." Brookings Institution. https://www.brookings.edu/blog/the-avenue/2018 /03/14/the-us-will-become-minority-white-in-2045-census-projects/.

Frey, William H. 2019a. "As Americans Spread Out, Immigration Plays a Crucial Role in Population Growth." Brookings Institution. https://www.brookings.edu/research/as -americans-spread-out-immigration-plays-a-crucial-role-in-local-population-growth/.

Frey, William H. 2019b. "Six Maps That Reveal America's Ethnic Diversity." Brookings Institution. https://www.brookings.edu/research/americas-racial-diversity-in-six -maps/?utm_campaign=Brookings%20Brief&utm_source=hs_email&utm _medium=email&utm_content=76509103.

Fry, Richard. 2015. "Millennials Surpass Gen Xers as the Largest Generation in U.S. Labor Force." Fact Tank, Pew Research Center, May 11. http://www.pewresearch.org /fact-tank/2015/05/11/millennials-surpass-gen-xers-as-the-largest-generation-in-u-s -labor-force/.

Fry, Richard. 2017. "It's Becoming More Common for Young Adults to Live at Home— and for Longer Stretches." Fact Tank, Pew Research Center, May 5. http://www .pewresearch.org/fact-tank/2017/05/05/its-becoming-more-common-for-young -adults-to-live-at-home-and-for-longer-stretches/.

Fuentes, Marisa J., and Deborah Gray White, eds. 2016. *Slavery and Dispossession in Rutgers History*. Vol. 1 of *Scarlet and Black*. New Brunswick, NJ: Rutgers University Press.

Fung, Esther. 2018. "Baby Boomers Are Living at Home. That's Bad News for Senior-Housing Developers." *Wall Street Journal*, October 30. https://www.wsj.com/articles /baby-boomers-are-living-at-home-thats-bad-news-for-senior-housing-developers -1540897200?shareToken=st6e7529fc02e54fce8d28d46c829867ce&ref=article _email_share.

Galenson, David W. 1984. "The Rise and Fall of Indentured Servants in the Americas: An Economic Analysis." *Journal of Economic History* 44, no. 1: 1–26.

Galenson, David W. 1996. "The Settlement and Growth of the Colonies: Population, Labor, and Economic Development." In *The Cambridge Economic History of the United States*, edited by Stanley Engerman and Robert E. Gallman, 135–207. Cambridge: Cambridge University Press.

Ganatra, Rupa. 2017. "The Rise of the Experience Economy." *Brand Quarterly*, May 23. http://www.brandquarterly.com/rise-experience-economy.

Gaquin, Deirdre A., and Mary Meghan Ryan, eds. 2015. *County and City Extra: Special Historical Edition 1790–2010*. Lanham, MD: Bernan Press.

Garland, Allen. 2002. "The Ideology of Elimination: American and German Eugenics, 1900–1945." In Nicosia and Huener 2002, 13–39.

Garmm, Carl H. 1938. *The Germans in New Brunswick, New Jersey . . . 1838 to 1888*. Cleveland: Central Publishing House.

Garreau, Joel. 1991. *Edge City: Life on the New Frontier*. New York: Anchor Books, 1991.

Garrow, David J. 2011. "The Legal Legacy of *Griswold v. Connecticut*." *Human Rights Magazine*, Spring. http://www.davidgarrow.com/File/DJG2011ABAGriswold.pdf.

Gates, Henry Louis, and Nellie Y. McKay, eds. 1997. *The Norton Anthology of African American Literature*. New York: Norton.

Gemery, Henry A. 2000. "The White Population of the Colonial United States, 1607–1790." In Haines and Steckel 2000, 143–190.

Gertner, Jon. 2012. *The Idea Factory: Bell Labs and the Great Age of American Innovation*. New York: Penguin.

Gibson, Campbell. n.d. "American Demographic History Chartbook: 1790 to 2010." Accessed October 8, 2019. http://demographicchartbook.com.

Gibson, Campbell, and Kay Jung. 2006. "Historical Census Statistics on the Foreign-Born Population of the United States." Population Division Working Paper No. 81 (February). Washington, DC: Bureau of the Census.

Gibson, Carrie. 2019. *El Norte: The Epic and Forgotten Story of Hispanic North America*. New York: Atlantic Monthly Press.

Gigantino, James J., II. 2010. "Freedom and Unfreedom in the 'Garden of America': Slavery and Abolition in New Jersey, 1770–1857." PhD diss., University of Georgia.

Gigantino, James J., II. 2014. "'The Whole North Is Not Abolitionized': Slavery's Slow Death in New Jersey, 1830–1860." *Journal of the Early Republic* 34, no. 3: 411–437. http://www.jstor.org/stable/24486906.

Gjelton, Tom. 2015. "The Immigration Act That Inadvertently Changed America." *The Atlantic*, October 2.

Goldman, Dan, Sophie Marchessou, and Warren Teichner. 2017. "Cashing In on the US Experience Economy." McKinsey & Company, December 11. https://www.mckinsey.com/industries/private-equity-and-principal-investors/our-insights/cashing-in-on-the-us-experience-economy.

Gordon, Thomas. 1834. *A Gazetteer of the State of New Jersey*. Trenton, NJ: Daniel Fenton.

Grabas, Joseph A. 2014. *Owning New Jersey: Historic Tales of War, Property Disputes, and the Pursuit of Happiness*. Charleston, SC: History Press.

Grant, Madison. 1916. *The Passing of the Great Race; or, The Racial Basis of European History*. New York: Charles Scribner.

"Great Ship Plant Needs Steel Men. Newark Yards Ready to Employ 12,000 Workers to Turn Out Vessels for War Use." 1917. *New York Times*, October 22.

Green, Victor H. 1940. *The Negro Motorist Green-Book*. New York: Victor H. Green Publisher. Prepared in cooperation with the United States Travel Bureau.

Greene, Evarts B., and Virginia D. Harrington. 1932. *American Population before the Federal Census of 1790*. New York: Columbia University Press.

Gregory, James N. 2005. *The Southern Diaspora: How the Great Migrations of Black and White Southerners Transformed America*. Chapel Hill: University of North Carolina Press.

Grieco, Elizabeth M., Yesenia D. Acosta, Patricia de la Cruz, Christine Gambino, Thomas Gryn, Luke J. Larsen, Edward N. Trevelyan, and Nathan P. Walters. 2012. "The Foreign-Born Population in the United States." American Community Survey Reports (ACS-19). Washington, DC: U.S. Census Bureau. https://www.census.gov/library/publications/2012/acs/acs-19.html.

Grubb, Farley. 1985. "The Incidence of Servitude in Trans-Atlantic Migration, 1771–1804." *Explorations in Economic History* 22:316–339.

Grubb, Farley. 2013. "Colonial New Jersey's Paper Money Regime, 1709–1775: A Forensic Accounting Reconstruction of the Date." Working Paper No. 19710, National Bureau of Economic Research.

Grubb, Farley. 2015. "Colonial New Jersey's Provincial Fiscal Structure, 1704–1775: Spending Obligations, Revenue Sources, and Tax Burdens during Peace and War." Working Paper No. 21152, National Bureau of Economic Research.

Gurowitz, Margaret. 2006–2008. "Kilmer House: The Story of Johnson & Johnson and Its People." https://www.kilmerhouse.com.

Hacker, Myra C. 1965. "Testimony before the U.S. Senate Subcommittee on Immigration and Naturalization of the Committee on the Judiciary. Washington, DC, February 10." Cited in Kammer 2015.

Haines, Michael R. 2000. "The White Population of the United States." In Haines and Steckel 2000, 305–369.

Haines, Michael R. 2006a. "Population by Sex and Race." In Carter et al. 2006, 1–48, 49.

Haines, Michael R. 2006b. "Population Characteristics." In Carter et al. 2006, 1–25.

Haines, Michael R., and Richard H. Steckel. 2000a. "Introduction." In Haines and Steckel 2000, 1–8.

Haines, Michael R., and Richard H. Steckel. 2000b. *A Population History of North America*. Cambridge: Cambridge University Press.

Hamilton, Brady E., Joyce A. Martin, Michelle J. K. Osterman, Anne K. Driscoll, and Lauren M. Rossen. 2018. "Births: Provisional Data for 2017." *NVSS Vital Statistics Rapid Release*, Report no. 004. https://www.cdc.gov/nchs/data/vsrr/report004.pdf.

Hansen, Marcus L. 1932. "Annex B: The Minor Stocks in the American Population of 1790." In *American Historical Association Annual Report: 1931* (Washington, DC, 1932), 360–397.

Harris, A. L. 1924. "Negro Migration to the North." *Current History Magazine of the New York Times*, 921–925.

Harrison, David. 2019. "Historic Asset Boom Passes by Half of Families." *Wall Street Journal*, August 30. https://www.wsj.com/articles/historic-asset-boom-passes-by-half -of-families-11567157400?mod=itp_wsj&mod=&mod=djemITP_h.

Hennelly, Robert. 2015. "Secret History of a Northern Slave State: How Slavery Was Written into New Jersey's DNA." *Salon*, July 29. https://www.salon.com/2015/07/29 /secret_history_of_a_northern_slave_state_how_slavery_was_written_into_new _jerseys_dna/.

Hess, William M. E. 1973. *On History's Trail*. Brick Township, NJ: Farley.

Hill, J. A. 1924. "Recent Northward Migration of the Negro." *Monthly Labor Review* (March):1–14.

Hill, N. Salomon. 1942. "The Negro in New Brunswick as Revealed by a Study of One Hundred Families." Master's thesis, Drew Theological Seminary.

Hirschman, Charles. 2014. "Immigration to the United States: Recent Trends and Future Prospects." *Malays Journal of Economic Studies* 51, no. 7: 69–85.

Hixson, Lindsay, Bradford B. Helper, and Myoung Ouk Kim. 2011. "The White Population: 2010." *2010 Census Briefs* (September). Washington, DC: U.S. Census Bureau.

Hobbs, Frank, and Nicole Stoops. 2002. *Demographic Trends in the 20th Century*. U.S. Census Bureau, Census 2000 Special Reports, Series CENSR-4. Washington, DC: U.S. Government Printing Office.

Hochschild, Adam. 2019. "Obstruction of Injustice." *New Yorker*, November 11, 28–34.

Hoeffel, Elizabeth M., Sonya Rastogi, Myoung Ouk Kim, and Hasan Shahid. 2012. "The Asian Population: 2010." *2010 Census Briefs* (March). Washington, DC: U.S. Census Bureau.

Hoffecker, Carol E., Richard Waldron, Lorraine E. Williams, and Barbara E. Benson, eds. 1995. *New Sweden in America*. Newark: University of Delaware Press and Associated University Presses.

Holt, Thomas C. 2010. *Children of Fire: A History of African Americans*. New York: Hill & Wang.

Horton, James Oliver, and Lois E. Horton. 2001. *Hard Road to Freedom: The Story of African America*. New Brunswick, NJ: Rutgers University Press.

Horwill, H. W. 1918. "Negro Exodus." *Contemporary Review* (September):299–305.

Howe, Neil, and William Strauss. 2000. *Millennials Rising: The Next Great Generation*. New York: Vintage Books.

Hsu, Madeline. 2015. *The Gold Immigrants: How the Yellow Peril Become the Model Minority*. Princeton, NJ: Princeton University Press.

Hughes, James W., and Joseph J. Seneca, eds. 1999. *America's Demographic Tapestry: Baseline for the New Millennium*. New Brunswick, NJ: Rutgers University Press.

Hughes, James W., and Joseph J. Seneca. 2000. *Anticipating Census 2000: New Jersey's Emerging Demographic Profile*. New Brunswick, NJ: Rutgers Regional Report Number 18, July.

Hughes, James W., and Joseph J. Seneca. 2003. *Housing Bubble or Shelter Safe Haven?* New Brunswick, NJ: Rutgers Regional Report Number 19, September.

Hughes, James W., and Joseph Seneca. 2004a. "Economy." In Lurie and Mappen 2004, 234–236.

Hughes, James W., and Joseph Seneca. 2004b. *Then and Now: Sixty Years of Economic Change in New Jersey*. New Brunswick, NJ: Rutgers Regional Report Number 20, January.

Hughes, James W., and Joseph Seneca. 2009. "The Economy." In Lurie and Wacker 2009, 152–156.

Hughes, James W., and Joseph J. Seneca. 2015. *New Jersey's Postsuburban Economy*. New Brunswick, NJ: Rutgers University Press.

Hughes, Langston. 1979. "One-Way-Ticket." In *Selected Poems of Langston Hughes*, 177. New York: Knopf.

Humes, Karen, and Howard Hogan. 2009. "Measurement of Race and Ethnicity in a Changing, Multicultural America." *Race and Social Problems* 1, no. 111 (September). https://doi.org/10.1007/s12552-009-9011-5.

Hunold, Janice. n.d. "Revolutionary Jersey Girls." *Crossroads of the American Revolution*. Accessed November 22, 2019. https://revolutionarynj.org/revolutionary-jersey-girls/.

Hunt, Mathew O., Larry L. Hunt, and William W. Falk. 2013. "Twenty-First Century Trends in Black Migration to the U.S. South: Demographic and Subjective Predictors." *Social Science Quarterly* 94, no. 5: 1398–1413.

Hunter, David. 1952. *Papermaking in Pioneer America*. Philadelphia: University of Pennsylvania Press.

Hunter, Richard W. 2009. "Early Milling and Waterpower." In Lurie and Wacker 2009, 170.

Hyginus, Huibert, and Pascalle Nusteling. 1993. "The Population of England (1539–1873): An Issue of Demographic Homeostasis." *Histoire & Mesure* 8, no. 2: 59–92.

IBM. n.d. "Chronological History of IBM: 1980s." IBM Archives. Accessed January 15, 2018. https://www-03.ibm.com/ibm/history/history/decade_1980.html.

"Indentured Servants in the U.S." n.d. *History Detectives*. Accessed January 6, 2020. https://www.pbs.org/opb/historydetectives/feature/indentured-servants-in-the-us/.

Iowa Community Indicators Program, Iowa State University. n.d. "Urban Percentage of the Population for States, Historical." Accessed March 1, 2019. https://www.icip .iastate.edu/tables/population/urban-pct-states.

Irving, Will. 2019. "Analysis of IPUMS (Integrated Public Use Microdata Series) from the National Historical Geographic Information System (NHGIS) for Indicated Years." IPUMS NHGIS, University of Minnesota. Accessed November 10, 2019. www.nhgis.org.

Irwin, Douglas A., and Richard Sylla. 2010. *Founding Choices: American Economic Policy in the 1970s*. Chicago: University of Chicago Press.

Irwin, Neil. 2018. "Is This a Mid-1990s Moment for the Economy? Three Reasons for Optimism," *New York Times*, September 9, BU5.

Jamison, Wallace N. 1964. *Religion in New Jersey: A Brief History*. Princeton, NJ: Van Nostrand.

Jasch, Mary. n.d. "Long Pond Ironworks: The Hills of Ramapo." *Skylands Visitor*. Accessed January 9, 2020. http://www.njskylands.com/hslongpond.

Jersey Promise. May 2019. *A Report on the State of Asian Americans in New Jersey*. New Providence, NJ: Jersey Promise. http://jerseypromise.org/wp-content/uploads/2019 /05/Jersey-Promise-Report-Final-5.5.2019.pdf.

Jones, Alice H. 1968. "Wealth Estimates for the American Middle Colonies, 1774." PhD diss., University of Chicago.

Jones, Alice H. 1980. *Wealth of a Nation to Be: The American Colonies on the Eve of the Revolution*. New York: Columbia University Press.

Kammer, Jerry. 2015. "The Hart-Celler Immigration Act of 1965." Center for Immigration Studies. Accessed November 20, 2019. https://cis.org/Report/HartCeller -Immigration-Act-1965.

Karasik, Gary, and Anna Aschkenes. 1999. *Middlesex County: Crossroads of History*. Sun Valley, CA: American Historical Press.

Karnoutsos, Carmela. n.d. "350th Anniversary of the Dutch Settlement of Bergen Colonial New Jersey." https://www.njcu.edu/programs/jchistory/Pages/D_Pages /Dutch_Settlement_Of_Bergen_Colonial_Jersey_City.

Keane, Katharine. 2016. "The Crossroads of the American Revolution." National Trust for Historic Preservation. Accessed August 8, 2019. https://savingplaces.org/stories /the-crossroads-of-the-american-revolution-new-jersey.

Kennedy, Lesley. 2019. "Building the Transcontinental Railroad: How Some 20,000 Chinese Immigrants Made It Happen." *History.com*. Accessed October 18, 2019. https://www.history.com/news/transcontinental-railroad-chinese-immigrants.

King, Charles. 2019. *Gods of the Upper Air: How a Circle of Renegade Anthropologists Reinvented Race, Sex, and Gender in the Twentieth Century*. New York: Doubleday.

King, Gregory. 1936. *Natural and Political Observations and Conclusions upon the State and Condition of England*. Edited by George E. Barnett. Baltimore: Johns Hopkins University Press. Cited in Thompson 1974, 161.

Kingsley-Hughes, Adrian. 2017. "Inside Apple's New A11 Bionic Processor." *ZD Net*, September 12. https://www.zdnet.com/article/inside-apples-new-a11-bionic-processor/.

Kitroeff, Natalie. 2018. "How Student Debt Can Ruin Home Buying Dreams." *New York Times*, May 25. https://www.nytimes.com/2018/05/25/business/how-student -debt-can-ruin-home-buying-dreams.html.

Klein, Herbert S. 2004. *A Population History of the United States*. Cambridge: Cambridge University Press.

Klett, Joseph R. 2014. *Using the Records of the East and West Jersey Proprietors*. Trenton: New Jersey State Archives.

Kliesen, Kevin L. 2003. "The 2001 Recession: How Was It Different and What Developments May Have Caused It?" *Federal Reserve Bank of St. Louis Review* (September–October):23–37. https://files.stlouisfed.org/files/htdocs/publications/review/03/09/Kliesen.pdf.

Klinghoffer, Judith Apter, and Lois Elkis. 1992. "'The Petticott Electors': Women's Suffrage in New Jersey 1776–1807." *Journal of the Early Republic* 12, no. 2: 159–193.

Kraft, Herbert C. 1986. *The Lenape: Archaeology, History, and Ethnography*. Newark: New Jersey Historical Society.

Kroeber, A. L. 1934. "Native American Population." *American Anthropologist* 36:1–25.

Kroeber, A. L. 1939. *Cultural and Natural Areas in Native North America*. Berkeley: University of California Press.

Krogstad, Jens Manuel, and D'Vera Cohn. 2014. "U.S. Census Looking at Big Changes in How It Asks about Race and Ethnicity." Pew Research Center, March 14. https://www.pewresearch.org/fact-tank/2014/03/14/u-s-census-looking-at-big-changes-in-how-it-asks-about-race-and-ethnicity/.

Krueger-Scott Cultural Center. n.d. "The Lost Years Recovered: Oral History of African Americans in Newark, New Jersey from 1910–1970." (Oral histories conducted between 1995 and 2000).

Krueger-Scott Oral History Collection. n.d. "Media Projects." Accessed November 28, 2019. https://kruegerscott.libraries.rutgers.edu/media-projects.

Lachman, M. Leanne, and Deborah L. Brett. 2011. *Generation Y: America's New Housing Wave*. Washington, DC: Urban Land Institute. http://uli.org/wp-content/uploads/ULI-Documents/GenY-Report-20110510.ashx_.pdf.

Lachman, M. Leanne, and Deborah L. Brett. 2013. *Generation Y: Shopping and Entertainment in the Digital Age*. Washington, DC: Urban Land Institute. https://uli.org/wp-content/uploads/ULI-Documents/Generation-Y-Shopping-and-Entertainment-in-the-Digital-Age.pdf.

La Gorce, Tammy. 2014. "How South Jersey Shaped Glass, and Vice Versa." *New York Times*, May 30. https://www.nytimes.com/2014/06/01/nyregion/how-south-jersey-shaped-glass-and-vice-versa.html.

Laky, S. 1921. "What the Hungarian People in This City Have Done to Help Develop New Brunswick." *New Brunswick Sunday Times*, April 24.

Lamiell, Patricia. 2008. "Rutgers Commemorates First Encounter between New Brunswick and Fukui, Japan." *Rutgers Today*, January 30. https://news.rutgers.edu/feature-focus/rutgers-commemorates-first-encounter-between-new-brunswick-and-fukui-japan/20080130#.Xc2rPS3Mxn4.

Ledesman, Ann. 1976. "City Park May Foster Unity." *Home News*, June 25.

Lee, Erika. 2015. *The Making of Asian America: A History*. New York: Simon & Schuster.

Lee, Francis. 1902. *New Jersey as a Colony and as a State*. New York: Publishing Society of New Jersey.

Lee, Sandra S. 2008. *Images of America: Italian Americans of Newark, Belleville, and Nutley*. Charleston, SC: Arcadia.

Leiby, A. Coulter. 1965. *The Early Dutch and Swedish Settlers of New Jersey*. Princeton, NJ: Van Nostrand.

Lemkin, Raphael. 2012. *Lemkin on Genocide*. Lanham, MD: Lexington Books.

Lepore, Jill. 2018. *These Truths: A History of the United States*. New York: Norton.

Levitt, James H. 1981. "For Want of Trade: Shipping and the New Jersey Ports, 1680–1783. Newark: New Jersey Historical Society, 224.

Listokin, David, Dorothea Berkhout, and James W. Hughes. 2016. *New Brunswick, New Jersey: The Decline and Revitalization of Urban America*. New Brunswick, NJ: Rutgers University Press.

Livingston, Gretchen. 2019. "Is U.S. Fertility at an All-Time Low? Two of Three Measures Point to Yes." Fact Tank, Pew Research Center, May 22. http://www.pewresearch.org/fact-tank/2018/01/18/is-u-s-fertility-at-an-all-time-low-it-depends/.

Lopez, Gustavo, Neil G. Ruiz, and Eileen Patten. 2017. "Key Facts about Asian Americans, a Diverse and Growing Population." Pew Research Center, September 8. https://www.pewresearch.org/fact-tank/2017/09/08/key-facts-about-asian-americans/

Lord, Lewis. 1997. "How Many People Were Here before Columbus?" *U.S. News and World Report*, August 18–25, 68–70.

Lotka, A. J. 1927. "The Size of American Families in the Eighteenth Century." *Journal of the American Statistical Association* 22:165.

Lukac, George J. 1966. *Aloud to Alma Mater*. New Brunswick, NJ: Rutgers University Press.

Lurie, Maxine. 1987. "New Jersey: The Unique Proprietary." *Pennsylvania Magazine of History and Biography* 111, no. 1: 77–97.

Lurie, Maxine, ed. 2010. *A New Jersey Anthology*. 2nd ed. New Brunswick, NJ: Rutgers University Press.

Lurie, Maxine, and Marc Mappen. 2004. *Encyclopedia of New Jersey*. Maps by Michael Siegel. New Brunswick, NJ: Rutgers University Press.

Lurie, Maxine, and Richard Veit, eds. 2012. *New Jersey: A History of the Garden State*. New Brunswick, NJ: Rutgers University Press.

Lurie, Maxine, and Richard Veit. 2016. *Envisioning New Jersey: An Illustrated History of the Garden State*. New Brunswick, NJ: Rutgers University Press.

Lurie, Maxine, and Peter O. Wacker, eds. 2009. *Mapping New Jersey: An Evolving Landscape*. Cartography by Michael Siegel. New Brunswick, NJ: Rutgers University Press.

Lyttle, Virginia M., Shirley J. Horner, Sally S. Minshall, and Jeanne H. Watson, eds. 1978. *Ladies at the Crossroads: Eighteenth-Century Women of New Jersey*. Morristown, NJ: Compton.

Mackum, Paul, and Steven Wilson. 2011. "Population Distribution and Change 2000 to 2010." *2010 Census Briefs* (March). Washington, DC: U.S. Census Bureau.

MacNutt, F. A. 1909. *Bartholomew de las Casas: His Life, His Apostolate, and His Writings*. New York: Putnam.

Madley, Benjamin. 2015. "Reexamining the American Genocide Debate: Meaning, Historiography, and New Methods." *American Historical Review* 120, no. 1 (February): 98–139.

Main, Gloria L. 2001. *Peoples of a Spacious Land: Families and Cultures in Colonial New England*. Cambridge, MA: Harvard University Press.

Malpezzi, Stephen. 2013. "Population Density: Some Facts and Some Predictions." *Cityscape: A Journal of Policy Development and Research* 15, no. 3: 183–201.

Malthus, Thomas. 1926. *An Essay on the Principle of Population*. Reprint. London: Royal Economic Society.

Mancall, Peter, Joshua Rosenbloom, and Thomas Weiss. 2008. "The Role of Exports in the Economy of Colonial North America: New Estimates for the Middle Colonies." Working Paper Series in Theoretical and Applied Economics, University of Kansas.

Mann, Charles. 2005. *1491: New Revelations of the Americas before Columbus*. New York: Knopf.

Manson, Steven, Jonathon Schroeder, David Van Riper, and Steven Ruggles. n.d. "IPUMS National Historical Geographic Information System: Version 14.0 [Database]." Minneapolis: IPUMS. 2019. https://doi.org/10.18128/D050.V14.0.

Maugham, Elisabeth. 1982. "The German Community." In *The Tercentennial Lectures, New Brunswick, New Jersey*, edited by Ruth Patt, 50–56. New Brunswick, NJ: City of New Brunswick.

McCormick, Richard P. 1964. *New Jersey from Colony to State, 1609–1789*. Princeton, NJ: Van Nostrand.

McCusker, John J. 1971 "The Current Value of English Exports, 1697 to 1800." *William and Mary Quarterly*, 3rd ser., 28 (October): 607–628.

McCusker, John J. 1981. "The Tonnage of Ships Engaged in British Colonial Trade during the Eighteenth Century." *Research in Economic History* 6:73–105.

McCusker, John J. 1984. "New Guides to Primary Sources for the History of Early British America." *William and Mary Quarterly*, 3rd ser., 41 (April): 277–295.

McCusker, John J. 1997. *Essays in the Economic History of the Atlantic World*. London: Routledge.

McCusker, John J. 2001. "Rethinking the Economy of Early British America." Paper presented at conference on the Past and Future of Early American Economic History, Philadelphia, April 20.

McCusker, John J. 2006a. "Colonial Statistics." In Carter et al. 2006, 5-627–5-746.

McCusker, John J. 2006b. "Population by Race and Colony or Locality: 1610–1780." In Carter et al. 2006, 5-651–5-653.

McCusker, John J. 2006c. "Population of New Jersey by Age, Sex and Race: 1726–1784." In Carter et al. 2006, 5-662.

McCusker, John J., and Russel R. Menard. 1991. *The Economy of British America, 1607–1789, with Supplemental Bibliography*. Chapel Hill: University of North Carolina Press.

McDaniel, Marie Basile. n.d. "Immigration and Migration (Colonial Era)." In *The Encyclopedia of Greater Philadelphia*. Accessed March 14, 2019. https://philadelphiaencyclopedia.org/archive/immigration-and-migration-colonial-era/.

McDonald, Forest, and Ellen Shapiro McDonald. 1980. "The Ethnic Origins of the American People 1790." *William and Mary Quarterly* 37, no. 3: 179–199.

McEvedy, Colin, and Richard Jones. 1978. *Atlas of World Population History*. Harmondsworth, UK: Penguin.

McGinty, J. C. 2019. "African-American History by the Numbers." *Wall Street Journal*, February 16–17, A.2.

McKearin, George S., and Helen McKearin. 1941. *American Glass*. New York: Crown.

McMahon, Lucia, and Deborah Schriver, eds. 2000. *To Read My Heart: The Journal of Rachel Van Dyke, 1810–1811*. Philadelphia: University of Pennsylvania Press.

"Migration of Negroes to Northern Industrial Centers." 1921. *Monthly Labor Review*, 201–203.

"The Migrations: From the 2nd Great Migration to the New Great Migration for African Americans (1940, 1960–2000)." 2016. Dartmouth University, History 90:01: Topics in Digital History, October 31. https://journeys.dartmouth.edu/censushistory/2016/10/31/the-migrations-from-the-2nd-great-migration-to-the-new-great-migration-for-african-americans-1940-2000/.

Miller, Chance. 2017. "iPhone X said to Cost Apple $357 to Make, Gross Margins Higher than iPhone 8." *9 to 5 Mac*, November 6. https://9to5mac.com/2017/11/06/how-much-iphone-x-costs-apple-to-make/.

Moller, Herbert. 1945. "Sex Composition and Corrected Culture Patterns of Colonial America." *William and Mary Quarterly* 2 (April): 113–153.

Montaigne, Fen. 2020. "The Fertile Shore." *Smithsonian* 50, no. 9 (January–February): 30–41, 110–112.

Moretta, John A. 2007. *William Penn and the Quaker Legacy*. New York: Pearson-Longman.

Morven Museum and Garden. n.d. Wall Plaque Description of Richard Stockton and Slave Ownership.

Mosher, W. D. 1988. "Fertility and Family Planning in the United States: Insights from the National Survey of Family Growth." *Family Planning Perspectives* 20, no. 5 (September–October): 207–217. https://www.ncbi.nlm.nih.gov/pubmed/3068068.

Mota, Tania, Luz Sandoval, and Laura Sandoval. n.d. *A Latino History of New Brunswick* [short video]. The Latino New Jersey History Project, Rutgers University Department of Latino and Caribbean Studies. Accessed November 8, 2019. https://latcar.rutgers.edu/about-us/the-latino-new-jersey-history-project.

Motow, R. R. 1923. "Migration of Negroes from Southern to Northern States and Its Economic Effects." *Economic World*, May 19: 688–691.

Mulholland, James A. 1981. *A History of Metals in Colonial America*. Tuscaloosa: University of Alabama Press.

Myers, William Starr. 1945. *The Story of New Jersey*. New York: Lewis Historical Publishing.

NAACP. n.d. "History of Lynchings." Accessed November 10, 2019. https://www.naacp.org/history-of-lynchings/.

Nash, Gary B., and Billy G. Smith. 1975. "The Population of Eighteenth-Century Philadelphia." *Notes and Documents*. https://journals.psu.edu/pmhb/article/view/43167/42888.

National Bureau of Economic Research, Business Cycle Dating Committee. 2010. *US Business Cycle Expansions and Contractions*. Cambridge, MA: National Bureau of Economic Research. https://www.nber.org/cycles.html.

National Center for Education Statistics. 2016. "Enrollment in Public Elementary and Secondary Schools, by Region, State and Jurisdiction: Selected Years, Fall 1990 through Fall 2023." *Digest of Education Statistics*. Table 203.20.

National Geographic Society. n.d. "Urban Area." Accessed August 24, 2019. https://www.nationalgeographic.org/encyclopedia/urban-area/.

National Park Service. n.d. "Did You Know: Women and African Americans Could Vote in New Jersey before the 15th and 19th Amendments." Accessed January 20, 2010. https://www.nps.gov/articles/voting-rights-in-nj-before-the-15th-and-19th.htm.

"Native Americans." n.d. Penn Treaty Museum. Accessed December 11, 2018. http://www.penntreatymuseum.org/history-2/.

Nelson, William. 1906. "Total Number of Persons in Families in New Jersey of Which the Names of Heads Indicated Specified Nationality, Computed upon the Basis of Estimated Proportions in 1790" and "Estimated Percent of the Population of New Jersey Contributed by Specified Nationalities: 1790." In Rossiter 1909, 119–120.

Newark Interracial Commission. n.d. "The Negro in Newark." https://riseupnewark.com/the-negro-in-newark-report-b.

Newark Public Library. 2016. "'We Found Our Way': Newark Portraits from the Great Migration." Exhibit, February 4–April 9, Newark Public Library.

Newark Sales and Advertising Co. 1916. *Newark, NJ* (Official Guide and Manual of the 250th Anniversary Celebration of the Founding of Newark, New Jersey).

"New Jersey and the Revolution." n.d. *Crossroads of the American Revolution*. Accessed November 22, 2019. https://revolutionarynj.org/learn/new-jersey-and-the-revolution/.

New Jersey Committee on Native American Community Affairs. 2007. *Report to Governor Jon S. Corzine*. December 17. Trenton, NJ: Office of the Governor. http://hdl.handle.net/10929/23742.

New Jersey Department of Labor. 2001. *New Jersey Population Trends 1790 to 2000*. NJSDC Census Publication, NJSDC-P2000-3.

New Jersey Department of Labor and Workforce Development. 2020a. "Population and Population Density by State: 2010 and 2018."

New Jersey Department of Labor and Workforce Development. 2020b. "Population Density by County and Municipality: New Jersey, 2010 and 2018."

New Jersey Historical Commission. 2002. *New Jersey's Underground Railroad Heritage: "Steal Away, Steal Away—": A Guide to the Underground Railroad in New Jersey*. Trenton, NJ: New Jersey Historical Commission.

New Jersey Historical Society. 1992. *New Jersey: The African-American Experience*. Reprint. Newark: New Jersey Historical Society.

New Jersey Office of State Planning (OSP). 1988. "Population Trends and Projections." Technical Reference Document OSP–54. https://nj.gov/state/planning/assets/docs/publications/054-population-projections-120188.pdf.

New Jersey State Data Center. 2001. *New Jersey Population Trends 1970 to 2000*. Trenton: New Jersey State Data Center. https://nj.gov/labor/lpa/census/2kpub/njsdcp3.pdf.

New Jersey State Library. n.d. "New Jersey Suffrage Time Line." Accessed January 20, 2020. https://libgrades.njstatelib.org/votesforwomen/timeline.

Newson, Linda A. 1993. "The Demographic Collapse of Native Peoples of the Americas, 1492–1650." *Proceedings of the British Academy* 81:247–288.

Nicosia, Francis R., and Jonathan Huener, eds. 2002. *Medicine and Medical Ethics in Nazi Germany: Origins, Practices, Legacies*. New York: Berghahn.

Noguchi, Paul. 1993. "Remember Bean-Picking at Seabrook." Seabrook Farms Oral History, August 25. https://njdigitalhighway.org/portalResults?q1=memoirs&q1field=mods%3Agenre&q1bool=AND&q2field=object&orderby=dateasc&ppage=50&key=NJDH&numresults=1&start=20.

Norris, Tina, Paula L. Vines, and Elizabeth M. Hoeffel. 2012. "The American Indian and Native Population: 2010." *2010 Census Briefs* (January). Washington, DC: U.S. Census Bureau.

Norwood, John R. 2007. *We Are Still Here! The Tribal Saga of New Jersey's Nanticoke and Lenape Indians*. Moorestown, NJ: Native New Jersey Publications.

NPR. 2008. "'Sesame Street' Changed Television for Children." *Morning Edition*, December 26.

Ogden, Evelyn Hunt, and Descendants of Founders of New Jersey. 2016. *Founders of New Jersey—First Settlements, Colonists, and Biographies by Descendants*. 3rd ed. N.p.: Descendants of Founders of New Jersey.

Okrent, Daniel. 2019. *The Guarded Gate: Bigotry, Eugenics, and the Law That Kept Two Generations of Jews, Italians, and Other European Immigrants out of America*. New York: Scribner.

O'Reilly, Margaret M. 2012. *The Story of New Jersey's Indians: New Jersey's State Museum's Archaeology and Ethnography Collections*. Trenton: New Jersey State Museum.

Ortega, Aracely. n.d. "Union City." The Latino New Jersey History Project, Rutgers University Department of Latino and Caribbean Studies. Accessed November 8, 2019. https://latcar.rutgers.edu/about-us/the-latino-new-jersey-history-project.

Osterud, Nancy, and John Fulton. 1976. "Family Limitation and Age at Marriage: Fertility Decline in Sturbridge, Massachusetts, 1730–1850." *Population Studies* 30, no. 3: 481–493.

"The Other African Americans." 2019. *Economist*, October 19, 26–27.

Otterman, Sharon. 2017. "In a City of Firsts, Hoboken Elects a Sikh as Mayor." *New York Times*, November 8. https://www.nytimes.com/2017/11/08/nyregion/hoboken -sikh-mayor-ravi-bhalla.html.

Palmer, Arlene. 1976. "Glass Production in Eighteenth-Century America: The Wistar-burgh Enterprise." *Winterthur Portfolio* 11:75–101.

Passel, Jeffrey S. 1997. "The Growing American Indian Population, 1960–1990: Beyond Demography." *Population Research and Policy Review* 16, no. 1–2 (April): 11–31.

Peck, Donald Johnstone. 2013. *An American Journey of Hope: Perth Amboy—The Capital and Port City on Raritan Bay 1683–1790*. Franklin, TN: Flying Camp Press–American History Press.

Peltier, Elian, and Nicholas Kulish. 2019. "Anti-immigrant Tale Retains Influence." *New York Times*, November 25, C1, C6.

Pendleton, Helen B. 1917. "Cotton Pickers in Northern Counties." *Survey* (February).

Perkins, Edwin J. 1988. *The Economy of Colonial America*. New York: Columbia University Press.

Perrone, Fernanda. 2017. "Invisible Network: Japanese Students at Rutgers during the Early Meiji Period." *Bulletin of Modern Japanese Studies* 34:448(23)–468(3).

Pew Research Center. 2015. "The Whys and Hows of Generations Research." Pew Research Center, September 3. http://www.people-press.org/2015/09/03/the-whys -and-hows-of-generations-research/.

Pew Research Center. 2018a. "At Least a Million Sub-Saharan Africans Moved to Europe since 2010." Pew Research Center, March 22. https://www.pewresearch .org/global/2018/03/22/at-least-a-million-sub-saharan-africans-moved-to-europe -since-2010/.

Pew Research Center. 2018b. "The Generations Defined." Pew Research Center, April 11. http://www.pewresearch.org/fact-tank/2018/04/11/millennials-largest -generation-us-labor-force/ft_18-04-02_generationsdefined2017_working-age/.

Philower, Charles A. 1931. "South Jersey Indians on the Bay, the Cape and Coast." *Proceedings New Jersey Historical Society* (January). Cited in Stewart 1972.

Pomfret, John. 1962. *The Province of East New Jersey, 1609–1702: The Rebellious Proprietary*. Princeton, NJ: Princeton University Press.

Pomfret, John. 1964. *The New Jersey Proprietors and Their Lands, 1664–1776*. Princeton, NJ: Van Nostrand.

Population Reference Bureau. n.d. "Milestones and Moments in Global Census History." Accessed January 13, 2020. https://www.prb.org/milestones-global-census-history/.

Potter, J. 1965. "The Growth of Population in America." In *Population in History: Essays of Historical Demography*, edited by D. V. Glass and D.E.C. Eversley, 631–688. Chicago: Aldine.

Prewitt, Kenneth. 2005. "Racial Classification in America: Where Do We Go from Here?" *Daedalus* 134, no. 1 (Winter): 5–17. https://www.jstor.org/stable/20027956 ?seq=1#metadata_info_tab_contents.

Price, Clement. 2005. "Newark and the Great Migration." Online lecture available in the "Great Migration" section of the New Jersey History Partnership Project website, https://www.nj.gov/state/njhistorypartnership/home_page.html.

Price, Jacob M. 1976. "Quantifying Colonial America: A Comment on Nash ['Urban Wealth and Poverty in Pre-Revolutionary America'] and Warden ['Inequality and

Instability in Eighteenth-Century Boston: A Reappraisal']." *Journal of Interdisciplinary History* 6, no. 4: 701–709.

Pruitt, Bernadette. 2005. "In Search of Freedom: Black Migration to Houston, 1914–1945." *Houston Review of History and Culture* 3, no. 1 (Fall): 48–57, 85–86.

Purvis, Thomas L. 1984. "The European Ancestry of the United States Population, 1790: A Symposium." *William and Mary Quarterly* 41, no. 1: 85–101.

Purvis, Thomas L. 1999. *Colonial America to 1763.* New York: Facts on File.

Quinn, Dermot. 2004. *The Irish in New Jersey: Four Centuries of American Life.* New Brunswick, NJ: Rutgers University Press.

Ramakrishnan, Karthick, and Farah Z. Ahmad. 2014. "State of Asian Americans and Pacific Islanders Series: A Multifaceted Portrait of a Growing Population." Center for American Progress and AAPI Data. Accessed October 10, 2019. https://www.api-gbv.org/resources/state-asians-americans-pacific-islanders-series-2014/.

Randall, William. 1975. *The Proprietary House in Amboy: Official Residence of William Franklin, New Jersey's Last Royal Governor.* Perth Amboy, NJ: Proprietary House Association.

Rastogi, Sonya, Tallese D. Johnson, Elizabeth M. Hoeffel, and Malcolm P. Drewery Jr. 2011. "The Black Population: 2010." *2010 Census Briefs* (September). Washington, DC: U.S. Census Bureau.

Ratcliffe, Michael. 2015. *A Century of Delineating a Changing Landscape: The Census Bureau's Urban and Rural Classification, 1910 to 2010.* Washington, DC: Geography Division, U.S. Census Bureau.

Reardon, Tim, and Sarah Philbrick. 2017. *The Waning Influence on Public School Enrollment in Massachusetts.* Chicago: Metropolitan Area Planning Council.

"Return of the Whole Number of Persons within the Several Districts of the United States according to 'An Act Providing for the Enumeration of the Inhabitants of the United States.'" 1793. Philadelphia: J. Philips.

Ripley, William Z. 1899. *The Races of Europe: A Sociological Study.* New York: Appleton.

Rizzo, Olivia. 2019. "First Female Muslim Mayor in the U.S. Calls This N.J. Town Home." *NJ.com*, May 21. https://www.nj.com/news/2019/05/first-female-muslim-mayor-in-the-us-calls-this-nj-town-home.html.

Rojas, Maria. 1981. "Hispanic Festival Rings with Pride." *Home News*, August 30.

Romm, Carl. 2014. "How the Transistor Radio with Music for Your Pocket Fueled a Teenage Social Revolution." *Smithsonian Magazine*, November 19. https://www.smithsonianmag.com/smithsonian-institution/sixty-years-ago-the-regency-TR-1-Transistor-Radio-Was-the-New-It-Gift-For-the-Holiday-Season-180953345/.

Rosado, Aziel. n.d. "Puerto Ricans in New Jersey: A Grandfather's Story." The Latino New Jersey History Project, Rutgers University Department of Latino and Caribbean Studies. Accessed November 8, 2019. https://latcar.rutgers.edu/about-us/the-latino-new-jersey-history-project.

Rosenblat, A. 1954. *La población indígena y el mestizaje en América.* Buenos Aires: Editorial Nova. Cited in Newson 1993.

Rosenblat, A. 1967. *La población de América en 1492: Viejos y nuevos cálculos.* Mexico City: Colegio de Mexico.

Rosenbloom, Joshua. n.d. "Indentured Servitude in the Colonial U.S." *EH.net.* Accessed January 1, 2020. https://eh.net/encyclopedia/indentured-servitude-in-the-colonial-u-s/.

Rosenbloom, Joshua L. 2018. "The Colonial American Economy." Economics Working Papers no. 18002, Iowa State University. https://lib.dr.iastate.edu/econ_ag_workingpapers/1.

Rosenbloom, Joshua L., and Thomas J. Weiss. 2011. "Economic Growth in the Mid-Atlantic Region: Conjectural Estimates for 1720 to 1800." Working Paper 17215, National Bureau of Economic Research.

Roserio, Kevin. n.d. "A Grandmother's Journey." The Latino New Jersey History Project, Rutgers University Department of Latino and Caribbean Studies. Accessed November 8, 2019. https://latcar.rutgers.edu/about-us/the-latino-new-jersey-history -project.

Rosetta, Robert. 2014. "New Jersey 350th—Fun Fact—So Where Did New Jersey Get Its Name and Why Nova Caesarea?" *AboutNewJersey.com Magazine*, June 15. https://magazine.aboutnewjersey.com/nj-history/new-jersey-350th-june-24-1664 -2014/new-jersey-350th-fun-fact-so-where-did-new-jersey-get-its-name-and-why -nova-caesarea/.

Rossiter, W. S. 1909. *A Century of Population Growth from the First Census of the United States to the Twelfth, 1790–1900*. Washington, DC: United States Bureau of the Census. https://permanent.access.gpo.gov/gpo115114/CenturyofPopulationGrowth /CenturyofPopulationGrowthComplete.pdf.

Ruggles, Steven. 2016. "Marriage, Family Systems, and Economic Opportunity in the USA since 1850." In *Gender and Couple Relationships*, edited by Susan M. Hale, Valerie King, Jennifer Van Hook, and Alan Booth, 3–41. Cham, Switzerland: Springer. http://users.hist.umn.edu/~ruggles/Articles/marriage.pdf.

Ruggles, Steven, Sarah Flood, Ronald Goeken, Josiah Grover, Erin Meyer, Jose Pacas, and Matthew Sobek. n.d. "IPUMS USA: Version 9.0 [dataset]. Minneapolis: IPUMS, 2019." https://doi.org/10.18128/D010.V9.0.

Russel, J. C. 1958. "Late Ancient and Medieval Population." *Transactions of the American Philosophical Society* 48, no. 3: 1–152.

Rutgers University, Department of Latino and Caribbean Studies. n.d. "The Latino New Jersey History Project." Accessed November 6, 2019. https://latcar.rutgers.edu /about-us/the-latino-new-jersey-history-project.

Rutgers University Libraries. 2017. "University and City Celebrate 150 Years of Friendship with Fukui, Japan." Accessed November 5, 2019. https://www.libraries .rutgers.edu/news/university-and-city-celebrate-150-years-friendship-fukui-japan.

Sanchez, Eladio, and Edwin Gutierrez. 1982. "The Hispanic Community." In *The Tercentennial Lectures, New Brunswick, New Jersey*, edited by Ruth Patt, 57–59. New Brunswick, NJ: City of New Brunswick.

Sandefur, Gary D., Ronald R. Rindfuss, and Barney Cohen, eds. 1996. *Changing Members, Changing Needs: American Indian Demography and Public Health*. Washington, DC: National Academy Press.

Sandoval, Luz. n.d. "From Cuba to New Jersey: Manuel Rey's Life Story." The Latino History Project, Rutgers University Department of Latino and Caribbean Studies. Accessed November 8, 2019. https://latcar.rutgers.edu/about-us/the-latino-new -jersey-history-project.

Sauer, Carl. 1966. *The Early Spanish Main*. Berkeley: University of California Press.

Schiff, Stacy. 2005. *A Great Improvisation: Franklin, France, and the Birth of America*. New York: Holt.

Schuessler, Jennifer. 2020. "The Jersey Exception." *New York Times*, February 25, C1.

Sebold, Kimberly R., and Sara Amy Leach. 1966. *Historic Times and Resources within the New Jersey Coastal Heritage Trail*. Washington, DC: U.S. Department of the Interior, National Park Service.

Seneca, Valarie. 2001. "Census Bureau 2000 Figures Reveal High Increase in Native American and Alaska Native Population." *Native American News* (June):24.

Shalhoub, Patrick, with Carmella A. Karnoutsos. 2001. "Chronology." *Jersey City Past and Present*. New Jersey City University. Accessed March 19, 2019. https://www.njcu .edu/community/jersey-city-past-and-present.

Shaw, Douglas. 1994. *Immigration and Ethnicity in New Jersey History*. Trenton: New Jersey Historical Commission.

Shoemaker, Nancy. 1999. *American Indian Population Recovery in the Twentieth Century*. Albuquerque: University of New Mexico Press.

Shuman, Eleanore. 1958. *The Trenton Story*. Trenton: MacCrellish & Quigley.

Siebert, Wilbur H. 1898. *The Underground Railroad: From Slavery to Freedom*. New York: Macmillan.

Skerry, Peter. 2000. *Counting on the Census? Race, Group Identity, and the Evasion of Politics*. Washington, DC: Brookings Institution Press.

Slesinski, Jason J. 2014. *Along the Raritan River: South Amboy to New Brunswick*. Charleston, SC: Arcadia.

Smith, Abbot E. 1947. *Colonists in Bondage: White Servitude and Convict Labor in America, 1607–1776*. Chapel Hill: University of North Carolina Press.

Smith, Daniel Scott. 1972. "The Demographic History of Colonial New England." *Journal of Economic History* 32, no. 1: 165–183.

Smith, Samuel. 1890. *The History of the Colony of Nova-Caesaria, or New Jersey . . . to the Year 1721*. In Samuel Smith, John D. McCormick, and William S. Sharp, *The Colonial History of New Jersey: A Reprint with Maps*. Trenton, NJ: William S. Sharp.

Snipp, C. Matthew. 1986. "Who Are American Indians? Some Observations about the Perils and Pitfalls of Data for Race and Ethnicity." *Population Research and Policy Review* 5:237–252.

Snyder, John P. 1969. *The Story of New Jersey's Civil Boundaries 1606–1968*. Reprint. Trenton: New Jersey Geological Survey, 2004.

Snyder, Timothy. 2010. *Bloodlands: Europe between Hitler and Stalin*. New York: Basic Books.

Soderlund, Jean R. 1985. *Quakers and Slavery: A Divided Spirit*. Princeton, NJ: Princeton University Press.

Spiro, Jonathon. 2008. *Defending the Master Race: Conservation Eugenics and the Legacy of Madison Grant*. Hanover, NH: University of Vermont Press.

Stannard, David E. 1992. *American Holocaust: Columbus and the Conquest of the New World*. New York: Oxford University Press.

Stansfield, Charles Jr. 1993. *A Geography of New Jersey: The City in the Garden*. New Brunswick, NJ: Rutgers University Press.

Steckel, Richard H. "The African American Population of the United States." In Haines and Steckel 2000, 433–482.

Sterbenz, Christina. 2015. "Here's Who Comes after Generation Z—and They'll Be the Most Transformative Age Group Ever." Business Insider, December 5. https://www .businessinsider.com/generation-alpha-2014-7-2.

Sternlieb, George, James W. Hughes, and Connie O. Hughes. 1982. *Demographic Trends and Economic Reality: Planning and Marketing in the '80s*. New Brunswick, NJ: Center for Urban Policy Research.

Stewart, Frank H. 1972. *Indians of Southern New Jersey*. Reprint. Port Washington, NY: Kennikat Press.

Stewart, J. H. 1949. "The Native Population of South America." In *Handbook of South American Indians*, edited by J. H. Stewart, 5:655–668. Washington, DC: Smithsonian Institution.

Still, William 1879. *The Underground Railroad*. Philadelphia: William Still.

Still, William. 1886. *Still's Underground Rail Road Records*. Philadelphia: William Still.

Sutherland, Stella H. 1966. *Population Distribution in Colonial America*. Reprint. New York: Columbia University Press.

Tavernise, Sabrina, and Robert Gebeloff. 2011. "Many U.S. Blacks Moving South, Reversing Trend." *New York Times*, March 25, A1.

Taylor, Alan. 2001. *American Colonies—The Penguin History of the United States*. New York: Viking.

Taylor, Gay Le Cleire. 2006. *The Fires Burn On: 200 Years of Glassmaking in Millville, New Jersey*. Millville, NJ: Museum of American Glass.

Taylor, Paul, and George Gao. 2014. "Generation X: America's Neglected 'Middle Child.'" Fact Tank, Pew Research Center, June 5. http://www.pewresearch.org/fact -tank/2014/06/05/generation-x-americas-neglected-middle-child/.

Terrell, Ellen. 2017. "Colonies in America: Commerce, Business, and the Economy." *Business and Economics Research Advisor* 27 (Spring).

Thomas, J. D. 2013. "The Colonies' First and New Jersey's Only Indian Reservation." Accessible Archives. Accessed September 5, 2019. https://www.accessible-archives .com/2013/08/colonies-first-new-jerseys-indian-reservation/.

Thompson, R. 1974. "Seventeenth-Century English and Colonial Sex Ratios: A Postscript." *Population Studies* 28, no. 1 (March): 153–165.

Thompson, Warren S., and P. K. Whelpton. 1943. *Estimates of Future Population of the United States, 1940–2000*. Washington, DC: National Resources Planning Board.

Thompson, Wilbur. 1974. "Economic Processes and Employment Problems in Declining Metropolitan Areas." In *Post-Industrial America: Metropolitan Decline and Inter-Regional Job Shifts*, edited by George Sternlieb and James W. Hughes, 187–196. New Brunswick, NJ: Center for Urban Policy Research.

Thornton, Russell. 1987. *American Indian Holocaust and Survival: A Population History since 1492*. Norman: University of Oklahoma Press.

Thornton, Russell. 2000. "Population History of Native North Americans." In Haines and Steckel 2000, 9–50.

Thorpe, Francis Newton, ed. and comp. 1909. *The Federal and State Constitutions, Colonial Charters, and Other Organic Laws of the States and Territories Now or Heretofore Forming the United States of America*. Vol. 5, *New Jersey–Philippine Islands*. Washington, DC: Government Printing Office. https://oll.libertyfund.org/titles/2678.

Tita, Bob. 2019. "Nucor to Replace CEO at Year-End." *Wall Street Journal*, September 6. https://www.wsj.com/articles/nucor-to-replace-ceo-at-year-end-11567788699 ?mod=itp_wsj&mod=&mod=djemITP_h.

Tolnay, Stewart E., and E. M. Beck. 1995. *A Festival of Violence: An Analysis of Southern Lynchings 1882–1930*. Urbana: University of Illinois Press.

Townsend, Camilla. 2016. "I Am Old and Weak . . . and You Are Young and Strong . . . :The Intersecting Histories of Rutgers University and the Lenni Lenape." In Fuentes and White 2016, 6–57.

Truesdell, Leon F. 1960. "Farm Population, 1880 to 1950." Technical Paper no. 3, U.S. Bureau of the Census.

Tuttle, Brad R. 2009. *How Newark Became Newark: The Rise, Fall, and Rebirth of an American City*. New Brunswick, NJ: Rutgers University Press.

Ubelaker, Douglas H. 1976. "Prehistoric New World Population Size: Historical Review and Current Appraisal of North America Estimates." *American Journal of Physical Anthropology* 45, no. 3: 661–665.

Ubelaker, Douglas H. 2000. "Patterns of Disease in Early American Populations." In Haines and Steckel 2000, 51–98.

"The Underground Railroad." n.d. *NJ.gov.* https://nj.gov/nj/about/history/underground_railroad.html.

United Nations. n.d. "Japan Population 1950–2020." *World Population Prospects.* Accessed January 5, 2020. https://www.macrotrends.net/countries/JPN/japan/population.

United Nations, Department of Economic and Social Affairs. 2019. *World Population Prospects 2019.* New York: United Nations. https://population.un.org/wpp/Publications/Files/WPP2019_Highlights.pdf.

Urban, Andy. n.d. "Chinese Exclusion and the Establishment of the Gate-Keeping Nation." Essay to accompany Rutgers University exhibition and video on "Chinese Exclusion in New Jersey: Immigration in the Past and Present." Accessed November 10, 2019. https://njdigitalhighway.org/exhibits/chinese_exclusion_portal#case:1.

U.S. Census Bureau. n.d.a. "1790 Census: Heads of Families at the First Census of the United States Taken in the Year 1790." Accessed December 30, 2019. https://www.census.gov/library/publications/1907/dec/heads-of-families.html.

U.S. Census Bureau. n.d.b. "History—1790 Overview." Accessed January 20, 2020. https://www.census.gov/history/www/through_the_decades/overview/1790.html.

U.S. Census Bureau. n.d.c. "History—Decennial Census." Accessed December 30, 2019. https://www.census.gov/history/www/programs/demographic/decennial_census.html.

U.S. Census Bureau. n.d.d. "History—Why Can't I Find 1890 Census Records?" Accessed January 2, 2020. https://www.census.gov/history/www/faqs/genealogy_faqs/why_cant_i_find_1890_census_records.html.

U.S. Census Bureau. n.d.e. "Measuring Race and Ethnicity across the Decades: 1790–2010." Accessed May 24, 2019. https://www.census.gov/data-tools/demo/race/MREAD_1790_2010.html.

U.S. Census Bureau. 1962. "Components of Population Change, 1950 to 1960, for Counties, Standard Metropolitan Statistical Areas, State Economic Areas, and Economic Subregions." *Current Population Reports*, Series P-23, No. 7 (November).

U.S. Census Bureau. 1996. *Population of States and Counties in the United States: 1790 to 1990.* Washington, DC: U.S. Government Printing Office.

U.S. Census Bureau. 2011. "Population Distribution and Change: 2000 to 2010." Census Briefs (March). Washington, DC: U.S. Census Bureau.

U.S. Census Bureau. 2012. "The Great Migration, 1910 to 1970." Accessed October 10, 2019. https://www.census.gov/dataviz/visualizations/020/.

U.S. Census Bureau. 2015. "Millennials Outnumber Baby Boomers and Are Far More Diverse, Census Bureau Reports." News Release, U.S. Census Bureau, June 25.

U.S. Census Bureau. 2016. "Income and Poverty: About." Accessed May 28, 2020. https://www.census.gov/topics/income-poverty/income/about.html.

Veit, Richard. 2009a. "Clay, Brick and Glass." In Lurie and Wacker 2009, 167.

Veit, Richard. 2009b. "Extractive Industries." In Lurie and Wacker 2009, 157.

Vinovskis, Maris A. 1979. *Studies in American Historical Demography.* New York: Academic Press.

Virginia Places. n.d. "How Colonists Acquired Title to Land in Virginia." Accessed January 17, 2019. http://www.virginiaplaces.org/settleland/headright.html.

Voicu, Alexandru, and David Listokin. 2018. *Who Lives in New Jersey Housing? Updated New Jersey Demographic Multipliers: The Profile of Occupants of Residential Development in New Jersey.* New Brunswick, NJ: Rutgers University Center for Urban Policy Research.

Wacker, Peter O. 1975. *Land and People: A Cultural Geography of Preindustrial New Jersey Origins and Settlement Patterns.* New Brunswick, NJ: Rutgers University Press.

Walker, Edwin R., Clayton L. Traver, and George A. Bradshaw. 1929. *A History of Trenton, 1679–1929: Two Hundred and Fifty Years of a Notable Town with Links in Four Centuries.* Princeton, NJ: Princeton University Press.

Wallman, Katherine K. 2012. "Foreword." In S. Wilson et al. 2012, iii.

Wallis, Michael. 2014. "The Other Road." *This Land* 5, no. 4 (February 15).

Walton, Gary M., and James F. Sheperd. 1979. *The Economic Rise of Early America.* Cambridge: Cambridge University Press.

Walton, Jean R. 2010. "New Jersey County Formation." New Jersey Postal History Society. Accessed January 20, 2020. https://njpostalhistory.org/media/pdf/NJCtyformation.pdf.

Wang, Ying, and Stefan Rayer. 2018. "Growth of the Puerto Rican Population in Florida and on the U.S. Mainland." Florida Bureau of Economic and Business Research, February 9. https://www.bebr.ufl.edu/population/website-article/growth-puerto-rican-population-florida-and-us-mainland.

Weiss, Harry. 1964. *Life in Early New Jersey.* Princeton, NJ: Van Nostrand.

Weiss, Harry B., and Grace M. Weiss. 1963. *The Old Copper Mines of New Jersey.* Trenton, NJ: Past Times Press.

Wells, Robert. 1971. "Family Size and Fertility Control in Eighteenth-Century America: A Study of Quaker Families." *Population Studies* 25, no. 1 (March): 73–82.

Wells, Robert. 1975. *Population of the British Colonies in America before 1776: A Survey of Census Data.* Princeton, NJ: Princeton University Press.

Wells, Robert. 1992. "The Population of England's Colonies in America: Old English or New Americans?" *Population Studies* 46, no. 1 (March): 85–102.

White, Deborah Gray. 2016. "Introduction: Scarlet and Black—A Reconciliation." In Fuentes and White 2016, 1–5.

Whitehead, William A., ed. 1880. *Documents Relating to the Colonial History of the State of New Jersey.* Vol. 1, *1631–1687.* Newark, NJ.

Widmer, Kemble. 1964. *The Geology and Geography of New Jersey.* Princeton, NJ: Van Nostrand.

Wigglesworth, Edward. 1775. *Calculations on American Population.* Boston. Cited in Potter 1965, 632n3.

Wilder, C. S. 2013. *Ebony and Ivy: Race, Slavery, and the Troubled History of America's Universities.* New York: Bloomsbury.

Wilkerson, Isabel. 2010. *The Warmth of Other Suns.* New York: Random House.

Williams, Lorraine E. 2010. "Caught in the Middle: New Jersey's Indians and the American Revolution." In Lurie 2010, 105–120.

Wilson, Harold, James Downes, Herbert Gooden, Francis Hopkins, Helen Shaw, and Charles Titus. 1950. *Outline History of New Jersey.* New Brunswick, NJ: Rutgers University Press.

Wilson, James. 1999. *The Earth Shall Weep: A History of Native America.* New York: Atlantic Monthly Press.

Wilson, Steven G., David A. Plane, Paul J. Mackon, Thomas R. Fischetti, and Justyna Goworowska. 2012. "Patterns of Metropolitan and Micropolitan Population Change 2000 to 2010." 2010 Census Special Reports, C2010SR-01, U.S. Census Bureau.

Wolfe, Alan. 1980. "The William Elliot Griffis Collection of Old and Rare Japanese Books, Olin Library, Cornell University." *Journal of East Asian Libraries* 63:40–47.

Woodward, Herbert P. 1944. *Copper Mines and Mining in New Jersey.* Trenton: Department of Conservation and Development, State of New Jersey.

Works Progress Administration. n.d. "African American Communities in the City's Third Ward." https://riseupnewark.com/the-third-ward-wpa-report-il.

World Bank. n.d.a. "Percentage of World Population That Is Urban." Accessed January 9, 2020. https://data.worldbank.org/indicator/SP.URB.TOTL.IN.ZS.

World Bank. n.d.b. "Population per Square Kilometer of Land Area." Accessed December 30, 2019. https://data.worldbank.org/indicator/EN.POP.DNST.

Worth-Baker, Marcia. 2014. "Witness to History: Diary of a Revolution." *New Jersey Monthly*, June 27. https://njmonthly.com/articles/jersey-living/witness-to-history -diary-revolution/.

Wright, Giles R. 1986. *Arrival and Settlement in a New Place.* Trenton: New Jersey Historical Commission.

Wright, Giles R. 1988. *Afro-Americans in New Jersey: A Short History.* Trenton: New Jersey Historical Commission.

Wright, Richard. 1993. *Black Boy.* New York: HarperCollins.

Wu, Sen-Yuan. 2011. "People from Many Nations Form New Jersey's Hispanic Population." *NJ Labor Market News*, no. 14. lwd.dol.state.nj.us/labor/lpa/pub/lmv/lmv_14.pdf.

Yamin, Rebecca. 2013. *Voices from Raritan Landing: An Educational Guide to a Colonial Port Community.* N.p.: Middlesex County Board of Chosen Freeholders and Middlesex County Cultural and Heritage Commission.

Zafar, Ramish. 2019. "Apple A13 for iPhone 11 Has 8.5 Billion Transistors, Quad-Core GPU." *WCCF Tech*, September 10. https://wccftech.com/apple-a13-iphone-11 -transistors-gpu.

Zelinsky, Wilbur. 1973. *The Cultural Geography of the United States.* Englewood Cliffs, NJ: Prentice-Hall.

Zimmerman, Andreas, Johanna Hilpert, and Karl Peter Wendt. 2009. "Estimations of Population Density for Selected Periods between the Neolithic and AD 1800." *Human Biology* 81, no. 2: 357–380.

Index

Act for the Gradual Abolition of Slavery (1804) in New Jersey, 280
Act Prohibiting Importation of Slaves (1807), 275
Adams, John, 317n10
adolescent, defined, 327n18
affluence, of post-World War II decades, 236–238
Africa: immigrants to New Jersey from, 126; immigrants to the United States from, 123–124
age characteristics, of New Jersey's colonial-era population, 45–46
age cohorts, generations and, 168–169
age distribution, as demographic multiplier, 294, 296, 297, 298–299
age of householder, income and, 243–245
age-restricted, active-adult communities: baby boomers and, 180, 186; Gen X and, 254
age-sex pyramid, 328n3
age structure, defined, 202
age-structure transformations, 6–7, 11, 202–217; changing age-structure distributions, 214–217; of New Jersey's population, 249; 1950–1960 period, 203–204; 1960s, 204–206; 1970s, 206–207; 1980–1990, 208–209; 1999–2000, 209–211; 2000–2010, 211–212; 2010–2018 (post-Great Recession period), 212–214
aggregate wealth, in 1790 United States, 67

aging of American society, 4
aging of baby boom, 247
aging of global population, 3
aging of New Jersey population, 216–217, 251
aging population, economic growth and, 316n6
agriculture: as basis of New Jersey's economy in eighteenth century, 68, 69; in eighteenth-century Massachusetts, 68
Alaska: land area, 304, 332–333n2; population density, 304, 306, 333
Allentown-Bethlehem-Easton metro area, 313
American colonies: overall population growth, 1600s to 1800, 35–36; population density of, 300–301; thirteen original, 319n1. See also *individual colonies*
American Community Survey (ACS), 89, 227, 228, 233, 235, 240, 294, 320–321n5, 329n7
American Council of Learned Societies (ACLS), national origins research, 52, 54, 56–57, 58–59
American dream, 236
American Eugenic Society, 119
American holocaust/American Indian holocaust, 94
American Indians and Alaskan Native (AIAN), population size in the United States and New Jersey 1800–2017, 95, 96

Americans with Disabilities Act (ADA), 327n7
ancestry, defined, 127
ancestry question on census, 323n12
Andros, Edmund, 17, 72
Annual Report of the American Historical Association, nationality research reported in, 56
area of enumeration, 332n2
Arizona, population growth in, 87
Arnold, Mildred, 103
Asada, Iddy, 107, 322n8
Asian and Pacific Islander (API): Census Bureau and, 105; population size in the United States and New Jersey 1800–2017, 95, 96
Asian Indians, 126, 127; Census Bureau enumeration of, 105; percent of Asian population in New Jersey, 106, 107
Asians: distribution of population in New Jersey, 130; immigration policy and, 103–105, 106; immigration to New Jersey, 125–126; median household income in 2017, 243; migrants passing over to North America via land bridge, 91–92; as New Jersey's fastest growing minority group, 9; percent of population of New Jersey in 2017, 130; population distribution in New Jersey, 129; population size in New Jersey, 106–107; population size in the United States, 105–106; racial profile, 103–108; rise in immigrants from after immigration law changes in the 1960s, 123; vignettes of life stories of Asians in New Jersey, 107–108
Atlanta Constitution (newspaper), 287, 289
Atlantic City-Hammonton metro area, 313
Atlantic colonies, slavery in, 278–279
AT&T, 195
Austria, immigrants to New Jersey from, 126
automobile-centric residential suburbanization, 82, 141

baby boom echo. *See* Generation Y (millennials)
baby boom generation, 1, 10, 37, 82, 173, 176; adaptation to digital technology, 193–194; age-structure disruptions and, 202; American dream and, 236; decade of the 1960s and, 204–206; development of

digital technology, 327n14; distinctions within, 169; diversity and, 183; emergence of aged society and, 4, 216–217, 247; ending date, 182–183; exodus from workforce, 6–7, 188; failure to reproduce itself, 207; first-time home ownership period, 185; impact of, 11, 203–204; imprint of, 179–181; in labor force, 210, 212; life-cycle stages, 183–184; malling of New Jersey and, 197; maturing seventy-somethings, 252–253; in 1990, 208–209; outmigration of retirees, 87; peak birth year, 182; predictions for postwar growth and, 181–182; replacement in the workforce by Gen X, 190–191; shelter eras, 184–186; starting date, 169–170; trading up in housing market, 147; in 2018, 214; in 2000, 210; in 2010, 212; in 2000–2010, 216; in twenty-first century, 186–187; withdrawal from large single-family homes, 188
baby bust, 146, 170, 173, 189, 205, 325n2. *See also* Generation X (Gen X)
baby bust echo, 170, 173, 198. *See also* Generation Z (postmillennials)
baby bust 2.0, 178
Barker, Howard, 56, 57
Bell Labs, 195
Bergen County: Black population in eighteenth-century, 42; international migration to, 165; national origins of colonial population, 53, 57; population growth in 1950s, 163–164
Berkeley, Lord, Sir John, 16, 17–18, 21
Bernard, Francis, 71
Berra, Yogi, 246, 247
Bhalla, Ravinder, 108
Bierstadt, Albert, 92
"big bang," baby boom, 187
Big Six cities (Camden, Elizabeth, Jersey City, Newark, Paterson, and Trenton), 10; growth of 1900–1930, 135–136; limited status of, 140–141; manufacturing and population growth in, 79; metropolitanization and, 134–140; new urbanism and, 150–154; population, 1860–1900, 133–134; population, 1900–1930, 324n5; population, 1940–1950, 324n6; population, 1950–1970, 142; population, 1970–1980, 144; population, 1980–2000, 146;

population, 2000–2010, 149–150;
population, 2010–2018, 151–154;
population density, 1950–2018, 311; rise
of, 133–134; suburban economic growth
corridors, 1980–2000, 146–147;
suburbanization, 1950–1970, 141;
turnaround, 2000–2010, 147–150
Bill (slave), on living in Raritan Landing, 73
birth dearth, 81, 169, 170, 181, 328n4; aging
of, 207, 209; defined, 173; in New Jersey,
214–216; in 1950–1960 period, 203; silent
generation and, 174, 175–176; in 2000, 211
birth patterns, age-defined population
cohorts and fluctuations in, 169
birth rates: age-specific, 316n7, 325n2; in
baby boom peak year (1957), 182; colonial
New Jersey, 44, 46–47; generation Alpha
and, 200; total fertility rate and, 326n8
births: in colonial-era New Jersey, 46–49; by
decade and year, 1924–2018, 170, 171; Gen
Y and, 177; in 2010, 177
Bishop, James, 128
Blacks: actions in New Jersey to enhance
civil rights, 281; ages of in colonial-era
New Jersey population, 45; count on
fractional basis in 1790 census, 62; in
eighteenth-century New Jersey, 41–43;
gender ratio in colonial New Jersey, 43;
Ku Klux Klan, 118; median household
income in 2017, 243; migration within the
south, 331n4; percent enslaved in 1790
census, 64–65; percent of total U.S.
population in 1790 census in, 64;
population distribution in New Jersey,
129, 130; population in all colonies,
1610–1780, 274–275; population in New
Jersey, 1790–1860, 277–278; population
in southern states, 1790–1860, 276;
population in United States, 1790–1860,
275; population of northeast, 1790–1860,
276–277; population share in New Jersey,
1800–2017, 98–99; population size in the
United States and New Jersey 1800–2017,
95, 96; racial profile, 97–103; rate of
natural increase in colonial era, 47;
slavery and, 273–281; slavery in New
Jersey, 277–278; undercount of in New
Jersey, 37. See also Great Migration;
Reverse Great Migration
Black suffrage, 318–319n21

Blair, Jean, 74
Bloomfield, Joseph, 281
Bloomfield, Moses, 281
Boardman, Samantha, 102, 287, 331n7
Boas, Franz, 117
boat production, in colonial New Jersey, 69
Bohr, Niels, 246
Bolivar, Parque, 113
Bonnell, Nathaniel, 71–72
Borbely, James, 129
Brail, Richard K., 327n10
Brookings Institution, 5, 313
Brotherton reservation, 37, 71
Brown v. Board of Education, 281
Brush, John, 46–47
Bureau of Indian Affairs (BIA), 320n5
Bureau of Labor Statistics, 330n7
Burlington, 22
business cycle, 7; Generation Alpha and,
201; Gen X and, 191–192; Gen Y and,
195–196
business cycle and demographics, 269–272;
expansions, 270, 271; recessions
(contractions), 269–271; structural and
cyclical economic shifts, 269–271
Business Cycle Dating Committee,
330–331n4
Byllynge, Edward, 21

Cabot, John, 90
calculator, electronic, 194, 195
California, urban population in,
308–309
Camden, 133; population density,
1950–2018, 311. See also Big Six cities
Camp Kilmer, 129
Camp of the Saints, The (Raspail), 116
Canada, immigrants to New Jersey
from, 126
Cape May County, gender ratio in
colonial, 43
capital cities, changing early New
Jersey, 22
Capnerhurst, Mary, 44
Carteret, George, 16, 17–18, 21, 22
Carteret, Philip, 17, 20, 72, 318n18
Casas, Bartolomé de las, 92
Cassidy, Dominic, 128
Castro, Fidel, 111
Celler, Emanuel, 119

Census Bureau: baby boom generation and, 176; definition of urban, 306–307; designation of persons of mixed Black and white blood, 119; enumeration of Asians, 105; generation categories, 174; household definitions, 221–222; identification of race and ethnicity, 88–89; metropolitan area, 311; net migration, 156; Population Estimates Program (PEP), 268

census counts, of New Jersey's colonial population, 37–40

Center for Urban Policy Research (CUPR), 173, 174

central region, 137, 139, 142; population, 1970s, 145; population growth, 1980–2000, 147; population, 2010–2018, 152

Century of Population Growth from the First Census of the United States to the Twelfth, 1790–1900, A (Rossiter), 24

CEO (chief executive officer), 190

CFO (chief financial officer), 190–191

Charles I, 19

Charles II, 17, 18

Chicago Forum Council, 118

Chinese: Census Bureau enumeration of, 105; migration to the United States in nineteenth century, 103–104; as one of top countries contributing to immigration to New Jersey, 127; percent of Asian population in New Jersey, 106, 107

Chinese Exclusion Act of 1882, 104

Chivukula, Upendra, 108

Church, Frederick, 92

cities: emerging dominant global superstar, 6; rise of New Jersey's, 133. *See also* Big Six cities

Civil Rights Act of 1884, 281

Clark Thread Mills, 128

Clopper, Cornelius, 73

cognitive skills, baby boom retirement and loss of, 187, 252

cohort, 328n2

cohort size variation, generations and, 169–170

colleges, pre-Revolutionary War, in New Jersey, 69. *See also* Princeton University; Rutgers University (Queens College)

Colombians, immigration to New Jersey from, 112, 126, 127

Colon, Otilio, 113

"Colonial Statistics" (McCusker), 24

Columbus, Christopher, 91–92, 93

Commerce Department, 62

Committee on Linguistic and National Stocks in the Population of the United States, 56

Commons, Michael, 307

compression, baby boom and, 182

Condict, Jemima, 44

Connecticut, 29; population density, 2000, 303; population density, 2018, 304

constant dollars, 329n4

Constitution, direction that federal census be undertaken every ten years, 59

Constitutional Convention, 59

consumer spending behavior, Gen Y and, 197

"continuing care," 325n3

contraception, access to, 189

COO (chief operating officer), 191

copper mines, in New Jersey, 68

core metropolis region, 136, 139, 142; internal state migration from, 146; population, post-2010, 151–152; population, 2010–2018, 153–154; population growth, 1980–2000, 147; population loss in 1970s, 144–145

Cornbury, Lord, 279

counties, number of in 1790 United States, 66

counties in New Jersey: East-West Jersey and evolving counties in the seventeenth and eighteenth centuries, 260; metropolitan area, 312–313; number and boundaries of, 318n12

county, population in New Jersey in the colonial era and as a state by, 259–268; county maps, 260, 262; historical data on county formation, 263; New Jersey counties and county boundaries, 259; population by county in New Jersey in the colonial era, 261; population by county, 1790–2018, 264–267; population counts and sources, 259, 268; 1790 census, 62

county components of population change: 1950–1960, 162–164; 2010–2018, 163, 165–166

county population in New Jersey, 40, 136–140; 1950–1970, 143–146; 1970–1980,

145; 1980–2000, 146–147, 148; 2000–2010, 149–150; 2010–2018, 151–154; distributional profile, 1900–2018, 153–154; population density, 2018, 310–311; racial differences in population in eighteenth century, 42–43

Covenhoven, Mary, 74

credit bubble, 85, 148

credit crisis, 85

Cubans in New Jersey, 111, 112, 113, 126

curb cuts, 327n7

current dollars, 329–330n4

Current Population Report (1962), 324n3

Current Population Survey (CPS), 237, 328n10, 329n7

cyclical economic shifts, 269–271; expansions, 270, 271; recessions (contractions), 269–271

Dating Committee of the National Bureau of Economic Research, 79

Daughters of the American Revolution, 18, 73

deaths, in colonial-era New Jersey, 46–49

Defalco, Mary, 128

Delaney, John, 18

Delaware Indians. *See* Lenni-Lenape

demalling of New Jersey, Gen Y and, 197

democracy, economy and, 7–8

demographic and socioeconomic profile of New Jersey in 1790, 59–70

demographic destiny, economic cycles and, 85–86

demographic geography, 146, 254, 330n1

demographic multipliers, 292–295; future New Jersey demographic change and, 299; summary of New Jersey, 295–299

demographic resurgence, between 1850 and 1870 in New Jersey, 79–80

demographic stagnation, in the United States, 4

Denevan, William, 92

dense sprawl, 332n1

Description of the Province of New Albion (Plowden), 19

de-suburbanization, 10

Dey, Horace, 128

digital technology: baby boomers adaptation to, 193–194; Generation Alpha and, 201; Gen Y and, 192–194; Gen Z and,

198–199, 256; redefining economy and generational transitions, 247

Dillingham, William, 117

Dillingham Commission, 117

dinks (double income, no kids), 183

direct baby boom housing demand, 185

disease, ravaging Native Americans, 91, 93

diversity: of Generation Alpha, 201; of Gen X, 190; of Gen Z, 198, 256; increasing in United States, 5; increasing racial and ethnic, 12; in New Jersey population, 9–10

diversity in New Jersey, 88–131; Asian racial profile, 103–108; Hispanic ethnic profile, 109–114; immigration and foreign-born profile, 114–129; Native American racial profile, 90–97; other races, 108–109; racial and ethnic minorities, 89; racial composition, 95, 96; racial, ethnic, and foreign-born differences within New Jersey, 129–131; white and Black racial profile, 95, 96, 97–103

divorce rates, household size and, 225

Dobbyns, H. F., 92

domestic migration, 156

domestic outmigration, 248

Dominican immigrants, 112, 127; in New Brunswick, 114

dot-com bubble, 85

Du Bois, W.E.B., 118

Dumont, John, 74

Dutch in early New Jersey, 15, 16, 20; in Bergen County, 53; slavery and, 42, 279

Dutch national origin: of white population of colonial America, 54, 56, 57, 58; of white population of colonial New Jersey, 53, 55, 57, 58; of white population of colonial New York, 55

Duyckinck, John, 74

Earth Shall Weep, The, 94

Easterlin, Richard, 120

East Jersey, 21; gender ratio in colonial, 43; map of, 260; population in eighteenth century, 40; refusal to participate in eumeration, 37; tension with West Jersey, 17

East Jersey-West Jersey division boundary, 317n7

Ebony and Ivy (Wilder), 280

echo boomers, 326n6

economic and demographic decentraliza-
    tion, 8
economic conditions, immigration and, 116
economic cycles: demographic destiny and,
    85–86; New Jersey's population and, 75
economic growth, aging population and,
    316n6
economies (global and national), forecasting
    future of New Jersey's population and, 246
economy: democracy and, 7–8; effect on
    immigration and swings of, 155; start-stop
    pattern of U.S. since 1973, 238
Ecuadorians in New Jersey, 112, 113
educational system (K-12): baby boom and,
    203, 326n9; excess capacity and shrinkage
    of school-age population, 208; Genera-
    tion Alpha and, 257
elder boom, 4, 249
electricity, rise of industrial metropolis and,
    7–8
Elizabeth, 133; population, 1900–1910,
    324n1; population density, 1950–2018, 311.
    See also Big Six cities
Elizabethtown (Elizabeth), 22; naming of,
    318n18; original grant, 317n5; voices of
    early settlers, 71–72
Ellis Island, 116
Emmons, William, 174
employment, link to recessions and
    expansions, 272
empty nesters, baby boom, 186
energy crises, 238
Englewood Academy, 101
English: claim of unpaid bills from former
    colonies, 70; conflict between colonists
    and proprietors, 16–17; in early New
    Jersey, 15–16; gender ratio in seventeenth-
    century, 44; immigrants to New Jersey
    from England, 126, 127; population
    density, 1790, 301–302; population
    density, 1800, 333n3; population increases
    1600s to 1800, 35; slavery in New Jersey
    and, 279
English national origin: of white population
    of colonial America, 54, 56, 58; of white
    population of colonial New Jersey,
    53, 57, 58
enumerations by county in New Jersey:
    1726, 1738, 1745, 1772, and 1784, 261
Escobar, Rebecca, 114

Essex County: gender ratio in colonial, 43;
    population change during 1950s, 163;
    population density in colonial, 51
ethnic differences in New Jersey, 129–131
ethnic diversity, in New Jersey in 2020s,
    249. See also diversity
ethnicity: Census Bureau identification of,
    89; median income and, 242–243
ethnic minorities, undercount in censuses, 89
ethnic profile in New Jersey, Hispanic,
    109–114
eugenics, 119
Europe: immigrants to New Jersey from,
    1850–1950, 125; voices of early settlers
    from, 71–72
European Union, 313
Evans, Tim, 306, 312–313
Excel spreadsheet, 327n11
expansions, economic, 270, 271; employment
    and, 272
experiential economy, Gen Y and, 197

family: Census Bureau definition of, 221;
    income and addition of more earners
    per, 238
family household, 221, 222; decrease in share
    between 2000–2010, 226; defined, 328n1;
    growth of in New Jersey, 1950–2000,
    230–231; increase in percentage share in
    New Jersey post–2010, 234
family incomes, 12, 238
farm population, rural population vs., 333n7
federal census, 315–316n4; Blacks and 1790,
    275; enumeration of foreign-born,
    114–115; population by county in New
    Jersey, 1790–2018, 264–267; population
    trends, 1790–2010, 76; 1790, 9, 24, 25–26,
    59–68, 76, 301–302, 315n3; 1900, 94; 2010,
    63–64
Federal Reserve, 85
Federal Reserve Bank of St. Louis, 174, 196,
    330n5
female householder (no spouse present) with
    children, median income in 2017,
    241–242
female householders (no spouse present),
    221; increase in number of, 1950–2000,
    222; increase in number of, 2000–2010,
    232; median income in 2017, 242
Fenwick, John, 21

fertility: age-defined population cohorts and fluctuations in, 169; in colonial America, 36; decline in post-Great Recession, 249

fertility rate: American Indians and, 320–321n5; baby boom and jump in, 176; in colonial-era America, 45; contraction of in United States, 4; by decade and year, 1933–2018, 170, 172; decline in in twentieth century, 220; declining contemporary, 247; falling global, 3; Generation Alpha and, 200, 257; Gen X and, 189; Gen Y and, 177; 2010, 177–178

Filipinos, 127; Census Bureau enumeration of, 105; percent of Asian population in New Jersey, 106, 107

first-generation, entry-level housing demand, 185

Ford, Theodeia Johnes, 73

foreign-born: current population of, 5; number of in New Jersey, 124–125; origins and fluctuating numbers of, 120–128; places of origin of in New Jersey, 125–127; population in New Jersey, 121; population in the United States by world region of birth, 122–124; profile of, 114–128; total population in the United States, 120–122; vignettes from, 128

foreign-born differences in New Jersey, 129–131

Fort Elfsborg, 16

Franklin, Benjamin, 35–36, 44, 47–48, 65, 116

Franklin, William, 35, 318n20

French: in Bergen County, 53; immigration to New Jersey, 126

French national origin: of white population of colonial America, 54, 56, 58; of white population of colonial New Jersey, 57, 58

Frey, William, 289

Frost Belt, 83

Fugitive Slave Act (1850), 101, 281

fully mature housing demand of baby boomers, 186

garden apartments, 180, 185

Garden State: digitally-influenced demographics and, 195; moniker, 22; narrative, 1–2. *See also* New Jersey

Garland, Claire, 97

Gates, Henry Louis, 282

Gaynor, Martha, 103, 288

Geary Act (1892), 104

Gemery, Henry, 48–49

gender, colonial-era population and, 43–44

gender ratio: of Blacks in colonial New Jersey, 43; in colonial New England, 43–44; in colonial New Jersey, 43; in 1790 in middle states, 66; in 1790 New England, 66; in 1790 South, 66; in seventeenth-century England, 44; in United States in 1790, 66

generation: as cohort, 328n2; defined, 168; by population and white non-Hispanic share for New Jersey, 2017, 175

generational framework, 10, 167–178; baby boom, defined, 167, 168, 176; cohort size variation and the generations, 169–170; early conceptualization of contemporary generations, 170–173; Generation Alpha/ Alphas, defined, 168, 178; Gen X, defined, 167, 176; Gen Y/millennials, defined, 167, 176–177; Gen Z/postmillennials, defined, 168, 177–178; newer conceptualizations of contemporary generations, 173–175; overview, 168–169; pre-baby boom, defined, 167, 175–176

Generation Alpha, 10, 11, 174, 200–201, 257–258; defined, 168, 178; ultimate size of, 251, 257

generational succession, 2

generational transformations, 6–7; in New Jersey, 75, 250

Generation X (Gen X), 1, 10, 11, 169, 173, 189–192, 315n1; age-structure disruptions and, 202; business cycle and, 191–192; defined, 167, 176; diversity of, 190; effect of, 205; as empty nesters, 253–254; excess capacity and, 207; expansion *vs.* shrinkage and, 190; immigration and increased number of, 190; impact of, 216; leadership of, 7, 253; maturing, 253–254; in 1990, 209; in 1990–2000, 210; replacing baby boomers in labor market, 190–191; in 2000, 211; in 2000–2010, 211–212, 216; in 2018, 214

Generation Y (millennials), 1–2, 10, 11, 147, 169, 173, 174, 176–177, 192–196, 315n1; baby boom rejoinder, 194–195; business cycle and, 195–196; defined, 167, 176–177;

Generation Y (millennials) (cont.)
digital-age advances and demographics,
192–194; Garden State effect, 195; Great
2007–2009 Recession and income of,
239; housing and, 188, 189; labor market
and, 188, 189, 190–191; maturing of,
254–255; in 1990, 209; in 1990–2000,
209–210; originally called echo boomers,
326n6; share of American workforce, 196;
termed baby boom echo, 147, 170, 173,
192, 325n1; in 2000–2010, 211, 216
Generation Z (postmillennials), 2, 10, 11,
174, 198–200, 211, 216, 325n4; defined,
168, 177–178; maturing of, 256–257;
termed baby bust echo, 170, 173, 198;
in 2000–2010, 211
genocide, loss of Native American life as, 94
German immigrants in New Jersey, 126, 127,
128; Germany as leading country of origin
for immigrants 1880 to 1920, 123
German national origin: of white population of colonial America, 54, 56, 57, 58; of
white population of colonial middle
colonies, 54–55; of white population of
colonial New Jersey, 53, 55, 58
GI Bill of Rights, 325n4, 328n6
Gini coefficient, 67
glassmaking, in colonial New Jersey, 68
global economic competitors, New Jersey's
population and, 83
global immigration, New Jersey and, 75
globalization, New Jersey's population and,
75–76
global macro trends, twenty-first, 3
Gloucester County: Black population in
eighteenth-century, 42–43; gender ratio
in colonial, 43
Goldwyn, Samuel, 246
goodbye babies, 170, 176
Gordon, Thomas F., 18
government: in 1790 United States, 66;
sources of revenue for colonial, 69–70
grandparenthood, baby boom and, 252
Grant, Madison, 116, 117, 118, 119
Great Depression, 270, 271; birth dearth,
169, 170, 173, 174, 175–176, 181, 203, 207,
209, 211, 214–215, 328n4; effect on
children of, 200; effect on population
growth, 155; effect on population of New
Jersey, 81

greatest generation, 173, 174, 175
"great household revolution," 221
Great Migration, 5, 9, 98–100, 282–289;
adverse conditions for migrants in the
north, 287–289; blacks living in New
Jersey, 1900–2017, 283, 286; experience of
journeying north, 287; experience of
migrants in New Jersey, 102–103; for
New Jersey, 1900–2017, 284; New
Jersey as destination in, 98–100; oral
history excerpts, 288, 331–332n7;
"push and pull" influences, 282,
286–287; southern places of origins
of migrants, 286
"Great Migration to Houston," 331n4
Great Trail, 91
Great Transmillennial Economic
Expansion, 85, 86
Great 2007–2009 Recession, 85–86, 211,
270–271, 272; economic change in
response to, 85; effect on pattern of
household change, 223–224; effect on real
family income, 239; Gen Y and, 195–196;
Gen Z and, 200; household formation
and, 330n2; New Jersey and, 148;
reurbanization following, 186; stabiliza-
tion of household size and, 224–225;
unemployment and, 272
Green, Jacob, 281
Green Book, 287
Greene, Evarts, 24, 25
Griffis, William Elliot, 107, 321–322n7
Grimké, Sarah, 101
Griswold v. Connecticut, 189
"grumpies," 183
Guarded Gate, The (Okrent), 116–117
Guatemalans in New Jersey, 112

Haines, Michael R., 117
Hall, Prescott, 118–119
Hamburg American Line, 115
Hamilton, Alexander, 131
Hansen, Marcus, 56, 57
Hardenbrook, Adolphus, 74
Harrington, Virginia, 24, 25
Hart-Celler Act of 1965, 84, 104–105, 117,
119–120, 121, 146, 190
Hawaii: land area, 304, 332–333n2;
population density, 309, 333
Hindus, 105

Hispanic heritage, Census Bureau measurement of, 89

Hispanics: census definition of, 110–111; identified as Some Other Race, 109; median household income in 2017, 242–243; national origins of in New Jersey, 112; in New Brunswick, 129, 323n11; percentage of population of various groups, 111–112; population distribution in New Jersey, 129–130; population size in the United States and New Jersey, 1850–2017, 110–111; racial profile, 109–114; share of New Jersey's population, 9

Hispaniola, population size in 1492 and early 1500s, 93

historical context of population trends, 2–3

Historical Statistics of the United States, Millennial Edition, 24

History of the Colony of Nova-Caesaria, or New Jersey . . . to the Year 1721, The (Smith), 18

Hitler, Adolf, *The Passing of the Great Race* and, 119

Hoboken, 134, 324n1; population density of, 311

household: American households in the twentieth century, 218–228; American households in twenty-first century by size and type, 223–224, 225–226; Census Bureau definitional framework, 221–222, 328n1; defined, 218–219, 221; New Jersey, 229–235; number of American, 1900–2000, 219; reshaping of, 6; 1950–2000 trendlines, 222–223

household-change parameters, 12

household characteristics, of New Jersey's colonial-era population, 44–46

household configuration: income and, 240–242; post-2010, 227–228, 277–288; 2000–2010, 226

household differentiation, baby boom and, 184

household diversification, 221; 2000–2010, 226

household diversity, 218

householder, 329n5; defined, 221

household formation: Gen Z and, 256–257; Great 2007–2009 Recession and, 330n2; increase in in twentieth century, 220

household incomes, 12; median, 2017, 242–243

household size, 220–221; age structure of population and, 225; in colonial-era New Jersey, 44–45; decrease in, 6, 218, 220–221, 249; decrease in New Jersey in the twenty-first century, 231–232; as demographic multiplier, 293, 294, 295; distribution, 2000–2010, 224–225; downward trend in, 292, 293; median, 329n4; post-2010, 227–228; in United States in 1790, 65–66

housing bubble, 85, 148

housing size (bedrooms), 296, 297

housing unit: defined, 328n2; demand for, 141–142

Howe, Neil, 174

Hudson, Henry, 20, 90

Hudson County: loss of population during 1950s, 162–163; population growth, 1900–1930, 139; population growth in 1950s, 164

Hudson River Gold Coast, 147, 149

Hughes, Langston, 282–283, 291

"hula hoop" generation, 183

Hungarian immigrants to New Jersey, 126; in New Brunswick, 128–129

Hunterdon County: national origins of colonial population, 57; population 2010–2018, 154

husband-wife households, 221

Hyatt Bearing plant, 141

Hyde, Edward, Lord Cornbury, 34, 35

IBM PC, 192–193, 194, 327n8

immigrants: hostility to, 115–116, 118–119; national origins of, 117–118; racial stereotypes of, 117–118; travel to United States, 115

immigration, 4–5, 114–128; changing Hungarian presence in New Brunswick, 128–129; demand for manufacturing labor and, 133, 247; economic conditions and, 116, 155; growth of Hispanic population in New Jersey and, 111–112; historical and legislative context, 114–120; New Jersey's population and waves of, 75; origins and fluctuating numbers of foreign-born, 120–128; population growth in New Jersey and first waves of, 80; population growth in New Jersey driven by, 84; profile of

immigration (cont.)
foreign-born and, 114–128; push and pull factors, 115; roadblocks to, 118–119; second great wave of, 247; surge in 1980s, 146; urban demographic stabilization and, 149. *See also* international immigration
Immigration Act of 1917, 104
Immigration and Nationality Act of 1952, 104
Immigration and Nationality (Hart-Celler) Act of 1965, 84, 104–105, 117, 119–120, 121, 146, 190
Immigration (Johnson-Reed) Act of 1924, 56, 104, 117, 118–119
immigration policy, Asians and, 103–105, 106
Immigration Restriction League, 118
income, 12, 236–245; affluence in United States, 236–238; age of householder and, 243–245; census money income defined, 329n1; contraction post-Great 2007–2009 Recession, 239; faltering trajectory in, 7; household configuration and, 240–242; New Jersey and the nation, 239–240; post-affluence intervals, 238; race and ethnicity and, 242–243; real median family, 330n5, 330n9; twenty-first century, 239; U.S. and New Jersey median family income, 1950–2017, 239–240, 241–245; U.S. median family income, 1950–2017, 237–238
indentured servants, 49, 62
industrial-based transformation and settlement patterns, 132–133
industrial decentralization, 247
industrial economy, 7–8
industrialization: Big Six cities and, 133–134; in early twentieth-century New Jersey, 80, 81; population growth in New Jersey and, 79
industrial-manufacturing clusters, New Jersey's population and, 75, 78
Industrial Revolutions: effect on settlement patterns, 132–133; manufacturing in New Jersey and, 246–247; population growth in New Jersey and, 75, 78–79, 80
inflation, impact on income, 238
inflation-adjusted incomes, 329n4
information-age economy, 83
information technology, 86, 193

in-migration: to colonial-era New Jersey, 48; gender ratio and, 43; growth of Hispanic population in New Jersey and, 111–112
in-movers, 156–157
innovation-based economy, 7
international immigration, 12, 156–157; boosting population 1990–2000, 209; as demographic growth engine, 248–249; multigenerational households and, 226; net, 158; pattern of settlement choices, 250; as source of population growth in Northeast, 159. *See also* immigration
internet connectivity, mobile, 193, 198, 199
interstate competition, New Jersey's population and, 75
iPhones, 193, 195, 327n9
Irish immigrants, 126, 127, 128; Ireland as leading country of origin for immigrants 1850 to 1870, 123
Irish national origin: of white population of colonial America, 54, 56, 57, 58; of white population of colonial New Jersey, 53, 55, 57, 58
ironworks furnace, in New Jersey, 68
Italian immigrants, 126, 127, 128; before and after Johnson-Reed Act, 118; Italy as leading country of origin for immigrants 1930 to 1970, 123

James, Duke of York, 17
James, Sharpe, 102, 288
Japan: curbing immigration from, 104; definition of urban in, 333n6
Japanese: Census Bureau enumeration of, 105; percent of Asian population in New Jersey, 106
Jefferson, Thomas, 62, 281
Jersey City, 133; Asian Indians in, 105; effect of new urbanism on, 151; population density, 1950–2018, 311; shelter spillover from New York City, 149. *See also* Big Six cities
Jersey Promise, 107
Jews, Nazi classifications of, 119
jobless economic growth, 272
Johnson, Lyndon, 119
Johnson, Reather Boswell, 288
Johnson-Reed Act (1924), 56, 104, 117, 118–119
Johnston, Annie Rose, 102–103

Kalm, Peter, 22, 36, 317n9
knowledge-based, information-age
    economy, 272
knowledge-based economy, 83
knowledge-dependent, innovation-based
    economy, 8
Koreans: Census Bureau enumeration of,
    105; percent of Asian population in New
    Jersey, 106, 107
Kraft, Herbert, 320n3
Krueger-Scott Cultural Center (Newark),
    102, 287, 288, 331n7
Ku Klux Klan, 118

labor force: baby boom and, 204, 212; Gen Y
    and, 188, 189, 196–197; Gen Z and, 256;
    mass exodus of baby boomers from,
    188, 252
land area: Alaska, 304, 332–333n2; Hawaii,
    304, 332–333n2; New Jersey, 301, 304,
    332–333n2
Latin Americans: immigrants to New Jersey
    from, 125–126; percent of population of
    New Jersey in 2017, 130; rise in immi-
    grants from after immigration law
    changes in the 1960s, 123
Latino. See also Hispanics
Latino, census definition of, 110–111
Latino heritage, Census Bureau measure-
    ment of, 89
"Latino New Jersey History Project, The,"
    excerpts from, 112–113
Lazarus, Emma, 119
Lenape: Archaeology, History, and Ethnogra-
    phy, The (Kraft), 320n3
Lenapehoking, 19
Lenix-Hooker, Catherine J., 331n7
Lenni-Lenape tribe, 18–19, 37, 96–97, 320n1;
    assimilation of, 71; profile of, 90–91
life-cycle stages, baby boom, 183–184
life plan communities, 187, 325n3
life-work-play (LWP) environments, 196
Listokin, David, 332n1
literacy test, for immigrants, 118
Little, Mageline, 102, 288
Lodge, Henry Cabot, 117
Long Depression, 79, 271
lottery, as source of revenue for colonial
    government, 69–70
Lotus Development Corp., 327n10

Louisiana Purchase, 78
Lovell, John, 73
Low, Cornelius, 74
Low, Johanna Gouverneur, 74
lynchings, of Blacks, 331n6

machine production, effect on settlement
    patterns, 132
macroeconomic structural changes,
    demographic geography and, 330n1
macro trends: global, 3; national, 4–8
Madley, Benjamin, 92
male householder (no spouse present), 221;
    increase in number of, 1950–2000, 222;
    increase in number of, 2000–2010, 232;
    increase in percentage share in New Jersey
    post–2010, 235
male householder (no spouse present)
    with children, median income in
    2017, 241
Malpezzi, Stephen, 332n1
Malthus, Thomas, 45, 47–48
Mann, Chief, 97
manufacturing, 324n3; in early twentieth-
    century New Jersey, 80; expansion of
    New Jersey, after World War II, 141;
    income in New Jersey and, 240; nascent
    in colonial New Jersey, 68–69
manufacturing centers, growth of early
    New Jersey cities and, 246–247
Mapson, Zaundria, 102, 103, 288
market segmentation, 185
marriage: age of in post-World War II
    America, 182; encouraging early, in
    colonial America, 36; post-World War II
    boom, 326n6
married-couple family, 221; changes in
    number of, 221; decrease in number in
    New Jersey, 2000–2010, 232; decrease in
    percentage share between 2000 and 2010,
    226; decrease in percentage share in New
    Jersey post–2010, 235; decrease in
    percentage share post–2010 in United
    States, 228; median income in New Jersey,
    2017, 241; percent of all households,
    1950–2000, 222–223
Married Women's Act of 1922, 118
Marx, Groucho, 246
Maryland, age distribution for whites in
    colonial-era, 45

Massachusetts: agriculture in eighteenth-century, 68; fertility rates in colonial-era, 45; lagging population growth in eighteenth century, 33; population density, 2000, 303; population density, 2018, 304; population density in colonial, 50, 51; as population leader in New England, 1700–1790, 29; urban population in, 307, 308, 309

Massachusetts Metropolitan Area Planning Council (MAPC), 299

mature in place, 257

maturing housing demand of baby boomers, 185

McCormick, Richard, 15

McCrindle, Mark, 325n1

McCusker, John, 15, 24–26, 29, 36

McKay, Nellie, 282

McMansions, baby boomers and, 180, 185

median age, 2018, 328n10

median family incomes, 7; 1950–2017, 237–240

median household incomes, 7; in New Jersey, 2017, 242–243

Menard, Russel R., 36

metropolis, electricity and rise of industrial, 7–8

metropolitan area, 311–313; defined, 312

metropolitan dispersion, concentration, and redispersion, 5–6

metropolitanization, 10; in Big Six cities, 1900–1930, 134–140; in early twentieth-century New Jersey, 80, 81; in Essex County, 139

metro south area of New Jersey, 137, 139

"Mexican," 109

Mexican immigrants, 111, 112, 126, 127; Mexico as leading country of origin since 1980, 123; in New Brunswick, 114

Meyer, Christopher, 128

microprocessors, 193

middle class, expansion of, 220

middle colonies (Delaware, New Jersey, New York, and Pennsylvania): migration to in seventeenth- and eighteenth-century, 48; percent of enslaved Blacks in 1790 census, 64, 65; population growth in, 28–33

Middlesex County, population growth in 1950s, 163–164

middle states: gender ratio in 1790, 66; national origin of colonial population, 54–55; newspaper ratio in 1790, 66; percent of total U.S. population in 1790 census in, 64; wealth inequality in 1790, 67; wealth in 1790, 67

Midwest: demographic stagnation in, 5; population change, 2010–2018, 157, 159; population density of, 1900–2018, 303; sluggish demography of, 248

migration, 3; in colonial-era New Jersey, 46–49; defined, 156; population growth and, 247; by region, 48–49

migration estimates, 324n1

migration flows, New Jersey and, 75

millennials. See Generation Y (millennials)

millennium (2000–2010), New Jersey's population growth in, 84–85

minor civil divisions (MCDs) in 1790 United States, 66

Minuit, Peter, 317n6

Morris, Lewis, 20

mortality rate, American Indians and, 320–321n5

Mosquito Castle, 16

multifamily housing, 293, 294, 295, 296, 297, 298

multigenerational households, 6, 226; increasing prevalence since Great Recession, 249–250

naming of New Jersey, 17–22

Nanticoke Indians, 96–97

national average density, 1790, 332–333n2

National Bureau of Economic Research (NBER), 270, 272, 330–331n4

national census, European, 14. See federal census

Nationality Act of 1790, 103

national origin: of colonial middle states population, 54–55; of colonial New England population, 54; of foreign-born population in the United States, 122–124; of Hispanics in New Jersey, 112; of immigrants to the United States, 117–118

Native Americans: conflict with Dutch in early New Jersey, 16; enumeration of population, 320–321n5; exclusion from 1790 census, 62; left out of censuses, 37; names or derivatives of in New Jersey, 19; population size in 1492 and 1900, 92–94; population size in New Jersey, 94–96; quote from Indian spokesman for the

Delaware on property ownership/land use, 70; racial profile, 90–97; war of extinction and, 91. *See also* Lenni-Lenape tribe
natural change, 156
natural increase, 10, 156; in colonial-era New Jersey, 46–48
natural increment, 156
natural origin: of colonial population in New Jersey, 51–59
Nazi Germany, racial classification and restrictions, 119
Neilson, James, 128
Nelson, William, 53, 57
net activity density, 332n1
net domestic migration, New Jersey, New York City, and Philadelphia, 159–160
net international migration, 156–157, 158
net migration, 10, 156, 324n3; within New Jersey, 162–166
net natural increase, 158
net outmigration, 166
net worth, 329n1
Nevada, urban population in, 309
New Albion, 19
New Amsterdam, 20
Newark, 133; as destination in Black Migration, 283; experience of Great Migration migrants in, 103, 287–289; Great Migration oral histories, 331–332n7; population density, 1950–2018, 311; settlement of, 316n4. *See also* Big Six cities
Newark Public Library, 331n7
New Brunswick: changing foreign-born population in, 131; as destination for Great Migration migrants, 287; Hispanics in, 112–114, 129, 323n11; hostility to abolitionists and escaped slaves in, 102; Hungarians in, 128–129
New England (Connecticut, Maine, Massachusetts, New Hampshire, Rhode Island, and Vermont): gender ratio in colonial, 43–44; gender ratio in 1790, 66; migration to and negative migration from in seventeenth- and eighteenth-century, 48–49; national origin of colonial population, 54; newspaper ratio in 1790, 66; percent of enslaved Blacks in 1790 census, 64, 65; percent of total U.S. population in 1790 census, 64; population growth in colonial, 28–34; wealth inequality in 1790, 67; wealth in 1790, 67

New Great Migration. *See* Reverse Great Migration
New Jersey: attracting settlers from other colonies, 34–35; competition with New York for settlers, 39–40; components of population change, 1950–1980, 2010–2018, 160–161; income and demographics in, 239–245; long-term diversity in, 9–10; microcosm of "immigration nation," 4; outmigration from, 78; percent of enslaved Blacks in 1790 census, 64–65; in 1790 census, 62–63; slavery in, 273–274, 277–278, 279–282; total area, 319n4; wealth inequality in 1790, 67–68
New Jersey, age structure: changing age-structure distributions, 214–217; 1950–1960, 203–204; 1960–1970, 204–206; 1970–1980, 206–207; 1980–1990, 208–209; 1990–2000, 209–211; 2000–2010, 211–212; 2010–2018, 212–213
New Jersey Coalition, 120
New Jersey Future, 306, 312, 332n1
New Jersey Historical Society (NJHS), 53
New Jersey households, 229–235; post-2010, 233–235; twentieth century, 229–231; twenty-first century, 231–232
New Jersey population: current share of national population, 87; 1970s, 83; 1980s, 83–84; 1990s, 83–84; population growth due to Industrial Revolutions, European immigration, and postwar suburbanization, 9; population growth in eighteenth century, 34; population growth of from 1670–1790, 9; share of national population in, 1700–1790, 33; share of national population in 1900, 80; in 2010, 9; in 2018, 76–77
New Jersey population, forecasting future of, 246–258; baby boom, 252–253; contextual dynamics, 247; demographic disconnects, 249; future of urban revival, 250–251; generational longwaves, 251–258; Generation Alpha, 257–258; Generation X, 253–254; Generation Y, 254–256; Generation Z, 256–257; household evolution, 249–250; international migration, 248–249; pre-baby boom, 251–252; racial and ethnic diversity, 249; slow-go/slow-grow New Jersey, 248

New Jersey population from the colonial
period to the early republic, 9, 14–74;
births, deaths, and migration, 46–49;
colonial-era census enumerations, 37–70;
colonial population estimates, 22–37;
demographic and socioeconomic profile
of New Jersey, the United States and
regions in 1790, 59–70; density, 49–51;
early history, 15–17; gender, 43–44;
household and age characteristics,
44–46; incompleteness of colonial
population censuses, 14–15; naming of
colony and state, 17–22; national origins,
51–59; oral histories, 70–74; population
by county, 40; population growth,
1790–2010, 76–78; racial composition,
41–43; uneven treatment of how African
Americans enumerated, 15
New Jersey Society for Promoting the
Abolition of Slavery, 280
New Jersey State Museum, 96
New Jersey State Plan, 313
New Jersey Women Suffrage Association,
319n21
New Netherlands, 20
newspaper ratio, in 1790 New Jersey, 66–67
New Sweden, 19–20
new urbanism (post–2010), 150–154
New York: early New Jersey and, 20–21;
gain in population, 1700–1790, 33;
population growth in eighteenth century,
33; urban population in, 307, 308, 309
New York City: industrialization in New
Jersey and proximity to, 319n7; links
between New Jersey's suburban communities and, 79; net domestic migration
and New Jersey and, 159–160; 1930
population, 140; 1950 population, 82; as
population magnet for millennials, 86;
resurgence of in 2000–2010, 84; as
superstar city, 6, 8
New York metro area, 312–313
New York Times (newspaper), 290
Noguchi, Paul, 107, 322–323n8
nominal dollars, 329–330n4
nonfamily households in New Jersey, 221;
decline in number of in post-2010, 234;
defined, 328n1; increase in, 1950–2000,
222, 230; increase in number of in
2000–2010, 232; increase in share

between 2000 and 2010, 226; lagging
median incomes in 2017, 242; percent of
all households, 1950–2000, 223
North Carolina, population growth in
eighteenth century, 33
North Central region, population change,
1950–2018, 157–159
Northeast: demographic stagnation in, 5;
population change, 1950–2018, 157–159;
population density of, 1900–2018, 303;
sluggish demography of, 248; state
comprising pre-Civil War, 331n3; waning
of slavery in, 276–277, 278
Northern American immigrants, 123, 126
Norwood, Pastor, 97
Nova Caesarea, 17, 18
Nova Caesarea: A Cartographic Record
of the Garden State, 1666–1888
(Delaney), 18
Nova Caesarea: A Cartographic Record of the
Garden State (Gordon), 18
Novelty Rubber Company, 128
nuclear families, 6
Nucor Corp., 326n2

"Observations concerning the Increase of
Mankind, and Peopling of Countries"
(Franklin), 36
occupations in America, 1670–1730, 68
Ocean City metro area, 313; growth of in
1970s, 146
Ocean County: net domestic migration
during 1950s, 164; population 2010–2018,
154
office building boom, 83, 146
office buildings, economic functions of, 86
Okrent, Daniel, 116–117
Oliver, Thomas Clement, 101
one-person nonfamily households: decline
in percentage share in New Jersey
post–2010, 233; increase in, 1950–2000,
221, 222; increase in post–2010, 228; share
of in New Jersey in the twenty-first
century, 231
"One-Way Ticket" (Hughes), 282–283
oral history, 70–74, 96–97, 112–113, 288,
331–332n7
Original Levittowners, 184
O'Rourke, Jeremiah, 128
Ousamequin, 320n2

outmigration, 43; of baby boom retirees, 87; from coastal states, 78

out-movers, 157

Owens, Jasmine, 290

Oyarzun, Jose, 113–114

Page Act (1875), 104

Panic of 1873, 271

Passing of the Great Race, The (Grant), 116, 117, 119

Paterson, 133; changing foreign-born population in, 131; influx of Hispanics and fluctuating population of Blacks, 291; population density, 1950–2018, 311. *See also* Big Six cities

Pauw, Michael Reyniersz, 316n2

Pendleton, Helen, 286, 287

Penn, William, 21–22

Pennsylvania: gain in population, 1700–1790, 33; population growth in eighteenth century, 33; William Penn and rights in New Jersey, 21–22

per capita wealth in 1790 United States, 67

Perez, Elsa, 113

personal computers, 192–193, 327n8

personal-consumption expenditures (PCE), on experience-related experiences, 197

Perth Amboy, 22, 134

Peruvian immigrants, 112

Pew Research Center, 3, 110, 168, 173

Pham, Co, 108, 323n9

Philadelphia: European population of, 318n14; industrialization in New Jersey and proximity to, 319n7; links between New Jersey's suburban communities and, 79; net domestic migration and New Jersey and, 159–160; 1930 population, 140; 1950 population, 82; as population magnet for millennials, 86

Philadelphia metro area, 313

Pitt, William, 73

Plowden, Edward, 19

Plymouth Colony, 91; Wampanoags and, 320n2

Poland, immigrants to New Jersey from, 127

population change: in eighteenth-century New Jersey, 28; estimated decennial population increase from colonial era to the 1790 census, 27

population change, components of, 10, 155–166; births, deaths, and migration, 156; national framework, 157–158; New Jersey, 159–161; within New Jersey, 162–166; regional setting, 158–159

population change, dimensions of, 2

population density: defined, 300; of United States in 1790, 65

population density, New Jersey, 300–306; calculating, 332–333n2; colonial, 49–51; metropolitan area, 311–313; within New Jersey, 309–311; urban and rural population, 306–309

population enumerations: colonial-era, 259, 268; for New Jersey American colonies through the 1790 census, 22, 23, 24; 1772, 259. *See also* federal census

population estimates from the colonial era to the 1790 census, 25

population geography, 7

population growth: all-colony, 28; migration in post–World War II era, 247; national, 1900–2000, 219; in New Jersey during post–World War II boom, 82–83; regional differentials, 5; slowing world, 3

population growth in New Jersey: early twentieth-century, 80–81; immigration and, 84; 1700–1790, 26, 28; 1850–1870, 319n9; 1860–1870, 319n8, 319n9; 1890–1910, 319n9; 1950–1970, 319n9; 1970–1980, 83, 206–207; 1980s and 1990s, 83–84; 1990–2000, 209; 2000–2010, 84–85

population pyramid, 328n3

Population Reference Bureau, 326n8

POSSLQs (unmarried couples), 184, 185, 221, 222

post–Great Recession millennials, 196–198

postindustrial economy, 8, 247; income in New Jersey and, 240; real income growth in United States and, 238

postmillennial generation, 174

post offices: number of in 1790 United States, 66; in 1790 New Jersey, 66

post–World War II: household formation and housing investment and end of, 141; population boom in New Jersey, 82–83; prediction of only modest postwar population growth, 181–182

post–World War II nesting generation, 184

pre-baby boom, 10, 174, 175–176; current and future decline in population of, 251–252

Price, Clement, 278, 331n7

Princeton University, 22, 69, 280

production facilities, deconcentration of wartime, 141

property claims, conflicting, in colonial New Jersey, 72

proprietary American colonies, 316n3. *See also* New Jersey

proprietors of early New Jersey, 16–17

Pruitt, Bernadette, 331n4

public school children (PSC), 293, 295, 296, 297, 298, 299; decline in number of, 292–294

public school enrollment, declining, 299

Public Use Microdata Sample (PUMS), 294

Puerto Rican Action Board, 114

Puerto Ricans, 111, 112, 113; in New Brunswick, 114

Purvis, Thomas, 50, 52, 54, 57–59

Quakers in West Jersey, 21, 42, 43; anti-slavery, 72, 101, 280

Queen Anne, 279

Quick, Thomas, Jr., 16

Quick, Thomas, Sr., 16

race: Census Bureau identification of, 88–89; median income and, 242–243

racial composition: of New Jersey's colonial population, 41–43; of the United States and New Jersey, 95

racial differences in New Jersey, 129–131

racial diversity in New Jersey in 2020s, 249

racial minorities: as engines of population growth, 5; undercount in censuses, 89

racial profiles in New Jersey: Asian, 103–108; Native American, 90–97; white and Black, 95, 96, 97–103

"Racism Is Everywhere, So Why Not Move South?," 290

railroads, New Jersey suburbs linked to New York City and Philadelphia, 135

Ramapough Lunaape (Munsee Delaware), 97

Raritan Landing, diverse inhabitants of, 73–74

Raspail, Jean, 116

RCA-Victor, 80, 140

real dollars, 329n4

real median family income, 330n5; 2007 and 2017, 330n9

recessions, 269–271; 2001, 239; comparison of twentieth-century, 326n5; definition of, 330n4; employment and, 272. *See also* Great 2007–2009 Recession

regional competition, New Jersey's population and, 75

regional distribution and growth of population, 1700–1790, 28–34

regional (national) components of population change, 157–159

regional population of New Jersey, 136–140; distributional profile, 1900–2018, 153–154; new urbanism (post-2010), 150–154; 1950–1970, 143–146; 1970–1980, 145; 1980–2000, 146–147, 148; 2000–2010, 150; 2010–2018, 151–154

regions of New Jersey, map, 138

replacement-level fertility, 316n7, 325n2

Report of the Council of the American Antiquarian Society, 22

residential housing in New Jersey, 292–299; aging baby boomers and, 188, 252–253; baby boomers trading up, 1990–2000, 210; choices of baby boomers, 180; demographic multipliers, 292–295; Gen X and, 253–254; Gen Y and, 188, 189, 254–255; summary of New Jersey demographic multipliers, 295–299

re-urbanization, 10

Reverse Great Migration, 5, 9, 99, 249, 289–291; migrants from New Jersey, 100, 285, 290–291; reasons underlying, 289–290

Revolutionary Jersey Girls, 318n20

Revolutionary War: conflicts in New Jersey, 34, 88–89; postwar boom in population following, 28, 33, 34; women's contributions to, 73

Rey, Manuel, 113

Rhode Island: colonial distribution of population, 30, 31, 45; colonial population, 32, 317n4; land area, 319n4; population density, 1960–2000, 300, 303–304; urban population in, 307, 308, 309

Richards, Edus, 73

Ripley, William, 117

Rodriguez, Benito, 113

Roosevelt, Franklin D., 325n4

Rossiter, William S., 15, 24–26, 29, 64, 332–333n2, 333n4; on national origins of foreign-born, 117–118; study on national origin of colonial population, 52–59

rural, definition, 307

rural/north/exurban region: population 2010–2018, 154

rural north/exurban region, 136, 139–140

rural population, 306–309; farm population *vs.*, 333n7

rural south region, 139

Russian immigrants, 126; before and after Johnson-Reed Act, 118

Rust Belt, 83

Rutgers University (Queens College), 69, 173; Japanese men studying at, 107, 321–322n7; slavery and, 101, 280

Salem County, differential migration flows 2010–2018, 165

Salvadorans, 112

Sand Hill Indian Historical Association, 97

Scarlet and Black (Fuentes & White), 280

Scheyichbi, 19

school-age children (SAC), 293, 294, 295, 296, 297, 298

Scott, Louise, 288

Scottish national origin: of white population of colonial America, 56, 58; of white population of colonial New Jersey, 53, 57, 58

Scottish settlers in Bergen County, 53

Seabrook Education and Cultural Center, 322n8

Seabrook Farm (Japanese-American internment camp), 107, 322–323n8

service-producing economy, 141

Sesame Street Generation, 189

settlement patterns, changing, 132; early industrial-based transformation, 132–133

Sheehan, Patricia, 113

shelter eras, baby boom and, 184–186

shipping of goods, colonial New Jersey, 69

Shoemaker, Nancy, 320n5

Sikhs, 108

silent generation, 173, 174, 175

Singer Sewing Machine, 80, 140

single-family attached (SFA; townhouses): baby boomers and, 180, 185; defined, 294; demographic multipliers by age cohort, 297; demographic school multipliers, 296, 298; household size and school multipliers, 295; persons of senior age in, 299; residential demographic multipliers for, 293

single-family detached (SFD) homes: decline in number of public school children in, 292–294; defined, 294; demographic multipliers by age cohort, 297; demographic school multipliers, 296, 298; household size and school multipliers, 295; residential demographic multipliers for, 293

single-family housing, 141; baby boomers and, 210; Gen Y and, 255

single-parent families, 185, 221. *See also* female householder (no spouse present); male householder (no spouse present)

slavery, 273–281; in the Atlantic colonies, 278–279; in New Jersey, 41–43, 101–102, 273–274, 277–278, 279–282; in the Northeast, 276–277, 278; Quakers and antislavery sentiment, 72, 101–102, 280; in the southern colonies, 275–276

"slow-go" demographic growth condition, 12

smartphones, 193, 198, 199

Smith, Samuel, 18

Snyder, John, 63

socioeconomic and demographic profile of New Jersey in 1790, 59–70

Some Other Race (SOR) federal census category, 108–109

Somerset County, national origins of colonial population, 57

South: gender ratio in 1790, 66; percent of enslaved Blacks in 1790 census, 64, 65; percent of total U.S. population in 1790 census in, 64; population change, 1950–2018, 157–159; population density, 1900–2018, 303; population growth in, 248; states comprising pre-Civil War, 331n2; wealth inequality in 1790, 67; wealth in 1790, 67

South Americans, 112; in New Brunswick, 114

South Carolina, population growth in eighteenth century, 33

southern colonies: colonies comprising, 331n1; migration to in seventeenth- and eighteenth-century, 48; population growth in, 28–33; slavery in, 275–276
southern shore of New Jersey, 139
Spanish American Civic Association, 114
Spanish Outreach Center, 113
Stacy, Mahlon, 317n8
stagnation, income, 238, 239
State Department, 62
state highway system, 135, 141
Statue of Liberty, 119
Stengel, Casey, 246
Still, William, 101–102
Stockton, Annis, 73
Stockton, Richard, 73, 281
Stone, Lucy, 319n21
Story of New Jersey's Civil Boundaries, 1606–1968, The (Snyder), 63
Strauss, William, 174
streetcar systems, spreading out from cities and, 8, 135
structural economic shifts, 7, 8, 269, 272
structural shifts, effect on population growth, 155–156
Stubbs, Bill, 102, 288
student debt, 196
suburban, family-raising environments, Gen Y and, 254–255
suburban economic growth corridors, 1980–2000, 146–147
suburbanization, 10, 135–136, 141, 247; abatement of in New Jersey, 84; of American population, 5; baby boom and, 203, 253; in early twentieth-century New Jersey, 80, 81; in New Jersey, 83, 114; New Jersey's population and, 75, 78; New York City and Philadelphia and New Jersey, 79–80, 82, 86, 135, 142–143, 145, 159, 180, 203, 250, 303; population density and, 303; renewal of, 250
suburban office campuses, 181
suburban office corridors, 83, 84
suburban subdivisions, baby boomers and, 180
suburban tract house model, 84
suburban tract houses, baby boom and, 183, 184
Sunbelt, 83, 155, 319n12
superregional malls, 181

superstar cities, 6, 8
Sussex County, differential migration flows 2010–2018, 165
Sutherland, Stella, 24
Suydam, Charles, 74
Swedish (includes Finnish) national origin: of white population of colonial America, 54, 56, 58; of white population of colonial New Jersey, 16, 19–20, 53, 55, 57, 58, 59

Taft, Howard, 116
Taro, Kusakabe, 107, 321–322n7
teacher shortage, 328n5
technological change: Gen Y and, 255–256; New Jersey's population and, 75–76; semiconductors, software, and desktop computing, 327n13; technology-driven transformation of New Jersey economy, 83
technology shaping Generation Alpha, 178
Texas: Asian population in, 106; land area, 304; Mexican immigrants to, 112; population density, 304
Thirteenth Amendment, 281
Thompson, Wilbur, 140–141
three-person households, increase in percentage share in New Jersey post-2010, 233
Tocqueville, Alexis de, 92
total fertility rate, 316n7, 325n2, 326n8
townhouses. *See* single-family attached (SFA; townhouses)
trading up in place, 255
transistor radio, 194, 195, 327n15
Trent, William, 317n8
Trenton, 133; as capital city, 22; founding of, 317n8; population density, 1950–2018, 311. *See also* Big Six cities
Trenton-Ewing metro area, 313
Tubman, Harriet, 102
Tuttle, Brad, 283
Twain, Mark, 246
twenty-first global macro trends, 3
two-person households: increase in percentage share in New Jersey post-2010, 233, 234; as most prevalent living arrangement, 228; share of in New Jersey in the twenty-first century, 231

unadjusted dollars, 329–330n4
Underground Railroad, 101–102
Union City, changing foreign-born
  population in, 131
United Nations, 3
United States: definition of urban, 333n6;
  macro trends, 4–8; percentage metropolitan population, 1910–2010, 312; percentage urban population, 1790–2010, 308,
  309; population density of, 1790–2018,
  301, 304–305; population of, 1790–2010,
  76–77
United States and regional components of
  population change: 1950–1960, 157–159;
  2010–2018, 157–159
U.S. Immigration Commission, 117
U.S. industry, absence of global competition
  for, 325n5
unmarried-couple households, 184, 185,
  221, 222
urban, definitions, 306–307, 333n6
urban boarding houses, 329n9
urban-centric environment, Gen Y and
  attraction to, 197
urban-centric millennial generation, 86
urbanization, 10; defined, 332n1; in early
  twentieth-century New Jersey, 81;
  population growth in New Jersey and, 75,
  79–80
urban population in New Jersey,
  306–309
urban profile within New Jersey, 309–311
urban reconcentration, 5–6
urban revival: future of, 250–251; Gen Y
  and, 254

Valenti, Blanquita, 113
Van Vorst, Cornelius, 15
Verrazano, Giovanni da, 90
Vietnamese, percent of Asian population in
  New Jersey, 106
Vineland-Millville-Bridgeton metro
  area, 313
Virginia: population growth in eighteenth
  century, 33; as population leader among
  southern colonies, 1700–1790, 29, 33;
  state population ranking, 87; status of
  first Blacks in, 49
VisiCalc, 327n10
Voices from Raritan Landing (Yamin), 73

"Voices of New Jersey's Contemporary
  American Indian Groups," excerpts from,
  96–97
Voicu, Alexandru, 332n1

Wacker, Peter: on colonial birth rates, death
  rates, and natural increase in West Jersey,
  47; on colonial diversity of New Jersey,
  88; on colonial population density of New
  Jersey, 51; colonial sex ratios, 43, 44; on
  cultural divide between East and West
  Jersey, 21; on natural increase and
  population growth, 48; New Jersey
  colonial history and, 15, 268; on Quakers
  and slavery in West Jersey, 42
Wall Street Journal (newspaper), 330n1
Wampanoags, 320n2
war babies, 170, 176
Warmth of Other Suns, The (Wilkerson), 282
Washington, George, 62
Washington, population growth in, 87
water-powered mills, colonial-era, 68
wealth accumulation, Gen Y and, 196
Wealth Belt, 137, 147
wealth inequality, 329n1; in 1790 United
  States, 67–68
wealth in 1790 United States, 66
Weld, Angelina Grimké, 101
Wells, Robert, 35, 39–40, 42, 44–45
Welsh national origin: of white population
  of colonial America, 54, 56, 58; of white
  population of colonial New Jersey,
  53, 57, 58
West: population change, 1950–2018,
  157–159; population density, 1900–2018,
  303; trend in population growth in, 248
West, Thomas, 320n1
Western Electric, 140
West Indies: population of as British colony,
  317–318n11; slavery in, 273, 279
West Jersey, 21; census counts in, 37; gender
  ratio in colonial, 43; map, 260; population in eighteenth century, 40; Quakers
  in, 21, 42, 43, 72, 280; rate of natural
  increase in colonial-era, 47; tension with
  East Jersey, 17
White, Hardis, 290
white-collar unemployment, twenty-first
  century recessions and, 272
white Gen Yers, as minority population, 254

Whitehead, Isaac, 71
Whitehead, Susanna, 71–72
whites: ages of in colonial-era New Jersey
    population, 45; in eighteenth-century
    New Jersey, 41; median household
    income, 2017, 242–243; natural increase
    and migration among in colonial America,
    48; national origins of colonial New
    Jersey population, 53; percent of total
    U.S. population in 1790 census in, 64;
    population distribution in New Jersey,
    129; population size in the United States
    and New Jersey, 1800–2017, 95, 96;
    racial profile, 97–103; rate of natural
    increase in colonial era, 47; ratio of slaves
    to in 1790, 65
Wigglesworth, Edward, 48
Wilson, Woodrow, 116
Wistar, Caspar, 68
Wistarburgh Glass Manufactory, 68
women: in the colonial era, voices of, 72–73;
    contributions to Revolutionary War
    effort, 73; suffrage, 73, 318–319n21
Woodstock generation, 183
Woolman, John, 72, 318n19

workforce: baby boom and, 210; Gen Y and,
    255–256; replacement of baby boomers by
    Gen X, 190–191
work-play environments, 1, 181, 196
Works Progress Administration (WPA),
    289
World Bank, 306
World Health Organization, 327n18
world population: density of, 306; increasing
    urbanization of, 309
Wright, Giles R., Jr., 331n7
Wright, Joseph, 73
Wright, Patience Lovell, 72–73
Wright, Richard, 282, 291

Yasohachi, Yagi (Kusakabe Taro),
    321–322n7
YOLO (You Only Live Once) generation,
    197
Yoshikami, Theodora, 107, 322n8
yuppies, 183, 185, 191

zones of millennial retention, 255
zones of suburban emergence, 255
zones of suburban millennial emergence, 255

About the Authors

JAMES W. HUGHES is a university professor and distinguished professor, and dean emeritus of the Edward J. Bloustein School of Planning and Public Policy, Rutgers University, in New Brunswick, New Jersey. His books include the coauthored *New Jersey's Postsuburban Economy* and the coedited *America's Demographic Tapestry: Baseline for the New Millennium* (both Rutgers University Press).

DAVID LISTOKIN is a distinguished professor and director of the Center for Urban Policy Research at the Edward J. Bloustein School of Planning and Public Policy, Rutgers University, in New Brunswick, New Jersey. His many books include *Landmarks Preservation and the Property Tax*, the coauthored *Development Impact Assessment*, and the coedited *Cities under Stress*.